1000 MAKERS OF THE TWENTIETH CENTURY

1000 MAKERS OF THE TWENTIETH CENTURY

edited by Godfrey Smith

TIMES NEWSPAPERS LIMITED

ISBN 0 7153 5441 8

Reproduced and printed in Great Britain by
Sir Joseph Causton and Sons Limited

PUBLISHER'S NOTE

The basis of this book was a series of articles that attracted universal attention when published in The Sunday Times weekly colour magazine between June 15 and September 21 1969.

Various changes have been made to bring the work up to date.

A

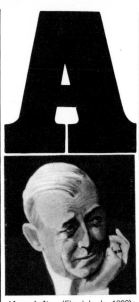

Alvar Aalto (Finnish, b. 1898): architect. Aalto has made Finland the Mecca of modern architecture, and has led the recent reaction against the technical utopias of 'functionalist' architects. He has had a profound influence as successor to Frank Lloyd Wright (q.v.) at the head of the 'humanist' or 'organic' wing of modern architecture. Although his sanatorium at Paimio (1929–33) was appropriately clinical, the library at Viipuri (1927–35) and newspaper offices at Turku (1929–30) already showed Aalto's poetic, freely flowing response to nature; so did his bentwood furniture for Finmar. In his postwar maturity, he has normally clothed his buildings with a warm red-brown skin of brick, copper and timber to harmonise with Finland's landscape and climate, within which he hides the air-conditioned womb of his synthetically furnished and tightly planned interiors. His major works in Helsinki include the Rautatalo office block (1952–4) with its indoor piazza of shops; the National Pensions Institute (1952–6), which was the canonical work of 'high density, low rise' layout; the House of Culture (1955–8); the Enso-Gutzeit offices (1959-62); the technical university at Otaniemi (1950–64); and the civic centre and opera house (designed 1964–8). Important works elsewhere are the town hall at Säynätsalo (1950–2), a delectable brick and timber piazza in a forest clearing; the church at Imatra (1956–8); flats at Bremen (1958–62); and the cultural centre for Volkswagen at Wolfsburg (1958–64). **N. J. W. T.**

'ALVAR AALTO', BY FREDERICK GUTHEIM (MAYFLOWER, 1960); 'GUIDE TO FINNISH ARCHITECTURE', BY J. M. RICHARDS (HUGH EVELYN, 1966).

King Abdullah of Jordan (1882–1951). The founder of modern Jordan was a member of the Hashimite family which had ruled Mecca under Ottoman suzerainty. He took part in the 'Arab revolt' led by his father King Hussein during the First World War, and as part of the post-war settlement became Amir (prince) of Transjordan under British Mandate, and later king when the country was granted independence. After the Arab-Israeli war of 1948, he incorporated part of Palestine into his kingdom which took the name 'Jordan'. A man of charm and traditional culture, he was more highly thought of by those of similar culture, by the Bedouin, and by the British, than by the educated Palestinians who from this time on formed a large section of his subjects. They and other Arabs criticised him for being too pro-British, for being willing to make too many concessions to Israel, and for not taking the Palestinian element into full partnership; he was assassinated by a Palestinian in 1951. But at least he created a political and administrative structure which gave Transjordan and the Arab part of Palestine a certain stability and a framework for economic development from 1948 to 1967; whether it will survive much longer the next few years may show. **H. H. A.**

'MEMOIRS' BY ABDULLAH, KING OF TRANS-JORDAN, ED. P. P. GRAVES (JONATHAN CAPE, 1950); 'JORDAN', BY A. DEARDEN (ROBERT HALE, 1958); 'A CRACKLE OF THORNS', BY SIR ALEC KIRKBRIDE (JOHN MURRAY, 1956).

Dean Acheson (U.S., b. 1893): statesman. Acheson personified the twin American policies of the mid-20th century: the Atlantic alliance and the containment of Communism. The son of an Episcopalian New England bishop and educated at Groton, Yale and the Harvard Law School, he was an upper-crust American if ever there was one. He publicly advocated American aid for Britain in 1940 and assisted the destroyer-bases deal. As Assistant Secretary of State from 1941 to 1946, and Under Secretary of State from 1945 to 1947, he accused the Soviet Union of retarding "the international pursuit of happiness", but proposed United Nations control of atomic energy. In 1949 he became 49th U.S. Secretary of State, just in time to be midwife to the North Atlantic Treaty Organisation (Nato). He explained that only a "colossal commitment" of American armies could have prevented the victory of Mao Tse-tung (q.v.) in China, but was second only to President Truman (q.v.) in responsibility for involving America in the Korean War. He was bitterly attacked as pro-Communist by Joseph R. McCarthy (q.v.) in his anti-Red campaign. He supported the first European steps towards the Common Market. **H. C. A.**

'THE CRUCIAL DECADE: AMERICA 1945–1955', BY E. F. GOLDMAN (KNOPF, NEW YORK 1956); 'AMERICAN FOREIGN POLICY SINCE WORLD WAR II', BY J. W. SPANIER (PRAEGER, NEW YORK, 1960); 'THE PATTERN OF RESPONSIBILITY', ED. MCGEORGE BUNDY (HOUGHTON MIFFLIN, BOSTON, 1952).

EDDA KOCHL

Christopher Addison, later Lord Addison (British, 1869–1951): politician. Addison, who initiated State-subsidised council housing in Britain, was originally a brilliant medical student, the discoverer of the 'Addison plane' (a reference point in anatomy) and Professor of Anatomy at Sheffield by the age of 27. Appalled by squalid East End conditions (he once delivered a mother who said, "Thanks, doctor, I'm afraid I can't do anything in return, but my sister will be glad to oblige you any time you like''), he turned to Liberal politics, and entered Parliament in 1910 at the height of the Liberal proto-Welfare State programme. He headed three of the key ministries which represented the new responsibilities undertaken by the State under stress of war: Munitions (1916), Reconstruction (1917), Health (1919). Addison's Housing Act (1919) for the first time directed State subsidies towards housing for the working classes. He was sacrificed by Lloyd George to placate the Tories, and joined the Labour Party. In the 1930s he entered the Lords and became leader there – ''a tiny atoll in the vast ocean of Tory reaction'' – during the critical period of Labour's Welfare State legislation after 1945. Addison harnessed medical knowledge, political finesse, and appreciation of the social potential of State action to further the building of the Welfare State. **A. M.**

'VISCOUNT ADDISON, LEADER OF THE LORDS', BY R. J. MINNEY (ODHAMS, 1958).

Konrad Adenauer (German, 1876–1967): statesman. There is an element of real romance in Chancellor Adenauer's political career. At the age of 69 he was still only a municipal official, the Chief Mayor of Cologne, his native city. He was summarily dismissed by a British brigadier in October 1945, and so returned to party politics, in which he had played an unexciting role before the Nazis seized power. Pure chance led to his becoming the candidate of the Christian Democratic Union, the post-1945 centre party which he helped to found, for the Chancellorship of the Federal German Republic. He was elected Chancellor by a majority of a single vote, his own, in September 1949. He held the post for the next 14 years, winning back full sovereignty for West Germany by stages. He brought his country into Western Europe – into the Common Market and Nato – and gave his people real friends and allies for the first time since Bismarck's day. He presided over economic recovery and the consolidation of democratic rule, and regarded as his own crowning success the signing of the Franco-German Treaty of Friendship in 1963, which formally ended a hundred years of bitter rivalry. He believed in the rule of law and a civilised way of life. His own loves were roses, Rhineland sunsets, good wine, a multitudinous family. His chief assets were a Roman clarity of mind and sense of logic. Sometimes impatient, even wilful, disliking opposition, his main achievements were to give a defeated nation hope for the future and help pave the way for a united Europe. **T. C. F. P.**

'KONRAD ADENAUER', BY PAUL WEYMAR (ANDRE DEUTSCH, 1957); 'GERMANY DIVIDED', BY TERENCE PRITTIE (HUTCHINSON, 1961); 'THE UNQUIET GERMANS', BY CHARLES THAYER (JOSEPH, 1958); 'MEMOIRS, VOL I', BY KONRAD ADENAUER (WEIDENFELD AND NICOLSON, 1966; VOL II DUE SOON).

Alfred Adler (Austrian, 1870–1937): psychiatrist. Adler was an early follower of Freud (q.v.) but his views were too far removed to be tolerated by Freud's Wednesday evening discussion circle. Adler broke away to found his own discipline – Individual Psychology. Adler's emphasis was on the world as the person saw it and his habitual reaction to it, or Life Style, rather than on the drives or the traces of past experience that Freud and Jung (q.v.) emphasised. The Inferiority Complex – Adler's most famous idea – is in his view the result of a person's attempts to compen-

sate for a perception of his inferiority. This perception can arise from a physical 'defect', e.g. being very short, like Napoleon, or from the natural dependent relationship of the child where the child feels overshadowed by the parents. It is perhaps ironic that Adler, who as a child suffered from rickets, and felt inferior to his elder brother, has also been overshadowed by Freud in the 20th century. He has, however, made a major contribution in the field of education, where his emphasis on the child's perception of the world has led to schools becoming more child-centred. **B. R. O.**

'ALFRED ADLER', BY L. WAY (PENGUIN BOOKS, 1956).

Lord Adrian (British, b. 1889): neurophysiologist. One of the great students of the nervous system, Edgar Adrian did pioneering work in the 1920s and 1930s which forms part of the basis of modern neurophysiology. He developed the then relatively crude techniques for recording the electrical activity in nerve fibres and was thus able to demonstrate how nerves respond to changes in stimulation. This led him to the fundamental discovery that a nerve transmits information about the intensity of a stimulus by frequency modulation. That is, as the intensity of stimulus increases, the number of discharges ('spikes') per second in the nerve also increases: the amplitude of the spikes remains the same. His later work, especially into the effect of drugs and other stimuli on the electrical rhythms of the brain, was also of extreme importance. He was Master of Trinity from 1951 to 1965, and is now Chancellor of Cambridge University. All students of the nervous system owe Adrian an enormous debt, but perhaps his establishment of the 'frequency code' was his greatest achievement. **J. B. M.**

'THE PHYSICAL BACKGROUND OF PERCEPTION', BY LORD ADRIAN (REVISED EDITION, O.U.P., 1967).

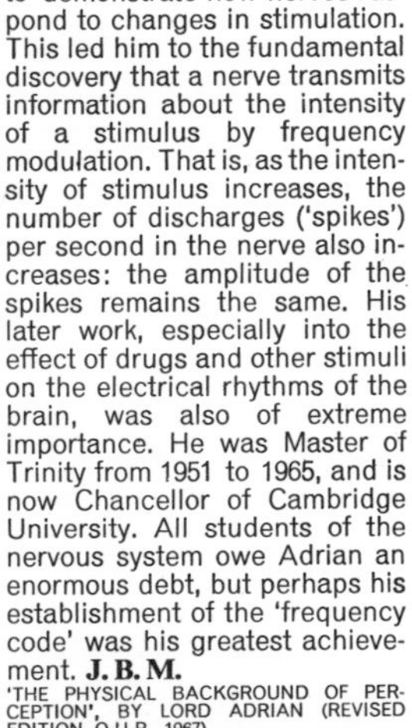

The Aga Khan (Indian, 1877–1957): religious leader. Hereditary chief of the Nizari branch of the Ismailis, Mohammed Shah Aga Khan was the Imam whom 20 million Muslims in Africa and Asia acknowledged as the legitimate heir of the authority of the prophet Mohammed. He played a part in Indian politics, as a Muslim leader, and Indian representative at the League of Nations, but he had no independent base from which to operate in an age of mass-politics. More lasting was his work for the education, social welfare and prosperity of his own community, not only in India and Pakistan but scattered throughout East Africa. He was, however, best known to the British public as a great figure in cosmopolitan society and a successful owner of racehorses, who weighed himself against a million pounds' worth of diamonds to celebrate the 60th anniversary of his Imamate. His *Memoirs* reveal a curious but attractive personality: with frank enjoyment of the good things of life there went a wide appreciation of the arts, a shrewd but charitable understanding of human beings, and a mystical interpretation of Islam. **A. H. H.**

'MEMOIRS OF AGA KHAN' (CASSELL, 1954).

Giovanni Agnelli (Italian, 1866–1945): motor manufacturer. In 1899, Agnelli became first secretary of the Fiat motor company (Fabbrica Italiana Automobili Torino) formed by a group of rich Italian enthusiasts to stand up to the menace of the nascent French car industry. Most of his fellow enthusiasts were interested in experimenting with wild, race-winning innovations, but Agnelli was already thinking in terms of thousands of cars coming off a mass-production line. As the others fell away, he laid the founda-

tions for what is now Italy's biggest industrial complex by far, turning Turin into what is still the biggest company town in Europe. Under his autocratic hand Fiat came to dominate motor manufacture, and dig itself into every form of heavy industry from dams and ball-bearings to naval ships and aeroplanes. He became a senator in 1923, and in 1932 went to Russia, to set up two vast factories for bearings and castings: a visit which finally paid off a few years ago when Fiat were chosen to build up, virtually single-handed, the Soviet Union's passenger car industry. **P. W.**

Howard Aiken (U.S., b. 1900): mathematician. The work of Aiken – "a simple man seeking simple answers", as he describes himself – has contributed a major part to one of the most vital technological advances of all time, the invention of the computer. In 1937 Aiken began work at Harvard on his Ph.D. in physics. Frustrated by seemingly endless complex mathematical calculations Aiken considered the possibility of carrying out such computations by machine, concluding that it was feasible for one general-purpose device to solve any number of mathematical problems. International Business Machines provided a team of engineers to assist him and work on the first computer – the Automatic Sequence Controlled Calculator, Mark I. An electro-mechanical device, it was designed to perform computations by following automatically a sequence of programmed instructions. Though the machine was rapidly superseded by a more sophisticated model, it featured many characteristics of today's equipment (including time sharing, whereby several users process information simultaneously). It operated for more than 15 years at Harvard, turning out mathematical tables still in use. Aiken, at 69, is now vice-chairman of Aiken Industries. **J. W. F.**

'THE ANALYTICAL ENGINE', BY JEREMY BERNSTEIN (SECKER AND WARBURG, 1965).

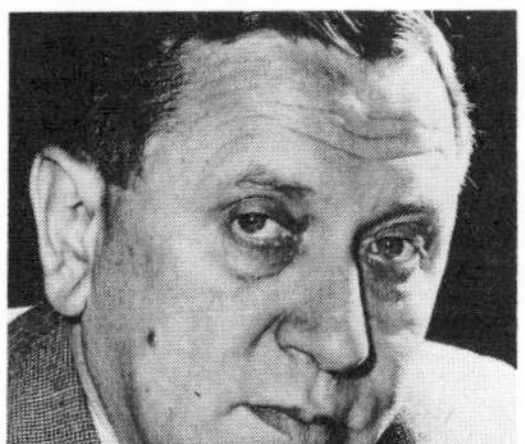

Kurt Alder (German, 1902–1958): organic chemist. Kurt Alder laid the foundation for many plastics and synthetic substances that are now so much a part of everyday life that it is almost impossible to imagine that man ever managed without them. For many years the great complexity and variety with which carbon atoms are joined together in natural substances from plants and animals had foiled chemists in their attempts to duplicate the products and processes of nature. With the 'diene' synthesis, Kurt Alder and Otto Diels (q.v.) opened the way to the simple and economical synthesis of a great many natural materials such as camphor and cantharidin, and Vitamin K substitutes. The theory behind the diene synthesis also opened up routes to the synthesis of giant molecules and thus formed one basis of the plastics industry. In the 1930s, Alder did fundamental work on the constitution and preparation of synthetic 'Buna' rubber for I. G. Farbenindustrie. **M. A. S.**

'NOBEL PRIZEWINNERS IN CHEMISTRY', BY EDUARD FARBER (REVISED EDITION, ABELARD-SCHUMAN, 1963); 'NOBEL LECTURES, CHEMISTRY 1942–62' (ELSEVIER, 1964); 'ORGANIC CHEMISTRY', BY DONALD J. CRAM AND GEORGE S. HAMMOND (McGRAW-HILL, 1959).

Field Marshal Earl Alexander of Tunis (British, 1891–1969): soldier and governor-general. At midnight on June 2, 1940, Major-General Alexander, who was later to defeat Mussolini (q.v.), satisfied himself by small boat that "no one was left behind at Dunkirk". It was Alexander's early fate to be appointed to campaigns *in extremis:* First World War at Mons; Dunkirk, succeeded by the retreat from Burma; Cairo and an army driven by Rommel from Cyrenaica. Some men emerge from unmerited adversity with an aura of defeat. Alexander's aura was the assurance of ultimate victory. At Alam Halfa Rommel was held again; at Alamein Montgomery broke him; at Tunis Alexander then eliminated the Axis armies of North

Africa. The conquest of Sicily followed. Militarily these things are vital, yet Alexander's place in history was secured by a political decision in distant Rome 15 days after the Sicilian landing, when the Fascist Grand Council, driven to despair by the endless succession of defeats, voted the deposition of Mussolini. Even the long bleeding of the German Army in Italy is irrelevant beside the historic fact that victory in Sicily shattered the first Fascist dictatorship and set a precedent for the West. Against the vacillations of the policy-makers, starved of amphibious craft, always short of manpower, he triumphed. It has been given to other generals to take Rome, as Alexander took it. It has been given to few men to extirpate a tyranny. **D. D.**

'THE ALEXANDER MEMOIRS', ED. JOHN NORTH (CASSELL, 1962); 'THE ITALIAN CAMPAIGN, 1943-45', BY G. A. SHEPPERD (ARTHUR BARKER, 1968); 'THE CAMPAIGN IN ITALY', BY ERIC LINKLATER (H.M.S.O., 1951).

Muhammad Ali (U.S., b. 1942): boxer. Cassius Clay was born in Louisville, Kentucky, where the famous baseball bat, the Louisville Slugger, comes from; they called Clay the Louisville Lip because he was a big sassy-talking black man and they like their black men soft-spoken down there, and in the fight world, too. He was Olympic light-heavyweight champion in 1960, took Sonny Liston's professional world heavyweight title in 1964, then K.O.-ed Liston in round one in 1965. Clay was angry owning a slave-owner's name, so he picked a new one: Muhammad Ali, a Black Muslim name. He was rubbing something in. He was hot, and the white men like their black men cool. He stopped Floyd Patterson in round 12, November 1965; outpointed George Chuvalo in March 1966; in May stopped Henry Cooper in the sixth; in August, K.O.-ed Brian London in the third; in September, stopped Karl Mildenberger in the twelfth; in November, stopped Cleveland Williams in the third. "A bum a month," Ali said. But he *would* keep calling white men devils; Vietnam was a white devils' war. In 1967 they took his title away because he would not serve his country. By the time he was allowed back into the ring, Ali had lost his twinkle-toed speed, and his successor, the bulldozing Joe Frazier, was too strong. **S. A. R.**

'AUTOBIOGRAPHY OF MALCOLM X' (PENGUIN, 1968); 'BLACK BOY', BY RICHARD WRIGHT (HARPER AND ROW, 1968); 'CASSIUS CLAY', BY JACK OLSEN (PELHAM BOOKS, 1967).

Roald Amundsen (Norwegian, 1872–1928): explorer. Amundsen was the first man to get to the South Pole, and is chiefly renowned in this country as the person who beat Scott (q.v.) to it. There has even been some sort of a hero/villain myth established, with Amundsen as the ruthless professional and Scott as the unsuccessful gentleman. Apart from this major achievement he led an adventurous life. In 1903 he planned to conquer the Northwest Passage, and sailed secretly with a crew of six to evade his creditors. He completed his mission successfully. In 1910 he left Norway, ostensibly for the North Pole. Only his brother knew that his real object was the Antarctic. He established a base 60 miles nearer the Pole than Scott and completed the final stage with dogs and with four companions. He later made various unsuccessful journeys in the Arctic. Finally, in 1926, together with Umberto Nobile, the Italian aviator, he crossed from Spitzbergen to Alaska in the dirigible Norge. There were disputes later about who should take the real credit. Even so it was in search of General Nobile, who had crashed in the Italia, that Amundsen lost his life. His plane was lost in the Arctic Ocean. **A. C. C.**

'AMUNDSEN', BY B. PARTRIDGE (HALE, 1953); 'ROALD AMUNDSEN, EXPLORER', BY C. TURLEY (METHUEN, 1935).

Lale Andersen (German, b. 1911): singer. Not a great singer – but she achieved the summit because she sang *Lilli Marlene,* the first and probably last genuinely 'international' war song hit. *Lilli* was also perhaps the luckiest hit song ever, for though its words were written in 1917 (by Hans Liep) and its melody in 1937 (by Norbert Schultze) it was not 'discovered' until the Germans were looking for records to beam over Radio Belgrade to Rommel's *Panzerarmee Afrika* in 1941. In the period 1941–44 some German stations were playing it 30 times a day. The 8th Army picked it up to make it *their* song, and so did every Allied nation in due course. Translated into 42 languages as well as innumerable ditty versions, this private little love song brought Lale around a million fan letters; but she had a shaky wartime career because Goebbels (q.v.) hated the song's sentiments and Lale (who had Jewish friends) was under Gestapo watch. Her post-war career was modestly successful. A film based on the song and featuring her was made in 1952 and in 1960 her *Never on Sunday* disc sold 800,000 copies. **D. J.**

'ALAMEIN AND THE DESERT WAR', ED. DEREK JEWELL (SPHERE, 1967).

Gabriele d'Annunzio (Italian, 1863–1938): poet. The most romantic figure of his day, d'Annunzio's vast output of poetry, drama and novels, though now scorned, was remarkable for rich diction, gorgeous imagery, and a sensualism that often tipped over into the morbid. In private life he was an unrestrained egoist, who brutally exploited his friends; his florid and rhetorical behaviour matched his writing. As a professional dilettante of the sensational and a self-styled Nietzschean superman, he took everything to extremes. He sat in the Italian parliament alternately on the extreme right and the extreme left, but felt out of place in between. For a while he lived in France to escape his debts, but in 1915 was summoned back by the Italian warparty to help push his country into the First World War. As a soldier, he served successively with the cavalry, the infantry, the navy and the air force, col-

lecting many medals (though he complained he should have had many more). In 1919–20 he ruled as dictator of Fiume, an independent state which he constructed as part of his plan for Italian dominance in the Adriatic, and this melodramatic example of international lawlessness made him a precursor of Fascism. He has been called the choreographer of the March on Rome in 1922, but he was too jealous of Mussolini (q.v.) to be a Fascist himself. **D. M. S.**

'THE POET AS SUPERMAN: A LIFE OF GABRIELE D'ANNUNZIO', BY ANTHONY RHODES (WEIDENFELD AND NICOLSON, 1959); 'D'ANNUNZIO', BY TOM ANTONGINI (HEINEMANN, 1933).

Jacques Anquetil (French, b. 1934): cyclist. By 1956 two riders had scored three wins in the Tour de France (founded 1903). Then came Jacques Anquetil, son of a Normandy strawberry grower. In 1964 he won the 2750-mile race for the fifth time, the last four in succession. Anquetil had not discovered a new way to cycle faster, just how to sustain speed over a distance. He has won few important one-day 'massed start' races, has never been world champion, but has rarely been beaten on his own against the stop-watch. He won nine Grands Prix des Nations time trials in nine attempts. This unpaced pedalling power explains Anquetil's domination of the Tour de France, whose winner is the man with the lowest total riding time. Before a Tour started he would calculate how many minutes he could afford to lose on mountain stages and then win it back – with enough over to give final victory – in time trial tests. Similar tactics won him two Tours of Italy and one Tour of Spain. In a group of racing cyclists Jacques Anquetil was consistently very good; on his own 'against the watch' he was, at his best, supreme. **J. B. W.**

'THE TOUR DE FRANCE', BY PETER CLIFFORD (STANLEY PAUL, 1965).

Michelangelo Antonioni (Italian, b. 1912): film director. Antonioni is as significant and central a figure to cinema as was Henry James to the novel, sharing James's acute and unnostalgic

awareness of a disturbed moral equilibrium and his scrupulous elaborations of style. He has yet, perhaps, to make his *Golden Bowl,* but his first feature film, *Cronaca di un· Amore,* in 1950, instantly marked him out as a director able to construct the most closely woven, novelistic sentences with a camera, a fastidious stylist, fascinated by themes of guilt, betrayal and moral ambiguity. The wildly controversial Cannes Festival screening of *L'Avventura* (1960) shot him to the top of the shaky international pyramid, as the film-maker who tracked alienated man through the most precise cinematic architecture, backed him against the whitest walls, the master-builder of contemporary *angst*. Antonioni has since made *La Notte*; his masterpiece *The Eclipse*; *The Red Desert*, with a landscape painted in the colours of neurosis; *Blow Up* (in London); and *Zabriskie Point* (in Death Valley). He has been endlessly imitated, chiefly for a particular style of placing figures in a landscape; and has made his central themes "the analysis of the sentiments", the gap in our society between technological advance and emotional paralysis, temperament in terms of environment. **P. H.**

'ANTONIONI', BY IAN CAMERON AND ROBIN WOOD (STUDIO VISTA, 1969); 'THE SCREENPLAYS OF MICHELANGELO ANTONIONI', (SOUVENIR PRESS, 1963); 'MICHELANGELO ANTONIONI', BY PIERRE LEPROHON (SIMON AND SCHUSTER, NEW YORK, 1963).

Guillaume Apollinaire (Polish-Italian, 1880–1918): poet, playwright, novelist, critic. Apollinaire, who was born Kostrowitzky in Rome but lived in France and wrote in French, was an innovator and prophet whose influence runs like quicksilver through the veins of the modern movement in literature. A mixture of personal legend and highly original poetic achievement (*Alcools,* 1913, and *Calligrammes,* 1918) leaves no doubt about his impact. He champions the Cubist painters, writes *Les Mamelles de Tirésias* as a "surrealist drama", composes a futurist manifesto for Marinetti, lectures on Poets and the New Spirit, praises Negro sculpture, Diaghilev and Chagall. At the still centre of this publicistic flurry is not only the poet of no punctuation but also of a traditionally French melancholy lyricism of love and war, of "grey silhouettes vanishing in the fog". His calligrams have taken on a new interest in the days of visual poetry. But his central importance to our century lies in his conception of a light, swift, truthful yet always surprising art which could lay together the incongruities of the world – rose, newspaper, aeroplane, burst tyre, "a hand digging into a pocket". **E. G. M.**

'APOLLINAIRE', BY MARGARET DAVIES (OLIVER AND BOYD, 1964); 'APOLLINAIRE', BY FRANCIS STEEGMULLER (HART-DAVIS, 1964); 'THE BANQUET YEARS', BY ROGER SHATTUCK (1958, REVISED ED. CAPE 1969).

Sir Edward Appleton (British, 1892–1965): physicist. Appleton was the discoverer of the layers of charged particles in the upper atmosphere of the Earth now called the ionosphere, which play a vital role in telecommunications as the 'mirror' from which long-distance radio signals are reflected. In 1924, with the aid of the BBC, he proved the existence of the first ionospheric reflecting layer by bouncing radio waves off it – which was the first application of radar. Appleton measured the height of this layer as 60 miles. In 1926, during a 12-year period at London University, he discovered a second, electrically stronger layer, now known as the Appleton· Layer, at a height of 150 miles. This layer reflects short radio waves. He later recorded the radio echoes on a cathode-ray oscilloscope, thus paving the way for the invention of the basic techniques of radar for aircraft detection developed during the Second World War. He received the Nobel Prize in 1947. His work has had great consequences both for radio communications and in laying the groundwork for the development of radar. **P. H. S. S.**

'NOBEL LECTURES IN PHYSICS 1942-1962' (ELSEVIER, 1965).

Elizabeth Arden (U.S. 1884–1966): beauty expert and cosmetics magnate. Elizabeth Arden, brought up in Canada but later a U.S. citizen, was the personification of the American career woman. Her only other interest was horse racing. She trained as a nurse but switched to beauty, opening her first salon in New York in 1912. Her first preparations were a small range of creams and lotions; at her death she was head of an empire manufacturing 450 preparations (in 1500 different shades) selling all. over the world. The British company alone sells to 80 countries. Her business was built on a theory of hygiene; exercise, diet, massage and good posture were essential to beauty and beauty preparations must be pure. She herself rose early, ate lightly and worked at a frenetic tempo. She took a highhanded attitude with her staff and did not like her managers to marry without her permission. Her real name was Florence Nightingale Graham; she was twice married and had· no children. Elizabeth Arden was a pioneer in an industry which was backward and insanitary when she entered it, and prosperous, modern and a real contribution to human happiness when she died. **A. S.-J.**

Louis Armstrong (U.S. 1900–1971): musician and singer. Louis Armstrong determined practically single-handed the course of jazz for three decades. Born in New Orleans, he was a professional musician by his mid-

teens and joined King Oliver's (q.v.) band in Chicago in ,1922. Joining Fletcher Henderson in 1924, he imbued a cumbersome dance band with jazz style. He returned to Chicago in 1925, and during multifarious club and theatre dates the Armstrong Hot Five and Seven made recordings which revolutionised jazz, bursting the limits of the New Orleans ensemble. His trumpet on *Cornet Chop Suey* (1926), *Potato Head Blues* (1927) and *West End Blues* (1928) were the jazz equivalent of breaking the sound barrier. In the 1930s he fronted big bands, applied his soaring imagination to 'concerto-style' improvisation and burnished his singing into a perfect vocal reflection of his trumpet-style. Even in his last years he retained incomparable beauty of tone and conception. **H. R. A. L.**

'SATCHMO – MY LIFE IN NEW ORLEANS', BY LOUIS ARMSTRONG (PETER DAVIES, 1955). RECORDS: LOUIS ARMSTRONG PLAYS W. C. HANDY (CBS REALM, M.52067); IN THE 30S, IN THE 40S (RCA VICTOR, RD. 7706); HIS GREATEST YEARS, VOLS. 1, 2 3, AND 4 (PARLOPHONE, PMC 1140, 1142, 1146 AND 1150).

Jean Arp (French, ex-German, 1886–1966): poet and artist. Wherever the terra incognita of art was being explored – in Zurich, Munich, Berlin, Paris – Arp was on hand as a pioneer among pioneers. Born in Strasbourg, he was a man without national prejudice who played with form, and played with language, and played with the physical materials of art, and came up in each case with something that was 20, 30 or even 40 years ahead of its time. By 1915 he was producing pictures which, like those of the 1960s, were, in his words, "their own reality, without 'meaning' or intellectual intention". He pioneered the principle of chance in art, perfected his own brand of concrete poetry, sponsored the notion of an expendable art, was in the thick of both Dada and Surrealism, and in middle life embarked on the free-standing sculptures which eventually brought him both fame and fortune. In these he continually invented forms that suggested, but did not describe, the whole range of Nature, from the hip-line of a beautiful woman to the snow-clouds that he had watched when he lived beneath the Rigi. A man of angelic nature, to whom vanity and rivalry were abhorrent, Arp had no enemies. **J. R.**

'ARP', BY HERBERT READ (THAMES AND HUDSON, 1968); 'JEAN ARP', BY CAROLA GIEDION-WELCKER (THAMES AND HUDSON, 1957).

Antonin Artaud (French, 1896–1948): theatrical director. The influence of Artaud on the modern theatre is inferior only to that of Brecht and Stanislavsky. Artaud was the originator of the Theatre of Cruelty which

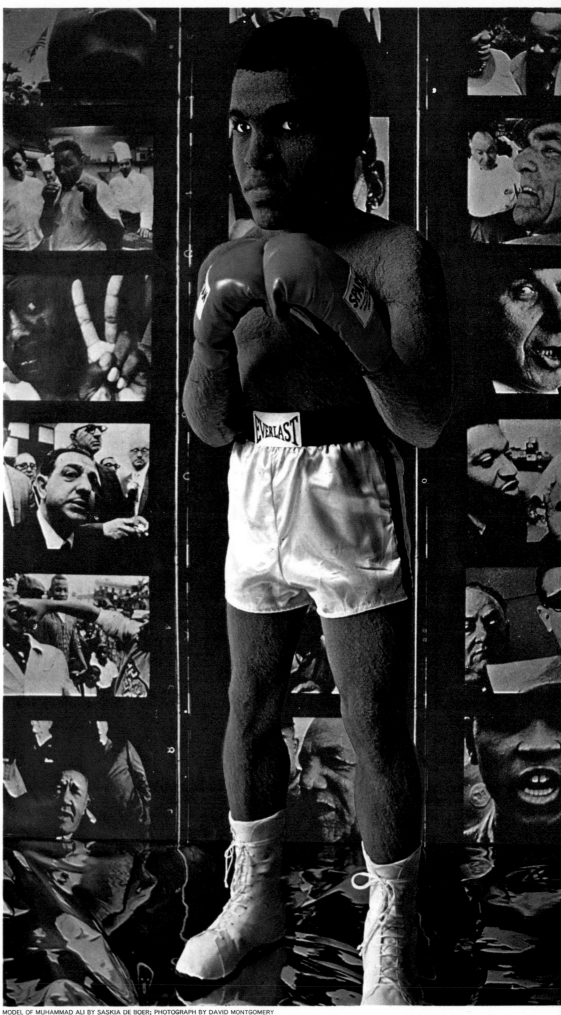

MODEL OF MUHAMMAD ALI BY SASKIA DE BOER; PHOTOGRAPH BY DAVID MONTGOMERY

has played a large part in contemporary British theatre, though in its own day it had little effect. Artaud demanded a theatre of screams, shrieks, violent physical gestures and sharp movements in which words, especially words placed in a rational order, played only a small part. The object of the Theatre of Cruelty as Artaud saw it was to release the unconscious feelings which people usually hold in check. Despite its name, it had little to do with the actual infliction of pain. While Artaud was alive it made scarcely any impression on his fellow-workers in the theatre. This was because he invented it chiefly to publicise his own play, *The Cenci*, which was a wretched failure. He did not succeed in giving it a wider connotation, and it would have been forgotten had not Peter Brook (q.v.) rescued it from oblivion, particularly in his production of Weiss's *Marat/Sade*, since when it has become a principal talking point of Western theatre. In 1936 Artaud went mad and was confined in a lunatic asylum until the end of the Second World War. **H. H.**

'NEW TRENDS IN TWENTIETH CENTURY DRAMA', BY FREDERICK LUMLEY (OXFORD UNIVERSITY PRESS, 1967); 'THE THEORY OF THE MODERN STAGE', BY ANTONIN ARTAUD, ED. ERIC BENTLEY (PENGUIN, 1968).

Herbert Henry Asquith (British, 1852–1928): politician. Asquith's political career spans the rise and fall of the post-Gladstonian Liberal Party. Born of Congregationalist parents in Yorkshire, he made his way to Balliol and Lincolns Inn. He developed a front-bench style almost from the moment he entered Parliament in 1886, was Home Secretary from 1892-5, Chancellor of the Exchequer from 1905-8 and Prime Minister from 1908-16. In the years just before 1914 he had to confront every kind of political problem and every style of political opposition. To his admirers he was like Pitt the Younger, "the captain who weathered the storm at home". But he did not weather the storm of the First World War, lost office in 1916 and his seat in the Commons in 1918. Lloyd George rose while Asquith fell, and the Liberal Party was broken in the process. Asquith briefly resumed its leadership in the 1920s when it seemed almost past restoration. "The last of the Romans", he received a peerage in 1925 and in the same year was rejected as Chancellor of Oxford University. His qualities best emerge in contrast. "He has no egotism, no jealousy and no vanity," it was claimed by a friend, but he lacked Lloyd George's genius. **A. B.**

'ASQUITH', BY ROY JENKINS (COLLINS, 1964); 'THE DOWNFALL OF THE LIBERAL PARTY', BY T. WILSON (COLLINS, 1966).

Fred Astaire (U.S., b. 1899): film actor. Fred Aslaire (born Frederick Austerlitz in Nebraska) revolutionised the making of screen musicals. Before his advent dancers were photographed 'in pieces': their feet, heads,

and torsos were fitted together in the cutting room. To preserve the line and logic of his dance, Astaire was filmed full-figure, which required lengthy rehearsals before shooting began. He plotted his routines, step by step, taking up to three months, with eight to 10 hours' rehearsal a day, before the blueprint was complete; he was a perfectionist, whose gloss was enlivened by what James Cagney (q.v.) admiringly called "a touch of the hoodlum". His first stage appearance, at five, with his sister Adèle, was appropriately in white tie and tails. Stage shows in the same tradition, such as *Stop Flirting* brought them to London in the 1920s where they adorned the Prince of Wales's set. But after 1933 the cameras revealed something more rakish in Astaire. His films with Ginger Rogers now seem tuneful but over-ornate trifles. But in *Easter*

Parade (with Judy Garland) and *The Band Wagon* (with Cyd Charisse – arguably the best of his screen partners) his style was sharp, sardonic, and impudently true to much tougher material. Astaire has appeared as a straight actor, notably as a scientist awaiting the end of the world in Stanley Kramer's *On the Beach*. But, for once, the prize-givers had the right idea when, in 1949, Astaire was presented with a Special Academy Award "for raising the standards of all musicals". **P. O.**

'STEPS IN TIME', BY FRED ASTAIRE (HEINEMANN, 1960).

Francis William Aston (British, 1877–1945): chemist. Aston invented the mass spectrograph, an instrument by which the stable chemical elements can be analysed in terms of their separate isotopes. Isotopes are varieties of the same element having the same chemical properties but different atomic masses – for example, uranium-235 and uranium-238 which have to be separated to make nuclear fuel or nuclear weapons. Aston, working with J. J. Thomson at Cambridge, set out to find if stable elements had isotopes like the known radioactive ones.

In 1919 he perfected a mass spectrograph in which isotopes were separated by an ingenious combination of electric and magnetic fields. He rapidly analysed some 50 of the 92 known elements and demonstrated that nearly all possessed isotopes. He discovered that the masses of these isotopes were not whole-number multiples of the mass of the simplest atom, hydrogen. Instead they showed a 'mass defect', accounted for (according to Einstein's famous equation $E = mc^2$) by the energy used up in binding the atomic nuclei together. For this significant development Aston was awarded the Nobel Prize for chemistry in 1922. Our understanding of isotopes is fundamental to our understanding of atomic structure. **P. H. S. S.**

'WORLD OF THE ATOM', ED. HENRY A. BOORSE AND LLOYD MOTZ, 2 VOLS (BASIC BOOKS, 1966); 'PHYSICS FOR THE ENQUIRING MIND', BY ERIC M. ROGERS (O.U.P., 1960).

Mustafa Kemal Ataturk (Turkish, 1881–1938): head of state. The founder of modern Turkey won fame as the defender of Gallipoli; he was the most successful Turkish general of the First World War. After the war he served as a leader for Turks who wished to resist Allied plans to divide and subject their country and Greek attempts to

occupy part of it. He re-made the Turkish army, defeated the Greeks, deposed the Sultan, and made a treaty with the Allies (Lausanne, 1923) which recognised the independence of his people, but in a new form: the nation-state of Turkey shorn of its Empire. He ruled it as President for the rest of his life and remoulded it. An unwavering 'westerniser', he separated state and religion, replaced Islamic by Western law, abolished the caliphate, emancipated women, and abandoned the Arabic for the Latin alphabet. He was a remarkable man, although whether he succeeded in taking Turkey out of the Middle East and inserting her in Europe it is too early to say. **A. H. H.**

'ATATURK', BY LORD KINROSS (WEIDENFELD AND NICOLSON, 1964); 'THE EMERGENCE OF MODERN TURKEY', BY B. LEWIS (O.U.P., 1964); 'TURKEY', BY G. L. LEWIS (3RD EDITION, ERNEST BENN, 1965).

Charles Atlas (U.S., b. 1893): strong man. As a seven-stone weakling Angelo Siciliano was beaten up by a thug with an ember-filled stocking. His vow that no one would ever hit him again brought hope, if not fulfilment, to the next five decades of seven-stone weaklings. Siciliano devised exercises based on the muscle-action of caged zoo animals and in 1921 was named by *Physical Culture* magazine "The World's Most Perfectly Developed Man". Then a wise copywriter named Charles Roman turned Siciliano into Charles Atlas, figurehead for a

mail-order bodybuilding empire; Roman coined legendary phrases such as "You Too Can Have a Body Like Mine!" and the enduring parable of the sunbathing weakling who has sand kicked in his face. The Atlas course, with its tedious work-outs, is issued in seven languages, reaches about 60,000 shrimps a year and is said to have helped a Peruvian Minister of War and a member of the British Royal Family not to have sand kicked in their faces. Recently the literature was still advising against "too much Jazz or Ragtime" and urging

"Banish all evil thoughts from your mind". Atlas appears in the photographs as he was decades ago; yet his frame, at 75, has not dwindled much from its peak of 47 in. chest, 32 in. waist, 17 in. neck, 17 in. biceps, $23\frac{3}{4}$ in. thighs. He lives, mostly on fruit, on Long Island. "I believe in using shapely muscles to make a better life and a better world," he says; an old philosophy when the world is dominated by peace-seeking fatties. But the runts still write in. **P. N.**

CHARLES ATLAS BROCHURE (FROM 10 CHITTY ST, LONDON W.1., OR 115 E. 23RD ST, NEW YORK).

Clement Attlee, later Earl Attlee (British, 1883–1967): statesman. Attlee was Deputy Prime Minister for five years during the Second World War (1941–5) and Prime Minister for six years afterwards (1945–51) – 11 consecutive years of exceptional strain. For 20 years he led one of the two great parties. No-one since Gladstone has equalled either record. He became Leader through an accident: the Labour Party crash of 1931. But once in control he beat off any attempts to unseat him. He was very much master of his own Cabinet. He is referred to, rightly, as the perfect chairman. More than any other Prime Minister he liked to work through leading colleagues and, except in a few chosen fields, left the initiatives to others. It is impossible, therefore, to disentangle his personal achievement in the British reconstruction after the war from that of his Party or Government. His patriotism, his caution, his respect for a wide variety of traditions, his devotion to national defence, determined the tone of his administration, in conjunction with his life-long concern for social justice and inflexible determination to give effect to the Labour Party programme. No-one could have presided over a social revolution and caused so little alarm. His name will always be especially associated with the liberation of India (1947), but the whole advance from Empire to Commonwealth owed almost as much to him. In his last years, to the surprise of many who thought they knew his limits, he dedicated himself to the cause of World Government. He remarked that if he was starting in politics at that time he would concentrate on nuclear disarmament. He remained as interested in youth as when he first began his social work in the East End of London. **L.**

'MR. ATTLEE', BY ROY JENKINS (HEINE-MANN, 1948); 'AS IT HAPPENED', BY EARL ATTLEE (HEINEMANN, 1954).

Wystan Hugh Auden (British, b. 1907): poet. After Eliot, the most important English poet between the world wars. His range of output and technical versatility is unparalleled, from grand opera and large-scale allegories to the fragile lyric or risqué limerick. Without any sacrifice of intelligence, Auden restored to poetry the honest dignity of variety, copiousness and the native vigour of traditional forms. His early poetry makes ironical use of Old English epic stoicism to underline the emotional insecurity of the matriarchal middle classes. His search for a key to the individual's unhappiness led him first to D. H. Lawrence (q.v.) and to psychologists like Homer Lane and W. H. Rivers; later (believing that humanism has no resources against a Hitler) to theologians like Kierkegaard and Reinhold Niebuhr. The major long poems of the 1940s are ambitious analyses of human weakness, ornate, dramatic and with beautifully controlled feeling. His greatest influence is a stylistic one, which has always transcended the boundaries of ideology; he is a master of observation and concise metaphor, and a master too of the assurance of tone that comes with a gravity of moral perspective. **J. L. F.**

'THE POETRY OF W. H. AUDEN', BY M. K. SPEARS (O.U.P., 1963); 'A READER'S GUIDE TO W. H. AUDEN', BY JOHN FULLER (THAMES AND HUDSON, 1969).

John Langshaw Austin (British, 1911–1960): philosopher. Between 1945 and 1960 Austin was the unquestioned leader of the school of ordinary language philosophers which dominated Oxford in this period and was the liveliest movement in technical philosophy in the English-speaking world. The main characteristics of the school are present in Austin's work to a very pronounced degree: lovingly exact fidelity to the details of the ordinary use of language and a piercingly common-sense scepticism about the speculative generalities of all kinds of previous philosophy. Austin, like Wittgenstein (q.v.), held that most of the more striking claims of the philosophy of the past were unfounded, being the outcome of insidiously attractive misunderstandings of the meaning of words. What was peculiar to him was the brilliant delicacy of his unravelling of the actual meaning of philosophically crucial terms and the fine deflationary wit with which he carried it out. His two main books, both posthumous, are *Sense And Sensibilia,* in which he showed the insubstantial foundations of the view, held by most previous philosophers, that material things are never the immediate objects of perception, and *How To Do Things With Words,* in which an apparatus is developed for distinguishing the many different ways in which, and the purposes for which, language is employed. Criticised for linguistic conservatism and too microscopic an approach, Austin has nevertheless bequeathed something of his caution and exactness to the many philosophers influenced by him. **A. Q.**

'SYMPOSIUM ON J. L. AUSTIN', ED. K. T. FANN (ROUTLEDGE, 1969); 'SENSE AND SENSIBILIA', BY J. L. AUSTIN, (O.U.P., 1964); 'PHILOSOPHICAL PAPERS', BY J. L. AUSTIN, (O.U.P., 1961); 'HOW TO DO THINGS WITH WORDS', BY J. L. AUSTIN (O.U.P., 1962).

Richard Avedon (U.S., b. 1923): fashion photographer. Uninterested in technicalities, Avedon's contribution to fashion photography has been to develop movement and action. Many of his pictures are small scenarios packed with drama. Born in Manhattan into a family of Jewish-Russian immigrants (his father owned a women's wear department store), from early childhood he kept a scrapbook of fashions and took portrait photographs. He left school at 17 to become errand-boy in a photographic concern, went into the U.S. Merchant Marine in 1942-4, and in 1945 took his collected pictures to *Harper's Bazaar,* which hired him on the spot. He remained 20 years until he left for *Vogue* on contract for a reputed million dollars. Avedon is renowned for his discovery of unusual models – many of whom he has made famous. The film *Funny Face* was based on his life and way of working. But apart from fashion, Avedon is an outstanding portraitist with an astringent style. Cutting out backgrounds, employing harsh, direct lighting, he achieves powerful – sometimes punitive – effects. In all fields of photography his aim is to plan everything. "Everything in my pictures is controlled – even the accidents." His achievement is to have exploited his immense success in fashion and advertising to subsidise his work as a portraitist – some of which is of permanent value. **T. H.**

'OBSERVATIONS', PICTURES BY RICHARD AVEDON, TEXT BY TRUMAN CAPOTE (WEIDENFELD AND NICOLSON, 1959); 'NOTHING PERSONAL', PICTURES BY RICHARD AVEDON, TEXT BY JAMES BALDWIN (ATHENAEUM, 1964).

B

Walter Baade (U.S., ex-German, 1893–1960): astronomer. Baade's discoveries increased the volume of the universe as we know it twenty-fold. He worked for 11 years at the University of Hamburg, where he discovered the planetoid (minor planet) Hidalgo. He emigrated to the United States in 1931. Taking advantage of the wartime black-out of Los Angeles, which cleared the night sky for the 100-inch telescope on Mount Wilson in California, Baade was able to resolve some of the stars in the inner region of Andromeda galaxy for the first time. He discovered that the brightest stars of the interior were not blue-white – as had previously been believed – but were reddish in colour. Baade reasoned that there were in fact two sets of stars with different structures and histories. He called the bluish (young) stars of the galactic outskirts Population I and the reddish (older) stars of the interior Population II. Later, examining the so-called Cepheid variable stars through the giant 200-inch Mount Palomar telescope, Baade found that previous calculations about the brightness – and hence distance – of Population I stars in distant galaxies had been underestimated considerably. The Andromeda galaxy, for instance, was not a mere 800,000 but 2 million light-years distant. **N. V.**

Isaak Babel (Russian, 1894–1941): author. Babel is one of the great writers of our century. He came from a poor Jewish family, and had seen pogroms as a child. He was the master of the short – the very short – story. He gives, not the enormous sweep and depth of Tolstoy or Dostoievsky, but the subtlety and humanity of Chekhov and Turgenev. But he fitted these to the new era, to the violence of the Revolution, of which he wrote: "It is eaten with gunpowder and the very best blood is poured over it." His masterpiece *Konarmiya* (Cavalry Army) is about his service with the Red Cossacks in the Civil War, an extraordinary blend of sentiment and cruelty, scepticism and tradition, violence and gentleness. As so often with Russian writers his achievement was in part a moral one. In 1934 he announced that writers would now have to practise "the heroism of silence" and he was hotly denounced for it. He was arrested in May, 1938 and by his death in March, 1941, in unknown circumstances in prison or labour camp, is perhaps the greatest single casualty of the Stalin Terror. Above all, he had carried the great Russian tradition through the fires of the new epoch. **G.R.A.C.**

'COLLECTED STORIES OF ISAAK BABEL', TR. W. MORISON (METHUEN, 1957); 'SOVIET RUSSIAN LITERATURE 1917–1950', BY GLEB STRUVE (UNIVERSITY OF OKLAHOMA PRESS, 1951).

Francis Bacon (British, b. 1909): painter. Bacon (right) has had a profound effect on the life of the imagination since 1945, when his *Three Studies for Figures at the Base of a Crucifixion* turned out to forecast and epitomise those forces in human nature which were revealed in full strength, a few weeks later, when Belsen was overrun by the Allied armies. Many later pictures which looked at first like thunder-flashes of private fancy turned out, once again, to have a universal import. It was found that many a key-figure in post-war demonology – the statesman on TV, the multiple murderer, Eichmann (q.v.) in his glass box – could already be found in Bacon's paintings, and with one skin less than their public image allowed. There were also huge set-pieces, of a multiple and ambiguous inspiration, in which Bacon brought the European 'grand manner' back into painting; and, as counter-weight to the sinister and calamitous aspect of human existence, he painted many portraits of close friends which are, in effect, metaphors for the resistance of the human personality to extreme stress. At a time when fashion ran quite the other way, Bacon thus kept alive an idea of human grandeur and, parallel to that, an idea of the enduring validity of the painted image. The fact that both ideas have the odds stacked against them is not, in Bacon's view, a reason to discontinue the game. **J. R.**

'FRANCIS BACON', BY ROTHENSTEIN AND ALLEY (THAMES AND HUDSON, 1964); 'FRANCIS BACON', BY JOHN RUSSELL (METHUEN, 1964).

ILLUSTRATION BY HOWIE KANOVITZ

Lord Baden-Powell (British, 1857–1941): founder of Scouting. "Military drill tends to destroy individuality, whereas we want, in the Scouts, to develop individual character"– Robert Baden-Powell, the founder of Scouting. It was a strange philosophy for a major-general (he was promoted at the age of 43, after Mafeking), but the only discipline he respected was self-reliance. He did not set out to organise a youth movement. But when the hero of Mafeking discovered that his book *Aids to Scouting* (1899) and a trial camp held in 1907 had stimulated the spontaneous formation of scout patrols and groups, he wrote *Scouting for Boys*, published in 1908. In 1910 Baden-Powell resigned from his post as Inspector-General of Cavalry and devoted himself full-time to Scouting. In 1920, he was acclaimed Chief Scout of the World at the first International Jamboree. He worked unremittingly, in spite of his advancing age, and spoke out loudly against totalitarianism and militarism, and the conditioning of the individual by mass media.
G. P. G. N.
'BADEN-POWELL', BY E. E. REYNOLDS (O.U.P., 1957); 'SCOUTING FOR BOYS', BY LORD BADEN-POWELL (PEARSON, 1968).

Leo Hendrik Baekeland (U.S., born Belgian, 1863–1944): chemist. Baekeland, the father of the plastics industry, was an early example of the European brain drain. Assistant Professor of Chemistry at the University of Ghent at 26, his interest in technological problems found no response either in his native country or in England. Emigrating from Belgium to the U.S.,

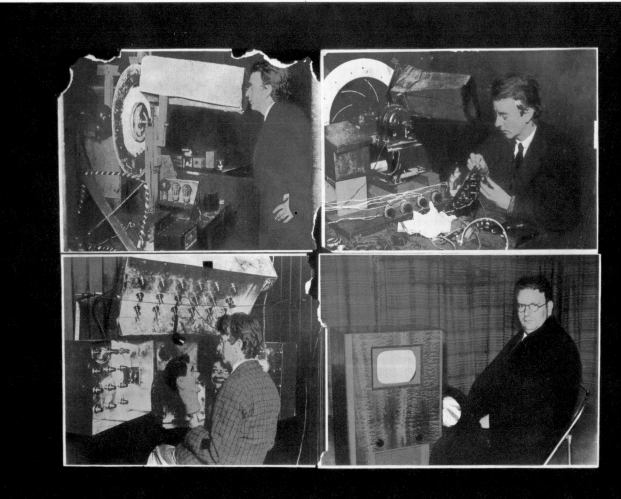

Baekeland entered industry, eventually to found his own consultancy service. His first £250,000 was made by selling his Velox photographic printing paper process – allowing contact printing in artificial light – to Kodak. He turned to the newly-developing plastics industry and systematically developed Bakelite – plastics based on phenol and formaldehyde. The idea of using these was not new, but the process of transformation to a tough, homogenous mass was technically poor and economically impossible before Baekeland. Bakelite is still used in very large quantities for many industrial products. Baekeland also made numerous other contributions to industrial chemistry, notably by developing the electrochemical cell. His work showed the importance of science-based technology in industrial processes. **P. J. F.**

'LANDMARKS OF THE PLASTICS INDUSTRY' (PUBLISHED BY PLASTICS DIVISION, ICI LTD, WELWYN GARDEN CITY, HERTS.); ARTICLE BY L. H. BAEKELAND IN JOURNAL OF CHEMICAL EDUCATION, VOL 9, 1932, P. 1000.

John Logie Baird (British, 1888–1946): inventor. The son of a Scottish minister, Baird (below left, with his experimental sets in various stages of completion) was an early developer of TV. In his youth he had tried several things, including the manufacture and sale of soap ('Baird's Speedy Cleaner'), but concentrated wholly on television from the early 1920s. He was soon the most widely known name in British television, although ironically not a single idea or design of his forms any part of the equipment used in today's TV services. His talents were for creating public interest rather than scientific endeavour; Gordon Selfridge was sufficiently impressed to put his equipment on show. Baird was officially transmitting in the early 1930s to a handful of viewers. However, in 1936 the BBC tested his rotating-discs system side by side with the all-electronic one developed by Shoenberg's (q.v.) team at EMI. Electronics won a crushing victory and Baird's system was dropped. Undaunted, Baird went on with his investigations, which now included colour and stereoscopic television, and continued to keep TV in the public eye. His contribution overall, though without much engineering merit, played a significant role in the development of TV in this country, which had the world's first high-definition public service by November 1936. **P. O. W.**

'TELEVISION'S STORY AND CHALLENGE', BY DEREK HORTON (HARRAP, 1951); 'ADVENTURE IN VISION', BY JOHN SWIFT (JOHN LEHMANN, 1950); 'HOW TELEVISION WORKS', BY W. A. HOLM (PHILIPS TECHNICAL LIBRARY, 1958).

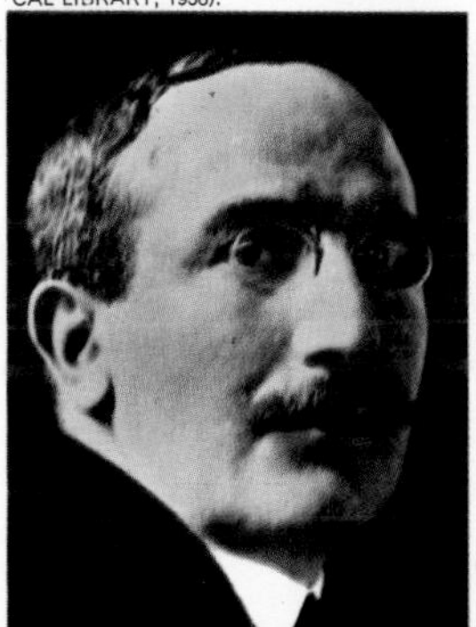

Léon Bakst (Russian, 1866–1924): scene-designer. As a young painter in pre-Revolutionary St Petersburg Bakst despised the ballet and found it odd that his cultivated friends – above all the portly and modish Sergei Diaghilev (q.v.) – should take it so seriously. Bakst was poor, Jewish, and had a large family to keep, and it seemed unlikely that he would realise the ambition – to be "the most famous painter in the world" – to which he confessed in 1897. But that is, very nearly, what he became when Diaghilev's Russian Ballet came to Western Europe from 1909 onwards. His decors were richer, stronger and more heady than any seen on stage before. It took 30 years to get this particular poison out of the bloodstream of dress-designers and interior decorators. Never had the stage had so decisive an influence on taste; and although Bakst excelled as much in the delicate insinuations of *Carnaval* as in *Schéhérezade* it was for the first glorious impact of a fabricated East that he was, and is, remembered. **J. R.**

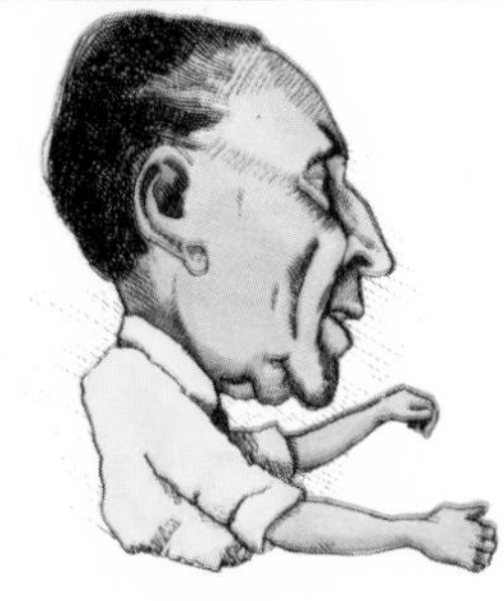

George Balanchine (U.S., ex-Russian, b. 1904): choreographer. Balanchine transplanted the Italo-Franco-Russian classical style of ballet to the U.S., and made it into something new and American. His early experimental choreography antagonised the Leningrad State Theatre directors; but in 1924 he was allowed to go on tour. Diaghilev (q.v.) engaged him in London for his *Ballets Russes* and at 21 Balanchine succeeded Nijinska as ballet master/choreographer; he created 10 ballets as well as dancing character roles. In 1934, invited to the U.S. by art patron Lincoln Kirstein, he founded the School of American Ballet in New York. This resulted in the formation of four companies, including (with Kirstein) the New York City Ballet (1948). Balanchine reacted against the drama and romanticism of Fokine (q.v.). Most of his greatest post-Diaghilev ballets were abstract. The most subtly musical of choreographers, he has been Stravinsky's (q.v.) closest collaborator. **R. B.**

'BALANCHINE', BY BERNARD TAPER (COLLINS, 1964); 'THE NEW YORK CITY BALLET', BY ANATOLE CHUJOY (KNOPF, NEW YORK, 1953); 'LOOKING AT THE DANCE', BY EDWIN DENBY (PELLEGRINI AND CUDAHY, NEW YORK, 1949); 'DANCERS, BUILDINGS AND PEOPLE IN THE STREETS', BY EDWIN DENBY (HORIZON PRESS, NEW YORK, 1965).

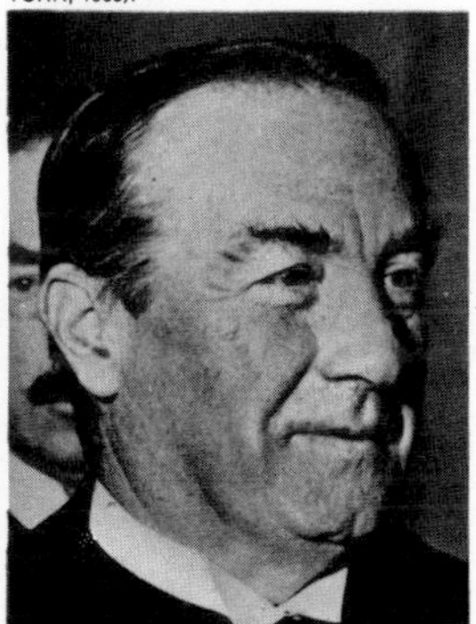

Stanley Baldwin (British, 1867–1947): statesman. Each age, we are told, gets the politicians it deserves, and war-weary England renounced Lloyd George's dynamic embrace for the soothing bedside manner of Stanley Baldwin. He was Prime Minister three times: 1923–4; 1924–9; 1935–7. Far more clearly than his abler contemporaries, he discerned and embodied England's longing for peace and relaxation. His pipe and his pigs, his cosy radio chats, his indolence and lack of ideas, all suggested the end of the strenuous phase of English life, and anticipated the day when image would supersede substance. From the moment he led the Tory backbench revolt against Lloyd George (q.v.) in 1922 Baldwin dominated inter-war politics – for eight years as Prime Minister, and a further four as effective head of MacDonald's National Government (1931–5). Baldwin has been praised for efforts at class reconciliation, and he certainly minimised the consequences of the 1926 General Strike. But his was the ultimate responsibility for the deflationary policies which produced it. He successfully handled the Abdication crisis in 1936, yet his lethargy was proof against solving the unemployment problem and promoting rearmament. He was a Walpole during a period when Britain increasingly required a Chatham. **R. Sk.**

'STANLEY BALDWIN', BY G. M. YOUNG (RUPERT HART-DAVIS, 1952); 'MY FATHER: THE TRUE STORY', BY A. W. BALDWIN (ALLEN AND UNWIN, 1955); 'A PATTERN OF RULERS', BY LORD FRANCIS-WILLIAMS (LONGMANS, 1965); 'THE BALDWIN AGE', ED. JOHN RAYMOND (EYRE AND SPOTTISWOODE, 1960).

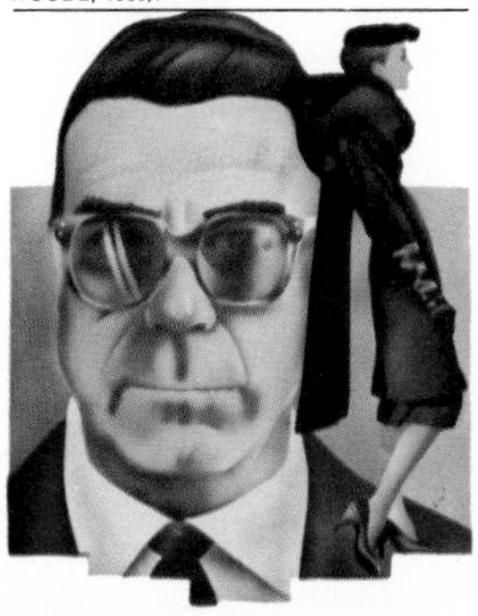

Cristobal Balenciaga (Spanish, b. 1895): dress designer. Balenciaga became fashion's greatest innovator, and was couturier to the world's most elegant women until his retirement in 1968. He was the son of a fishing-boat captain of Guetaria, and his intense interest in women's clothes was encouraged by the Marquesa de Casa Tores who placed him in a Madrid tailoring house. Later he opened his own shops in Madrid, San Sebastian, Barcelona. The Civil War sent him to Paris, where, in 1937, he opened a couture house at 10 Avenue George V. The initial collection won acclaim. His first innovation was to abolish the fitted line, remodelling the body with concave front, loose back, sloping shoulders. This led logically to the loose tunic, the sack, the chemise, the shift. His basic silhouette changed only gradually, yet he stayed ahead of other designers. They might proliferate new ideas, but always found themselves returning to the Balenciaga direction. Because of this he was called 'the designers' designer'. Courrèges (q.v.), fashion's next great innovator, worked under him for 10 years. Balenciaga shaped the silhouette of the mid-20th-century woman. **A. A.**

'IN MY FASHION', BY BETTINA BALLARD (SECKER AND WARBURG, 1960); 'PARIS A LA MODE', BY CELIA BERTIN (GOLLANCZ, 1957).

Arthur James Balfour (British, 1848–1930): politician. Balfour succeeded his uncle, the third Marquess of Salisbury, as Unionist Prime Minister in 1902. During a political career of more than 50 years, he was a minister for 32. He outlived most of his contemporaries, and was

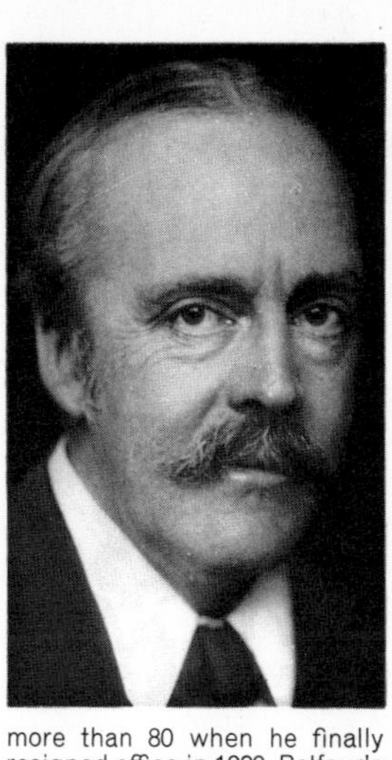

more than 80 when he finally resigned office in 1929. Balfour's political career spans the last years of aristocratic government, and he was an aristocrat by temperament as well as by birth. His subtlety of mind was often too much for his followers, and his range of interests, philosophical and historical, was always far wider than was customary in High Society; Keynes (q.v.) said of him that he was "the most extraordinary *objet d'art* our society has produced". The high spots of his career included his handling of the Education Bill in 1902 and his chairmanship of the Committee of Dominion Prime Ministers in 1926 which pointed to new Commonwealth relationships. Yet he had to resign from his leadership of the Conservative Party in 1911 on grounds of lack of forcefulness. He is best remembered for the 'Balfour Declaration' which he signed as Foreign Secretary in 1917: it favoured the establishment of a Jewish 'national home' in Palestine. **A. B.**

'ARTHUR JAMES BALFOUR', BY K. YOUNG (BELL, 1963).

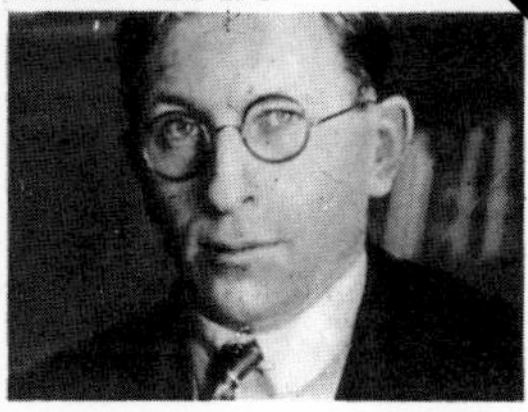

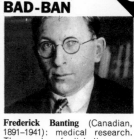

Frederick Banting (Canadian, 1891–1941): medical research. Thousands of diabetics owe their lives to this largely self-trained scientist. Before insulin treatment became available diabetes killed the young and shortened the life of the elderly. The existence of insulin and its origin from the pancreas (which also produces digestive ferments) was deduced more than 20 years before its discovery, but all attempts to isolate it had failed. Banting had a patient in whom disease had destroyed the digestive part of the gland, yet diabetes did not follow. This suggested that previous attempts to extract insulin had failed because, in the process, digestive ferments had destroyed the insulin. His experiments showed this to be correct, and from his findings other scientists were able to devise the modern process which extracts insulin, unharmed, in large quantities. Banting's ability to see the point others had overlooked was characteristic, and his discovery attracted increasing numbers of able men to medical research. **H. P. H.**

'LIVES OF THE FELLOWS OF THE ROYAL COLLEGE OF PHYSICIANS', VOL V, BY R. R. TRAIL (PUBLISHED BY THE COLLEGE, LONDON, 1968); 'SIR FREDERICK BANTING', BY L. G. STEVENSON (HEINEMANN, 1947).

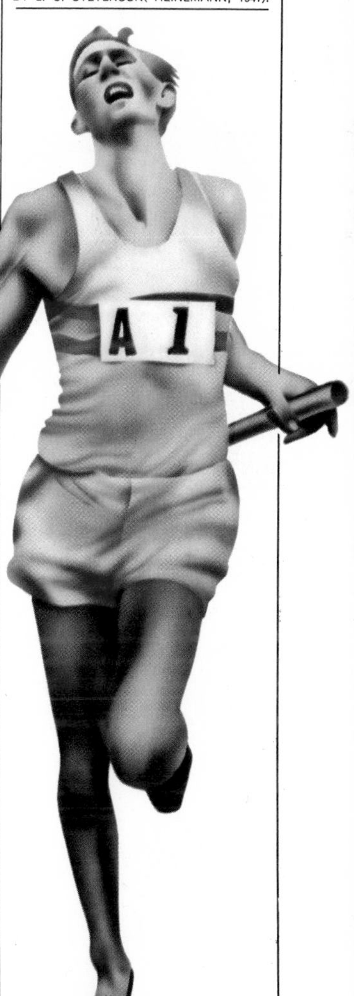

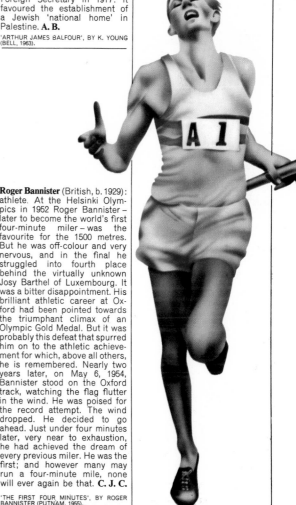

Roger Bannister (British, b. 1929): athlete. At the Helsinki Olympics in 1952 Roger Bannister – later to become the world's first four-minute miler – was the favourite for the 1500 metres. But he was off-colour and very nervous, and in the final he struggled into fourth place behind the virtually unknown Josy Barthel of Luxembourg. It was a bitter disappointment. His brilliant athletic career at Oxford had been pointed towards the triumphant climax of an Olympic Gold Medal. But it was probably this defeat that spurred him on to the athletic achievement for which, above all others, he is remembered. Nearly two years later, on May 6, 1954, Bannister stood on the Oxford track, watching the flag flutter in the wind. He was poised for the record attempt. The wind dropped. He decided to go ahead. Just under four minutes later, very near to exhaustion, he had achieved the dream of every previous miler. He was the first; and however many may run a four-minute mile, none will ever again be that. **C. J. C.**

'THE FIRST FOUR MINUTES', BY ROGER BANNISTER (PUTNAM, 1955).

Brigitte Bardot (French, b. 1934): film actress. The 20th-century *femme fatale* is determined by the cinema. In the Fifties, the period of Nabokov's nymphet, the child-woman appeared, a paradoxical combination of innocence and knowingness, and the archetype was Brigitte Bardot. She entered films, after a brief career as a model, in 1952. By the time *La Lumière d'en Face* appeared she had achieved international recognition as an erotic symbol. After *Et Dieu Créa la Femme,* directed by her Svengali-like first husband Roger Vadim, she became the world's best-known film star outside America. Her acting ability was rarely tested: it was enough, as Vadim put it, that she existed. BB (the punning *bébé* in French) was impulsive, sensual, passionate, uncaring for the future. Her uniform was the bikini, her weaponry cascading blonde hair and pouting lips. She has had three husbands, three divorces, a suicide attempt and a succession of lovers, each discarded with the regularity of the Paris collections. In her mid-thirties, her attractions undiminished, she still promises to continue to delight and scandalise us for some years to come. **G. C. P.**

'BRIGITTE BARDOT AND THE LOLITA SYNDROME', BY SIMONE DE BEAUVOIR (DEUTSCH /WEIDENFELD AND NICOLSON, 1959); 'THE STARS', BY EDGAR MORIN (EVERGREEN PROFILE 7, GROVE PRESS/CALDER, 1960).

Christiaan Barnard (South African, b. 1922): cardiac surgeon. The man who performed the first heart transplant is a man of modest origins from a small town in the semi-desert scrubland of South Africa. He trained at Cape Town University in the early 1940s. He was a quiet, well-liked, hardworking medical student – not a pacesetter, either academically or socially. In the late 1950s he went to Minneapolis to train under the eminent cardiac surgeon Walt Lilliehei. Once back in South Africa, he worked on straightforward cardiac surgery, and was in the forefront of all cardiac surgical development. He made a further visit to the States in the mid-1960s to study their latest operative techniques. Before he did a human heart transplant, Barnard did many experimental operations on dogs. Dr Shumway, in the States, had announced his intention to do a heart transplant back in August 1967. Dr James Hardy had transplanted a baboon's heart into a patient before that. But Chris Barnard was the surgeon who, on December 3, 1967, actually did the first one, and broke the ice; since then, more than a hundred other heart transplants have been done. Barnard's own second patient, Philip Blaiberg, lived for 594 days after the operation. As a surgeon, he would be in the international class even if he had not done the world's first human heart transplant. But he was to become the right man in the right place at the right time. **D. N. R.**

Sydney Barnes (British, 1873–1967): cricketer. Bowlers have been the innovators in the long history of cricket's progress, but Sydney Barnes, greatest of all contributors to the craft of bowling, was a perfecter rather than an inventor. Born at Smethwick in 1873, by his twenties he was a large strong man and a rather moderate fast bowler, who had played for Warwickshire without much success, and was locally known as 'Bumping Barnes'. He was, however, blessed with a beautiful action, a keen brain, and a determined nature. He soon knew what he wanted, which was to bowl the leg-break at a fast pace, a feat no-one had so far completely mastered. It was clear to him that the accepted method of bending the wrist to a right angle would not achieve this so he adopted his own method, palm toward the batsman, wrist cocked as for the off-break. This is simplicity itself – in theory – but only Barnes perfected it. When he had done so, everything else stemmed from this foundation – swerve, flight and even subtlety of pace. No other combination has proved so successful in all conditions. And he nursed his resources. When he was 58 the South African tourists thought him the best bowler they met in England. At 80 he bowled the first over in a match for his benefit, refusing a new ball on the grounds that he 'didn't want to get the game over too quickly'. **I. A. R. P.**

'S. F. BARNES: THE MASTER BOWLER', BY L. DUCKWORTH (THE CRICKETER LTD, 1967); 'A HISTORY OF CRICKET', BY H. S. ALTHAM AND E. W. SWANTON (ALLEN AND UNWIN, 1963).

Murray Barr (Canadian, b. 1908): anatomist. The 'Barr body', now universally used as a marker in a simple screening test for the sex of an individual, takes its name from a discovery made jointly in 1949 by Barr and by Bertram, a graduate student who was working with him in the medical school of London, Ontario. Their project was primarily concerned with fatigue in nerve cells, but they noted that a small mass of chromatin found in the nuclei of some nerve cells was peculiar to female animals. They soon confirmed this in women. This "sex chromatin" was later shown to be characteristic of a female (XX) sex chromosome constitution. Coupled with the development since 1956 of methods of displaying chromosomes, this inspired finding has been responsible for a new epoch of understanding in a whole range of disorders, including infertility, spontaneous abortion, mental deficiency and many forms of developmental abnormality. Though not devoid of danger when employed for this purpose, the test made possible by their discovery can be used to determine the sex of a child before birth. In this way, children with a high risk of being affected by sex-linked hereditary disorders can be identified long before birth. Much of the importance of this test lies in its very simplicity: not only has it helped to identify genetic errors associated with a wide variety of relatively common developmental disabilities, but it has also provided a new and important link between biology and medicine. **J. A. S.**

'THE SEX CHROMATIN', BY K. L. MOORE (SAUNDERS, 1966).

James Matthew Barrie (British, 1860–1937): author. Without *Peter Pan*, Barrie would have no lasting importance. His early success in the novel was achieved in the 1880s by writing up his mother's nostalgia for a pre-industrial Scotland of the

1840s, and his post-1900 theatrical successes (*The Admirable Crichton, Dear Brutus, Mary Rose*) are in themselves mainly a negative comment on English 'taste' of the period. His ironic, pessimistic, but ultimately undisturbing commentary, unaffected by contemporary thought, was without real seriousness. But *Peter Pan* (1904) has representative significance. Childhood experience had produced in him a disturbed, oedipal psyche, which, he himself said, made "desperate attempts to grow up, but couldn't". In this sense, he apotheosised his own resigned self in Peter Pan – "the boy who wouldn't grow up". Generations were brought up inside Barrie's Wendy House in the 'Never Land'. He mythologised the cult of immaturity into which the Romantic image of the child had largely resolved. He expressed an elemental retreat from reality, pervasive in a disintegrating civilisation; and foreshadowed the whole 'growing-up' maturation problem which is central to 20th-century culture. Peter Pan's "I'm youth; I'm joy; ... No-one is going to catch me and make me a man" suggests a major regressive reference behind the infantilism of our own mid-century. **P. C.**

'THE STORY OF J. M. B.: A BIOGRAPHY', BY DENIS MACKAIL (PETER DAVIES, 1938); 'BARRIE AND THE KAILYARD SCHOOL', BY GEORGE BLAKE (ARTHUR BARKER, 1951); 'THE IMAGE OF CHILDHOOD', BY PETER COVENEY (PELICAN, 1967).

Karl Barth (Swiss, 1886-1968): theologian. Barth was the theologian who said No to the early 20th century at its worst crisis.

His own teachers, the big names of liberal Protestantism in Germany, supported the Kaiser's war. But equally shocking to the young Barth was his own failure to preach effectively in a Swiss village when all that he could produce was their mild version of Christian optimism. He turned to the strange new world of the Bible, and his commentary on St Paul to the Romans (1919) burst like a bomb in the theologians' playground. Recalled into German academic life, he studied the medieval, Lutheran and Calvinist theologians whom so many despised, and launched himself into the writing of a multi-volumed work, *Church Dogmatics* (still incomplete when he died). He proclaimed Christ as the only Word of God, the only revelation of the nature and destiny of man, the only Lord. This theology provided a rallying point for Protestants in Germany who refused to accept Hitler as the new Messiah. Barth returned to Switzerland. His growing enthusiasm about the humanity of God embodied in the Christ of Easter did not conceal his continuing No to the evil embodied in the men who had made our century. **D. L. E.**

'KARL BARTH'S CHURCH DOGMATICS', SELECTIONS BY H. GOLLWITZER (T. AND T. CLARK, 1961); 'DOGMATICS IN OUTLINE', BY KARL BARTH (S.C.M. PRESS, 1949); 'EVANGELICAL THEOLOGY', BY KARL BARTH (COLLINS, 1965).

Guy Bartholomew (British, 1885–1962): newspaper company chairman. Bartholomew joined the *Daily Mirror* in 1904 as a picture engraver. He left as chairman in 1951, having turned the *Mirror* into a paper with the biggest circulation in the Western world. From 1934 he took control of the *Mirror*, and by putting the emphasis on pictures he jerked the paper away from the idea that it was news that really mattered. In came the thickest and blackest of headlines – often leading with a story of sex or human interest. Privacy was shamelessly invaded. In, too, came many strip cartoons, 'live letters' (those not printed were carefully analysed to see what readers wanted), sport and pin-ups. 'Bart' was said never to read a book, he cared nothing for art or politics, he wrote nothing himself. Yet his *Mirror* was also an impressive – and often feared – radical voice. **G. P. G. N.**

'DANGEROUS ESTATE', BY FRANCIS WILLIAMS (LONGMANS, 1957).

Béla Bartók (Hungarian, 1881–1945): composer and pianist. Bartók is one of the century's few established musical classics. He first composed at the age of eight and first appeared in public as a pianist at the age of ten. He grew into an outstanding virtuoso – a "second Dohnányi". Bartók's strongest early influence was Richard Strauss (hear his first big orchestral work, the *Kossuth* Symphony, which, at the same time, shows the first unmistakable sparks of genius). A crucial year was 1905, when he started his studies of Magyar (as distinct from Gipsy) folk music – together with Kodály, who became a close friend. After the First World War, Europe and America gradually came to know him; after the outset of the Second World War, he emigrated to America and died an 'American composer' like – i.e. as little as – Schoenberg (q.v.). His enormous output includes stage and choral works, orchestral music, concertos, songs, duo and piano music: much has become midstream repertoire. Above all, perhaps, there are the six towering string quartets, a monument to a monumental medium. Bartók's stylistic influence on minor masters such as Mátyás Seiber was lasting; his aesthetic influence as a truthful, rather than playful, genius is overwhelming – or if it isn't it certainly ought to be. **H. K.**

'HUNGARIAN FOLK MUSIC', BY BELA BARTOK (TRANS. M. D. CALVOCORESSI, O.U.P., 1931); 'THE STRING QUARTETS OF BELA BARTOK', BY MATYAS SEIBER (BOOSEY AND HAWKES, 1945); 'BELA BARTOK: HIS LIFE IN PICTURES', BY BENCE SZABOLCSI (BOOSEY AND HAWKES, 1964).

Count Basie (U.S., b. 1904): bandleader. For more than 30 years Count (actually, William) Basie has led one of the great big bands in jazz. As a child he studied music first with his mother and later with Fats Waller, and developed his highly personal piano style, rhythmically relaxed and deceptively simple, with Bennie Moten's band in the early Thirties. When Moten died and Basie turned bandleader, he took the best of Moten's musicians with him, including the great Walter Page on bass. Relying heavily on the 12 bar blues form and uncluttered arrangements, the band has always enjoyed a surfeit of brilliant soloists including Joe Newman, J. J. Johnson, and the immortal tenor saxophonist Lester Young (q.v.), whose recorded solos with the Basie band remain glorious examples of the art of jazz. Although some of Basie's later records have shown a tendency to aim at a more commercial market than is good for his music, he nevertheless still has an orchestra capable of producing fine big band jazz. He remains, along with Duke Ellington (q.v.), a man to whom almost every big jazz band since the early Forties owes allegiance. **R. S.**

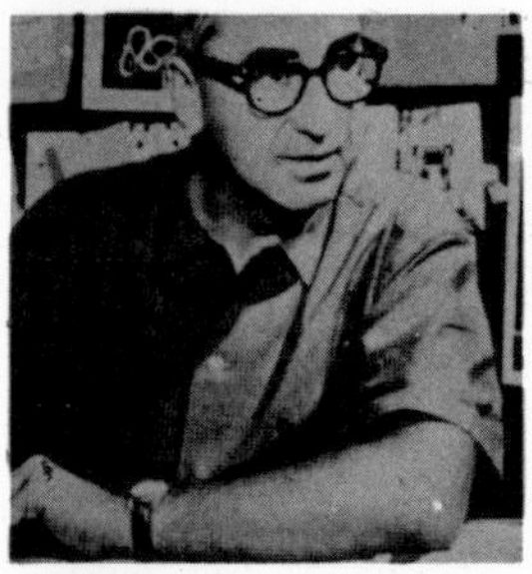

Saul Bass (U.S., b. 1920): graphic designer. Saul Bass pioneered graphic film titles. After working as a competent, though far from pre-eminent, graphic designer, he shot to public notice in the mid-Fifties with his animated film credit sequences and end titles. Until then credit titles were usually a roll of honour on a blank screen, but Bass made them into a positive introduction to a film, suggesting what was to come and setting the atmosphere. The opening and closing sequences of *The Man With The Golden Arm, The Big Knife, The Seven Year Itch, A Walk on the Wild Side, West Side Story*, etc. have become as famous as the films themselves and inspired many imitators. **G. D. A.**

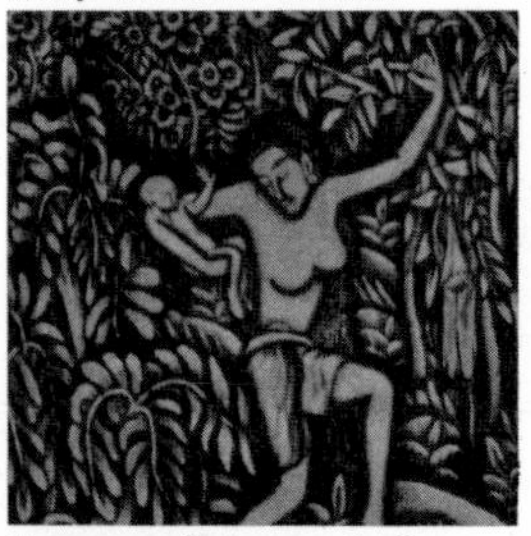

Gregory Bateson (U.S., ex-British, b. 1904): anthropologist. This communications scientist was a son of William Bateson – himself of immense stature in 20th-century genetics. At Cambridge his interest in behaviour led him from physical into cultural anthropology, the study of societies and communication within them. He worked in New Guinea and later studied Balinese life and art (above). In 1936 he published *Naven*, about ceremonial transvestite behaviour in a New Guinea tribe. This was not just an analysis of a complex piece of behaviour: Bateson also tried to examine the way his data were handled to form theories. The development of cybernetics in the 1940s provided the conceptual framework adequate to describe Bateson's thesis. Studying 'feedback' between groups of individuals in closed systems led him ultimately to psychology, where he developed the famous 'double bind' theory of schizophrenia (1951), an illness he sees as essentially one of communication failure. **J. B. M.**

'NAVEN' BY G. BATESON (2ND ED. STANFORD UNIVERSITY PRESS, 1958)

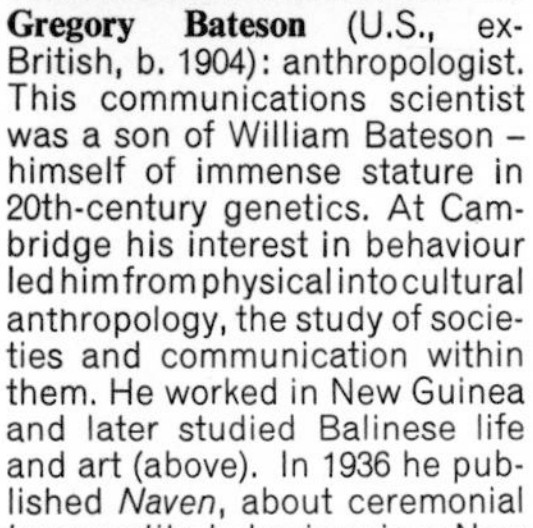

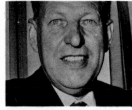

Sir Frederick Bawden (British, b. 1908): virologist. A student of plant viruses and virus diseases, Sir Frederick Bawden has done work of great practical implication over the last 30 years at Rothamsted Experimental Station, where he is now Director. His most important single achievement was to isolate, with Pirie, the tobacco-mosaic virus in crystalline form. Research on this virus (which causes the brown areas on diseased tobacco leaves) led to our first discoveries of virus structure and multiplication. Special tests with X-rays and the electron microscope showed that the virus is a hollow tube made out of a spiral of ribonucleic acid and protein. It was found that if this ribonucleic acid was injected into uninfected cells, it would cause them to produce new viruses. This led to discoveries about the way in which new proteins are produced, a process which underlies the creation of life itself. **J. B. M.**

'THE NEW INTELLIGENT MAN'S GUIDE TO SCIENCE', BY I. ASIMOV (NELSON, 1967).

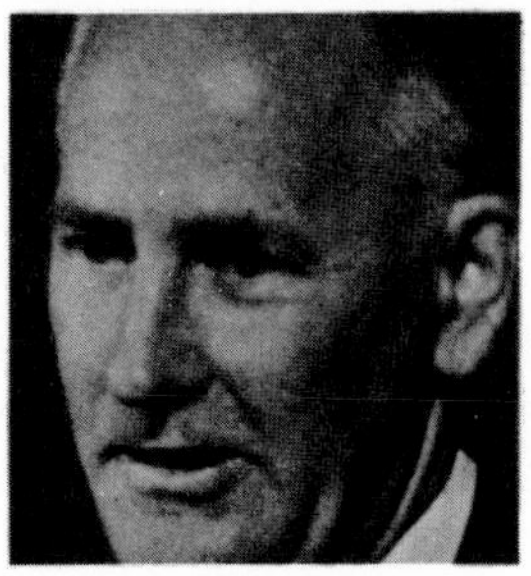

George Beadle (U.S., b. 1903): geneticist. The son of a Nebraskan farmer, Beadle was the first scientist to study closely the chemistry of genetics. He began by making important studies on the genetics of maize and fruit flies, involving the hitherto unheard of refinement of transplanting flies' eyes to unravel the complex process of transmission of hereditary characteristics. This work led to the idea that each gene performed its function by forming a particular chemical substance. In 1937 he joined forces with Tatum (q.v.) at Stanford University, where they carried out ingenious and highly significant researches on the salmon-pink bread mould, Neurospora, and they were at last able to show that each gene controlled one particular biochemical process. This 'one gene, one enzyme' concept has since become a cornerstone of modern biology. For their discovery, Beadle and Tatum shared the 1958 Nobel Prize for medicine and physiology with Joshua Lederberg (q.v.). Their work led ultimately to the present far-reaching research on the genetic code. **P. H. S .S.**

'THE MESSAGE OF THE GENES', BY NAVIN SULLIVAN (ROUTLEDGE & KEGAN PAUL, 1968); 'THE LANGUAGE OF LIFE', BY GEORGE AND MURIEL BEADLE (PANTHER, 1969).

Lord Beaverbrook (British, 1879–1964): newspaper proprietor and politician. William Max Aitken, better known as Lord Beaverbrook of the *Daily Express*, was born in Canada and spent his first 30 years becoming a millionaire. In the summer of 1910 he came to Britain – and by December he was Tory M.P. for Ashton-under-Lyne. But after his key role in engineering the 1916 coup which installed Lloyd George (q.v.), he was kicked upstairs with a peerage at 37. Out for ever from the competitive centre of politics, he found that, having acquired the *Daily Express*, he might well have an instrument in his hands to make and break ministries and to push through his dream of a Customs Union for the British Empire. He directed the paper personally, legendarily, down a battery of telephones. By 1936, the *Express* had the largest daily net sale in the world. A formula of making politics and high life a gin-fizz for the masses was the tonic which raised its circulation. Politically it failed. Even

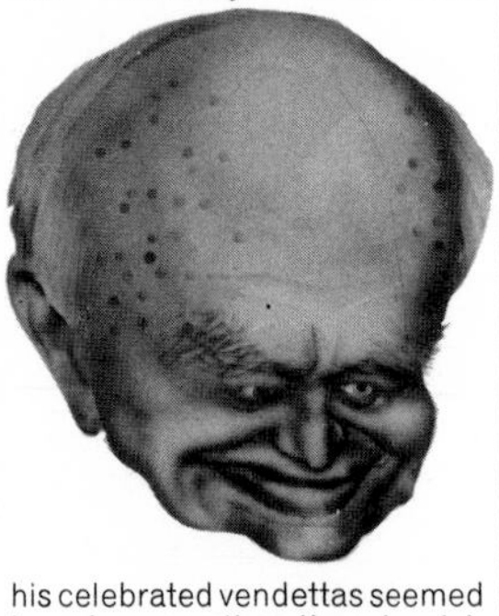

his celebrated vendettas seemed to enhance rather than tarnish the image of his enemies. Summoned by Churchill to be Minister of Aircraft Production in the Second World War he used his titanic energies to get the planes built. He was a showman of genius, but his simplistic chauvinism never took root. **G. P. G. N.**

'THE TRUE HISTORY OF BEAVERBROOK', BY ALAN WOOD (HEINEMANN, 1965); 'DANGEROUS ESTATE', BY FRANCIS WILLIAMS (LONGMANS, 1957); BEAVERBROOK'S OWN BOOKS, PARTICULARLY 'POLITICIANS AND THE WAR' (COLLINS, 1966).

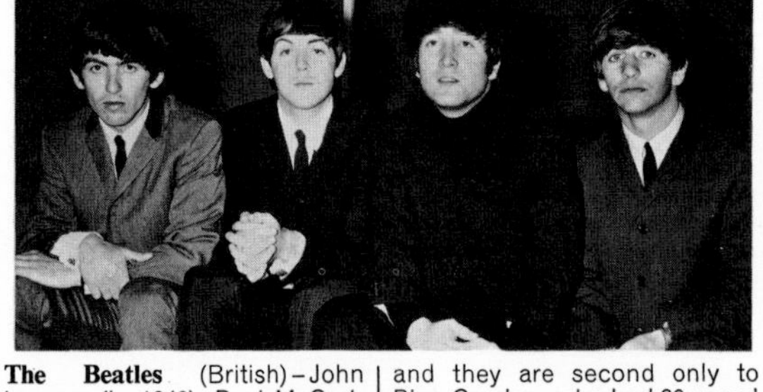

The Beatles (British) – John Lennon (b. 1940), Paul McCartney (b. 1942), Ringo Starr (b. 1940), George Harrison (b. 1943): singers and composers. The Beatles were the most influential figures of the 1960s in musical fashions and life-style for the young. After playing around Liverpool in the late 1950s, Lennon and McCartney finally teamed up with the other two to get their first gold disc (million-seller) in 1963 – *She Loves You*, which harnessed the hard beat of rock music to their fresh-sounding melodic and harmonic approach. Thereafter virtually every disc-sale record fell to them. In April 1964 the five top positions in the U.S. charts were all held by Beatles discs, and they are second only to Bing Crosby – who had 30 years' start – and perhaps Presley in total discs sold. Beatlemania has come and gone; they've been paid £1m. plus for a tour; they've made ever more interesting and 'advanced' records which serious music critics revere; they've done movies (e.g. *Help!*) and dabbled in mysticism; formed a business company (Apple); taken wives. By 1971 the group had split up, in personal and financial confusion, but the individual members had embarked on successful recording careers of their own. **D. J.**

'THE BEATLES', BY HUNTER DAVIES (HEINEMANN, 1968); RECORDS: LPs: 'A COLLECTION OF BEATLES OLDIES' (PARLOPHONE); 'SERGEANT PEPPER'S LONELY HEARTS CLUB BAND' (PARLOPHONE).

Samuel Beckett (Irish, b. 1906): novelist and playwright. *Waiting for Godot* (1953) – one of the few works of the century to take mythic status, as did once *Gulliver's Travels* or *Robinson Crusoe* – is a memorial to the patient martyrs of a world tantalised by a god who has cruelly been imagined. Who now but Beckett does justice (and

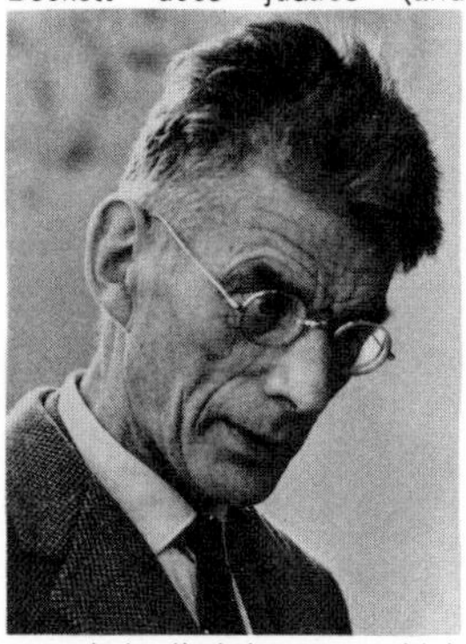

mercy) to that in man which aches for oblivion? Beckett is the only true heir of T. S. Eliot and James Joyce (Joyce even conceded "I think he has talent"). And is there another 20th-century writer whom two national literatures (in different languages – English and French) would insist on claiming as their own? He was born in Dublin of Protestant Anglo-Irish parents; he had a distinguished academic career including two years in Paris (1928–9), when he became closely associated with James Joyce; he settled permanently in Paris in 1937. Without bitterness or elation, he has lived through two decades of neglect and nearly two decades of acclamation, plainly his own man and plainly a man of supreme loyalty to his art: from his first novel *Murphy* (1938), through the plays *Endgame* and *Krapp's Last Tape* to *Play* (1964), it has been his drama of stoic wit that has established his international reputation. "To know you can do better next time, unrecognisably better, and that there is no next time, and that it is a blessing there is not, there is a thought to be going on with." **C. R.**

'THE NOVELS OF SAMUEL BECKETT', BY JOHN FLETCHER (CHATTO AND WINDUS, 1964); 'SAMUEL BECKETT: A COLLECTION OF CRITICAL ESSAYS', ED. MARTIN ESSLIN PRENTICE-HALL, 1966.

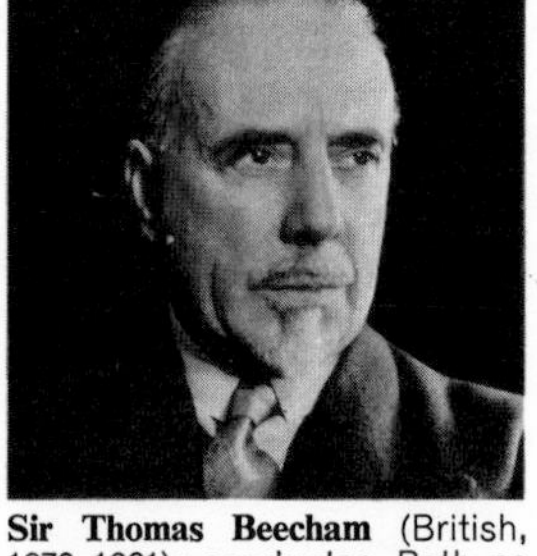

Sir Thomas Beecham (British, 1879–1961): conductor. Both as interpreter and patron, Beecham was the greatest single force for musical good in his native country during his lifetime and before the days of State subsidies for the Arts. Virtually a self-taught musician, he was the grandson of the founder of the pill-manufacturing firm. Two orchestras he created (the London Philharmonic and Royal Philharmonic) still survive. He initiated the cult for Mozart in England, introduced the operas of Strauss here, and promoted festivals of Delius (q.v.) and Sibelius. **F. A.**

'A MINGLED CHIME', BY THOMAS BEECHAM (HUTCHINSON, 1952); 'THOMAS BEECHAM', BY CHARLES REID (GOLLANCZ, 1961); 'THOMAS BEECHAM', BY NEVILLE CARDUS (COLLINS, 1961).

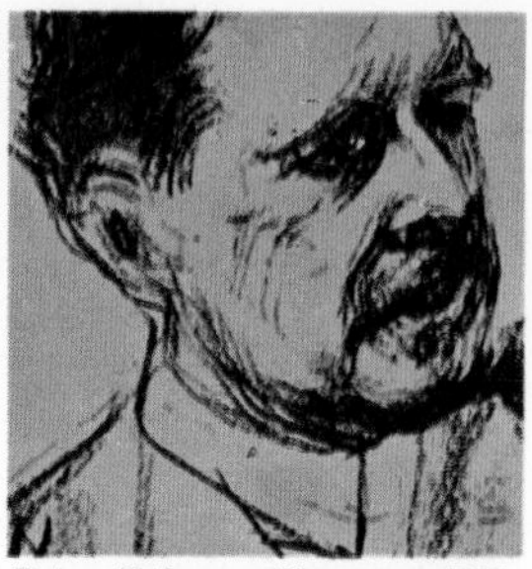

Peter Behrens (German, 1868–1940): architect and designer. Behrens, originally an Art Nouveau painter, was the midwife of modern architecture. Equally important was his complete design service from 1907 for the firm of AEG (the German General Electric Co.), where he established the architect's role as an industrial designer in humanising the entire technological environment. For AEG he designed cookers and catalogues, letterheads, posters – and buildings ranging from shops to the Turbine Factory of 1908–9. His architecture was at first semi-traditional, in the kind of 'stripped classicism' which a generation later was to be adopted by the Nazis; but he moved with the times, his Hoechst Dyeworks (1920–5) being a major example of Expressionist sculpture in brick and his later houses emulating the white-walled International Style of his pupils. Among his other major works were the German Embassy at St Petersburg (1911–12) and the Mannesmann offices, Düsseldorf (1913–23). **N. J. W. T.**

'PIONEERS OF MODERN DESIGN' BY NIKOLAUS PEVSNER (PENGUIN, LATEST EDITION 1968); 'THEORY AND DESIGN IN THE FIRST MACHINE AGE', BY REYNER BANHAM (ARCHITECTURAL PRESS, 1960).

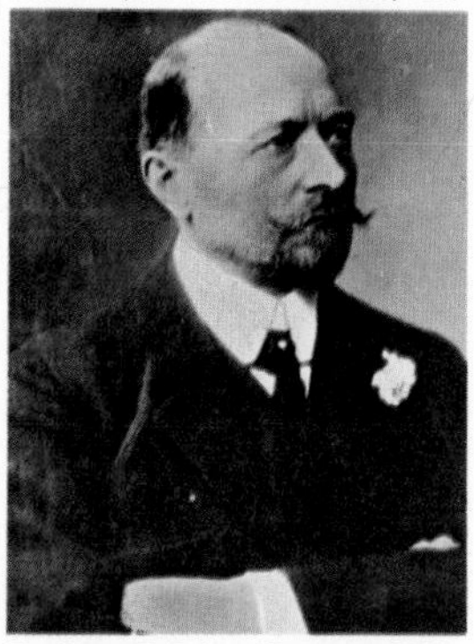

Emil von Behring (German, 1854–1917): immunologist. Von Behring was a pioneer of diphtheria immunisation, though it was for his work on serum therapy (he had introduced the treatment of diphtheria and tetanus with antitoxins) that he won his Nobel Prize in 1901. In the field of prevention, however, he pioneered mass diphtheria immunisation in 1913. Modern vaccines are safer and better than his, but the end result of his work has been the virtual elimination of diphtheria as a killer disease. Great success attended the British national immunisation campaign, begun in 1940 and continued energetically ever since (an alum-containing toxoid – a British discovery – deserves most of the credit). Since 1940, the incidence of diphtheria in this country has fallen from a yearly average of 58,000 cases with 2800 deaths in the years 1930–39, to approximately 12,000 cases with 472 deaths in 1946, and only 24 notifications with no deaths in 1966. Von Behring also worked on tuberculosis, but with less success. **H. J. P.**

'A HISTORY OF IMMUNIZATION', BY H. J. PARISH (LIVINGSTONE, 1965); 'A SHORT HISTORY OF MEDICINE', BY SINGER AND UNDERWOOD (CLARENDON PRESS, 1962).

Bix Beiderbecke (U.S., 1903–1931): cornetist and pianist. Leon Bismarck Beiderbecke had a short career but a massive legend. The son of a middle-class German family in Davenport, Iowa, he made his first appearance as a cornetist with the youthful Wolverines in Chicago (1923). Contemporaries wax maudlin in recollection of first hearing him. Wolverine recordings reveal a very cool-headed, lyrical improviser with bell-like tone and attack. An ambitious, restless musician, he moved on through a series of commercial bands – Charlie Straight, Gene Goldkette and eventually Paul Whiteman (q.v.) – leaving a trail of gem-like solos amidst cumbersome backing (*Dardanella, Sweet Sue* with Whiteman). His best records were made with Frankie Trum-bauer (*Singin' the Blues, I'm coming, Virginia*) or with his own 'Gang', over whom he towered (*Jazz-me Blues, Jazz Band Ball*). He developed an absorption with impressionist composers like Debussy and Holst (q.v.) – cf. his own composition, *In a Mist*. After an increasingly erratic professional life he died of pneumonia-cum-alcoholism. Beiderbecke remains an enigmatic figure, enshrined in myth. Apart from his direct influence on a whole school of trumpet players – Bobby Hackett, Billy Butterfield and Jimmy MacPartland – he gave to white musicians their first hero, to Scott Fitzgerald's Jazz Age its perfect artist figure and to jazz fans a rich legend. **H. R. A. L.**

'THE JAZZ MAKERS', BY HENTOFF AND SHAPIRO (PETER DAVIES, 1957). RECORD: THE BIX BEIDERBECKE LEGEND (RCA VICTOR, R.D. 27225).

Saul Bellow (U.S., b. 1915): novelist. Bellow's main achievement is to have defined and explored the anxieties, preoccupations and responses of the contemporary urban American in quest of meaning and comprehension in the congested modern world. Bellow's main characters are usually Jewish but in their intelligence and impotence, their torments and resilience and humour, they were recognised as being prototypical; and their experience, with its particular moments of dread and wonder, was felt to be profoundly representative. *The Adventures of Augie March* (1953) and *Herzog* (1964) are his most famous novels. A writer of immense stylistic resources who rejects the stance of alienation, he has shown how the novel can confront the bewildering complexity of modern American experience. **T. T.**

'SAUL BELLOW', BY TONY TANNER (OLIVER AND BOYD, 1965); 'THE NOVELS OF SAUL BELLOW', BY KEITH OPDAHL (PENNSYLVANIA U.P., 1967); 'RADICAL INNOCENCE', BY IHAB HASSAN (PRINCETON U.P., 1961).

Eduard Benes (Czech, 1884–1948): statesman. The uniquely civilised record of the Czechs in the first half of the 20th century owes much to Eduard Benes' leadership (their two catastrophes were due to forces beyond his control). He began his political career as an organiser of illegal Czech resistance to the Austrians in 1914–15, then as the main exiled Czech spokesman in Western Europe in 1917–18. In the First Czechoslovak Republic he was continuously Foreign Minister until he succeeded Thomas Masaryk (q.v.) as President in 1935. He was an outstanding figure at League of Nations meetings. the best known spokesman of the small nations. The Munich Agreement of September 1938 brought his fall and his second exile. In the Second World War Benes again won international prestige as the exponent of the view that the Czechs, with their liberal traditions and Slav sympathies, could act as a 'bridge' between the Western nations and Russia. This hope was crushed by the Soviet-inspired Czech Communist putsch of February 1948. Benes' reputation suffered unduly because his successes were followed by such dramatic failures. Nobody could have saved the Czechs from disaster when faced by the implacable will to total power of first Hitler and then Stalin; and by the indifference and abdication of will of the leaders and nations of France, Britain and America. **H. S.-W.**

'WAR MEMOIRS', BY EDUARD BENES, 2 VOLS. (ALLEN AND UNWIN, 1928); 'MEMOIRS FROM MUNICH TO NEW YEAR AND NEW VICTORY', BY EDUARD BENES (ALLEN AND UNWIN, 1954); 'BENES OF CZECHOSLOVAKIA', BY GODFREY LIAS (ALLEN AND UNWIN, 1940).

David Ben Gurion (Israeli, b. 1886 in Poland): statesman. The 'Lloyd George of Zionism', David Ben Gurion was the first Jewish leader to see that the German Final Solution destroyed Weizmann's (q.v.) dream of a harmonious Arab-Jewish community in Palestine. His Zionism and socialism are indivisible, sprung from a well of populist nationalism and watered with the blood of Russian pogrom and Arab massacre. In the 1920s and 1930s he urged self-reliance on the Jewish settlement in Palestine and built up the Jewish Defence Force (the Haganah) and the General Federation of Labour (the Histadruth). In 1942 he carried the Zionist movement to accept the establishment of a Jewish State and six years later, as Israel's first Prime Minister, read her Declaration of Independence. Until 1963, Ben Gurion presided over Israel's troubled infancy and led her to victory in 1948 and 1956 against overwhelming odds, but also to division in peace. His greatest accomplishment has been to give back to the Jews the knowledge that "the Archimedes lever lay in their own hearts". **S. S.**

'BEN GURION', BY MAURICE EDELMAN (HODDER AND STOUGHTON, 1964); 'THE JEWS IN THEIR LAND', BY DAVID BEN GURION (ALDUS BOOKS, 1961); 'CROSSROADS TO ISRAEL', BY CHRISTOPHER SYKES (COLLINS, 1965).

William Benton (U.S., b. 1900): advertising pioneer. Benton founded the Benton and Bowles advertising agency, now one of the Madison Avenue big four, and counts as one of the key figures in the development of modern advertising. Yet he sold out all his interests at the age of 35: "I'd been taking three or four hundred thousand dollars a year out of it. Any business where a kid can make that kind of money is no business for old men." Marketing and common-sense, not memorable slogans, were his great contribution. Market research on Maxwell House coffee, one of his first big accounts, showed that people liked the product but not the price. So Benton told his clients to cut the advertising so they could cut the price; and Maxwell House became the world's most successful instant coffee. In 'retirement' Benton became vice-president of the University of Chicago; Senator for Connecticut; and Assistant Secretary of State (1945–7). **P. W.**

'MADISON AVENUE, USA', BY MARTIN MAYER (HARPER AND ROW, NEW YORK, 1958).

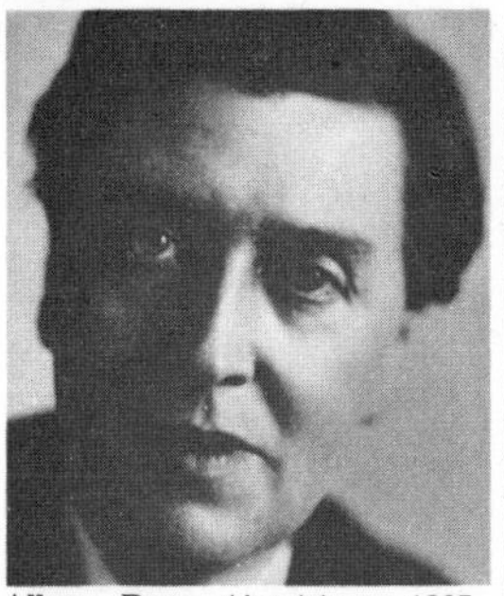

Alban Berg (Austrian, 1885–1935): composer. He is one of our time's acknowledged classics. His crucial year was 1904, when he became Schoenberg's (q.v.) pupil. As an artist and as a man, Schoenberg remained Berg's ego-ideal throughout his short life, and three major works – the *Three Orchestral Pieces*, the *Chamber Concerto* and the opera *Lulu* – are dedicated to the master. According to musical world opinion Berg's *Wozzeck* (1921) is one of the few of our age's operas which, like Britten's (q.v.) *Peter Grimes* (1945), have come to stay. The Violin Concerto (1935), likewise, is beginning to penetrate even the conservative star virtuoso's repertoire. In parts of the *Lyric Suite* for string quartet (1926), Berg first used the 'method of composing with twelve notes' which Schoenberg had introduced in the early Twenties. His works also include the masterly early Piano Sonata (1908), 14 songs, an earlyish string quartet, *Four Pieces* for clarinet and piano, and important compositions for voice and orchestra. Berg's influence, especially on the tonally-minded atonalists, is one of our time's paradoxes. **H. K.**

'ALBAN BERG: THE MAN AND HIS MUSIC', BY HANS F. REDLICH (CALDER, 1957).

Ingmar Bergman (Swedish, b. 1918): film director. Noted equally as stage and film director in Sweden since 1945, Bergman struck gold in the mid-Fifties with an extraordinary trio of films: *Smiles of a Summer Night, The Seventh Seal, Wild Strawberries.* Distributors rushed to meet the demand for more Bergman, any Bergman, old or new. Inevitably, a reaction set in: despite leavenings of airy, enchanting comedy, the spiri-

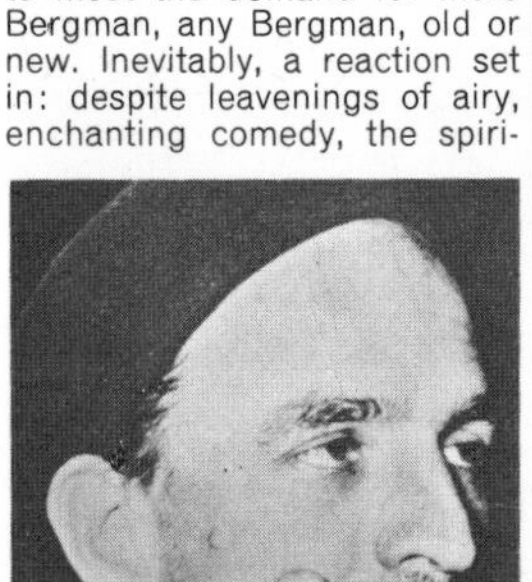

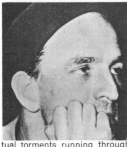

tual torments running through his work in a welter of dreams, death personified and speculations on love and death soon led to jokes about that old Swedish *angst.* Also reacting, Bergman hit back with a new mastery and control, exploring the role of art and the artist with searing honesty in a series of films from *The Silence* to *Persona, Hour of the Wolf* and *The Shame.* With them, Bergman retains his unique position as a film-maker who has for over 20 years written his own scripts and picked his own mouthpieces from his own stock company of actors. **T. M.**

'THE PERSONAL VISION OF INGMAR BERGMAN', BY JORN DONNER (INDIANA UNIVERSITY PRESS, 1964); 'FOUR SCREENPLAYS OF INGMAR BERGMAN' (SECKER AND WARBURG, 1960).

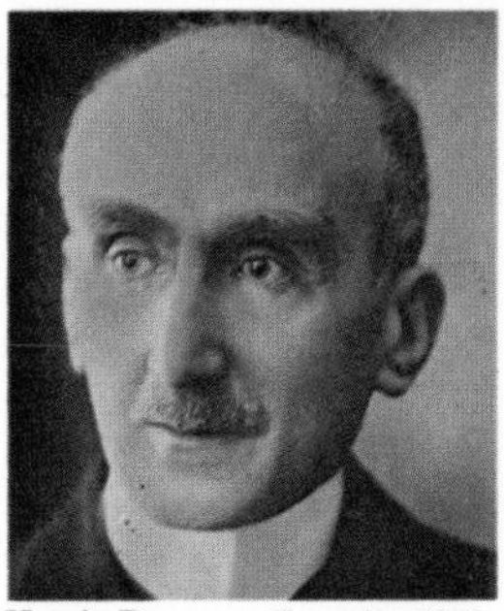

Henri Bergson (French, 1859–1941): philosopher. Bergson's philosophy is a protest on behalf of life, novelty and uniqueness against the picture of the world as a dead, mechanical system given by 19th-century science. Its basic principle is his distinction between intellect and intuition. Intellect represents things in spatial terms, distinct from one another and subject to abstract universal laws. Its account of the world as a great closed system is the content of most science and much metaphysics. Intuition is the inarticulate but direct awareness we have of the continuous flux of life and consciousness within us. The findings of the intellect are convenient for the practical purposes of action, but intuition alone grasps reality as it really is. Time, in particular, is not the linear sequence of separate events seen by the intellect; it is the interpenetration of past and present revealed to intuition. True reality is a continuous vital process (*élan vital*), an irresistible surge into novelty of which matter is a kind of waste product. Bergson ingeniously used the findings of science to discredit its claims to yield final truth. **A. Q.**

'INTRODUCTION TO METAPHYSICS', BY HENRI BERGSON (MACMILLAN, 1913).

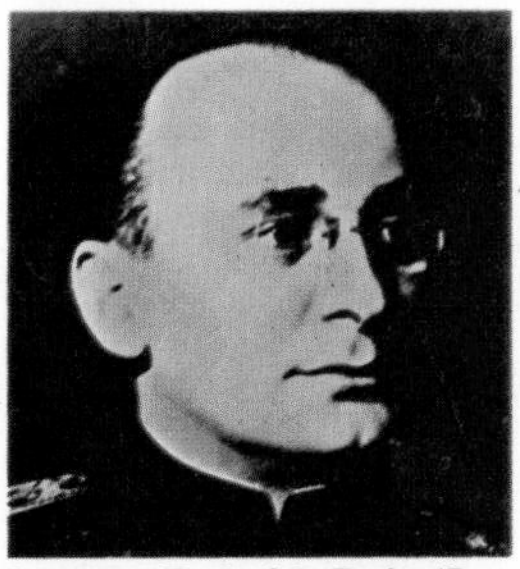

Lavrenty Pavlovich Beria (Russian, 1899–1953): politician, police chief. For 15 years Beria was Stalin's (q.v.) secret police chief. A Communist at 18, he started his career in the secret police in Georgia and became First Secretary of the Communist Party in 1931. He served his fellow Georgian Stalin by exterminating his Socialist and Communist opponents. He was appointed People's Commissar of the Interior (NKVD) in 1938, and Deputy Chairman of the Council of People's Commissars in 1945. He remained overlord of police, security, espionage and forced labour camps until his death. Beria inherited the slave labour force from his predecessor, Ezhov, but added to its millions by vast deportations within Russia and from occupied territories. After Stalin's death, he shared supreme power with Khrushchev (q.v.) and Malenkov, but was arrested in 1953. He was allegedly tried and executed – but more probably shot by his colleagues. He was in truth neither worse nor better than those who killed him, but a victim of the lawless tyranny he did much to build up. **L. B. S.**

'THE GREAT TERROR', BY R. CONQUEST (MACMILLAN, 1968); 'THE KREMLIN SINCE STALIN', BY W. LEONHARD (O.U.P., 1962).

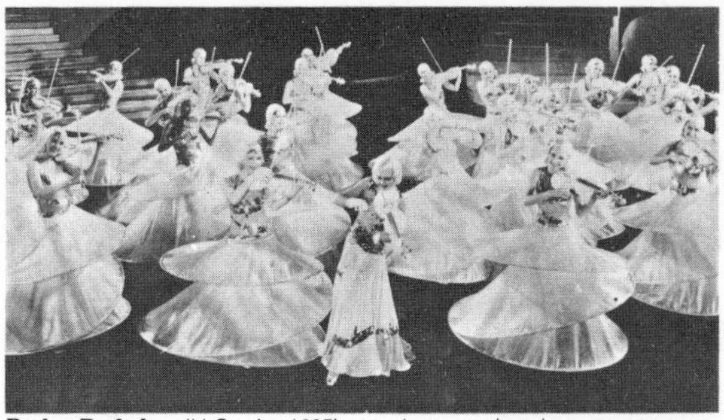

Busby Berkeley (U.S., b. 1895): film director. William Berkeley Enos was raised in a theatrical family, and after a tentative start as an actor graduated to directing Broadway musicals. With the talkies Hollywood looked desperately to New York and in 1930 Berkeley was invited by Sam Goldwyn to direct musical sequences in Eddie Cantor pictures. Until then film musicals looked as if a stage performance had been shot from the stalls. Berkeley drilled scores of dancers to perform to the camera and created intricate effects. He worked on *42nd Street*; then followed with *Gold Diggers of 1933, Footlight Parade, Dames* and others. Berkeley used massive sets, a sleeping-car express split down the middle, a waterfall using 20,000 gallons a minute, a hundred gyrating grand pianos played by a hundred girls. He built monorails across studio roofs to shoot overhead shots of dancers making kaleidoscopic patterns. He made stars out of such unpromising material as Ruby Keeler and Dick Powell. He gave chorus jobs to Ginger Rogers, Lucille Ball, Betty Grable and Paulette Goddard. He made Gene Kelly's first film *For Me and My Gal.* Television has resurrected his spirited contribution to film history. **G. C. P.**

'ALL TALKING, ALL SINGING, ALL DANCING', BY JOHN SPRINGER (CITADEL, 1966).

Irving Berlin (U.S., ex-Russian, b. 1888), composer. Irving Berlin is certainly the only composer to set two world wars to music. His First War revue *Yip, Yip Yaphank* contained the song *Oh How I Hate to Get Up in the Morning*; the second revue was *This is the Army* for the Second World War in which he sang the title song. The show netted $10 million for Army Emergency Relief. His *God Bless America*, written in 1918 but not brought out until 1941, stood a good chance for a while of knocking out the *Star Spangled Banner* as

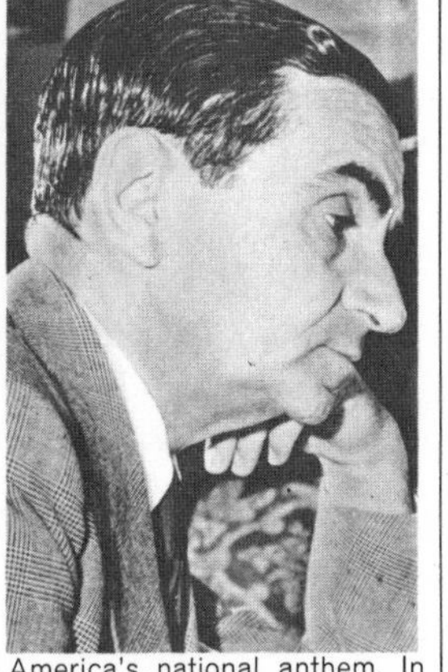

America's national anthem. In 1911, though he could neither read nor write music, he wrote his first big hit: *Alexander's Ragtime Band* was the first 20th century popular song influenced by jazz rhythms and melodies – and in turn influenced everything that followed in pop. Berlin has possibly the largest catalogue of multi-million hits of any composer. And in films his name on the score equalled the star's in box office importance – *Top Hat* for Fred Astaire (q.v.), *Annie Get Your Gun* for Ethel Merman, *Holiday Inn* for Bing Crosby (q.v.). He may or may not be forgiven for the ubiquitous and inescapable *White Christmas*, possibly the largest selling song in history. But it is a safe assumption that right at this moment some radio or TV station somewhere is broadcasting *Alexander's Ragtime Band, Blue Skies, Easter Parade* or *Cheek to Cheek.* **L. A.**

Hans Bethe (U.S., b. Germany, 1906): theoretical physicist. This brilliant physicist was the first to put forward the theory of how the Sun and other stars burn by nuclear fusion. His work paved the way indirectly to the hydrogen bomb, but also to the present hope of unlimited power supplies from the use of controlled nuclear fusion in future thermonuclear devices. Bethe's researches, however, extended far and wide over the quantum theory of the atom, the theory of atomic nuclei and atomic collision processes, and the theory of metals. He left Nazi Germany for America, becoming professor at Cornell University, in 1937. Chadwick (q.v.) had discovered the neutron – the uncharged particle in the atomic nucleus – three years earlier. Bethe, with the mathematician Peierls, showed that the neutron could fuse with the proton, the positively-charged particle in the nucleus, to form a heavier stable particle, the deuteron. In the process a lot of energy was released. Neither

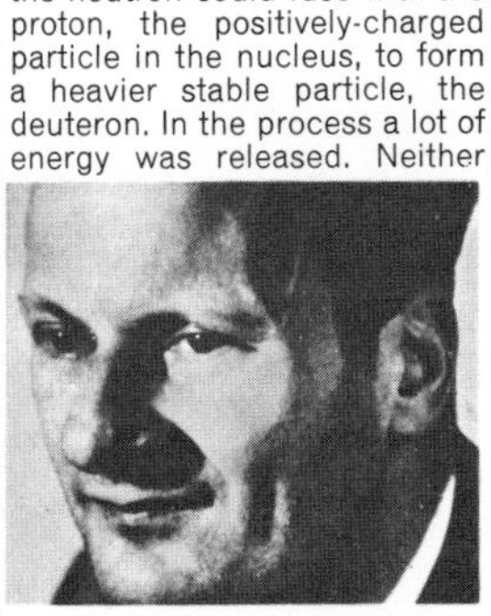

chemical reactions nor gravitational energy can account for the enormous heat and light output of the stars and Bethe proposed a version of the nuclear fusion process as the answer. His researches have left us thermonuclear weapons – and the promise of unlimited supplies of energy. **P. H. S. S.**

'WORLD OF THE ATOM', ED. HENRY A. BOORSE AND LLOYD MOTZ, 2 VOLS. (BASIC BOOKS, 1966); 'PHYSICS FOR THE ENQUIRING MIND', BY ERIC M. ROGERS (O.U.P., 1960).

Theobald von Bethmann Hollweg (German, 1856–1921): statesman. He was made Chancellor of the German Empire in 1909, despite the Kaiser's doubts, for lack of a better alternative. An able, hard-working, conservative intellectual, his freedom of action was limited by the need to satisfy the Kaiser (q.v.), the aristocracy, the army and Parliament, where Socialist strength was growing. He tried to get agreement with Britain over the reduction of naval strength but could not carry the Kaiser against Tirpitz (q.v.). He came to the conclusion that war was inevitable and judged that the Sarajevo murder provided the occasion most favourable to Germany. He urged action on the Austrians throughout July 1914, until it was too late to halt the soldiers. Ready for Germany to make considerable gains in war at non-Germans' expense, he gradually saw that a compromise peace and internal reform were essential; but he lacked the power to achieve

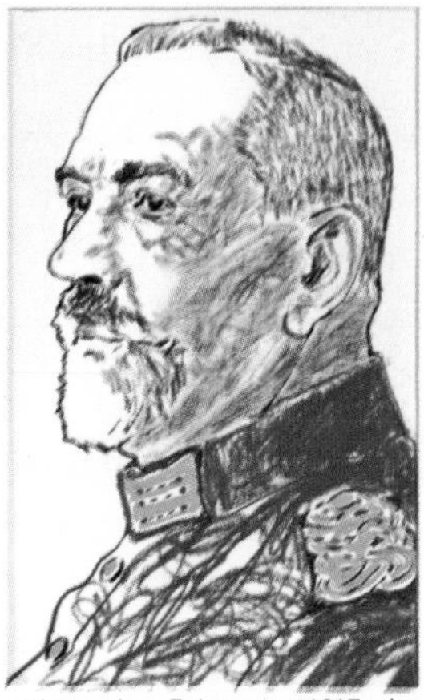

either. In February 1917 he agreed to the submarine campaign against his better judgment. His resignation was finally insisted on by Hindenburg and Ludendorff (qq.v.) in July 1917. **M. L. G. B.**

'REFLECTIONS ON THE WORLD WAR', BY T. VON BETHMANN HOLLWEG (BUTTERWORTH, 1920); 'JULY 1914, THE OUTBREAK OF THE WORLD WAR', ED. I. GEISS (BATSFORD, 1967).

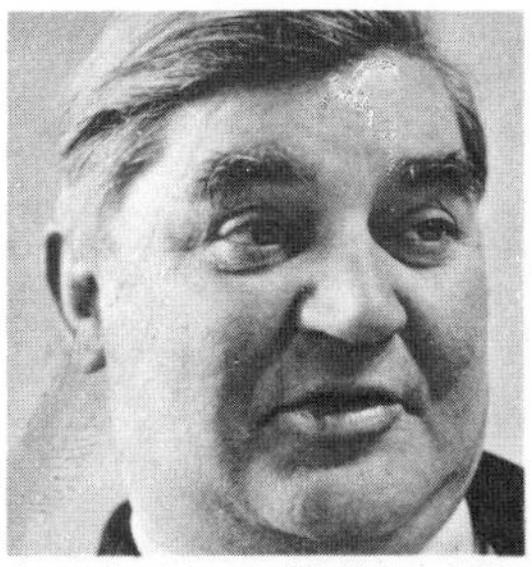

Aneurin Bevan (British, 1897–1960): politician. Chiefly remembered as the architect of the National Health Service, Aneurin Bevan shared with Hugh Gaitskell (q.v.) a tragic destiny. Each was cut off as he drew near his supreme opportunity. Nye Bevan resigned from Attlee's Cabinet over Hugh Gaitskell's Budget. They fought one another for the soul of the Labour movement and crucified one another in the process. Before the end they had come together as allies. Today Nye Bevan's reputation stands probably higher than ever. Among the Labour rank and file he is almost deified. Even those Tories who, with Churchill, regarded him as "a squalid nuisance" for his criticism of the Government during the war, and did not quickly forgive his reference to them as "vermin", recognise him now as one who loved his country. His lack of academic training in the ways of orderly thought must, as in the case of Churchill, be set against the fact of his genius. As an orator he stands alone with Churchill during our time. Yet no contrast could be sharper than that between Churchill's grand literary compositions and Nye Bevan's improvised magic. Nye Bevan's phrases – "The commanding heights of the economy," "The religion of socialism is the language of priorities" – helped to form the outlook of an entire generation. The Health Service built during his Ministry (1945–51) is his lasting monument, and the Labour Movement treasures him as the most eloquent prophet of the new society. **L.**

'ANEURIN BEVAN', BY VINCENT BROME (LONGMANS, 1953); 'ANEURIN BEVAN', BY MICHAEL FOOT, VOL I, 1897–1945 (MACGIBBON AND KEE, 1962).

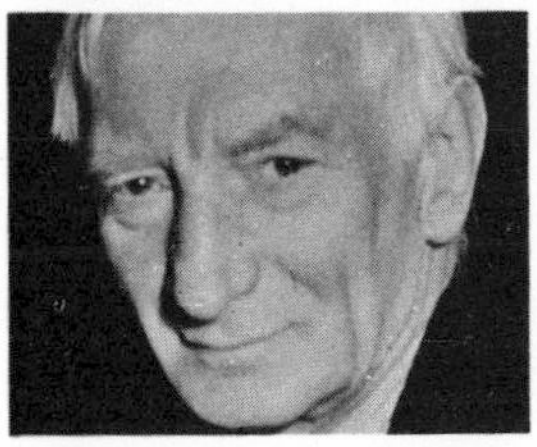

William Beveridge, later Lord Beveridge (British, 1879–1963): public servant. A social worker and journalist turned civil servant, Beveridge was one of the first, in the Edwardian period, to present a realistic analysis of unemployment and to suggest remedies. He pioneered labour exchanges and associated with Churchill and Lloyd George (qq.v.) in other social reforms. After a distinguished backroom career in the First World War, particularly at the vitally important Ministry of Food, he became a director of LSE in the post-war expansionist phase when it was "that part of the University of London on which the concrete never sets", and chaired various commissions. Conceited and unpopular, he was, early in the Second World War, shunted off on to a committee "to survey existing social services and make recommendations". His triumph was to turn this limited assignment into the Beveridge Report, a vivid blueprint for a co-ordinated Welfare State, which caught the imagination of all the peoples engaged in the struggle against Hitler. His programme, implemented by the post-1945 Labour Government, effectively changed the social face of Britain. **A. M.**

'POWER AND INFLUENCE', BY LORD BEVERIDGE (HODDER, 1953); 'LORD BEVERIDGE, 1879-1963', BY LORD SALTER (O.U.P., 1965); 'BRITAIN IN THE CENTURY OF TOTAL WAR', BY ARTHUR MARWICK (BODLEY HEAD, 1968).

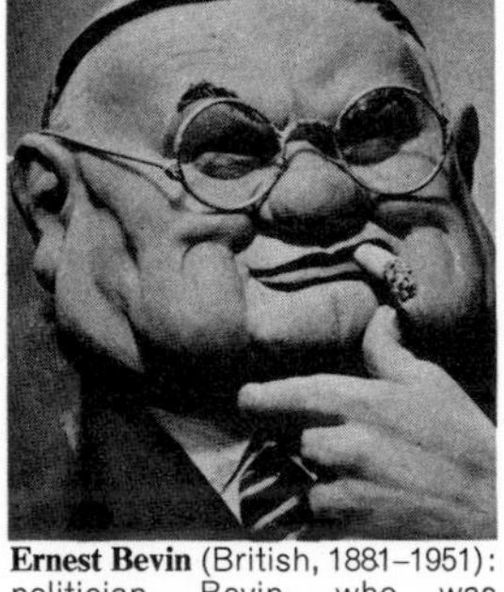

Ernest Bevin (British, 1881–1951): politician. Bevin, who was British Foreign Minister from 1945–51, had no illusions about the Russian threat to the very existence of the West. In the conception of Nato and the whole Western defence system, the U.S. may have been the senior partner, but Bevin was the strongest individual force. He made England's voice count for more among the nations than her strength seemed to make possible. His defects revealed themselves in a scepticism towards the new Israel and a wider European community. As Minister of Labour and National Service (1940–45) his organisation of the Labour force during the war was a glorious achievement. And if he had never entered a government he would still be remembered as the architect of the Transport and General Workers' Union and the most influential trade union leader. He was a granite-like antagonist (when someone said of an opponent "He is his own worst enemy", Ernest Bevin replied, "Not while I am alive he ain't") but his loyalties were wide and binding. He could have supplanted Attlee in 1947, but to him such a course was unthinkable. Without any educational advantages whatever he could hold his own on any plane of discussion. When King George VI asked him where he had gained so much knowledge, he replied: "Your Majesty, I plucked it from the 'edgerows of experience." **L.**

'THE LIFE AND TIMES OF ERNEST BEVIN', BY ALAN BULLOCK (HEINEMANN, VOL I 1960, VOL II 1967).

Georges Bidault (French, b. 1899): politician. Bidault sees himself as the defender of France against two great betrayals: the humiliation of Vichy and the abandonment of Algeria by de Gaulle. A history teacher who joined the French resistance in February 1942, he became President of the National Council of the Resistance in August 1943. De Gaulle (q.v.) made him Foreign Minister in 1944 and he held this post without interruption until 1948 except for a brief period as Prime Minister in 1946. The hopes of post-war France were centred on him. He was a new man; a patriot; a Catholic and a progressive; the principal figure in the new Social Catholic party (MRP); in favour of European unity. But he was not as effective as had been hoped.

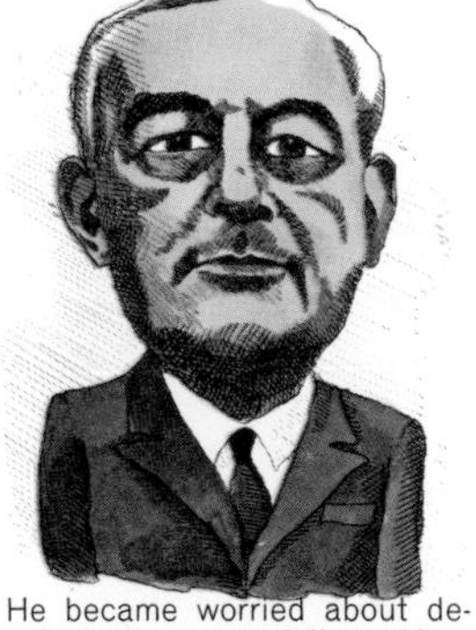

He became worried about decolonisation, especially in Algeria. He supported the return to power of de Gaulle (1958), believing he would keep Algeria French. But when de Gaulle accepted Algerian independence, Bidault opposed him and organised a new National Council of the Resistance. Exiled in 1962, he returned to France only in 1968. An honourable man, but not always right, Bidault illustrates how nationalism is the means in politics whereby one moves from the Left to the Right. **D. W. J. J.**

'RESISTANCE, THE POLITICAL AUTOBIOGRAPHY OF GEORGES BIDAULT', BY GEORGES BIDAULT (WEIDENFELD AND NICOLSON, 1967).

Sir Rowland Biffen (British, 1874–1949): plant breeder. When Biffen was appointed botany lecturer in Cambridge University's newly founded department of agriculture in 1899, plant breeding was aptly described as "a game of chance between man and plants". Biffen's early attempts to improve breadmaking quality in English wheat convinced him that chance favoured the plants. In 1900 a fellow scientist at Cambridge unearthed Mendel's 50-year-old paper on heredity, hitherto overlooked. Biffen

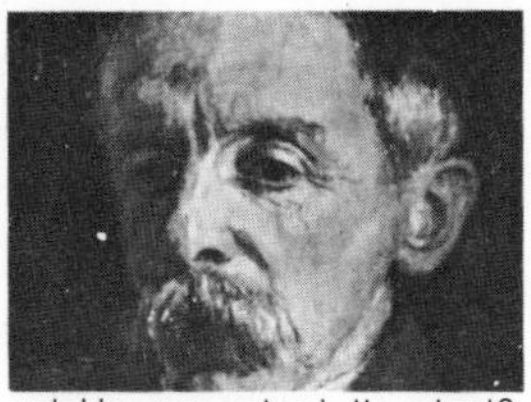

quickly recognised its significance and successfully applied Mendelian principles to produce improved cereal varieties, thus establishing plant breeding as a science. His first wheat, *Little Joss,* was unsurpassed for 40 years. Biffen also demonstrated (1905) that disease-resistance in plants is heritable – a discovery which has had worldwide application in combating crop losses. He directed the Cambridge Plant Breeding Institute from 1912 until 1936, and his scientific acumen and consummate skill started the flow of improved crop plants that have helped agricultural production everywhere. **S. L.**

'PLANT BREEDING', BY W. J. C. LAWRENCE (EDWARD ARNOLD, 1968); 'ESSAYS ON CROP PLANT EVOLUTION', ED. J. B. HUTCHINSON (C.U.P., 1965).

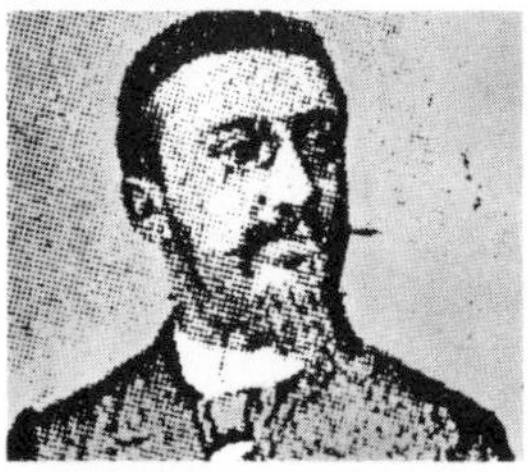

Alfred Binet (French, 1854–1911): psychologist. Binet is father of the Intelligence Test as we know it today. He also pioneered projective tests which have been developed to give insight into personality. He was impressed by Galton's idea for standardised tests to measure individual differences on psychological dimensions, and so he created such a test when asked to devise a method for separating defective from educable children. He had a healthy contempt for elaborate apparatus – "the brass instruments of the German band." The result was a paper and pencil test with some illustrations and other simple material. The performance of suspected defective children on this test could be compared to the obtained performance of a sample of children drawn from the general population. The first scale was published in 1905 and there have been numerous revisions since. The Stanford version of the scale, which was standardised on a large American sample, was last revised in 1960 and is still in use throughout the English-speaking world. **B. R. O.**

'ALFRED BINET', BY R. MARTIN (PRESSES UNIVERSITAIRES DE FRANCE, 1925).

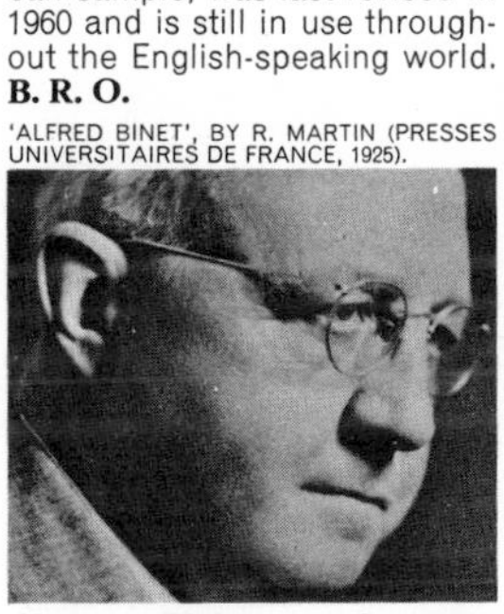

Clarence Birdseye (U.S., 1886–1956): food processer. Without Clarence Birdseye fish fingers would probably not be a national dish. He was a young naturalist with the U.S. Department of Agriculture who became a Labrador fur trader and then an expert in Arctic fishery. On a hunting trip in the early 1920s he observed how food was preserved by natural freezing, and worked for seven years to perfect an industrial process to do the same thing. Birdseye found that if freezing was slow, big crystals formed which broke down the cell structure of the food and ruined the taste. He wedged fresh vegetables and food between freezing metal plates top and bottom, cooled the food from 32° to 25° F. in a few minutes (as against two or three hours the old way), which preserved the taste better, and sold the first packs in 1930. Birdseye was not the first man to freeze food but his idea made money. **T. F. C.**

'BIRDS EYE: THE EARLY YEARS', BY W. J. READER (PRIVATELY PUBLISHED, 1963).

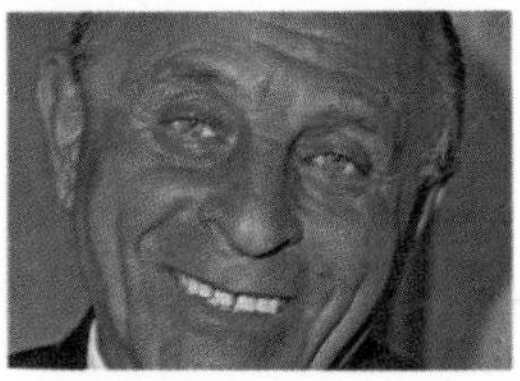

Lázlo Biró (Hungarian, now Argentinian, b. 1900): inventor. Lázlo Biró is the man who noticed the advantages of quick-drying ink and had the idea of combining the ink and some kind of pen. He produced the first crude prototype, and patented it in 1938. Just before the outbreak of war he fled from Hungary's Fascist government to Argentina, where a company was set up. In 1944 he patented a new principle using capillary action and gravity, and the pen was perfected. It could write under water or on wet paper, and the U.S. armed forces took the invention up. After the war, the first 'Biros' sold in Britain for £2 15s. They now cost as little as 3p, and perhaps some 200 million are made in this country every year. **G. P. G. N.**

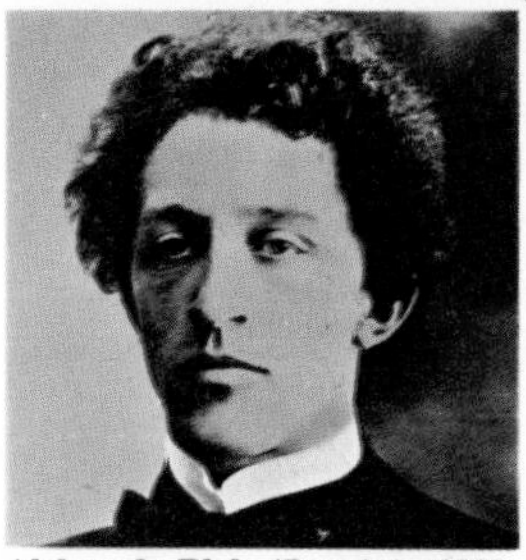

Aleksandr Blok (Russian, 1880–1921): poet. "A poet graced by God, and a man of fearless integrity" (Gorky), Blok was a romantic whose work is the intimate diary of a search for the unattainable. In early poems the ideal is purely personal; later he believed that "in the poetic experience of the world there is no rift between the individual and the general"; he must express not only the music within himself, but also the music that is "the essence of the world". Moreover, the poet's task is active: to change "our false, filthy, boring, ugly life" into a "just, pure, joyful and splendid life". The Russian Revolution seemed to promise just this: in 1918 he wrote his greatest poem, *The Twelve*, to "the sound of the old world crumbling". In this poem Christ, symbol of the "great music of the future", leads his unwitting disciples – 12 Red Guardsmen – towards a new world. Blok did not live to see the form this world was to take; and with his death an epoch ended. He could have no successors.' **T. J. B.**

'MODERN RUSSIAN POETRY', BY VLADIMIR MARKOV AND MERRILL SPARKS (MACGIBBON AND KEE, 1966); 'THE POETS OF RUSSIA 1890–1930', BY RENATO POGGIOLI (HARVARD UNIVERSITY PRESS, 1960);

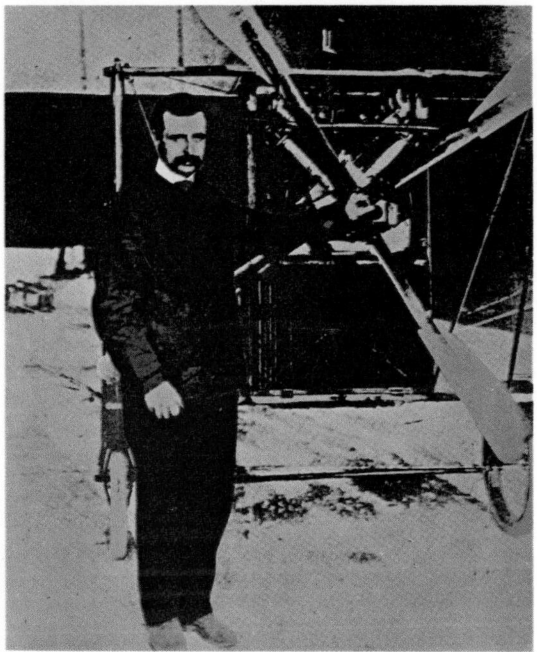

Louis Blériot (French, 1872–1936): aviator. In 1909, amid general hilarity, Lord Northcliffe (q.v.) offered a prize of £1000 for the first flight across the English Channel between sunrise and sunset. On a windless Sunday morning, on July 25, Blériot was helped into his plane; he had burnt his foot in an accident a few days before. "Where is Dover?" he asked, just before he took off at the official sunrise hour of 4.41 a.m. His plane weighed 600 lb., with a 22–25 h.p. engine. Thirty-seven minutes later he landed at Dover, to be met by two bewildered policemen. His engine failed as he landed, and earlier a shower had providentially cooled his engine. The Wright brothers had flown in 1904, and Wilbur Wright had gone 74 miles in 54 minutes in 1908. But Blériot, by making the first flight over water between two countries, dramatised fully the arrival of the aeroplane, and secured glory for France in the process. All the early aviators took great risks. But by one dramatic coup Blériot achieved the most fame and his name will therefore always be synonymous with the dawn of flying. **A. C. C.**

'A HISTORY OF FLYING', BY CHARLES GIBBS-SMITH (BATSFORD, 1953); 'BRITISH AVIATION, THE PIONEER YEARS', BY HARALD PENROSE (PUTNAM, 1967).

Léon Blum (French, 1872–1950): statesman. Though now remembered as the leading French socialist of the last 50 years, Blum was originally a literary and dramatic critic. He entered active politics at the age of 47. Elected deputy after the First World War, he quickly established himself as leader of the French Socialist party. His major achievement was the reconstruction of the party after the Communist Party gained control of Socialist funds and organisation. In 1936–7 he was France's first Socialist prime minister; his Popular Front government introduced paid holidays and the 40-hour week, began the nationalisation of armaments industries, and brought the Bank of France under state control. He earned the hostility of the French Right, and was imprisoned by the Vichy regime during the Second World War, but he survived to become one of the Fourth Republic's elder statesmen. **C. M. A.**

'LEON BLUM', BY L. E. DALBY (THOMAS YOSELOFF, 1963); 'FOR ALL MANKIND', BY LEON BLUM (GOLLANCZ, 1946).

Umberto Boccioni (Italian, 1882–1916): painter and sculptor. Boccioni joined Marinetti, author of the Futurist Manifesto of 1909, in his attempt to bury the glorious past of Italy and concentrate on forms of art appropriate to the modern age. In paintings like *The City Rises* (1910), and sculptures like *Muscles at Speed* (1913) Umberto Boccioni rendered the ethos of Futurism in ways still instinct with the excitement of the time. He made palpable the aggression, controlled or otherwise, which was an important element in Futurism; and when the Futurists provoked their opponents to physical violence (as they often did) Boccioni never avoided the fight. In principle the 1914–18 war was the culmination of all that the Futurists had lived for (see Boccioni's *Charge of the Lancers*, 1915); but his own military experience was a disappointment to him, and just before his accidental death he wrote that, after all, "Art is the only thing that exists". **J. R.**

'CONCISE HISTORY OF MODERN PAINTING', BY H. READ (THAMES AND HUDSON, 1968).

Humphrey Bogart (U.S., 1900–1957): film actor. Bogart's screen character was the hero for disillusioned liberals. Not surprisingly, his legend looks more authentically durable every year. He began life as 'the original Maud Humphrey Baby'. His mother painted in watercolours, his father was a doctor. Bogart started as one of a matching set of patent-leathered Broadway juveniles, actually speaking on stage the deathless words: "Tennis, anyone?" The transition from Humphrey to Bogey was on the way by 1936, when he repeated for Hollywood his stage role as the gangster Duke Mantee in *The Petrified Forest*. But although Bogart became a star as a gangster, he never quite fitted that era. His world and his legend were found in the sour, smokily romantic films of the 1940s: playing Sam Spade for John Huston, Philip Marlowe for Howard Hawks, patrolling his spy-infested nightclub in *Casablanca*, whistling for Lauren Bacall in *To Have and Have Not*, mad for gold in *Treasure of Sierra Madre*. He was the great tarnished incorruptible, and the audience knew that the tarnish wouldn't rub off like studio make-up; he corroded the romantic adventurer's image, played it defensively, sardonically, with a wincing smile, and it emerged as more romantic than ever. **P. H.**

'THE BOGEY MAN', BY JONAH RUDDY AND JONATHAN HILL (SOUVENIR PRESS, 1965); 'BOGEY: THE GOOD-BAD GUY', BY EZRA GOODMAN (LYLE STUART, NEW YORK, 1965); 'BOGEY: THE FILMS OF HUMPHREY BOGART', BY CLIFFORD McCARTY (CITADEL PRESS, NEW YORK, 1965).

Enid Blyton (British, 1897–1968): children's writer. The creator of Noddy trained as a Froebel teacher and worked in educational publishing. Her first book, *Child Whispers,* a collection of verse, was published in 1922, but she did not begin writing prolifically until the late 1930s. Her works include various series of books about favourite characters, including the Famous Five, the Secret Seven, Mr Meddle, and Noddy. She also edited various magazines and undertook school readers and books on nature study and religious subjects. She published around 400 books, of which 200 are constantly in print, and after Agatha Christie and Shakespeare is the most translated British author. Noddy became a major British industry and appeared on soap, china, chocolate, pyjamas, breakfast cereals, curtains. Miss Blyton took her work seriously, and held that she catered for all ages and tastes and that her stories were packed with ethical and moral teaching. Librarians and teachers disagreed, and deplored her flat style and her compulsive hold over children. The most popular children's writer of all time, she was consistently ignored by the adult intelligentsia who simultaneously reviled her and pretended she did not exist. **G. E. A.**

'DEAR LITTLE NODDY', BY COLIN WELCH ('ENCOUNTER', JAN. 1958).

Niels Bohr (Danish, 1885–1962): physicist. Bohr's model of the atom is a cornerstone of 20th century science. He left Copenhagen University in 1911 to work in the Cavendish Laboratory at Cambridge. Six months later he moved to Lord Rutherford's (q.v.) laboratory at Manchester University; he quickly finished his studies on the absorption of alpha rays and turned to the study of the structure of the atom based on Rutherford's discovery of the atomic nucleus. By 1913 he had built up a picture of the hydrogen atom as consisting of a central nucleus surrounded by an electron that could circle it in a variety of different orbits. If the electron dropped into a lower orbit it radiated a quantum of energy; to move to a higher orbit it had first to absorb a quantum of energy. This scheme won Bohr the Nobel Prize for Physics in 1922. During the Nazi occupation of Denmark, he escaped to neutral Sweden and spent the last two years of the war in Britain and America. After the war, he devoted much of his life to furthering peaceful uses of atomic energy. His views are set forth in his Open Letter to the United Nations written in June 1950. **N. V.**

'NIELS BOHR', ED. S. ROZENTAL (NORTH HOLLAND, AMSTERDAM, 1967); 'ESSAYS 1958–62 ON ATOMIC PHYSICS AND HUMAN KNOWLEDGE', BY NIELS BOHR (JOHN WILEY, 1964); 'THE UNITY OF KNOWLEDGE', ED. L. G. LEARY (DOUBLEDAY AND CO, NEW YORK, 1955).

David Bomberg (British, 1890–1957): painter. Bomberg's was the one utterly original voice in the glittering turmoil of pre-1914 painting in London. His near-abstract *The Mud Bath* and *In The Hold* – have stood up to the years as no other English painting from that period. But the First World War smashed that atmosphere of untrammelled experiment and he was never again to recapture the poise, optimistic and dogmatic, from which these pictures had been made. Still less could he recapture the recognition that had greeted them. His unique later style, in which the demanding structures of the early works are rediscovered in a subjective relationship with landscape or figure, was not an easy or a fashionable one. Bomberg brought an almost Mosaic dedication to his work which was not at all what the English art world was used to, and but for a time in the mid-1930s he was unbought. During the last 12 years of his life he put most of his energy into teaching. He died in poverty at the very moment public attention was coming to recognise this noble and uncompromising work. **A. M. F.**

'BOMBERG', BY W. LIPKE (EVELYN ADAMS AND MACKAY, 1968).

Hermann Bondi (British, b. 1919): mathematician. Professor Bondi is one of the three originators of the so-called 'steady state' theory of the Universe. Born in Vienna, he came to Britain in 1937 and was naturalised 10 years later. Until recently he was Director General of the European Space Research Organisation which in 1968 launched three highly successful satellites. In 1948 at Cambridge, Bondi with Thomas Gold (and Fred Hoyle independently) produced a theory in which the Universe, instead of originating in a single primordial fireball (the 'Big Bang'), was regarded as having existed in the same condition since time immemorial. Because the Universe appears to be continuously expanding, this theory demanded an entirely new additional concept – that new matter is being created spontaneously and continuously throughout space. The steady-state theory introduced the 'Perfect Cosmological Principle', which maintains that "every observer must at all times have the same overall impression of the Universe". **P. H. S. S.**

'THE NATURE OF THE UNIVERSE', BY FRED HOYLE (2ND EDITION; BLACKWELL, 1960); 'THE UNIVERSE AT LARGE', BY H. BONDI (HEINEMANN, 1962).

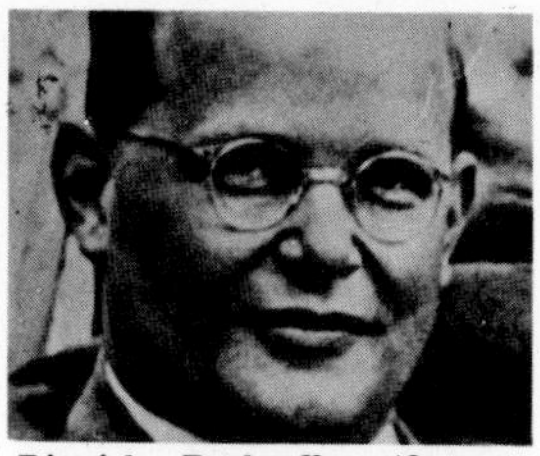

Dietrich Bonhoeffer (German, 1906–1945): theologian. It fell to this Protestant theologian in a Nazi prison to herald the "coming of age" of mankind. But the message of Dietrich Bonhoeffer was not as paradoxical as it seemed. His posthumously published letters formed only one in a series of books where he had meditated on the challenge to the Christian Church of the drama of the 20th century. His anti-Nazi statements made it prudent for the young Bonhoeffer to spend time as a pastor to Germans in South London, and as a critical visitor to the United States. But he chose not to stay abroad, and not to confine himself to professional religion; he became a worker for the political plot against Hitler. In a time of tragedy, he regarded the Christian's discipleship as a share in the suffering of God, and stood and suffered alongside secular men. He expected, however, a time when the Church would have to come to terms with the problems of peace, including secularisation. Would it be necessary, or possible, to work out a 'religionless' Christianity? He was hanged for his part in the plot after writing a few pages about the Church's need to accept man's new dignity, pages which have fascinated post-war Christians. The emphasis in the 1960s on a 'secular Christianity' has treated Bonhoeffer as a major prophet. **D. L. E.**

'THE LIFE AND DEATH OF DIETRICH BONHOEFFER', BY MARY BOSANQUET (HODDER AND STOUGHTON, 1968); 'I KNEW DIETRICH BONHOEFFER', ED. R. GREGOR SMITH (COLLINS, 1966); 'THE COST OF DISCIPLESHIP', BY DIETRICH BONHOEFFER (REVISED EDITION, S.C.M. PRESS, 1959); 'LETTERS AND PAPERS FROM PRISON', BY DIETRICH BONHOEFFER (REVISED EDITION, S.C.M. PRESS, 1967).

Pierre Bonnard (French, 1867–1947): painter. In any list of the great secret professionals Bonnard would come at the top. As a young man he was a member of an outstandingly gifted and amusing group of young people who were involved in painting,

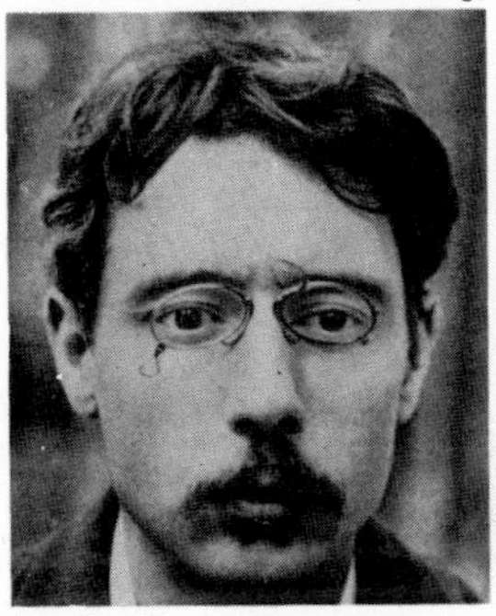

the theatre, music and literature and had something to contribute to all of them. Bonnard was one of the great French social observers: he was able to characterise a man by his eyebrows or a woman by the set of her hat. But as a participant in life he was easy game for anyone – so incurious that he lived with a woman for 40 years without finding out her real name, and so timid that he allowed her to separate him from all his friends until finally his world was bounded almost entirely by the studio, the view from the window, and the bathroom in which his wife would seem to have lolled away a great part of the day. All his audacity went into his painting: till the day of his death he went on raising the stakes, heightening his colour or taking risks with composition which would have made anyone else's pictures fall apart, re-creating the world in a series of small, ugly, inconvenient suburban rooms. **J. R.**

'BONNARD', BY A. VAILLANT (THAMES & HUDSON, 1966).

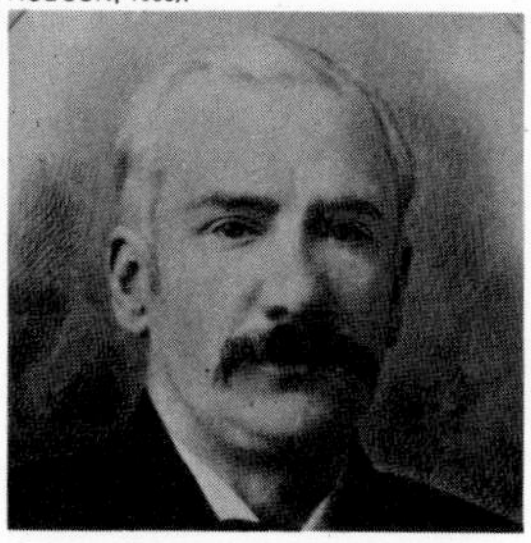

Jesse Boot, later Lord Trent (British, 1850–1931): cash chemist. Jesse Boot was a 19th-century figure who set a marketing pattern which has survived far into the 20th. His father, a Nottingham herbalist, died when Jesse was 10, leaving a shop, and the boy started work there at 13. At 27 he owned it and started a 50-year fight with other chemists by advertising 'Drugs and Proprietary Articles at Reduced Prices'. He stamped ahead (later he took a jackboot for the crest on his coat of arms), sent 200 of the first telegrams to his customers, telling them to "Visit our exceptional display of sponges at Goose Gate", and in 1888 registered the Boots Pure Drug Company. In 1896 he started the first of the great chain of Boots manufacturing plants. By then he had 60 shops in 28 towns – and was virtually ready with the business we know today. At 50 his muscles began to ossify, and eventually he had to be carried everywhere like a baby, but nothing stopped him, and by 1933, two years after his death, the chain was already 1000 strong. **P. W.**

Carl Bosch (German, 1874–1940): chemical engineer. At the turn of the century, scientists realised that man was rapidly outstripping his ability to grow enough food. The problem was nitrogenous fertilisers – there appeared to be a limited supply dependent on the reserves of the Chile saltpetre beds. The first

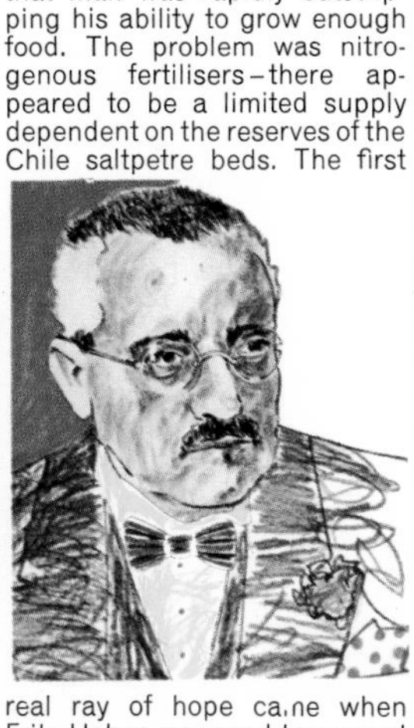

real ray of hope came when Fritz Haber managed to convert nitrogen from the air and hydrogen into ammonia – an important raw material for fertilisers – in his laboratory at Karlsruhe. In 1908, the German chemical giant Badische Anilin-und Soda-fabrik acquired the rights to this process and set Bosch the task of making the laboratory process work on an industrial scale. Working with Alwin Mittasch, Bosch improved on the catalysts used by Haber. These speeded up the reaction and made it possible; but to make it work well, high gas pressures were needed and the chemical Industry had no experience of work at such pressures. By 1913, Bosch had taken the process through all the steps necessary to make it feed the world and he had shown the chemical industry that it was not merely a large-scale laboratory dream. **M.A.S.**

'AN INTRODUCTION TO CHEMICAL INDUSTRY', BY JOHN MANNING (PERGAMON, 1965); 'NOBEL PRIZEWINNERS IN CHEMISTRY', BY EDUARD FARBER (REVISED EDITION, ABELARD-SCHUMAN, 1963); 'NOBEL LECTURES: CHEMISTRY 1922-41' (ELSEVIER, 1966).

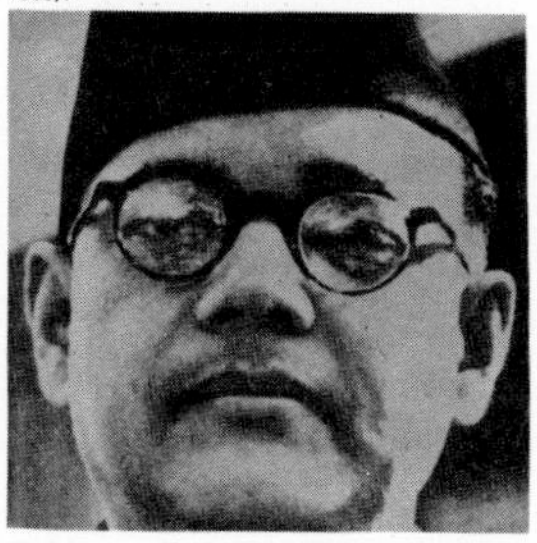

Subhas Chandra Bose (Indian, 1897–1945): politician. 'The Springing Tiger' was 20th-century Bengal's greatest hero. After studying at Cambridge he entered politics in 1921 under C. R. Das, the Bengal Swarajya leader, and ran the Calcutta Corporation. In 1927 he assumed Das's mantle. He was jailed twice (1930 and 32) for his part in Gandhi's (q.v.) civil disobedience movements and then lived in Europe (1933-36). From there he condemned Gandhi's tactics, and evolved a militant programme that veered between socialism and totalitarianism. Back in India, he joined with Nehru and other Left-wingers in attacking Gandhi's Old Guard who, in an effort to appease the criticism, let Bose become Congress President in 1938; however, they soon forced him out when he openly challenged Gandhi's leadership. Bose then formed the Forward bloc, and urged India to take advantage of Britain's war difficulties to win independence; but he failed even in Bengal to upset Gandhi's dominance. Early in 1941 Bose fled to Berlin. He tried and failed to get Germany and Italy to declare for Indian independence, but satisfied his taste for soldiering by organising an Indian Legion. In 1943 he threw in his lot with the Japanese, formed a Provisional Government of Free India, and organised an Indian National Army (of POWs) which fought in the Burma Campaign. He died in a plane crash in Formosa (though some admirers still believe he is alive). Bose's career is a commentary on the political decline and fall of Bengal in the 20th century, as well as on the failure of the Left Wing and the militants to capture the Indian National Congress. **A. S.**

'AN INDIAN PILGRIM' BY SUBHAS CHANDRA BOSE (ASIA PUBLISHING HOUSE, LONDON, 1965); 'SUBHAS CHANDRA BOSE, THE SPRINGING TIGER', BY HUGH TOYE (CASSELL, 1959).

Horatio Bottomley (British, 1860–1933): demagogue. Swindler, publisher, on-and-off millionaire, politician, super-spiv, crusader-journalist, spellbinder, racehorse owner – Bottomley was an arch-rogue who was almost a great man. Millions believed he would become Prime Minister and conjure easy times for the workers in his own mode of kippers and champagne for breakfast before the races. He was raised in a Birmingham orphanage, became a Law Courts shorthand writer, developed as mob orator, and was elected M.P. for South Hackney in 1906. (Unseated because of bankruptcy, he was triumphantly re-elected in 1918.) He bought a London evening newspaper, launched *John Bull*, floated a multitude of crooked companies and lotteries, and mulcted the poor he championed of £20 million. In 1922 he was imprisoned for seven years for fraudulent conversion. His last part was as a walk-on at the Windmill Revudeville, and he died a pauper in a public ward. The mystery of Bottomley is not that he fooled so many for so long, but that he couldn't be bothered to seize the power available to him. He anticipated Hitler and Mussolini as a 20th century mob-ruler, and had a Kennedy charisma. His mass magic was that of a serviceman's tribune, the workers' hero; but he also bewitched men of rank. His preference for being a playboy rather than a Führer possibly saved democracy from sinister pressures. **K. A.**

'HORATIO BOTTOMLEY: A BIOGRAPHY OF AN OUTSTANDING PERSONALITY', BY S. THEODORE FELSTEAD (MURRAY, 1936); 'THE RISE AND FALL OF HORATIO BOTTOMLEY', BY "TENAX" (ARCHER, 1933); 'HORATIO BOTTOMLEY: A BIOGRAPHY', BY JULIAN SYMONS (CRESSET PRESS, 1955).

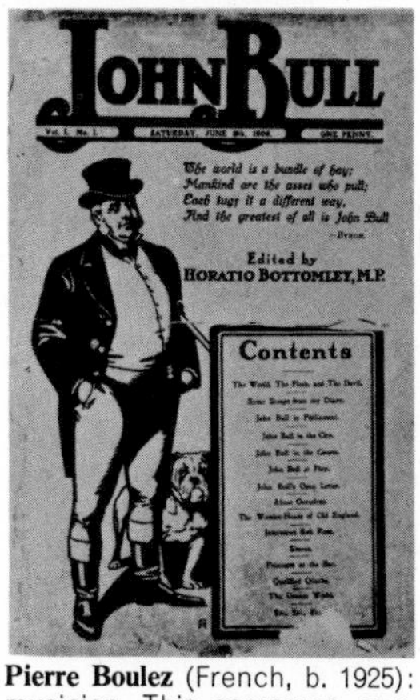
JOHN BULL
The world is a bundle of hay:
Mankind are the asses who pull;
Each tugs it a different way,
And the greatest of all is John Bull
Edited by
HORATIO BOTTOMLEY, M.P.
Contents

Pierre Boulez (French, b. 1925): musician. This composer, conductor and self-taught pianist was a student of mathematics until he became Messiaen's pupil in 1944 and, in due course, spiritual pupil of Debussy, Stravinsky, Schoenberg and Webern (qq.v.). Boulez's attitude to Schoenberg has been ambivalent; in fact, he has profited greatly from his love-hates towards father figures. From total serialism to partial and controlled indeterminacy ultimately inspired by John Cage (q.v.), his brilliant compositions have been searching for contrasting methods of construc-

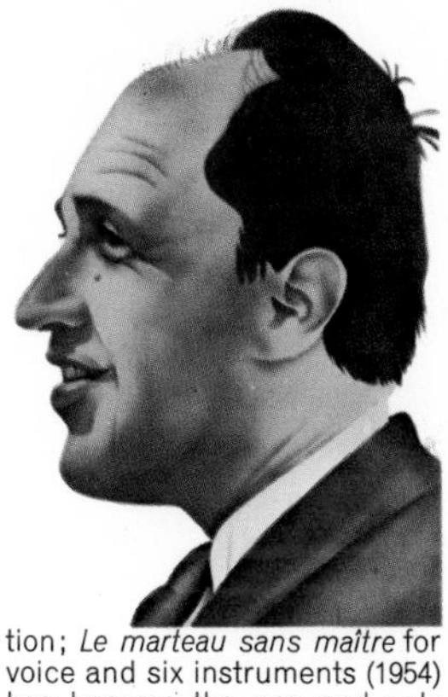

tion; *Le marteau sans maître* for voice and six instruments (1954) has become the one and only top-of-the-pop avant-garde work. In recent years, he has developed into a virtuoso conductor and has become Chief Conductor of the BBC Symphony Orchestra. His intense re-creative activities may be indicative of a creative crisis. He has only published about half his output. He has acted as a continuous stimulator on mid-century music; our own Richard Rodney Bennett was his pupil. **H. K.**

'THOUGHTS ON MUSIC TODAY', BY PIERRE BOULEZ, TRANS. SUSAN BRADSHAW AND RICHARD RODNEY BENNETT (FABER, COMING 1970); 'IN SEARCH OF BOULEZ', BY SUSAN BRADSHAW AND RICHARD RODNEY BENNETT, IN 'MUSIC AND MUSICIANS' JANUARY 1963 and AUGUST 1963.

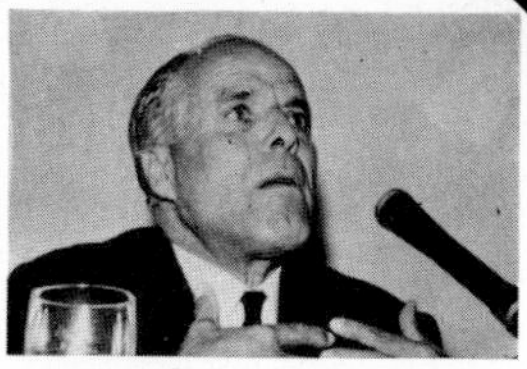

Habib Bourguiba (Tunisian, b. 1903): head of state. This French-educated intellectual founded the neo-Destour party in the 1930s, and in 20 years of organising, negotiating, exile and imprisonment, secured independence for Tunisia (1956). He became Prime Minister; then, after deposing the Bey, President of the Republic. Before independence, his personal contribution lay in the skill with which he created a disciplined party with roots in every town and village, and his tactics of accepting what the French offered and using it as a basis for further demands. Since independence, he has given Tunisia more than a decade of firm government, economic development and honest administration. He has used the party as a channel of communication between ruler and ruled. Bourguiba's tragedy has been to be a great man in a small country. Until 1962, his policy was overshadowed by the Algerian national revolt, which was largely directed from Tunisian territory. In the Middle East, his suggestions that the Arabs should follow towards Israel the policy he had adopted towards France – accept less than they wanted, practise co-existence and wait patiently – fell between two stools; other Arab rulers denounced him, and the Israelis made no response. **A. H. H.**

'TUNISIA', BY A. SYLVESTER (BODLEY HEAD, 1969).

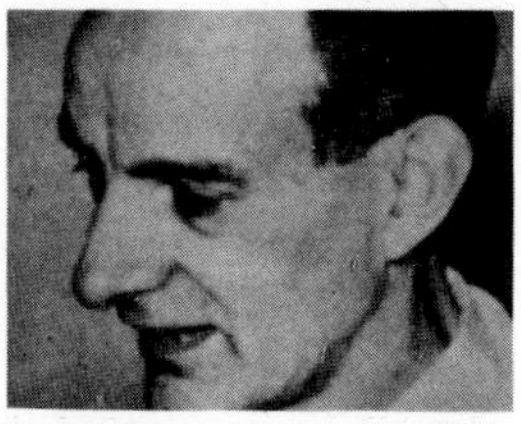

Daniel Bovet (Swiss, b. 1907): pharmacologist. Sufferers from hay fever and travel sickness have reason to be grateful to Daniel Bovet. In the 1920s and 1930s a great deal had been discovered about histamine, acetylcholine and adrenaline, substances which are made in the body and have important functions. Histamine, for example, is released from affected tissues in various allergic diseases, such as urticaria and hay fever, and acetylcholine is the transmitter substance at many types of nerve terminals, including those of motor nerves to voluntary muscle. Bovet began his work in the 1930s and for 20 years looked for new compounds with structural resemblances to naturally occurring ones, with the idea of finding substances that would block the effects of histamine, acetylcholine or adrenaline. His plan succeeded brilliantly and resulted in the introduction into medicine of several series of completely new types of drugs. The general approach to drug synthesis which this Nobel Prize-winner (1957) pioneered has been and continues to be extremely fruitful. **A. H.**

'SELECTIVE TOXICITY', BY A. ALBERT (4TH. ED., METHUEN, 1968); 'CURARE AND CURARE-LIKE AGENTS', BY D. BOVET, F. BOVET-NITTI AND G. B MARINI-BETTOLO (ELSEVIER, 1959); 'NOBEL LECTURES IN PHYSIOLOGY OR MEDICINE, 1942–1962', ED. NOBEL FOUNDATION, PP 549–580 (ELSEVIER, 1964).

Clara Bow (U.S., 1905–1965): film actress. The original 'It' girl was raised in poverty in Brooklyn. At the age of 17 she won a beauty competition which took her to Hollywood and – in the space of a dozen films – to stardom. As an actress she was capable, vivacious, charming, and would still have been a star even if she had never made *It* (1927); but it was this film, based on Elinor Glyn's novel and supervised by the formidable Madame Glyn herself, that seemed to focus Bow's particular and potent kind of sexuality. She was the quintessence of the Flapper, the New Girl of the Jazz Age – smoking, drinking and dancing till dawn, in revolt against the old morality and the old hypocrisy, withal good-natured and gritty. Significantly her career did not really survive the Twenties, which she, more than anyone else, symbolised. Her own dream-wish career; the roles she played; the scandals of her private life; the high spirits that were in her later years to turn to mental disorder, seemed to sum up the feverish optimism and the poignant disillusion of America between the First World War and the Wall Street crash. **D. R.**

'THE PUBLIC IS NEVER WRONG', BY ADOLPH ZUKOR (PUTNAM, 1953); 'THE CELLULOID SACRIFICE', BY ALEXANDER WALKER (MICHAEL JOSEPH, 1966, PUBLISHED AS 'SEX IN THE MOVIES' BY PENGUIN, 1968).

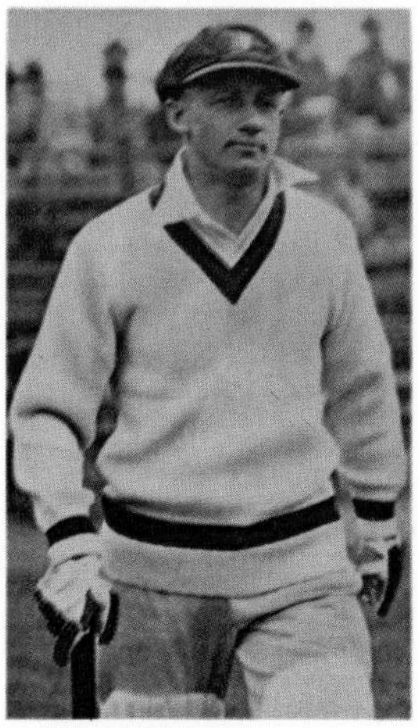

Sir Donald Bradman (Australian, b. 1908): cricketer. Most men need a god, and for those who revere batsmen the figure up there is a little man in a baggy green cap: Bradman, The Don, Sir Donald; a lonely boy for whom practice (with golf ball and stump) made perfect. If this man had hit one more boundary in any one of 80 Test matches he would have averaged 100. Footwork he had, and shots – like his trademark, the pull to leg, right knee bent, ball never off the ground. He was fielder too, and a winning captain. Contemporaries called him a batting engine, a machine without a soul: the lonely boy, we are told, became a man admired but not loved. But re-read the story of body-line – his trial by fire. Learn of the pride and courage great cricketers share with generals and politicians. Beat Bradman and we've won, said Jardine. Right. From that moment cricket changed: it was no longer merely a game to be savoured and enjoyed. And for Bradman there was no joy in being second. That was 1932. Since then many other games have seen the screw of competition tighten. And Bradman gave that screw its biggest twist. **R. G. M.**

'WISDEN CRICKETERS' ALMANACK' (1949); 'FAREWELL TO CRICKET', BY DON BRADMAN (HODDER AND STOUGHTON, 1950); 'BRIGHTLY FADES THE DON', BY J. H. FINGLETON (COLLINS, 1949); 'CRICKET – THE GREAT ONES', ED. JOHN ARLOTT (PELHAM BOOKS, 1967).

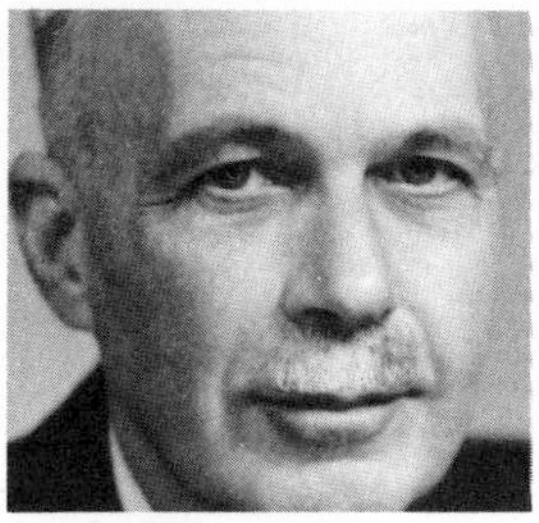

Sir Lawrence Bragg (British 1890–1971): crystallographer. Son of W. H. Bragg (q.v.) with whom he revealed the molecular architecture of crystals, Bragg was born in Adelaide and came to England with his parents in 1909. He took a first in physics at Trinity, Cambridge, in 1911, and that year started his classic work on the 'von Laue phenomenon'. For three years he collaborated closely with his father, with whom he shared the Nobel Prize for Physics in 1915 for "services in the analysis of crystal structure by means of Röntgen (X-) rays". After the war (in which he won the M.C.), Bragg became Professor of Physics at Manchester University, where he stayed until 1937, then director of the National Physical Laboratory for a year before moving to Cambridge. Professor Emeritus at the Royal Institution until his death, he directed research until 1966 on X-ray analysis of the structure of protein molecules – work which is fundamental to the understanding of the complex molecules of living matter. The Braggs, father and son, provided the tools for visualising the intricate architecture of molecules. **N. V.**

'AN INTRODUCTION TO CRYSTAL ANALYSIS', BY SIR WILLIAM BRAGG (G. BELL AND SONS, 1929); 'AN INTRODUCTION TO CRYSTALLOGRAPHY' BY F. C. PHILLIPS (LONGMANS, 1963).

Sir William Bragg (British, 1862–1942): physicist. The man who with his son Lawrence (q.v.) revealed the molecular architecture of crystals studied mathematics at Trinity College, Cambridge, before settling for physics in the Cavendish Laboratory. He became Professor of Mathematics at the University of Adelaide when only 23. He re-

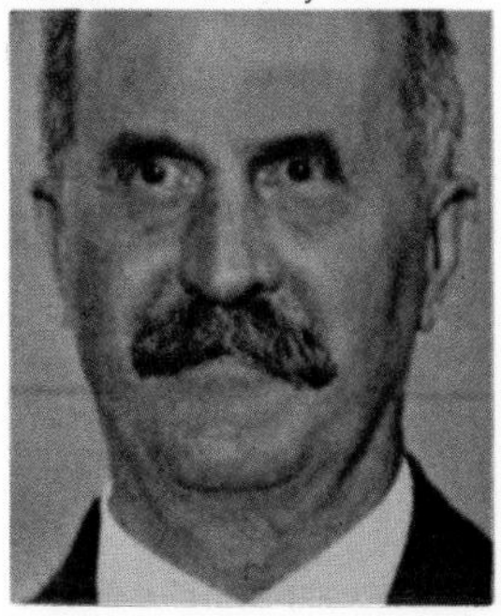

turned to Britain in 1909, to become Professor of Physics at Leeds; by 1923 he had become Director of the Royal Institution in London. He was highly adept at picking up subjects casually, making important contributions and then dropping them; but he is remembered largely for the brilliant work done with his son Lawrence on the analysis of crystal structures using X-ray beams. Father and son were awarded the Nobel Prize for Physics in 1915. Knighted in 1920 for his scientific eminence and work done during the war on the detection of U-boats, Bragg was in short a man of astonishing productiveness who, with his son's assistance, developed the branch of science known as X-ray crystallography. **N. V.**

BIBLIOGRAPHY: SEE PREVIOUS ENTRY.

Constantin Brancusi (Rumanian, 1876–1957): sculptor. Brancusi invented modern sculpture, bringing it with his own two hands from stage-coach to satellite. Yet no one could have been further from 'modern man' than Brancusi, who at seven was a shepherd boy in the Carpathian mountains, and at 18 an apprentice carver just teaching himself to read and write. He came to Paris in 1904 from a countryside still sunk in

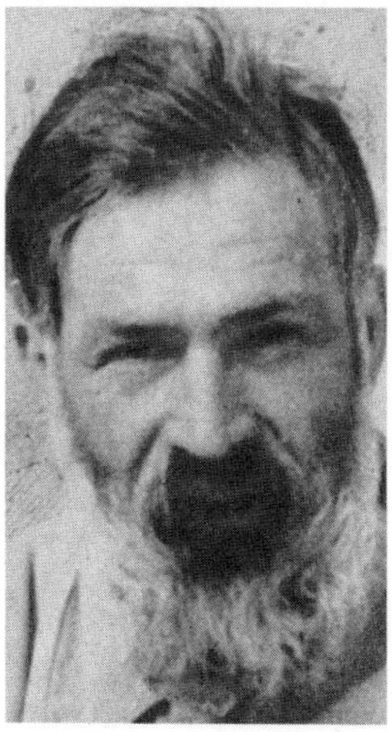

prehistory; once in Paris, he pioneered the reductive principle which was eventually to dominate in our century in every department of life, from architecture to electronics and from interior design to space-travel. Faced with an art that had barely moved forward since Bernini, he went after the irreducible, "the essence of things, and not their outward form". He kept to a primeval rhythm, working and re-working each sculpture for years, searching for the lines of force that would release its maximum potential, and "meditating", as Ezra Pound (q.v.) noted, "on pure form, free from all terrestrial gravitation". What resulted was often archaic in its massive simplicity and its disdain for compromise. Prehistory was reborn in these blocks of wood and stone; and much of what had passed for sculpture was dwarfed. But Brancusi also did things which we have not quite caught up with even today; he made speed visible, he found emblems for weightless flight, and he produced an "infinitely extendable steel tower which, if enlarged, would support the vault of Heaven". **J. R.**

'BRANCUSI: STUDY OF A SCULPTOR', BY S. GEIST (STUDIO VISTA, 1968); 'BRANCUSI', BY C. GIEDION-WELCKER (ZWEMMER, 1959); 'CONSTANTIN BRANCUSI', BY DAVID LEWIS (TIRANTI, 1957); 'BRANCUSI', BY I. JIANOU (ZWEMMER, 1963).

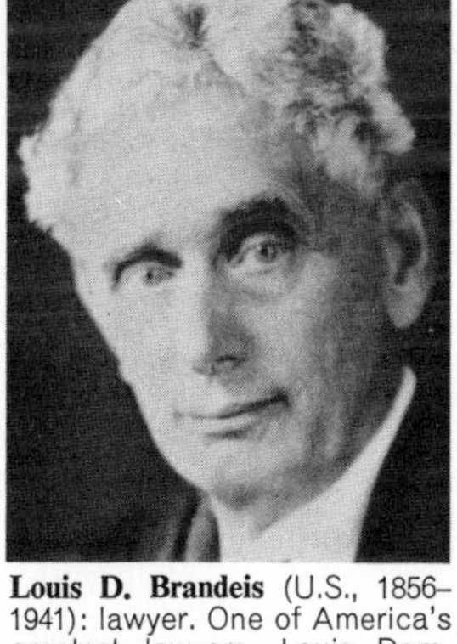

Louis D. Brandeis (U.S., 1856–1941): lawyer. One of America's greatest lawyers, Louis Dembitz Brandeis was the first Jew to be appointed to the United States Supreme Court. The bitter opposition to his appointment in 1916 was as much the result of his progressive views as of his religion. Of middle-class, middle-Western, middle-European immigrant background, he graduated from the Harvard Law School with the highest marks ever attained. He soon became a millionaire by his law practice but cared more for his public work, which earned him the name 'The People's Attorney'. He was deeply devoted to Civil Service reform, antitrust legislation, the rights of labour, and freedom of thought. He was a close adviser of President Wilson (q.v.), and is often credited with that Administration's increasing radicalism. An ardent Zionist, he was instrumental in obtaining the Balfour Declaration which promised a Jewish national home in Palestine. His forceful progressive opinions had a deep effect on American socio-political development. He was an ardent supporter of Franklin D. Roosevelt (q.v.) and of much of the New Deal. A fearless, tireless and masterly advocate of liberal causes, he embodied two familiar American combinations – Jewish Liberal and political lawyer. **H. C. A.**

'OTHER PEOPLE'S MONEY, AND HOW THE BANKERS USE IT', BY LOUIS D. BRANDEIS (STOKES, NEW YORK, 1914); 'BRANDEIS: A FREE MAN'S LIFE', BY A. T. MASON (VIKING PRESS, NEW YORK, 1946); 'THE AGE OF REFORM, FROM BRYAN TO F. D. R.', BY RICHARD HOFSTADTER (KNOPF, NEW YORK, 1955); 'JUSTICE LOUIS D. BRANDEIS', BY E. RABINOWITZ (PHILOSOPHICAL LIBRARY, NEW YORK, 1968).

Marlon Brando (U.S., b. 1924): actor. Brando's mumbling, psychopathic Stanley Kowalski in the Broadway production of *A Streetcar Named Desire* and his re-creation of the role in his second movie in 1951 made him America's first major post-war star. As the foremost exponent of 'The Method', Brando helped shape the character of a new wave of actors and, through his restless, non-conformist behaviour, became an emblematic figure to a new generation of rebellious youth. For five years there was a consonance between the idiosyncratic private Brando and his screen persona in an outstanding series of movies (*Viva Zapata!, Julius Caesar, On the Waterfront, The Wild One, Guys and Dolls*), which revealed his immense range. Subsequently his complex, self-tortured personality was rarely realised, except perhaps in *One-Eyed Jacks* which he directed himself. The greatest screen actor of our day, Brando remains an enigma, who at 47 may still surprise those who regard him as a spent force: a victim of our society, who has had too much demanded of him and has failed to find the right vehicles to contain the immense demands he makes on himself. **P. N. F.**

'MARLON BRANDO AND THE GHOST OF KOWALSKI', BY HOLLIS ALPERT IN 'THE DREAM AND THE DREAMERS' (MACMILLAN, NEW YORK, 1962); 'THE DUKE IN HIS DOMAIN', BY TRUMAN CAPOTE IN 'SELECTED WRITINGS OF TRUMAN CAPOTE' (HAMISH HAMILTON, 1963); 'BRANDO', BY CHARLES HAMBLETT (MAY FAIR BOOKS, 1962).

Willy Brandt (German, b. 1913): politician. Willy Brandt, now Leader of the Social Democratic Party, is one of the most exciting personalities in West German politics. From the humblest beginnings – he was born illegitimate – he has risen to be Foreign Minister of West Germany. And he achieved this after having to leave Germany in 1933 as an opponent of the Nazis, working in both the German and Norwegian 'undergrounds' against them, and returning to Germany in 1945 as a Norwegian citizen. He took back German nationality, worked in the Berlin administration, and rose to be its Governing Mayor in 1957. He became chairman of the opposition S.P.D. in 1964, and Social Democratic candidate for the Chancellorship in 1961 and 1965. In December 1966 he became Foreign Minister under the Christian Democratic Chancellor Kiesinger. He showed flair and judgment in governing Berlin for nearly a decade. He

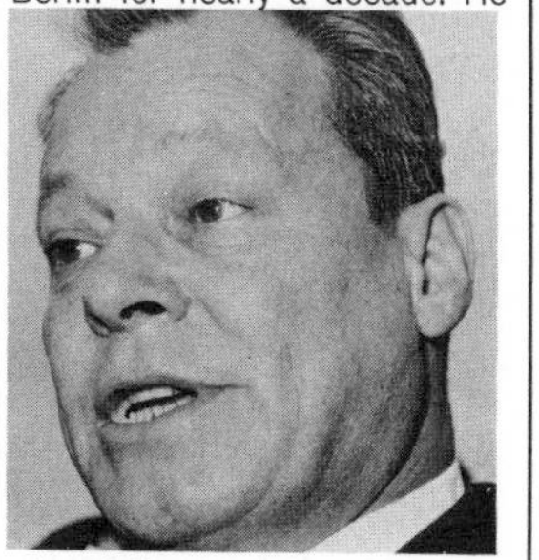

played the biggest part in inducing his Party to 'think European', supporting a German contribution to Nato and membership of the Common Market, and to pursue pragmatic and not ideologically-based policies. He is a keen supporter of British membership of the Common Market, and of expanding it to include Scandinavian and other applicants. He was the natural choice for Chancellor after the Social Democratic Party's triumph in the 1969 elections. **T. C. F. P.**

'WILLY BRANDT', BY JOHN HYND (LINCOLNS PRAGER, 1966); 'SOCIETY AND DEMOCRACY IN GERMANY', BY RALF DAHRENDORF (WEIDENFELD AND NICOLSON, 1968); 'MY ROAD TO BERLIN', BY WILLY BRANDT (PETER DAVIES, 1960).

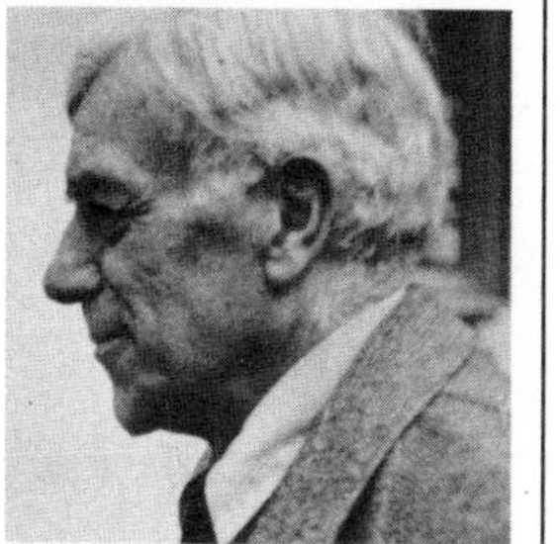

Georges Braque (French, 1882–1963): painter. Braque in his work has a triple identity. He was the last of the great French decorative painters. A still life of oysters or peaches or red mullet by Braque was the picture that nearly everyone most wanted to have – benign but never insipid, resourceful but never 'clever', delectable but never merely ingratiating: intelligent, above all things. But he was also, with Picasso, the co-founder of cubism: a tough-minded, tough-acting revolutionary who called perspective "a ghastly mistake which it has taken four centuries to redress", and the author of the austere, monumental canvases of 1911 which can hold their own with any pictures painted anywhere and at any time. Thirdly, he was the man who went on inventing in old age, when others foundered in narcissism and lucrative self-imitation. In Braque's great symphonic interiors of 1948-56 the very idea of painting a room is re-invented from scratch. Space has a mysterious ambivalent quality, objects wind in and out of one another, the paint itself takes on a richness and particularity which have no precedent, and a great European tradition is taken to a point beyond which it can go no further. Braque was the end of something; but that end upheld man's dignity. **J. R.**

'BRAQUE', BY JOHN RICHARDSON (PENGUIN, 1959); 'GEORGES BRAQUE', BY JOHN RUSSELL (PHAIDON, 1959); 'BRAQUE', BY E. MULLINS (THAMES AND HUDSON, 1968).

BRA-BRO

Wernher von Braun (U.S., b. Germany 1912): engineer. The rockets that have put men – both Russian and American – into space have been made possible by the work of Wernher von Braun. While still at school von Braun wrote a thesis on the theory of long-range rockets, and at university was inspired by Hermann Oberth (q.v.), who 20 years earlier had made a detailed study of space flight. Von Braun became Technical Director of the German Army's rocket establishment at Peenemünde at 25, and within two years had fired an experimental liquid propellant rocket in a stable and controlled trajectory. By 1942, he had developed the V2 ballistic missile weighing 13 tons, using liquid oxygen and alcohol as fuel, and over 5000 of these missiles were launched against London from bases in Holland. The V2 was the prototype for all subsequent liquid-fuelled rockets both in Russia and America. After the war von Braun went to the United States and developed the Redstone rocket which was selected as the only booster reliable enough for launching the one-man Mercury space capsule in 1961. His eight-engined Saturn was chosen for the orbital flight test of the Apollo command module, and his Saturn V for the manned lunar landing. The phenomenal successes of the Apollo missions have set entirely new standards of reliability. Continued planetary exploration is now limited not by engineering but by the resources which can be made available. It is von Braun, more than any other man, who has brought this about. As General Dornberger (q.v.) commented when the V2 made its first flight in October 1942: "Today the spaceship was born." **R. C.**

'ROCKETS, MISSILES AND SPACE TRAVEL', BY W. LEY (VIKING PRESS, 1957).

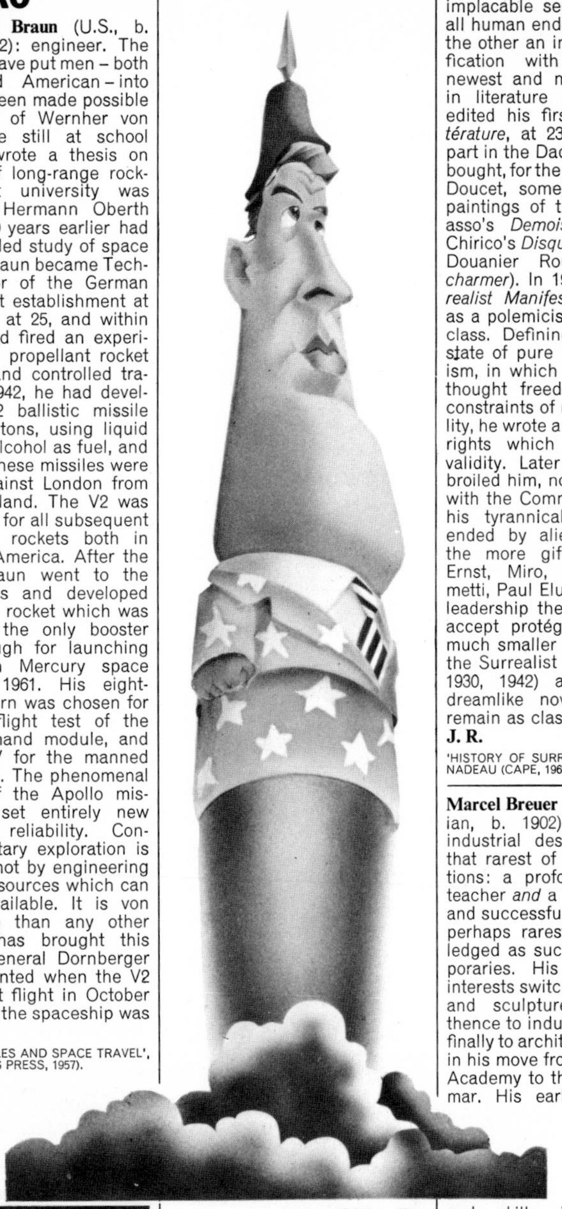

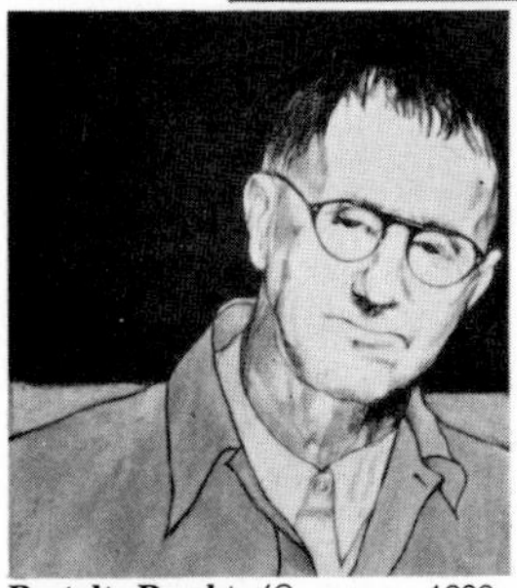

Bertolt Brecht (German, 1898–1956): dramatist and poet. This Marxist used the theatre for spreading Communism, at first directly (*The Mother*, 1932), later by inviting his audiences to draw the obvious conclusion from the facts (*Mother Courage*, 1941: capitalism as the cause of war). His alienation theory of presentation was meant to induce reflection in the audience, not acquiescence – "Change the world, it can do with it!" – but the relevance of his facts was questionable (Mother Courage is not a capitalist, the causes of war are not explored, and though *The Caucasian Chalk Circle* of 1948 was apparently a parable of rational agricultural policy its political moral seems an afterthought to the anarchistic high jinks). Brecht enjoyed worldwide success in front of the Iron Curtain, but was not popular in the USSR. *The Threepenny Opera* (1928) is his best-known work. Some illiberalism and brutality in plays of his middle period (*The Measures Taken*, 1930) disappeared in later plays (*Galileo*, 1943) which were mellower and less strident. His lyric poetry is now praised by some more than the plays – which, though an outstanding attempt at making literature directly relevant to politics, suggest to some that it can't be done. **R. D. G.**

'THE THEATRE OF BERTOLT BRECHT', BY J. WILLETT (METHUEN, 1959); 'BRECHT: A CHOICE OF EVILS', BY M. ESSLIN (EYRE AND SPOTTISWOODE, 1959); 'BRECHT', BY RONALD GRAY (OLIVER AND BOYD, 1961); 'BRECHT, A COLLECTION OF CRITICAL ESSAYS', BY P. DEMETZ (PRENTICE-HALL, 1962).

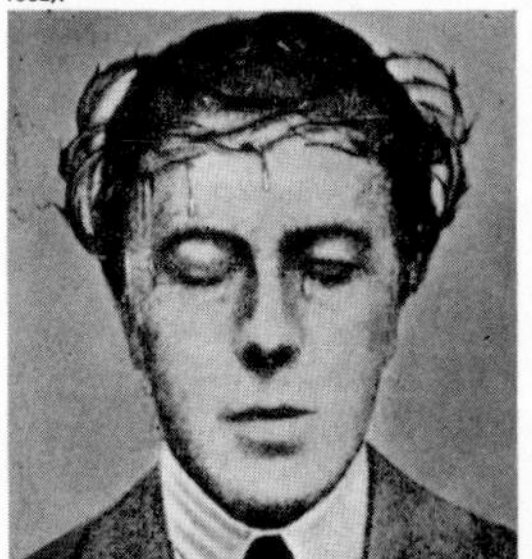

André Breton (French, 1896–1966): surrealist leader. Befriended in youth by two great poets, Valéry and Apollinaire, Breton took from the one his implacable sense of quality in all human endeavours and from the other an imaginative identification with whatever was newest and most adventurous in literature and art. Breton edited his first magazine, *Littérature*, at 23, took a leading part in the Dada movement and bought, for the collector Jacques Doucet, some of the greatest paintings of this century (Picasso's *Demoiselles d'Avignon*, Chirico's *Disquieting Muses*, the Douanier Rousseau's *Snake-charmer*). In 1924 his *First Surrealist Manifesto* revealed him as a polemicist of the very first class. Defining Surrealism as a state of pure psychic automatism, in which for the first time thought freed itself from the constraints of reason and morality, he wrote a charter of human rights which still has much validity. Later manifestos embroiled him, not always happily, with the Communist Party, and his tyrannical turn of mind ended by alienating many of the more gifted Surrealists – Ernst, Miro, Magritte, Giacometti, Paul Eluard. The habit of leadership then caused him to accept protégés who were of much smaller calibre. But both the Surrealist Manifestos (1924, 1930, 1942) and the strange dreamlike novel *Nadja* (1928) remain as classics of their kind. **J. R.**

'HISTORY OF SURREALISM', BY MAURICE NADEAU (CAPE, 1968).

Marcel Breuer (U.S., ex-Hungarian, b. 1902): architect and industrial designer. Breuer is that rarest of mortal combinations: a profoundly influential teacher *and* a highly practical – and successful – designer; and, perhaps rarest of all, acknowledged as such by his contemporaries. His early aesthetic interests switched from drawing and sculpture to craft-work, thence to industrial design, and finally to architecture – reflected in his move from the Vienna Art Academy to the Bauhaus, Weimar. His early preoccupation and skills in experimental furniture design and modular unit systems resulted in his appointment as head of the Bauhaus furniture department at 24. His steel tubular designs for chairs, desks, tables brought him wide technical renown (perhaps the best known is his steel-and-leather chair, below); these 40-year-old designs have retained their validity and, more surprising, their popularity among architects and designer-decorators, particularly in

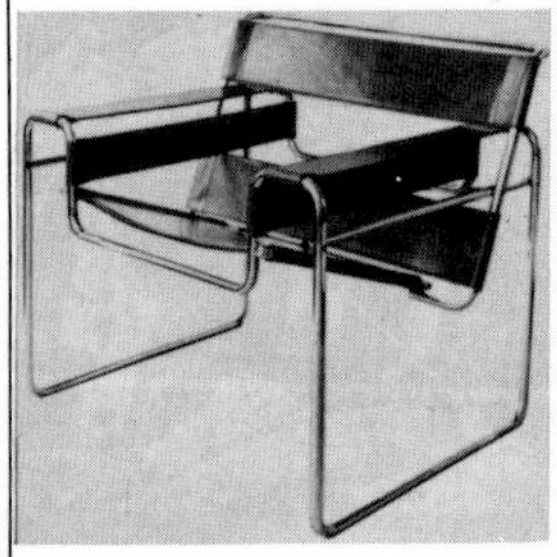

Europe (in England, thanks to the enthusiasm of Zeev Aram and other younger men). Breuer left Nazi Germany in 1933, was briefly a partner with the English architect F. R. S. Yorke, but left four years later to join, as co-teacher and partner in practice, the ex-Bauhaus head Walter Gropius (q.v.), then teaching at Harvard. They received many notable joint commissions for houses and collegiate buildings. In 1946 Breuer moved to New York and set up a practice designing colleges, factories and offices in the U.S., town-planning projects in Latin America, and Unesco buildings (with the Italian Nervi and Frenchman Zehrfuss) in Paris. **R. H.**

'MARCEL BREUER: SUN AND SHADOW – THE PHILOSOPHY OF AN ARCHITECT', ED. BY PETER BLAKE (LONGMANS GREEN, NEW YORK, 1956); 'FORTY YEARS OF BREUER, 1924–1964', BY KENNETH FRAMPTON (ARCHITECTURAL DESIGN, SEPTEMBER, 1964).

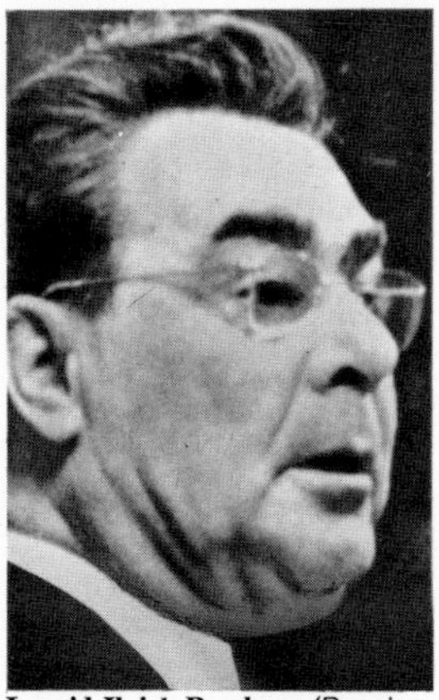

Leonid Ilyich Brezhnev (Russian, b. 1906): Soviet politician. Like Khrushchev (q.v.) to whom he owed his rise in the Party hierarchy, the Russian leader who sent tanks into Czechoslovakia in 1968 comes from the Ukraine. Brezhnev's political career began to flourish during Stalin's (q.v.) last years when he was made an alternate member of the Party Praesidium. With Khrushchev's ascendancy, he rose further – as a secretary of the Central Committee and, between 1960 and 1964, Head of State. Though probably not an originator of the coup which overthrew Khrushchev in 1964, he was its chief beneficiary. By the 23rd Party Congress in 1966 he had emerged as the strongest (though not unchallenged) member of the collective leadership. Rarely identified publicly with specific policies until the recent enunciation of the 'Brezhnev Doctrine' of intervention, he generates a cautious and unimaginative but reliable image, not unlike Stalin's in the mid-1920s. Whether his response to the Soviet Union's current problems (economic reform, intellectual unrest, China, relations with Eastern Europe) will be as drastic as Stalin's was, remains to be seen. His handling of the Czechoslovakian episode suggests that it may be rather less successful. **A. Q. D.**

'POLITICAL SUCCESSION IN THE U.S.S.R.', BY MYRON RUSH (COLUMBIA UNIVERSITY PRESS, 1965); 'POWER IN THE KREMLIN', BY M. TATU (VIKING PRESS, NEW YORK, 1968).

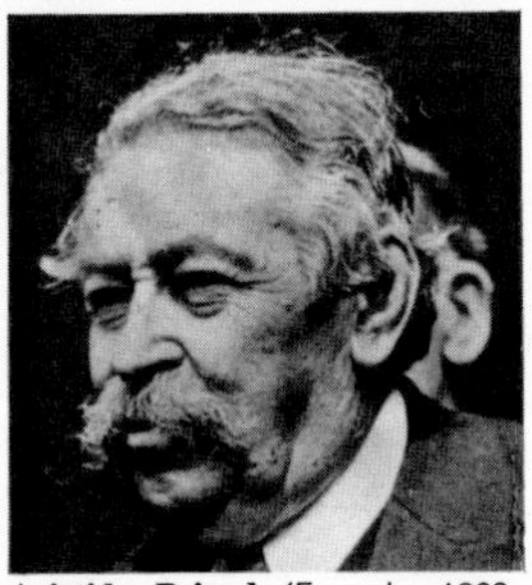

Aristide Briand (French, 1862–1932): statesman. Briand was Prime Minister more often than any French politician of his time, though never for any term of more than 20 months. He is chiefly remembered, however, as Foreign Minister: a post which he held in no fewer than 16 cabinets. Briand was a born negotiator with a remarkable gift for emotional rhetoric which he displayed to great effect in both the Chamber of Deputies and the League of Nations. He achieved great popularity during the 1920s as the 'archangel of peace' and was regularly depicted by French cartoonists in the act of turning swords into ploughshares. One of his main aims was a reconciliation between France and Germany, and his co-operation with Stresemann (q.v.), his German opposite number, was one of the most hopeful signs in the period of optimism in international relations during the later 1920s. Briand's most spectacular success was his initiative in bringing about the Kellogg Pact, a renunciation of war signed by more than 60 states. He was a strong advocate also of European unity, proposing on one occasion a 'United States of Europe'. His success, however, was short-lived. When he died in 1932, the failure of his hopes for Franco-German reconciliation and European co-operation was already becoming clear. **C. M. A.**

'A SHORT HISTORY OF INTERNATIONAL AFFAIRS, 1920-1939', BY G. GATHORNE-HARDY (4TH EDITION, O.U.P., 1950); 'THREE MEN TRIED', BY E. STERN-RUBARTH (DUCKWORTH, 1939).

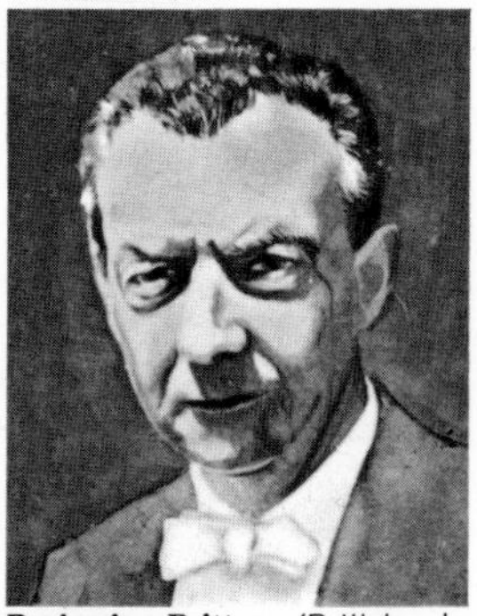

Benjamin Britten (British, b. 1913): composer and pianist. Britten is one of the century's few towering composers who, like Shostakovich (q.v.) and Henze, has bypassed the crisis of 20th-century music and is in touch with his audiences as if ours were another age. A pupil of Frank Bridge, he also wanted to study with Berg (q.v.), a wish which the Royal College of Music met with disdain. Passages like the opening of the development section of his Second Quartet, however, show that he studied with Berg without having to meet him. Eclectic like Mozart, he has, in fact, creatively responded to every available influence – expectedly to Stravinsky (q.v.) and unexpectedly to Schoenberg (q.v.), whose serial technique he applied humorously in the *Cantata Academica: Carmen Basiliense*, and utilised seriously in *The Turn of the Screw* which, despite the worldwide popularity of *Peter Grimes*, may be the profoundest and most masterly of his 15 operas, children's, chamber, and church operas included. There are 87 opus numbers to date – and plenty of pieces and arrangements without opus numbers: Britten has covered the whole of music, though he remains at his most personal when inspired by the human voice, and by poetry. **H. K.**

'BRITTEN', BY IMOGEN HOLST (FABER, 1966); 'BENJAMIN BRITTEN: A COMMENTARY ON HIS WORKS BY A GROUP OF SPECIALISTS', ED. DONALD MITCHELL AND HANS KELLER (ROCKLIFF, 1953); 'ORPHEUS IN NEW GUISES', BY ERWIN STEIN (ROCKLIFF, 1953); 'BENJAMIN BRITTEN: A SKETCH OF HIS LIFE AND WORKS', BY ERIC WALTER WHITE (REVISED EDITION, FABER AND BOOSEY & HAWKES, 1969).

Wallace Reed Brode (U.S., b. 1900): spectroscopist. Brode was a pioneer in developing the use of spectroscopy, one of the most useful tools of the physical scientlst. By irradiating chemical substances with light of various wavelengths, the changes induced in the compounds examined give an important indication of their nature and constitution. These techniques can be applied to a wide variety of systems. The various spectroscopic techniques were independently developed during the first 30 years of this century, but

Brode, Professor of Chemistry at Ohio State University from 1938-1948, later Associate Director of the National Bureau of Standards, Washington DC, and till recently President of the American Chemical Society, contributed by his writings in a major way to the establishment of general acceptance for these techniques among the scientific community. The use of spectroscopic techniques enabled major advances to be made in all areas of the physical sciences. **P. J. F.**

'CHEMICAL SPECTROSCOPY', BY W. R. BRODE (JOHN WILEY, 1939).

Prince Louis de Broglie (French, b. 1892): theoretical physicist. The son of one of the grandest families in France, de Broglie, who had started a literary career before turning to science, became fascinated with the work in theoretical physics done by his elder brother, Maurice, and began to specialise in quantum mechanics. His doctoral thesis (1924) contained a series of important findings which were received with astonishment: the ideas put forward, later confirmed by other scientists, led to the general theory now known as wave mechanics – a theory which utterly transformed the understanding of physical phenomena on the atomic scale. He was awarded the Nobel Prize for Physics in 1929 "for his discovery of the wave nature of electrons". In more recent years de Broglie has been fairly successful in the search for a causal interpretation of wave mechanics using classical concepts of space and time, a task he first tried in 1927 but abandoned in the face of stiff scientific opposition. He suggested that matter had not only corpuscular properties but also a wave nature. **N. V.**

'THE CURRENT INTERPRETATION OF WAVE MECHANICS: A CRITICAL STUDY', BY LOUIS DE BROGLIE (ELSEVIER, AMSTERDAM, 1964); 'NON-LINEAR WAVE MECHANICS: A CAUSAL INTERPRETATION', BY LOUIS DE BROGLIE (ELSEVIER, AMSTERDAM, 1960).

MODEL OF MARLON BRANDO BY SASKIA DE BOER PHOTOGRAPHED BY DAVID MONTGOMERY

Peter Brook (British, b. 1925): theatrical director. Peter Brook's insatiable energy, aesthetic curiosity, disinclination to remain prisoner of any static theory, and his great powers of assimilation as well as creativity have made him the chief intermediary between Britain and the Continent. As a theatre director he has been everything by turns and nothing overlong. In his early days he was brilliantly colourful; in *Titus Andronicus* (1955) he discovered blood and guts. A year later when he directed *Cat on a Hot Tin Roof* with Jeanne Moreau in Paris he discovered Europe. Since then he has kept up a continuous dialogue with the Continent. In his *Lear* for the Royal Shakespeare Company, of which he has been a director since 1962, he used the ideas of the Polish scholar, Jan Kott. In Weiss's *Marat/Sade* he began a long innings with Artaud's Theatre

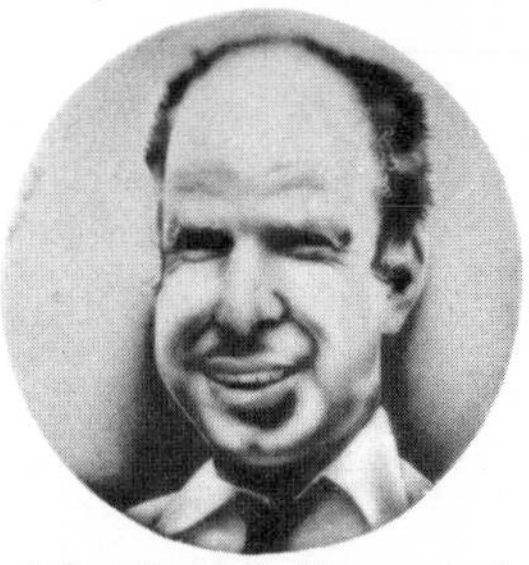

of Cruelty (q.v.). More recently he has translated Grotowski's Theatre of Ritual into his experimental treatment of *The Tempest* at the Round House (1968). His films, particularly *Lord of the Flies*, have also established him as a major creative force in the cinema. **H. H.**

'THE EMPTY SPACE', BY PETER BROOK (MACGIBBON AND KEE, 1968); 'NEW TRENDS IN TWENTIETH CENTURY DRAMA', BY FREDERICK LUMLEY (ROCKLIFF, 1967).

Rupert Brooke (British, 1887–1915): poet. In the years just before 1914 Rupert Brooke achieved a limited fame, both as a poet and as an inordinately handsome young man who was the darling of a distinguished circle of admirers in London and Cambridge. His talents as a poet were modest, even by the unexacting standards of the Georgians, and his probable future was as an academic teacher of literature at Cambridge. Yet the First World War transformed his career and turned him into a mythic figure of the martyred poet and hero. Brooke saw very little of the war; he died in the Aegean from blood-poisoning on his way to the Gallipoli campaign, at precisely the moment in which his patriotic '1914' sonnets, and particularly *The Soldier* ("If I should die, think only this of me . . . "), had suddenly become popular in England. This combination of events was sufficient to ensure for Brooke a reputation that still endures. His real importance lies in his contribution to English cultural history rather than to literature. **B. B.**

'RUPERT BROOKE', BY CHRISTOPHER HASSALL (FABER, 1964); 'THE GEORGIAN REVOLT', BY ROBERT H. ROSS (FABER, 1967).

Avery Brundage (U.S., b. 1887): President, International Olympic Committee. Avery Brundage is the Colossus of the Olympic Games, having dominated it with an inflexible will for the past 17 years. It is hard to imagine the movement without him, but he has said he will not stand again as president after the Munich Games of 1972. By then he will be 85 – though no doubt still a man of imposing physique, firm tread and clear mind. It has been Brundage's misfortune to be in command of affairs during the most testing period in Olympic history, bedevilled by two Germanys, two Koreas, two Chinas, a divided South Africa, rampant nationalism and mounting commercialisation. But under his leadership the Olympic movement succeeded for a time, where the United Nations failed, in uniting Germany under a

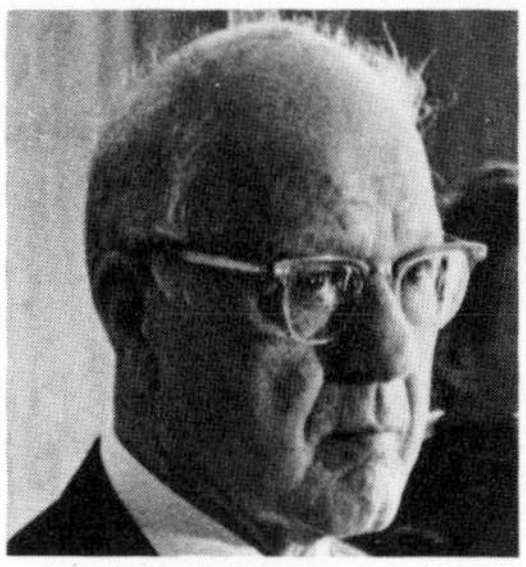

common flag. Of late, however, east and west have become separate entities. Thus one of Brundage's proud claims – of political success where politicians had failed – has foundered. More seriously, his attitude to professionalism, however sincerely motivated, has been anachronistic. For at least two decades some compromise in a materialistic world has been needed, but Brundage has been unable to modify his attitude, so that the movement is rife with hypocrisy on what it most holds dear, amateurism. **J. J. H.**

'THE FOUR DIMENSIONS OF AVERY BRUNDAGE'. BY HEINZ SCHOBEL (EDITIONS LEIPZIG, AVAILABLE FROM THE IOC. LAUSANNE, SWITZERLAND); 'PROFILES', BY R. SHAPLEN (NEW YORKER, JULY 1960).

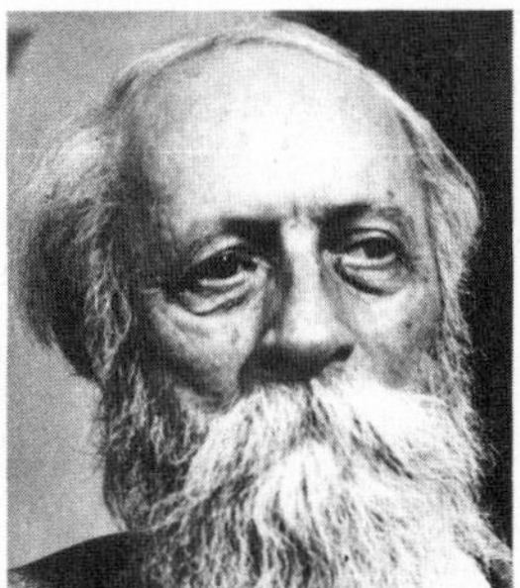

Martin Buber (Israeli, 1878–1965): philosopher. Buber was also a theologian, Bible exegete, educationist, Zionist thinker, and touched 20th-century life at many points. His most important contributions were the introduction of Western man to the East European Jewish mystical movement of Hasidism, and the philosophy of dialogue. A totally self-centred man, if such be possible, would be for Buber less than human. Man's 'I' acquires its significance in relationship with other beings and things so that there are two 'primary' words: 'I-It' and 'I-Thou'. In the 'I-It' relationship man *uses* others. He investigates, he surveys, he studies. He is detached – standing, as it were, outside the life around him. This is essential if there is to be scientific and technological progress. In the 'I-Thou' relationship, on the other hand, man *meets* others. These *speak* to him. In saying 'Thou' to them his own 'I' is enriched. He becomes a person encountering other persons. Buber's interpretation of the golden rule was: 'Thou shalt love thy neighbour [not as a thing but] as thyself [as a person just as you are]'. God is the 'Thou' behind all particular 'Thous' and is to be encountered in true meeting with them. Buber is uneasy about the concept of a divine law imposed from without since this does not necessarily speak to man, and here he parts company with the mainstream of Judaism. **L. J.**

'I AND THOU', BY MARTIN BUBER (SCRIBNER'S, N.Y., 1937); 'TALES OF THE HASIDIM', BY MARTIN BUBER, 2 VOLS. (THAMES AND HUDSON. 1956); 'THE PHILOSOPHY OF MARTIN BUBER', EDITED BY SCHILPP AND FRIEDMAN (C.U.P., 1969).

Frank Buchman (U.S., 1878–1961): evangelist. Frank Buchman, the founder of Moral Re-Armament, was to many an apostle and leader of a revitalised Christian faith, changing the lives of individuals and influencing the development of nations. Others remember him as the man who, between the wars, is alleged to have said: "Thank Heaven for Adolf Hitler who built a front line of defence against the anti-Christ of Communism." He was born and brought up in Pennsylvania by Lutheran parents of Swiss descent against a background of Protestant hymns, teetotalism

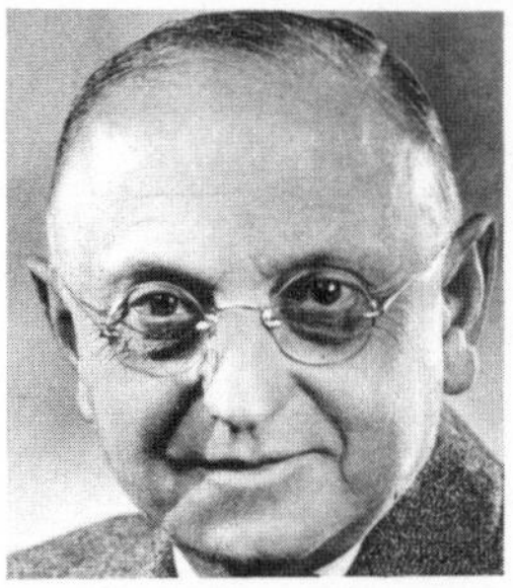

and an emphasis on sexual purity. After an alleged "vision of the Cross" in a Lake District church (1908) he founded a revivalist movement, the 'First Century Christian Fellowship' which later, after his work among Oxford students, became the 'Oxford Group', finally to be named 'Moral Re-Armament'. He based his movement on the idea of a "new Social Order under the dictatorship of the Spirit of God". The movement, with many adherents among the social and financial elite, while underlining its Christian content, became a vehicle for an anti-Communist ideology with a ruthless publicity, financed by lavish donations from various sources. Although disclaiming any interest in money Buchman was surrounded by luxury. "And why not?" he said. "Isn't God a millionaire?" **J. A.**

'THE MYSTERY OF MORAL RE-ARMAMENT', BY TOM DRIBERG (SECKER AND WARBURG, 1964); 'REMAKING THE WORLD', THE COLLECTED SPEECHES OF FRANK BUCHMAN (BLANDFORD, 1961).

Nikolai Ivanovich Bukharin (Russian: 1888–1938): Soviet statesman. Next to Lenin (q.v.), Bukharin was the most intellectually gifted of the Russian

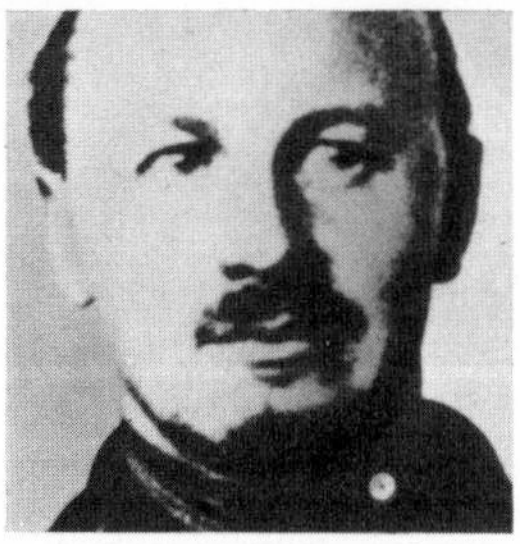

Revolutionary leaders of 1917, and his pre-revolutionary writings on imperialism and the state anticipated many conclusions Lenin later reached and acted upon. *The Theory of Historical Materialism* is the only important account of Marxist sociology by any Bolshevik: and *The ABC of Communism* (written with Preobrazhensky) is still the most visionary description of the Communist Utopia. His political career was less successful. He joined Stalin in the mid-1920s as the chief ideological spokesman of Socialism in One Country, but when in 1928–29 his gradualist, pro-peasant economic policy collapsed he rejected Stalin's solution of forced collectivisation and followed Trotsky and Zinoviev into opposition and defeat. Out of power from 1929 until his liquidation in 1938, he nonetheless drafted much of the 1936 Constitution, which still enshrines the democratic promise of Soviet Socialism. In easier circumstances, Bukharin might have led the achievement of this promise. As it was, the stormy construction of Socialism in Russia cast him aside, though Soviet society may yet be able to afford to recognise him as one of its most talented founders. **J. D. B.**

'THE ABC OF COMMUNISM', BY N. BUKHARIN AND E. PREOBRAZHENSKY, WITH AN INTRODUCTION BY E. H. CARR (PENGUIN, 1969); 'SOCIALISM IN ONE COUNTRY', BY E. H. CARR, 3 VOLS (MACMILLAN, 1958–64); 'THE PROPHET UNARMED: TROTSKY 1921–1929', BY ISAAC DEUTSCHER (O.U.P., 1959).

Luis Buñuel (Spanish, b. 1900): film director. Buñuel broke into the cinema at the very end of the silent era with a double-barrelled Surrealist scandal: *Un Chien Andalou* (the film in which an eyeball was slashed with a razor) and *L'Age d'Or* (a paean to *l'amour fou* in which lovers wallowed ecstatically in the mud under indignant ecclesiastical eyes). Then, with true Surrealist thoroughness, he disappeared entirely from view, re-emerging in Mexico 20 years later with *Los Olvidados*, a cruel, ferociously unsentimental study of delinquent youth which showed that he was still scabrous, scathing and scandalous. Still Buñuel, in fact. Masterpiece has since followed masterpiece with almost clockwork regularity: *Robinson Crusoe, El, Nazarin, Viridiana, The Exter-*

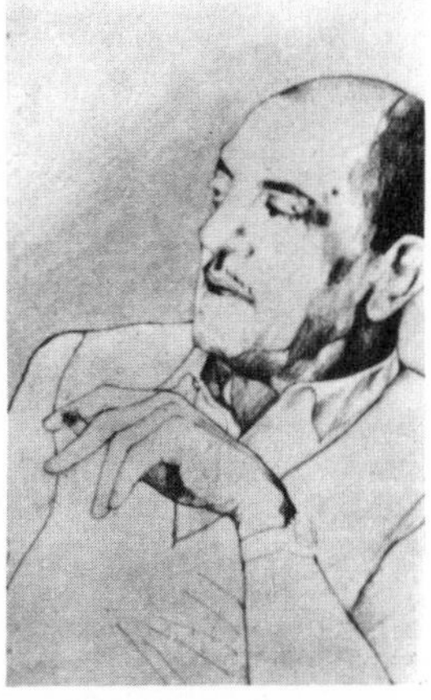

minating Angel, Simon of the Desert, Belle de Jour, and now *La Voie Lactée*. Time has mellowed Buñuel's technique, but not his temperament: he remains the cinema's most unrelenting gadfly, from whom no public prudery, no private perversion and, above all, no ecclesiastical pretension is safe. **T. M.**

'LUIS BUNUEL', BY ADO KYROU (SIMON AND SCHUSTER, NEW YORK, 1963).

Sir MacFarlane Burnet (Australian, b. 1899): immunologist, virologist. Burnet has contributed much to the control of many human diseases such as polio and influenza, but his greatest influence has been in the field of ideas: he has the rare gift of being able to extend his detailed observations on disease to generate broad biological principles. Twenty-five years ago he showed how the presence of one virus in the body might hinder the growth of another – which we now know to be due to the production of the substance called interferon. He also showed how changes in virus virulence were due to the selective growth of the more vicious individuals from a mixed infection, rather than to the creation of a quite new strain. This principle of selection rather than new creation he applied to the genesis of antibodies, the body's protective substances,

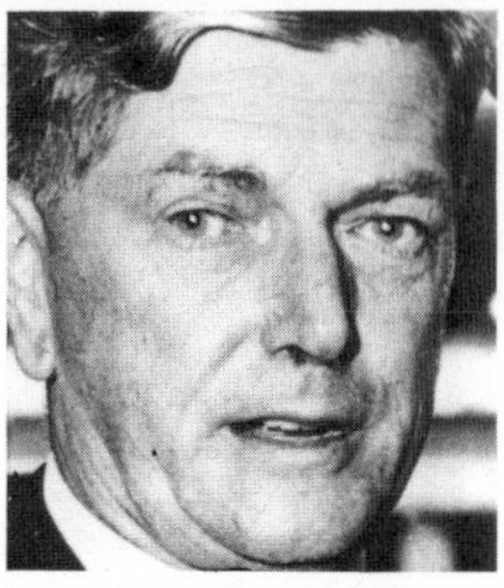

in his Clonal Selection Theory. Problems of how the body recognises substances as 'foreign' led to prediction of 'tolerance', which fitted in so elegantly with Medawar's (q.v.) concurrent work on homografts; and to theories of auto-immune diseases which are still a stimulus to research. Current work on how to make human organ grafts tolerated by the body owes much to the stimulus he and his pupils have given. By turning immunological theory upside down he has kept the world's immunologists busy and happy for the last decade: his ideas have not always stood up to test but have always been worth testing – they can never be safely ignored: so often they turn out to be pure gold. **P. G. H. G.**

'VIRUS AS ORGANISM: EVOLUTIONARY AND ECOLOGICAL ASPECTS OF SOME HUMAN VIRUS DISEASES', BY SIR MACFARLANE BURNET – MONOGRAPH IN 'MEDICINE AND PUBLIC HEALTH' (O.U.P., 1945).

Sir Montague Burton (British, 1885–1952): tailor. Montague Burton put the British working man into a decent suit. He started his first store in 1900 on £100 borrowed from a relative. He aimed to bridge the gap between the product of the high-quality gentleman's tailor and the shapeless ready-made. Helped by the trend towards simplicity in men's clothes after the First World War, he prospered. And Burtons now have over 600 retail stores in the U.K. In 1945, they made over a quarter of all the demob suits in their factories at Leeds and elsewhere. Burton also provided decent facilities for his work

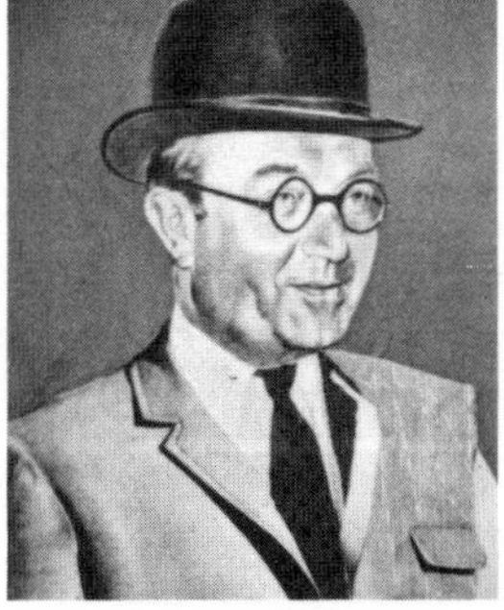

people. He published two books, *Ideals in Industry* (largely a random scrap-book on the progress of his business) and *The Middle Path*, an excursion into international affairs. He was extremely generous to Leeds and other universities, and became a prophet of moderation in business: "A business must have a conscience as well as a counting house." **G. P. G. N.**

Sir Matt Busby (British, b. 1909): football manager. Matt Busby has been the most successful manager of the postwar era. When he took over Manchester United in 1945 he inherited a bombed ground and a Nissen hut; today they are one of the half dozen most glamorous teams in world football. Under Busby, now United's managing director, the club has become the most successful in British football since the war: twice F.A. cup winners (and twice losing finalists); five times league champions and six times runners-up; and the first English club to win the European Cup (in 1968). And all this was achieved despite the Munich air disaster of 1958 in which eight of the 'Busby Babes' died and Busby himself barely escaped with his life. He is a rare bird, a visionary who saw the value of international club games and sought them against the advice of the soccer hierarchy. One of the few managers in British football to believe in individual class and skill as opposed to collective method, he has made Manchester United the biggest crowd puller in British soccer. A grandfather, a family man and a Catholic, he is also a magnificent public relations man. **M. P.**

'THE FOOTBALL MAN', BY ARTHUR HOP-CRAFT (COLLINS, 1968).

Vannevar Bush (U.S., b. 1890): engineer and administrator. He is best known as one of the leading people in the giant Manhattan project that made the first atomic bomb. And he was involved in discussions that in the event decided how much secret information should be shared between Britain and the U.S. Dr Bush became Associate Professor of Electric Power Transmission at Massachusetts Institute of Technology in 1919 and eventually chairman. Among his lesser claims to fame is the fact that he pioneered the use of computers and designed the 'differential analyser' (not a digital machine) at MIT in 1925, the advanced model of which was used in the Second World War for the computation of artillery firing tables. In 1940 and 1941 he was in charge of the National Defence Research Committee and afterwards (until 1946) of the parent body, the Office of Scientific Research and Development. It was Vannevar Bush who saw the need for expanding the efforts to make military use of atomic energy and getting away from the limited, though extensive, laboratory research. He became one of the Top Policy Group with President Roosevelt and others. It was Bush's report in 1942 that decided President Roosevelt to go ahead with atomic bomb development with full support and on an unlimited scale. **C. L. B.**

'PRINCIPLES OF ELECTRICAL ENGINEERING', BY V. BUSH (JOHN WILEY, NEW YORK, 1922); 'NOW IT CAN BE TOLD', BY LESLIE R. GROVES (DEUTSCH, 1963).

Ferruccio Busoni (Italian, 1866–1924): musician. Busoni was one of the greatest pianists of his age, and a composer whose work is still too little known and valued, although there have been many recent signs of renewed interest. His divided nationality (Italian father, half-German mother) affected his development as a composer; like Rachmaninov (q.v.), he was further torn between his brilliant career as a concert pianist and his longing for creative solitude and leisure. Such keyboard works as the large-scale Piano Concerto and the superb *Fantasia contrappuntistica* on an unfinished fugue of Bach show a highly personal blend of German romanticism and complexity and of Italian fire and lyrical feeling. His masterpiece is *Doktor Faust*, the last of his four operas. **D. S.-T.**

'FERRUCCIO BUSONI: A BIOGRAPHY', BY E. J. DENT (OXFORD, 1933).

Richard Austen Butler (British, b. 1902): politician. From 1932 until 1964 Butler held office in every Conservative or Coalition administration, a period in office of more than a quarter of a century. His most remarkable legislative achievement was the Education Act of 1944, the most valuable contribution by the Coalition to the social reforms inspired by the desire to make a better post-war Britain. Lord Butler (made a life peer in 1965) had a greater record of social reform than any Conservative leader of his generation. He became an immensely skilled politician; as Leader of the House of Commons or as Home Secretary he was able to deal with the most sensitive political

situations with an astonishing facility and good humour. As Chancellor, he was responsible for the economic success of the first post-war Conservative Government. He was never made Leader of the Conservative Party because Right-wing Conservatives did not like or trust him. They found him too clever and his sense of social compassion was a quality they did not particularly admire. They distrusted instinctual responses more complex than their own. Since he retired (to become Master of Trinity College, Cambridge) the Conservative Party has lacked anyone with his sense of political possibilities or his skill in avoiding political dangers. His constructive record in home politics is unmatched by any of his contemporaries. **W. R.-M.**

'RICHARD AUSTEN BUTLER', BY FRANCIS BOYD (ROCKLIFFE, 1956); 'POLITICS WITHOUT PREJUDICE', BY RALPH HARRIS STAPLES, 1956).

Sir Billy Butlin (British, b. 1899): holiday camp tycoon. Billy (William Edmund Heygate Colbourne) Butlin put an annual holiday by the sea within the reach of millions. Born in South Africa, he spent his boyhood in England and Canada, and in 1921 returned to England with £5 as his total assets. After a spell of travelling with a hoop-la stall, he had a side stall at Bertram Mills; then he set up four stalls at Skegness. There he introduced dodgem cars to England. His Skegness amusement park grew, and he conceived the idea of a holiday camp, which opened some miles away in 1936. The pattern of communal holidays where the price included basic accommodation, food, recreational facilities and a wide range of entertainment was soon established. By 1939, Skegness could take 5000 campers. Clacton followed; then seven others after the war. In 1950 he tried to attract Americans to a super-Butlins on Grand Bahama island, but the venture was a financial disaster. However, his monetary affairs recovered, and he was knighted in 1964. **G. P. G. N.**

'THE BUTLIN STORY', BY REX NORTH (JARROLDS, 1962).

James Byrnes (U.S., b. 1879): politician. 'Jimmy' Byrnes made practical politics of F. D. Roosevelt's (q.v.) programmes for economic recovery from the Depression and for economic mobilisation for the Second World War. During the New Deal, Byrnes negotiated the passage of F.D.R.'s emergency legislation. During the transition from isolation to the realities of war, Byrnes became the crucial link between the President and Congress; even after his elevation to the Supreme Court in June, 1941 he remained the overseer of all national defence legislation. He resigned from the Court in 1942 to become virtually Assistant President, responsible for the entire home front from price stabilisation to war production. When Harry Truman (q.v.) succeeded to the presidency, he named Byrnes Secretary of State; during the following 18 months Byrnes presided over the onset of the Cold War, before he retired in 1947. Essentially a moderate conservative, Byrnes saw the need for the concentration of emergency government powers during 13 years of non-stop crisis. As Secretary of State, he was one of the first to recognise the impossibility of reasonable political dealings with Stalin (q.v.). **W. H. J.**

'ALL IN ONE LIFETIME', BY J. F. BYRNES (HARPER, ROW, 1961); 'SPEAKING FRANKLY', BY J. F. BYRNES (HEINEMANN, 1947).

From a photograph by Sherril Schell   Emery Walker Ltd

Rupert Brooke

1913

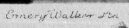

C

John Cage (U.S., b. 1912): composer. In 40 years as a composer John Cage has done more than anyone, ever, to change the nature of musical experience. (His teacher, Schoenberg [q.v.], once said: "Cage is not a composer but an inventor – of genius.") As early as 1937 Cage foresaw that "any and all sounds that can be heard" would one day be part of music. In 1938 his 'prepared piano' endowed the player with a whole encyclopaedia of new sounds. By 1939 sound engineers, not Conservatoire musicians, were his natural collaborators. His *Imaginary Landscape No. 5* (1952) was the first composition on magnetic tape. In the 1940s he pioneered the principle of indeterminacy by which chance was accepted as integral to musical experience. In 1952 he initiated the multi-media Happening, a mix of art, poetry, dance, concert, lecture. More recently Cage has made music into a metaphor for what he regards as the most urgent of human tasks: adaptation to an environment which is changing too fast and too radically for the conscious mind to keep up with it. Working in "an indeterminate interrelated field of awareness", he aims "not to bring order out of chaos or to suggest improvements in creation, but simply to wake up to the very life we're living". **J. R.**

'SILENCE', BY JOHN CAGE (CALDER AND BOYARS, 1968).

James Cagney (U.S., b. 1904): film actor. Cagney, born in Hell's Kitchen, New York, gave a face, a code, and style to American gangster movies. What he synthesised was cocky, murderous charm, notably on show in *Public Enemy* (1931) in which anti-hero Cagney, with umpteen murders to his credit, ended an argument with his moll by grinding a grapefruit in her face. A chunky 5 ft. 8 in, Cagney trained as a dancer, and moved with a precise, finicky grace. His voice, too, was a staccato whisper. There were no loose ends about him. He was an all-purpose actor and appeared in Westerns, musicals and comedies, including *The Bride Came C.O.D.* in which he performed the notable feat of plucking cactus spines from Bette Davis's rump. A long-time radical, he was once accused of being a Communist. Cleared by the Dies Committee in 1940, he was starred as George M. Cohan in *Yankee Doodle Dandy* at the instigation of his brother, who advised the studio to put Cagney in a film "playing the damndest patriotic man in the country". His image, however, remained that of the smiler with a gun. The violent ambiguities first patented by Cagney are still cherished. With Billy the Kid, bootleggers, and Babe Ruth they are part of the American Dream. **P. O.**

Maria Callas (Greek, ex-U.S., b. 1923): singer. An authoritative, if now vocally erratic interpreter, Maria Callas has long established her right to be considered one of the world's greatest singers, of this or any other age. Born in New York of Greek parents, she went to live and study in Greece when she was 13. Her truly international career began with her Italian debut 11 years later. January 1949 saw Callas, already established in some of the heaviest operatic soprano roles, singing Elvira, in Bellini's *I Puritani*, shortly after a *Walküre* Brunnhilde. Before long, she began to relinquish the Wagnerian and heavier parts in favour of the *bel canto* operas and more agile roles. The vocal tone of Callas, sporadically beautiful, but never easily or artlessly produced, takes second place to the sheer power of her interpretative abilities. And although she has sung less in recent years, her proved command of the classical style, her magnetic stage personality and her passionate and conscientious artistry have made her the outstanding *diva* of our time. **F. A.**

'CALLAS, LA DIVINA', BY STELIOS GALATO-POULOS (DENT, 1966).

Charles Calmette (French 1863–1933): bacteriologist. Nearly 250 million people have been vaccinated against tuberculosis with the BCG vaccine developed by Calmette. A disciple of Louis Pasteur, he was the first director of the Pasteur Institute in Lille (1895–1917), and later assistant director of the Pasteur Institute in Paris. With Guerin, he pre-

pared a protective vaccine against TB, Bunyan's 'Captain of the Men of Death'. An ordinary vaccine of dead tubercle microbes was useless. Consequently, they applied Pasteur's principles and spent 13 years in perfecting a living, attenuated (weakened) vaccine, which did not recover its lost virulence and was, therefore, stable and safe. Vaccinated animals resisted challenge by virulent organisms. BCG was first used in a baby in 1921. The vaccine has had its ups and downs. It was almost still-born: the Germans who occupied Lille in the 1914–18 war nearly executed Calmette because he kept laboratory pigeons. Between the wars, progress was made, although certain influential scientists outside France opposed its use. Nevertheless, Calmette's claims were completely vindicated – although, alas, mainly after his death. **H. J. P.**

SEE UNDER VON BEHRING.

Melvin Calvin (U.S., b. 1911): chemist. Calvin discovered how plants use the sun's energy to make sugars and starches from water and carbon dioxide – the process of photosynthesis. The process is known as the Calvin cycle. At the University of California, Calvin became preoccupied with the way photosynthesis works in plants. In a series of classical experiments, he and his colleagues exposed microscopic one-celled plants ('chlorella') to carbon dioxide containing traces of radioactive carbon-14, and analysed the subsequent uptake of the 'labelled' carbon dioxide by the various chemicals within the cells. For deciphering the reactions involved in photosynthesis, Calvin was awarded the Nobel Chemistry Prize in 1961. **N. V.**

Sir Malcolm Campbell (British, 1885–1949): speedster. Most of Sir Malcolm Campbell's life was expended in attempts to go faster than anyone else, and his records on land and sea stood for a season, gratifying to both

himself and his country. He scorned a crash helmet and survived, as might be expected, many crashes. The son of a diamond merchant, he was proud he had "lived a man's life". As well as achieving high speeds on land and sea he searched for buried treasure, unsuccessfully, built aeroplanes, and set spring traps with blank cartridges in his garden to discourage trespassers. Through this device one of his employees lost a leg. Between 1923 and 1935, often in rivalry with Sir Henry Segrave, he gradually raised the world land speed record from 137 mph to 301.129 mph at the Bonneville Salt Flats in Utah. He announced that he would rest content with this achievement, unless it was beaten by a foreigner. Interested in speed on water as well, in 1937 he raised the water speed record from 124.86 mph to 129.91 mph. He later achieved, in 1939, 141.74 mph on Coniston Water. He was one of the creators of a 20th-century mania and not the least of his achievements was that, unlike his son Donald, he survived it. **A. C. C.**

Mrs Patrick Campbell (British, 1865–1940): actress. As Mrs Patrick Campbell, Beatrice Stella Tanner was known as a tempestuous actress of great range and power, who first became famous as Paula Tanqueray in Pinero's *The Second Mrs Tanqueray* (1893), for the

first time in the history of the British theatre creating a *realistic* portrait of the hitherto romantic character of "the woman who had sinned". She was also at home in Ibsen, in the Symbolist drama of Maeterlinck (*Pelleas and Melisande*), and in Shaw (*Pygmalion*). She had a celebrated semi-erotic friendship with Shaw, which resulted in a fulgurant exchange of literarily

passionate letters. She was a devastating wit in private life, and of a richly bohemian temperament. "How glorious to have £700 one week," she exclaimed, "and nothing the next." She was excitingly beautiful, and seemed destined by nature to become a great star of the popular, lush, romantic drama of her day. But just as unexpectedly as the rich and lovely Countess of Warwick espoused Socialism, so Mrs Campbell became the luscious banner-bearer of the pre-1914–18 war intellectual drama. She died in poverty. **H. H.**

Albert Camus (French, 1913–1960): writer. Camus emerged from an obscure Algerian background to become an increasingly international figure, as writer and moralist, after the Second World War. He worked for the clandestine newspaper *Combat* during the French Occupation and continued writing independent and humane editorials on social and political questions between 1945 and 1948. His first major novel, *The Outsider*, was followed by *The Plague*, and both works remain impressive in terms of their technical skill and challenging intellectual content. They revealed Camus as an important spokesman of his generation and commentator on its problems. A third novel, *The Fall*, is another artistic *tour de force* containing stinging attacks on the hypocrisy of the Left Wing as well as the bourgeois varieties. His rejection of nihilism and defence of an anti-Marxist political liberalism are outlined

in the essays *The Myth of Sisyphus* and *The Rebel*. Although his plays are generally less admired, the overall quality of Camus' writing and his position as an exemplary figure remain remarkably high. **J. Cr.**

'CAMUS', BY G. BRÉE (HARCOURT BRACE, 1964); 'ALBERT CAMUS AND THE LITERATURE OF REVOLT', BY J. CRUICKSHANK (O.U.P., 1960).

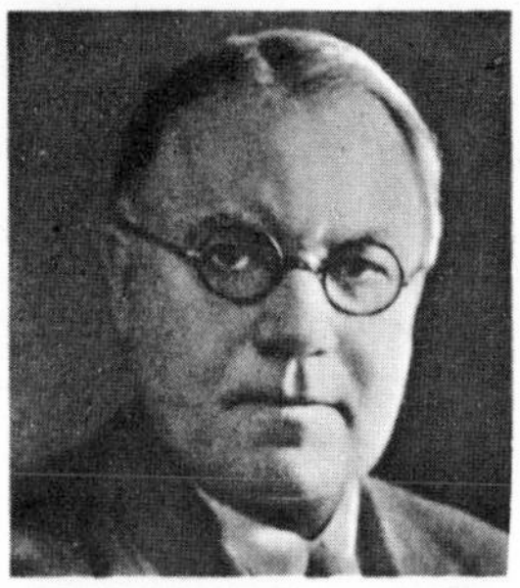

Walter Cannon (U.S., 1871–1945): physiologist. Cannon's first major discovery was that the movements of parts of the alimentary canal could be seen under X-rays after a meal containing a barium salt had been swallowed. This was the precursor of the 'barium meal' that is so important in diagnostic medicine. He then realised that the movements were interrupted after disturbances that caused fright or anger, and this in turn led him to appreciate the significance of adrenaline in liberating the body's reserves. Investigating the way that the living body maintains a steady state in its body fluids despite wide variations in the environment, he coined the word *homeostasis* to describe this self-regulation. This concept has been developed in the modern study of cybernetics. While working at a casualty clearing station in the First World War he originated a major contribution to the study of shock by suggesting that the effects of shock were caused by release of poison in the body. **J. B. M.**

'THE WISDOM OF THE BODY', BY W. B. CANNON (KEGAN PAUL, 1938).

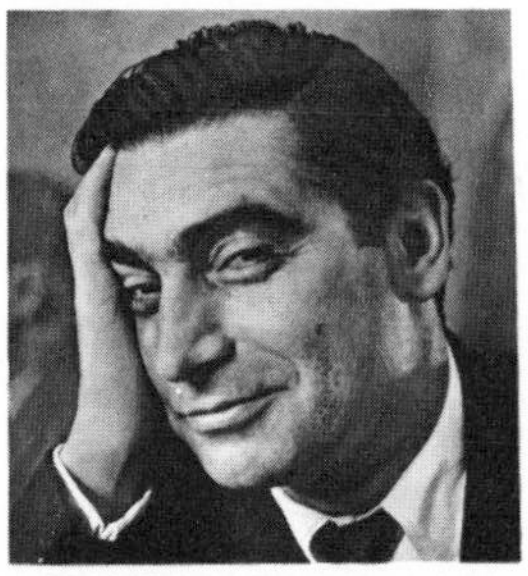

Robert Capa (Hungarian, 1914–1954): war photographer. Robert Capa was a man of great courage and great charm. He hated war. His ambition, he said, was to be "an unemployed war photographer". He took his pictures to make us see what war is like, what we are doing to each other. He was born André Friedmann in Budapest. At 18 he left for Paris where he took eagerly to Bohemian life, found work as a darkroom assistant, and began to develop his photographic talent. He also became "devoted to the ideals of freedom". This led him in 1936 to try to record the Spanish Civil War. Refused a visa under his real name, he contrived a new one – and was admitted. His pictures made an instant impact on the world's picture magazines. One of them, *Death of a Spanish Loyalist*, is still the most dramatic war picture ever taken. For the next 18 years Capa was in most of the beachhead landings and besieged strongholds of a troubled world. In May 1954, walking up a road in Indo-China to find exactly the right distance and angle for his picture, he trod on a landmine and was killed instantly. **T. H.**

'IMAGES OF WAR', BY ROBERT CAPA (HAMLYN, 1964); 'DEATH IN THE MAKING', BY ROBERT CAPA (COVICI, 1938); 'SLIGHTLY OUT OF FOCUS', (O.U.P., 1947); 'RUSSIAN JOURNAL', BY JOHN STEINBECK, PHOTOGRAPHS BY ROBERT CAPA (MACMILLAN, 1948).

Al Capone (U.S., 1899–1947): gangster. 'Scarface' was the hoodlum of the century. An Italian barber's son, he was working as a union strong-arm man when he was summoned to Chicago in 1919 by Johnny Torrio, a gangster whose main source of income was brothel keeping and gambling machines. In January 1920, when Prohibition came in, Torrio made Capone his partner and their poisonous bootleg booze was soon bringing in over two million dollars profit a year. Other 'alky cookers' had territory in Chicago: Dion O'Banion, the Genna brothers, Bugs Moran. In November 1924, O'Banion was shot to death in a florist's, and the gang war began in which 135 gangsters were shot or tortured to death in three years. Torrio backed out and left the field to Capone, who called the gangs together in 1926 and arranged for co-operation. But two gangs – Aiello's and Bugs Moran's – refused and made periodic attempts to kill Capone. The Aiello gang were gradually eliminated; five of Moran's gang were massacred by Capone gangsters dressed as policemen in their garage and liquor store on St. Valentine's Day, 1929. Later that year Philadelphia police succeeded in jailing Capone for a year for carrying a gun; so he operated from prison. In 1931, the F.B.I. managed to jail him for tax evasion until 1939. He lived on for eight years, dying on his Palm Island estate of apoplexy, aged 48, having become one of the most notorious characters of U.S. history, and a model for gangland in the future. **C. W.**

'THE BOOTLEGGERS', BY KENNETH ALLSOP (HUTCHINSON, 1961); 'PROHIBITION', BY ANDREW SINCLAIR (FABER, 1962).

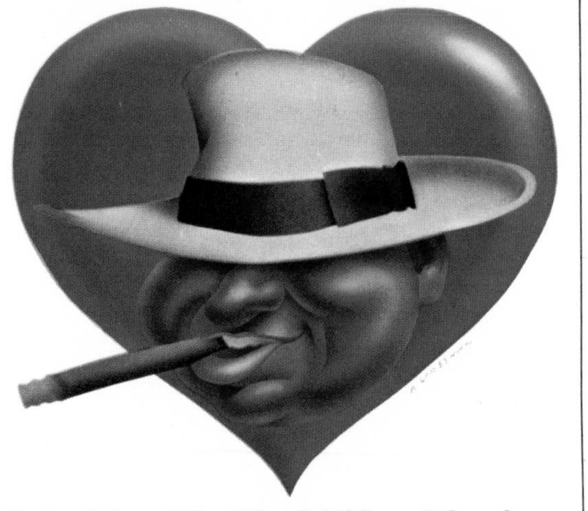

Chester Carlson (U.S., 1906–1968): inventor. The man who invented xerography was a physicist and patent agent. He once wrote: "I grew up in poverty. During the Depression I decided that making and selling an invention was one of the few possible avenues through which one could rapidly change one's economic status." And he therefore sat down to invent the xerographic, or dry-copying, machine which has been almost certainly the single most lucrative discovery in the mid-20th century. In 1930, Carlson lost his research job at Bell Telephone. Realising the need for an easy, cheap, non-messy, nonphotographic copying machine he systematically combed the literature in New York Public Library. After three years he worked out the principle – electrostatic deposit of powder on ordinary paper – and took out patents. In 1938 he printed the first xero-copy – '10-22-38 Astoria' from a glass slide to waxed paper. It took another 12 years to get a commercial machine out, via the then tiny Haloid Corporation – now, as Xerox, valued at over $6 billion. Carlson died worth around $50 million. **P. W.**

'THE SOURCES OF INVENTION', BY JOHN JEWKES (MACMILLAN, 1958).

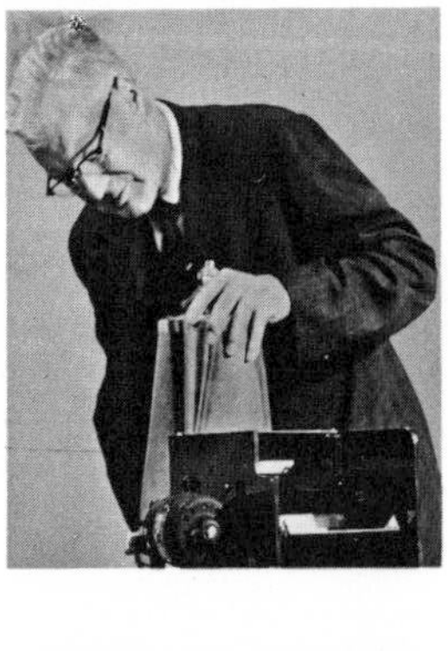

Rudolf Carnap (U.S., ex-German, (1891–1970): philosopher. Carnap was one of the original leaders of the Vienna Circle, the group of thinkers who created logical positivism, and he became the most productive and perhaps most influential of its members. Like most of the Vienna Circle he was trained not as a philosopher but as a scientist. His logical positivism is a scientifically orientated philosophy for which the ideal standard of signifi-

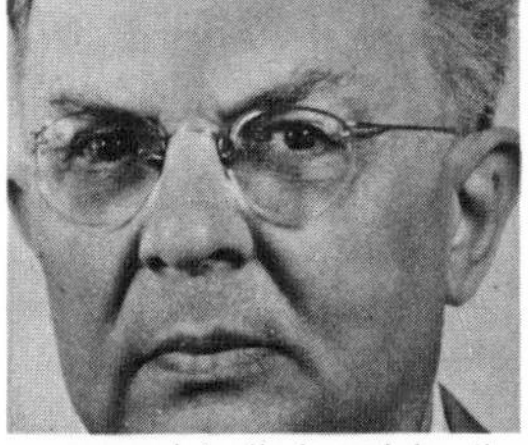

cance and truth is set by the propositions of mathematics and natural science. There are two kinds of truth for Carnap: the empirical truth of statements that can be verified, directly or indirectly, by observation; and the analytic truth of statements of logic and mathematics, which depends simply on the meaning of the terms they contain. The utterances of metaphysics, theology and ethics, and so the main content of traditional philosophy, cannot be verified in either of these ways and are, therefore, strictly meaningless. What philosophy should be is a logical investigation into mathematics and science, and this Carnap consistently practised, first in central Europe, but from 1936 in the U.S. His writings were expressed in a scientific way: lucid and impersonal. **A. Q.**

'THE PHILOSOPHY OF RUDOLF CARNAP', EDITED BY P. SCHILPP (C.U.P., 1965).

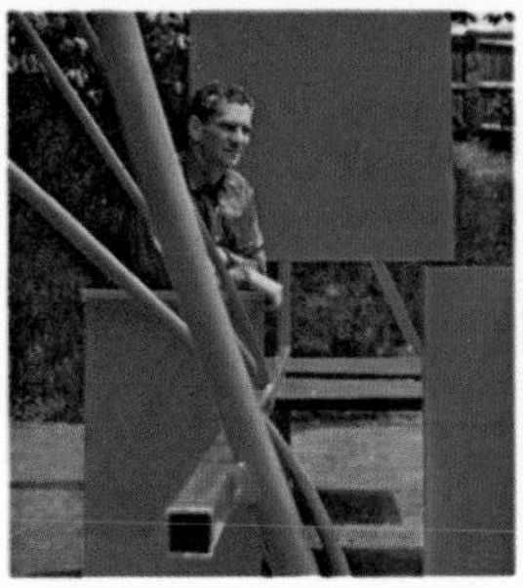

Anthony Caro (British, b. 1924): sculptor. Caro's contribution to the history of art is that he single-handedly got British sculpture out of the long and rightly-venerated shadow of Henry Moore and proved that it could begin again with new materials, new techniques and new ambitions. As assistant to Moore (q.v.) from 1951–1953 he saw at first hand that what Moore had done could not be done better: as Nietzsche said, "Every great man is a finale". Teaching under Frank Martin at the St Martin's School of Art from 1953, he persuaded a whole generation of British sculptors to explore a new area for sculpture: one in which the work would exist in and for itself, without echoes of landscape or the human body, without narrative impulse, without reference to earlier art. He himself began again with standard industrial sections of steel and aluminium, bolted and welded; the results, first shown in 1961, did not look at all like 'art' but have turned out to have in them every shade of feeling from a rugged and undifferentiated power to a fastidious delicacy of touch and imagination. Caro's is a classic English background, and he has shown classic English powers of leadership; but it is for the fearless forays in his work that he is a front-rank figure in the U.S. as much as at home. **J. R.**

Wallace Carothers (U.S., 1896–1937): chemist. The inventor of nylon forsook university life, where he was a brilliant lecturer in organic chemistry, to join Du Pont, the American chemical company – probably because industry could more readily provide the resources to enable him to follow his chosen field of pure research, the study of polymerisation. One of Carothers' incidental discoveries was that some of the polymers he succeeded in synthesising were fibre-forming, and it was a short step to the formation of a specific polymeric synthetic fibre to which Du Pont gave the name nylon. When the discovery was announced in 1938,

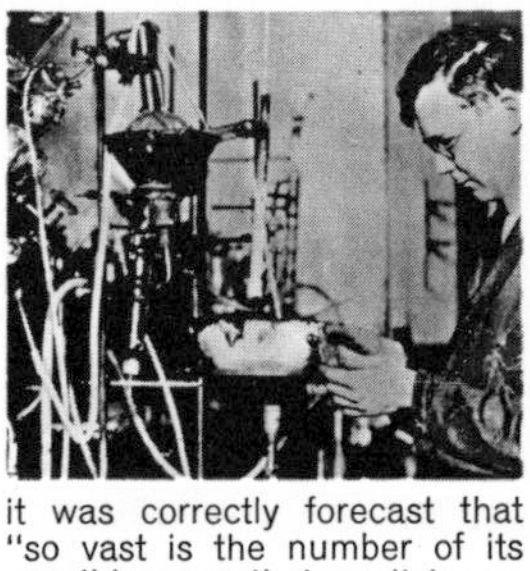

it was correctly forecast that "so vast is the number of its possible uses that no list . . . can include them all". By ringing the changes on the fibre's characteristics, it has been possible to develop uses in spheres as far apart as lingerie and motor tyres, international haute couture and conveyor belts. Sadly, he had lived long enough to see only the earliest beginnings of the world textile revolution his discovery was to cause. **P. C. A.**

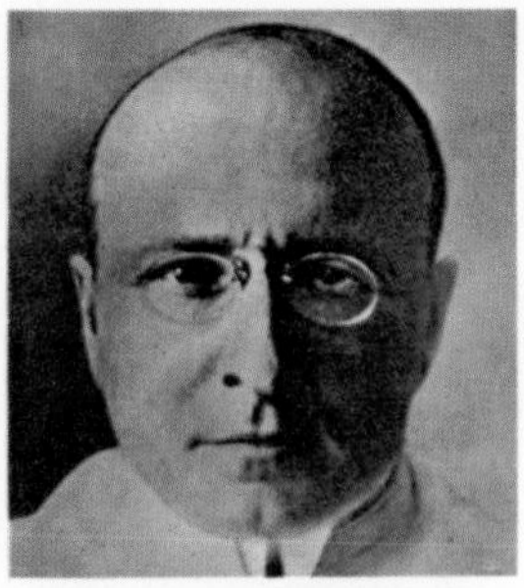

Alexis Carrell (French, 1873–1944): surgeon. Alexis Carrell was the father of blood vessel surgery and organ transplantation. He graduated as a doctor at Lyons in 1900, and his first paper, 'The operative technique of vascular anastomoses and the transplantations of organs', appeared two years later. This was the first publication of a successful surgical method for joining major blood vessels. Carrell described the need for meticulous care, the use of very fine needles and sewing material, the 'triangulation stitch' and other points, all of which remain the basis of present-day vascular surgery. This biological plumbing made organ transplantation technically practicable. Moving to the Rockefeller Institute, New York, he transplanted in animals such diverse organs as the heart, lungs, kidneys, thyroid and ovaries, and even entire limbs. He also recognised and described the immune rejection reaction which caused the eventual failure of these grafts. For these works he was awarded the Nobel Prize in Medicine in 1912. In 1935, with the aviator Charles Lindbergh (q.v.), he constructed a mechanical heart capable of keeping the isolated kidney or other organs alive on the laboratory bench, thus anticipating the organ storage problem currently important in transplantation research. Carrell's brilliant technical achievements, half a century ahead of their time, ensured the ultimate development of clinical vascular surgery and organ transplantation. **G. W. T.**

'NOBEL PRIZEWINNERS IN MEDICINE OR PHYSIOLOGY 1901–1950', BY L. G. STEVENSON (HENRY SCHUMAN, NEW YORK, 1953).

Willis Carrier (U.S., 1876–1950): engineer. Carrier was the man who 'invented' air conditioning. Before him it was a crude hit-and-miss affair of ice blocks and Punkah fans, but he made it a scientific process. The term 'air conditioning', first suggested by Carrier, meant the process of treating air to control simultaneously its temperature, humidity, cleanliness, and distribution to meet the requirements

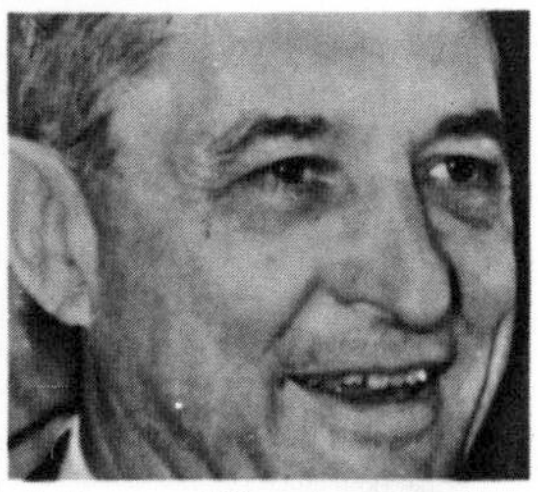

of the conditioned space: i.e., the complete control of internal climate. The essence of air conditioning is full humidity control, and Carrier showed how this could be achieved in practice. Air conditioning is now indispensable to many industrial processes – and the QE2's air conditioning was installed by the British firm that Carrier helped to found in 1921. **H. S.**

'CLIMATE AND THE ENERGY OF NATIONS', BY S. F. MARKHAM (O.U.P., 1947); 'MODERN AIR CONDITIONING', BY WILLIS H. CARRIER ET AL. (PITMAN, 3RD EDITION, 1959).

Sir Edward Carson (British, 1854–1935): statesman. This Southern Irish Unionist became the organiser of the Ulster Orange movement and contrived the political circumstances which made the partition of Ireland inevitable. It was Carson who, in 1912, anticipating the passage of Asquith's Home Rule Bill, promoted the Ulster Covenant and pledged the Northern people to refuse recognition to any Irish parliament which might be created under its terms. In 1913 he employed his immense legal capabilities as a member of both Irish and English bars to construct a provisional government for Ulster, of which he

was himself the head. It was backed by a volunteer force of 100,000 men in arms. By the outbreak of the First World War, therefore, with the army at The Curragh evidently sympathetic to Ulster unilateral action, the British Constitution was brought to its most critical test in modern times. Compromise, of course, prevailed, and in the Act of 1920 Ulster separatism was legalised. Carson had himself joined Lloyd George's Coalition Cabinet in 1916. He was the plumber, rather than the architect, of Northern Ireland. **E. R. N.**

'THE LIFE OF LORD CARSON', 3 VOLS. BY E. MARJORIBANKS AND I. COLVIN (GOLLANCZ, 1932–6); 'CARSON: THE LIFE OF SIR EDWARD CARSON', BY H. MONTGOMERY HYDE (HEINEMANN, 1953).

Henri Cartier-Bresson (French, b. 1909): photographer. As an international-ranking, globetrotting photographer since 1933, Cartier-Bresson is one of the half-dozen men to persuade us that photography can be an art. He has done it by consistently outstanding *reportages* as a photo-journalist; a dozen books running into international editions; countless major exhibitions in museums and art galleries across the world. Every photograph betrays an extremely subtle, unusual sensibility. Among picture-editors he is a legendarily awkward customer and a 200 per cent. stickler over standards. He doesn't believe colour photography works;

never sets up a phoney incident; never retouches his negatives; never after-edits the frame of his picture; never allows his pictures to be cropped. Ignoring sport, fashion, war, politics, or even physical objects, he is interested only in people, their spatial relationships, and in landscape as space. He is quite prepared to come back empty-handed from a magazine assignment if he didn't get the feeling, from any particular instant, of summatory significance. Usually in fact he comes back loaded with unforgettable images – completely baffling us how he was there, camera ready, at the precise, most revelatory moment – be it from Europe, America, Russia, India, China. He is a nonpareil spotter of ironic moments – like his two nuns amazed by Matisse's *Dancers* – and yet he is never heavy-handed about it. **C. H.**

Enrico Caruso (Italian, 1873–1921): singer. Half a century after he flourished, Caruso remains, thanks to the gramophone, the best-known of all operatic tenors. His voice, rich, rounded, golden and smooth, lent itself to recording, so that he is the first great singer to have left an adequate legacy of song by which his art may still be judged and enjoyed. His records show, as well as the ample girth and sonority of his voice, its fine flexibility. More than merely an exceptional instrument, it reflected in vocal sound its owner's involvement in the emotions of the music he sang. This covered a wide range of French and Italian operatic music, lyric and dramatic, as well as his native Neapolitan folksongs which he communicated unforgettably and inimitably. His own definition of the attributes of a great singer as "a big chest, a big mouth, 90 per cent. memory, 10 per cent. intelligence, lots of hard work and something in the heart" about sums him up, except that his heart was big too. Familiar at Covent Garden before the First World War and the mainstay of the New York 'Met' from 1903, he died in Naples, his birthplace, at the age of 48. **F. A.**

'ENRICO CARUSO, HIS LIFE AND DEATH', BY DOROTHY CARUSO (LAURIE, 1946); 'THE GREAT SINGERS', BY HENRY PLEASANTS (GOLLANCZ, 1967).

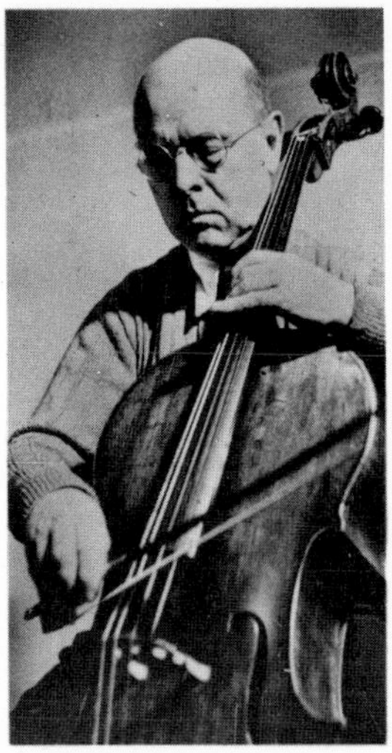

Pablo Casals (Spanish, b. 1876): cellist. Possibly the greatest ever, certainly the greatest of his time, Casals married a highly individual virtuoso cello technique (unfailing at the height of his powers) to his broad, deep, and wholly unexhibitionistic musicality. He studied the piano, organ and violin by the age of six; violin-fingering was to influence his original development of cello technique. He decided to become a cellist at the age of 11, and made his debut as a virtuoso at the Lamoureux concerts in Paris in 1898. In 1905 he founded the Thibaud-Casals-Cortot trio, one of the age's great chamber groups; its interpretations of the two Schubert Trios have remained unequalled. In 1919 he founded the *Orquestra Pau Casals* (Barcelona), which he last conducted in 1936 before leaving Spain for ever (during and after the 1939 war he lived in Prades, in the French Pyrenees). He introduced Bach's unaccompanied suites into the living repertoire, evolved novel principles of cello technique (expounded in Diran Alexanian's *Traité Théorique et Pratique du Violoncelle*), taught outstanding cellists (Gaspar Cassado and Maurice Eisenberg amongst them) and composed a great deal – though perhaps nothing lasting. **H. K.**

'PABLO CASALS', BY LILLIAN LITTLEHALES (DENT, 1949).

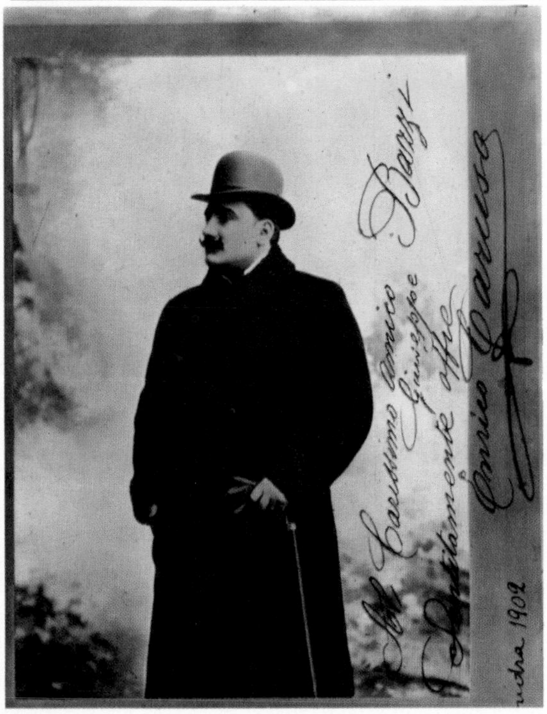

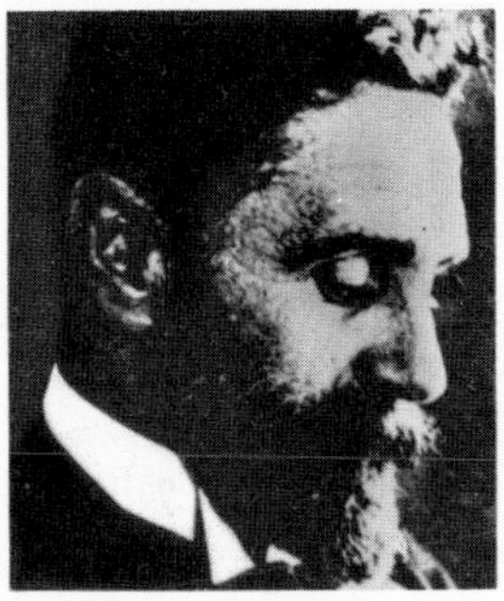

Sir Roger Casement (Irish, 1864–1916): Irish nationalist. One of the early gestures of Harold Wilson's premiership was to send back to Ireland what were believed to be Roger Casement's remains. The action was suitable: Casement symbolises the forlorn idealism of the Irish struggle for independence. His actual contribution, however, was slight. On retirement from the British consular service in 1913 he had gone back to his native Ireland and involved himself with militant nationalism. At the start of the First World War he took himself to Germany and toured the prisoner-of-war camps recruiting an Irish brigade to fight against the British in Ireland. The outcome was unhappy. Casement was ignored by the prisoners and distrusted by the Germans. Realising that German support for a rebellion was unforthcoming, and in the hope of warning the Irish Nationalists, he got himself repatriated just before Easter, 1916. He was arrested on the Kerry coast when he landed from a U-boat. It was Good Friday. Casement was sent to London, convicted of treason and executed in Pentonville prison. **E. R. N.**

'SIR ROGER CASEMENT', BY DENIS GWYNN (CAPE 1930); 'ROGER CASEMENT: A NEW JUDGMENT', BY RENE MACCOLL (HAMISH HAMILTON, 1956); 'ROGER CASEMENT' (FAMOUS TRIALS, 9) BY H. MONTGOMERY HYDE (PENGUIN, 1964).

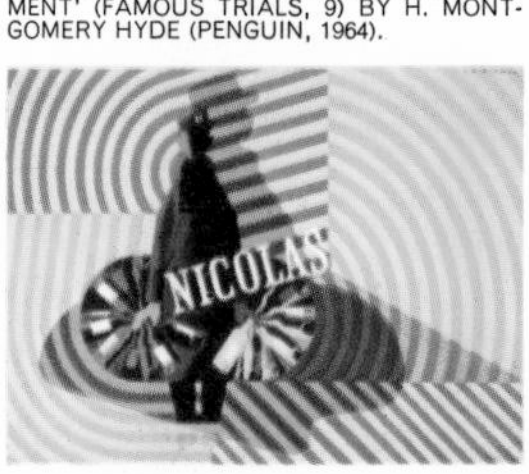

A. M. Cassandre (French, 1901–1968): poster designer. The work of Cassandre paved the way for the acceptance of avant-garde art. His first poster was designed in 1923 for a furniture shop: *Le Bûcheron* ('The Woodcutter'). It was a simple V design in which a stylised woodcutter (left branch) felled a tree (right branch). With Cassandre (and Paul Colin's *Bal Nègre*) the avant-garde stormed the hoardings of Paris. His success stemmed from his central idea that "the poster is solely a means of communication rather like the telegraph. Like the telegraphist, the poster designer does not issue the message, he passes it on. All that is required of him is a clear, powerful and precise communication." Those tough principles renovated the poster and renewed the looks of metropolitan hoardings. His best known posters were *Le Bûcheron, Etoile du Nord, L.M.S., The Davis Cup, Dubonnet, Angleterre, Prunier* and *Nicolas* (shown above). His best known stage sets were for *Amphitryon '38, Mirages* and *Don Giovanni*; his best known type faces were Acier, Bifur and Peignot. **Ph. G.**

'A. M. CASSANDRE: POSTERS' (ZOLLIKOFER, SWITZERLAND, 1948).

Fidel Castro (Cuban, b. 1926): politician. The revolutionary leader of Cuba, reputedly the illegitimate son of a landowner, first became prominent as a militant leader against Batista's dictatorship during his days as a law student at Havana University. In his trial after his failure to take the Moncada barracks in Santiago on July 26, 1953, he declared Batista's rule unconstitutional. Released under amnesty in 1955, he trained as a guerrilla in Mexico and landed in Cuba in December 1956 with 12 survivors from 82 men. From his mountain base in the Sierra Maestra, Castro eroded Batista's power, entering Havana in triumph in January 1959. He moved steadily to the Left, and as his relations with the 'Imperialist' U.S. worsened he drew closer to the Soviet camp, announcing in 1961 his acceptance of Marxist-Leninism. But he never accepted the Soviet-inspired legalism of Latin American Communists; the missile crisis showed him that the USSR would settle a 'Cuban' issue over his head, and his insistence on Cuban independence made him quarrel with Red China. He made serious economic blunders in his early attempts to industrialise, but he now recognises the importance of Cuba's sugar crop and has rectified mistakes with boundless energy. He is a television ruler, and the secret of his hold lies in his speeches and in his posture as the revolutionary leader of the whole of Latin America. **R. Ca.**

'CASTRO – A POLITICAL BIOGRAPHY', BY HERBERT L. MATTHEWS (A. LANE, 1969); 'THE CUBAN REVOLUTION AND LATIN AMERICA', BY B. GOLDENBERG (ALLEN AND UNWIN, 1965); 'CUBA: CASTROISM AND COMMUNISM 1959–66', BY A. SUAREZ (M.I.T. PRESS, CAMBRIDGE, MASS., 1967).

Edith Cavell (British, 1865–1915): nurse. If history and propaganda had left Edith Cavell alone, she would have been modestly remembered for what she was – an austere, respected but wholly friendless Englishwoman who introduced skilled lay nursing into Belgium. Instead she died a popular martyr before a German firing squad in occupied Brussels. As founder-matron of the city's Berkendael Nurse Training Institute, she had sheltered over 200 French, Belgian and British soldiers on their way to rejoin Allied lines. She was legally executed for "conveying troops to the

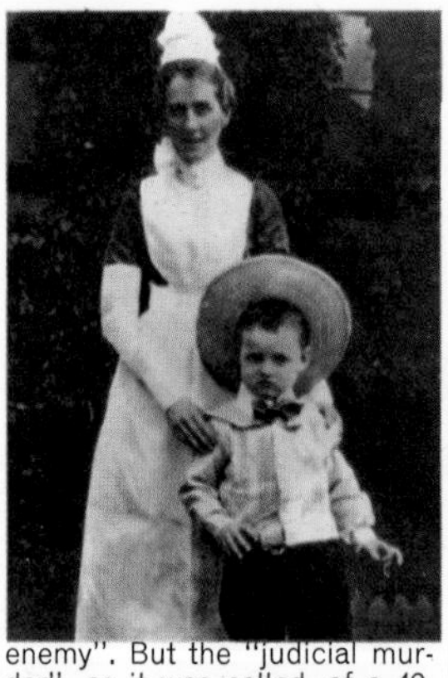

enemy". But the "judicial murder", as it was called, of a 49-year-old woman in the uniform of mercy scandalised neutral countries, ruined her judges and helped tip America into the war. Her last words – "I realise that patriotism is not enough" – puzzled everyone. In fact, her Resistance work was bungled. She felt unable to refuse runaway soldiers at her almost empty institute, let them get drunk in Brussels and when arrested incriminated 11 co-workers. **E. J. E.**

'EDITH CAVELL: PIONEER AND PATRIOT', BY A. E. CLARK-KENNEDY (FABER, 1965).

Sir James Chadwick (British, b. 1891): nuclear physicist. Chadwick discovered the unchanged elementary particle called the neutron, and showed that all atomic nuclei consist of a mixture of protons and neutrons; he is hence the father of the nuclear physics which led ultimately to uranium fission, the atom bomb, and the atomic reactor. He began research at Manchester under Rutherford, continued under Hans Geiger (qq.v.) in Berlin and, after the First World War, returned to Cambridge to work again with

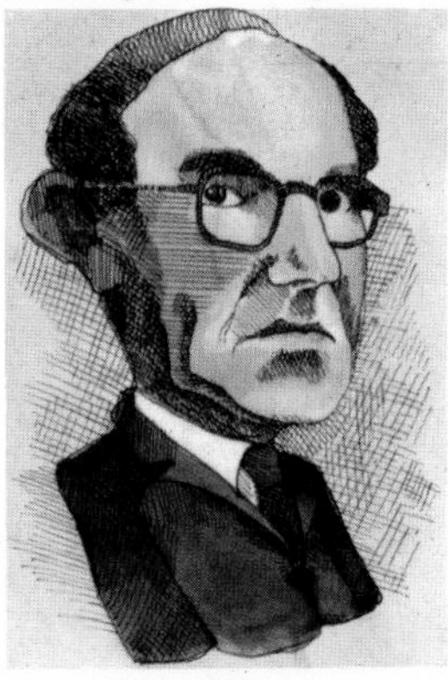

PAINTING BY BURTON SILVERMAN

Rutherford. After important atom-splitting experiments he began looking for an electrically neutral particle in the atomic nucleus – whose discovery Rutherford had predicted. Others had been puzzled by a strange type of radiation excited from the metal beryllium by alpha-particle bombardment. In 1932 Chadwick conclusively proved that it was made up of the neutral particles, or neutrons, he was seeking. In the Second World War he headed the British Mission attached to the Manhattan Project to develop the atom bomb. **P. H. S. S.**

'WORLD OF THE ATOM', ED. HENRY A. BOORSE AND LLOYD MOTZ, 2 VOLS (BASIC BOOKS, 1966).

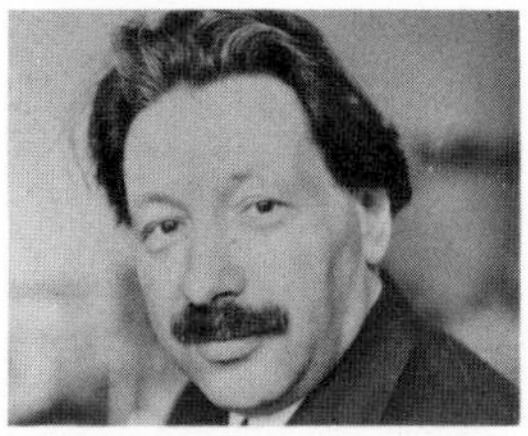

Sir Ernst Chain (British, ex-German, b. 1906): biochemist. Chain, who became professor of biochemistry at Imperial College, London, in 1961, received the Nobel Prize in 1945, together with Fleming and Florey (qq.v.) for the work on penicillins which led to the large-scale production of this antibiotic during the Second World War. Trained as a chemist, Chain worked at the Friedrich Wilhelm University in Berlin until Hitler made him a refugee. His work continued at Cambridge and later at Oxford under Florey. Penicillin was the first fruit of their general researches into antibiotics. It achieved great successes where the already introduced sulpha drugs had proved powerless. It is very effective against pneumonia, and against staphylococci and streptococci in general. Penicillin has limitations – against particular ranges of bacteria; through its side-effects; and because it can cause bacterial mutations – but it and other antibiotics are among the most beneficial discoveries of modern medicine. **P. J. F.**

'NOBEL LECTURES IN PHYSIOLOGY OR MEDICINE', (ELSEVIER, 1964); 'THE CHEMISTRY OF PENCILLIN' ED. H. T. CLARKE, J. R. JOHNSON AND R. ROBINSON (PRINCETON UNIVERSITY PRESS, 1949).

Fyodor Chaliapin (Russian, 1873–1938): bass singer and actor. No-one, not even Caruso (q.v.), made a greater impact on the world of opera than this astonishingly gifted peasant, who came from the banks of the Volga near Kazan. He was built on the heroic scale: huge of stature as of voice, with magnificent dramatic and musical powers and the autocratic temperament of a boyar. Making his way from the humblest origins, he scored his first great success in 1896 with the Private Opera in Moscow. Here began that gallery of memorable character portraits which brought Russian history and legend to life for the operatic world: among them Ivan the Terrible in Rimsky-Korsakov's *Maid of Pskov*, the two roles of Prince Galitzky and the Tartar chief, Khan Kontchak, in Borodin's *Prince Igor*, and

above all the guilty and tormented Tsar in Mussorgsky's *Boris Godunov*. Besides these roles, he became world-famous also as Mephistopheles (both Boito's and Gounod's), Mozart's Leporello, Rossini's Don Basilio and Massenet's Don Quixote. His semi-dramatised concert recitals were unique: the dark splendour of his voice and the intensity of his style are unmistakable in his numerous gramophone recordings. **D. S.-T.**

'CHALIAPIN', BY MAXIM GORKY (MAC-DONALD, 1967).

Neville Chamberlain (British, 1869–1940): politician. Neville Chamberlain, the man who led the 'appeasers' in the late Thirties and who signed the Munich Agreement with Hitler, was never groomed for high office by his thrusting father as his half-brother Austen (below) was. Yet he followed his father's example in serving as Lord Mayor of Birmingham (1915) before entering the House of Commons in 1918. Having established a reputation as a prudent and sensible Minister (local government reform and sound finance) he succeeded Baldwin (q.v.) as Prime Minister in May 1937. The last three years of his political life were packed with more excitement than all the years before. Pursuing an active foreign policy designed to prevent war, Chamberlain set out to 'appease' Italy and Germany while rearming Britain. Yet the Munich Agreement of 1938 which followed the Czech crisis was a Pyrrhic victory, and within less than a year European war had broken out. Chamberlain's policies, which brushed aside moral criteria, had aroused such opposition that he was ill-equipped to serve as an effective national leader, and he was replaced by Churchill (q.v.) in 1940. **A. B.**

'THE LIFE OF NEVILLE CHAMBERLAIN', BY KEITH FEILING (MACMILLAN, 1946); 'NEVILLE CHAMBERLAIN', BY IAIN MACLEOD (MULLER, 1961).

Sir Paul Chambers (British, b. 1904): civil servant/industrialist. Paul Chambers is the archetypal clever civil servant who swapped horses in mid-stream and went into industry. After the City of London College and London School of Economics, he went out to India to advise on income tax; then came back, during the war, to the Board of Inland Revenue, and is widely credited with devising the now-hallowed 'pay-as-you-earn' method of tax collection. He spent a period running the finances of the British Control Commission in Germany, and then departed, to considerable Whitehall surprise, to join Imperial Chemical Industries. He was chairman of ICI from 1960 to 1968, a period of huge expansion and investment for the company, but his whole period at the top was shadowed by the abortive take-over bid which ICI made for Courtaulds in 1962. This was one of the most bitterly-fought commercial battles in recent history (Courtaulds held a thanksgiving service after they had won) and ICI's policies towards the vital and profitable textile sector have never fully recovered. Sir Paul now heads the Royal Insurance Group and also Spey Investments. **P. W.**

Raymond Chandler (U.S., 1888–1959): novelist. Dashiell Hammett was the Onlie Begetter of the American private eye crime story; Chandler thought so himself. But Chandler refined, polished, subtilised; sentimentalised a little too, as any comparison of Sam Spade with Philip Marlowe shows. But he was a conscious literary artist as few crime writers have been. He had a wonderful eye for the Californian scene, its toughs, eccentrics and phoneys, a wonderful ear for American as it's spoken. He made a fortune out of his seven books, the first of which appeared when he was 50, and deserved it for preserving personal and literary integrity in a difficult business and a hard world. He cocked a snook at Hollywood, and wasn't deeply concerned with money. Once he had fully discovered his talent, after long years as a magazine writer, he never wrote at less than his best, and he knew exactly the limits of what he could do. He wrote his own epitaph in a letter: "To accept a mediocre form and make something like literature out of it is in itself rather an accomplishment." That's over-modest, really. The American crime story, which means Hammett and Chandler, is part of 20th-century literature. **J. G. S.**

'RAYMOND CHANDLER SPEAKING', EDITED BY DOROTHY GARDINER AND KATHRINE SORLEY WALKER (HAMISH HAMILTON, 1962); 'THE BIG SLEEP', BY RAYMOND CHANDLER (HAMISH HAMILTON, 1939).

Coco Chanel (French, c. 1883–1971): dress designer. Coco – otherwise Gabrielle Bonheur – Chanel was distinguished in a business over-burdened with chi-chi by the simplicity of her approach to everything concerning fashion. She first made a name for herself in the 1920s and 1930s by putting the Cunarder Set into glamorous interpretations of workers' clothes. She made feminine versions of trench coats, sailor's reefer jackets and matelot blouses; she made grown-up versions of schoolgirl uniforms and soft easy cardigan suits. Most of the fabrics she used moved with the body – Linton tweeds and silk

jersey. She always said she was flattered rather than furious when she was copied; and this intelligent, as opposed to intellectual, approach to fashion has done a great deal to democratise the business. After retiring in 1938, she made a triumphant comeback in 1954. Until she died she still ran her house in the Rue Cambon and produced collections each year. **M. McC.**

'THE FASHIONABLE SAVAGES', BY JOHN FAIRCHILD (DOUBLEDAY, NEW YORK, 1965); 'THE GLASS OF FASHION', BY CECIL BEATON (WEIDENFELD AND NICOLSON, 1954).

MAN. UN'TD

Bobby Charlton (British, b. 1938): footballer. Charlton is a great international star. To many abroad, he personifies many of the best English qualities. A miner's son from Ashington in Northumberland, he is regarded with affection and admiration by his countrymen. Diffident, taciturn, unaffected, and apparently unemotional – but when Manchester United won the European Cup in 1968, he left the field in tears. As a player for Manchester United and England, Charlton is highly gifted, cool and unselfish – a strong and elusive mover, with a shot of startling force and accuracy. He was voted Europe's Footballer of the Year in 1966, and has scored more goals than anyone else for England. In his competitive and often violent world, he controls his nerves and his temper, never fouls, never retaliates, never throws punches. He survived the Munich air crash in 1958, which wiped out a wonderful young Manchester United and changed him, at 20, from a junior to a veteran. He is an extraordinary ordinary man, who has given both excitement and a fine example. **T. D.**

Austen Chamberlain (British, 1863–1937): politician. Though he held many high political posts, including those of Chancellor of the Exchequer (1903–5: 1919–21) and Foreign Secretary (1924–9), Austen Chamberlain was never a real political leader. With eyeglass and orchid, he looked like his famous father, Joseph, who did everything he could to promote Austen's career. Austen was always in danger as a young man, therefore, of being considered not as a voice but as an echo of a voice; and as one political journalist put it, "no one ever girded on his sword to follow an echo". Rugby and Cambridge had softened the Birmingham in him and his temperament was as different from his father's as his features were similar. He reached the peak of his career at the time of the Locarno Pact of 1925, which seemed a reasonable pledge of peace in our time. Ten years later, however, there was some talk of Austen as a successor to Baldwin (q.v.) at the time of the Hoare-Laval Pact. Birkenhead (q.v. F. E. Smith) summed up Austen pithily: "Austen always played the game and always lost it." **A. B.**

'LIFE AND LETTERS OF AUSTEN CHAMBERLAIN', BY SIR CHARLES PETRIE, 2 VOLS. (CASSELL, 1939, 1940).

Charles Chaplin (British, b. 1889): film director and actor. After a slum childhood and music-hall training Charles Chaplin went in 1914 to Hollywood, where a star was born – a dandified tramp with cane, seedy bowler, baggy trousers, and outsize boots. Chaplin's short comedies were anarchic, robust in mood and exquisite in performance: *The Pawnshop, Easy Street, Shoulder Arms*; next, with the anarchism softened by pathos, came the classic feature films, *The Kid, The Pilgrim* and, with imperishable memories – Charlie dining off boiled boot and using bread rolls for a mock dance – *The Gold Rush*. Then the talkies arrived. The great clown was stylistically conservative; in the beautiful *City Lights* (1931) and *Modern Times* (1936) he remained, except for hiccups and nonsense rhymes, obstinately mum. At last in *The Great Dictator* (1940) with its parody of Hitler he spoke – and dropped the tramp-figure who had made him an international idol. As a result the satirical brilliance of *Monsieur Verdoux*, incomparably the best of his later works, has been undervalued. His genius lies in the creation of a universal tragi-comic figure. **D. P.**

'MY AUTOBIOGRAPHY', BY CHARLES CHAPLIN (BODLEY HEAD, 1964; PENGUIN, 1966); 'CHARLIE CHAPLIN', BY THEODORE HUFF (CASSELL, 1952).

1000
CHA-CHU

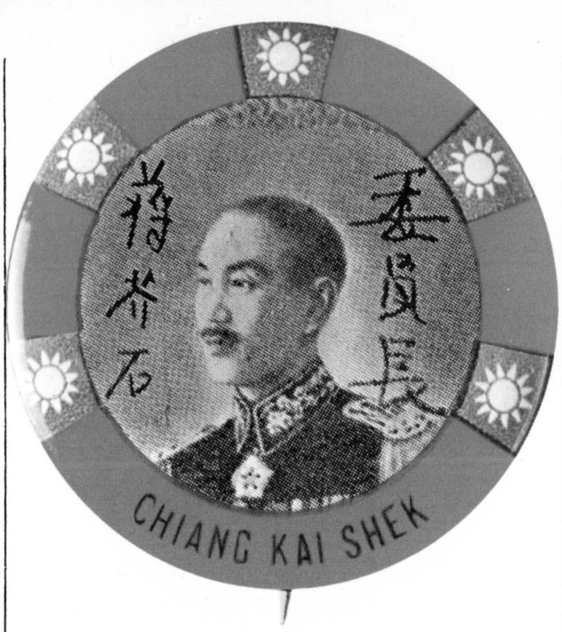

Chiang Kai-shek (Chinese, b. 1887): head of state. The defeat and exile to Formosa of the Chinese Nationalist Party in 1949 considerably reduced Chiang Kai-shek's status as an Asian statesman, and may also diminish, in the eyes of future historians, his role as a nationalist leader in the 1930s. Trained in Japan, Chiang first met there his mentor, Sun Yat-sen (q.v.), and was converted to the latter's revolutionary theories. In 1926 he launched his successful northern expedition to give China a veneer of unity, but his rise to power was not purely military. It was also due to the financial contributions of businessmen and landlords, popular support, and ideological authority. Ruling China from 1928 to 1949 he sadly misunderstood the needs of true unity (demobilisation and nationalisation of the fighting forces), of the urgent need for agrarian rehabilitation after decades of warlords' appropriations, and of rural reconstruction. But the defects of his power structure were ruthlessly exposed and aggravated during the anti-Japanese war of 1937–45, and thereafter his efforts in controlling the Communist opposition, even with limited American aid, were doomed to failure. Since 1950 Chiang's rule in Formosa has been more effective than it was on the continent and his agrarian reform has had a measure of success. **J. C.**

'THE MODERN HISTORY OF CHINA', BY HENRY McALEAVY (WEIDENFELD AND NICOLSON, 1967).

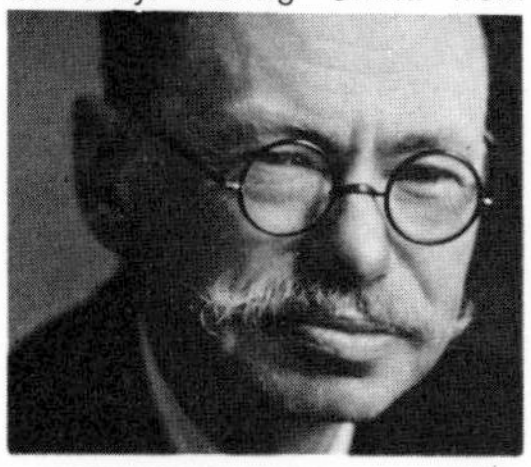

Gordon Childe (Australian, 1892–1957): archaeologist. The publication of Childe's *Dawn of European Civilisation* (1925) marked a new starting point in prehistoric archaeology and a revolution in the understanding of prehistory. Previously archaeologists postulated a simple, unilateral culture sequence for early man – one culture overtaking another, diffused from one source by a master race. Childe was the first to offer an alternative. He set out complex culture schemes covering small regions and time spans, which seemed to deny formal pattern, but which made sense in man's inability to comply with rigid theory. Childe's *Danube in Prehistory* (1929), *Bronze Age* (1930) and *Prehistoric Communities of the British Isles* (1940) demonstrate perfectly the logical application of his belief in how different culture elements could combine to form compound civilisations. Today scientific skills and interest in the psychology of man's development have widened archaeological horizons, but our understanding of the synthetic nature of prehistoric cultures was inspired by Gordon Childe's work. **P. G. St. B. C.**

'WHAT HAPPENED IN HISTORY', BY V. GORDON CHILDE (PENGUIN, 1942); 'THE IDEA OF PREHISTORY', BY GLYN DANIEL (C. A. WATTS, 1962); 'ARCHAEOLOGY AND SOCIETY', BY GRAHAME CLARKE (METHUEN, 1960).

Giorgio de Chirico (Italian, b. 1888): painter. Born in Greece, the son of a railway engineer, Chirico grew up in Athens, Munich, Florence, Turin: cities notable for arcades many times man-size, huge open spaces landmarked by equestrian statues, echoing railway-stations and sudden vistas of a distant countryside. All this Chirico turned into a dreamland as

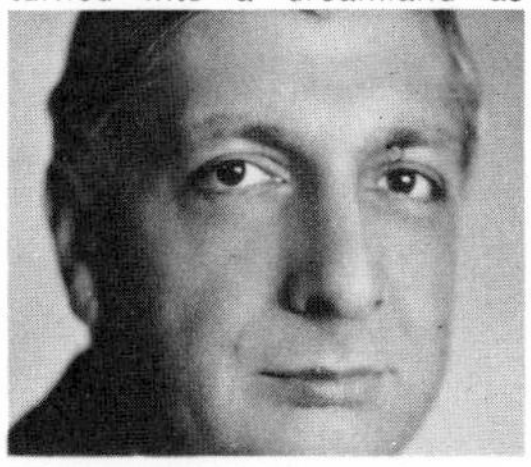

fraught with menace as any in European art. He saw the city as a dictionary of omens. "One of the strangest and deepest sensations that prehistory has left with us," he once wrote, "is the sensation of *knowing something beforehand* . . ." That is what we feel when he tips the arcades on end, or convinces us that the little girl bowling her hoop across the uninhabited piazza is somehow in mortal danger. From 1912 to 1919 Chirico was one of the supreme masters of the poetic imagination in European painting, but in 1919 he was convinced by a mysterious vision that he was altogether on the wrong tack and should revert to straightforward academic painting. He did so, and thereafter remained for 50 years – industrious, magniloquent, irascible – a Lost Leader of modern art. **J. R.**

'GIORGIO DE CHIRICO', BY J. T. SOBY (MUSEUM OF MODERN ART, N.Y., 1955).

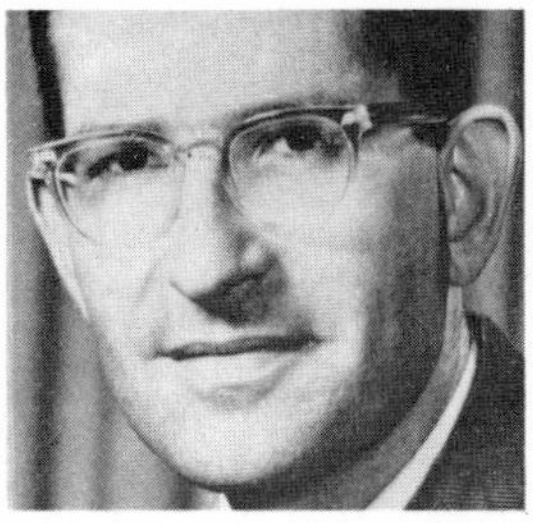

Noam Chomsky (U.S., b. 1928): theoretical linguist. Chomsky's *Syntactic Structures* revolutionised linguistics, hitherto a somewhat pedestrian classificatory discipline. A Chomsky 'Transformational Generative Grammar' consists of a sequence of exactly formulated rules specifying the form of sentences in a language. Its aim is to define the knowledge of that language acquired by human beings in childhood, enabling them to produce and interpret an infinite variety of sentences, most of which they have not previously met. The readiness with which children acquire this 'rule-governed creativity' of language is held by Chomsky to depend on innate properties of the mind. He rejects the positivism and behaviourism of the last 150 years as an aberration, and opposes the application of Skinner's (q.v.) 'operant conditioning' to distinctively human behaviour. Though personally a gentle, dispassionate, quiet-spoken, even unworldly man, he is an uncompromising intellectual polemicist and radical political activist, believing grass-roots political enlightenment to be one of the intellectual's responsibilities to society. **J. L. M. T.**

'LANGUAGE AND MIND', BY NOAM CHOMSKY (HARCOURT, 1968); 'AMERICAN POWER AND THE NEW MANDARINS', BY NOAM CHOMSKY (PANTHEON PRESS, NEW YORK, 1969).

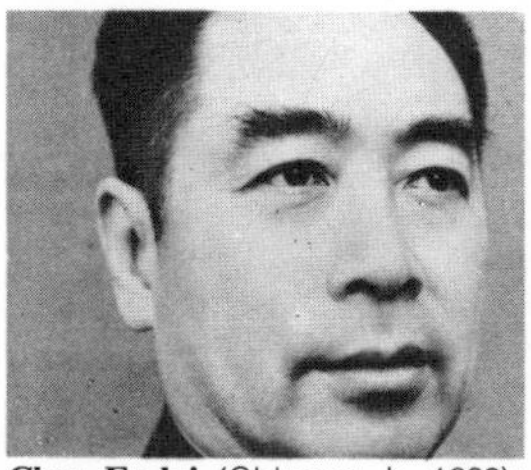

Chou En-lai (Chinese, b. 1898): statesman. Prime Minister of Communist China since 1949, Chou En-lai has always appeared to the outside world as the leader of a moderate force or view in his party. When he was a student in post-war Paris he embraced Communism, and in 1927 was selected to command the famous Nanch'ang Uprising, which failed. From 1928–34 he faithfully supported whatever party leadership Moscow favoured, and from 1932 onward he wielded more military power in the Red Army than anyone else. Yet under Chou the Red Army suffered disastrous reverses in 1934, and was forced on the Long March. According to one source, at the Tsunyi Conference in January 1935 Chou thoroughly examined his own mistakes and handed military power to Mao Tse-tung (q.v.), never again to resume strategic command. Not an original thinker, he seems to have an uncanny ability in assessing the relative strengths of the contending factions of the Communist Party, thereby always emerging on the side of the victor. In 1966, on the eve of the Cultural Revolution, he was the only man capable of preserving China's administrative continuity. **J. C.**

'CHOU EN-LAI', BY KAI-YU HSU (DOUBLEDAY, 1968).

Arthur Christiansen (British, 1904–1963): editor. Leaving, perforce, policy to Beaverbrook (q.v.) Christiansen, from 1933–1956, dynamited the *Daily Express* into millions of homes with an acute mixture of news, human interest and opinion presented every morning like a package tour, highly formalised, brilliantly displayed. Style and rewriting were all-important. He structured page one around column one, the important story,

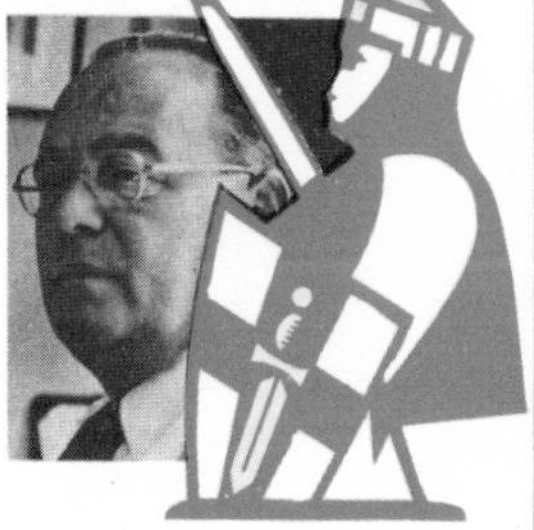

necessary for status but too heavy, too lacking in human interest, for the readers; the lead, which alternated between high policy or the big news of the day; an outside lead which on policy days took over the role of the lead; and a centre-column, a unique sugar-coated *Express* diversion – amusing, often glossy, always well written but irrelevant to the news. Christiansen's compulsive control of editorial techniques was his real strength. In his early days it enabled him to scoop Fleet Street, if not the world, on the R.101 disaster. During the war, after a top-level briefing, he would have written, subbed, headlined and displayed the news while other editors were still dictating the gist of the briefing to their secretaries. **R. P. W.**

'HEADLINES ALL MY LIFE', BY ARTHUR CHRISTIANSEN (HEINEMANN, 1961).

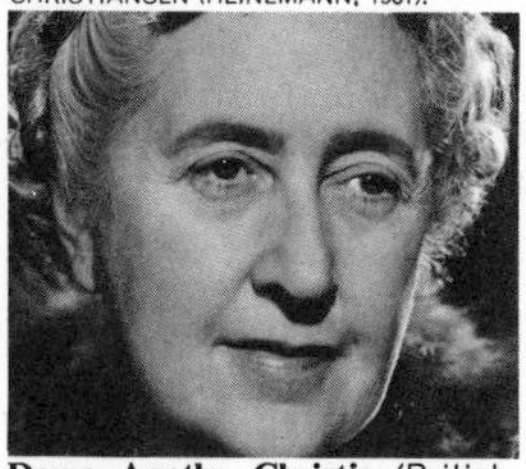

Dame Agatha Christie (British, b. 1890): novelist. Choose one name among living crime writers and which would it be? Agatha Christie. Choose one book – and for many people it would be *The Murder of Roger Ackroyd* (1926). This work is one of the most ingenious exercises in detection ever written, a conjuring trick that even after nearly half a century mustn't be revealed because there are always new readers to be astonished. Other books she wrote in the Twenties and Thirties are almost as cunningly deceptive (*The ABC Murders*, *N or M?*, *Lord Edgware Dies*). *The Mousetrap* (1951) is not her best play, not even a good play in its genre, yet it's been going over 18 years. Why does a mousetrap run? The Christie legend, yes, but also her natural knowledge of what makes theatre audiences kin – the cosy mixed with hints of something nasty. It's cosiness she loves, preferring Miss Marple to Poirot, never letting real violence get into her books; yet her own fascination with domestic crime seeps through to her millions of readers. They know that when she poisons it is always in jest, that the blood of her victims will leave no stain on the imagination. She is the undisputed Queen of Impossible Crime. **J. G. S.**

'AGATHA CHRISTIE: MISTRESS OF MYSTERY', BY G. C. RAMSEY (COLLINS, 1968).

Sir Winston Churchill (British, 1874–1965): statesman. Churchill emerged from a lonely, but not unhappy, childhood to find his feet in war. He took part in five campaigns before he was 25 and became a national figure when he escaped from the Boers. His precociousness made him enemies. When he entered Parliament as a Tory in 1900, he behaved like a cabinet minister

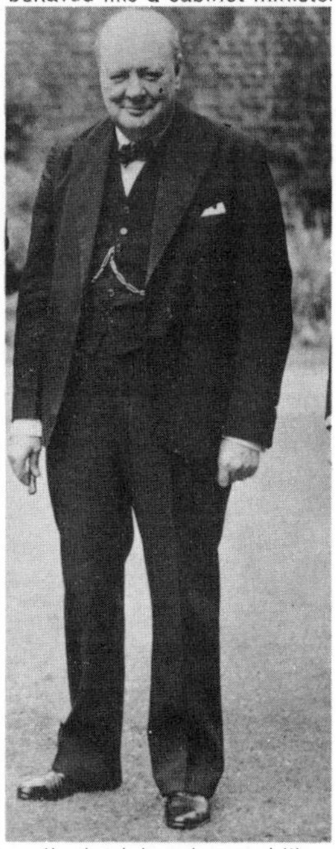

on the back benches and like a prime minister when he first entered the Government. They called him the Blenheim pup. His youthful achievements as President of the Board of Trade, Home Secretary, and above all as First Lord (1911–15) made his critics seem merely jealous. The Dardanelles unfairly revived the legend of irresponsibility, and he took, literally, to the trenches. After the war he was Colonial Secretary, Secretary of State for War, and Chancellor of the Exchequer. His offices still read like battle-honours. In political exile in the Thirties he wrote and painted at Chartwell, and found in Hitler an adversary worthy of his obstinacy, individuality and patriotism and in 1940, at the age of 65, he reached his destination. He became undeclared dictator, by his supremacy of character and the force of his parliamentary gifts. His ebullient optimism paid off. A considerable strategist, an adventurous diplomatist, his success was due to his inner conviction of what was right and possible, and to the opportunity gained when his opponents attacked Russia and the United States. Then in 1945, having won the race, he was warned off the course. Instinctively the British people felt that he was not the right man to reconstruct the country. He remained at heart a late Victorian aristocrat. No Free India for him, no Beveridge, no industrial charter. He had the magnificent conception of a Europe united under Britain's leadership, but he failed to press it home, defeated, he said, by the Party machine. But it was not true. His second premiership was an anti-climax. His genius was like his painting – splashes of colour – and old age dimmed the highlights. He had little sympathy with the new world he had inadvertently created by saving the old. **N. N.**

'WINSTON S. CHURCHILL', BY RANDOLPH CHURCHILL – TWO VOLS. UP TO 1914 (HEINEMANN, 1966-67).

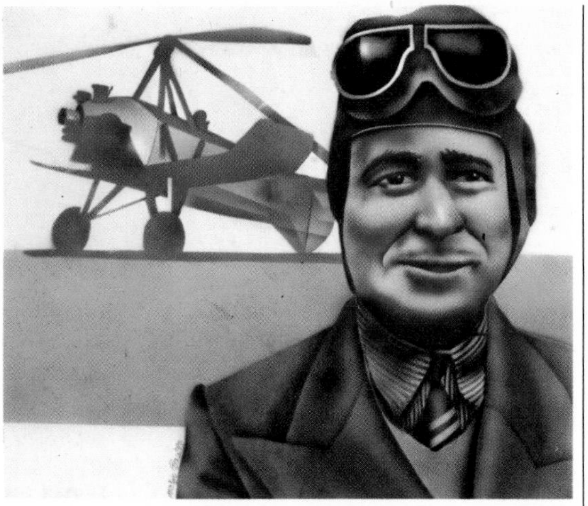

Juan de la Cierva (Spanish, 1895–1936): engineer. The man who invented the autogyro was born into an aristocratic family at the turn of the century. Brooding over the crash of his first aeroplane, he set out to design an aircraft that would be stall-proof and capable of flying very slowly. Four years of experiment led to the first successful flight of his so-called 'autogyro' – an aircraft with freely-revolving, unpowered rotors – in 1923. His earlier machines had shown an alarming tendency to roll over on take-off – an effect caused by the rotor blades advancing into the airstream on one side of the plane and moving downstream on the other, which resulted in 'asymmetric lift'. Cierva's ingenious solution to this 'capsizing' problem was to make the rotor blades as flexible as possible so that they could flap and thus naturally balance the lift on the left and right side of the rotor. In 1927 he invented the 'drag hinge' which allowed the blades of the rotor to drag behind a little as they turned, so helping to off-load the massive stresses built up in the hub. In all, some 500 autogyros were built, many in Britain, but by the mid-1930s the first true helicopters – with their fully-powered rotors – were taking to the air with rotors and components developed by Cierva's 'Spanish windmill'. His machines were the flying test-beds for today's helicopters. **N. V.**

'HELICOPTERS AND AUTOGYROS', BY CHARLES GABLEHOUSE (FREDERICK MULLER, 1968).

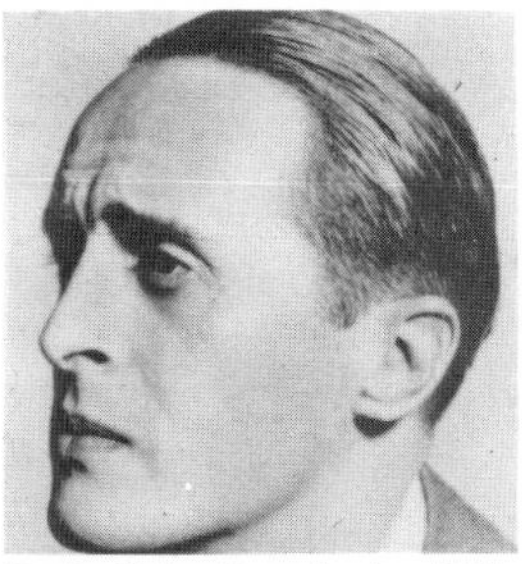

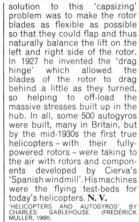

René Clair (French, b. 1898): film director. René Clair's early experiments with motion and immobility (*Paris Qui Dort*) and fantasy (*Entr'acte*) foreshadowed a lifelong fascination by the visual properties of cinema; in 1927 his brilliant *The Italian Straw Hat* showed a delighted command of absurdity. After his first talkie, *Sous les Toits de Paris*, Clair became a pioneer in the witty narrative handling of music, and *Le Million* (1931) is still among the most elegant comedies ever made. A satire on mechanised labour, *A Nous la Liberté* (said to have influenced Chaplin's *Modern Times*), *Quatorze Juillet* and the less successful *Le Dernier Milliardaire* followed, then work in Britain (*The Ghost Goes West*) and, during the war, in America (*The Flame of New Orleans* and *It Happened Tomorrow*). Back in France, he made a nostalgic comedy about the silent cinema, *Le Silence est d'Or*; a Faust-story, *La Beauté du Diable*; a dream-fantasy, *Les Belles-de-Nuit*; and in *Summer Manoeuvres* used colour with a delicate sense of its potentialities. His later work lost the early impetus, but no film-maker has made a greater contribution to the marriage of music and movement in humane, ironic comedy. **D. P.**

'REFLECTIONS ON THE CINEMA', BY RENE CLAIR (WILLIAM KIMBER, 1953); 'RENE CLAIR: AN INDEX', BY CATHERINE DE LA ROCHE (BRITISH FILM INSTITUTE 1958).

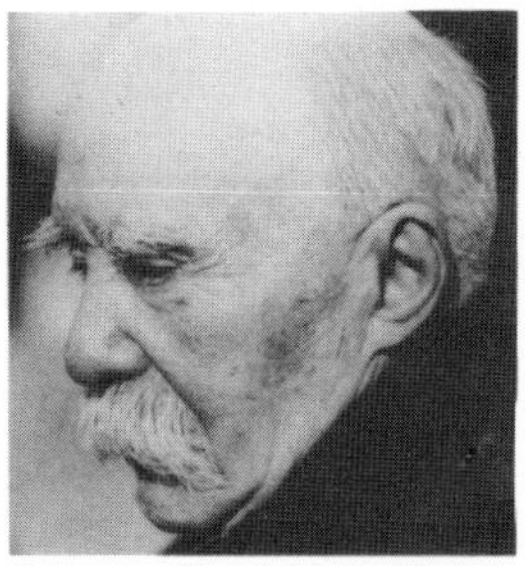

Georges Clemenceau (French, 1841–1929): statesman. Clemenceau stood for the principles of the French Revolution – authoritarian, democratic, patriotic; he was a 20th-century Jacobin. The French politician who had the most nicknames (*le tombeur des ministères, le Tigre, Père la victoire*) and fought the most duels, he began his career as a radical deputy and outspoken journalist, in continuous conflict with Catholics, royalists, moderates, socialists. His greatest moment came in 1917 when, Prime Minister for the second time, elderly and deaf, he still became the symbol and inspiration of the French determination to win the war. In the peace negotiations he tried to get security for France against Germany, yet was attacked for not being more successful; he was defeated in the Presidential elections of 1920 and retired. He was an independent character (in 1919, en route for some ceremony, he met Balfour in the lift – Balfour was wearing a top hat and Clemenceau his battered deer-stalker. A puzzled Balfour : "But they told me that I had to wear a silk hat." Clemenceau: "They told me that too"); and a sardonic wit ("*si seulement je pouvais pisser comme Lloyd George parle*"). **D. W. J. J.**

'CLEMENCEAU AND THE THIRD REPUBLIC', BY J. HAMPDEN JACKSON (TEACH YOURSELF HISTORY LIBRARY, E.U.P., 1946); 'FOCH VERSUS CLEMENCEAU', BY J. C. KING (HARVARD UNIVERSITY PRESS, 1960).

John Cobb (British, 1899–1952): speedster. Unlike Sir Malcolm Campbell (q.v.) John Cobb – the first man to exceed 400 mph on land – did not survive his enthusiasm for speed. In 1952 his jet-propelled boat hit a ripple on Loch Ness (believed by some to have been caused by the monster) and disintegrated. He was going faster than anyone else had on water (about 250 mph) but did not establish a formal record. Cobb symbolises as much as anyone else the great speed craze, superseded by the present zest for feats of solitary circumnavigation. It was a constant source of pride to some of his countrymen that on some occasions Britain held almost all such records. A fur broker, he was on one occasion commissioned by the Russians to sell their annual pelt stock, but on another, just before a

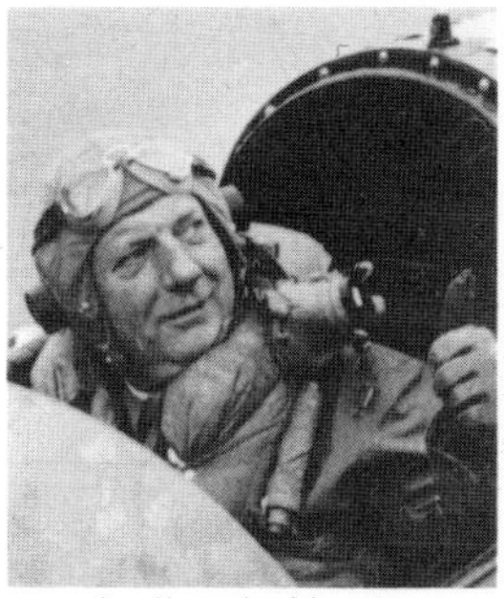

record attempt, his car was almost in the hands of the receivers. The first great landmark in his sporting career was when he broke the world land speed record at Bonneville Flats in 1938, at 350.20 mph. The following year he went at 369.7 mph. Finally, in 1947, in one direction only, he managed to drive at 403.135 mph. **A. C. C.**

Sir Charles Cochran (British, 1873–1951): impresario. C. B. Cochran made entertainment a glittering word, and he died before serious sociological dramatists tarnished it. As a theatrical manager he promoted all kinds of shows from plays by Ibsen to Wild West rodeos and presented Max Reinhardt's spectacular *The Miracle*. But the genre in which he achieved significance was the revue, a light form of entertainment which consisted of a series of sketches united by songs and

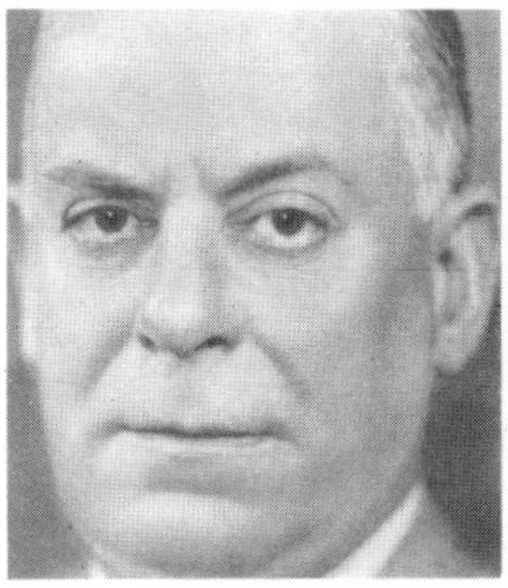

dances, and celebrated for their attractive choruses. Mr Cochran's Young Ladies and Gentlemen, attired respectively in Ascot dresses and top hats and tails, were the very glass of fashion and the mould of form in the late 1920s and early 1930s. Cochran's most famous revues, *This Year of Grace* and *Wake Up and Dream*, were miracles of delicacy and taste. His productions might have been painted by Watteau or Fragonard. In their exquisite fragility they might have been designed for a nation of Marie Antoinettes. **H. H.**

'SECRETS OF A SHOWMAN', BY C. B COCHRAN (HEINEMANN, 1930); 'COCK-A-DOODLE-DO', BY C. B. COCHRAN (DENT, 1941); 'COCKIE', BY SAM HEPNER (LESLIE FREWIN, 1969).

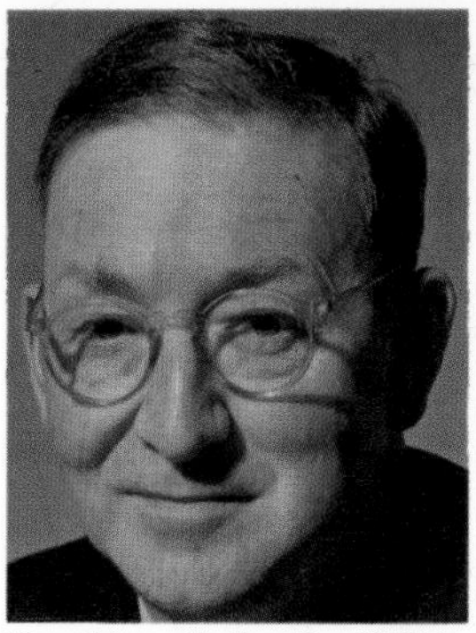

Sir John Cockcroft (British, 1897–1967): physicist. Cockcroft produced with Ernest Walton (q.v.) the first atom-smashing machine. Rutherford (q.v.), with Chadwick (q.v.) and others, had already split the atom and fulfilled the dream of the alchemists by transmuting one element into another, but they had used natural alpha-particles produced by radioactive decay for the purpose. Cockcroft, who started out as an electrical engineer, switched to mathematics at Cambridge and subsequently joined Rutherford in the Cavendish Laboratory. In 1928 he turned his thoughts to the problem of how to accelerate protons artificially to high enough energies to break open atomic nuclei. By 1932 he and Walton had produced a machine based on rectifying high-voltage electric currents created simply with a transformer. Simultaneously in America, Van de Graaf was working on a high-voltage electrostatic generator, and Lawrence and Livingston were working on their cyclotron, which was to prove the best way of accelerating particles. But Cockcroft and Walton got there first. Starting with lithium they managed to split a number of light atoms at energies only one-millionth that of the currently proposed European 300-GeV accelerator. They shared the Nobel Prize in 1951. Among many important offices Cockcroft filled was that of the UK Atomic Energy Research Establishment's first director. His work marked the first step towards the world of modern particle physics. **P. H. S. S.**

'THE WORLD OF THE ATOM', BY HENRY A. BOORSE AND LLOYD MOTZ, 2 VOLS. (BASIC BOOKS, NEW YORK, 1966); 'PHYSICS FOR THE ENQUIRING MIND', BY ERIC M. ROGERS (O.U.P., 1960).

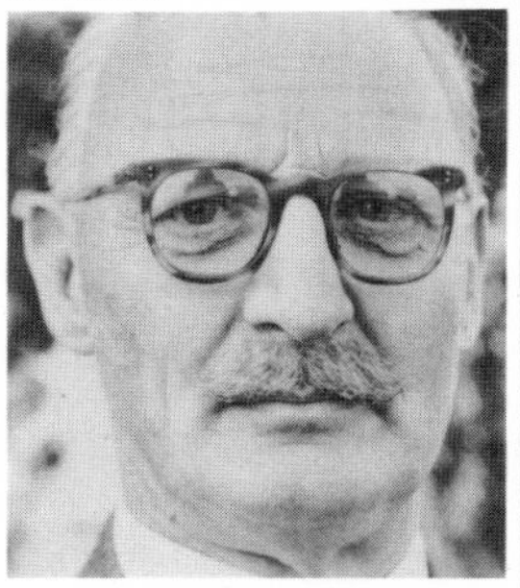

Sir Christopher Cockerell (British, b. 1910): engineer. The invention of the Hovercraft can be traced back to the purchase of a boatyard by Cockerell on the Norfolk Broads in 1950, and his subsequent difficulties in improving the performance of his boats. Somehow there had to be a way of overcoming wave resistance and the friction created by water passing around a hull. Cockerell conceived the idea of riding a craft on a cushion of air. There were many technical snags, particularly the problem of holding his air cushion in place beneath the craft, and no less frustrating was the inventor's need of official recognition for this entirely new form of transport. Eventually, in 1958, the Hovercraft – as Cockerell and his wife named it – was patented. Ten years later the giant 150-ton SRN4 Mountbatten class entered into the first cross-Channel commercial passenger and car ferry service. But Cockerell had not merely invented a new amphibious transport. The air cushion concept has already a wide variety of industrial applications. Medical science has appreciated its use in serious burn cases by literally floating a patient on a bed of air, with consequent relief from pain and faster recovery. The impact of Cockerell's invention is only beginning. **P. H. E. B.**

'HOVERCRAFT', BY ANGELA CROOME (BROCKHAMPTON PRESS, 1965); 'ABOUT HOVERCRAFT' (BRITISH PETROLEUM, 1969); 'THE HISTORY OF AIR CUSHION VEHICLES', BY LESLIE HAYWARD (KALERGLI-MCLEAVY, 1963).

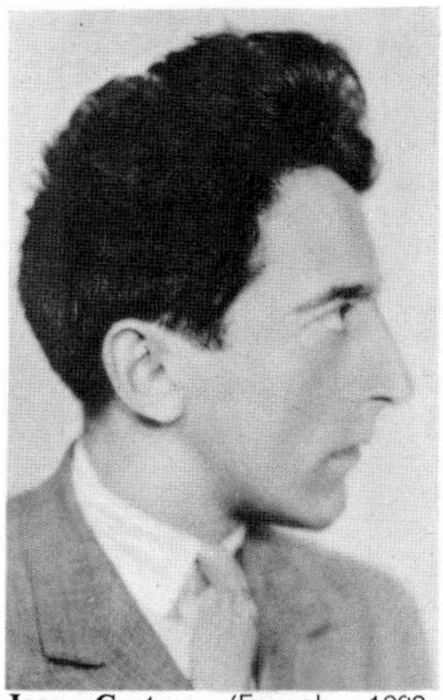

Jean Cocteau (French, 1889–1963): poet. During his lifetime the darling of gossip-writers, and abiding with us in death as he promised (*Je reste avec vous*), Cocteau – dramatist, novelist, artist, cineast – remains the archetypal poet of our time. Yet all his life he was obsessed by the legends of ancient Greece: his favourite hero was Orpheus, and among his best work are *Orpheus* and its sequel *The Testament of Orpheus*, both films, like *The Blood of a Poet*, which meditate upon the quasi-divine status of the poet. The poet cannot die because the sound of his lyre pleases the gods too much. All Cocteau's work (and he wrote a lot) is *poésie*: fiction-poetry, criticism-poetry, theatre-poetry, film-poetry, graphic-poetry, as well of course as poetry-poetry (the titles are his). He has a depth which you have, perhaps, to be something of a poet yourself to appreciate: poet enough to sense, at least, that poetry is not necessarily deadly serious. Although he was no mean draughtsman and novelist, Cocteau's influence on 20th-century theatre and cinema will remain the more profound and lasting. In drama he foreshadowed developments in the Theatre of the Absurd. He was fascinated by what he called the "good absurd", manifested in a "logical sequence of illogical events": his plays show a deliberate anti-naturalism subverting a naturalistic framework. His films, similarly, veer from the mundane to the mythical: Death loves the middle-class, happily-married Orpheus and abducts him in a limousine. Her radio station broadcasts poetry and her gloves dissolve mirrors and stop time. This sensitivity to mystery and wonder keeps Cocteau's work fresh today. **J. W. J. F.**

'SCANDAL AND PARADE', BY NEAL OXENHANDLER (CONSTABLE, 1958); COCTEAU', BY ELIZABETH SPRIGGE AND JEAN-JACQUES KIHM (GOLLANCZ, 1968).

Ornette Coleman (U.S., b. 1930): jazz musician. Ornette Coleman, alto saxophonist, violinist, composer, achieved some recognition as a player of modern jazz in the more accepted style in the Fifties, but soon created great controversy by making a breakaway which rejected the chordal and harmonic structure then regarded as essential. His attempts to apply atonality to jazz, as well as his experiments with collective free improvisation, brought down the wrath of many of the critics. His world-wide touring activities have engendered a number of disciples among younger players and, whatever his eventual standing, attempts such as his to equate the rejection of restrictions in notation, form, key and harmony in formal music with a similar departure in jazz have caused all serious exponents of the music to stop and think. Variously evaluated as a confidence trickster or a Messiah, he will probably emerge as neither, but as a musician of moderate talent courageous enough to break a strong taboo in what is sometimes a very conservative branch of music. **J. P. W. D.**

RECORDS: 'ON TENOR . . . ORNETTE COLEMAN' (ATLANTIC, 588121); 'AN EVENING WITH ORNETTE COLEMAN' (INTERNATIONAL POLYDOR DOUBLE ALBUM, 6232446/7); 'ORNETTE!' (LONDON ATLANTIC, LT2-K15241).

Colette (French, 1873–1954): writer. Colette wrote of vegetables as if they were love objects and of sex as if it were an especially delightful department of gardening. Her concrete, always intelligent, never intellectualised prose lifts sensuousness to the pitch of sanctity. Born Sidonie-Gabrielle Colette, one-sixteenth Negro, into the middle class of Burgundy, she married the journalist 'Willy' and became, if not the *belle*, the *jolie laide*, of Paris in the Nineties. Her first books, the four Claudine novels (1900–03), were published as Willy's work but later reclaimed. She divorced Willy, went on the music halls, lived with a transvestite *marquise*, remarried and bore a daughter. After another divorce she married (1935) Maurice Goudeket and settled to a hard-working, arthritic, famous old age. Her large *oeuvre* – fiction, non-fiction and a mixture of the two – has for its chief themes her music-hall experiences, her mother, the individuality of animals and, most classically in *Chéri* (1920), the sadnesses of love. **Br. Br.**

'EARTHLY PARADISE', COLETTE'S AUTOBIOGRAPHY DRAWN FROM THE WRITINGS OF HER LIFETIME, BY ROBERT PHELPS (SECKER AND WARBURG, 1966); 'CLAUDINE AT SCHOOL', BY COLETTE, TR. ANTONIA WHITE (PENGUIN, 1963); 'CHÉRI' AND 'THE LAST OF CHÉRI', BY COLETTE, TR. ROGER SENHOUSE (PENGUIN, 1955); 'THE PURE AND THE IMPURE', BY COLETTE, TR. H. BRIFFAULT (SECKER AND WARBURG, 1968)

Michael Collins (Irish, 1890–1922): Irish nationalist. Like Ché Guevara, Collins preferred people when they were dressed up in uniforms. This provided the context for the only sort of politics he found tolerable. It was largely his achievement to have diminished the influence of the moderates in the Sinn Féin movement by rigging the election of extremists to the convention of 1919. He had originally proposed to steal the Stone of Destiny from Westminster Abbey, but – this seeming inadequate – he turned his considerable talents to the systematic assassination of British intelligence officials in Dublin. During the Anglo-Irish troubles of 1920–1, Collins emerged as a formidable military organiser. In the autumn of 1921 he was sent off by the Dáil cabinet as one of the Irish delegates to the Treaty negotiations in London; as a result he was landed with the defence of the negotiated Free State, and after the death of Arthur Griffith in August 1922 he became head of the Government. In this role he lasted less than two weeks – before his own death in a Republican ambush in his native County Cork. **E. R. N.**

'MICHAEL COLLINS AND THE MAKING OF A NEW IRELAND', BY PIARAS BEASLAI (HARRAP, DUBLIN, 1926); 'THE BIG FELLOW', BY FRANK O'CONNOR (CORGI, 1969); 'MICHAEL COLLINS', BY REX TAYLOR (FOUR SQUARE, 1961).

Joseph Conrad (British, ex-Polish, 1857–1924): novelist. One of the century's greatest novelists, Józef Teodor Konrad Nalecz Korzeniowski was the son of a Polish landowner exiled for conspiring against Poland's Russian rulers. He joined the

English merchant navy and only started learning English when he was 21. His first novel was published 17 years later. Many of his books deal with life at sea, but he is more than a writer of adventure stories. Hardship and the isolation of command bring to the surface the stresses and strains we all feel. Conrad's heroes face normal human problems, but in acute forms and in a great loneliness. His knowledge of many countries and his Polish experience give great force to his tales of politics and colonialism. *Nostromo* is about revolution and civil war in South America and the effect of invested capital on an underdeveloped country; *The Secret Agent* concerns anarchist plotters in London; 'Heart of Darkness' (from *Youth and other stories*) describes exploitation and megalomania in the Congo. Technically, these are complex books, with ornate prose and sudden shifts of viewpoint. His best works probe our feelings about order and disorder, tyranny and rebellion; they are disturbingly prophetic of what has come in our day. **D. J. H.**

JOSEPH CONRAD: A CRITICAL BIOGRAPHY', BY JOCELYN BAINES (WEIDENFELD AND NICOLSON, 1960); 'CONRAD THE NOVELIST', BY ALBERT J. GUERARD (HARVARD U.P., 1959, DISTRIBUTED BY O.U.P.); 'CONRAD: A REASSESSMENT', BY DOUGLAS HEWITT (BOWES AND BOWES, CAMBRIDGE, 1952, REVISED EDITION, 1969); 'JOSEPH CONRAD', BY J. I. M. STEWART (LONGMANS, 1968).

Jacques Copeau (French, 1878–1949): theatrical manager and director. Of the great theatrical directors of the 20th century, the one whose work is most eclipsed by current tendencies is Jacques Copeau. At the *Vieux Colombier* in Paris he preached that in the beginning was the Word, and the Word was with the Theatre, and the Word was Theatre. Contrary to the theories of Craig (q.v.) he diminished the importance of scenery and setting in the theatre, concentrating on perfect clarity of speech. He brought an ascetic simplicity into the French theatre, and raised a band of disciples. His theories were exemplified in the *Compagnie des Quinze*, which was managed by his nephew, Michel Saint-Denis. When it came to London in the middle 1930s it created an immense im-

pression by the beauty of its speaking. Almost the only company in the West that continued Copeau's theories was that of Jean-Louis Barrault. Copeau's day may, however, return. But that there is no prospect of this at the moment is shown in Terry Hands's instructions to the Royal Shakespeare Company not to worry if the audiences chattered since listening is less important than looking. **H. H.**

'THE CONTEMPORARY FRENCH THEATRE', BY JOSEPH CHIARI (ROCKLIFF, 1958).

Le Corbusier (Swiss-French, 1887–1965): architect. Le Corbusier unquestionably made the most versatile contribution to 20th century architecture. Charles-Edouard Jeanneret first settled in Paris as a Purist painter. His Domino system of prefabricating housing (1914) explored the possibility, in framed concrete, of eliminating the conventional wall, and a series of houses in the 1920s established the synthesis of modern architecture known as the International Style. He said a house was "une machine à habiter", but, never a narrow 'functionalist', he showed panache in his prize-winning design for the League Building, Geneva (1927) which was, however, not accepted. His massive concrete became emotively sculptural at the pilgrimage chapel of Ronchamp (1950–4), and in the rough-textured roof-structures of the Unité d' Habitation flats, Marseilles (1947-52). He revived thick walls of dark brick at the brutalist Maisons Jaoul, Neuilly (1952–7). His planning dogmas were fulfilled in the Punjab at Chandigarh (from 1950). His masterpiece is probably the monastery of La Tourette (1956–60), while his single-storey hospital for Venice (designed 1964–5) continues the Mediterranean neoclassical tradition. **N. J. W. T.**

'THE COMPLETE ARCHITECTURAL WORKS, 1910-1965, BY LE CORBUSIER, 7 VOLS. (THAMES AND HUDSON, 1967); 'TOWARDS A NEW ARCHITECTURE', BY LE CORBUSIER, TRANS. BY F. ETCHELLS (ARCHITECTURAL PRESS, LONDON, 1927).

André Courrèges (French, b. 1923): dress designer. As the man who launched the miniskirt, Courrèges has played an essential part in the change which has overtaken fashion in the 1960s. His earliest ambition was to be a civil engineer, and he was a student of engineering for a time – a training which led him to apply architectural principles to fashion. For the first two years after he set up on his own (in 1961, after 11 years with Balenciaga) he found few buyers for his clothes, for his approach to fashion was very different from that of the great figures of the past. But in 1964 he showed his space-age version of the trouser suit and cut his skirts a good four inches shorter than anyone else, and caused a sensation. Since then he has been one of the most significant designers and his influence has been as revolutionary as was that of Christian Dior (q.v.) 20 years ago. **J. L.**

Jacques-Yves Cousteau (French, b. 1910): underwater explorer. An icy day in January 1943: a car with a strange balloon on top stops on the banks of the Marne. Two men get out. One is Cousteau. He straps a cylinder to his back with a rubber tube leading to his mouth; he wades into the water and submerges. Man had definitively entered the underwater world of 'Inner Space'. Cousteau and Gagnan – the other man on the river bank – had created the Aqualung, a portable compressed-air cylinder with a regulator valve, that freed the aquanaut from the hoses of boot-and-helmet diving and from the deadly effects of oxygen that military frogmen risk when below 33 ft. All of Cousteau's work has been with teams, and they have carried out numerous underwater researches – among the most dramatic being a one-mile descent in the bathyscaphe underwater vessel and a colony that was established for one month under the Red Sea. Most of the earth's surface is water and is capable of yielding untold riches of minerals, energy and food. Cousteau's importance in the 20th century is not only in opening up these resources, but in his life-style where teamwork, technical precision and humanity combine to create the ideal approach to using these resources. **B. R. O.**

'THE SILENT WORLD', BY J-Y. COUSTEAU AND F. DUMAS (HAMISH HAMILTON, 1952); 'WORLD WITHOUT SUN', BY J-Y. COUSTEAU (HEINEMANN, 1965).

Sir Noël Coward (British, b. 1899): actor, dramatist, composer, theatrical director. All proportions kept, Coward is the Leonardo da Vinci of the stage. As an actor his clipped pronunciation is famous, and recognised all over the world as something distinctively English. As a cabaret artist, his elegance, wit, and modish cynicism make him the idol of the sophisticated. As a patriot, he prefers to live in Switzerland, far from the grimy realities of the Welfare State. As a critic, he is almost as harsh on critics as he is on the yesterday dramatists of the kitchen sink. His plays, which represent a body of work perhaps unrivalled in the modern theatre, are of wide scope. There is no more violent condemnation of family life and drug-taking than *The Vortex*, which he wrote as long ago as 1924. *Bitter Sweet* (1929) and his film *Brief Encounter* show his expertise in the romantic. He was the greatest master of revue when this form of art was at its apex, composing both words and music of *This Year of Grace* (1928). He is also skilful in farce (*Blithe Spirit*, 1941, having the then record run for a straight play of 1997 performances). And he was one of the first English dramatists to take advantage of increasing liberty to discuss homosexuality (*A Song at Twilight*, 1966). **H. H.**

'PRESENT INDICATIVE', BY NOEL COWARD (HEINEMANN, 1937).

Gordon Craig (British, 1872–1966): theatrical director. Edward Gordon Craig was the most successful failure in the history of the theatre, and possibly the happiest man whose projects came to nothing. He led a tumultuous and passionate life, always short of money (his mother, Ellen Terry, helped him when he was young), but hedonistic as a Renaissance prince. He translated his scenic fantasies into stage designs that were nearly always impracticable and inordinately expensive. For this reason he did little actual work in the theatre, though in 1926 he designed *The Pretenders* in Copenhagen. He saw the director as the real creative force in the theatre, capable of writing the play, designing the scenery, and even composing the music. He reduced the actor to little more than a puppet. He lived an indulgent and passionate life in Florence and on the Riviera –

Lorraine Crapp (Australian, b. 1938): swimmer. Lorraine Crapp was the first of the great world record-breaking swimmers of the modern era in this sport of teenage kings and queens. Her man-size swipes at the world 400 metres free-style record took her through the apparently impassable five-minute barrier and women's swimming has never looked back. This epic swim was on August 25, 1956, in Townsville, Queensland. The incredulous timekeepers clocked her at 4 minutes 50.8 seconds, nearly ten seconds faster than the previous mark which had stood for 16 years. She broke 16 world records from 100 m. to 880 yards and won the 1956 Melbourne Olympic 400 m. title by 7.9 seconds. She also opened the flood-gates of modern swimming record-breaking. Never again were women in the pool looked upon as second-rate. **P.B.**

Francis Crick (British, b. 1916): molecular biologist. Together with J. D. Watson (q.v.), Crick proposed the now well-known model for the structure of DNA, the chemical that carries some of the instructions that determine heredity. It depended on many other brilliant molecular biologists' work, but was unique in that it pulled together wide areas of biology. With its publication in 1953 molecular genetics could begin in earnest. It had been known for some time that the nucleic acids (DNA) in the chromosomes were somehow responsible for carrying genetic instructions. Crick and Watson suggested that the DNA molecule comprised a double spiral strand, with base-groups arranged linearly along each strand. In replication the two strands separated and synthesised new halves identical with the old ones. Thus in cell division one molecule of DNA would give rise to two precisely identical molecules of DNA so that the two new cells would have the same set of instructions. Here was the physical basis for Mendelian genetics and, confirmed experimentally, it enabled studies on the genetic code to begin. Crick and Watson shared a Nobel Prize in 1962. **J. B. M.**

'THE DOUBLE HELIX', BY J. D. WATSON (WEIDENFELD AND NICOLSON, 1968)

Hawley Harvey Crippen (U.S., 1862–1910): poisoner. The century's most celebrated wife-murderer was born in Coldwater, Michigan; he obtained a medical degree of sorts but was never, strictly speaking, a doctor. His first wife died when he was in his late twenties, and Crippen then married a girl of 17. He worked for a patent medicine company, which in 1900 opened offices in London; Crippen was installed as manager. By this time he was finding his marriage a strain; Cora – as his wife was known – was oversexed and vain. She had had her voice trained with the idea of becoming a music hall artist and Crippen found his shy, anaemic little secretary, Ethel Le Neve, better for his ego. He bought hyoscine – used in American hospitals as a sexual depressant – in 1910, but whether to kill his wife or moderate her nymphomania has never been determined. Mrs Crippen died on or about February 1, 1910, and was dismembered and buried in the cellar. Acquaintances were told that Cora had returned to America, and Ethel Le Neve moved into 39 Hilldrop Crescent, and began to wear Cora's jewellery. Crippen now made his mistake; when the police became mildly curious, he panicked and fled; with Ethel dressed as a boy, they sailed for America on the SS. Montrose. The police, now suspicious, dug and found bits of a body, and the SS. Montrose was telegraphed – the first time wireless telegraphy had been used in a murder case. Because he was so obviously not the murderer type, he aroused widespread sympathy; but, largely on Sir Bernard Spilsbury's evidence, was found guilty and hanged. **C. W.**

'THE TRIAL OF CRIPPEN', ED. FILSON YOUNG (NOTABLE BRITISH TRIALS, 1912).

Sir Stafford Cripps (British, 1889–1952): politician. Labour's greatest Chancellor of the Exchequer was originally a prosperous, well-connected barrister. He moved slowly towards the Labour Party and joined in 1929. He became Labour's Solicitor-General in 1930 with a knighthood and a parliamentary seat, but after 1931 moved far towards Marxism as leader of the Socialist League. He was expelled from the Labour Party in 1939 for supporting the Popular Front Campaign against Chamberlain, but seeing him as a man of "force and fire", Churchill appointed him Ambassador to Moscow in May 1940. During the war Cripps was the only politician to rival Churchill in the public eye, serving as Leader of the House and Minister of Aircraft Production. His mission to India in March 1942 failed when Gandhi refused his "post-dated cheques on a bankrupt empire". As Chancellor of the Exchequer after 1947 he helped to restore confidence in the crumbling Labour administration through tough austerity policies and pioneering attempts at income restraint and genuine economic planning; he was, however, forced to devalue in 1949. Cripps was the embodiment of the Christian conscience in politics, and he gave authority and moral fibre to the epoch-making post-war Labour Government. **A. M.**

'THE LIFE OF RICHARD STAFFORD CRIPPS', BY COLIN COOKE (HODDER AND STOUGHTON, 1957); 'STAFFORD CRIPPS', BY ERIC ESTORICK (HEINEMANN, 1949).

Benedetto Croce (Italian, 1866–1952): philosopher and scholar. Croce was almost certainly the greatest Italian of our century, a vastly erudite scholar and literary critic who had a tremendous influence on several generations of his fellow countrymen. As a master of European literature, he did a great deal to de-provincialise Italian culture through the magazine *La Critica*, which he founded in 1903. Though his fine prose suffers in translation, he was celebrated everywhere as the leading figure in neo-idealist philosophy, as the developer of a new theory of aesthetics, and as a historian. His philosophy was non-academic, non-metaphysical; he thought of it as a way to understand history which to him was always contemporary history, an illumination of the present by means of the past and of the past by the present. Never was Croce more influential than in preserving some liberty of thought under Fascism. In politics he was a conservative. He was Minister of Education in 1920-21, and in 1944-7 he led the Italian Liberal Party. **D. M. S.**

'BENEDETTO CROCE, MAN AND THINKER', BY CECIL J. S. SPRIGGE (BOWES AND BOWES, CAMBRIDGE, 1952).

Herbert Croly (U.S., 1869–1930): political thinker and journalist. Herbert Croly was the man of one book. He had other claims to distinction, notably that of

founding the *New Republic*, America's not very close equivalent of the *New Statesman*; but is remembered today as the author of *The Promise of American Life*, which appeared in 1909. At one level this was an attempt to veneer with intellectual respectability the political opportunism, bullying and buffoonery of that pseudo-reformer, Theodore Roosevelt (q.v.); but his book is still worth reading today as a highly intelligent attempt to think out the principles and strategies essential to modern liberal democracy. In American terms, he demonstrated that traditional democratic ends could nowadays only be attained by the means of a strong national government. **D. H. V. B.**

'THE PROMISE OF AMERICAN LIFE', BY HERBERT CROLY (HARVARD UNIVERSITY PRESS, 1965)

Bing Crosby (U.S., b. 1904): singer. Though Al Jolson (q.v.) rivalled him at first, Crosby swiftly became the first of the super-star crooners – and has held his position, despite Sinatra (q.v.), Andy Williams *et al* ever since. He's sold more records than anybody else has (well over 300 million), has recorded more titles than any other singer (nearing 3000) and made the best-selling disc of all time (Irving Berlin's [q.v.] *White Christmas*). His strong, resonant voice (like a man singing into a rain barrel, one critic said in the 1930s) is highly individual and his style ('The

---

Isadora Duncan (q.v.) bore him a child – and his impossible dreams have enormously influenced the theatre, especially on the Continent. **H. H.**

'ON THE ART OF THE THEATRE', BY E. G. CRAIG (HEINEMANN, 1911); 'EDWARD GORDON CRAIG', BY E. A. CRAIG (GOLLANCZ, 1968).

Groaner') has remained instantly recognisable down the years. Many copied his wonderful phrasing and his tone as the race of crooners grew. After the movie *King of Jazz* (1930) his solo break came with *I Surrender Dear*, and the hits followed year after year, together with the inevitable movies. He won an Oscar, oddly enough, for his straight role as a priest in *Going My Way* (he's a devout Roman Catholic) but will be better remembered for the classic *Road To . . .* movies made with Bob Hope and Dorothy Lamour in the 1940s and 1950s. He's variously estimated to be worth between £25m. and £50m. and has innumerable business interests (banking, oil, TV, real estate, a baseball team, etc). **D. J.**

RECORDS: 'BING CROSBY IN HOLLYWOOD 1930/4' (DOUBLE ALBUM C.B.S.); 'BING CROSBY' (MUSIC FOR PLEASURE); 'MERRY CHRISTMAS' (M.C.A.).

Aleister Crowley (British, 1875–1947): writer and 'magician'. A prophet of freedom, sensuality and black magic, Edward Alexander Crowley (who changed his name to Aleister) liked to call himself "the Great Beast" and "the wickedest man alive". Crowley could have been a fine novelist and poet; but his spirit of showmanship was too strong; he hungered for notoriety. Swept into the 'magical revival' of the late 19th century, Crowley became a member of Yeats's Order of the Golden Dawn. Jealous of Yeats, he settled for a time near Loch Ness, and tried to conjure demons, then moved restlessly on to America, Mexico, Egypt and Hong Kong, where he abandoned his wife and baby. The baby died of typhoid in Rangoon; his wife later became an alcoholic, and then insane. Most people who became closely associated with 'the Beast' died tragically. In 1920, he set up an 'Abbey of Theleme' in Cefalu, Sicily, where drug-taking, sexual orgies and 'magical ceremonies' were the order of the day; his motto was Rabelais's "do what you will". In 1921, a series of exposures of him in the *Sunday Express* brought him the universal notoriety he craved and the title "the wickedest man in the world"; his novel *Diary of a Drug Fiend* was its immediate cause. The magic, sex and general exhibitionism continued until his death in 1947. **C. W.**

'THE GREAT BEAST', BY JOHN SYMONDS (RIDER, 1951); 'THE MAGIC OF ALEISTER CROWLEY', BY JOHN SYMONDS (MULLER, 1958); 'ALEISTER CROWLEY', BY CHARLES CAMMELL (RICHARDS PRESS, LONDON, 1951); 'THE MAGICAL DILEMMA OF VICTOR NEUBERG', BY JEAN OVERTON FULLER (ALLEN, 1965).

Ely Culbertson (U.S., 1891–1955): bridge player. If there have been better bridge players than Ely Culbertson, there has been none so sharp. Vanderbilt made Contract respectable, Culbertson made it pay. What Ford (q.v.) did for the motor car, Culbertson did for bridge: he standardised it and made it accessible to millions. Millions were his reward. His *Blue Book* and its frequent supplements acquired, for middle class America, the immutable force of a morality. In the Twenties, women accused their husbands of adultery; in the Thirties, "playing Culbertson", they could be no less outraged by a man who opened the bidding on less than two-and-a-half honour tricks. Culbertson's brilliantly publicised success as a champion – in partnership, of course, with his wife, Josephine – swept aside probably more gifted but less determined rivals, like Lenz and Hal Sims, and left him the unquestioned Ace. His calculated choice of vocabulary ("approach bid" and "forcing bid" were

typical) had an underlying sexiness which appealed to the new respectability. Culbertson had wider ambitions. He wrote passionately in favour of world government, but there is only one sense in which he will be remembered as the man who got everyone round a table – and that was playing bridge. **F. R.**

'THE BLUE BOOK' (FABER, 1930); 'THE RED BOOK' (J. C. WINSTON, 1934); 'THE GOLDEN BOOK' (J. C. WINSTON, 1936).

Michael Cullen (U.S., 1884–1936): retailer. Cullen was the man who started mass cut-price self-service retailing. 'King Kullen', as his store signs proclaimed, opened one of the world's first supermarkets in August 1930 in Jamaica, Long Island, and in two years had eight outlets, in spite of the raging Depression, which he actually turned to his advantage. King Kullen Markets started the 'cheapy'. They had no expensive fittings, goods were littered in huge piles, signs were compellingly tasteless. The markets were established in low-rent premises, bankrupt department stores, factories or warehouses. Cullen sold about a quarter of his goods at cost, and leased out part of his 'cheapy' to outside concessionaires whose payments covered the rent. Kullen Markets and their slogans – "The World's Greatest Price Wrecker", "Why pay more?",

"How does he do it?" – continue to immortalise Michael Cullen's name in and around New York. **G. P. G. N.**

'SUPERMARKETING', BY FRANK J. CHARVAT (MACMILLAN, NEW YORK, 1961); 'THE SUPERMARKET', BY M. M. ZIMMERMAN (MCGRAW-HILL, NEW YORK, 1955).

Marie Curie (French, ex-Polish, 1867–1934): physicist. Quiet, dignified and unassuming, Marie Curie was the first to develop methods for separating radium from radioactive residues in quantities large enough for detailed scientific studies. After early education in Warsaw she became a governess for several years. Gradually she saved enough to go to the Sorbonne, in Paris. There she met Pierre Curie, professor in the School of Physics, whom she married in 1895. Inspired by Henri Becquerel's discovery of radio-activity in 1896, the Curies embarked on their brilliant and painstaking researches with pitchblende, culminating in the

isolation of polonium (named after Marie's native country) and radium. For this they shared the 1903 Nobel Prize in Physics with Becquerel. After Pierre was killed in 1906, Marie took his place as professor in the Sorbonne Faculty of Sciences – first woman to hold such a post as she was the first woman Nobel prizewinner. She also developed methods for separating radium from radioactive residues in sufficient quantities to carry out detailed studies of its properties. She won a second Nobel Prize, this time in Chemistry, in 1911 – an achievement only Linus Pauling has matched. Throughout her life, she promoted the medical uses of radium to alleviate suffering, but her years of work on radio-active materials finally took their toll and she died of leukaemia in 1934. **N. V.**

'MADAME CURIE', BY EVE CURIE (HEINEMANN, 1938).

Curnonsky (French, 1872–1956): writer and journalist. One of the great 'good food' crusaders, Curnonsky was born Maurice Edmund Saillant in Angers. A brilliant conversationalist, a prolific novelist and a very successful journalist, he had perhaps the finest palate of his time. This would have given him only ephemeral importance as a gastronomic arbiter had he not done something more. Between 1921 and 1928 he produced, in collaboration with Marcel Rouff, the 28 volumes of *La France Gastronomique*; with Austin de Croze, *Le Trésorier Gastronomique de France* in 1933; with P. Andrieu, *Les Fines Gueules de France* in 1935; and, without a collaborator, *Cuisine et Vins de France* in 1953. In 1940 he founded the serious and important journal of that name. He also edited, as a rival to *Michelin*, a *Guide des Touristes Gastronomes* with maps of each *département* of France and lists of finest raw materials, the dishes created from them and the restaurants that served them. This classification and codification ensured the perpetuation of regional French cooking and made the recipes accessible to everyone. Curnonsky's work has had an immense influence on other writers. He himself claimed that his tastes were formed in childhood by the food served by the family cook: "regional, simple, honest and good'. **M. M. C.**

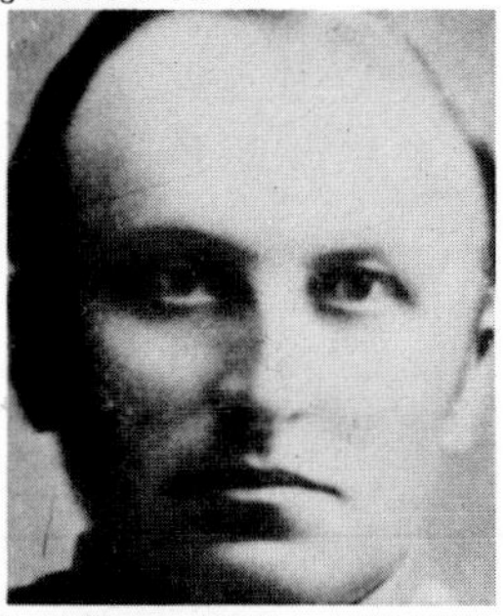

Lord Curzon (British, 1859–1925): Viceroy of India 1898–1905. The present-day image of the British Raj in India derives from Curzon's viceroyalty – much the most significant period of his political career, though he was Foreign Secretary from 1919 to 1924. He made it both a spectacle, splendid as never before, and an efficient machine. Fired by that masochistic dedication to hard work which the late-Victorians too often confused with high-minded philanthropy, and with a very aristocratic belief in the mollifying value of justice and good government for the masses, Curzon was the model of the benevolent despot. But the brilliance of his reign was that of a meteor's final immolation. He despised and discounted the infant Indian National Congress – representative, he said, only of their middle-class selves. He alone knew what was good for the masses. Maybe he was right about Congress. But by disregarding and provoking it he only antagonised and strengthened it, and so prepared the soil in which it was soon to flourish. His partition of Bengal (1905) was justifiable on grounds of administrative efficiency. But it gave birth to a turmoil of nationalistic resentment and religious antagonism between Moslem and Hindu. Curzon's actions had been designed to make the Raj eternal. Ironically their chief significance was the impetus they gave its disruption. **B. J. P.**

'BRITISH POLICY IN INDIA 1858–1905', BY S. GOPAL (C.U.P. 1965); 'HIGH NOON OF EMPIRE', BY MICHAEL EDWARDES (EYRE AND SPOTTISWOODE, 1965); 'THE GUARDIANS', BY PHILIP WOODRUFF, FROM 'THE MEN WHO RULED INDIA' (JONATHAN CAPE, 1954).

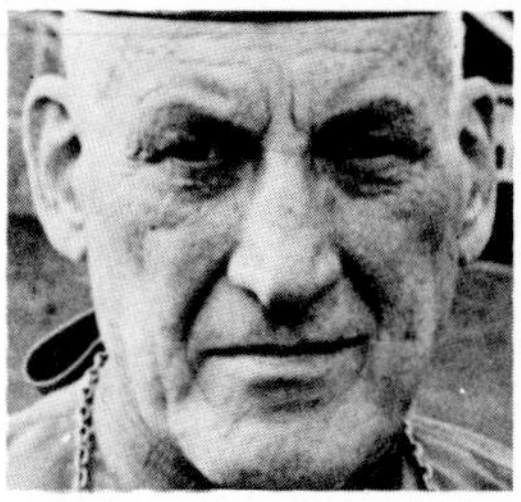

Cardinal Richard Cushing (U.S., 1895–1970): religious leader. The local boy who became Archbishop of Boston was also the first Roman Catholic prelate to offer the official prayers at the inauguration of a U.S. President. A prominent liberal, so enthusiastic was his espousal of the new learning at the Vatican Council that he made himself ill, and the Pope himself, at their final meeting, had to recommend the Cardinal to take bicarbonate of soda. In the late Sixties he became a leading exponent of Catholic liberalism in the western world, and a forthright advocate of civil justice in America. He enjoyed a long relationship with the Kennedy family, which received international press-coverage when he defended the Onassis match in 1968. **E. R. N.**

'RICHARD, CARDINAL CUSHING', BY ARAKELIAN RYAN (HARVARD UNIVERSITY PRESS, CAMBRIDGE, MASS, 1959); 'OUR AMERICAN PRINCES', BY FRANCIS B. THORNTON (PUTNAM, NEW YORK, 1963).

D

Sir Henry Dale (British, 1875–1968): pharmacologist. Dale found that extracts of the fungus ergot reversed the actions of adrenaline, and discovered the first use of the many adrenaline-blocking agents now widely used in medicine. He found that pituitary extracts contract the uterus muscle, a discovery which probably led to their most frequent application in practical medicine – to prevent haemorrhage after birth. Without his work on histamine, the discovery of the antihistamine drugs used to treat allergic disorders such as hay fever would scarcely have been possible. During the First World War his work on histamine also led to recogni-

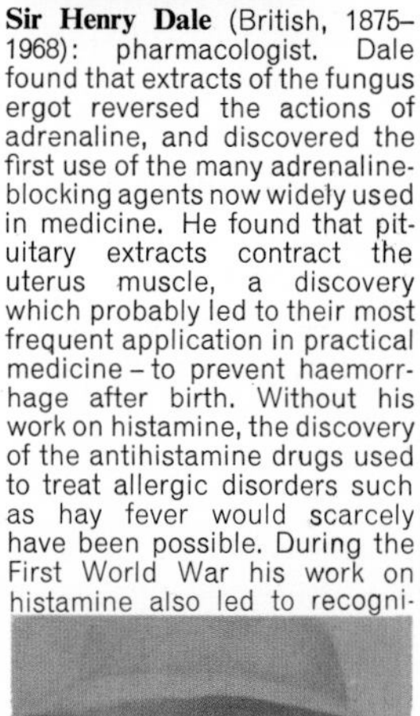

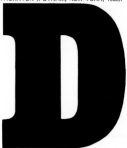

tion of the fact that the best way of treating 'secondary wound shock' was with blood or plasma transfusion. Dale showed that nerve impulses were transmitted to skeletal muscle and autonomic ganglion cells via an agent called acetylcholine, and that the electrical variation of the nerve impulse itself was not sufficient to activate these structures. This work brought about a revolutionary change in our views on nerve transmission and had a profound impact on brain physiology. **W. F.**

'ADVENTURES IN PHYSIOLOGY', BY SIR HENRY DALE (THE WELLCOME TRUST, 1965).

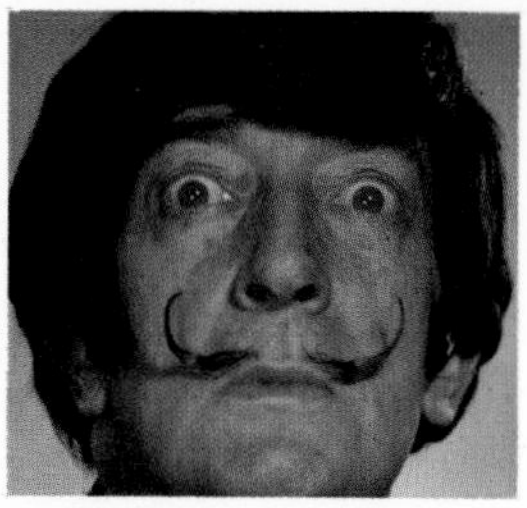

Salvador Dali (Spanish, b. 1904): painter. At art school in Madrid the most notorious of all the Surrealists displayed a precocious dexterity in his studies. He had a genuine gift for the manipulation of imagery; and when he went to Paris in 1928 and Miro (q.v.) presented him to the Surrealists he quickly established himself as the dazzling newcomer from whom everything could be expected. Between 1929 and 1936 he produced a long series of minutely detailed canvases in which cryptic and phantasmagorical events went forward beneath a high-arched sky and against, as often as not, the recognisable landscape of northern Spain. Dali at this time was a true visionary: it was possible to believe that psychic pressures of an altogether extraordinary kind were dictating the images that somehow got down on the canvas. But, as André Breton (q.v.) had foreseen, the time came when Dali "could not tell the sound of his own voice from the creak of his patent-leather shoes"; and for the last 30 or more years there has been little to compare with the urgency, the compulsion to "tell it how it is", of 1929–36. **J. R.**

Raymond Dart (Australian, b. 1893): anthropologist. Dart's discovery and naming of *Australopithecus africanus* (South African ape) near Taungs in Bechuanaland in 1924 was the centre of great controversy. Dart concluded the fossil was from a six-year-old member of "an extinct race of apes intermediate between living anthropoids and man". Other anthropologists were sceptical but

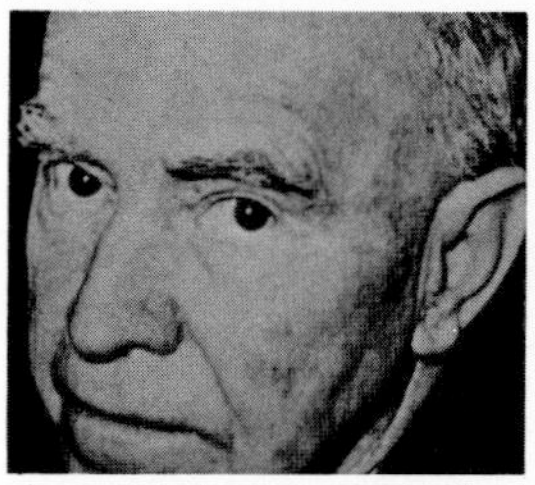

close examination emphasised the fossil's human affinities. Dart later tried to prove that *Australopithecus* used tools. Many fossil baboon skulls which had been badly damaged were found with the man-ape. From a statistical analysis Dart concluded that the man-ape had inflicted the damage. He also thought that they used tusks and teeth as cutting tools and jaws as saws; he thus postulated a Bone Age prior to the Stone Age. Fragments of charcoal also led him to believe that the man-ape had used fire. These later theories are not now widely accepted, but it was Dart's work that has, according to Robert Ardrey, "made possible our present knowledge of human origins". **J. H.**

'AFRICAN GENESIS', BY ROBERT ARDREY (COLLINS, 1961).

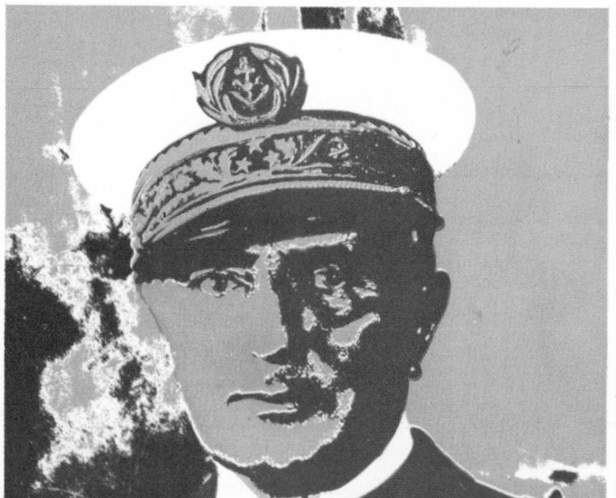

François Darlan (French, 1881–1942): admiral and politician. Admiral Darlan became one of the most anti-British members of the Vichy Government, and in February 1941 became Premier. At first he attempted to follow a policy whereby France, through limited collaboration, could keep its Empire, its fleet and a semblance of a free government; but by spring 1942, when German victory was less certain, Darlan's lack of co-operation made the Germans demand his replacement by Laval (q.v.). Darlan became C.-in-C. and his chance presence in North Africa in November, when French forces remained loyal to Vichy, made it essential for the Americans to negotiate with him. After much indecision he signed an armistice and soon headed the French forces in their new anti-German role. A month later he was assassinated and de Gaulle (q.v.) eventually took command, but Darlan was the man whose authority brought the French North African Army into the Allied camp. **R. M. G.**

'THE MURDER OF ADMIRAL DARLAN', BY PETER TOMPKINS (SIMON AND SCHUSTER, NEW YORK, 1965); 'DARLAN: A STUDY', BY GEORGE MIKES (CONSTABLE, 1943).

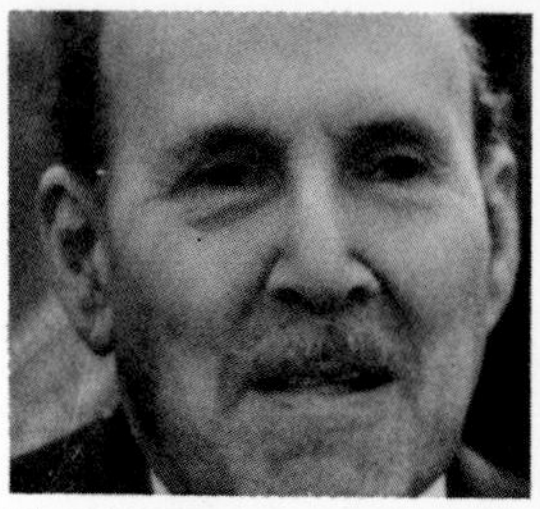

Marcel Dassault (French, b. 1892): aircraft manufacturer. The designer of the great French Mirage and Mystère jet fighters made his debut during the First World War with the invention of an improved propeller. After the war he produced the Languedoc quadromotor and military planes. In 1937 the Popular Front nationalised his plants but Dassault was hired as a civil servant to run the firm. Under Vichy, Dassault, who was a Jew, was offered the chance to become an honorary Aryan if he would make planes for the Nazis. He refused, went into hiding, was caught and finished the war in Buchenwald. With his business restored to him he re-launched his empire with first Mystère jets, and then the famous family of Mirages, all of which he helped design. Besides a swing-wing version of the Mirage which is now in production, Dassault Aviation also produced the American businessman's favourite personal plane, the Falcon fan-jet. A Gaullist Party financial backer, Dassault also ran a bank and construction company, and launched a parallel career in journalism as publisher of the weekly *Jours de France*. **V. L.**

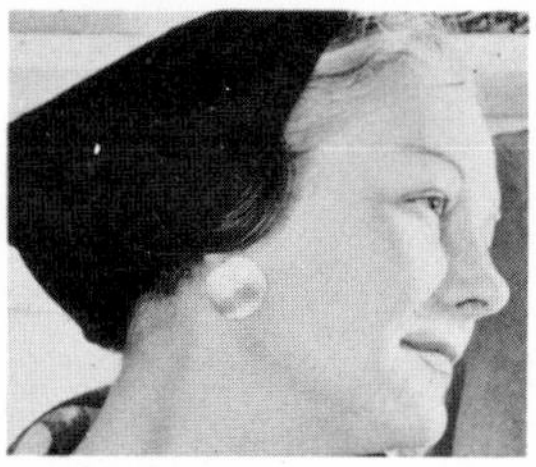

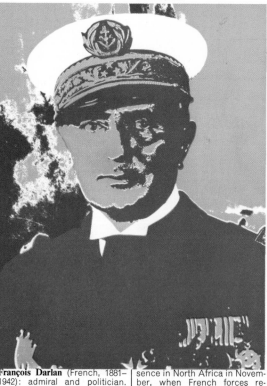

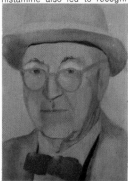

Elizabeth David (British, born *c.* 1914): cookery writer. Elizabeth David's first book appeared in 1950 in the grey, rationed, restricted period that succeeded the Second World War. *A Book of Mediterranean Food* (1950) reminded its servantless and dispirited readers of the excitement of travel and of the still accessible pleasures of the table. Four more books – each enthusiastic, far-ranging, the recipes authentic and accurate, each stamped with the author's integrity – were to appear within the decade; *French Provincial Cooking*, which appeared in 1960, has sold over 220,000 copies. They gave those who cooked at home new courage, as well as new ideas, confidence and prestige; their success has been responsible for an endless stream of lesser books. And the hundreds of small amateur restaurants up and down the country would probably never have opened at all without her inspiration. "The feeling of our time," she once wrote, "is for simpler food, simply presented . . . It demands less time and less expense than *la haute cuisine* but . . . a more genuine feeling for cookery and a truer taste." **M. M. C.**

SELECTED BOOKS BY ELIZABETH DAVID: 'A BOOK OF MEDITERRANEAN FOOD' (J. LEHMANN, 1950); 'SUMMER COOKING' (MUSEUM PRESS, 1959); 'FRENCH PROVINCIAL COOKING' (MICHAEL JOSEPH, 1960); ALL REISSUED BY PENGUIN

Bette Davis (U.S., b. 1908): film actress. One of the most powerful and individual personalities produced by the cinema, Bette

PHOTOGRAPH OF BETTE DAVIS FROM THE JOHN KOBAL COLLECTION

Davis came to Hollywood via successes on Broadway. Her screen career falls into five phases: in the early Thirties the Warner Studios attempted, without much success, to mould her into current glamour-girl patterns; *Of Human Bondage* (1934; with Leslie Howard) asserted her as an actress of stature, and inaugurated her best period, which culminated in her films with William Wyler (*Jezebel, The Little Foxes*); through the Forties she seemed to find it harder to find suitable vehicles; and after her brilliant performance in Mankiewicz's *All About Eve* (1950) she entered a period of infrequent and often weird roles (*The Virgin Queen, Pocketful of Miracles*). In the Sixties, however, she began a successful new career with a run of female monsters, the first in *Whatever Happened to Baby Jane?* Never beautiful, her striking features, huge eyes and clipped speech, and her preference for extravagant screen make-up have made her the delight of impersonators and cartoonists, while her demand for creative independence has given her an off-screen reputation for temperament. She is nevertheless a film star who is also an actress gifted enough to assimilate mannerisms and extravagances into characterisations of outstanding intelligence. **D. R.**

'THE LONELY LIFE', BY BETTE DAVIS (MACDONALD, 1963).

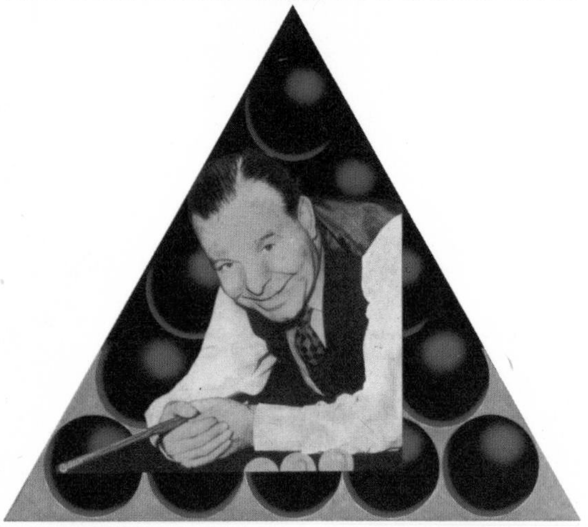

Joe Davis (British, b. 1901): snooker player. Snooker crept upon the professional scene in the Twenties when the odd frame of crude knockabout was supplied as a makeweight if a billiards session finished early. Alone in his high assessment of its potential mass appeal, and evolving, virtually in a vacuum, the complex strategies, techniques and sequences of the modern game, Joe Davis persuaded the Billiards Association to organise the first world championship in 1927, duly won it and retained it until 1947. He retired from championship play in that year, but his remarkably sustained level of performance in tournaments and exhibitions, his commanding personality and his vast influence in all aspects of professional snooker enabled him to establish a pre-eminence which could never be threatened. Tough, aggressive, imperious and immensely self-assured, Davis at his best went close enough to infallibility to leave snooker fans with an abiding image of unique sporting perfection as reds and colours disappeared magnetically into pockets while the referee, white-gloved and deferential, tolled the score like an inexorable cash register. **C. E.**

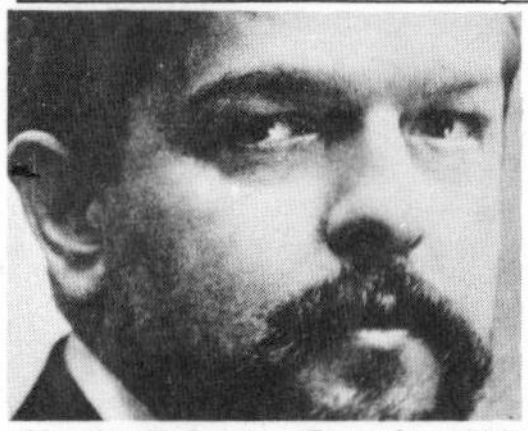

Claude Debussy (French, 1862–1918): composer. The most original voice in 20th-century music, Claude Debussy was trained at the Paris Conservatoire, won its coveted *Premier Grand Prix de Rome*, but, soon displeasing the Jury by the modernity of his work, went on his own way to extend the language of music. His *Prélude* (1894) affected directly or indirectly all music written after it, just as his only completed opera, *Pelleas et Melisande* (1902), proved a landmark in operatic writing. Such scores as the *Nocturnes*, *La Mer*, the *Images* and *Jeux* evoke scenes in colour as surely as the Impressionist canvases of which they are the musical counterpart. He also enriched the literature of song and of music for the piano, his own instrument. Three chamber sonatas written towards the end of his life show extreme refinement and new directions which his death from cancer prevented him from exploring further. Debussy's music, unlike that of his precursors, embraces the archaic and the oriental, monody and nascent harmonies being used empirically in sequences or as points of colour. His orchestral textures are conceived in terms of timbre or instrumental colour, so that this is felt to be as important an element as the pitch, density and rhythmic progress of the music. In this his influence on the music of our time has been paramount. **F. A.**

'DEBUSSY', BY EDWARD LOCKSPEISER (DENT, THE MASTER MUSICIANS, 1963); 'DEBUSSY, HIS LIFE AND MIND', BY EDWARD LOCKSPEISER, 2 VOLS (CASSELL, 1962, 1965); 'DEBUSSY, MAN AND ARTIST', BY OSCAR THOMPSON (CONSTABLE, 1968).

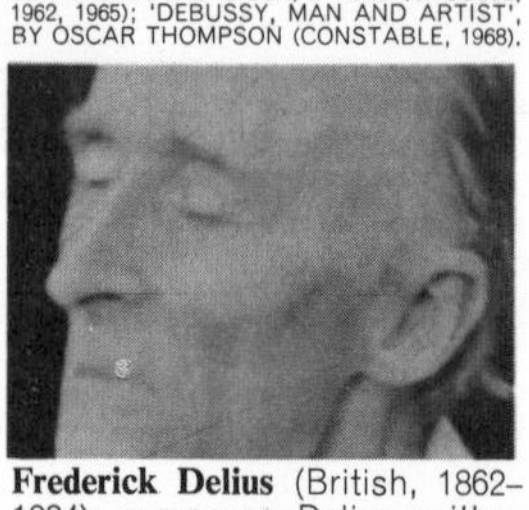

Frederick Delius (British, 1862–1934): composer. Delius neither came from nor founded a musical school. He remains a solitary musical poet, whose work has shown its ability to survive the death of its greatest interpreter, Thomas Beecham (q.v.). Bradford-born of German parentage, Delius was a cosmopolitan in the truest sense. He went to Florida as a young man, then studied music briefly at Leipzig, became attached to Scandinavia and its culture, but lived and composed in France for the greater part of his life. Delius was essentially self-taught as a composer. A harmonic sense of pronounced individuality colours his music and gives it its peculiarly moving quality. While such works as *A Mass of Life* (1905) show him capable of writing vigorously, most of his music is nostalgic and autumnal in feeling. Much of it deals with the transcience of things. This mood permeates not only works like the opera *A Village Romeo and Juliet* (1906), *Sea Drift* (1903), *Songs of Sunset* (1907) and *Arabesk* (1911) but also many of Delius's orchestral and chamber works. Blind and paralysed in his last years, Delius was fortunate in having as amanuensis a young Yorkshireman, Eric Fenby, who, from Delius's dictation, was able to help him complete his final works, including the *Idyll* and *Songs of Farewell* (1930). **F. A.**

'FREDERICK DELIUS', BY PHILIP WARLOCK (BODLEY HEAD, 1952); 'DELIUS AS I KNEW HIM', BY ERIC FENBY (ICON BOOKS, 1966); 'FREDERICK DELIUS', BY SIR THOMAS BEECHAM (HUTCHINSON, 1959).

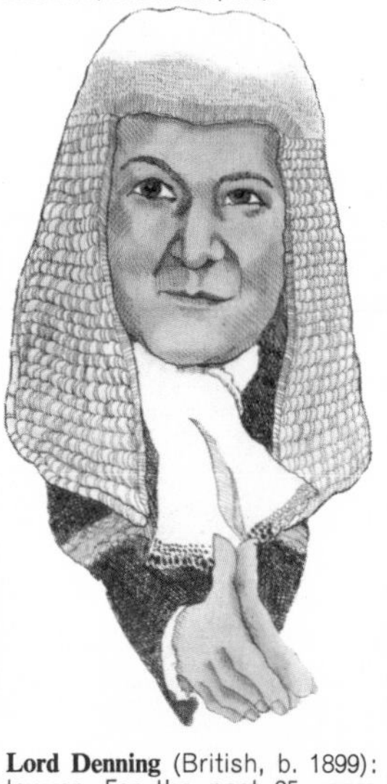

Lord Denning (British, b. 1899): lawyer. For the past 25 years Lord Denning has been one of the most original and controversial judges on the English Bench. Alfred Thompson Denning was appointed a trial judge in 1944, and soon gave evidence of his clarity of thought and expression, and his anxiety to produce a fair and sensible result, refusing to be bound by the niceties and absurdities of precedent. He became Lord Justice of Appeal in 1948, Lord of Appeal in 1957, and Master of the Rolls in 1962. Many of his judgments, regarded as heterodox when delivered, have been subsequently approved by higher courts or by Parliament. In 1951, for instance, he advocated a general principle of liability for careless advice; this was substantially accepted by the House of Lords in 1963. His campaign for the right of the deserted wife to occupy the matrimonial home led to legislation in 1967; his persistent attempts to make 20th-century sense out of the 19th-century tangle of family property law will almost certainly lead to statutory reform in the near future. He has fought doughtily against the excessive dominance of precedent; and, particularly since his appointment as Master of the Rolls, his influence in modernising the law has been profound and all-pervasive. **P. F.**

'FREEDOM UNDER THE LAW', BY LORD DENNING (STEVENS, 1949).

Eamon De Valéra (Irish, b. 1882): statesman. As the only survivor of the commandants of the 1916 Rising – his brigade occupied Boland's Flour Mills – De Valéra personifies the heroic age of modern Irish nationalism. He escaped execution thanks to his then American citizenship, and was subsequently sprung from Lincoln Gaol after a succession of keys had been sent to him in

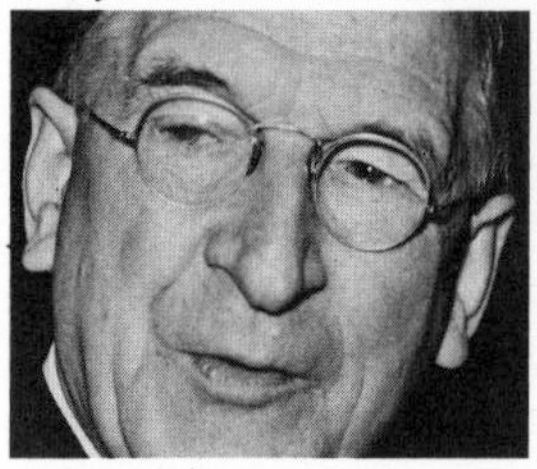

a succession of cakes. An austere intellectual insistence on pure republicanism prompted his resignation as first president of Dáil Eireann when he disagreed with the majority vote in favour of the Anglo-Irish Treaty in 1922. For a year he was imprisoned by the new government, and there then followed an interlude of distant opposition until 1932, when the Fianna Fáil party was elected under him to more or less permanent government. First as *Taoiseach* and latterly as President, De Valéra managed to scoop up a number of political successes: the preservation of Ireland's neutrality during the 1939–45 War and the early gestures towards economic reconstruction. **E. R. N.**

'EAMON DE VALERA', BY M. J. MACMANUS (TALBOT PRESS, DUBLIN, 1944); 'THE IRISH REPUBLIC', BY DOROTHY MACARDLE (CORGI, 1968); 'DE VALERA', BY MARY BROMAGE (HUTCHINSON, 1956).

John Dewey (U.S., 1859–1952): philosopher. Pragmatism – the label often given to Dewey's philosophy – stresses the consideration of practical consequences of ideas, and he applied this in ethics, in psychology and in educational and social reform – adding the important corollary that practical outcomes are best determined by experimentation. In education he considered 'Problem Solving' the basic method. The child, coming to a problem, is encouraged to clarify the difficulty, gather data and test the proposed solution by comparing actual and predicted outcomes in an experimental situation. This approach was contrasted with the traditional subject-centred, formal approach current in American schools at the

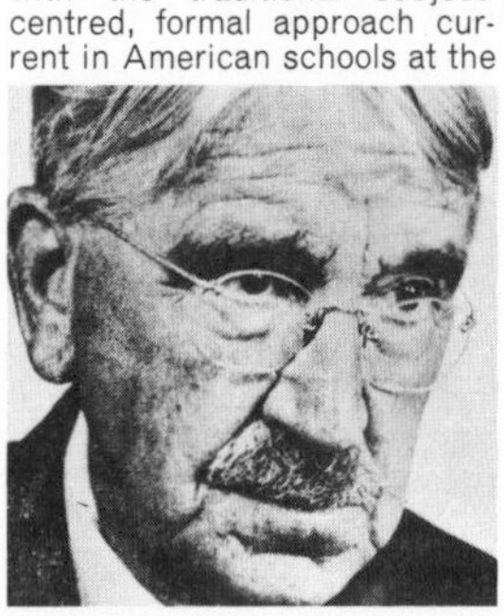

beginning of the century and it set off a wave of educational reform which at times embarrassed Dewey with its excessive zeal. Dewey saw education as a vehicle of social reform, and the good, democratic society was one in which problems were solved by high intercommunication and pooling of resources. His influence on the 20th century has been to provide a rallying point for educational reform, especially in the USA. **B. R. O.**

'RECONSTRUCTION IN PHILOSOPHY', BY JOHN DEWEY (HENRY HOLT, NEW YORK, 1920, REVISED BEACON PRESS, BOSTON, 1948); 'EXPERIENCE AND EDUCATION', BY JOHN DEWEY (MACMILLAN, N.Y., 1938).

Melville Dewey (U.S., 1851–1931): librarian. Dewey worked out a system for arranging books by subject which is used in more than nine out of ten libraries in Britain and America, and which is behind most subject arrangements in bibliographies. First published in 1876, the Dewey Decimal System was the best arrangement of subjects available then, and was also

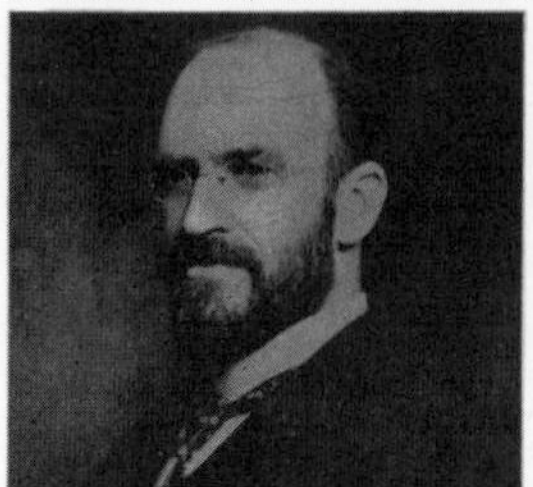

easy to administer and understand; it made it possible to let non-librarians loose among the books instead of making them queue for things they had heard of but not seen. Previous systems numbered places on shelves, making additions and re-arrangement difficult; Dewey's numbered the books, like the subjects, decimally, allowing limitless scope for additions. His classification caught on with the library boom of the late 19th century, and what we owe him is part of what we owe public libraries: something incalculable. **A. E.**

BOOKS ON LIBRARIANSHIP (DEWEY NUMBER 020); BOOKS ON LIBRARY CLASSIFICATION (025.4); 'INTRODUCTION TO THE DEWEY DECIMAL CLASSIFICATION', BY C. D. BATTY (CLIVE BINGLEY, 1967).

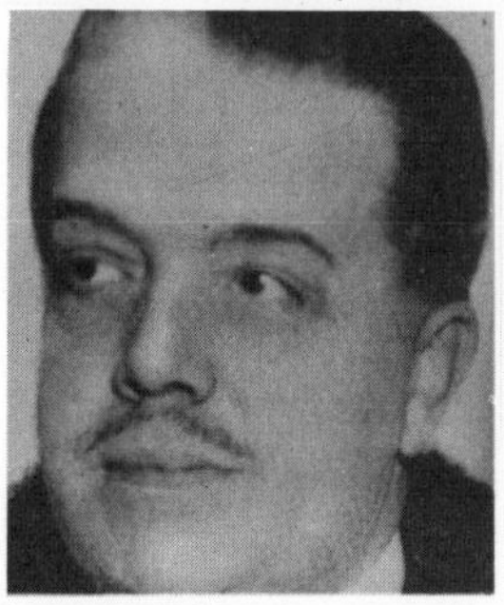

Sergei Diaghilev (Russian, 1872–1929): impresario. Diaghilev revived ballet as an art in Western Europe. Born of Russian nobility, he began by revealing Russia to itself and to the world, and went on to change the course of the performing and visual arts everywhere. His talent lay in encouraging the genius of others. He organised exhibitions, edited *The World of Art* and brought exhibitions of Russian art (1906), concerts of Russian music (1907) and Mussorgsky's *Boris Godounov* (1908) to Paris. His first 'Russian Season' of opera and (particularly) ballet conquered Paris in 1909 and from 1911 till Diaghilev's death in 1929 his permanent company performed in Western Europe, South America and the USA. He initiated close collaboration between composers, painters, choreographers and dancers, commissioning scores from Stravinsky, Debussy, and Ravel (qq.v.), decors from Benois, Bakst, Picasso, Braque, Matisse, Chirico (qq.v.), Larionov and Gontcharova, and worked with choreographers Fokine, Nijinsky, Balanchine (qq.v.), Massine and Nijinska. His company could not survive him, but his collaborators, Rambert, de Valois (qq.v.), Massine, Dolin, Lifar and Balanchine, carried on the succession. **R. B.**

'THE DIAGHILEV BALLET 1909–1929', BY S. L. GRIGORIEV (CONSTABLE, 1953); 'DANCING FOR DIAGHILEV', BY LYDIA SOKOLOVA, ED. RICHARD BUCKLE (JOHN MURRAY, 1960).

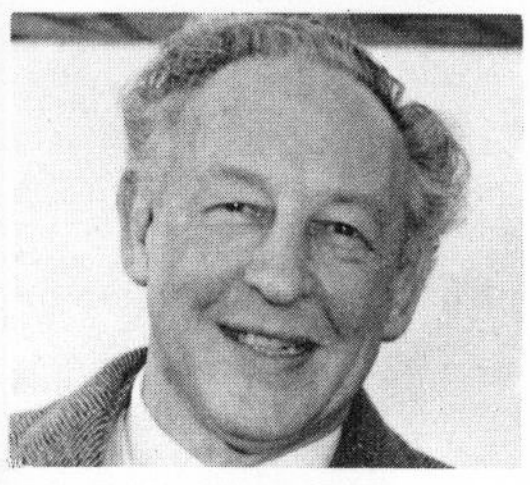

Grantly Dick-Read (British, 1890–1959): obstetrician. Dick-Read was the man who helped dispel the old wives' tales that had clustered round generations of pregnant women. At the end of his career he was able to write: "By the employment of elementary ante-natal education, physical relaxation and an understanding of the total phenomena of labour, fear, pain and unnecessary anaesthesia have been eliminated." For much of his life, he was a prophet crying in the wilderness, as far as the British medical profession was concerned, although Princess Elizabeth was alleged to have read *Childbirth Without Fear* before the birth of Prince Charles, and the Pope gave it his endorsement in 1956. As a boy, he had not understood why animals should give birth easily while human mothers suffered; and a woman in Whitechapel, whom he attended while he was a student at the London Hospital, finally confirmed him in his vocation. She refused the chloroform he offered; and when her baby was born, she said: "It didn't hurt. It wasn't meant to, was it, Doctor?" Countless thousands of women have reason to be grateful to her and, more directly, to Dick-Read. He took the hard labour out of labour, and even – according to his more fortunate disciples – made it fun. He himself believed that childbirth should, and could, be a truly happy event, and by the end of his life he saw this view accepted, and welcomed, by women all over the world. **S. M. R.**

'NATURAL CHILDBIRTH', BY GRANTLY DICK-READ (HEINEMANN, 1933); 'REVELATION OF CHILDBIRTH' (LATER CALLED 'CHILDBIRTH WITHOUT FEAR'), BY GRANTLY DICK-READ (HEINEMANN, 1942; 5TH EDITION, PAN, 1969); 'WHAT EVERY WOMAN SHOULD KNOW ABOUT CHILDBIRTH', BY JESSICA DICK-READ AND PRUNELLA BRIANCE (HEINEMANN, 1965).

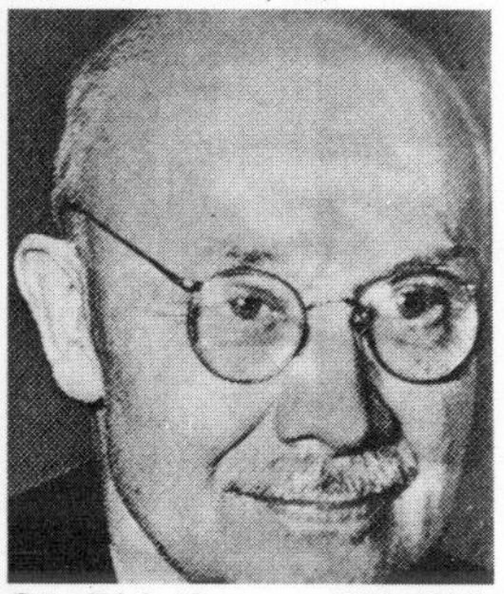

Otto Diels (German, 1876–1954): chemist. Diels, Professor of Chemistry at the University of Berlin and subsequently at Kiel, discovered an elegant way of making a large class of compounds, where (in the words of his Nobel Prize presentation in 1950) "a chain of atoms catches its own tail and forms itself into a ring". An important part of organic chemistry deals with the synthesis of new compounds. They may be theoretically or practically important, but synthesis also provides unambiguous proof of structure – what the compound really looks like. Especially among naturally occurring substances, most of them very complicated ones, laboratory synthesis is the final proof. The cause of the 'chain of atoms' was elucidated by Diels and his collaborator Alder (q.v.). The Diels-Alder reaction, or diene synthesis, opened up new fields of organic chemistry and made possible the production of large numbers of complex structures. Its use has been significant in university and industrial chemistry. Diels's discovery is important for knowledge of biologically vital compounds such as cholesterol, oils and resins; it has also proved valuable to research on new plastics and the range of products obtained from petrochemicals. **P. J. F.**

'NOBEL PRIZEWINNERS IN CHEMISTRY', BY EDUARD FARBER, REVISED EDITION (ABELARD SCHUMAN, 1963).

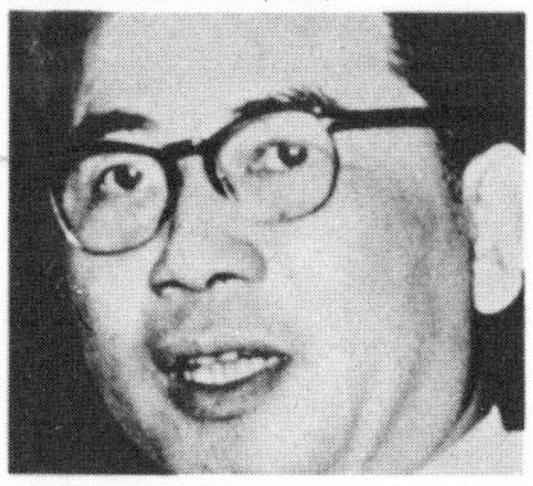

Ngo Dinh Diem (Vietnamese, 1901–1963): politician. Diem's career and demise highlight not only the failure of American policy in South East Asia, but also the senseless strategy of sponsoring an autocrat and expecting him to behave like a democrat. He assumed power in June 1954 as the first Prime Minister of the State of Vietnam. Following a referendum in October 1955, he deposed the head of state, Bao Dai, to proclaim the Republic of Vietnam of which he became President. Motivated by a Confucian heritage, a deep and abiding Roman Catholic faith and a doctrinaire anti-Communism, he was a mandarin-ruler. His own ruthless determination to exercise the mandate of heaven against all opposition alienated autonomous forces within South Vietnam from his regime. He was an aloof, ascetic figure, distant from those problems which an organised insurgency were quick to exploit. He initially consolidated his position through American benefaction and when this was withdrawn – against a background of Buddhist self-immolation and a deteriorating security situation – he was overthrown in a military coup and murdered. **M. L.**

'GOVERNMENT AND REVOLUTION IN VIETNAM', BY DENNIS J. DUNCANSON (O.U.P., 1968); 'THE TWO VIETNAMS', BY BERNARD B. FALL (REVISED ED., PALL MALL, 1965); 'SOUTH VIETNAM: NATION UNDER STRESS', BY ROBERT SCIGLIANO (HOUGHTON MIFFLIN, BOSTON, 1964); 'EIGHT NATION MAKERS', BY WILLARD A. HANNA (ST MARTINS PRESS, NEW YORK, 1964).

Marlene Dietrich (German, born *c.* 1901): film actress. Indifferent to convention, a legend in her own lifetime, Dietrich is the 20th-century symbol of the erotic unattainable. Her origins and date of birth ("say I am 75 and let it go at that") are open to question; what is certain is that she appeared in many German films and played on the stage under Reinhardt's (q.v.) direction before Joseph von Sternberg saw her leaning "with cold disdain" against the wings and knew he had found his Lola for *The Blue Angel* (1930). Submitting absolutely to his direction, Dietrich became the spectacular partner in a triumph which continued in Hollywood with *Morocco, Dishonoured, Shanghai Express, Blonde Venus, The Scarlet Empress, The Devil is a Woman.* Exploiting the disdain, playing lights and shadows on her cheekbones and eyesockets and the incomparable legs von Sternberg created an exquisite erotic myth. The partnership dissolved, but Dietrich had toughness and brilliance enough to survive on her own, whether in films – the rough-and-tumble *Destry Rides Again* (1939), the sardonic *A Foreign Affair* (1948), the anti-Nazi *Judgment At Nuremburg* (1961) – or employing her thrilling, masculine, non-singing voice as a cabaret singer. **D. P.**

'MARLENE DIETRICH', BY JOHN KOBAL (STUDIO VISTA, 1968); 'FUN IN A CHINESE LAUNDRY', BY JOSEPH VON STERNBERG (SECKER AND WARBURG, 1966).

Christian Dior (French, 1905–1957): couturier. In February 1947, Christian Dior opened his luxurious couture house on the Avenue Montaigne in Paris and changed the face of Western

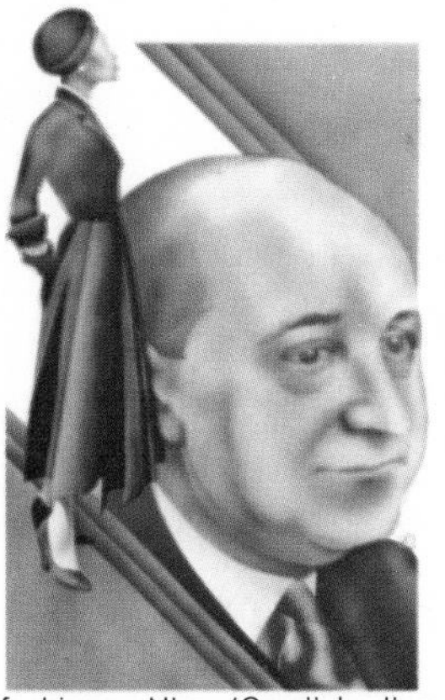

fashion. His 'Corolle' line, which America dubbed the New Look, was instantly bought, copied, and publicised all over the Western world. It was criticised in Britain by pompous officials and Mrs Grundies on the grounds of its extravagant use of cloth, but the criticism was ignored; women wanted and wore it. The success of the Corolle line (a tight bodice shaped into a tiny waist below which a long skirt burst into fulness like a flower) was due to its extreme femininity. Women were weary of the mannish clothes of the war period and Dior was exactly the man for the hour. A true professional, Dior designed all his own beautiful accessories. His talent never stood still; after the New Look, he created the Umbrella, Scissor, Horseshoe, H and A lines, all influential and commercially successful. His achievement was to bring back elegance, colour, fine workmanship and a sense of quality to a scene where they had been long forgotten. **A. S.-J.**

'DIOR BY DIOR' (WEIDENFELD AND NICOLSON, 1957).

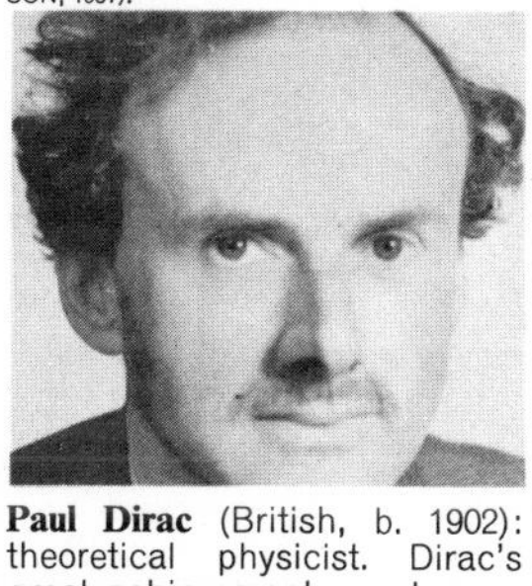

Paul Dirac (British, b. 1902): theoretical physicist. Dirac's great achievement was to provide physics with the modern mathematics now used universally to cope with its most fundamental problems. The son of a Swiss father and English mother, he became Lucasian Professor of Mathematics at Cambridge in 1932. Excitement about the new quantum theory of matter and radiation was then at its peak. Two versions were proposed in the 1920s – one due to Bohr and Heisenberg, the other to de Broglie and Schroedinger (qq.v.) – neither of which took Einstein's (q.v.) theory of relativity into account. Between 1926 and 1932 Dirac proved, with characteristic elegance, that each of these theories was a different aspect of a more general mathematical concept of the atom. In 1928 he produced his relativistic theory of the electron for which he received the 1933 Nobel Prize with Schroedinger. This theory predicted the positive electron or 'positron' and the other anti-particles' which exist for each of the many elementary particles now known. **P. H. S. S.**

'QUANTA', BY J. ANDRADE E SILVA AND G. LOCHAK (WEIDENFELD AND NICOLSON, 1969); 'PHYSICS FOR THE ENQUIRING MIND', BY ERIC M. ROGERS (OXFORD UNIVERSITY PRESS, 1960); 'THE WORLD OF THE ATOM', ED. HENRY A. BOORSE AND LLOYD MOTZ, 2 VOLS (BASIC BOOKS, NEW YORK, 1966); 'PRINCIPLES OF QUANTUM MECHANICS', ED. P. A. M. DIRAC (CLARENDON PRESS, OXFORD, 1930).

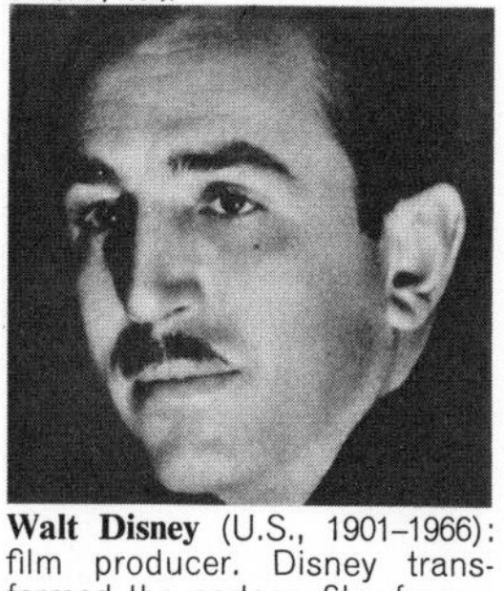

Walt Disney (U.S., 1901–1966): film producer. Disney transformed the cartoon film from a primitive comic strip into a brilliant narrative form, and the denigration of his work prompted by the sophistication of later animators has been largely unfair. He was first to introduce sound into cartoons, and created in *Steamboat Willie* (1928) a figure universally famous, Mickey Mouse (who was followed by such other celebrated inventions as Donald Duck, Goofy, Pluto, and Ferdinand the Bull). He was also the first to make a cartoon in three-colour Technicolor (*Flowers and Trees*). *The Ugly Duckling, Three Little Pigs, Mother Goose Goes Hollywood, Peculiar Penguins* – scores of short pieces capable of pathos, satire, wit and, let's face it, both cruelty and archness showed that cartoons could achieve tension, and in 1937 Disney and his team ventured on a feature-length tale, *Snow White and the Seven Dwarfs*. The human figures were insipid, but fantasy blossomed in *Pinocchio, Dumbo* and an essay teetering between success and vulgarity in the illustration of serious music, *Fantasia*. Disney continued with cartoons; experimented with nature films (e.g. *The Living Desert*, a mixture of genuine observation and fake drama); made undistinguished live-action films; and in *Mary Poppins* (wildly over-praised) followed earlier pioneering work in simultaneous use of cartoon figures and living players. **D. P.**

'THE ART OF WALT DISNEY', BY ROBERT D. FEILD (COLLINS, 1944); 'WALT DISNEY', BY RICHARD SCHICKEL (WEIDENFELD AND NICOLSON, 1968).

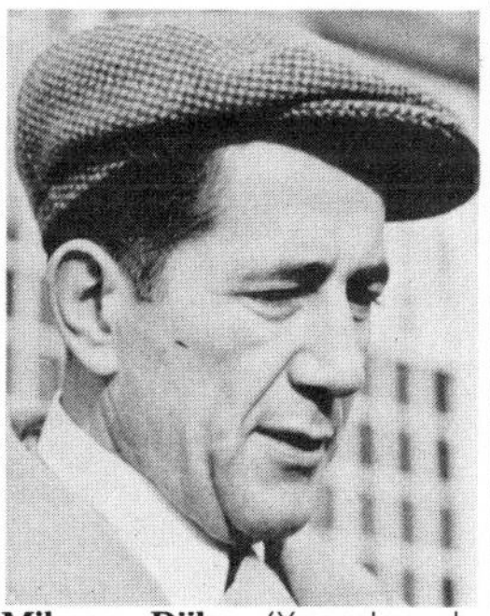

Milovan Djilas (Yugoslav, b. 1911): political theorist. Djilas's 'heresies' strike at a basic dilemma of Yugoslav Communism and a major issue of this century: the measure of political democracy compatible with collectivist society. Following the break with Moscow in 1948, Yugoslavia under Marshal Tito (q.v.) embarked on a programme of decentralisation and democratisation. But devolution of political authority did not keep pace with expansion of socio-economic autonomy. In 1953 Djilas argued that an obsolete party threatened the revolution and concluded that the political bureaucracy must "wither away". "The new enemy," he declared, "bureaucracy, is even more dangerous than the old one, capitalism." The party leadership rejected Djilas's thinking and expelled him from their ranks. Shortly afterwards Djilas took his original heresy a step further with *The New Class*, an outright condemnation of contemporary Communism. Turning Marxism-Leninism against its proponents, Djilas exposed a new class of owners and exploiters whose legitimacy derived from tyrannical exercise of absolute power. He has been twice imprisoned by the Tito regime. As a revolutionary, soldier and politician Djilas contributed much to Communism. As a heretic he has contributed even more. For his heresy is the soul of Tito's revisionism. **J. M. K.**

'THE NEW CLASS', BY MILOVAN DJILAS (PRAEGER, N.Y., 1957); 'CONVERSATIONS WITH STALIN', BY MILOVAN DJILAS (RUPERT HART-DAVIS, 1962); 'LAND WITHOUT JUSTICE', BY MILOVAN DJILAS (METHUEN, 1958): 'TITOISM IN ACTION', BY FRED WARNER NEAL (CALIFORNIA U.P., 1958).

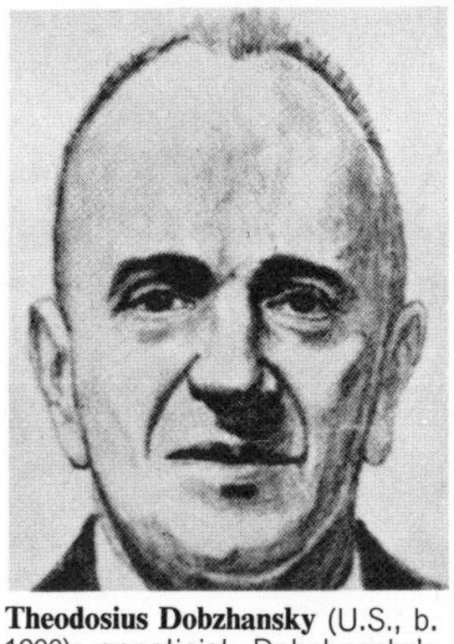

Theodosius Dobzhansky (U.S., b. 1900): geneticist. Dobzhansky's book *Mankind Evolving* has been dubbed the "most judicious scientific treatise ever written on the nature of man". He began his research on the fruit fly *Drosophila* but soon became interested in the evolution of human populations. This led him to a study of race and later to the attempt "to understand mankind as a product of evolution and as an evolving whole". In 1959, while Da Costa Professor of Zoology at Columbia University, he was invited to deliver the Silliman Lectures which formed the basis of *Mankind Evolving*. He stressed that the most important point of Darwin's evolutionary theory had been missed – man not only has evolved but is still evolving. He argued that man, by changing the world, also changes himself both culturally and physically. He saw in this the hope that changes resulting from knowledge could also be directed by knowledge. "Evolution need no longer be a destiny imposed from without; it may conceivably be controlled by man." **J. H.**

BOOKS BY DOBZHANSKY: 'MANKIND EVOLVING' (YALE U.P., LONDON AND NEW-HAVEN, CONN, 1962); 'GENETICS AND THE ORIGIN OF SPECIES' (COLUMBIA U.P., 1959); 'HEREDITY, RACE AND SOCIETY' – WITH L. C. DUNN (MENTOR 1952 AND NEW ENGLISH LIBRARY, 1965).

Karl Doenitz (German, b. 1891): admiral. Doenitz, the German Grand Admiral who sank some 15 million tons of Allied shipping in the Second World War, was in his earliest service sceptical of surface fleets, visualising war basically in terms of submarines. When convoys in the First World War defeated the U-boat, he conceived revolutionary forms of concentrated attack. As Flag Officer U-Boats at the outbreak of the Second World War, he had the nascent U-boat fleet already trained in his wolf-pack tactics. Professional opinion was then against submarines – the Royal Navy, disastrously over-confident in Asdic, their sonic submarine-detecting system, had neglected alternative counter-measures. Despite inadequate numbers and political restrictions, Doenitz sank 2,187,000 tons of Allied shipping in 1940 and two years later, free of restrictions, 6,266,000. Improved defences cut the losses to 700,000 tons in 1944, but Doenitz responded with astonishing constructional innovations which were ready, but too late, in 1945. His masterful command had three consequences: the enduring effects of Britain's gargantuan loss in ships and cargoes; renewed confidence in the future of the submarine leading logically to Rickover's (q.v.) triumph with the nuclear Nautilus, and Raborn's (q.v.) stupendous Polaris concept; and swift development, partly as a consequence of captured material, of the Russian submarine fleet to its present strength of 350 ships. **D. D.**

'THE DOENITZ MEMOIRS' (WEIDENFELD AND NICOLSON, 1959); 'HITLER AND HIS ADMIRALS', BY ANTHONY MARTIENSSEN (SECKER AND WARBURG, 1948); 'THE WAR AT SEA 1939–1945', BY CAPT. S. W. ROSKILL, 3 VOLS (H.M.S.O., 1954–61); 'SEA WARFARE 1939–1945', BY VICE ADMIRAL FRIEDRICH RUGE (CASSELL, 1957).

Gerhard Domagk (German, 1895–1964): biochemist. Gerhard Domagk's discovery of the therapeutic effects of the sulpha drugs revolutionised the management of infectious diseases – infection after childbirth, for instance, and streptococcal infection of the ear with meningitis. As early as 1920 the German company I. G. Farbenindustrie postulated the preparation of a substance later to be called prontosil, but not until 1932 did Domagk discover, in a systematic search, its extraordinary chemotherapeutic effects. He drew attention to the harmlessness of the preparation and its pharmacological inertness – though chemotherapeutically it had a remarkable effect in the animal in protecting from or curing streptococcal infection which would kill within two days if untreated. He also noticed that this effect occurred only in the animal; it showed little activity when studied in the test tube. Although this work was completed in 1932, Domagk did not publish his work until 1935. In the meantime a number of clinical papers had appeared demonstrating the chemotherapeutic activity of prontosil in

man, and indeed it seems certain that Domagk had in fact treated his own daughter successfully during this time. The immediate effect of Domagk's discovery was the revolution in the treatment of streptococcal and some other forms of infection. The mortality and disability of streptococcal infection rapidly declined. For the first time a weapon had been produced which could materially influence the course of bacterial infection. The development of further sulpha drugs rapidly followed, and widened the scope of control of bacterial infections. **E. F. S.**

Walter Dornberger (German, b. 1895): engineer. The inventor of the V2 was a mere artillery captain when the Reichswehr appointed him to establish an experimental unit for military rockets. With his most celebrated recruit, Wernher von Braun (q.v.), he produced four successive marks of rocket with varying degrees of failure. Hitler (q.v.) gave no encouragement until the fourth prototype of the fourth mark flew accurately 118 miles, when his unbalanced enthusiasms promptly became an embarrassment. Yet despite

them and the RAF's gigantic raid on Peenemünde, Major-General Dornberger succeeded. On September 8, 1944, the first operational V2 – *Vergeltungswaffen Zwei* – fell on London at Chiswick. It was a missile triumph, but, because of the lack of a commensurate warhead, a military failure. Barely 11 months later, a nuclear warhead was proved possible at Hiroshima. The marriage of the two was – with Dornberger's assistance after he moved to the States in 1947 – inevitable; the speed of escalation shattering. Twelve years later the first Intercontinental Ballistic Missiles had permanently changed the material, the methods and the principles of war. **D. D.**

'V-2', BY MAJOR-GEN. WALTER DORNBERGER (HURST AND BLACKETT, 1954); 'THE DEFENCE OF THE UNITED KINGDOM', BY BASIL COLLIER (H.M.S.O., 1957); 'THE MARE'S NEST', BY DAVID IRVING (WILLIAM KIMBER, 1964, CORGI, 1966).

Norman Douglas (British, 1868–1952): writer. Norman Douglas might be called the Grand Old Man of expatriates; he spent the last half of his life in Italy and France. He toured the Tirol, Calabria, Tunisia or the Appennines to satisfy the energy which he turned into travel books. These were among the first modern travel books, particularly *Siren Land* (1911), *Old Calabria* (1915), *Alone* (1920) and *Together* (1923). They helped to establish the modern sensibility – just as *South Wind* (1917) set the tone for the novel of conversation and expatriate hedonism. Douglas's intellectual outlook was pagan, cosmopolitan and steeped in Mediterranean culture. He was scientifically minded, and a passionate pleader for toleration, good sense and cosmic irresponsibility. To know him was to fall permanently under his spell:

he was an intoxicating companion. His disjointed autobiography is unduly neglected, his reputation, especially in America, is rather wobbly. Fundamentally an essayist, he lacked intensity: his grace was never pressurised to the heat we look for now. He was a mixture of erudition, fun, curiosity, robust castigation of somewhat obvious targets, rational selfishness. His last words were "Love, love, love". **C. C.**

'GRAND MAN', BY NANCY CUNARD (SECKER AND WARBURG, 1954); DOUGLAS'S BOOKS WERE PUBLISHED BY SECKER.

Giulio Douhet (Italian, 1869–1930): strategist. Douhet, an Italian General in the First World War, was a prophet of the view that future wars would be determined by bombing alone. He suggested that heavy, sudden and ruthless attack on main centres of civil population and industry would bring even major powers to defeat and capitulation. His ideas were reflected, spontaneously or otherwise, in Trenchard's view when he was Chief of British Air Staff in the inter-war years that the best defence was attack and that the moral effect of bombing was more important than the physical; in that of Mitchell (a U.S. Air Corps General) that air power rendered naval and military operations obsolete; and also in Baldwin's statement (1932) that "the bomber will always get through". Douhet's theories were shown in the Second World War to be defective, especially in the fate of the 'self-defending' formations of U.S. day bombers which were shot to pieces by the Germans. Douhet had overestimated the power of bombing, ignored the possibility of effec-

tive air defence, and overlooked the surviving importance of naval and military operations. Nevertheless, as champion of air power, Douhet represented in persuasive style the philosophical background to diplomacy and military planning in the critical period between 1920 and 1939. **N. F.**

'THE COMMAND OF THE AIR', BY GIULIO DOUHET, TRANSLATED BY DINO FERRARI (COWARD-McCANN, NEW YORK, 1942).

Alexander Dovzhenko (Russian, 1894–1956): film director. One of the most individualistic artists in the cinema, Dovzhenko was the child of illiterate Ukrainian peasants. Having been a student, a soldier, a diplomat, a cartoonist and a painter he decided at the age of 34 that

painting was the art of the past and that he would try the cinema. Early experiments led to *Zvenigora*, "an astonishing mixture," said Eisenstein (q.v.), "of reality with a profoundly natural poetic imagination. Quite modern and mythological at the same time. Humorous and heroic. Something Gogol about it." The poetry and the paradoxical juxtapositions were to mark all his later work: *Arsenal* (1928–9); his masterpiece *Earth* (1930); and four sound films *Ivan* (1932), *Aerograd* (1935), *Shchors* (1939) and *Michurin* (1948). The most deeply committed of Soviet directors, Dov-

zhenko dealt with all aspects of Soviet achievement (*Earth* is ostensibly about collectivisation; *Ivan* about the Dnieper Dam project and so on) but his vision was infinitely broader than political tract-making. The humanism and pantheism of his best work and his poetic and philosophical perception of man's relation to the living world give his films – particularly *Earth* – a universal significance beyond the Soviet Union. **D. R.**

'KINO', BY JAY LEYDA (ALLEN AND UNWIN, 1960).

Sir Hugh Dowding, later Lord Dowding (British, 1882–1970): Air Chief Marshal. The victor of the Battle of Britain saw action as a Royal Flying Corps observer and pilot on the Western Front in the First World War. In the 1930s he encouraged the development of the monoplane all-metal eight-gun fighter specification which produced the Hurricane and the Spitfire, and in 1936 he approved the expenditure asked for by the Tizard Committee to develop a radar early-warning chain. Later in 1936 he was appointed first C-in-C, Fighter Command; due to him Fighter Command was operationally better prepared for war than other elements in the British forces. Dowding's determination and persuasive power checked the drain on Fighter Command in the Battle of France in May and June 1940. If the Luftwaffe had knocked Fighter Command out before September 17, 1940, invasion would have followed. Dowding's victory saved Britain and opened the way for the defeat of Hitler's Germany. **N. F.**

'LEADER OF THE FEW', BY BASIL COLLIER (JARROLDS, 1957).

Theodore Dreiser (U.S., 1871–1945): writer. Dreiser, the first novelist to be at home among squalid American actualities, is still controversial, still unavoidable despite outrageous imperfections, stylistic infelicities, banal sentiments, primitive philosophising and bogus science. Alternately crushed and exhilarated by the human spectacle, he used as literary material family scandals, newspaper stories and his own amatory adventures. From a poverty-ridden household in Indiana and an unconfident, auto-erotic youth, he set out to discover the City, a milieu he sounded and savoured. After apprentice days as a Mid-Western reporter, he became a magazine editor in New York. *Sister Carrie* (1900), his first and (some think) best novel, was suppressed by his publisher. He wrote more than 25 other books, among them *Jennie Gerhardt, The Financier* and *An American Tragedy*, which in 1925 was the last and the most widely discussed. During the Thirties, he 'exposed' social injustice and defended the Soviet Union. He joined the Communist Party in 1945. Dreiser's fictional characters portray contrary facets of himself: power-seeking sensual supermen and dingy failures pitifully equipped to survive in their native jungle. He was, in Mencken's phrase, "the Hindenburg of the American novel", who smashed genteel barriers, opened up tabooed literary terrain, and cleared the way for iconoclastic successors. **D. A.**

'DREISER AND THE LAND OF THE FREE', BY DOROTHY DUDLEY (WISHART, 1933); 'THEODORE DREISER', BY F. O. MATTHIESSEN (METHUEN, 1951); 'DREISER', BY W. A. SWANBERG (CHARLES SCRIBNER'S, 1965); 'THE STATURE OF THEODORE DREISER', ED. A. KAZIN AND C. SHAPIRO (UNIVERSITY OF INDIANA, 1955).

Carl Dreyer (Danish, 1889–1968): film director. Majestic is really the only word for Dreyer's films, yet it is a misleading one. When people think of Dreyer, they usually conjure up *The Passion of Joan of Arc*, with its relentless portrayal of suffering as Joan is driven remorselessly to the stake; or *Day of Wrath*, with its

implacably doom-laden tale of a 17th-century witch-hunt. Yet in a career spanning 35 years and 14 films, Dreyer ranged far and wide. Ribald pastoral comedy in *The Parson's Widow*, gentle domestic comedy in *Master of the House*; a brilliant study of psychological decadence in *Mikael*; lyrical romance amid the log cabins and rolling hills of Norway in *The Bride of Glomdal*; and arguably the greatest horror film ever made, with the ethereal, haunted landscapes and wraith-like characters of *Vampyr*. Through all of them runs a mysterious radiance which reaches its apogee in his last film, *Gertrud*, the serenely melancholy story of a woman whose appeals for love go unanswered, and who yet can say, grown old and tranquil, "I have known love". Majestic, yes. **T. M.**

'CARL TH. DREYER: DANISH FILM DIRECTOR', BY IB MONTY (MEMORIAL PAMPHLET, MINISTRY OF FOREIGN AFFAIRS, COPENHAGEN, 1968).

Alexander Dubcek (Czechoslovak, b. 1921): statesman. Dubcek will go down in history for one of the most courageous acts of this century. Born in Slovakia, he spent his youth in the Soviet Union. The family returned to Slovakia shortly before the outbreak of the war: young Alexander, a pattern-maker by trade, joined the illegal Communist Party and later the partisan movement. He was wounded twice in the uprising against the Germans. He became a full-time Party official in 1949 and spent the years 1955–8 at the Moscow Party school. He became the First Secretary of the Slovak Communist Party in 1963 and, in January 1968, he reached the top position in the Czechoslovak organisation, from which he was demoted 15 months later. Nevertheless, in those 15 months Dubcek became the leader of the Czechoslovak Communist reform movement. He introduced a new style into Communist politics: a light touch, flexibility, sensitivity and responsiveness to popular mood. He tried to humanise socialism by loosening the grip of state bureaucracy. **Z. A. B. Z.**

'PRAGUE SPRING, A REPORT ON CZECHOSLOVAKIA 1968', BY Z. A. B. ZEMAN (PENGUIN 1969).

William Du Bois (U.S., 1868–1963): writer. The most dynamic American Black leader to bridge the gap between Booker T. Washington and Martin Luther King (q.v.), Du Bois was always more of a firebrand than either. From 1900 he was an ardent advocate of Pan-Africanism, prophesying that "the problem of the 20th century is the problem of the colour line". From 1909 he was an officer of the National Association for the Advancement of Coloured People (NAACP), and after Washington's death in 1915

challenged the moderate policies he had followed, saying: "The African movement means to us what the Zionist movement must mean to the Jews – the centralisation of race effort and the recognition of a racial fount." When the colour problem became really acute after the Second World War he became a figure of national importance. Du Bois embraced Communism in the Cold War and emigrated to Ghana in 1960 as Director of the *Encyclopedia Africana*, becoming a member of the Communist Party in 1961 and a Ghanaian citizen in 1963. The prophet of Black Power, he was the leading American advocate of the world-wide unity of the Black race, declaring: "The real essence of this kinship is its social heritage of slavery, the discrimination and insult." **H. C. A.**

'BLACK RECONSTRUCTION', BY W. E. B. DU BOIS (HARCOURT, NEW YORK, 1935); 'THE AUTOBIOGRAPHY OF W. E. B. DU BOIS', (INTERNATIONAL PUBLISHERS, NEW YORK, 1963).

Jean Dubuffet (French, b. 1901): painter. Dubuffet was known in Paris from 1918 onwards as a wine-merchant who played the bagpipes, made marionettes, corresponded with lunatics and their keepers, got sent to the glasshouse for indiscipline when in the army, wrote like a caustic angel and poured scorn on Art with a capital A. In 1944, when pre-war standards of ingratiation still dominated the Parisian art scene, Dubuffet turned up as a full-time painter whose work was nearer to the graffiti of factory-wall ("the art of the ordinary man") and mental home than to conventional painting. His art came in at the back door of life and sought out materials so crude, and so close to everyday life, that people had discarded them as irredeemable. Dubuffet reacted to a blank wall, or a patch of northern earth, or a beat-up table-top, as other painters reacted to the Montagne Ste Victoire. All chance aggregations of physical matter fired his imagination; and as he had also a prehensile intelligence and a colossal capacity for work, it turned out over the next 25 years that he was not a blasphemer after all, and that his collocations of anthracite, vine stalks, salad baskets, butterfly-wings, steel wool, straw and tar were the appointed successors to the paintings of Bonnard and Matisse. **J. R.**

CATALOGUE OF DUBUFFET EXHIBITION, BY A. BOWNESS (ARTS COUNCIL 1966).

Marcel Duchamp (French, 1887–1968): artist. Duchamp throughout his long life personified the idea of definitive invention in art. By 1913 he had added something to caricature, something to post-Impressionism, something to Futurism. He touched – lightly, but once and for all – on the potential of Dada, Surrealism, Pop art, and Op art. He was a master of the concise statement that left nothing unsaid: among many such that have achieved legendary status, the signed urinal (*Fountain*, 1917) and the moustached Mona Lisa (1919) stand out. He redefined the whole notion of 'art'; many of his ideas gained universal currency in other and feebler hands, but Duchamp saw to it that his larger and more complex works – above all, that panorama of his intentions which is known as the *Large Glass* (1915–23) – would resist all attempts at analysis. A man of seraphic and disinterested nature, Duchamp was honoured in Paris, in New York and in London as much for his personal example as for what he did. And it was revealed after his death that for 20 years he had been working in secret on a complete room – a synthesis of all his preoccupations – which scotched the legend that he had abandoned art in middle life. **J. R.**

'MARCEL DUCHAMP', BY R. LEBEL (TRIANON PRESS, 1959).

John Foster Dulles (U.S., 1888–1959): diplomat. Appropriately, Eisenhower's Secretary of State was born and died in Washington, D.C. He was a lifelong member of the executive establishment, shuttling between Government diplomatic service and a large practice as an international lawyer. From Versailles (1919) to San Francisco (1945) and beyond, Dulles was there. Eisenhower made him Secretary of State in 1953. With the nation for client, he displayed a lawyer's virtues (canniness, thoroughness) and a lawyer's vices (dryness, distrust, addiction to fine print). Eisenhower (q.v.) said nice things about world peace: Dulles said hard things about the menace of world Communism. His words carried further; he travelled 500,000 miles to put his point across. Dulles was the prophet of 'brinkmanship', of 'liberation' for Iron Curtain countries, of an 'agonising reappraisal' of U.S. policy. At times his State Department seemed merely the visible tip of that mainly invisible iceberg the CIA (run by his brother Allen Dulles). Two ironies, though. First, episodes like the abortive Hungarian rising showed his theories to be without substance. Second, in retrospect his kind of sanctimonious bluff looked innocent when compared with the actual realism of American foreign policy in the 1960s. Dulles as Secretary of State spoke loudly yet did not carry a very big stick. **M. F. C.**

'THE WARFARE STATE', BY FRED J. COOK (MACMILLAN, NEW YORK, 1962); 'JOHN FOSTER DULLES: A REAPPRAISAL', BY RICHARD GOOLD-ADAMS (APPLETON-CENTURY-CROFTS, NEW YORK, 1962).

Isadora Duncan (U.S., 1878–1927): dancer. Isadora Duncan was the pioneer of the free dance as opposed to the classical ballet. She developed a simple system of movement "springing from the soul". The novelty and sincerity of this, plus the magic of her generous personality, captivated Europe. She danced to the music of Schubert, Gluck, Wagner and Beethoven, and her visit to Russia in 1905 influenced Fokine (q.v.) to develop freer movement and use 'serious', i.e. non-ballet, music. Believing noble movement made people live better lives, she established a free school in Germany which later moved to France, to the U.S. during the war, and back. Her many lovers included Gordon Craig (q.v.) and the millionaire Paris Singer. (Her two children by Craig and Singer were drowned.) She accepted an official invitation to the USSR in 1921 to found a school there, but was obliged to embark on desperate tours abroad to subsidise it (in vain). After a scandal on one such American tour she and her husband, the Russian poet Yessenin, were asked to leave the U.S. as 'Bolsheviks'. Her ambition was to perform Beethoven's Ninth Symphony with 1000 dancers; but she died poor, strangled by her scarf caught in the wheel of a motor-car at Nice. Isadora's influence is increasing every day. **R. B.**

'MY LIFE', BY ISADORA DUNCAN (GOLLANCZ, 1930, REISSUED 1966); 'DUNCAN DANCER', BY IRMA DUNCAN (WESLEYAN U.P., CONNECTICUT, 1966); 'THE TECHNIQUE OF ISADORA DUNCAN', BY IRMA DUNCAN (KAMIN, NEW YORK, 1937); 'ISADORA DUNCAN, THE RUSSIAN YEARS', BY ILYA ILYICH SCHNEIDER, TRANSLATED BY DAVID MAGARSHACK (MACDONALD, 1968).

Emile Durkheim (French, 1858–1917): sociologist. The questions Durkheim asked, the methods through which he investigated them and the answers he arrived at, laid the foundations of modern sociological thinking. What is the relationship between the individual and society? Durkheim's work – notably his classic study of suicide – made it clear that social phenomena exist independently of and externally to individual lives, and that social norms and pressures constrain individual behaviour into regular and, in aggregate, predictable patterns. What is the basis of social cohesion – why do societies hold together rather than disintegrate into anarchy? Durkheim emphasised the importance of some minimum degree of *moral* consensus, capable of underpinning all specific agreements or contracts, formal laws or regulations. From the inadequacy of such consensus in modern societies – their state of *anomie* – stemmed both persisting social problems (e.g., industrial unrest) and the high incidence of personal disequilibrium. How can modern society gain a more effective moral basis? Durkheim rejected a religious solution and urged institutional reforms. Social life could be transformed only by changing social structures, not by attempts to change men or revive gods. **J. H. G.**

'EMILE DURKHEIM AND HIS SOCIOLOGY', BY H. ALPERT (RUSSELL AND RUSSELL, NEW YORK, 1961); 'EMILE DURKHEIM, 1858–1917', ED. KURT WOLFF (OHIO STATE UNIVERSITY PRESS, 1960); 'EMILE DURKHEIM', ED. ROBERT NISBET (PRENTICE-HALL, NEW YORK, 1965).

Bob Dylan (U.S., b. 1941): singer, composer. A major influence on the contemporary era of popular music, Dylan re-emphasised (after the 'soft' pop decade 1945–1955) the folk and blues elements of popular music, using them to comment socially, to protest and arouse. Artists from the Beatles to Jimi Hendrix show his influence. Beginning by reworking traditional folk melodies, Dylan made his mark in 1962. His songs ("stories" he calls them) quickly became the anthems of civil rights and nuclear bomb protesters: e.g. *Blowin' in the Wind*, and *The Times They Are A'Changin'*. Shouting against social injustice, racial discrimination, war and the U.S. establishment, he was soon able to fill concert halls with hushed, reverent teenagers, and to earn £100,000 a year. Latterly he has shifted his emphasis from specific protest to generally broody melancholy, with the words of his songs – always more important than the tunes, which he intones in a cross and elderly drone – becoming more personal, mysterious and poetic. He also runs a line in simple country sounds. **D. J.**

RECORDS: 'THE FREEWHEELIN' BOB DYLAN', 'THE TIMES THEY ARE A'CHANGIN', 'JOHN WESLEY HARDING', 'BLONDE ON BLONDE' 'NASHVILLE SKYLINE', (ALL LPs ON CBS).

Charles Eames (U.S., b. 1907): architect and industrial designer. With Marcel Breuer (q.v.), Eames has been the great furniture designer-innovator-liberator of our time. Yet, unlike most industrial designers, he has shown himself deeply and consistently concerned with the requirements of human comfort. He cut short formal architectural training at Washington University, St Louis, and was in his forties before making his major breakthrough – winning first prize, with Eero Saarinen (q.v.), in an international designs competition sponsored by the New York Museum of Modern Art for a moulded plywood chair (ply forming the seat, arms and back over a light metal underframe). Eames's further designs for chairs were shown in 1946 at

the Museum. His most influential design, prototype for countless international imitations, is his lounge chair and ottoman': moulded rosewood plyshell, black hide upholstery and steel base – the complete tycoon's comfort chair and status symbol. **R. H.**

'EAMES, CELEBRATIONS': A SPECIAL ISSUE OF 'ARCHITECTURAL DESIGN', SEPTEMBER 1966 (STANDARD CATALOGUE CO.).

George Eastman (U.S., 1854–1932): industrialist. George Eastman made photographers of most of us, but at the same time did more than any single man to make photography a vital tool of medicine, science, industry and education, as well as an art and entertainment. He found it in the wet plate era, and in the late 1880s introduced the first commercial transparent roll film. In 1900 the first of his famous Kodak Brownie cameras brought photography to the man in the street, with the slogan: "You press the button – we do the rest." In 1923 amateur home movies became practicable with the marketing of the Ciné-

MODEL OF BOB DYLAN BY SASKIA DE BOER; PHOTOGRAPH BY DAVID MONTGOMERY; LIGHTS BY SENSUAL LABORATORY

MODEL OF GEORGE EASTMAN BY ROGER LAW; PHOTOGRAPH BY DAVID MONTGOMERY

Kodak 16mm motion picture camera and projector, followed in 1932 by 8mm equipment. Eastman was inventor, technologist, organiser, leader and philanthropist. He gave away all his wealth – more than 100 million dollars – to art, medical, education and scientific institutions. **R. F. T.**

'GEORGE EASTMAN', BY CARL W. ACKERMAN (CONSTABLE, 1930).

Friedrich Ebert (German, 1871–1925): statesman. Ebert was the first President of Germany's Weimar Republic, so-called after the constitution adopted by the National Assembly of 1919 at Weimar, which lasted until the advent of Hitler in 1933. Trained as a saddler, Ebert

succeeded Bebel as leader of the Social Democrats in 1913. After the outbreak of the First World War, he was instrumental in obtaining Socialist support for the Kaiser's government. He strongly opposed social revolution and the proclamation of the Republic, but on Nov. 10, 1918, he was elected co-chairman of the Council of People's Representatives by the Workers' and Soldiers' Councils. On that day he also concluded the famous alliance with the High Command to preserve law and order and to fight Bolshevism; this alliance became the Weimar Republic's cornerstone. In January 1919 he was elected President of Germany, which he remained until 1925. The Workers' and Soldiers' Councils were defeated and all extremist coups drowned in blood. In 1923 executive power was transferred by Ebert to the war minister, to cope with growing extremism on the Left and Right, vast currency inflation, French occupation of the Ruhr, and Separatism in south and west. That the Weimar Republic survived was largely his merit: vitriolic attacks from the Right were his reward. **F. L. C.**

'A HISTORY OF THE GERMAN REPUBLIC 1918–1930', BY ARTHUR ROSENBERG (METHUEN, 1936); 'A HISTORY OF THE WEIMAR REPUBLIC', BY ERICH EYCK (HARVARD U.P., 1962); 'THE REICHSWEHR AND POLITICS 1918–1933', BY F. L. CARSTEN (O.U.P., 1966).

Sir John Eccles (Australian, b. 1903): neurophysiologist. Eccles has made especially important contributions to our knowledge of the way in which nerves interact in the spinal cord. He has also worked extensively on the cerebellum, that part of the brain which regulates posture and locomotion. Cells in the nervous system are not continuous: they make functional

contact with each other only at tiny localised areas, the synapses. These are gaps across which a nerve impulse must 'jump' to pass from one cell to another. Eccles inserts fine micro-electrodes into single cells in the spinal cord and records the very small electrical potential present. He can then measure precisely how this potential changes when the cell is excited via the synapses – or, even more interesting, when it is inhibited. The idea that some synapses are inhibitory instead of excitatory is an old one, but Eccles has shown inhibition physiologically as well as providing evidence about the physico-chemical events that underlie synaptic transmission. Together with recent electron-microscope studies, this work has enormously advanced our understanding of the working of the central nervous system.
J. B. M.

'NERVE, MUSCLE AND SYNAPSE', BY B. KATZ (MCGRAW HILL, 1966); 'THE PHYSIOLOGY OF SYNAPSES', BY J. C. ECCLES (SPRINGER, BERLIN, 1966).

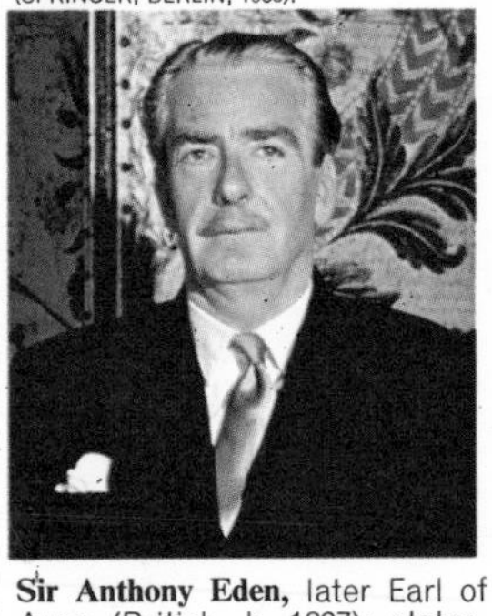

Sir Anthony Eden, later Earl of Avon (British, b. 1897): statesman. It is quite wrong to think of Eden in terms of Suez and the final disaster, for he was not born to be a Prime Minister. Even before Suez he was too determined to prove his political virility; and Churchill's manner did not suit him. One should remember him as one of the greatest Foreign Secretaries Britain has ever had: great not only in diplomatic technique, but in policy, in making the most of Britain's limited influence. A great persuader – remember the early days of the League of Nations, the Spanish Civil War (the proto-Vietnam), Greece, Trieste, the United Nations. At conferences and Foreign Affairs debates he was at his best, better than on platforms, where he received an adulation that he did not court. The highpoint of his career was not his resignation in 1938 (in protest against Chamberlain's attitude to Mussolini), for his motives were not understood by the public and he had supported Chamberlain (q.v.) in the Rhineland crisis, but in 1954, when he saved Europe by his diplomatic initiatives. **N. N.**

'THE EDEN MEMOIRS', 3 VOLS. (CASSELL, 1960–1965); 'DIARIES AND LETTERS', BY HAROLD NICOLSON, 3 VOLS. (COLLINS, 1966–68).

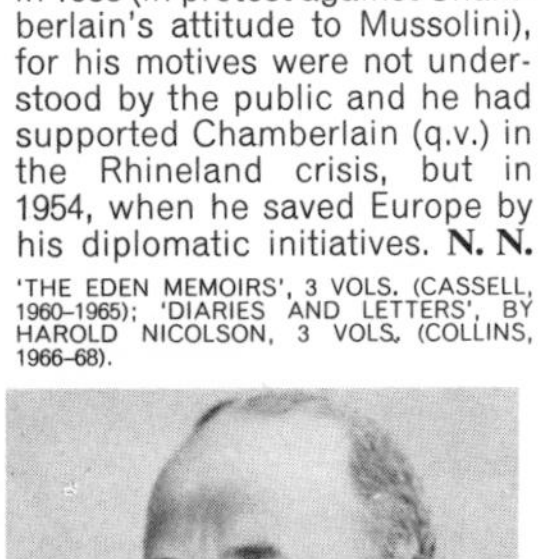

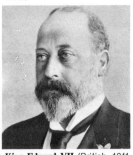

King Edward VII (British, 1841–1910): head of state. The exercise of social sovereignty was Edward VII's principal occupation during a 60-year apprenticeship as Prince of Wales. Denied access to cabinet papers upon which his mother Queen Victoria worked in seclusion, his pursuit of pleasure aroused criticism, but he put duty first upon becoming King in 1901. Impatient and genial, King Edward hated desk work and loved the gay world. He idolised his shy heir, George V, to whom he opened all official secrets. His tastes were earthy, like the man in the street's, but he staged a splendid show with inimitable panache, and few British sovereigns have been more popular, although some have earned greater respect. Edward VII inaugurated a self-adjusting British pattern of representative sovereignty which suited a society in process of ever more rapid transformation. But he was dismayed by Asquith's (q.v.) head-on clash with the hereditary principle in the House of Lords. He became profoundly despondent about the monarchy's prospects, and would have been cheered and surprised to know that he had strengthened its foundations substantially in 20th-century public opinion. **P. M.**

'KING EDWARD THE SEVENTH', BY PHILIP MAGNUS (JOHN MURRAY, 1964; PENGUIN BOOKS, 1967); 'KING EDWARD VII', BY SIR SIDNEY LEE, 2 VOLS. (MACMILLAN, 1925–1927); 'EDWARD VII AND HIS CIRCLE', BY VIRGINIA COWLES (HAMISH HAMILTON, 1956).

Edward VIII, later Duke of Windsor (British, b. 1894): exile. The great-grandson of Queen Victoria, Edward Albert Christian George Andrew Patrick David was called David by the members of his family: Queen Victoria insisted on the Albert.

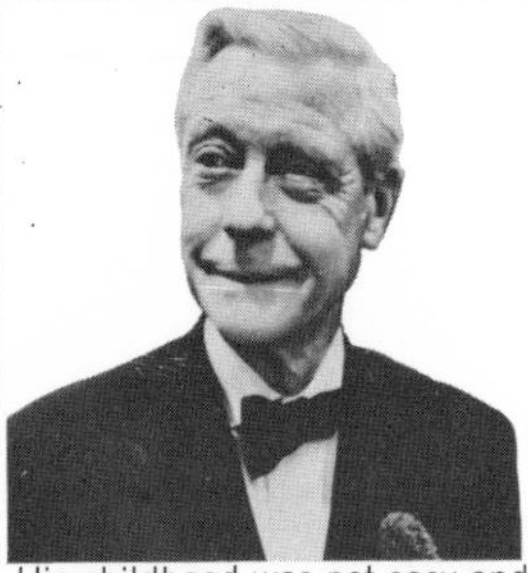

His childhood was not easy and his education was inadequate. Thereafter he had three public lives. The longest has been the last, since from December 1936 he has lived, mainly in exile, as Duke of Windsor. The shortest was his brief reign as Edward VIII. When he succeeded his father, George V, in January 1936, he was the first bachelor of mature years to ascend the throne since William Rufus. He was never crowned. As Prince of Wales (the 19th Prince but the first to seek to learn Welsh), he had become well known everywhere not only to his fellow-countrymen but in all parts of the world. He set something of a new style, and prided himself on meeting people "under all conditions and circumstances". His friendship with the American Mrs Simpson, who secured a divorce from her husband in October 1936, the second of her life, had turned into a love story which could only end in abdication. The 'abdication crisis' was dramatic and painful, but brief. Duty triumphed in Britain, and love abroad. Social divisions were revealed, but the monarchy was not weakened. **A. B.**

'THE KING'S STORY', BY THE DUKE OF WINDSOR (CASSELL, 1951); 'ABDICATION', BY B. INGLIS (HODDER, 1966).

Ilya Ehrenburg (Russian, 1891–1967): writer. Ehrenburg was for half a century the most durable link between the intellectual worlds of Russia and the West. Born into a middle-class Jewish family, by 17 he was a political

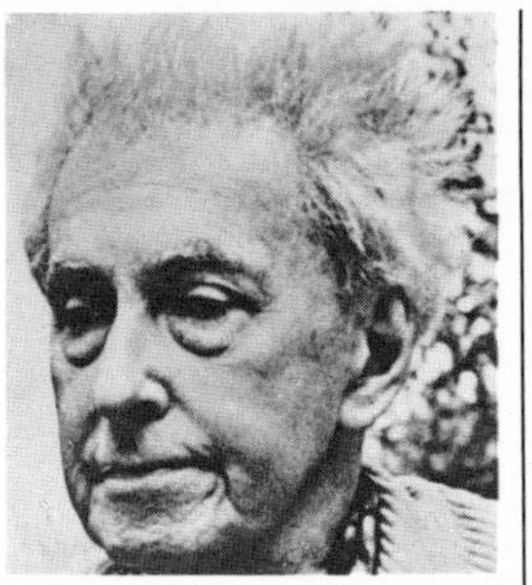

exile. In Paris, he met Lenin and wrote poetry. Like many artists his attitude to the Revolution was ambiguous, and he spent most of the next 20 years in the West as a sympathetic emigré – retaining Soviet citizenship and writing several novels around Socialist themes. In 1940 he returned to settle in Russia, where he gained enormous popularity (not least with Stalin) for his brilliant and prolific anti-Nazi war journalism. This helped him later when, despite his 'cosmopolitan' background, he survived Zhdanov's purge unscathed. During the 1950s he emerged as one of the leading liberals in the Soviet literary establishment. His novel *The Thaw* set the tone for the post-Stalin period, and his memoirs are among the most important products of recent Soviet literature. In them he rehabilitated many figures, argued for greater artistic freedom, and challenged Khrushchev's claim that at the time no-one had known of Stalin's crimes. **A. Q. D.**

'MEN, YEARS – LIFE', BY ILYA EHRENBURG, 6 VOLS. (MACGIBBON AND KEE, 1962–6); 'LITERATURE AND REVOLUTION IN SOVIET RUSSIA', BY M. HAYWARD AND L. LABEDZ (O.U.P., 1963); 'KRUSHCHEV AND THE ARTS', BY P. JOHNSON AND L. LABEDZ (M.I.T. PRESS, CAMBRIDGE, MASS., 1965); 'SOVIET RUSSIAN LITERATURE', BY MARC SLONIM (O.U.P., 1964).

Paul Ehrlich (German, 1854–1915): immunologist. Paul Ehrlich is not only the father of modern chemotherapy, his work has also led to today's scientists being able to tailor-make drugs to kill particular bacteria. In his

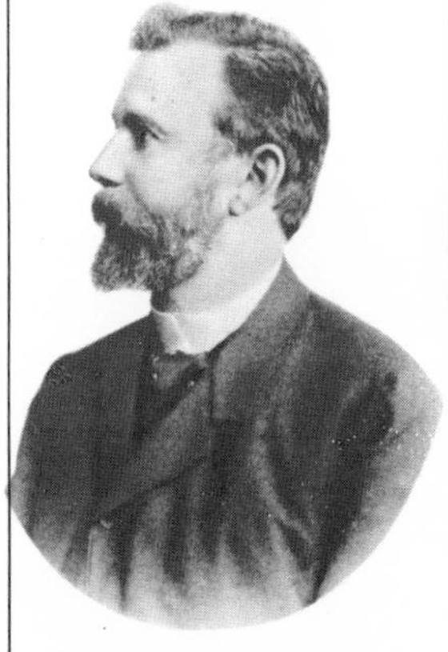

student days this visionary enthusiast used the synthetic aniline dyes, discovered by Perkins in Manchester, to stain the blood cells and other body tissues. His finding that the dyes coloured the various parts of the cells in different ways laid the foundation for the laboratory science of haematology. Even more important, since aniline dyes were known to kill bacteria in the laboratory, the next step was to see whether they kill them in the body without harming it. He expressed himself thus: "Antitoxins and antibacterial substances are, so to speak, charmed bullets which strike into those objects for whose destruction they have been produced." This selective chemical approach he pursued with fanatical devotion, using variants of organic arsenicals synthesised by his colleague Bertheim, to treat protozoal and spirochaetal infections in animals. At the age of 55, in 1909, his long search was rewarded by the discovery of salvarsan, or '606', which was effective in killing spirochaetes within tissues and which reigned supreme in the treatment of syphilis until the introduction of penicillin.
R. G. W.

'PAUL EHRLICH', BY M. MARQUARDT (HEINEMANN, 1949); 'THE HISTORY OF BACTERIOLOGY', BY W. BULLOCH (O.U.P., 1938); 'STUDIES IN IMMUNITY', BY P. EHRLICH ET AL. (JOHN WILEY, NEW YORK, 1910).

Adolf Eichmann (German, 1906–1962): Nazi administrator. Eichmann was the time and motion man of genocide. Personally squeamish, he noted on one of many visits to Auschwitz that flesh "cooked like stewing meat". Proud of his Teutonic efficiency, happy in his work if impatient for promotion, he thought "the worst offence a man can commit is to break his oath of loyalty". Established as an expert on the 'Jewish question' his moment came in 1941 when Heydrich, the head of his Main Security Office, received the order from Goering (q.v.) to implement the 'Final Solution'. For the next three years Eichmann's model bureaucracy ran the annihilation of European Jewry with unexampled speed and effectiveness; even under pressure from advancing Russians and a panicking Himmler (q.v.), Eichmann deported and exterminated 400,000 Hungarian Jews in two months in 1944. Abducted from oblivion in the Argentine in 1960, Eichmann sat before the world's curiosity and Israeli judges behind a bullet-proof glass booth, a slight twitch creasing his otherwise impassive face. Gnomic, contradictory, uncomprehending, unsuccessfully appealing for clemency; it was difficult to suppose that he went to his execution boasting, as he once had done, that he would die happy in the knowledge that he despatched five million enemies of the Reich.
S. S.

'THE FINAL SOLUTION', BY GERALD REITLINGER (VALLENTINE MITCHELL, 1968); 'THE CAPTURE AND TRIAL OF ADOLF EICHMANN', BY MOSHE PEARLMAN (WEIDENFELD AND NICOLSON, 1963); 'EICHMANN IN JERUSALEM', BY HANNAH ARENDT (FABER 1963); 'JUSTICE IN JERUSALEM', BY GIDEON HAUSNER (NELSON, 1967).

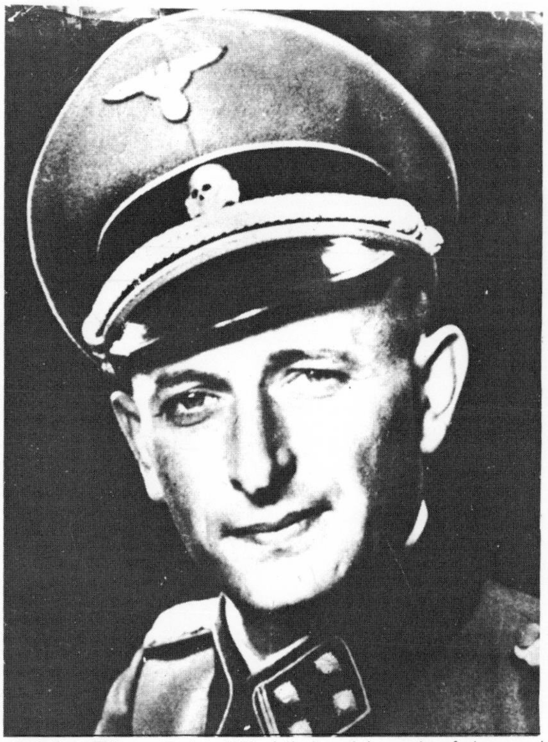

Christiaan Eijkman (Dutch, 1858–1930): bacteriologist. While studying beri-beri in the East Indies at the end of the 19th century, Christiaan Eijkman made an accidental observation that was to result in the discovery and isolation of the antineuritic Vitamin B_1. He noticed that hens in the chicken run of his laboratory had contracted a disease similar to human beri-beri. Search for infection proved fruitless, but suddenly the sick hens got better and no new cases appeared. Food was suspected: and it was discovered that the laboratory attendant had started using cooking rice from the hospital as chicken-feed three to four weeks before symptoms appeared; and that the hospital cook had been replaced and his successor objected to military rice going to chickens. The chickens' diet had reverted to normal a couple of weeks before the symptoms began to clear up. This was the clue that Eijkman needed, and a long series of feeding experiments showed that certain parts of rice – and other grain cereals – contained the antineuritic principle (now known as vitamin B_1) which could be used as a remedy by mouth or by injection. But it was many years before the practical value of Eijkman's observations were appreciated – he received his Nobel Prize only in 1929. Eijkman was among

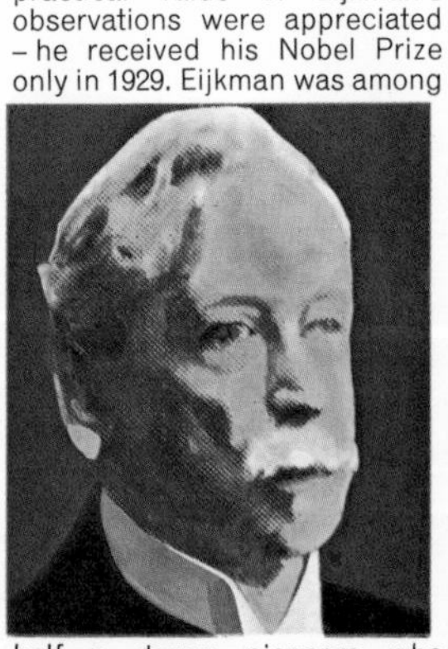

half a dozen pioneers who opened a vitally important field in human health: beri-beri is now treatable. **P. G. R.**

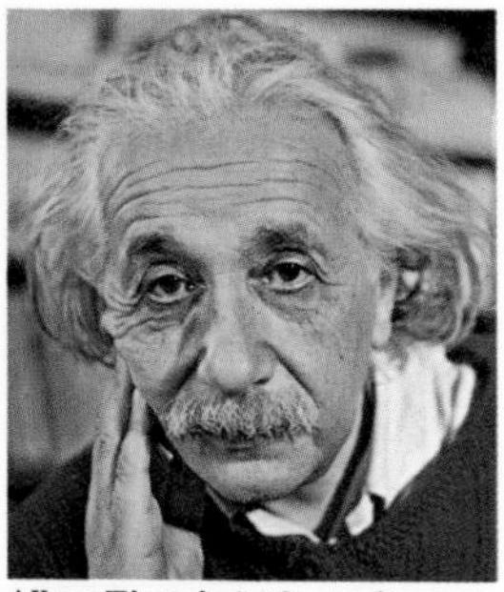

Albert Einstein (U.S., ex-German, 1879–1955): mathematician. The greatest scientist since Newton was refused a teaching post in Switzerland, so he joined the Swiss Patent Office as a technical assistant at the beginning of the century. It was during this time that Einstein produced much of his remarkable work. His special theory of relativity was an attempt to reconcile the laws of mechanics with the laws of electromagnetism. Working in the evening, after spending the day at the Patent Office, Einstein also became engrossed in the classical problems of statistical mechanics and their application to quantum theory: the result was a perfect explanation of the Brownian motion of molecules. He also looked into the thermal properties of light and his observations laid the foundation for the modern photon theory of light. In 1909 Einstein was made Professor Extraordinary at Zurich University, and in 1914 he was appointed director of the world-famous Kaiser Wilhelm Physical Institute and professor in the University of Berlin. There he was to make his most staggering contribution of all – his monumental paper announcing the general theory of relativity, which was published two years later in 1916. Einstein renounced his German citizenship in 1933 for political reasons and emigrated to America. After the Second World War he was an active figure in the World Government Movement, and was offered the Presidency of Israel (which he declined). **N. V.**

'ALBERT EINSTEIN: PHILOSOPHER-SCIENTIST', ED. P. A. SCHILPP (CAMBRIDGE UNIVERSITY PRESS, 1950); 'ALBERT EINSTEIN AND THE COSMIC WORLD ORDER', BY CORNELIUS LANCZOS (JOHN WILEY, 1965).

William Einthoven (Dutch, 1860–1927): electrophysiologist. After years of painstaking work, William Einthoven published in 1903 the design of his string galvanometer which was sufficiently sensitive to record the

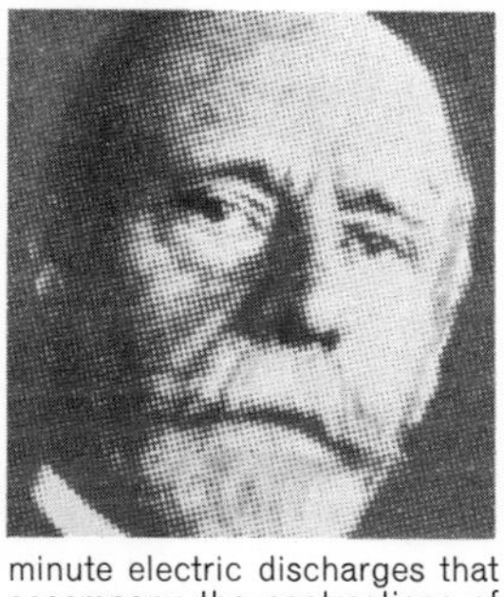

minute electric discharges that accompany the contractions of the heart. It consisted of a fine wire suspended between the poles of a magnet: the tiny oscillations of the wire were magnified some 600 times by a beam of light and its shadow registered on moving photographic plate or film. Einthoven then proceeded to formulate the basis of electrocardiography as practised in every hospital in the world today. He and Sir Thomas Lewis, of University College Hospital, used these tiny action currents of the heart to study and solve problems of rhythm so thoroughly that little more has been added in the last 50 years. They had not envisaged, however, the value of their instrument for the diagnosis of coronary artery disease, nor, perhaps, the artificial production of tiny electric currents mimicking the electrocardiogram and used to pace the heart when the human conducting system has failed. **A. L.**

'A HISTORY OF ELECTROCARDIOGRAPHY', BY G. F. BURCH AND N. P. DEPASQUALE (YEAR BOOK MEDICAL PUBLISHERS INC., CHICAGO, 1964).

Dwight D. Eisenhower (U.S., 1890–1969): general and statesman. In January 1961, at the end of his eight years in the White House, Eisenhower delivered a farewell address, warning the United States against the "military-industrial complex". The gesture was typical: benevolent, sincere yet second-hand, rhetorical, belated. He entrusted the address to speechwriters, who themselves coined the famous phrase. And, though a former general, he was willing to sound off on the dangers of the warfare state. American military heroes divide into the Ikes and the Macs: those who

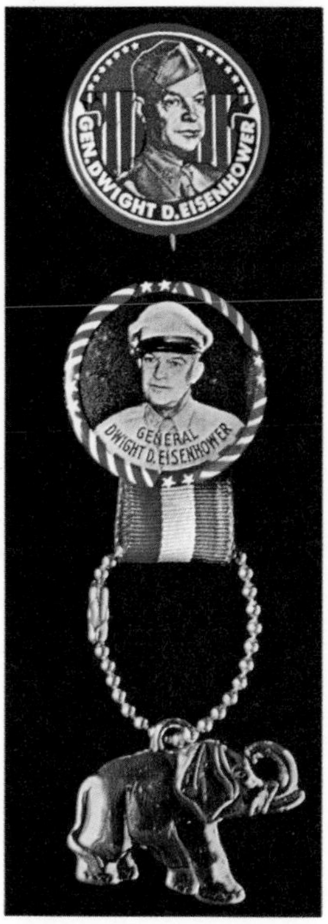

remain civilian in outlook, and those who like MacArthur (q.v.) play the generalissimo. West Point turned Eisenhower into a professional, who rose rapidly when the Second World War supplied the opportunity. But his ability was of the board-chairman variety, not that of the warrior-martinet. Luck and genial reliability brought him command of the coalition campaigns that terminated the war in Europe. Then eventually he yielded to the wooing of the Republicans – who saw him as a dream vote-getter. He was an unbeatable candidate and an unmemorable President: amiable, peaceloving, platitudinous. America could have done better and might have done worse. Ike was a nice guy plucked from Abilene, Kansas, to preside over the destinies of half the world for eight years. **M. F. C.**

'AMERICAN PRESIDENTS AND THE PRESIDENCY', BY MARCUS CUNLIFFE (EYRE AND SPOTTISWOODE, 1969); 'EISENHOWER AS PRESIDENT', EDITED BY DEAN ALBERTSON (HILL AND WANG, 1963); 'THE ORDEAL OF POWER: A POLITICAL MEMOIR OF THE EISENHOWER YEARS', BY EMMET J. HUGHES (MACMILLAN, 1963).

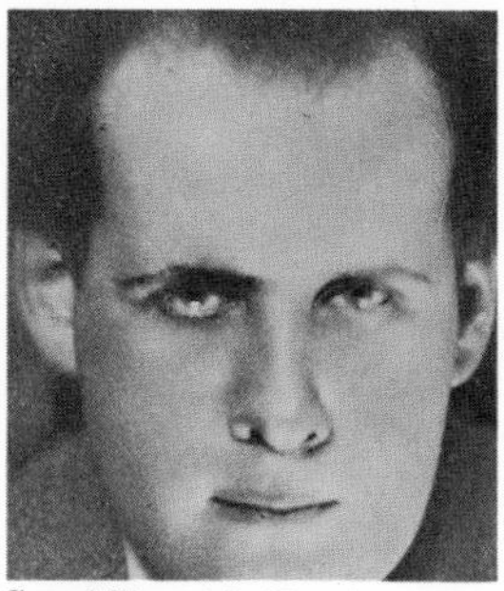

Sergei Eisenstein (Russian, 1898–1948): film director. Despite his frustrated career, Eisenstein remains the most influential artist in the cinema – through his films, his vivid theoretical writings, his teaching, and above all his personal dynamism and the wide cultural experience he applied to a cinema still, when he found it, in a comparatively unlettered stage of development. He became deeply involved in the avant-garde theatre of the heroic period of Soviet Revolutionary art and his first full-length film, *Strike* (1924), has all the vitality and extravagance of the avant-garde; but it equally reveals Eisenstein's life-long ability to associate influences as disparate as Leonardo, the Chinese theatre, Freud, and the fairground. *The Battleship Potemkin* – a reconstruction of an incident in the 1905 Revolution, which combined realistic material and dramatic and cinematic means – was electrifying, wholly original, and established a world-wide reputation. After this, however, Eisenstein succeeded in completing only one film (*Alexander Nevsky*, 1938) as he intended it. *October* (1927) and *The General Line* (1928) were revised to accord with changes in official policy. In Hollywood two scripts for Paramount were abortive. In Mexico *Que Viva Mexico* remained unfinished because of quarrels with its producer, Upton Sinclair. Back in the USSR many projects were rejected while *Bezhin Meadow* was halted and its director charged with 'formalism'. Only two of the three parts of the grandly operatic *Ivan the Terrible* (1942–6) were completed. **D. R.**

'KINO', BY JAY LEYDA (ALLEN AND UNWIN, 1960); 'WITH EISENSTEIN IN HOLLYWOOD', BY IVOR MONTAGU (SEVEN SEAS, 1968).

Sir Edward Elgar (British, 1857–1934): composer. Apart from some violin lessons in London, England's greatest musical laureate was self-taught, but in and around his native Worcestershire he gained practical experience in playing and writing for musical instruments as a young man. With his *Enigma Variations*, completed just before the turn of the century, Elgar established himself as the most significant English composer since Purcell with a work that still survives in the international as well as native repertory. Elgar's setting of Cardinal Newman's *The*

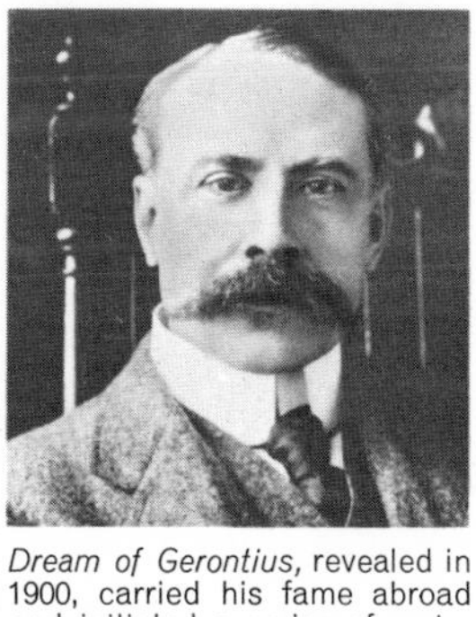

Dream of Gerontius, revealed in 1900, carried his fame abroad and initiated a series of major scores including two more oratorios, two symphonies, two concertos and *Falstaff*, one of the greatest of all symphonic poems. Inevitably Elgar's music reflected the Edwardian era, and he himself felt the times out of joint for his music in the last 15 years of his life. But Elgar was the undisputed leader of the renaissance of English music in our time. Although his work typifies a more opulent part of the 20th century, it has proved its powers of survival. **F. A.**

'PORTRAIT OF ELGAR', BY MICHAEL KENNEDY (O.U.P., 1968); 'EDWARD ELGAR', BY DIANA M. MCVEAGH (DENT, 1950); 'ELGAR, O. M.', BY PERCY YOUNG (COLLINS, 1955); 'LETTERS AND OTHER WRITINGS OF EDWARD ELGAR', ED. P. M. YOUNG (BLES, 1956).

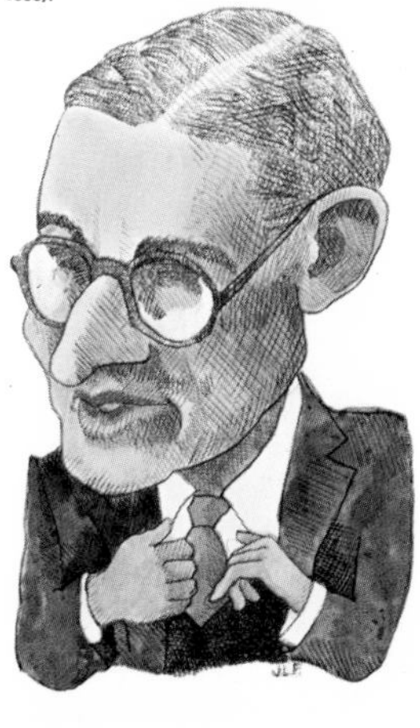

Thomas Stearns Eliot (British, ex-U.S., 1888–1965): poet and critic. Harvard-trained, with a particular interest in the French symbolist poets, in philosophy and Eastern religions, Eliot restored to poetry its intellectual respectability. Despite his anti-romantic bent and cult of impersonality, his verse betrays powerful feelings only partly disguised by the cultivated precision of tone and the sometimes ostentatious literary allusiveness and abstruseness. Eliot was the first to chart a 20th-century intellectual's troubled route from Ninetyish ennui and rueful wit through a grotesque sexual disgust to a final quasi-mystical Anglicanism. His poetry is vivid and dramatic in the imagist tradition. As publisher, editor and literary pundit, too, his influence upon younger writers was profound. His criticism exhibited a new interest in imagery rather than in ideas in poetry, and he was largely responsible for a revival of verse drama in the 1930s. He is the 20th century's great critic-poet in the tradition of Coleridge and Arnold. **J. L. F.**

'A READER'S GUIDE TO T. S. ELIOT', BY GEORGE WILLIAMSON (THAMES AND HUDSON, 1955); 'T. S. ELIOT'S POETRY AND PLAYS', BY GROVER SMITH (CAMBRIDGE UNIVERSITY PRESS, 1956).

Queen Elizabeth II (British, b. 1926): head of state. From her accession in 1952, the Queen has had to try and reconcile the claims of a modern and critical age with the traditions of an ancient and pomp-encrusted monarchy. Substantially helped and guided by her husband, Prince Philip, Duke of Edinburgh, she has gone some way towards giving a 20th-century look to the throne. But the context remains unmistakably British. The Queen – rather small, with beautiful eyes and a peaches-and-cream complexion, and a high, somewhat childlike voice – remains a conscious guardian of the rights due to a Sovereign: no bicycling among her people, on the Dutch model. In public, she often seems shy and distant; in private, though no intellectual, she can be charming, witty and wise, with an enviable memory for and grasp of the affairs of state which daily pass through her hands. Though by the end of the Sixties she had not been called upon to exercise her royal prerogative in the choice of a First Minister, it is still practically possible for her, in a crisis, to do so. Everything about her training and her personal view of her responsibilities suggests she would carry out this duty with disinterested concern for the unwritten Constitution. **F. T. R. G.**

'THE WORK OF THE QUEEN', BY DERMOT MORRAH (WILLIAM KIMBER, 1958).

Duke Ellington (U.S., b. 1899): bandleader, composer, pianist. Edward Kennedy Ellington is the greatest artist yet known in the jazz-popular music field, and is arguably the greatest artist in *any* musical field this century. He has been compared wtih Delius and Debussy, Mozart and Bach. Since 1927–8 he has led the world's No 1 jazz orchestra. The key players in the band (Johnny Hodges, Harry Carney, Lawrence Brown etc.) have stayed more or less continuously and Ellington writes for them as individuals. "Ellington's instrument is not his piano, but his orchestra," said Billy Strayhorn, who from 1939 until his death in 1967 collaborated almost telepathically with Ellington. As a composer Ellington has a wide range – from brilliant popular songs (*Solitude, Sophisticated Lady*) to major tone-poems and suites. Ellington (or Ellington/Strayhorn) has composed at least 2000 works but it could be 5000 since many pieces are not committed to manu-

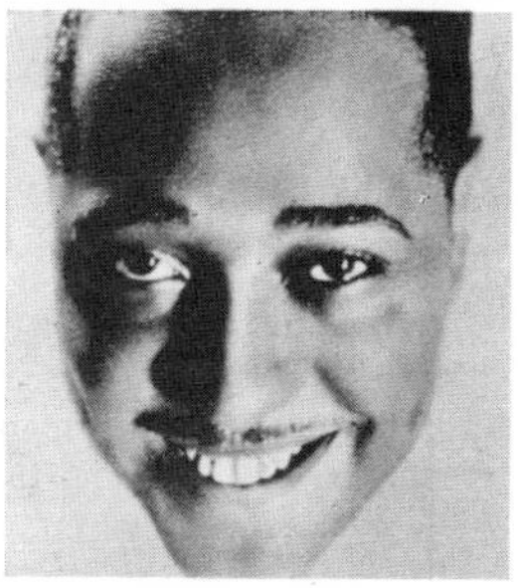

script. Major works include celebrations of Negro history (*Black, Brown and Beige*), 'programme' works (his Shakespearian suite, *Such Sweet Thunder*), semi-oratorios (*My People*), re-created classics (*Tchaikowsky's 'Nutcracker Suite'*), suites about places (*Far Eastern Suite*) – all created in the dust and heat of non-stop world touring and one-night stands. His band has the most *personal* sound of any this century. **D. J.**

'DUKE ELLINGTON, HIS LIFE AND MUSIC', ED. PETER GAMMOND (PHOENIX, 1958). RECORDS: ANY ELLINGTON LP, OF WHICH THERE HAVE BEEN ABOUT 100.

Havelock Ellis (British, 1859–1939): sexologist. The psychology of sexuality became a fit subject for scientific research through the books of Havelock Ellis. His brilliant and original gifts led him while still a medical student to launch and edit 'The Contemporary Science Series' of books. Many of them became classics, including his own *Man and Woman: A Study of Human Secondary Sexual Characters*. He put his Finals on one side and qualified in medicine through the London Society of Apothecaries. For years most medical men looked askance at his publications. But not all: he was elected FRCP. By everyday standards his marriage was remarkable: his wife was a lesbian and he had women friends. So there were crises. At one point she demanded and obtained a legal separation. But this made no perceptible

difference; their mutual devotion continued. Ellis said his marriage was successful because he and his wife met only at intervals. She lived in Cornwall, he, usually, in London. *Studies in the Psychology of Sex,* in seven volumes, was his life-work. It transformed the public attitude towards sexuality and made a tremendous impact on educated opinion. *Sexual Inversion,* the first volume – issued soon after the Oscar Wilde case – was judged to be obscene and publication of the *Studies* was banned in England; but it was arranged in America. Ellis's work did much to dispel 19th-century prudery. **E. A. B.**

'MY LIFE', BY HAVELOCK ELLIS (REVISED EDITION, NEVILLE SPEARMAN, 1967).

Charles Elton (British, b. 1900): ecologist. One of the most significant developments of 20th century biology has been a new emphasis on studying living animals instead of preserved specimens. Two important disciplines to emerge from this have been animal behaviour (or ethology) and ecology – the study of animals (and plants) in their natural environments; and Elton – Linnaean Society gold medallist in 1967 – is one of the world's greatest ecologists, especially significant for starting work on animal populations – crucial in developing the modern concept of evolution (his *Animal Ecology and Evolution,* 1930, was a landmark). The Bureau of Animal Population at Oxford, which he directed from 1932 to 1967, is now a world-renowned centre for sophisticated ecological studies. **J. B. M.**

BOOKS BY CHARLES ELTON: 'ANIMAL ECOLOGY' (SIDGWICK AND JACKSON, 1927); 'ANIMAL ECOLOGY AND EVOLUTION' (CLARENDON PRESS, OXFORD, 1930); 'THE PATTERN OF ANIMAL COMMUNITIES' (METHUEN, 1966).

John Enders (U.S., b. 1897): microbiologist. Professor Enders's outstanding contribution to the study of viruses began with his work on mumps (1943–46) when he showed that this virus could be grown in chick embryo, and after successive cultivations would lose the capacity to cause disease while retaining the ability to immunise against it. In this way the modified virus could then be used in the preparation of vaccines for the control of disease. The poliomyelitis viruses, until 1949, could be propagated in the laboratory only by inoculating monkeys. Enders showed that the viruses could be grown in cultures of non-nervous tissue of monkeys and man, and eventually, by this technique, an inactivated vaccine for poliomyelitis (Salk vaccine) was developed. The application of Enders's techniques in tissue culture led to the discovery of many other viruses and in 1954, the year he received the Nobel Prize for Physiology or Medicine, he succeeded in isolating the measles virus, which led to the development of a vaccine now widely used in measles prophylaxis. **D. G. E.**

Ludwig Erhard (German, b. 1897): politician. Conventionally depicted as the symbol of bourgeois prosperity and respectability, Erhard deserved better of his country and of Europe. Before 1945 his life was that of a successful businessman who opposed Nazism and spent difficult years as a result. In

1946 he was a founder-member of the Christian Democratic Union, and in 1949 he became the Federal Republic's first Minister of Economics. His brilliant success in this post, which he held until 1963, helped to ensure the 'German Economic Miracle'. His subsequent two-and-a-half years' tenure of the Chancellorship was no more than a postscript to his active political career. He combined an astonishing flair for timing with his liberal trade policies. By explaining the facts of the economic situation fully to the public he built up good relations with the trade unions, avoided strikes and kept wages and prices steady; he was given a completely free hand by Chancellor Adenauer (q.v.). A firm believer in European integration and the Western Alliance, Erhard's own Chancellorship was wrecked by Adenauer's bitter criticism, forcing his premature resignation. As an economist he had genius. **T. C. F. P.**

'THE ECONOMICS OF SUCCESS', BY LUDWIG ERHARD (THAMES AND HUDSON, 1963); 'GERMANY'S COMEBACK IN THE WORLD MARKET', BY LUDWIG ERHARD (ALLEN AND UNWIN, 1954).

Max Ernst (French, ex-German, b. 1891): painter. By 1919, when he made the wood relief called *Fruit of a Long Experience,* and by 1920, when he completed a long series of mixed-media pictures in Cologne, Max Ernst had pioneered much of what was to pass, over the next 40 years, as the newest thing in art. The work in question combined an outstandingly nimble and imperious fancy with the ability to outwit and render obsolete the ponderous procedures of conventional art. Ernst displayed further aspects of these same traits when in the 1920s, newly resident in Paris, he was in the van of the Surrealist movements as painter, inventor of the collage-novel, and the

master of a wide range of improvisatory or chance-dictated techniques. Born a German, he had the inwardness and the myth-making capacity of the German Romantics; but he had, too, the quicksilver wit and the lightning adaptability which characterise a French intelligence. Gifted from the outset with hallucinatory good looks, Max Ernst had also the ability to live up to them and to uphold the supremacy of the individual imagination. **J. R.**

'MAX ERNST', BY JOHN RUSSELL (THAMES AND HUDSON, 1967).

Edith Evans (British, b. 1888): actress. Dame Edith Evans is a shining example of the fact that great artists often owe their greatness to disadvantages which they turn to use. She has a difficult, swooping voice which she has made one of the wonders of the stage. Sometimes, as in Wilde's Lady Bracknell (*The Importance of Being Earnest*), it expresses shocked astonishment; sometimes, as in *The Late Christopher Bean,* the gentlest and tenderest love; sometimes, as in Shaw, brilliant argument. Her first famous part was Millamant in Congreve's *The Way of the World* (1924). Whatever she does, she flashes

and gleams. Though not conventionally pretty, her face, as James Agate said in a famous phrase, "is like a city in illumination". She is the greatest mistress in our day, perhaps in any day, of intellectual fascination and enchantment, the supreme example of the brilliance of brains. **H. H.**

'THE OXFORD COMPANION TO THE THEATRE', ED. PHYLLIS HARTNOLL (O.U.P., 1967).

Douglas Fairbanks Snr. (U.S., 1883–1939): film actor. The best-known photograph of Douglas Fairbanks shows him nattily clad in boots and riding breeches with Mary Pickford and Charles Chaplin (q.v.) perched on either shoulder. It represents, with some accuracy, the structure of United Artists, the company formed by the three stars, with the director D. W. Griffiths (q.v.) as fourth partner. Fairbanks came to Hollywood as a minor Broadway star. A series of comedies established him as the all-American male, a prophet of optimism and clean living, and his marriage to Mary Pickford, America's Sweetheart, was a triumph of sentimental logic. The swashbuckling hero of a long line of costume romances (*Robin Hood, The Thief of Baghdad,* and *Son of Zorro*), Fairbanks bounded exuberantly through elaborate and costly sets, righting wrongs and putting villains to the sword. "The good artist," he said, "has three things – enthusiasm, courage, and imagination. I have the first two." He was being uncommonly modest. *The Black Pirate* (1926) was the first Hollywood film to use the Technicolor process throughout, and his daring screen athletics raised movie stunts to the level of ballet. His last film, *Don Juan,* was made in England for Alexander Korda (q.v.), and was a qualified failure. With Fairbanks, the capering became the man. Words, however witty, were no substitute. **P. O.**

Juan Manuel Fangio (Argentinian, b. 1911): racing driver. Fangio is probably the greatest racing driver since the war – indeed of all time. An Italian, born in Argentina, he won five World Championships, and was team leader of Mercedes-Benz, Alfa Romeo, Ferrari and Maserati. He had unusual concentration, fantastic stamina, and great ability to keep his car balanced under all conditions. Like many at the top of their field, he is humble and sensitive: easy to approach, but difficult to know – almost like a cat. His greatest race was possibly the German Grand Prix of 1957. He didn't seem to stand a chance, having dropped 48.5 seconds behind due to a pit stop. He rallied round by beating the lap record of the 14.8-mile circuit time and again, and finished up by catching and overtaking his main competitors, Mike Hawthorn and Pete Collins, who were entering a corner behind the pits. He passed Pete on his left, and Mike on his right, within 200 yards of each other. This demonstration of brave, forceful brilliance was typical. It showed why – until he retired in 1958 – Fangio was the man that other drivers used as a yardstick to judge their own performances. **S. C. M.**

'FANGIO – RACING DRIVER', BY OLIVIER MERLIN (BATSFORD, 1961); 'MY TWENTY YEARS OF RACING', BY JUAN MANUEL FANGIO (TEMPLE PRESS, 1961).

ELL-FIS

King Farouk (Egyptian, 1920–1965): head of state. Farouk became king of Egypt in his teens, was deposed after the military revolution of 1952, and died in exile. It was his misfortune to be ruler of Egypt during the last era of a decaying social system, and regarded as the embodiment of the decay. He inherited a political structure based on a complex relationship between three forces: the monarchy (founded by his ancestor Muhammad Ali), the British (in occupation of Egypt since 1882), and the Wafd (the nationalist party whose aim was to end the

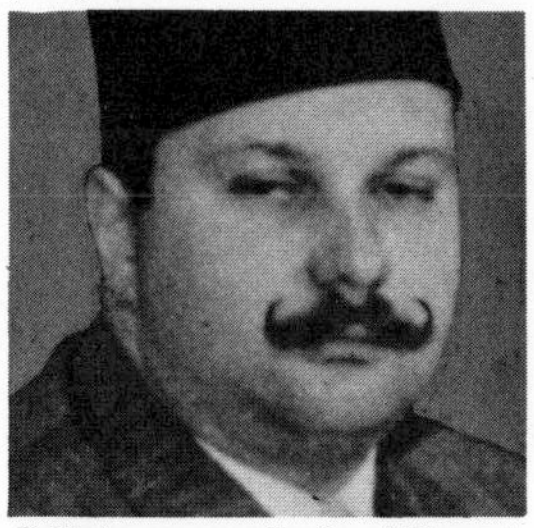

British occupation). Although he was intelligent and witty, the development of Egyptian society overtook him: the growth of population – of peasants and unskilled workers – the rise of a new educated class, and the spread of new political ideas on both Right and Left overwhelmed him. He himself contributed to the collapse: by his decision to involve Egypt in the unsuccessful war with Israel in 1948, and by the flamboyant vulgarity of his way of life. **A. H. H.**

'THE MODERN HISTORY OF EGYPT', BY P. J. VATIKIOTIS (WEIDENFELD AND NICOLSON, 1969); 'FAROUK OF EGYPT', BY B. S. MCBRIDE (HALE, 1967).

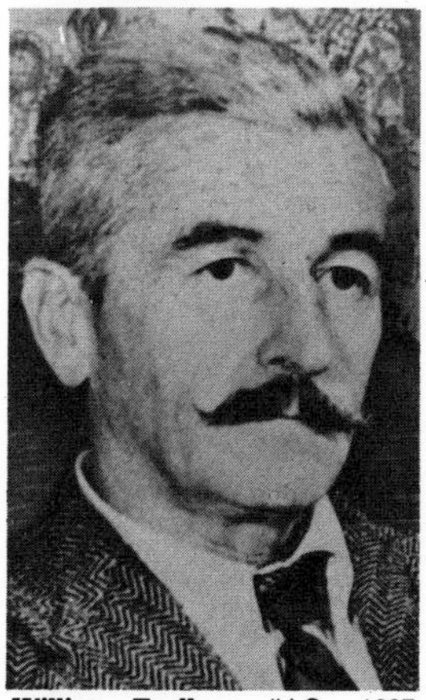

William Faulkner (U.S., 1897-1962): novelist. Faulkner aspired to create an "intact world of his own" like Balzac; yet his imaginary Yoknapatawpha County is not at all a fictional picture of his native Lafayette County, Mississippi, but a real place where he set his universally human legends. His characters (apart from the idiots) are all manically wilful and individualistic: typically, if they sell horses, the horses are unbroken killers, tied together with barbed wire, not rope. Moreover, his characters are normally too proud to explain themselves. Besides excelling at dark descriptions of physical experience he is ominous and dramatic without revealing some essential fact straight away, so the effect may come at the end, shatteringly. He was an uneven and sometimes pretentious writer, and paternalistic about civil rights, but he wrote five very good books: *As I Lay Dying; The Sound and the Fury; Light in August; Absalom, Absalom!* and *The Hamlet*. **A. E.**

'WILLIAM FAULKNER', BY MICHAEL MILLGATE (OLIVER AND BOYD, 1961).

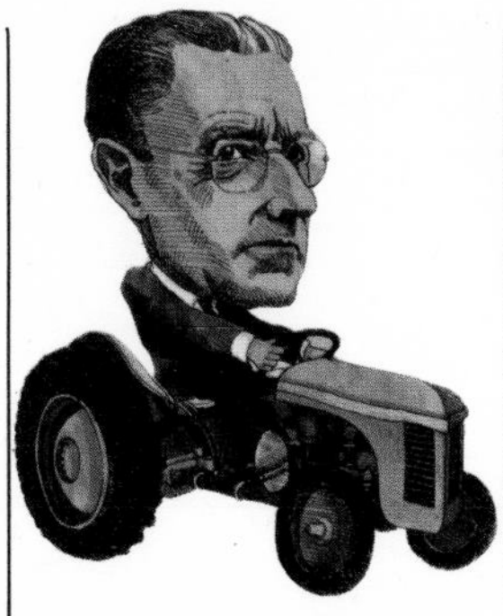

Harry Ferguson (British, 1884–1960): engineer. While supervising the maintenance of Northern Ireland's farm tractors during the First World War, Harry Ferguson saw the limitations of existing machines and determined to design improved ones. He succeeded brilliantly with the 'Ferguson system' – an ingenious 3-point linkage for attaching farm implements and tools to the tractor, combined with a hydraulic control system which gave finger-tip control from the driver's seat. The first prototypes were built in Belfast in 1933 and mass-production started at Huddersfield in 1936. Ferguson's revolutionary designs transformed the farm tractor into a mobile power unit, integrated with tools or implements, having great versatility and making possible rapid, widespread adoption of mechanised farming. **S. L.**

'FARM MACHINERY', BY C. CULPIN (REVISED ED., CROSBY LOCKWOOD, 1963); 'FARM MACHINERY', BY B. BELL (2ND ED., CASSELL, 1965).

Enrico Fermi (U.S., ex-Italian, 1901–1954): nuclear physicist. Fermi became interested in the neutron as soon as its discovery was announced by the British physicist James Chadwick (q.v.) in 1932. As Professor of Physics at Rome University, Fermi discovered that neutrons were particularly effective in triggering nuclear reactions when they were passed first through water or paraffin; such 'thermal' neutrons stayed in the vicinity of the atomic nucleus in question for a longer fraction of a second, and were therefore more easily absorbed than 'fast' neutrons. In 1934 he carried out the fateful experiment concerning the bombardment of uranium with neutrons in an attempt to create an artificial element heavier than uranium. Fermi did not then realise it, but he had a much bigger tiger by the tail – nuclear fission.

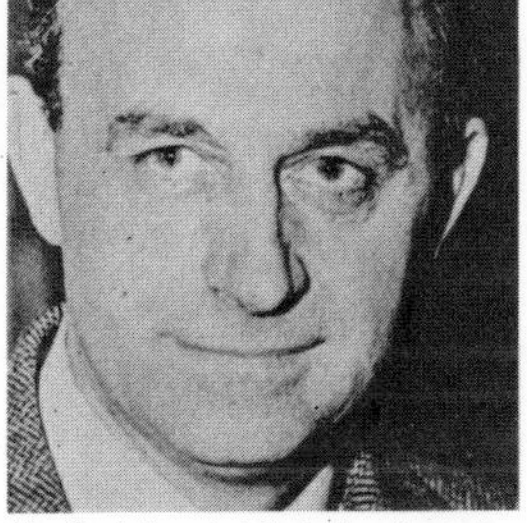

He fled Fascist Italy for America in 1938, and began to speculate about the possibility of a chain reaction. Although an enemy alien, Fermi was placed in charge of the U.S. Government wartime effort to construct the first self-sustaining nuclear reactor. Their experimental pile, in a squash court beneath the sports stadium at the University of Chicago, went critical for the first time on December 2, 1942, and thus opened the nuclear age. **N. V.**

'ATOMS IN THE FAMILY', BY LAURA FERMI (ALLEN AND UNWIN, 1955); 'ENRICO FERMI', BY PIERRE DE LATIL (SOUVENIR PRESS, 1965); 'ILLUSTRIOUS IMMIGRANTS', BY LAURA FERMI (CHICAGO U.P., 1968).

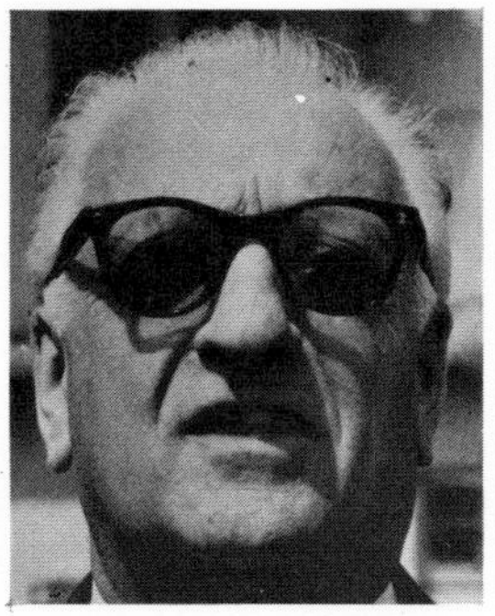

Enzo Ferrari (Italian, b. 1898): motor manufacturer. Racing Ferraris are bright red and synonymous with indifference to death. Born in Modena, Ferrari, able to drive by the time he was 13, grew up to have a more profound effect on snorty, glamorous, high-performance automobiles than any of his contemporaries. During the First World War, he shod horses for the cavalry and, afterwards, became a racing driver. Ferrari moved to the famous Alfa Romeo in the early Twenties, where he took over the running of the racing. In 1929, Alfa Romeo withdrew from the sport, and Ferrari formed his legendary 'scuderia Ferrari' as a small autonomous division of Alfa Romeo. The prancing horse symbol, carried proudly on all Ferrari cars since 1929, was presented to him by the parents of Francesco Baracca, Italy's First World War air ace. After the Second World War, Ferrari moved his factory to Maranello, producing in 1947 the first of his world-beating cars: they have won six Grand Prix Formula I world championships and a glittering galaxy of sports car races. Ferrari, the Napoleon of his sport, became a more secluded, enigmatic personality upon the death of his beloved son, Dino. But his singleminded obsession with cars and engines kept him going and has made him unique. When he dies the Ferrari racing car will probably become a ghost. **D. S. J.**

'MY TERRIBLE JOYS', BY ENZO FERRARI (HAMISH HAMILTON, 1963).

Louis Feuillade (French, 1873–1925): film director. Entering the cinema in its childhood in 1905, Feuillade made literally hundreds of films as Gaumont's artistic supervisor: everything from farces, burlesques, historical reconstructions and low-life dramas to literary, mythological and biblical adaptations. But his

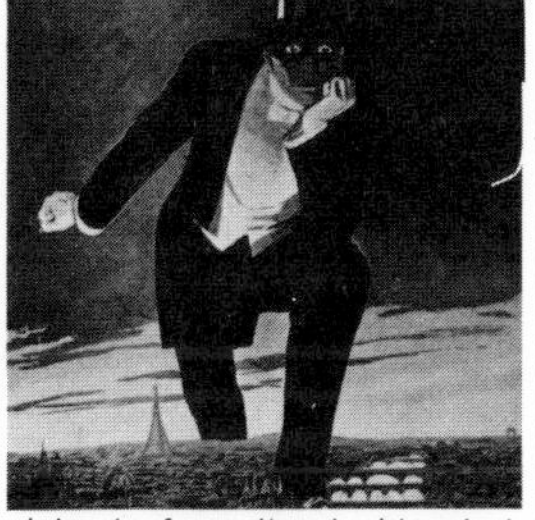

claim to fame lies in his gloriously preposterous, fantastically beautiful serials, where arch-criminals plotted the end of society, dispensing poisoned handshakes and terrible dooms with the gravest courtesy, while slinky heroines stalked the rooftops in tight black tights and miraculous escapes were a dime a dozen. Without *Fantômas, Les Vampires, Judex, Tih Minh* and *Barrabas*, there would probably have been no *Perils of Pauline* and no *Flash Gordon*. But Feuillade was also a supreme visual stylist, and under his hands the Paris and the Côte d'Azur of *la belle époque* become weird, haunted moonscapes of crumbling buildings, deserted streets and lurking menace. His films have been variously – and justly – hailed as the cinema's first masterpieces, as Surrealism incarnate, as poetic documentaries, and as criminal attempts to glorify crime. **T. M.**

'LOUIS FEUILLADE', BY FRANCIS LACASSIN (ARTICLE IN 'SIGHT AND SOUND', WINTER, 1964/65).

Gracie Fields (British, b. 1898): singer. Gracie Fields was the last great figure of the British music hall. With her pure soprano voice, with which she performed the most sensational loops and leaps, her overwhelming good nature, and her Rochdale accent, she exemplified the spirit of the provinces, being one of the first to bring its vitality and democratic exuberance to the metropolis. She is one of the most popular and admired figures in the British theatre, but has lived abroad, chiefly in Capri, since the beginning of the Second World War. Her generosity to charitable causes has become legendary. **H. H.**

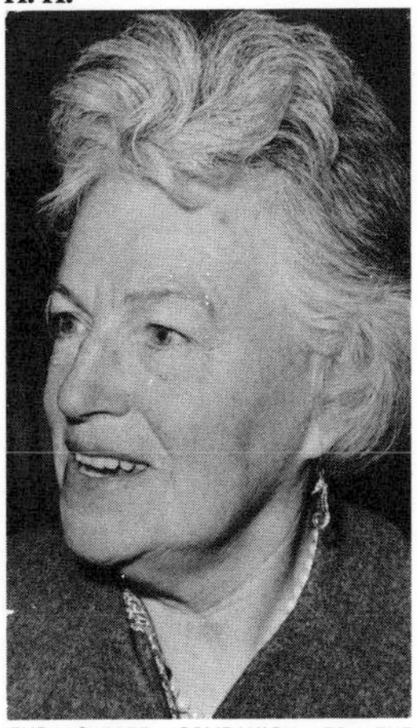

'THE OXFORD COMPANION TO THE THEATRE', ED. PHYLLIS HARTNOLL (O.U.P., 1967).

W. C. Fields (U.S., 1879–1946): film actor. The comedy of W.C. Fields was – and remains – the ultimate in screen misanthropy. He genuinely disliked and distrusted most people – especially bankers, cops, wives, mothers-in-law, children, animals and Negroes. Throughout 42 films, only 30 of which have survived, he waged war on a world which he felt, with some justice, had done him wrong. He was born William Claude (a name he loathed) Dukinfield, and fled home when he was 12, leaving his father knocked out cold in the barn. He became a superb juggler, toured the world – hob-nobbing on the way with Edward VII (q.v.), whom he called Ed – and sauntered into movies with *Sally of the Sawdust*. He made two-reelers for Mack Sennett, then with infinite guile negotiated a contract with Paramount which installed him as writer, star, and unofficial director of a number of brilliant, malevolent comedies including *It's a Gift* and *The Man on the Flying Trapeze*. His languid, rasping delivery was unique. His balefulness was inimitable. Fields was a con-man of genius out to bilk the society which habitually cheated lesser men. He feared death – "that fellow in the bright nightgown" – but, even as he lay dying, he remained bilious and intractable. Visitors hemmed his bedside, waiting for the pickings. Fields gathered his strength and spat in their faces. He died with perfect timing in the season which pained him most of all with its sentimentality and synthetic good cheer. It was Christmas Day. **P. O.**

'THE ART OF W. C. FIELDS', BY WILLIAM K. EVERSON (ALLEN AND UNWIN, 1969).

Hans Fischer (German, 1881–1945): biochemist. Fischer's main achievement was to investigate the biologically important pigments that occur in both animal and vegetable life: notably haemin in the blood and a range of pigments related to the green chlorophyll in plants. Blood is the main carrier of oxygen in all animals: without this function, life would cease. The oxygen carrier in blood is a compound called haemin that forms, together with a protein, haemoglobin. Fischer not only deduced

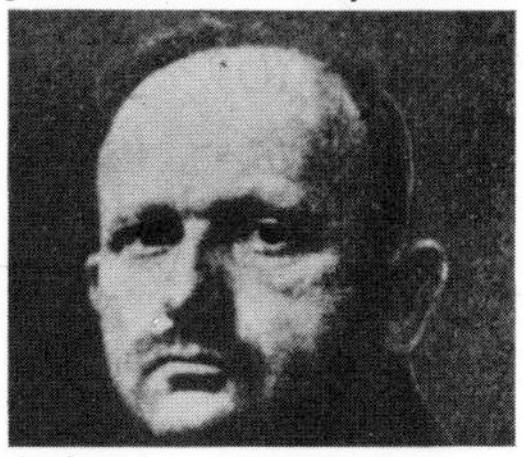

what the haemin part of haemoglobin is like: he synthesised it and so confirmed our knowledge beyond doubt. He also demonstrated that although biologically important pigments and their functions are immensely complicated, they are all related and can be dealt with logically. His researches on haemin and bile pigments are still being actively pursued. **P. J. F.**

'NOBEL PRIZEWINNERS IN CHEMISTRY', BY EDUARD FARBER (ABELARD-SCHUMAN, 1964).

Lord Fisher (British, 1841–1920): admiral. Thanks to Sir John Fisher, British naval primacy lasted through the first two decades of the 20th century. As a boy he had served on a sailing ship in the Crimean War; and he then played a prominent part in the modernisation of the Navy during the late 19th century. In 1904 the British Government decided that the Navy – increasingly challenged after a long peace – needed a powerful

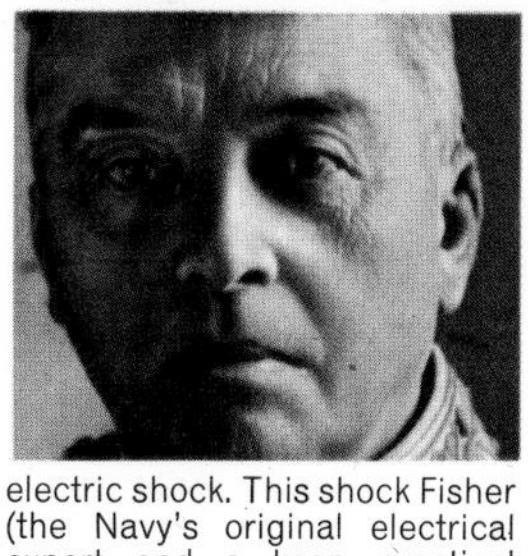

electric shock. This shock Fisher (the Navy's original electrical expert and a keen practical joker) jubilantly applied. His genius was for organisation, simplification, and the elimination of obsolescence and waste. He heightened tensions all round – between Britain and Germany, between the British Services and within the Navy itself. Fisher's Fleet sufficed in the day of trial: it sealed off the formidable Germans in the North Sea and safeguarded the blockade. Against much opposition Churchill (q.v.) restored Fisher as First Sea Lord (he had retired in 1910) in 1914. At the age of 73, Fisher destroyed von Spee, planned to land troops in the Baltic and created an armada; but in 1915 he opposed the Dardanelles expedition, walked out of the Admiralty, and demolished the Government. He was frustrated as head of the Board of Invention (1915–18), though his scientists shared the discovery of 'Sonar', a system for detecting submarines. **R. F. M.**

'FROM THE DREADNOUGHT TO SCAPA FLOW', BY A. J. MARDER, 3 VOLS. (O.U.P., 1961-66).

W.C. FIELDS in *Never Give a Sucker an Even Break* with GLORIA JEAN

A UNIVERSAL PICTURE

Sir Ronald Fisher (British, 1890–1962): statistician. R. A. Fisher fundamentally clarified and improved the statistical methods used in biological research. He developed the analysis of variance which makes it possible to disentangle and quantify reliably the contributions of numerous different factors to the outcome of an experiment. It provided a powerful means of separating the sources of variation in agricultural field trials, and it is also equally valuable in medical and operational research. As well as introducing the principle of randomisation, Fisher also did more than anyone to establish the use of significance tests in the evaluation of experimental

results. And of his major contributions to genetics the greatest was his theory of the genetical basis of natural selection. This satisfyingly combined Darwinian theory with genetics which, until then, had seemed to contradict one another. **W. A. O.**

'STATISTICAL METHODS FOR RESEARCH WORKERS', BY R. A. FISHER (OLIVER AND BOYD, 1958); 'THE DESIGN OF EXPERIMENTS', BY R. A. FISHER (OLIVER AND BOYD, 1960).

Sir Warren Fisher (British, 1879–1948): civil servant. Rich, handsome and occasionally explosive, Fisher from his schooldays devoted himself to preparation for the public service, which he entered in 1903. In 1919, not yet 40, he became Permanent Secretary to the Treasury and Head of the Civil Service, where he was happy to remain throughout the inter-war years. Since the great 19th-century reforms, the Civil Service had been steadily fragmenting into its separate parts. Fisher's great achievement was reunification under the Treasury as "a sort of General Staff". He shared in the standard passion of his class for economic retrenchment and forced through reforms which

ensured that departmental heads were strictly accountable for departmental expenditures. He was largely responsible for the regional and civil defence plans of the Second World War. If Fisher accepted the tradition that the Civil Service should be amateur and inward-looking, he also maintained and developed the vital aspects of that tradition; in an era when British

governments were slowly extending their influence in all walks of life, thanks to Fisher they had to hand the indispensable tool, an efficient and loyal Civil Service. **A. M.**

'CENTRAL ADMINISTRATION IN BRITAIN', BY W. J. M. MACKENZIE AND J. W. GROVE (LONGMANS, 1957); 'CIVIL DEFENCE', BY T. H. O'BRIEN (HMSO AND LONGMANS, 1955).

Ella Fitzgerald (U.S., b. 1918): singer. Discovered while singing at an amateur show in Harlem in 1934, Ella has since become that rarity, a singer that all jazz musicians respect and admire. Blessed with a flawless technique and impeccable intonation, she has the ability to transform the tritest pop song into a minor work of art. Her first hit record was *A-tisket A-tasket* in 1938. In 1946 she began working for Norman Granz – an association which was to prove of the greatest benefit to her, particularly as she became more selective in her choice of material under his personal management. She visits England annual-

ELLA FITZGERALD

ly, often appearing with the Oscar Peterson Trio (from 1948–52 she was married to the Trio's erstwhile bassist, the great Ray Brown). Her ability to sing ballads with exquisite taste and her prodigious natural technique at faster tempos – in particular her famous version of *Lady Be Good* – has set a standard almost impossibly high. **R. S.**

RECORDS: ELLA FITZGERALD, MUSIC FOR PLEASURE (MFP 1203); ELLA AND LOUIS, MUSIC FOR PLEASURE (MFP 1296).

Scott Fitzgerald (U.S., 1896–1940): writer. The American version of the myth of the Dying God flowered with the Jazz Age he helped to create and then wilted in obscurity till his death. His books are light-hearted adolescent day dreams, brilliantly observed, with increasingly tragic undertones. "It was fun when we all believed the same things. It was more fun to think we were all going to live together or die together, and none of us anticipated this great loneliness." *This Side of Paradise* (1920) was a best-seller; his stories include some of his best work (*The Rich Boy, Baby-*

lon Revisited). *The Great Gatsby* (1925) is one of the most perfect American threnodies on lost youth and the Prohibition era. Then followed the slow decline for which his wife Zelda was partly responsible. "She wanted me to work too much for her and not enough for my dream . . . I struggled on . . . till my heart collapsed, and all I cared about was drink and forgetting" (to his daughter in 1938). In those last years he wrote his near-masterpiece, *Tender is the Night*, faithfully depicting the break-up of his marriage, and was at work on an unfinished Hollywood novel, *The Last Tycoon*, when he died. His wife was burnt to death in a fire in a mental home in 1947. His blend of irony, regret and lyrical enjoyment, Gatsby's "neat sad waltz", has appealed to many other writers. **C. C.**

'THE FAR SIDE OF PARADISE', BY ARTHUR MIZENER (EYRE AND SPOTTISWOODE, 1951); 'SCOTT FITZGERALD', BY ANDREW TURNBULL (BODLEY HEAD, 1962, MAYFLOWER 1965); 'THE LETTERS OF SCOTT FITZGERALD', ED. A. TURNBULL (BODLEY HEAD, 1964).

Kirsten Flagstad (Norwegian, 1895–1962): soprano. Flagstad was the reigning Wagnerian sop-

rano from the mid-1930s to 1951, when she sang her last Isolde at Covent Garden. She came late to the big Wagner roles and international fame, and the lasting freshness of her voice had grown naturally through a long Scandinavian apprenticeship in the lighter roles and even in operetta. Her big chance came when she was invited to sing Sieglinde at Bayreuth in 1934; her triumph when she gave her first mature Isolde at the Metropolitan in 1935. During the following years she conquered Covent Garden, especially as Isolde and Brünnhilde; and when she reappeared in London after a 10-year interval it was wonderful to discover the vocal ease and buoyancy unimpaired and the golden notes as full as ever. Her temperament was placid, sensible, northern; she was an exceptionally accurate musician and made herself into an adequate and dignified actress; but it was the heroic power and radiant quality of the voice itself that made her unique and unforgettable. **D. S.-T.**

'THE FLAGSTAD MANUSCRIPT', BY LOUIS BIANCOLLI (HEINEMANN, 1953).

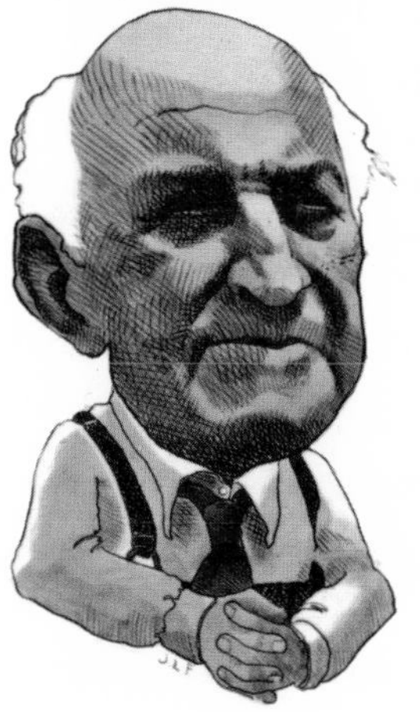

Robert Flaherty (U.S., 1884–1951): film director. Robert Flaherty never called himself a 'documentary' film maker but his credo of "showing life the way it is" was adopted, and often misunderstood, by admirers who seized on the term as a timely social slogan. Flaherty was a poet and a romantic. His first film, *Nanook of the North*, grew out of four expeditions he led into the Hudson Bay area of Northern Canada. The film was an immense success, and the commercial studios attempted to cash in on the new primitive style: The results, *Moana*, which was filmed in the South Seas, and *Tabu* were discouraging. But Flaherty rediscovered his true theme – man against nature – with *Man of Aran* in which his hero battled with breakers and basking sharks in waters off the Irish coast. He filmed *Elephant Boy* in India (and created a star in Sabu) but studio alterations made him feel rejected. What was out of fashion was his way of looking. His savage pastorals were no longer relevant. In 1948 his reputation was restored by his beautiful *Louisiana Story*, but the only solid offer of work it brought was that of making travelogues for Cinerama. The worst never happened. Flaherty died before completing his first Cinerama assignment. It was to have been a 60-minute newsreel of General MacArthur's (q.v.) triumphant return from Korea to Chicago—in 3-D and wide-screen colour. **P. O.**

'THE INNOCENT EYE', BY ARTHUR CALDER-MARSHALL (W. H. ALLEN, 1963).

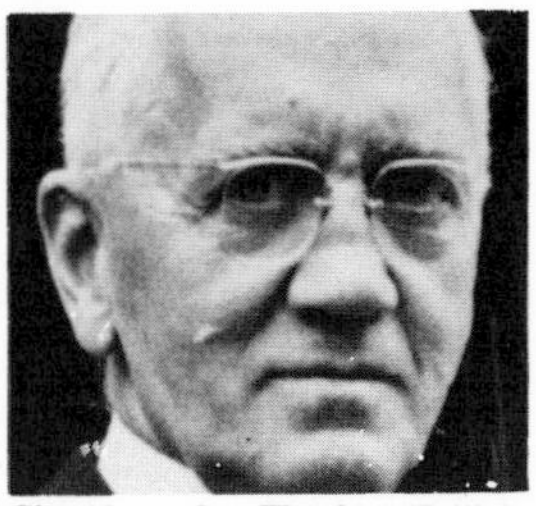

Sir Alexander Fleming (British, 1881–1955): bacteriologist. The discoverer of penicillin was an Ayrshire Scot who came to London in his teens and entered a business firm, but left to study medicine at St Mary's Medical School. He began research in the laboratory of Almroth Wright and soon showed his ability doing important work during the First World War on the bacteriology of infected wounds. In 1922 he discovered lysozyme, an important defence-agent in the human body. In 1928 he noted that an intruding mould, *Penicillium notatum*, that had contaminated a culture, was strongly antagonistic to many pathogenic microbes; even when diluted a million times the mould-juice (which he called penicillin) destroyed its microbic enemies. In 1929 he published details of its properties and prophesied its future clinical use. In 1940–41 purified penicillin was made available by Florey (q.v.) and others, and Fleming's prophesies were fulfilled. **V. Z. C.**

'THE LIFE OF SIR ALEXANDER FLEMING', BY ANDRE MAUROIS, TRANSLATED BY GERARD HOPKINS (JONATHAN CAPE, 1959).

Sir John Fleming (British, 1849–1945): engineer. Fleming's invention of the radio valve in the early years of the century was vital to the development of wireless. Edison had noticed in 1884 that if a metal plate was inserted in an electric light bulb and a connection made to the filament, then an electric cur-

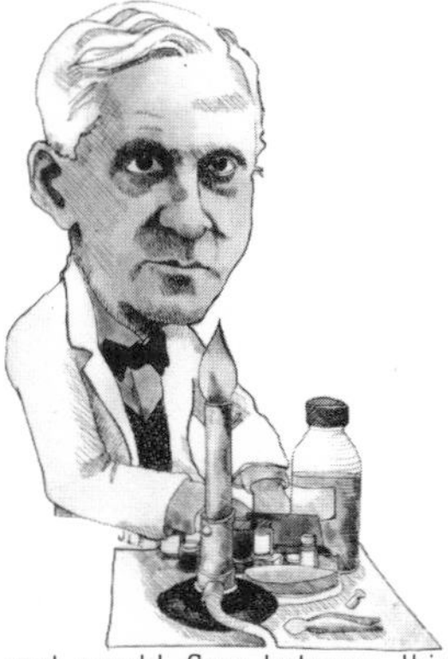

rent would flow between this plate and the lamp filament – and that the current would flow in one direction only. Fleming developed this 'Edison effect' and showed that it was because negative charges of electricity were emitted from the hot filament and could be collected by making the plate positive. In 1904 he invented the first 'thermionic' valve and used it as a rectifier for wireless signals. This worked better than the methods then in use, but it was left to Lee De Forest (q.v.) to invent the all-important amplifying valve. It was curious that the idea of a controlling mesh or grid of wires between the filament and the plate did not apparently occur to Fleming; but he must be given credit for the first patent on a thermionic valve. After some 65 years, several hundred million radio valves are switched on every day in the U.K. in domestic radio and TV equipment. **P. O. W.**

'FOUNDATIONS OF WIRELESS', BY M. G. SCROGGIE (ILIFFE, 1958).

Carl Flesch (Hungarian, 1873–1944): violinist. Flesch may emerge as the important figure in the history of violin teaching. A pupil of S. M. Grün and Marsick and hence, technically, a member of the Franco-Belgian school, Flesch made his first public appearance in Vienna in 1895, when his thoughtful musicality and the purity of his tone

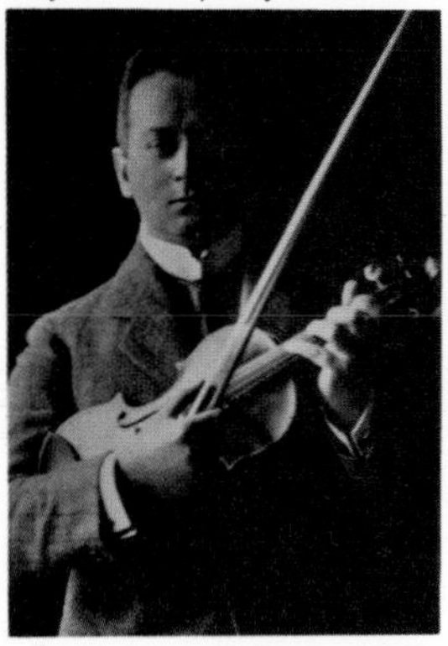

made an overwhelming impression. In 1911, Ysaye heard him play Nardini's D major Sonata and commented: "Ah, si j'avais la tranquillité de votre archet!" (Ah, if I only had the tranquillity of your bow!) He combined important teaching positions in various countries with an international solo and chamber-musical career. As a player, he was admired and respected rather than loved. His intense intellectual control may have resulted in a certain lack of spontaneity: he never quite succeeded in his double life. His works include what have become classical technical and educational writings, as well as numerous new editions of violin music and studies. A short list of his pupils summarises his influence on our age: Szymon Goldberg, Ida Handel, Ginette Neveu, Ricardo Odnoposoff, Max Rostal (q.v.) and Henryk Szeryng. **H. K.**

'THE ART OF VIOLIN PLAYING', BY CARL FLESCH, TRANSLATED BY FREDERICK H. MARTENS (CARL FISCHER, NEW YORK, 1924); 'THE MEMOIRS OF CARL FLESCH', TRANSLATED AND EDITED BY HANS KELLER (ROCKLIFF, 1957).

Friedrich Flick (German, b. 1884): tycoon. Flick, now the richest man in Germany, was born the son of a farmer and timber merchant in the Siegerland, east of Bonn. He went into steel, which was then controlled by the 19th-century dy-

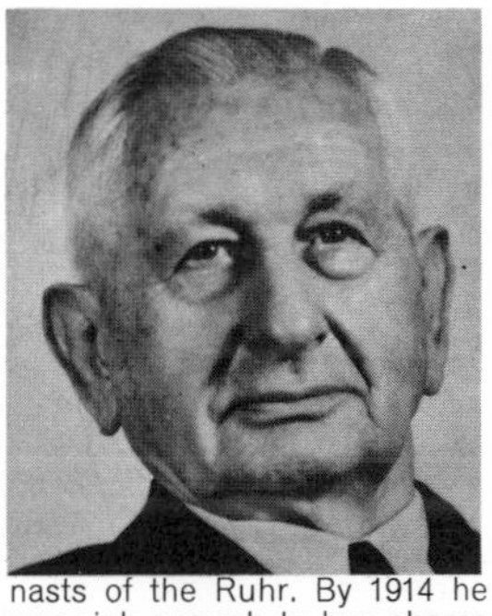

nasts of the Ruhr. By 1914 he was rich enough to buy shares and in 1919 he introduced highly profitable scrap techniques, but the Thyssens and Krupps (q.v.) were too tough. He went East to Silesia, and helped by ramping inflation (borrow, buy and pay back in virtually worthless currency) he built up huge coal and steel holdings. At the peak he controlled 10 per cent. of German steel, 8 per cent. of coal and 6 per cent. of lignite, before selling out in the 1930 slump. A close friend of Goering, and a major contributor to Himmler's funds, he ran the vast *Vereinigte Stahlwerke* complex for two years. He was sentenced to seven years' imprisonment at Nuremberg for using slave labour. Released in 1950, he skilfully used coal and steel compensation money to found his post-war empire – chemicals, paper, engineering and the dominant stake in Daimler-Benz and Mercedes. **P. W.**

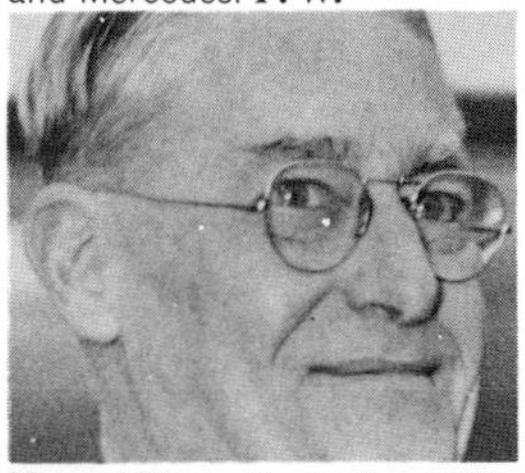

Howard Florey (Australian, 1898–1968): pathologist. Florey did much to make pathology in this country an experimental science and was a key figure in the discovery of penicillin. Early in his career he became interested in lysozyme, a substance present in a number of body fluids which brings about the dissolution of certain bacteria. He brought chemists into the Sir William Dunn School of Pathology, the first being E. B. Chain (q.v.), with whom he planned a systematic study of antimicrobial substances produced by microorganisms (antibiotics). The first substance to be looked at was Fleming's (q.v.) penicillin, which in 1938 was still uncharacterised. With the help of a group of workers penicillin was purified. As Professor of Pathology at Oxford, Florey carried out crucial experiments which demonstrated that it had remarkable therapeutic properties, and directed the treatment of the first patients to receive it systemically. **E. P. A.**

'ANTIBIOTICS', VOLS. I AND II, BY H. W. FLOREY ET AL. (O.U.P., 1949).

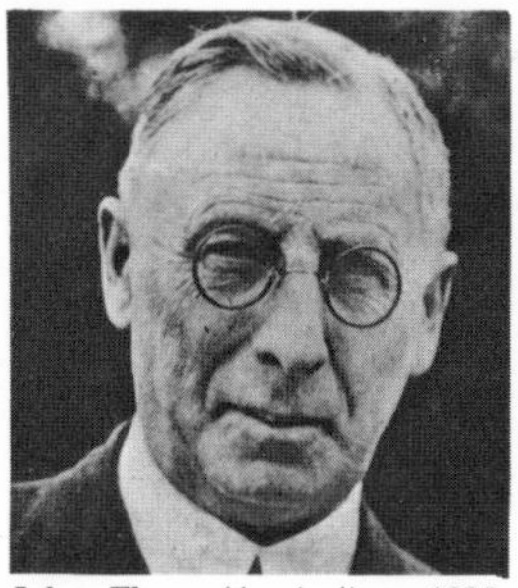

John Flynn (Australian, 1880–1951): missionary. The Rev. Dr John Flynn was the pioneer of the flying doctor service in the Australian outback. As a Presbyterian missionary, working with the sheep shearers and travelling by camel, he heard how during the First World War wounded were being transported by aeroplane. He immediately saw this was the answer for the outback's problem: a flying ambulance and a flying doctor. He inspired a young electrician, Alfred Traeger, to design a cheap radio transmitter, worked by pedals, and in 1928 the first flight was made by the Aerial Medical Service. The pedal radios were slowly distributed throughout the isolated homesteads of the outback, a network that today covers over 2 million square miles. Everyone in that huge area can be confident that medical help will be on hand within hours. **G. P. G. N.**

'FLYNN OF THE INLAND', BY ION IDRIESS (ANGUS AND ROBERTSON, SYDNEY, 1965); 'JOHN FLYNN – APOSTLE TO THE INLAND', BY W. S. MCPHEATT (HODDER AND STOUGHTON, 1963); 'FLYING DOCTOR CALLING', BY ERNESTINE HILL (ANGUS AND ROBERTSON, SYDNEY, 1947).

FIS-FON

Michel Fokine (Russian, 1880–1942): dancer and choreographer. Fokine's ideas and reforms made possible the success of the Russian ballet in the West. He was influenced by Isadora Duncan's (q.v.) freer movement and use of symphonic music. He drew up reforms of ballet, which he saw as decadent: ballet was to be an organic unity of music, painting and movement; male dancers and the *corps* were to have important roles; music and dancing should reflect accurately character, period and place. The Imperial Theatre was slow to adopt his ideas, but Pavlova (q.v.), Karsavina and Nijinsky (q.v.) followed him. He choreographed *La Mort du Cygne* for Pavlova. Diaghilev (q.v.) based his Ballets Russes in the West on Fokine's reforms and engaged him as *maître de ballet*. His ballets for Diaghilev included *Prince Igor*, *Les Sylphides*, *Cleopatra*, *Schéhérazade*, *Firebird*, *Petrushka*, *Le Spectre de la Rose* and *Thamar*. After a disagreement he left Diaghilev, returning briefly in 1914 to

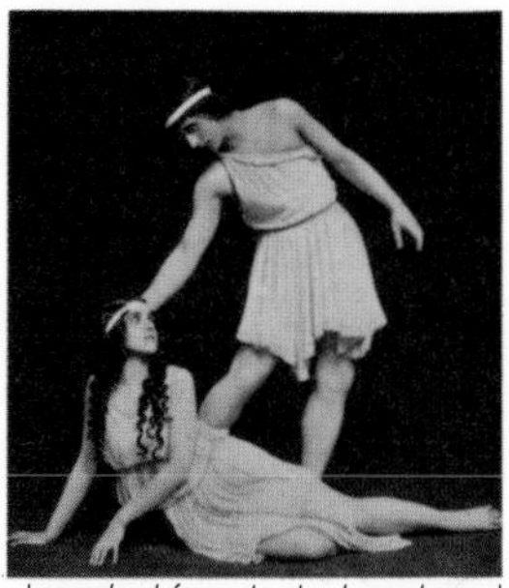

stage *La Légende de Joseph* and *Coq d' Or*, then worked in Russia, Denmark, Monte Carlo, and the Americas. He remained a respected teacher and choreographer till his death. **R. B.**

'MICHEL FOKINE AND HIS BALLETS', BY CYRIL W. BEAUMONT (BEAUMONT, 1935).

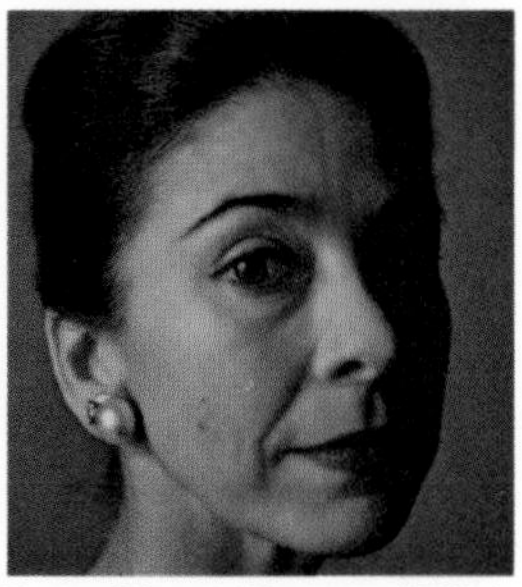

Dame Margot Fonteyn (British, b. 1919): ballet dancer. Fonteyn, besides being the most celebrated dancer in the world today, is the first and greatest British-trained prima ballerina. Her career has spanned almost the entire history of our native ballet. Three years after Ninette de Valois (q.v.) had founded the Vic-Wells Ballet in 1931, Fonteyn (born Hookham) joined the school at Sadler's Wells. When Markova left in 1935, de Valois promoted the 16-year-old Fonteyn to dance with Robert Helpmann: their partnership lasted for many years. Fonteyn took on the roles of Odette-Odile and Giselle. Her widely praised Aurora in *The Sleeping Beauty* followed in 1939. Fonteyn has gained much from her partners: Helpmann was succeeded by Michael Somes: then, in 1961, began the third great period of her career with Rudolf Nureyev. Her greatest artistic collaboration has been with Sir Frederick Ashton, who found her ideal for his choreography. She has acute musical sense, perfect control, subtle powers of characterisation. **R. B.**

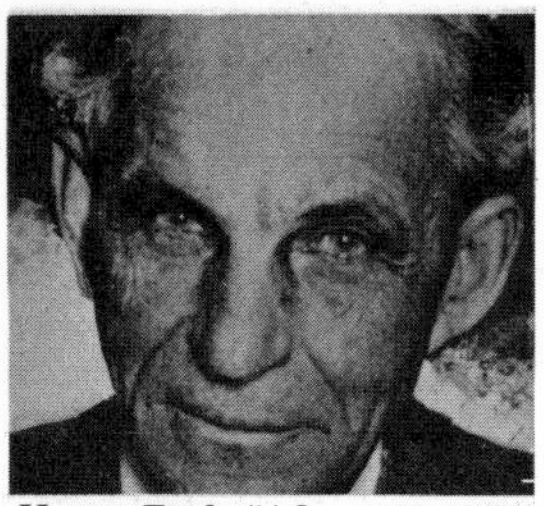

Henry Ford (U.S., 1863–1947): motor manufacturer. A farmboy who hated farming but loved machines, Ford built his first two-cylinder bicycle-wheel car in 1896, while working for Edison in Detroit. In 1904 he set up Ford Motor Company with a capital of $100,000 and in 1904, after breaking the world speed record on ice at Lake St Clair at a speed of 91.4 mph, he started planning the Ford Model T. It was the car that changed America, made every ploughboy a motor mechanic, launched large-scale mass production ("Bring the work to the man – waist-high") and sold 15 million units before General Motors knocked the bottom out of the market in 1927. Ford was tough and peculiar; he gave a $5 a day minimum wage in 1914, but in 1937 was still resisting trade unions (Walter Reuther, now head of United Auto Workers, was brutally beaten by Ford's private police force at "The Battle of the Overpass"). Ford fought off patent suits and dissident shareholders (in 1919 he resigned as president of Ford's and threatened to set up in competition). He ran the 1916 Ford Peace Ship mission (a flop), said "History is bunk" but built a vast historical collection, and was once pushed for President of the United States. And when he died, 100,000 people came to look at his body. **P. W.**

'FORD', BY ALLAN NEVINS, 3 VOLS. (SCRIBNER, NEW YORK, 1954–63).

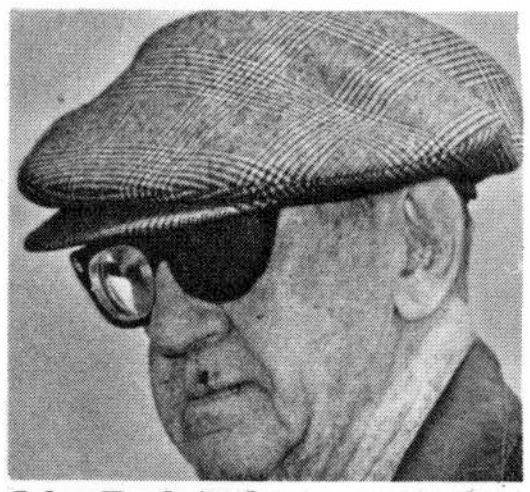

John Ford (U.S., b. 1895): film director. He who says "Westerns" says John Ford. Anyone who has ever been to the cinema has heard of *Stagecoach*, that classic tale of flight across the desert, Indians whooping in pursuit, cavalry charging to the rescue with all bugles blaring. Before it, Ford had made some 90 films; after it, another 35. Although he tackled everything from stark tragedy (*The Informer*) to Shirley Temple seducing the Indian Army (*Wee Willie Winkie*), from man's inhumanity to man (*The Grapes of Wrath*) to Graham Greene's whisky-priest (*The Fugitive*), most of the films are Westerns or tales of backwater American history, and it is there his genius lies. The story of the Mormon trek to Utah in *Wagonmaster*; of the moulding of a President in *The Young Mr Lincoln*; of old men dreaming of days of glory and the Confederate South in *The Sun Shines Bright*; of love, simple faith and loyalties in a whole string of films from *Fort Apache* to *The Horse Soldiers*, as lines of cavalry sweep stirringly over the skyline and bugles mourn as an old comrade dies. Pick your own favourite from *My Darling Clementine*, *She Wore a Yellow Ribbon*, *The Searchers*, or where you will. Each proves that Ford is the great legend-maker of America's pioneer past. **T. M.**

'JOHN FORD', BY PETER BOGDANOVICH (STUDIO VISTA MOVIE PAPERBACKS, 1968).

Lee De Forest (U.S., 1873–1961): inventor. De Forest's autobiography published in 1950 is entitled *Father of Radio*, and this is probably no exaggeration. Whereas Fleming (q.v.) in 1904 simply adapted an effect noticed by Edison to produce a

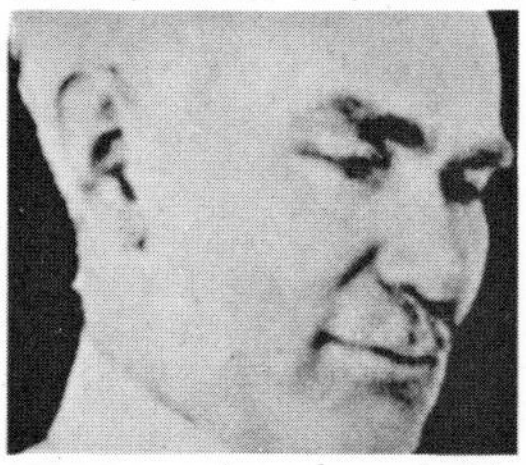

one-way valve for electric currents, De Forest two years later, invented the much more important amplifier valve. He did this by inserting a wire mesh, or 'grid' as it was called, to control the current. By this means the feeble signals from a radio aerial could be magnified to fill the Albert – or in his case Carnegie – Hall. It was this three-electrode, or triode, valve which really opened up the possibilities for broadcasting and electronics as they are today. There was wrangling over patents – both here and in the U.S. – in the early days of the valve. Yet there seems no reasonable doubt of the truth of De Forest's claims to originality, and his development was of immense significance. Without it we would not have had the modern systems of electronic communications: radio, radar and television. **P. O. W.**

'FOUNDATIONS OF WIRELESS', BY M. G. SCROGGIE (ILIFFE, 1957); 'INVENTION AND INNOVATION IN THE RADIO INDUSTRY', BY W. R. MACLAURIN (MACMILLAN, N.Y., 1949); 'FATHER OF RADIO', BY LEE DE FOREST (WILLCOX AND FOLLETT, CHICAGO, 1950).

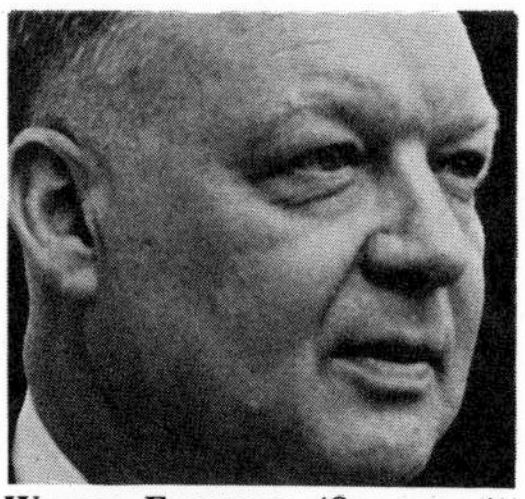

Werner Forssman (German, b. 1903): surgeon. Forssman's pioneering work in the diagnosis of heart disorder began in 1929 when he became concerned about the risks of direct injection of medicaments into the heart by thrusting a needle through the chest wall. These intracardiac injections were often given when the heart suddenly stopped during the induction of general anaesthesia. Forssman thought it would be safer to make the injections through a fine tube passed through an arm vein into the heart, and asked a fellow doctor to do it on him. The tube was passed as far as the armpit when Forssmann's colleague took fright, but Forssmann himself, with the catheter in this position, walked to the radiological department and, with a radiographer holding a mirror in front of the screen so that he could see his chest, he completed the insertion and took X-ray pictures of the catheter in his own heart. He showed how, with radio-opaque injections, he could outline the chambers and blood vessels of the right side of the heart. His work met with official disapproval in Germany, but it was developed in Portugal, then in the U.S. and Britain. Forssman's method has now become routine in the precise diagnosis of the complex defects of the heart in 'blue babies,' as well as in many other heart disorders, and it has made modern cardiac surgery possible. **J. McM.**

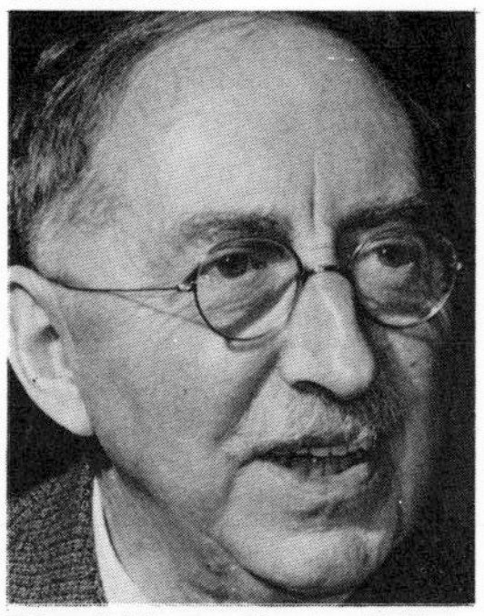

Edward Morgan Forster (British, 1879–1970): writer. E. M. Forster began writing fiction amid the turmoils of liberalism at the beginning of the century. When he finished in 1924, to turn to essays and journalism, he had created five novels that are major contributions to modern English fiction. The first three – *Where Angels Fear to Tread* (1905), *The Longest Journey* (1907), *A Room with a View* (1908) – are tough-minded social comedies. *Howards End* (1910) attacked contemporary society at its heart, hunting for a common culture for an England divided between its new businessmen and its new intellectuals. The best came after the war: *A Passage to India* (1924), a magnificent social novel about the meeting of races, and a complex symbolist work. All these books, and his other writings, carry the ferment of the liberal-humanist view of art and life, centred in duty to culture, love, the true voice of feeling, honesty and integrity of mind. But in our age liberalism is a paradox, threatened by its own generosity; Forster's work is shot through with its ironies, social, cultural and economic. He still stands for some of the best values of literary humanism. **M. S. B.**

'E. M. FORSTER', BY K. W. GRANSDEN (OLIVER AND BOYD, 1962); 'THE ACHIEVEMENT OF E. M. FORSTER', BY J. B. BEER (CHATTO AND WINDUS, 1962); 'FORSTER: A COLLECTION OF CRITICAL ESSAYS', ED. MALCOLM BRADBURY (PRENTICE HALL, N.Y., 1966); 'ASPECTS OF E. M. FORSTER', ED. OLIVER STALLYBRASS (ARNOLD, 1969).

James Franck (U.S., ex-German, 1882–1964): physicist. Franck was the outstanding experimentalist who with Gustav Hertz (q.v.) in 1914, published the results of researches clinching Bohr's (q.v.) quantum theory of the atom. At the Kaiser Wilhelm Institute of Physical Chemistry at Berlin-Dahlem they devised a very simple apparatus in which electrons bombarded gas atoms.

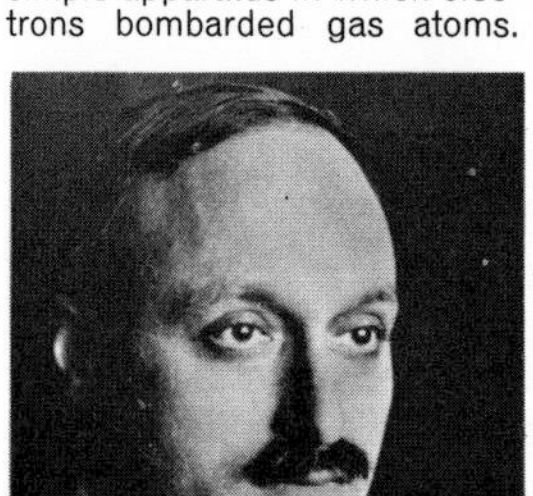

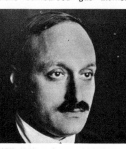

With it they demonstrated conclusively that the atoms could only take energy from the electrons – that is, become excited by them – in quite definite 'packets' or multiples of the fundamental quantum. Their work established that Bohr's theory applied not only to radiant energy but also to the energy of mechanical motion, as both Bohr and Einstein (qq.v.) had suspected earlier. Franck and Hertz received the Nobel Prize in 1925 for this important contribution to physics. Franck left Nazi Germany for the U.S. in 1935, and worked as one of the scientists on the Manhattan Project to manufacture the atom bomb; and he led the group who signed the 'Franck Petition' urging President Truman to demonstrate the bomb before allowing its use. Franck did important research on the structure of molecules, photochemistry and photosynthesis, but he is primarily remembered for providing one of the major experimental buttresses of the quantum theory. **P. H. S. S.**

'THE WORLD OF THE ATOM', ED. HENRY A. BOORSE AND LLOYD MOTZ (BASIC BOOKS, 1966); 'PHYSICS FOR THE ENQUIRING MIND', BY ERIC M. ROGERS (O.U.P., 1960).

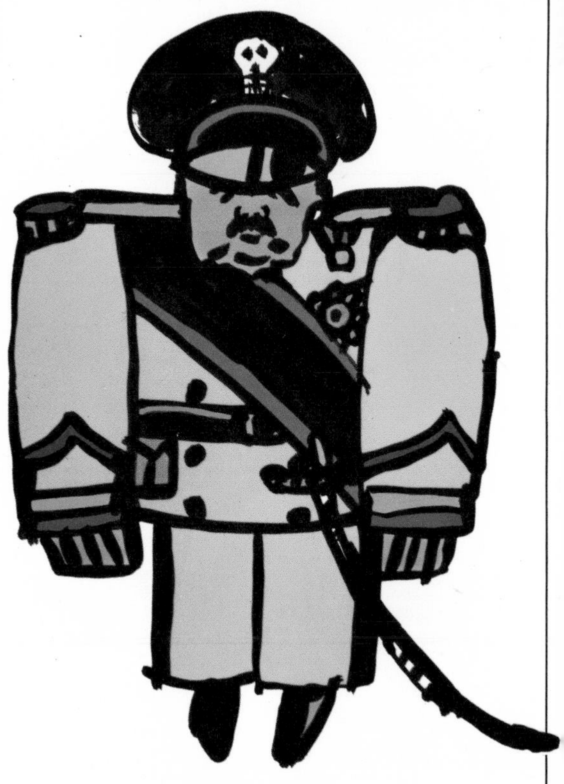

General Franco (Spanish, b. 1892): head of state. Francisco Franco Bahamonde, Caudillo of Spain, made a brilliant career in the Moroccan wars of the 1920s in which he was noted for his extreme bravery and administrative efficiency. He kept his politics to himself and, though a monarchist, accepted the Second Republic, joining the conspiracy against it late in the day. By 1937 he was uncontested political and military leader of Nationalist Spain. In the Civil War of 1936–9 he showed himself a good painstaking general who stood up to his German and Italian allies; and though in the Second World War he drove Hitler to distraction by his refusal to side with Germany, he was nevertheless ostracised by the victorious allies. As ruler of Spain from 1939 to the present day he has been a military autocrat in the 19th-century tradition rather than a Spanish edition of Fascist rulers; he secures his power by balancing political factions – monarchists, Falangists, technocrats, Christian Democrats – against each other, and by his undisputed hold over the army. He kept the domestic peace which was a precondition of economic revival in the 1960s, because no-one can face the prospect of another Spanish Civil War, but has failed to find a permanent political solution for Spain. His guarded attempts at liberalisation were suspended after student troubles in January 1969. **R. Ca.**

'FRANCO, A BIOGRAPHICAL HISTORY', BY BRIAN CROZIER (EYRE AND SPOTTISWOODE, 1967); 'FRANCO, THE MAN AND HIS NATION', BY GEORGE HILLS (HALE, 1967); 'THE SPANISH CIVIL WAR', BY HUGH THOMAS (EYRE AND SPOTTISWOODE, 1961).

Anne Frank (German, 1929–1945): diarist. Anne Frank wanted "to live even after my death", and through her diary she remains the most vivid and poignant symbol of Jewish suffering in the 20th century. Refugees in Holland since 1933, the Franks sheltered above an office in Amsterdam for three years before discovery and deportation. Anne died from sickness and starvation in Belsen. But for the threat of the Gestapo in the wings, the events Anne described would be unremarkable, yet her prose flashes with candour, charm and an understanding which, by her 15th birthday, had ripened into astonishing sagacity and detachment – she was perfectly aware of her probable end. Canonised with vapidity by Broadway and Hollywood, her diary endures, full-blooded, unselfpitying, a perpetual reminder that the enormity of the Nazi crime amounted not to the abstraction of 'genocide' but the murder of six million individuals. **S. S.**

'THE DIARY OF A YOUNG GIRL', BY ANNE FRANK (VALLENTINE MITCHELL, 1952); 'THE FOOTSTEPS OF ANNE FRANK', BY ERNST SCHNABEL (LONGMANS, 1959).

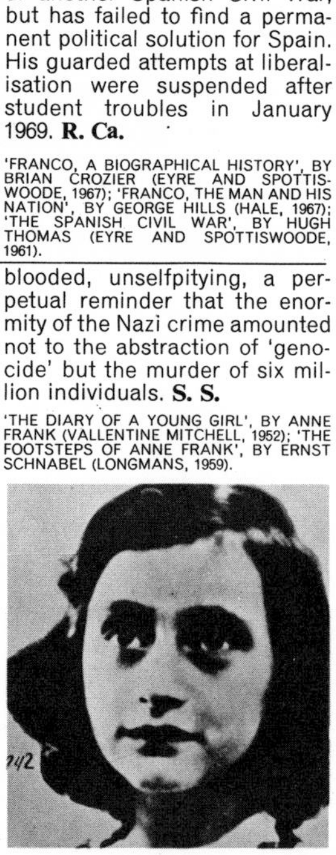

FRE-FUL

Charles Burgess Fry (British, 1872–1956): cricketer. C. B. Fry changed cricket into a matter for much ratiocination. He made runs as though by the book of arithmetic – 30,886 of them, averaging more than 50 an innings. He played his every stroke thoughtfully, yet with a rare athletic manliness. He was, in fact, an athlete; but he took sport in his lithe commanding stride. When he wasn't getting first-class honours in Classical Moderations at Wadham, establishing a world long-jump record, fishing, hunting and representing England at soccer, he was memorising hexameters, running a boys' training ship, editing his own magazine and declining an offer of the Kingdom of Albania. He was taken as an example of 'physical culture' (as the term was then used) by schoolboys of his epoch; *C. B. Fry's Magazine* was as influential on youth in the 1900s as the Beatles are today. His gifts were perhaps too versatile; he might have attained eminence as a literary critic, states-

man, or lawyer. After his 70th birthday, he entered his club, saw his friend Denzil Batchelor, and said he was sighing for new worlds to conquer, and was now proposing to interest himself in the Turf and attach himself to a stable. Batchelor, summing up greatness, actual and potential: replied: "In what capacity, Charles – trainer, jockey or horse?" **N. C.**

'LIFE WORTH LIVING', BY C. B. FRY (EYRE AND SPOTTISWOODE, 1939).

Buckminster Fuller (U.S., b. 1895): designer. Not an architect, but a philosopher and inventor, Buckminster Fuller has pursued the future forms of our environment with a mathematical logic reminiscent of the 18th-century Enlightenment. In 1927 he devised the Dymaxion House (dymaxion = dynamic + maximum efficiency), in which the modern home was seen not in terms of walled structure, but primarily in terms of mechanical services, the ducts branching out from a single central shaft. Fuller's Dymaxion Three-Wheeled Auto of 1932 similarly rejected the traditional coach-maker's craft-

work of Gropius's (q.v.) car body designs in favour of a totally machine-made streamlining. Fuller's fascination with mathematics led him in the Forties to the perfection of geodesic domes, built up from prefabricated metal frames of octahedron or tetrahedron shape; these covered the maximum floor area (384 ft diameter for the repair shop of the Union Tank Car Co. at Baton Rouge, Louisiana, 1958)

Sigmund Freud (Austrian, 1856–1939): psychoanalyst. Freud belongs to that very small group of men of genius who have revolutionised the way men think about themselves. His influence has spread far beyond psychiatry to affect our ideas of education, sociology, literature, painting and criticism. Some of his theories are contradictory, others incomplete, still others impossible to prove or disprove; but he provided us with so immense and so original a theory of mental functioning that even attempts to demolish it are themselves the source of new concepts. He did not invent the idea of the unconscious mind; but he certainly put it on the map. He asserted that children have a sexual life, and that, in this sphere as in others, the child is father to the man. He began unravelling the meaning of dreams. He first discerned the phenomena of transference. By his invention of free association he taught doctors to listen, to understand and to interpret, rather than to persuade or cajole their patients. Freud was the rationalist who realised that men are governed by emotion; the humanist who dismissed the bulk of mankind as trash, yet taught us compassion and tolerance; the pessimist who yet held out new hope for the relief of human suffering. As W. H. Auden put it: "To us he is no more a person/Now but a whole climate of opinion." **C. A. S.**

'AN AUTOBIOGRAPHICAL STUDY' BY SIGMUND FREUD (HOGARTH PRESS AND INSTITUTE OF PSYCHOANALYSIS, 1935); 'SIGMUND FREUD. LIFE AND WORK', BY ERNEST JONES, 3 VOLS. (HOGARTH PRESS 1953-57); 'FREUD AND THE CRISIS OF OUR CULTURE', BY LIONEL TRILLING (BEACON PRESS, BOSTON, 1955); 'AN OUTLINE OF PSYCHOANALYSIS', BY SIGMUND FREUD (HOGARTH PRESS), 1949); 'COMPLETE PSYCHOLOGICAL WORKS', BY SIGMUND FREUD, 24 VOLS. (HOGARTH 1951).

Robert Frost (U.S., 1874–1963): poet. Frost will be remembered with Pound, Eliot, and Lawrence (qq.v.) as a poet who broke with the polite and the poetic and restored the urgency of daily speech to poetry in English. Like Yeats (q.v.), Frost was a late Romantic who drew strength from a tradition his poetry tacitly rejected. Even in *A Boy's Will* (1913) subtle subversions of tone set him apart from the early Yeats and the Georgians. He entered the new century by the American back-door, almost without realising it. London reviewers, notably Pound, recognised the novelty and created an audience. In the best of Frost, tough-mindedness and a sense of the terrible qualify the poetry of natural things and the drama of man and wife in a country world. Frost gives himself to the familiar Romantic subjects – a brook, a tree, a bird's song – but only with reservations. Alone and unconsoled he looks into the night or glimpses in nature "design of darkness to appal". **R. A. Br.**

ROBERT FROST: 'THE EARLY YEARS, 1874-1915', BY LAWRANCE R. THOMPSON (JONATHAN CAPE, 1967); 'SELECTED LETTERS OF ROBERT FROST', ED. LAWRANCE R. THOMPSON (JONATHAN CAPE, 1965); 'POETRY AND THE AGE', BY RANDALL JARRELL (FABER, 1955); 'THE POETRY OF ROBERT FROST: CONSTELLATIONS OF INTENTION', BY REUBEN A. BROWER (O.U.P., 1963); 'IN THE CLEARING,' BY ROBERT FROST (HOLT, RINEHART AND WINSTON, 1962).

with the minimum area of enclosing surface – light, cheap and easy to dismantle. Fuller has since developed what he calls Tensegrity Structures (=tensional integrity). But the aesthetic implications of his obstinate belief in the harmonising power of reason are almost neoclassical, as in his glitteringly translucent dome for the U.S. Pavilion at the Montreal Expo in 1967. **N. J. W. T.**

'THE DYMAXION WORLD OF BUCKMINSTER FULLER', BY ROBERT W. MARKS (CHAPMAN, 1960).

Wilhelm Furtwängler (German, 1886–1954): conductor, pianist, composer. While Toscanini is a legend, Furtwängler has become a myth, and so influences those who never heard him. In 1920 he became Strauss's successor as conductor of the Berlin Opernhaus Concerts; in 1922 Nikisch's successor at the Leipzig Gewandhaus (at the same time he was conductor of the Berlin Philharmonic); in 1930 conductor of the Vienna Philharmonic. He refused the New York Philharmonic. In 1931 he was at Bayreuth, with Toscanini; in 1933 Director of the Berlin State Opera; in 1939 with the Vienna Philharmonic again. He conducted at many Salzburg festivals. A courageous opponent of the Nazis, he was described by Hitler as "one of the most unpleasant contemporaries I know"; yet he stayed in Germany as a conscious German and had to be de-Nazified – with the crucial help of Yehudi Menuhin. Among conductors, Furtwängler is recognised by many as the outstanding figure of the century. Those who played under both Mahler and Furtwängler have told of the uncanny similarity of approach; their utter commitment to the music, and spontaneity in performance. **H. K.**

'CONCERNING MUSIC', BY WILHELM FURTWÄNGLER, TRANSLATED BY L. J. LAWRENCE (BOOSEY AND HAWKES, 1953); 'WILHELM FURTWÄNGLER: A BIOGRAPHY', BY CURT RIESS, TRANSLATED BY M. GOLDSMITH (FREDERICK MULLER, 1955).

G

Clark Gable (U.S., 1901–1960); film actor. Clark Gable survived more bad films than any other star of his generation. Only three out of 90 offered him memorable roles: *Gone With the Wind, Mutiny on the Bounty,* and *It Happened One Night.* For the rest he gave his screen personality – tough, sexy, wise-cracking – another run-through. It was not altogether synthetic. Gable was a some-time farmer, ex-oilfield roughneck and lumberman – whose hefty physique had been developed long before he entered a studio gym. On top of the genuine fabric, however, was imposed a pulp fiction raffishness which could be tailored to fit any one of his interchangeable roles as gambler, gangster, oil rigger, test pilot, or war correspondent. His greatest asset was a natural magnetism which, in promotional hands, became sex appeal. It was shown in action with screen partners ranging from Jean Harlow (an equal match) to Norma Shearer (a snow-woman to be melted). MGM tended his image devotedly, and his elevation to the movie peerage – for years he was called King of Hollywood – was triumphant proof that the star system worked. Endearingly, Gable knew his limitations. He was unpretentious, workmanlike, and free of temperament. He was also completely a product of his time. When he turned freelance in 1954 he was asked if he planned to try directing a film as so many of his contemporaries had done. "Hell, no", he replied. "I haven't even learned how to act yet." He was an honest man too. **P. O.**

Dennis Gabor (British, ex-Hungarian, b. 1900): engineer. Professor Gabor first received wide attention for his flat, shallow 'picture rail' television receiver to hang on the wall and on which research is still being pursued; but in the world of technology he is better known for his invention of holography, a technique of reconstructing an image in three dimensions from a flat plate or film specially prepared by an optical-interference method. In 1949 his paper on 'Microscopy by Reconstructed Wavefronts' followed up his previous exposition that if an object were illuminated with a narrow beam of monochromatic light, the light waves would

interact to produce a pattern from which it would be possible to build up a complete three-dimensional picture of the object – a holograph. It was necessary to have 'coherent' light – that is, light with all the waves in step; and it was the coming of the laser in 1960 as a source of coherent light of great intensity that accelerated interest in Professor Gabor's ideas. **C. L. B.**

'MICROSCOPY BY RECONSTRUCTED WAVE-FRONTS', BY DENNIS GABOR (PROCEEDINGS OF THE ROYAL SOCIETY, 1949).

Yuri Gagarin (Russian, 1934–1968): cosmonaut. The first man in space was born of peasant parents in Smolensk, and had bitter experience of the Nazi occupation when two sisters were taken by the retreating German army. At the age of 17 he went to Moscow to attend a foundrymen's school and in 1955 enrolled at a flying school, got a licence and went on to jets all within the year. He applied for cosmonaut training in 1959 and joined the team at Tyuratam Cosmodrome near the Aral Sea the following spring. During a training session trainee cosmonauts were asked to rate one another as to who should be sent into space first and why. Sixty per cent. voted for Gagarin because of his "fitness, principles, modesty and simplicity". Three months later he became the first man in space, when he made one orbit in Vostok on April 12, 1961, and landed to a welcome fit for a Tsar. He died on March 27, 1968, when his MIG-15 training aircraft crashed in a field 30 miles east of Moscow. As the first human guinea pig, he showed that man could survive the gruelling journey into space, the extended period of weightlessness and the inferno of re-entry. **N. V.**

'ROAD TO THE STARS', BY YURI GAGARIN (THE FOREIGN LANGUAGES PUBLISHING HOUSE, MOSCOW, 1962); 'HISTORY OF ROCKETRY AND SPACE TRAVEL', BY WERNHER VON BRAUN AND F. I. ORDWAY III (THOMAS Y. CROWELL CO, NEW YORK, 1966); 'SOVIET SPACE EXPLORATION', BY WILLIAM SHELTON (ARTHUR BARKER LTD, LONDON, 1969).

Hugh Gaitskell (British, 1906–1963): politician. Hugh Gaitskell led the Labour Party in Opposition for seven years and died within sight of the Premiership. The tributes were heartfelt and world-wide. The conviction was unmistakable that here was one who stood on the verge of greatness. Chancellor of the Exchequer at the end of Clement Attlee's (q.v.) Government, he was soon recognised as a first-rate practical economist, fine parliamentary expositor, and admirable public servant. But he never really impinged on the public until he challenged the Labour Party Conference in 1960. He vowed

that, if defeated, he would "fight and fight and fight again''; and a year later he signally triumphed. This charming, civilised, unaggressive Wykehamist found himself engaged in a series of tremendous clashes with the Conservatives over Suez, with his own Party over nationalisation, Unilateral Disarmament and the Common Market. The passion of his morality, or (if one prefers) the morality of his passion, seems today to belong to a different world from ours. He set out to modernise the Labour Party, to render it responsible and practical, but he was just as concerned to carry on traditional ideals. He loved efficiency much, but justice a great deal more. Compared with Attlee (q.v.) he was a less astute politician, but a more articulate exponent of ethical principles. In integrity there was nothing to choose. **L.**

'HUGH GAITSKELL, 1906-63', ED. W. T. RODGERS (THAMES AND HUDSON, 1964).

George Gallup (U.S., b. 1901): pollster. Dr Gallup's name has been attached to a new dimension in modern politics. A psychologist by training, he left his Professorship in Journalism in 1932 to be director of research for a New York advertising agency. As a side-line he launched, in 1935, the American Institute of Public Opinion to undertake regular 'Gallup' surveys on public issues, using the established techniques of market research, for syndication across the States in a variety of newspapers. It was the presidential election of 1936 which put 'Gallup' polls on the map. Till then election-forecasting had been monopolised by the 'straw-vote', notably the *Literary Digest's.* That year, on the basis of more than two

million postal ballots, the *Digest* predicted a defeat for Roosevelt. Gallup, and others, by interviewing diminutive but 'representative' samples, correctly predicted Roosevelt's victory. This taught people that bigger opinion polls are not necessarily better. The discomfiture of the pollsters came in 1948 when they all wrongly predicted a defeat for Truman, but their subsequent record redeemed their reputation. **R. J. E. S.**

'GAUGING PUBLIC OPINION', BY HADLEY CANTRIL (PRINCETON U.P., 1944); 'SURVEY METHODS IN SOCIAL INVESTIGATION', BY C. A. MOSER (HEINEMANN, 1958).

John Galsworthy (British, 1867–1933): novelist. The author of *The Forsyte Saga* did not begin his literary career until he was nearly 30, after a highly conventional education: Harrow, New College and the Bar. *The Man of Property* (1906) was his first novel to achieve wide-popularity, and it remains an effective satirical exposure of late-Victorian bourgeois attitudes, seen both in the Forsytes' love of property and over-furnished houses, and in Soames Forsyte's proprietorial attitude to his wife, Irene. Yet, in D. H. Lawrence's words, "Galsworthy had not quite enough of the superb courage of his satire. He faltered and gave in to the Forsytes." In the later volumes that make up *The Forsyte Saga* and *A Modern Comedy* we see him writing in an increasingly sentimental and indulgent way

about Soames and the whole well-loved clan of the Forsytes, disconcertingly contradicting his original intentions. The nostalgic appeal of Galsworthy's novels is, however, likely to endure for a long time, even though the particular promise of *The Man of Property* was not fulfilled. **B. B.**

'THE MAN OF PRINCIPLE', BY DUDLEY BARKER (HEINEMANN, 1963); 'SELECTED LITERARY CRITICISM', BY D. H. LAWRENCE (MERCURY BOOKS, 1961); 'FOR SOME WE LOVED', BY R. H. MOTTRAM (HUTCHINSON, 1956); 'GALSWORTHY THE MAN', BY RUDOLF SAUTER (PETER OWEN, 1967).

Indira Gandhi (Indian, b. 1917): politician. The Prime Minister of India was the only child of Jawaharlal Nehru (q.v.). As a child, she organised a children's Vanar Sena, or Monkey Brigade, which helped Congress by carrying clandestine messages during the civil disobedience movement. In 1942 she married Feroze Gandhi, a Parsi (and no relation of the Mahatma), from whom she was later separated. In 1946 she joined her father in Delhi, remaining with him as his official hostess until his death in 1964. Although she did not enter Parliament until 1964, she moved steadily up the hierarchy of the Congress Party. In 1959 she was elected Congress Party President, and in 1964 she became Minister of Information and Broadcasting, serving under Lal Bahadur Shastri. In 1966 she succeeded Shastri as Prime Minister. By a combination of political sense, luck, tact and feminine skills, Indira Gandhi has held together a varied set of colleagues and states with increasingly divergent interests. Her succession to power has vindicated the democratic process in one of the world's largest countries, confirms the strength of the Nehru tradition, and strikingly illustrates the new and important role of women in modern India. **A. S.**

'INDIRA GANDHI', BY ANNE CUBLIER (GONTHIER, PARIS, 1966).

Mahatma Gandhi (Indian, 1869–1948): statesman. India's greatest man of the 20th century, Gandhi, by superb political skill and charismatic authority, held together an increasingly diverse nationalist movement, gave to India an ideal of *Swaraj* (self

rule) that was as much an individual moral purpose as a national political objective, and to the world a new philosophy and technique of political agitation: civil disobedience. When he went to South Africa in 1893 and became the unquestioned leader of the Indian community there, organising its protest against discrimination, he came to reject the material civilisation of the West and to advocate *Ahimsa* (non-violence) and *Satyagraha* (soul-force, or passive resistance). He returned to India in 1915 and skilfully captured the Indian National Congress in 1920. Under his leadership, the Congress became a mass party organisation, capable of mobilising new regions and new ranges of the population. It declared for independence to be achieved through non-co-operation and in 1930 and 32 Gandhi launched his two great civil disobedience movements. In October 1934 he formally resigned from Congress, ostensibly to devote himself to social work, but in effect he continued to be its leader until independence in 1947. On January 30, 1948, Gandhi was assassinated by a Hindu extremist. Staunch advocate of Hindu-Muslim unity, he in fact helped to divide India by his Hindu style of politics and his unwillingness to treat with the Muslim League. **A. S.**

'MAHATMA GANDHI: A BIOGRAPHY', BY B. R. NANDA (ALLEN AND UNWIN, 1958); 'THE STORY OF MY EXPERIMENTS WITH TRUTH', BY M. K. GANDHI, 2 VOLS. (NAVA-JIVAN PRESS, AHMEDABAD, INDIA, 1927–1929).

Greta Garbo (Swedish, b. 1905): film actress. Garbo's career seemed to happen without any conscious direction on her part: from a poor childhood in Stockholm to shop assistant, model, bathing beauty in slapstick comedy, discovery by Mauritz Stiller and stardom in *The Atonement of Gösta Berling*. After study at the Royal Dramatic School in Stockholm, and a role in Pabst's *Joyless Street* in Berlin, she was recruited to MGM where she spent the rest of her career till her definitive retirement in 1941. Her art, likewise, seems as involuntary and as inexplicable. Few of her vehicles were in essence better than *kitsch* – even *Anna Karenina* could be substantially diminished in translation to the screen – yet she seemed always to transform them. No Garbo film is inconsiderable: even in those that have dated most over 30 or 40 years, Garbo's own performances seem unaltered. Large-boned, awkward, with a nose too long to be classical, she nevertheless seems always the most beautiful and graceful creature in the world. Her languour seems to come from the exhaustion of too intense passion. She is incapable of even momentary untruth in her playing. **D. R.**

'GARBO', BY JOHN BAINBRIDGE (FREDERICK MULLER, 1955); 'GARBO', BY FRITIOF BILLQUIST (ARTHUR BARKER, 1960).

Charles de Gaulle (French, 1890–1971): soldier and statesman. Ambitious, proud, patriotic, courageous; it is not yet clear whether de Gaulle's is the greatest success story of the 20th century or one of the near misses. His military career had

languished, in spite of some advanced ideas on warfare, until, refusing to accept the French surrender, he came to London in 1940 as the leader of Free France. Various people – Churchill and Roosevelt among them – tried to get rid of him, but it was de Gaulle who triumphed. Then the political leaders of liberated France tried to get rid of him and succeeded from 1946 to 1958. But he returned at a time when it seemed that France might collapse into civil war; and he stayed until defeated in the referendum of April 1969. His long-held guiding beliefs still stood firm: that life is a constant struggle; that the state must be strong and must have a leader; that there must be direct contact between him and the people; that there is only one political reality, the nation-state, and that people identify with it above ideology. Concerned with France, her unity and her greatness, he believed French unity was only attained when France was engaged in a great enterprise, and that therefore the importance of France in the world must be constantly emphasised. **D. W. J. J.**

'DE GAULLE', BY ALEXANDER WERTH (PENGUIN, 1965); 'AN EXPLANATION OF DE GAULLE', BY ROBERT ARON (HARPER AND ROW, NEW YORK, 1966).

Sir Patrick Geddes (British, 1854–1932): biologist, sociologist, and planner. This professor of botany at Dundee from 1888, whose special field was the evolution of sex, exerted an influence on town planning equal to that of Ebenezer Howard (q.v.). A pupil of T. H. Huxley, he saw civic design in terms not of aesthetically authoritarian boulevards in the Nash or Haussmann tradition, but of evolutionary equations, scientifically observed, of population/

FUR-GEM

environment/employment – or, as Geddes himself put it, of folk/place/work. He used data from archaeology, anthropology and social psychology (all infant disciplines at the time) to define the laws of behaviour which underlie the surface appearance of cities. Only an evolutionary approach to city planning, he realised, could keep pace with the increasingly rapid changes in modern society – an approach since developed by Lewis Mumford (in *The Culture of Cities*) and Constantine Doxiadis (in *Ekistics*). Geddes himself advised on the planning of Ramsay Gardens, in Edinburgh, where the tenements express his evolutionary ideas in a 'Scottish vernacular' style like C. R. Mackintosh's. **N. J. W. T.**

'PIONEER OF SOCIOLOGY': LIFE AND LETTERS OF PATRICK GEDDES', ED P. MAIRET (LUND HUMPHRIES, 1957); 'CITIES IN EVOLUTION', BY P. GEDDES (WILLIAMS AND NORGATE, 1915).

Hans Geiger (German, 1882–1945); physicist. Together with Ernest Marsden, Geiger carried out the crucial experiment that led to our modern picture of the atom. When Rutherford (q.v.) arrived at Manchester University in 1907, the young Geiger was already working in the laboratory. Rutherford first

asked this very able experimentalist to design an electrical device for counting alpha-particles emitted by radioactive elements. Geiger's early research eventually gave birth, in 1928, to the famous 'Geiger counter' so widely employed in atomic and particle physics and for cosmic-ray work. Marsden and Geiger went on to examine how alpha-particles were scattered by the atoms in thin metal foils. Their results revealed unexpected peculiarities in the way particles emerged from the foil. They were quite inconsistent with the prevailing picture of the atom as a 'pudding' of positive electrical charge in which electrons were embedded like sultanas. The alpha-particle scattering experiment caused Rutherford to search for a different kind of atomic structure. As a result he proposed the modern concept of a highly compact, positively-charged nucleus, surrounded by negatively-charged electrons moving in orbits. Geiger verified this model in 1911. His research, backed by the genius of Rutherford, thus marks one of the greatest achievements of 20th-century physical science. **P. H. S. S.**

'WORLD OF THE ATOM', ED. HENRY A. BOORSE AND LLOYD MOTZ, 2 VOLS. (BASIC BOOKS, 1966); 'PHYSICS FOR THE ENQUIRING MIND', BY ERIC M. ROGERS (O.U.P., 1960).

Carl Gemzell (Swedish, b. 1910): gynaecological endocrinologist. Gemzell's work has given new hope of childbirth to infertile women. Some women are infertile because they lack the hormone which stimulates ovarian follicles to mature so that subsequently one of them can rupture and release its ovum to be fertilised. In 1958 Gemzell and his colleagues Diczfalusy and Tillinger at the Karolinska Hospital extracted this follicle-stimulating hormone (FSH) from human pituitary glands collected post-mortem, and Gemzell was soon able to report that two women to whom he had given this extract had conceived and given birth to twins. This was a milestone in the history of gynaecological endocrinology and more than half the women suffering from this type of infertility are now able to conceive when given this treatment. A compound, clomiphene, has subsequently been developed which, though not so successful, needs less meticulous supervision. Gemzell was also the first person to show that the gland could be used for the extraction of both FSH and growth hormone; the latter can be subsequently used to treat cases of pituitary dwarfism. And in 1960 Gemzell and a colleague, Leif Wide, introduced an immunological pregnancy test that superseded previous tests in that it no longer required the use of animals such as mice, rabbits or toads. **P. M. F. B.**

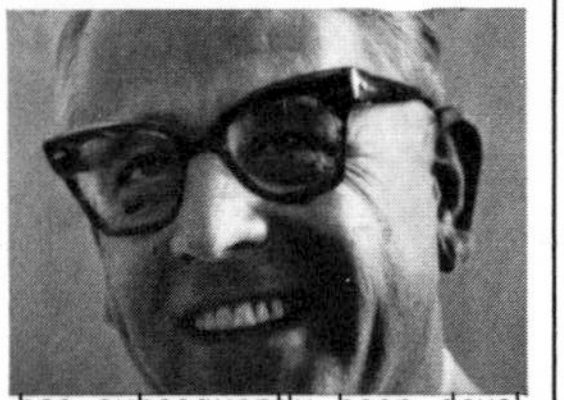

'FSH AGAINST INFERTILITY', BY P. M. F. BISHOP (NEW SCIENTIST, AUGUST 5, 1965).

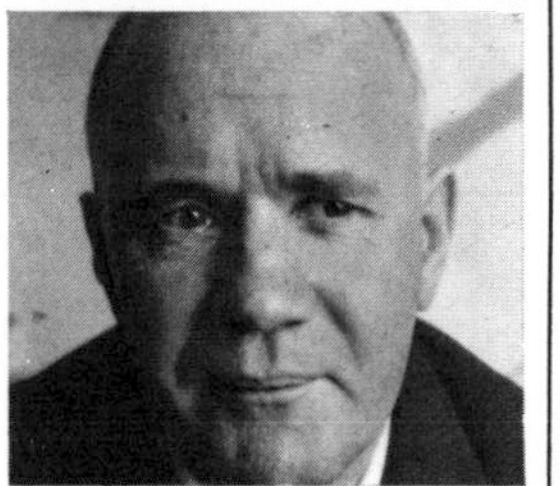

Jean Genet (French, b. 1910): novelist and playwright. Jean Genet has 'reinvented literature', according to Jean-Paul Sartre. His subject-matter – theft, murder, convict camps, homosexuality – is not new, but he writes of it in a revolutionary way: he makes himself a spokesman for it, he exalts it. He sees the world of crime as a sacred domain, with its own creed, rites, and saints. Absolute evil is its goal, and its heroes are condemned murderers. A foundling himself, Genet spent his youth mostly in reformatories, and his early manhood in penal colonies and the criminal quarters of seaports. In prison he commenced a series of novels – the first and most famous, *Our Lady of the Flowers,* a reverie about homosexual prostitutes living with hoodlum toughs in the Paris underworld – which won the astonished attention of the French literary intelligentsia. A group of notables among them succeeded in obtaining his release from jail after he had been locked up for life. Genet then turned to the theatre, transferring his perverse fantasies to the stage. Plays like *The Maids, The Balcony* and *The Blacks* made him an international figure, and a guru of the drop-out youth movement. **J. A. B.**

'SAINT GENET, ACTOR AND MARTYR', BY JEAN-PAUL SARTRE, TRANS. B. FRECHTMAN (MUSEUM OF MODERN ART, NEW YORK, 1963); 'JEAN GENET', BY PHILIP THODY (HAMISH HAMILTON, 1967).

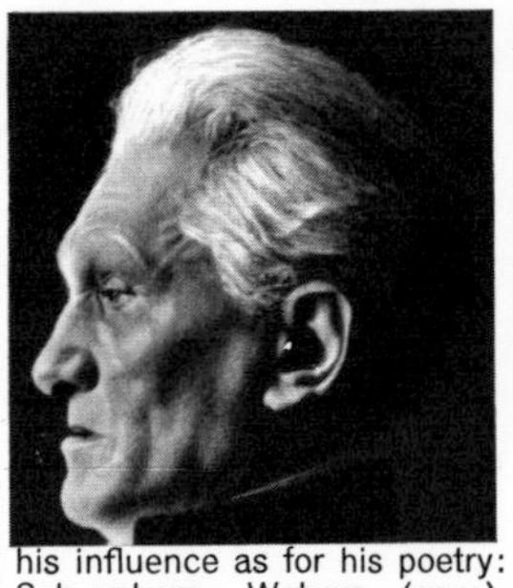

Stefan George (German, 1868–1933): poet. After Nietzsche, George was considered to be the great megalomaniac of German literature: he used to dress up as Caesar or Dante. He was almost as important for his influence as for his poetry: Schoenberg, Webern (qq.v.), Mallarmé, Verlaine, Hugo von Hofmannsthal, the English musician Cyril Scott, and Claus von Stauffenberg (q.v.) who died in the abortive coup against Hitler – all fell under his spell. He wrote no novels, no plays, almost no criticism: his devotion to poetry was totally single-minded. He restored dignity and grace to German poetry, harmonising strength with beauty: "Sparta's steel-bound courage wedded to Ionia's grace", in the words of *Der Siebente Ring.* He demanded a chant-like diction which emphasised the elements of magic in his verse. He caused a scandal by dedicating a cycle of poems, *Maximin,* to the young Maximilian Kronberger, who died of meningitis in 1904 at the age of 16 – Beatrice to his Dante. George's aesthetic passion for manly beauty was part of his re-creation of a new classicism in the early part of the century, which captured the imagination of a whole generation of Germans before the First World War. From an esoteric circle it broadened into a cultural movement which affected many European intellectuals. **A. C.**

'STEFAN GEORGE' BY E. K. BENNETT (BOWES AND BOWES, CAMBRIDGE, 1954); 'THE GENIUS OF THE GERMAN LYRIC', BY A. CLOSS (THE CRESSET PRESS, 1965); 'STEFAN GEORGE, FRIEDRICH GUNDOLF AND THE MAXIMIN MYTH', BY D. J. ENRIGHT (GERMAN LIFE LETTERS 1952); 'THE WORKS OF STEFAN GEORGE, RENDERED INTO ENGLISH', BY OLGA MARX AND E. MORWITZ (NORTH CAROLINA U.P., 1949).

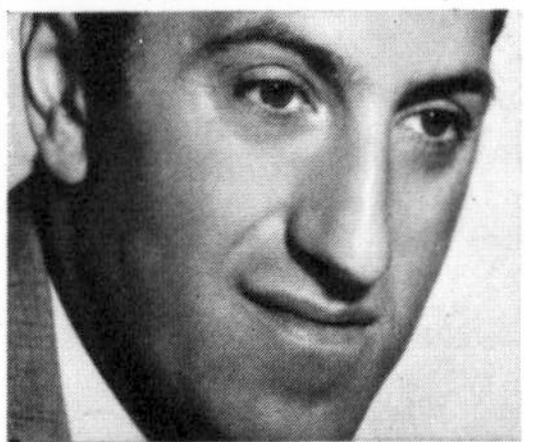

George Gershwin (U.S., 1898–1937): composer. In 21 years, from his first song in 1916 to his last, *Our Love Is Here To Stay,* in 1937, George Gershwin wrote 30 musicals and four films. His compositions are played by jazz and classical musicians alike: Miles Davis has recorded *Porgy and Bess* while Toscanini (q.v.) has conducted the Concerto in F. Gershwin began as a song-plugger at $15 a week, accompanied singers, was hired out as a rehearsal pianist, and made piano rolls. His first big hit was *Swanee* for Al Jolson. Then in 1924 Paul Whiteman asked him to write a work for a concert at Carnegie Hall. Gershwin wrote it in four weeks and called it *Rhapsody in Blue.* Not yet 23, he became the first composer to cross the barriers between light and serious music. But his greatest work, *Porgy and Bess* (1935), was unsuccessful at first – making up for it later. The supreme accolade was a 20-minute standing ovation at La Scala in Milan, where a George Gershwin room was set aside – he is the only American so honoured. **L. A.**

'GERSHWIN', BY ROBERT PAYNE (ROBERT HALE, 1962). RECORDS: 'RHAPSODY IN BLUE', BY REID NIBLEY AND THE UTAH SYMPHONY ORCHESTRA (MUSIC FOR PLEASURE 2107); 'PORGY AND BESS' FILM SOUNDTRACK (CBS S70007).

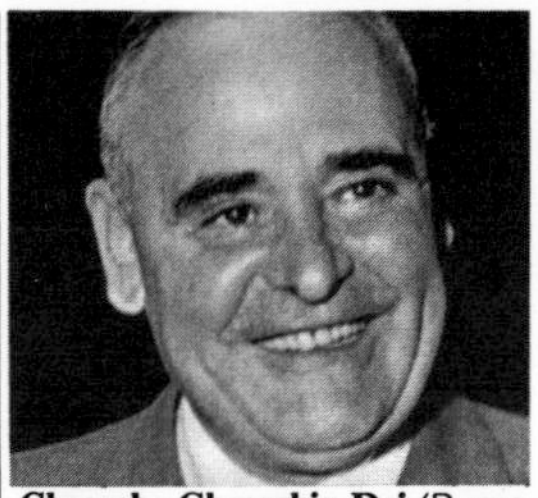

Gheorghe Gheorghiu-Dej (Rumanian, 1901–1965): statesman. For 20 years Gheorghiu-Dej ruled Rumania with prudence and cunning. Under his leadership Rumania eventually emerged an independent state. But Gheorghiu-Dej challenged Soviet authority only after years of careful preparation. And he sought to establish 'new type relations', avoiding a breach. First he asserted his supremacy; removed sources of Soviet influence; strengthened the economy; and broadened international contacts. Then in 1960 Rumania's quarrel with the U.S.S.R. began. Defying Soviet plans for co-ordination among specialised economies, Rumania determined to pursue integrated national development. For this Soviet assistance was vital. Hard bargaining in Comecon (East Europe's 'Common Market') reached deadlock by 1963. Gheorghiu-Dej seized on the Sino-Soviet rift. Exploitation of dissension in the international Communist movement soon reaped major economic rewards. Now he pressed to secure the political gains derived from his economic success and Rumania declared its independence in April 1964. That summer the Kremlin yielded. Rumania's national sovereignty within the Warsaw pact and Comecon was won. When he died Gheorghiu-Dej left an independent Socialist Rumania, founded on solid socio-economic achievements. **J. M. K.**

'THE NEW RUMANIA', BY STEPHEN FISCHER-GALATI (M.I.T. PRESS, CAMBRIDGE, MASS., 1967). 'COMMUNISM IN RUMANIA, 1944–1962', BY GHITA IONESCU (O.U.P., 1964).

Alberto Giacometti (Swiss, 1901–1966): sculptor. Born in the mountains of Italian Switzerland, the son and nephew of distinguished painters, Giacometti began sculpting at 14 and went on for ever after. From 1922 onwards he worked in Paris. Despairing of being able to render the model exactly as he saw it, he began in 1925 on imaginative pieces, more dreams-made-visible than sculptures, which exert to this day an intact and undiminished fascination. (*The Palace at 4 a.m.* is probably the most influential of all sculptures of its date, as much for its way of opening out a given space as for the bizarre family of objects which inhabits its all but transparent architecture.) The sculptures made between 1925 and 1934 were visionary pieces: "sculptures which presented themselves to my mind in a finished state. Whenever I have attempted to work out a sculpture consciously," he said in 1933, "it has always been a failure." In 1935 all this changed – he reverted to the living model, and there began a 30-year struggle to set down what really happens when one human being looks at another. The human being as captive, the human being as fortress, the human being as ritual offering – all take a turn as the search for an impossible completeness in human relations continues – and, with it, the search for an impossible truth in the telling. **J. R.**

'ALBERTO GIACOMETTI' BY JACQUES DUPIN (MAEGHT, PARIS, 1962); 'ALBERTO GIACOMETTI' (ARTS COUNCIL, 1965).

Vo Nguyen Giap (Vietnamese, b. 1912): soldier. Originally a teacher, Giap formed the first Communist guerrilla bands in Tonkin with American aid during the Second World War, ostensibly to fight the Japanese, and later commanded the Viet Minh guerrilla army under Ho Chi Minh (q.v.) in the first Indo-China War (1946–54). Having had his nose bloodied by Marshal de Lattre de Tassigny in a premature offensive in 1951, he is now renowned for his subsequent decisive victory over the French at Dien Bien Phu in 1954. He has reputedly directed Viet Cong and North Vietnamese military operations in South Vietnam since 1959, and he was the architect of the traumatic Tet offensive in 1968 which did much to topple President Johnson (q.v.). Without winning a military victory, Giap has refined Mao's (q.v.) protracted revolutionary war to achieve its political aim by developing a situation where costs in manpower indefinitely acceptable to him impose costs (in men, money and dissent) unacceptable to the United States. He believes in world revolution, and that, if North Vietnam wins in Vietnam, "we shall win everywhere". No one knows whether he is just one of a team or is himself a novel military genius, but we have certainly not heard the last of him. **R. G. K. T.**

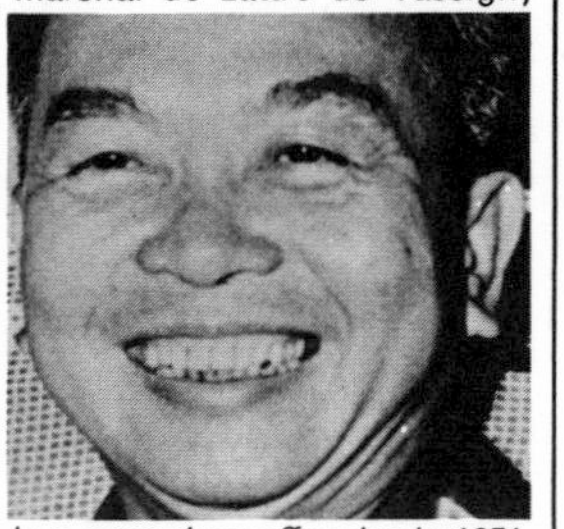

'GENERAL GIAP – POLITICIAN AND STRATEGIST', BY ROBERT J. O'NEILL (CASSELL, 1969); 'PEOPLE'S WAR, PEOPLE'S ARMY', BY GENERAL VO NGUYEN GIAP (PALL MALL, 1963).

André Gide (French, 1869–1951): writer. When the Great War ended the foremost French writers were Claudel, Valéry (q.v.), Proust (q.v.) and Gide. The first three were each pre-eminent in one literary form. It cannot be claimed that Gide excelled in any one genre, but his spirit permeated the entire literary climate in the years following the War. He was a moralist, less a model than a ferment, and there was definitely an atmosphere which can be termed 'Gidism'. Curtius called him "The Voice of the European Mind", and he became the spokesman for the new *Mal du Siècle,* the symbol of the angst of the post-war generation. Gide considered that, in his attempt to conform, the individual was obliged to develop a counterfeit personality which crippled him, which must be discarded. He was, however, accused of destroying what had been built up by centuries of tradition, of squandering the spiritual capital of the past. However, towards the end of his life he came to believe that culture needed, for its survival, a developing tradition. Gide's ultimate fate will be to be considered as a moralist, whose integrity and nobility of thought, whose purity and harmony of style give him an immortal place amongst the great masters of French literature. **E. M. S.**

'ANDRE GIDE', BY GEORGE PAINTER (WEIDENFELD AND NICOLSON, 1968); 'PORTRAIT OF ANDRE GIDE', BY JUSTIN O'BRIEN (ALFRED KNOPF, NEW YORK, 1953); 'GIDE', BY GERMAINE BREE (RUTGERS UNIVERSITY PRESS, N. J. 1963); GIDE AND THE HOUND OF HEAVEN', BY HAROLD MARSH (O.U.P., 1952); NOVELS BY ANDRE GIDE: 'THE IMMORALIST' (CASSELL, 1953); 'STRAIT IS THE GATE', TR. D. BUSSY (SECKER AND WARBURG, 1948); 'SYMPHONIE PASTORALE', ED. SHACKLETON (HARRAP, 1951); 'THE VATICAN CELLARS' (CASSELL, 1953).

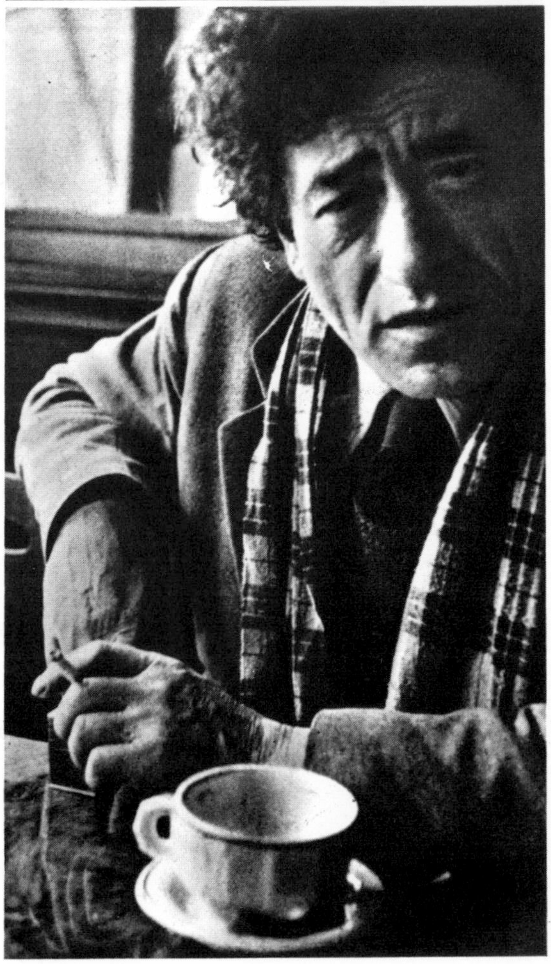

GP. 69

come the popular modern jazz Elder Statesman, the first U.S. jazz ambassador with State Department-sponsored tours of the Middle East, Far East and Latin America. Said Norman Granz in the mid-Forties: "Even the drummers sound like Dizzy Gillespie." **H. R. A. L.**

'THE JAZZ MAKERS', BY SHAPIRO AND HENTOFF (HOLT, RINEHART, NEW YORK, 1957). RECORDS: 'DIZZY GILLESPIE' (RCA-VICTOR RD 7827); 'DIZZY GILLESPIE AT NEWPORT' (COLUMBIA 33 CX 10105); 'AN ELECTRIFYING EVENING WITH THE DIZZY GILLESPIE QUINTET' (HMV CLP 1586).

Giovanni Giolitti (Italian, 1842–1928): statesman. Giolitti was Prime Minister of Italy five times between 1892 and 1921. He was a good liberal and a great administrator who had to preside over a difficult period of considerable change. Many radical measures were introduced under him, including national insurance in 1911 and a wider suffrage, but his name was associated with corruption and intimidation in parliamentary elections. It was also associated with transformism, a practice by which, instead of a two or three-party system, a single man held office by means of a continuously changing succession of broad coalitions. Giolitti tried to bring the new forces of Socialism, political Catholicism and Nationalism inside his transformist coalition, but without much success. In 1911 he followed public opinion and led Italy into a debilitating war against Turkey, but the experience left him strongly averse to entering the First World War in 1914, and hence he lost control of the Liberal Party. In 1920 he tried to revive a policy of social reform and to withstand the strong currents of reactionary, chauvinistic hysteria. But when the Socialists and Catholics would not join him, he favoured Fascism instead. His resignation in 1921 marked the eclipse of Italian liberalism. **D. M. S.**

'MEMOIRS OF MY LIFE', BY GIOVANNI GIOLITTI, TRANS. E. STORER (CHAPMAN AND DODD, 1923); 'ITALY FROM LIBERALISM TO FASCISM 1870-1925', BY C. SETON-WATSON (METHUEN, 1967).

Lillian Gish (U.S., b. 1896): film actress. On the stage from the age of six and in films at 16 – a fellow-veteran, Mary Pickford (q.v.), introduced her to D. W. Griffith (q.v.) – Lillian Gish was the ideal interpreter of Griffith's frail romantic heroines (Birth of a Nation, Hearts of the World, Broken Blossoms, Way Down East, Orphans of the Storm). From the start, however, her own great talent went far beyond the limits of Griffith's high Victorian sentimentality. Work with other directors like Henry King (Romola, The White Sister), King Vidor (La Bohème) and Victor Sjöstrom (The Scarlet Letter, The Wind) showed how complete was her mastery of the complex art of acting for the silent screen. Usurped both as MGM's top star and America's ideal of womanhood by Greta Garbo (q.v.), Gish retired to the theatre at the end of the Twenties, but since the Forties has reappeared in films as a fine character actress. Her special quality is for "thinking out a character directly and concretely and then executing

it in terms of semi-vague suggestion" (George Jean Nathan). Gish was the first actress to apply conscious and intense professional intelligence to developing a specifically cinematographic technique. **D. R.**

'LIFE AND LILLIAN GISH', BY A. BIGELOW PAINE (MACMILLAN, NEW YORK, 1932); 'HOLLYWOOD IN THE TWENTIES', BY DAVID ROBINSON (ZWEMMER/BARNES, 1968); 'THE MOVIES, MR. GRIFFITH AND ME', BY LILLIAN GISH WITH ANN PINCHOT (PRENTICE-HALL, NEW YORK, 1969).

Montague Gluckstein (British, 1854–1922): caterer. In the late 1880s Gluckstein, a travelling partner in a tobacco business, found that it was almost impossible to get refreshment in Britain other than in licensed premises, and suggested to a number of relatives that this was a gap that they could fill. One of them, Joseph Lyons, became chairman of the syndicate which they had set up to open tea-shops and cater for shows and exhibitions. In 1909 the first Corner House, in Coventry Street, was opened, and there followed two London hotels – the Strand Palace and the Regent Palace – and more Corner Houses and teashops. The Lyons establishments were particularly popular with unaccompanied women, and as more women went out to work, so Lyons increased in prosperity. The Lyons waitress, the 'nippy', soon became a symbol of quick service in establishments which were convenient and which gave value for money. Gluckstein's company also entered the mass production field and marketed packaged food, particularly tea and cakes such as their legendary Swiss Rolls. **G. P. G. N.**

Jean-Luc Godard (French, b. 1930): film director. Godard became almost inadvertently the spearhead of the French New Wave with A Bout de Souffle in 1959, when he reinvented the jump-cut by lopping off the beginning and end of each scene in order to tighten up an easy-paced thriller. Since then, with films like Vivre sa Vie, Une Femme Mariée, Pierrot le Fou, Masculin-Féminin, La Chinoise and Weekend, he has developed a highly idiosyncratic style: a kind of off-the-cuff collage in which plots snatched from headlines, from gangster movies or from political and social data are fleshed out with intellectual comment, literary quotations, puns, jokes and television-style interviews, all bound together by a dazzling sense of visual composition. A later film, One Plus One, interspersed shots of the Rolling Stones with scenes of Black Power militants in a Battersea automobile junkyard. Believing films to be expendable after they have served their purpose, he works quickly, cheaply and without advance preparation, capturing his thoughts on celluloid almost exactly as a writer does on paper. The results, greeted with admiration and derision, have unquestionably stirred up a small revolution in film-making: Godard, along with Resnais

Sir John Gielgud (British, b. 1904): actor. John Gielgud is the outstanding representative of the aristocratic spirit in the theatre. Of commanding presence and high intelligence, with great generosity of spirit and a noble voice, he is nevertheless quickly responsive to emotion. His early fame was based on his deeply emotional Richard II in Gordon Daviot's Richard of Bordeaux (1931). As Shakespeare's Richard II (one of his most celebrated parts) he combined electrifying emotional instability with command of formal verse-speaking. The spirit of the age has been against him, and he regards with disfavour the most influential developments of modern drama, such as they are revealed in the work of Beckett and Genet, though he committed himself wholeheartedly to the name part in Peter Brook's (q.v.) startling version of Seneca's Oedipus at the National Theatre. **H. H.**

'EARLY STAGES', BY SIR JOHN GIELGUD (FALCON PRESS, 1953).

Eric Gill (British, 1882–1940): typographer. Gill left an indelible mark on the history of type. His analytical approach to the whole field of lettering in the context of our society, his highly original typeface designs (his Perpetua and Gill Sans founts, with their clean functional appearance, expressed the power of industrialism combined with the humanity of craftsmanship) can still be seen reflected in every newspaper, advertisement or public inscription. "Craftsmanship," he says in his famous Essay on Typography, "will always be with us – like the poor." He was a persistent advocate of social reforms and put his name to countless protests and pamphlets against social injustice and the servility of the arts. He was an eminent engraver, illustrator and sculptor. Many of his carvings are familiar to Londoners – notably his Stations of the Cross in Westminster Cathedral. He designed and carved his own epitaph: "Pray for me Eric Gill stone carver, 1882–1940. **J. A.**

'AN ESSAY ON TYPOGRAPHY', BY ERIC GILL (SHEED AND WARD, 1931); AUTOBIOGRAPHY', BY ERIC GILL (CAPE, 1940); 'THE LIFE OF ERIC GILL', BY ROBERT SPEAIGHT (METHUEN, 1966).

Dizzy Gillespie (U.S., b. 1917): jazz musician. John Birks Gillespie played the leading part in the 'bop' revolution, the greatest impact on jazz since Louis Armstrong (q.v.) in the Twenties. Featured as a trumpet soloist with Cab Calloway (1939-41) he began to display personal idiosyncrasies of style (Pickin' the Cabbage, Bye Bye Blues). Early in the 1940s he met saxophonist Charlie Parker (q.v.). A loose partnership was formed through which Gillespie and Parker became known as the twin founders of 'rebop', 'be-bop', 'bop' (rhythmic shorthand for an across-the-board shake-up of jazz thinking). Parker-Gillespie recordings in 1945-6 (Groovin' High, Shaw 'Nuff, Dizzy Atmosphere) hold the same watershed significance as the Armstrong Hot Fives of 20 years before. Parker provided the legend, Gillespie the leadership, attracting hero-worship and vituperation. He weathered the storm, leading a succession of bands big and small to be-

and Antonioni (qq.v.), has become one of the most imitated modern directors in the cinema. But, nevertheless, he remains

Robert Goddard (U.S., 1882–1945): engineer. Goddard is credited with being the father of the rocket in the United States. While the Russian Tsiolkovsky (q.v.) first published calculations on liquid-fuelled rockets, Goddard first put speculation into practice. Not having the facilities for making liquid hydrogen fuel, he turned his attention instead to paraffin and liquid oxygen ('lox' in missile slang). On March 16, 1926, he fired his first successful liquid-fuelled rocket – to a height of 200 feet. By 1935 his small experimental rockets had achieved heights of 7500 feet and speeds of up to 550 mph. He developed steering devices and gyroscopes to keep rockets pointing the right way and also

patented the important idea of the multi-stage rocket. Because each stage sheds part of the original weight when it finishes burning, a rocket divided into a series of stages can reach higher speeds and altitudes than one with the same amount of fuel stored in a single stage. Goddard was a rocket visionary who built the ancestors of today's three-stage boosters. **N. V.**

'ROBERT GODDARD, SPACE PIONEER', BY ANNE PERKINS DEWEY (LITTLE, BROWN, BOSTON, 1962); 'AMERICAN SPACE EXPLORATION: THE FIRST DECADE', BY WILLIAM SHELTON (LITTLE, BROWN, 1967).

Josef Goebbels (German, 1897–1945): propagandist. The chief propagandist of the Nazi Party – indeed the greatest master of propaganda in this century – Goebbels was the one man of genuine intellect in the Nazi leadership, and the only one from an industrial background (a Rhenish Catholic artisan family). Initially Goebbels belonged to the 'left' wing of the Nazi Party, which predominated

inimitable. **T. M.**

'JEAN-LUC GODARD', BY RICHARD ROUD (SECKER AND WARBURG/B.F.I., 1967); 'THE FILMS OF JEAN-LUC GODARD', ED. IAN CAMERON (STUDIO VISTA, 1967).

in North and West Germany, and he retained his anti-bourgeois resentments even after going over to Hitler's more conservative line. Hitler acknowledged his populist verve in 1927 by making him the regional boss (*Gauleiter*) of Berlin with its Left-dominated mass politics. He battled it out with the Communists "for the conquest of the streets", which the traditional Right had never attempted, and edited *Der Angriff* (*The Attack*), "for the oppressed, against the exploiters". He managed Hitler's election campaigns, and in 1933, becoming Minister for Propaganda and Public Enlightenment, gained centralised control over radio, press, cinema and foreign publicity. But he became primarily a

censor: the regime's few creative artists (e.g. Leni Riefenstahl) escaped his net. The first mass communicator, Goebbels specialised in oratory, mass rallies, posters and films. Alone with Bormann he stayed with Hitler to the end. **P. G. J. P.**

'DOCTOR GOEBBELS', BY ROGER MANVELL AND HEINRICH FRAENKEL (HEINEMANN, 1960); 'THE GOEBBELS DIARIES', ED. LOUIS P. LOCHNER (HAMISH HAMILTON, 1948); 'GOEBBELS AND NATIONAL SOCIALIST PROPAGANDA, 1925–1945', BY ERNEST K. BRAMSTED (MICHIGAN STATE U.P., 1965).

Hermann Goering (German, 1893–1946): politician. Goering aspired to be the Falstaff of the Nazi movement, swaggering, genial, *bon vivant*, despising his colleagues' anti-semitic crudities, and a lover of (other people's) pictures. He was the

'salon Nazi', acceptable to landowners and industrialists before the take-over, to foreign diplomats afterwards. A Bavarian, the son of a diplomat, he was a fighter ace in the First World War whom defeat and a pugilistic streak turned into an extreme nationalist. He was wounded during Hitler's 1923 beer-hall *putsch*. As President of the Reichstag (1932) he put the final touches to the parliamentary pandemonium of the Weimar Republic. As Prussian police chief (1933) he set up the first concentration camps and stage-managed the Reichstag Fire trial. As creator and Commander of the *Luftwaffe* and Plenipotentiary for the

"NO MORE RACE TRACK LOSSES"

PLACE TWO DOLLARS IN BETTING MACHINE AND PULL HANDLE – WHEN MONEY PASSES THROUGH MACHINE YOUR COAT IS GENTLY LIFTED AND YOUR DOUGH IS DROPPED INTO YOUR BACK POCKET – AFTER YOUR HORSE LOSES, YOU REACH IN BACK POCKET FOR HANDKERCHIEF TO DRY YOUR TEARS AND DISCOVER **YOU** ARE STILL EVEN !

Rube Goldberg (U.S., 1883–1970): cartoonist. When an American talks about a Rube Goldberg set-up he's referring to some botched-up, implausible piece of improvised mechanics which more often than not manages to work. The man whose name has passed into American dictionaries was also a leading exponent of the great American daily strip cartoon, one of their chief contributions to the century's newspapers. Graduating as an engineer in 1904, Goldberg turned from designing sewers to sports cartooning for the *San Francisco Chronicle*. Shortly after he moved over to New York he started the long-running and goonish comic strip Boob McNutt. His surrealistic inventions, with

Peter Goldmark (U.S. ex-Hungarian, b. 1906): engineer. Dr Peter Goldmark invented and, with a team of assistants, developed the long-playing record. Annoyed like many others at the need for changing records on the gramophone he suggested to the Columbia Broadcasting System's record department that he should develop a long-playing record (though it was a sideline for him). He had the advantage over previous experimenters that vinyl plastic had been used during the war because of Japan's control of shellac, and vinyl had been proved to produce less surface noise and better high frequency response. Dr Goldmark worked out ideas for a stylus that would make grooves fine enough to accommodate some 300 to the inch. He worked out the speed reduction to 33 revolutions per minute. The

Four-Year Plan (1936) he directed Germany's mobilisation, and initiated conscription of slave labour. A better actor than administrator, his decline began with the Battle of Britain, and was completed by supply failures in Russia. He withdrew into a morphine haze, draped in his toga. Goering demonstrated that one could not be a gentleman Nazi. He was the parasite of a parasitic revolution, the big flea's little flea. He took poison after his death sentence at Nuremberg. **P. G. J. P.**

'HERMANN GOERING', BY ROGER MANVELL AND HEINRICH FRAENKEL (HEINEMANN, 1962); 'GOERING', BY WILLI FRISCHAUER (ODHAMS, 1951); 'THE GERMAN AIR FORCE', BY ASHER LEE (DUCKWORTH, 1946); 'THE BREAKING WAVE', BY TELFORD TAYLOR (WEIDENFELD AND NICOLSON, 1967).

their frightening disregard for the laws of nature but drawn with an arrogant air of engineering authority, are his best-known work, although his broad humorous range also enabled him to win a Pulitzer prize for political cartooning and in advanced years to take up with great energy the exacting art of sculpture. The National Cartoonists Society in America each year presents the Reuben, a Goldberg fantasy statuette, to the leader of the profession. In 1968 the winner was Rube Goldberg. **M. C.**

'COMIC ART IN AMERICA', BY STEPHEN BECKER (SIMON AND SCHUSTER, NEW YORK, 1959); 'COMICS AND THEIR CREATORS', BY MARTIN SHERIDAN (RALPH T. HALE, BOSTON, 1942); 'THE PENGUIN BOOK OF COMICS', BY GEORGE PERRY AND ALAN ALDRIDGE (PENGUIN, 1967); 'RUBE GOLDBERG VS. THE MACHINE AGE' (HASTINGS HOUSE, N.Y.).

combination thus made about six times the recording or playing time of a 78 rpm disc. He and his team then developed the lightweight pick-up, high-compliance cartridge and slow-

speed turntable. The new records were announced to the Press in June 1948. Thus Dr Goldmark founded a new industry and made high quality music available to everyone in comfort at home. **C. L. B.**

'THE FABULOUS PHONOGRAPH', BY ROLAND GELATT (CASSELL, 1956); 'TIN FOIL TO STEREO', BY O. READ AND W. L. WELCH (BOBBS-MERRILL INC., NEW YORK, 1959).

Wladyslaw Gomulka (Polish, b. 1905): statesman. The leader of Communist Poland from 1956–70 is a man of peasant origins with little formal education who joined the Polish Communist Party in 1926, but spent five years in Polish prisons before war broke out in 1939. After the German attack on Russia he became an underground leader – soldier, politician and journalist – writing many of the basic tenets of the new Polish Workers' Party, which now rules Poland. He played his part in the liquidation of anti-Communist resistance after the new Communist government took over in July 1944, but differed from some of his comrades by resisting collectivisation of land and insisting on Poland's internal independence from Russia. For this he was accused, dismissed and finally (in 1951) imprisoned. Released in 1954, he was seized upon by Polish liberal reformers and carried to power by popular acclaim in 1956. Until his fall in 1970, precipitated by economic problems, he largely decollectivised agriculture, preserved a certain freedom of speech and restored many of Poland's traditional links with Western Europe, though suppressing many of the hopes under which he was originally elected. **N. B.**

'THE INDEPENDENT SATELLITE', BY HANS-JAKOB STEHLE (PALL MALL, 1965); 'POLAND, BRIDGE FOR THE ABYSS?', BY RICHARD HISCOCKS (O.U.P., 1963); 'GOMULKA, HIS POLAND AND HIS COMMUNISM', BY NICHOLAS BETHELL (LONGMANS, 1969).

Benny Goodman (U.S., b. 1909): jazz musician. Born of a poor Chicago Jewish family, Benny Goodman rose to fame as a clarinet prodigy; he was a sort of counterpart to the rise of Menuhin in formal music. His personal style was formulated in traditional jazz days, but Goodman was quick to see the commercial possibilities of a large jazz orchestra mixing jazz standards and popular songs of the day in its repertoire. Thus he became the part instigator and figurehead of the Swing Era, which in 1936 was to be the last big upheaval in popular music before the rock era of Presley and Beatlemania. But Goodman remains one of the few popular musicians who retained the highest musical standards. Bartok (q.v.) and Copland both wrote music dedicated to him. He is now considerably less active as a jazz musician but the final years of his heyday nevertheless contributed to later jazz developments. Goodman made history in the middle Thirties by including Negro musicians (Teddy Wilson, Lionel Hampton) in a field of music hitherto segregated. **J. P. W. D.**

RECORDS: 'BENNY GOODMAN AND THE SMALL GROUPS' (RCA-VICTOR, R.D. 7775); 'SWING, SWING, SWING' (CAMDEN: CDN, 148). BOOK: 'THE KINGDOM OF SWING', BY BENNY GOODMAN (STACKPOLE, PENN., 1939).

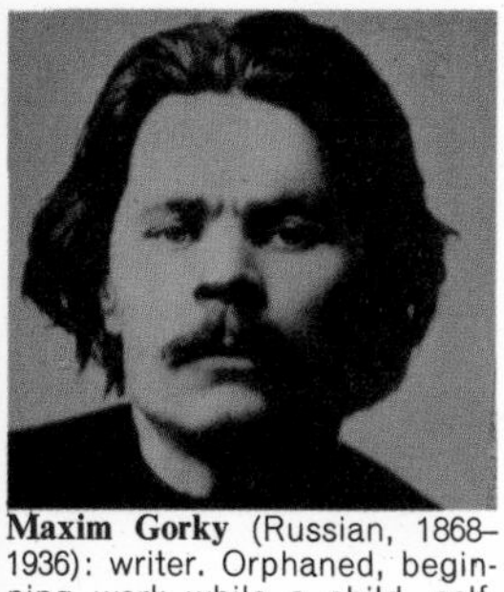

Maxim Gorky (Russian, 1868–1936): writer. Orphaned, beginning work while a child, self-educated, politically suspect at 21 and wandering in south Russia among other outcasts. Maxim Gorky was probably saved, by his desire to write, from the social abyss whose life style and religion he described. His writing soon made him famous (though even more a revolutionary), and public opinion gained his release when in 1905 he was arrested for pamphleteering. However, he left Russia then for some years, a self-exile ironically repeated when, after the Revolution, his friend Lenin (q.v.) had to persuade him to leave again: his newspaper had been banned for criticising the *Pravda* line, the Bolshevik monopoly and the reign of terror. Maybe his country (and the world) should be most grateful for his revolutionary work, his care for writers and artists during those hard years, his innumerable private kindnesses, his contributions to Bolshevik funds and his humane opposition to Lenin. But surely Gorky will be remembered for those images which haunt literature still: the thief, those tramps, the poor, even the frogs he saw kicked down on to his father's coffin and buried alive by the gravediggers, in the pouring rain, a century ago. **A. E.**

'MY CHILDHOOD', BY MAXIM GORKY (PENGUIN, 1966); 'LOWER DEPTHS AND OTHER PLAYS', BY MAXIM GORKY (YALE U.P., 1959); 'MAXIM GORKY: THE WRITER', BY F. M. BORRAS (O.U.P., 1967).

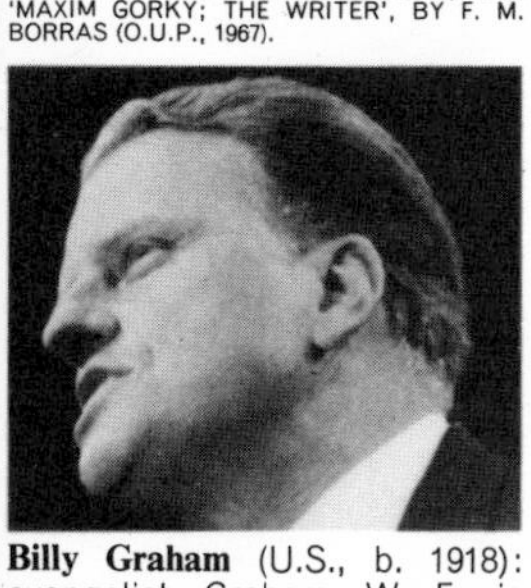

Billy Graham (U.S., b. 1918): evangelist. Graham, W. F., is an employee (salary £8000 p.a.) of the Billy Graham Evangelistic Association, founded in 1950 with its headquarters in Minneapolis. He claims to have preached the gospel to "more millions than anyone in history", specialising in Crusades to great cities; he has descended on London four times. He is a blond, blue-eyed Southern Baptist, raised in North Carolina – with hickory stick and Bible – and converted at 16. He is fundamentalist, predictably puritan, given to brimstone warnings on sex and Communism: he "thanked God" in the early Fifties for Joe McCarthy (q.v.), and since then has been noticeably cautious on issues like race and Vietnam. Many Christians think his 'gospel' inadequate or perverse. Graham himself is an anachronism, the latest in a declining line of Bible Belt gospellers; his success is principally a triumph of public relations and managerial techniques. His headquarters staff number 345, his Crusade 'teams' are masters of the soft sell. It works – subject to diminishing returns. The Harringay Crusade (1954) was a phenomenon; Wembley (1955) a "disappointment", Manchester (1961) a "disaster". In 1969 Graham's career looks like an inevitable back-lash against secularisation – spectacular but transitory. **V. P.**

'BILLY GRAHAM, THE AUTHORISED BIOGRAPHY', BY JOHN POLLOCK (HODDER, 1967); 'EVANGELISM INC', BY G. W. TARGET (ALLEN LANE, 1968).

A scene from Intolerance *(left), directed by D. W. Griffith (inset, left) in 1916. Lillian Gish (q.v., above left) was one of the stars*

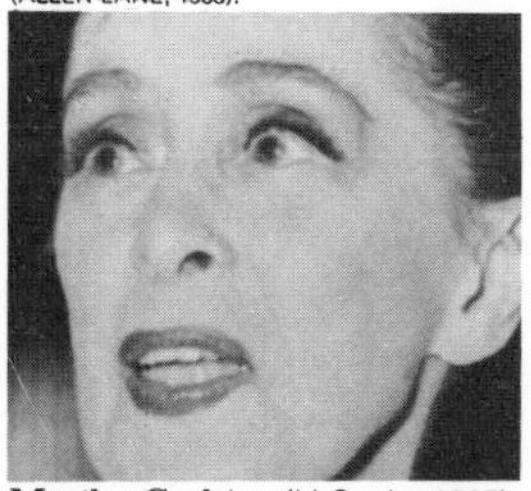

Martha Graham (U.S., b. 1895): dancer, choreographer. Martha Graham has been the greatest innovator in the modern or 'free' dance since Isadora Duncan (q.v.). After a brief period in vaudeville and revue, she made her independent debut in Manhattan in 1926 with a varied programme of interpretative dances to classical and early modern music. Eventually she founded a company trained in her method (now used as a teaching medium in schools), which involves the unity of body and mind, muscular co-ordination and controlled movement and breathing so that the body is an instrument for dramatic use. Her ballets are in fact poetic plays, and her dancers actors. They are a unity of music, décor, choreography – and sometimes the spoken word. Her early interest was in Red Indian mysticism and tribal life: this gave way to a concern with social and psychological problems and with the American pioneer spirit, culminating in *Appalachian Spring*. From the Thirties she used only original music. Plot in her ballets is a framework for the expression of feelings: passions, fears, dreams. Since the war she has reinterpreted ancient myths and historical characters in her individual post-Freudian way. **R. B.**

'MARTHA GRAHAM', BY LEROY LEATHERMAN, PHOTOGRAPHS BY MARTHA SWOPE (KNOPF, NEW YORK, 1966); 'LOOKING AT THE DANCE', BY EDWIN DENBY (PELLEGRINI AND CUDAHY, NEW YORK, 1949).

Günter Grass (German, b. 1927): writer. Günter Grass is one of Germany's foremost avant-garde authors. He does not offer a 'poetic message', but he views the artistic destiny with a critical awareness of human absurdities. With masterful buffoonery and linguistic ingenuity, using anti-poetic expressions, he unmasks hypocrisy and pomposity. In his grotesques he meticulously records smells, obscenities or sexual aberrations. Grass selects physical and social misfits as central characters, for instance, in his world-famous novel *The Tin Drum*. The dwarfish Oskar, who because of a fall has stopped growing, witnesses with the eyes of a misshapen creature contemporary events. His *Dog Years* presents society from a dog's eye view. Grass's virtuosity in blending linguistic banality with formal subtlety is less effective in his dramas, like *The Plebeians Rehearse a Revolt*. Much of Grass's poetry displays black humour. The very titles of his verse-books are puzzling: *The Merits of the Wind-chicken, Gleisdreieck* (a Berlin railway station between East and West). In *Questioned*, Grass tells us what is in store for mankind: a "new mysticism". "Now we need not think any longer but only obey." **A. C.**

'TWENTIETH CENTURY GERMAN LITERATURE', BY AUGUST CLOSS (CRESSET PRESS, 1969); 'ASPECTS OF G. GRASS'S NARRATIVE TECHNIQUE', BY IDRIS PARRY (FORUM FOR MODERN LANGUAGE STUDIES III, 1967); 'GUNTER GRASS', BY A. SUBIOTTO IN 'ESSAYS ON CONTEMPORARY GERMAN LITERATURE', EDITED BY B. KEITH-SMITH (WOLFF, 1966); 'MALICE IN WONDERLAND', BY W. E. YUILL (UNIVERSITY OF NOTTINGHAM, 1967).

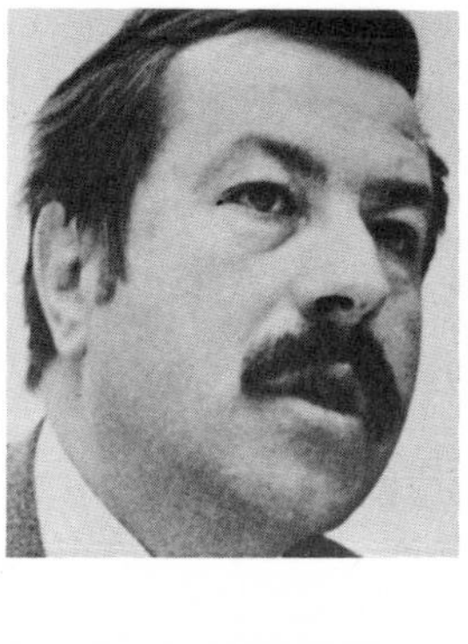

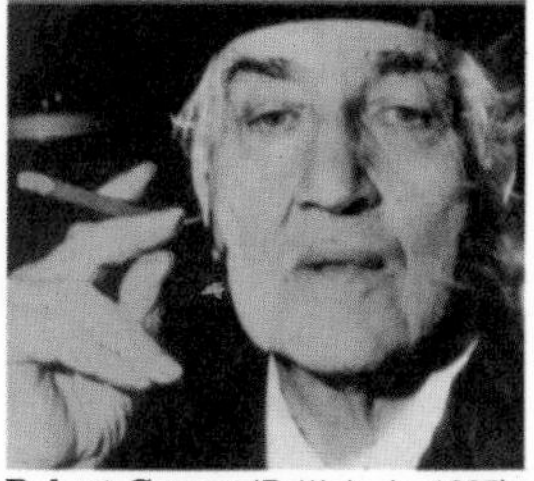

Robert Graves (British, b. 1895): writer. The son of an Irish songwriter, Robert Graves first came to public notice as a contributor to Edward Marsh's *Georgian Poetry* (1916–17). Rescued from tepid whimsy by his experience of trench warfare (he tells the whole story in his autobiography *Goodbye to All That*) Graves did not embrace the fashionable alternative – Eliot-Pound (q.v.) modernism – but evolved instead the curious vein of cerebral romanticism which can be seen as the characteristic of his verse. Wit, irony, epigrammatic sharpness: odd qualities to predominate in the work of a professed romantic but they are Graves's most valuable assets. He has taken pains throughout his career to keep himself aloof from poetic movements. His traditionalist technique, his disdainful treatment of his contemporaries, his bizarre scholarship, and in particular his espousal of the White Goddess doctrine (which, put crudely, equates the Muse of Poetry with the Goddess worshipped in prehistoric matriarchal societies) – these factors have conspired to keep him from the mainstream of English poetry. But Graves's devotees are right to claim for him an important niche in English poetry. **I. H.**

'COLLECTED POEMS', BY ROBERT GRAVES (CASSELL, 1965); 'THE CROWNING PRIVILEGE', BY ROBERT GRAVES (PENGUIN, 1959); 'I, CLAUDIUS', BY ROBERT GRAVES (METHUEN, 1939); 'THE WHITE GODDESS', BY ROBERT GRAVES (FABER, 1952).

Sir James Gray (British, b. 1891): zoologist. Gray has altered our way of looking at animals. Until the mid-Twenties zoology was the study of dead specimens, the object of which was to find relationships between animals – a hangover from the 19th-century preoccupation with evolution. Between the wars this outlook changed and James Gray, at Cambridge, was a leading voice in developing the new experimental zoology, which sought to discover how living animals worked. Gray himself worked extensively on animal locomotion and his elegant studies (often with Hans Lissmann) forced us to think of backbones and legs in a new way – rather as an engineer would. Consideration of an animal's skeleton in terms of struts, pivots or girders proved profitable when analysing its movements, and also showed how certain morphological features could be explained in operational terms. Gray's influence extended beyond his department, but within it functional studies of the most varied kind flowered: insect physiology, the nervous systems and behaviour, experimental embryology. Despite the excellence of his own work it is as an intellectual force that he is most important. **J. B. M.**

'THE CELL AND THE ORGANISM', ED. SIR V. B. WIGGLESWORTH AND J. A. RAMSAY (C.U.P., 1961); 'ANIMAL LOCOMOTION', BY SIR JAMES GRAY (WEIDENFELD AND NICOLSON, 1968).

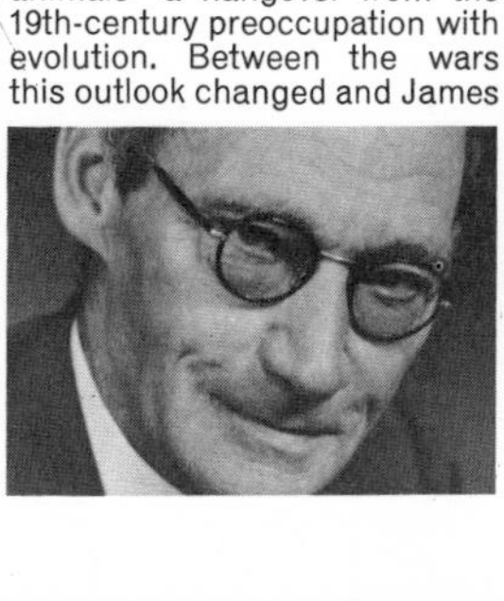

Graham Greene (British, b. 1904): novelist. Over the past 40 years Greene has published more than 20 volumes of novels, short stories and plays, as well as books of travel and criticism. Although he uses the word 'entertainment' to characterise his fiction when it borrows the form and technique of the thriller, all his books are entertaining. His heroes are obsessed men who undergo an experience of change with regard to their feelings about God, other men and themselves. A highly topical writer, he examines this change against the circumstances of particular times and places: London, Mexico, West Africa, Haiti, Indo-China. Influenced by Henry James, Conrad (q.v.), Stevenson and Maugham, his voice is by turns terse and relaxed, but always metaphorical and usually ironic and knowing. If at times his novels suggest, as George Orwell (q.v.) remarked, that there is something *distingué* in being damned, they also fascinate and ensnare us: we must

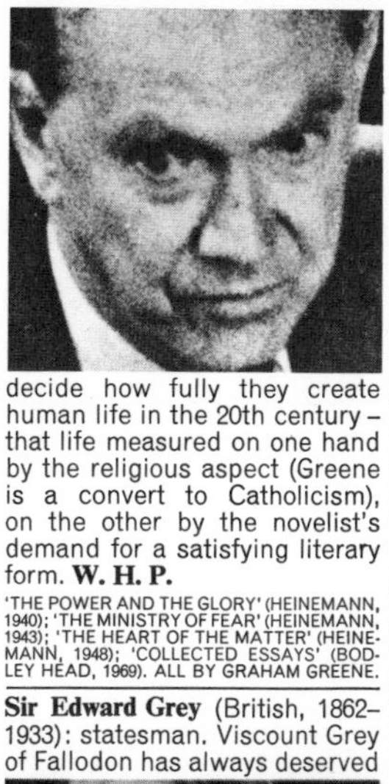

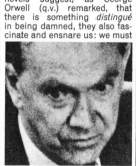

decide how fully they create human life in the 20th century – that life measured on one hand by the religious aspect (Greene is a convert to Catholicism), on the other by the novelist's demand for a satisfying literary form. **W. H. P.**

'THE POWER AND THE GLORY' (HEINEMANN, 1940); 'THE MINISTRY OF FEAR' (HEINEMANN, 1943); 'THE HEART OF THE MATTER' (HEINEMANN, 1948); 'COLLECTED ESSAYS' (BODLEY HEAD, 1969). ALL BY GRAHAM GREENE.

Sir Edward Grey (British, 1862–1933): statesman. Viscount Grey of Fallodon has always deserved

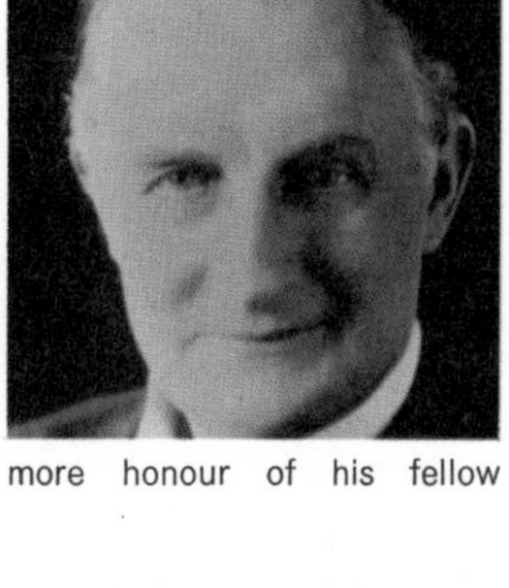

more honour of his fellow countrymen than he has in fact received. He was Foreign Secretary from 1905–1916; he took Britain into the First World War on the French side; and there have always been enough of his countrymen to regard this as a uniquely wicked abandonment of Britain's traditional policy of isolation from Continental disputes. As Foreign Secretary he maintained the *ententes* with France and the United States and negotiated one with Russia in 1907. He tried to revive the Concert of Europe; but it could no longer contain a Germany intent on dominion and he committed Britain to secret staff talks with France and Belgium so as to balance Germany diplomatically, without realising that he was morally committing her to fight on their side. He inspired the transformation of Britain's colonies into dominions. **D. C. W.**

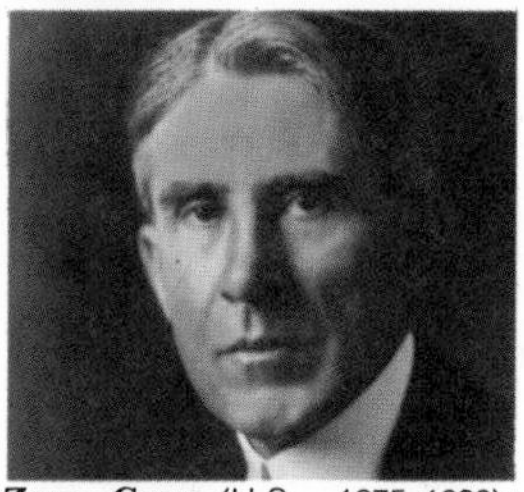

Zane Grey (U.S., 1875–1939): novelist. Zane Grey was the novelist of the Old West – the mythopoeic landscape of the American dream. The great Western themes – man against nature, the law of the gun, an easily apparent Good versus patent Evil – remain part of the tissue of American thought, anachronistic though they are; but the West never found a poet or novelist as big as itself who could re-create its cowboys, lawmen and brigands in giant forms. Instead, it produced a genre of sub-literary pulp fiction. The audience for Zane Grey's Western romances numbered tens of millions; he is still avidly read out of an atavistic yearning for wide-open spaces. But the film-makers bypass the written word and magnificently render the myth in visual terms – perhaps it is not amenable to conventional literary forms, anyway. Nevertheless, the enormous appeal of Grey's books, for all their lack of style, served to make American nostalgia for lost heroic innocence a significant part of the 20th century. **A. O. C.**

'COWBOY SONGS AND OTHER FRONTIER BALLADS', COMPILED JOHN A. LOMAX (REISSUED MACMILLAN, NEW YORK, 1966). 23 ZANE GREY WESTERNS HAVE BEEN PUBLISHED BY CORGI BOOKS.

David Wark Griffith (U.S., 1875–1948): film director. A stage actor and aspiring playwright who entered the cinema in 1908, D. W. Griffith is generally acknowledged as the father of the cinema, the man who invented everything from cross-cutting to the close-up. Though rival claims may be pressed – for Louis Feuillade (q.v.) and Benjamin Christensen, among others – the fact remains that Griffith, with his unbounded ambition and taste for grandeur, did more than anyone else to make the cinema realise its own potential. His two most famous films, *Birth of a Nation* (1915) and *Intolerance* (1916), still stun with their epic scale, fantastic set-pieces and almost biblically lofty sentiments. It is a pity that the inspirational claims of these masterworks have tended to overshadow the more endearing merits of the small, unassuming sagas of rural America such as *True Heart*

Susie. Here, inimitably, Griffith preserved an age of lost innocence, a world of white-fenced houses and sunlit orchards where ragged youths and demure maidens with rosebud lips dreamed their dreams of pure romance. **T. M.**

'D. W. GRIFFITH, AMERICAN FILM MASTER', BY IRIS BARRY (MUSEUM OF MODERN ART, NEW YORK, 1965); 'THE MOVIES, MR. GRIFFITH, AND ME', BY LILLIAN GISH (WITH ANN PINCHOT) (PRENTICE-HALL, N.Y., 1969).

Grock (Swiss, 1880–1959): clown. He was born Charles Adrien Wettach, son of a Swiss watchmaker and acrobat; but to the world, who laughed at the futility of his struggles with a reticent reality, at his efforts to push the piano to the stool, at the battered chair through which he would invariably fall while brilliantly playing the concertina, at his trickery and final triumph over all adversity, he was Grock the king of clowns. At least 30 million people must have seen him during his six decades of clowning. He appeared with Mistinguett (q.v.) in the Folies-Bergère in Paris, and in Cochran's (q.v.) famous productions in London. His native tongue was French, but he spoke English so well that, at a party in London, Winston Churchill told him that only an Englishman could be so great a clown. He came to England before the First World War, but left in 1924 after a disagreement with the theatre management. He never came back. After the Second World War he travelled with his own circus in Germany where, in 1954, he retired for good, only to perform occasionally on Italian television. During his final appearance he fell ill, but the king of clowns finished his last act before collapsing. **J. A.**

AUTOBIOGRAPHIES: 'LIFE'S A LARK' (HEINEMANN, 1931); 'GROCK, KING OF CLOWNS' (METHUEN, 1957).

Walter Gropius (U.S., ex-German, 1883–1969): architect. Although not an outstanding individual creator like Le Corbusier or Mies van der Rohe, whom he met as fellow pupils of Peter Behrens (qq.v.), Gropius has a pre-eminent place as the teacher of the professional and technical system of teamwork in modern architecture and industrial design. As founder-director in 1919 of the Bauhaus at Weimar, he harnessed diverse talents (Klee, Kandinsky [qq.v.], Itten, Feininger, Moholy-Nagy [q.v.]) to the common task of training designers for a total environment, with a stress on basic formal training and regard for the innate qualities of materials. Gropius himself specially exploited the spatial transparency of glass within the classic

framework of the Fagus shoelace factory at Alfeld (1911), in the circular staircases of the Werkbund administration building at the Cologne Exhibition (1914) and in the curtain walling of the Bauhaus workshops at Dessau (1925–6). He pioneered ideas of modern drama in the Total Theatre project (1927), of education in the village college at Impington near Cambridge (1936–9), and of low-cost housing in the Siemensstadt area of Berlin (1930) and in the New Kensington estate near Pittsburgh (1941). After moving in 1938 to Harvard, he founded the Architects' Collaborative, which designed the U.S. Embassy in Athens (1957–61). **N. J. W. T.**

'WALTER GROPIUS, WORK AND TEAM-WORK', BY SIGFRIED GIEDION (ARCHI-TECTURAL PRESS, 1954); 'WALTER GROPIUS', BY JAMES MARSTON FITCH (MAYFLOWER, 1960); 'THE NEW ARCHITECTURE AND THE BAUHAUS', BY WALTER GROPIUS (FABER AND FABER, 1965); 'BAUHAUS 1919-1928', ED. HERBERT BAYER AND WALTER AND ILSE GROPIUS (CHARLES T. BRANFORD, BOSTON, 1952).

Heinz Guderian (German, 1888–1954): soldier. Guderian was the creator of the Panzer divisions which formed the decisive element of the German army during the Second World War. His idea of establishing hard-hitting armoured formations was inspired by the need to offset Germany's inferior strategic position after the First World War by lightning, or *Blitzkrieg*, operations. It was fostered by the example of the original massive employment of British tanks in 1917–18 and the arguments in favour of mechanised forces

advanced in Britain by Fuller and Liddell Hart (q.v.). It was finally realised with the backing of Hitler. Having helped train them, Guderian led Panzer divisions into battle. In 1940 his Panzer corps achieved the decisive break-through at Sedan and he led one of the Panzer armies which drove to the gates of Moscow in 1941. His ideas and actions made a major contribution to German successes during the first part of the Second World War and spurred on the mechanisation of armies throughout the world. **R. M. O.**

'PANZER LEADER', BY HEINZ GUDERIAN (MICHAEL JOSEPH, 1952); 'PANZER BATTLES', BY F. W. VON MELLENTHIN (CASSELL, 1955).

Che Guevara (Argentinian, 1928–1967): guerrilla. Ernesto Guevara's death in 1967 and his romantic revolutionary extremism made him the symbolic hero of young revolutionaries the world over. The asthmatic son ("puny", his father called him) of an upper-class Argentinian family of bohemian tastes, Guevara interrupted his medical studies for a hitch-hiking tour of Latin America which convinced him of the necessity for violent revolution as the solu-

tion to the problems of that continent. He was in Guatemala when the revolutionary Government of Arbenz was toppled by a CIA-backed invasion. Then he met Castro in Mexico in 1955 and joined Castro's expedition, becoming the most noted guerrilla leader and theoretician, taking charge of the breakout from the Sierra Maestra. In revolutionary Cuba he became head of the National Bank and Minister of Industry, and was responsible for the early failures of industrial development. Never an orthodox Marxist, he

Charles Edouard Guillaume (Swiss, 1861–1938): physicist. Guillaume made the first accurate standards of length. He joined the International Bureau of Weights and Measures at the age of 22 and remained there all his working life, retiring as director in 1936. His early work resulted in much improved mercury thermometers, but above all he is remembered for his chance observation of the almost zero thermal expansion of certain steels. Guillaume's discovery of 'invar' – steel containing 36 per cent nickel – led to a host of accurate measuring applications. Never varying in

length, no matter what temperature, the material was quickly adopted for measuring geodetic baselines. It is also widely used in precision instruments like thermostats and pendulums for astronomical clocks. A closely related alloy called 'elinvar' became the hairspring of high grade watches and chronometers. Awarded the Nobel Prize for Physics in 1920 "in recognition of the service rendered to precision measurements in physics by his discovery of anomalies in nickel steel alloys", Guillaume made possible the 20th-century sense of precision. **N. V.**

was more concerned with the morality of a new Socialist man than the efficiency of a new Socialist economy. In 1965 he left Cuba to start a Latin American revolution – not through urban Left-wing parties but by revolutionary guerrilla activity in the countryside; after several abortive attempts at guerrilla action he was wounded in a skirmish in eastern Bolivia and shot by his captors. **R. Ca.**

'REMINISCENCES OF THE CUBAN REVOLUTIONARY WAR', BY CHE GUEVARA, TRANSLATED BY V. ORTIZ (ALLEN AND UNWIN, 1968); 'THE COMPLETE BOLIVIAN DIARIES OF CHE GUEVARA', EDITED BY DANIEL JAMES (ALLEN AND UNWIN, 1968).

Earle C. Haas (U.S., b. 1885): doctor. Early in the 1930s Dr Haas realised that the shortcomings of the conventional sanitary towel could be overcome. Why, he wondered, should a woman be burdened with a bulky external pad?

Knowing the surgical principle of tamponage, in which a cavity is filled with a tightly-inserted absorbent plug, he adapted it for use by women. His efforts culminated in the development of the modern compressed tampon for intra-vaginal use. Patents were granted, and his invention was marketed under the brand name of 'Tampax tampons' from 1937, with the formation of Tampax Incorporated. Three other Americans, Thomas F. Casey, Earle A. Griswold and Ellery W. Mann developed the invention and made it generally available. Tampax mounted a considerable educational compaign on menstruation and general biology, and tampons, which were not popular at first, are now used all over the world. **G. P. G. N.**

Fritz Haber (German, 1868–1934): chemist. Haber's greatest achievements were the discoveries resulting in the fixation of nitrogen which in turn led to the manufacture of synthetic fertilisers. To produce efficient, economical fertilisers the nitrogen in the atmosphere has to be fixed, or made available for growing plants. The Haber, or Haber-Bosch, process turns nitrogen into ammonia which can be further processed. Haber's method is still the basis for producing over 20 million tons of ammonia a year, and is the basis of all manufacture of artificial fertiliser. In the First World War Haber worked on poison gases, and after the war he sought to extract gold from sea water to help with Germany's war reparations. The process is feasible, but winning gold from the sea costs more than its value. In 1933 Haber, whose Nobel Prize of 1918 was disputed by allied scientists for his involvement with poison gas manufacture, was declared an unwanted Jew by the Nazis. He took refuge in Cambridge. **P. J. F.**

'THE STORY OF FRITZ HABER', BY MORRIS GORAN (BAILEY BROTHERS AND SWINFEN, FOLKESTONE, 1967).

Otto Hahn (German, 1879–1968): chemist. The reluctant father of the nuclear age studied chemistry at Marburg and Munich. He achieved early fame with the discovery of the radioactive isotope of thorium while working at University College London. Later, he studied under Rutherford (q.v.) in Canada and discovered radioactive actinium. In 1907 he teamed up with the brilliant Viennese physicist Lise Meitner (q.v.), a close collaboration resulting finally in a Nobel Prize for Hahn in 1944. His crowning – and shattering – contribution was made just before the 1939-45 War. Working in Nazi Germany, Hahn had not dared to voice his thoughts. But Meitner, having fled to Stockholm (she was Jewish), published a letter in *Nature*. The crucial experiments involved the formation of a 'middle weight element (barium) from a heavy weight element (uranium). Breakthrough came when it was realised that the nuclei of uranium atoms were being split into two nearly equal bits. The process became known as nuclear fission. Two months after Hahn's ideas were published by Meitner the awesome possibility of the nuclear chain reaction had dawned upon the scientific world. **N. V.**

'OTTO HAHN: A SCIENTIFIC AUTOBIOGRAPHY', TRANSLATED AND EDITED BY WILLY LEY (MACGIBBON AND KEE, 1967).

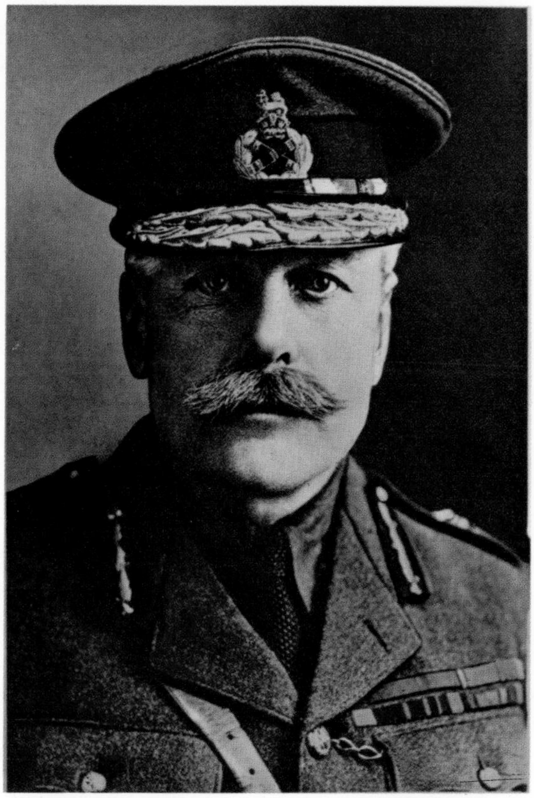

Field Marshal Earl Haig (British, 1861–1928): soldier. It is the tragedy of Haig, and of Britain, that he was the man best fitted for command of the British Army in the First World War. The typical product of a military system that had disregarded the first quarter of a century of the technological development of arms, he, like his contemporaries, was forced to substitute for the war of manoeuvre the trench, barbed wire and human lives. The machine-gun was inadequately appreciated in the Army of 1915. Even in the field two per battalion was thought sufficient. The Germans used 80. When, fortuitously, the tank developed, he regarded it as an adjunct to cavalry, unable to surrender his belief in "the horse – the wellbred horse". Yet when tanks appeared in numbers in the summer of 1918, he displayed effective generalship. Because of his impassivity in the face of losses in mud battles like Passchendaele, he has been elevated to a symbol of callous command. Clearly he accepted losses; by accepting them he bought time after the collapse of Russia, the French mutinies, and the U-boat campaigns. Others also accepted losses. It is pertinent in any assessment to remember that German losses were 2,000,000 against Britain's 743,000, and that Russia in the Second World War had 7,500,000 military dead and 17,500,000 civilian. **D. D.**

'HAIG', BY DUFF COOPER (FABER AND FABER, 1935).

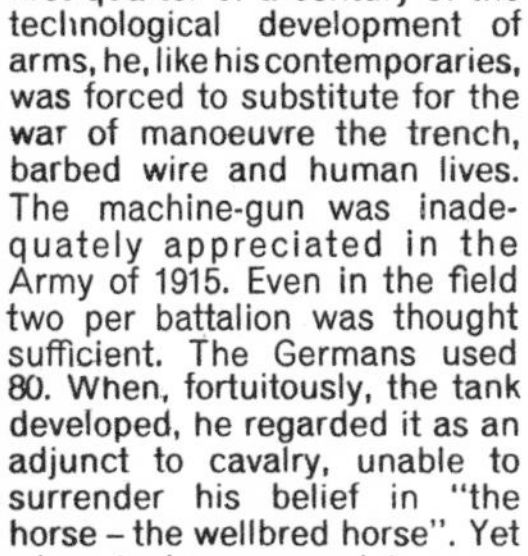

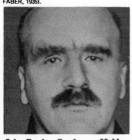

John Burdon Sanderson Haldane (Indian, ex-British, 1892–1964): geneticist and physiologist. Haldane was recognisably very much larger than life, even in a nation that expects its geniuses to be eccentric. He probably knew more science than anyone of his time. He would argue and even fight with opponents, but he sometimes ran after people he had insulted so that he could apologise (he did not always catch up with them). His family was distinguished in science – at nine he was a guinea-pig for some of his father's experiments on mine gases. After Eton he went to Oxford where he got first class degrees in both mathematics and classics. Science was for use, he considered, and risked his own life finding out how death had occurred when the submarine Thetis sank; he campaigned for air raid shelters before the Second World War and against atmospheric nuclear testing after it. Equally, as Professor of Biometry at University College, London, he was a distinguished academic scientist who, with R. A. Fisher (q.v.), virtually invented the mathematical study of population genetics. Although he was a Communist for many years, and a superb populariser of science for the *Daily Worker*, he was gradually driven from the party by its politically-based adoption of Lysenko's genetic theories. Later, he emigrated to India where he died of cancer shortly after writing perhaps the only poem by a scientist celebrating the removal of a tumour. **W. A. O.**

'JBS: THE LIFE AND WORK OF J. B. S. HALDANE', BY RONALD CLARK (HODDER AND STOUGHTON, 1968).

Sir William Haley (British, b. 1901): editor. Reading *The Street of Adventure* (the newspaper novel by Philip Gibbs) as a boy determined William Haley to become a journalist. Immediately after the First World War (in which he was a Merchant Service wireless operator), he got a job on *The Times* as a telephonist. Northcliffe soon sent him to Brussels to organise a news service, and it was in Manchester that he won his national reputation for brilliance on both the editorial and business sides of newspaper work. His ruthlessness and his capa-

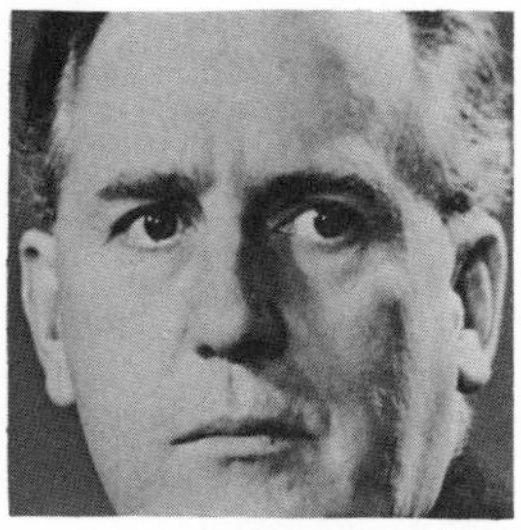

city for keeping prodigiously long hours brought him both admirers and critics. Early in the Second World War he became Editor-in-Chief, then Director General, of the BBC. Politicians and other pillars of the Establishment, seeking to bend programmes in their own interests, found him a nut too hard to crack. He carried this spirit of independence to his editorship of *The Times*. Now in the chair of Delane and Dawson, its ex-telephonist gave 'The Thunderer' a new look, including news on the front page. Haley did not hesitate to ruffle susceptibilities; controversy and pressure, no matter how high the level, never caused him to budge an inch on a point of principle. Patient in hearing all sides of an argument, once his mind is made up he is inflexible. He moved in January 1968 to the Encyclopaedia Britannica, from which he resigned in 1969. **A. P. R.**

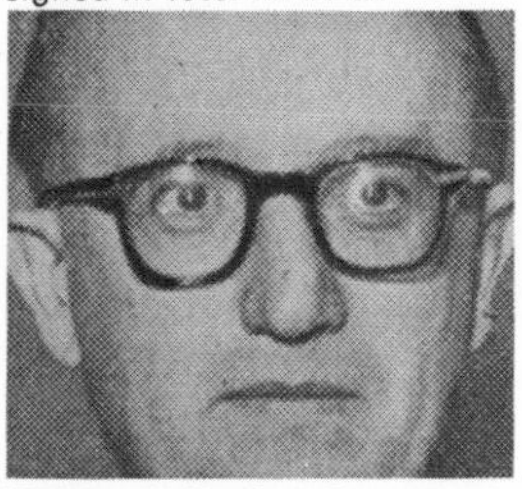

Walter Hallstein (German, b. 1901): statesman. 'The first Pope of the Common Market', Hallstein has been the most formidable champion of European unity since the Treaty of Rome. A professor of law, Hallstein lent his name, as State Secretary of the West German Foreign Office, to the 'Doctrine' which threatened diplomatic rupture with any state (except the USSR) which recognised East Germany. As President of the EEC Commission from 1958–67, he directed the nascent community towards federalist unity with unprofessorial panache. After the French veto on Britain in 1962 Hallstein set a collision course with de Gaulle (q.v.) in 1965 by linking farm finance with proposals to strengthen the political authority of the Commission and the European Parliament. Provoking the French 'empty chair boycott' and even demands for Treaty revision, the President's rashness brought the EEC within an ace of collapse. The compromise which brought the French back to Eurocracy marked a setback to unity; it included deliberately vindictive ostracism of Hallstein at the Rome anniversary celebrations in 1967 and his removal from the Presidency. The victim of an authority without power, Hallstein's weaknesses were those of the EEC, but his assertion of an independent European sovereignty will endure long after Gaullism has been relegated to the last footnote of French chauvinism. **S. S.**

'UNITED EUROPE', BY WALTER HALLSTEIN (O.U.P., 1962); 'THE NEW EUROPEANS', BY ANTHONY SAMPSON (HODDER, 1968); 'THE EUROPEAN COMMON MARKET AND COMMUNITY', BY UWE KITZINGER (ROUTLEDGE, 1967).

Dag Hammarskjöld (Swedish, 1905–1961): statesman. Hammarskjöld consolidated Trygve Lie's (q.v.) work in expanding the role of the Secretary General of the United Nations, adding his own great personal authority to the post from 1953–61. Brought in as the quiet administrator, he soon showed his calibre in negotiations with Chou En-lai (q.v.) for the release of imprisoned U.S. airmen. At first, nothing followed. He told the Americans to be patient. A few months later, the airmen were released. "Leave it to Dag" had begun. The Middle East crisis of 1956–7 showed him the role the U.N. can play among uncommitted countries. He developed his theory of "filling vacuums" and he coaxed Nasser (q.v.) into accepting UNEF, which kept the peace for 10 years. He declared in reply to a Soviet onslaught: "It is not the Soviet Union, or indeed any of the other big powers who need the

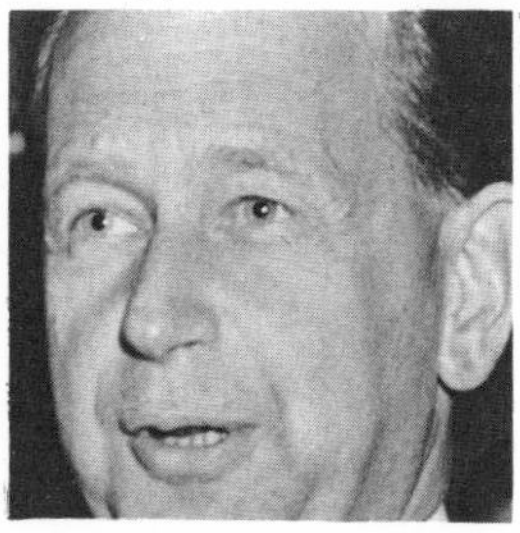

United Nations for their protection. It is all the others." Consequently, Hammarskjöld grew interested in the newly independent African countries. He saw that the U.N. must help prevent threats to territorial unity there. Thus a U.N. force entered the Congo and subsequently Katanga after the province had seceded; and, flying to see Tshombe, he was killed. Hammarskjöld brought to his role an unprecedented subtlety of method, a scrupulous sense of international morality, and a new insight into the problems facing the world. **H. J. B.**

'SERVANT OF PEACE', ED. WILDER FOOTE (HARPER AND ROW, NEW YORK, 1962); 'THE MYSTERIOUS DEATH OF DAG HAMMARSKJOLD', BY ARTHUR L. GAVSHON (WALKER, NEW YORK, 1962); 'MARKINGS', BY DAG HAMMARSKJOLD (FABER ,1964); 'DAG HAMMARSKJOLD', BY JOSEPH LASH (CASSELL, 1962).

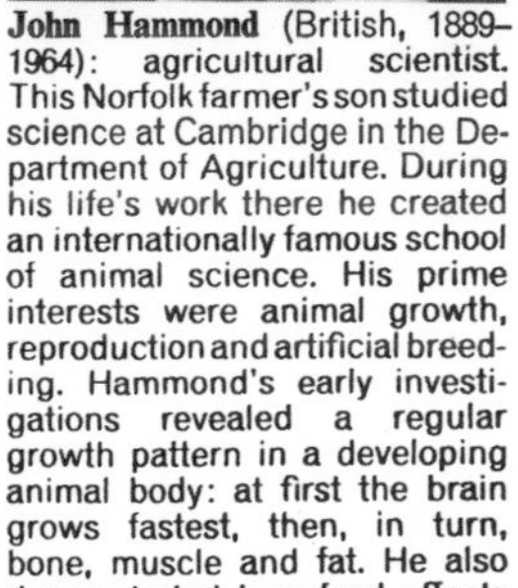

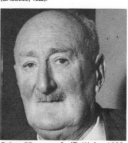

John Hammond (British, 1889–1964): agricultural scientist. This Norfolk farmer's son studied science at Cambridge in the Department of Agriculture. During his life's work there he created an internationally famous school of animal science. His prime interests were animal growth, reproduction and artificial breeding. Hammond's early investigations revealed a regular growth pattern in a developing animal body: at first the brain grows fastest, then, in turn, bone, muscle and fat. He also demonstrated how food affects carcass characteristics. This work has influenced livestock management and feeding programmes ever since. He pioneered artificial insemination of cattle in Britain, overcoming heavy opposition with skilful advocacy. Pilot centres at Cambridge (1942) and Reading (1943) showed that the scheme was workable; the national network followed. Within 14 years 10 million cattle had been bred by artificial insemination (AI) in Britain, and under the Milk Marketing Board's organisation AI has radically improved Britain's dairy herd and beef production. Hammond has greatly advanced world food production through livestock improvement because he believed theories less valuable than their application and sought always to help farmers understand scientific findings. **S. L.**

'FARM ANIMALS, THEIR BREEDING, GROWTH AND INHERITANCE', BY JOHN HAMMOND (EDWARD ARNOLD, 1960); 'MODERN ASPECTS OF ANIMAL PRODUCTION', BY N. T. M. YEATES (BUTTERWORTH, 1965); 'THE SEMEN OF ANIMALS AND ARTIFICIAL INSEMINATION', BY J. P. MAULE (COMMONWEALTH AGRICULTURAL BUREAU, 1962).

Keir Hardie (British, 1856–1915): politician. No other British

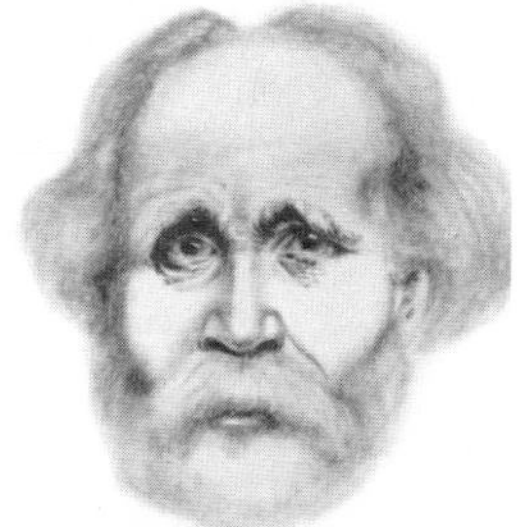

labour leader is so firmly established in both Labour mythology and in Labour history as Keir Hardie, the quintessential pioneer of the Golden Age. Hardie (a miner from the age of 10) graduated in Labour politics via the Temperance Movement, trade unionism and journalism. His appeal was essentially moral – impatience with suffering, anger at inequality, scorn for poverty in the midst of plenty. In 1892 he was elected M.P. for West Ham: he arrived at Westminster wearing a cloth cap and tweed jacket and escorted by his constituents in a charabanc complete with trumpeter. In 1893 he presided over the founding conference of the Independent Labour Party in Bradford. After the general election of 1906, when 29 'Labour' M.P.s recognised his leadership, he was for five years in charge of the infant Parliamentary Labour Party. Ramsay MacDonald (q.v.) succeeded him, but Keir Hardie, less ambitious, never lost Labour's affections. In 1915 he died, broken-hearted because of the First World War whose onset he had worked vainly to oppose. **A. B.**

'J. KEIR HARDIE', BY WILLIAM STEWART (CASSELL, 1921); 'THE ORIGINS OF THE LABOUR PARTY, 1880-1900', BY H. PELLING (OXFORD UNIVERSITY PRESS, 1965).

Jean Harlow (U.S., 1911–1937): film actress. The original Platinum Blonde – and significantly one of her earliest bit parts was in *The Saturday Night Kid* (1929), whose star, Clara Bow (q.v.), Harlow was to replace as the American sexual archetype. Discovered by Ben Lyon, she first starred in Howard Hughes's (q.v.) *Hell's Angels* (1930), but it was *Red Dust* (1932) which defined her future screen character, and with little essential variation, until the last year of her life and career, when she tried to break out of the image established for her. Her luminous skin, shimmering platinum hair, voluptuous figure (she was credited with restoring to the breast its primary erotic interest), her provocative attitudes and movements, her very apparent habit of not wearing underclothing, and the echo

JEAN HARLOW · WILLIAM POWELL

RECKLESS

FRANCHOT **TONE**
MAY **ROBSON**
TED HEALY
NAT PENDLETON
ROBERT LIGHT

PRODUCED BY
DAVID O. SELZNICK

DIRECTED BY
VICTOR FLEMING

A Metro-Goldwyn-Mayer Picture

THE *Giant* MELODY DRAMA!

---

of her turbulent off-screen life, brought to the American cinema a new frankness in sexuality. At the same time her square, cleft chin, assurance, metallic voice and deft handling of a wise-crack betrayed the toughness that made her the most equal of Clark Gable's screen partners (*Red Dust, Hold Your Man, China Seas, Wife versus Secretary, Saratoga*). Brassy, bold, good-natured; a pal as well as a tramp; with a physique ideally designed for art-deco interiors, she was the supreme sex symbol of the early Thirties. **D. R.**

'HARLOW: AN INTIMATE BIOGRAPHY', BY IRVING SHULMAN (MAYFLOWER-DELL, 1964); 'THE CELLULOID SACRIFICE', BY ALEXANDER WALKER (MICHAEL JOSEPH, 1966).

Gayelord Hauser (U.S., ex-Austrian, b. 1895): dietitian. Hauser has popularised the 'natural food' cult and has himself remained remarkably well-preserved for a man now in his mid-seventies; he claims wonder properties for such foods as honey, fruit and vegetable juices, yoghurt, yeast, wholemeal bread and wheat germ. These are good nutritious foods for those who like them, but there is no scientific foundation for the claim that they have special health-

giving properties that could not be provided by most other foods available. Hauser makes extensive reference to carefully selected scientific information about food and nutrition. The scientific basis he propounds would often not stand up to critical analysis; nevertheless, a considerable amount of his advice is sound good sense, which has psychological as well as nutritional overtones. He is a successful 'beauty farmer' and popular author who demonstrates what dedicated enthusiasm, common sense and clever publicity can achieve. **A. C. F.**

'LOOK YOUNGER, LIVE LONGER', BY GAYELORD HAUSER (FABER AND FABER, 1951).

Sir Geoffrey de Havilland (British, 1882–1965): engineer. Probably the most outstanding figure among the early British aviation designers, de Havilland, the son of a clergyman, taught himself to fly in 1910 on a plane whose frame and engine he had designed and largely built himself, on a £1000 gift from his grandfather. After the First World War the de Havilland Aircraft Co. (founded 1920) produced the Tiger Moth, which was one of the best light planes ever built

and on which thousands first learned their flying. In 1934 the de Havilland Comet, with a wood frame, won the England to Australia air race, and provided the know-how for the immensely versatile Mosquito fighter-bomber, built virtually off the drawing-board in 1940. By 1945 de Havilland (who was a technician rather than a businessman – he never became either chairman or managing director of his company) realised that Britain needed a real commercial breakthrough to keep ahead of the Americans. The result was the Comet jet, with its two years of triumphant success and then tragedy, when metal fatigue, then little understood, sent two of the planes plunging into the Mediterranean, and caused complete withdrawal from service. Finally Comet IV came into service over the Atlantic just ahead of Boeing, but the big lead had been lost. In 1961, de Havilland's became part of the Hawker-Siddeley complex. **P. W.**

'OUTLINE OF DE HAVILLAND HISTORY,' BY C. MARTIN SHARP (FABER AND FABER, 1960); 'SKY FEVER', BY GEOFFREY DE HAVILLAND (HAMISH HAMILTON, 1961).

Coleman Hawkins (U.S., 1904–1969): jazz musician. Coleman Hawkins began his career in an era when the saxophone was already a basic necessity of the dance-band, but when still a rarity in jazz. He achieved his fame with Fletcher Henderson's orchestra in the late Twenties, as the first great exponent of the tenor saxophone as a jazz solo instrument. From then till the early Forties his was the only style widely accepted on the instrument, and was emulated

throughout the world. At the height of his fame he left the U.S. and worked in England with Jack Hylton and elsewhere on the Continent with a number of groups. There he also made records, the most famous being with fellow American saxophonist Benny Carter and French gipsy guitarist Django Reinhardt (q.v.). During the late Forties Hawkins managed to up-date his style to attune with the new sounds of modern jazz without losing his highly individual character. But gradually his exoticisms were eclipsed by the 'dry' tenor style instigated by Lester Young (q.v.). Nevertheless he may well have been the man Adolf Sax had in mind when he presented the world with the saxophone in 1840. **J. P. W. D.**

RECORDS: 'DJANGO AND HIS AMERICAN FRIENDS,' VOL. 1 (HMV CLP 1920); 'HAWK IN HOLLAND' (ACE OF CLUBS ACL 1247); 'FURTHER DEFINITIONS' (WORLD RECORD CLUB, T.864); 'THE HAWK AND THE HUNTER' (ACE OF HEARTS, AH 174); 'HINES PLUS ELDRIDGE WITH SPECIAL GUEST STAR COLEMAN HAWKINS' (MERCURY SMWL 21031)

Howard Hawks (U.S., b. 1896): film director. Howard Hawks has made every kind of movie, and among the best of every kind. Comedy: *Bringing Up Baby*. Western: *Rio Bravo*. Gangster: *Scarface*. Musical: *Gentlemen Prefer Blondes*. War: *Air Force*. Thriller: *The Big Sleep*. Hawks's movies are primarily concerned with individual heroism – ironic and often comic. Professionals fascinate him: a man doing his job is always interesting to watch. But Hawks never ceases to point out that when it comes to ordinary life we are all amateurs. Women, particularly, make professional men seem confused and helpless in Hawks's films. His style is cool and un-cluttered visually. There are no camera effects, no traces of expressionism. He defines a good film director as "a man who doesn't annoy you". More than anyone Hawks has used the various genres of Hollywood cinema for their true purpose: to satisfy the audience on the level of myth, of stories told and retold for enjoyment and instruction. There's no need to talk about art. **P. Ma.**

'HOWARD HAWKS', BY ROBIN WOOD (SECKER AND WARBURG, 1968).

Sir Norman Haworth (British, 1883–1950): organic chemist. Haworth established the way in which carbon, hydrogen and oxygen atoms are arranged in space in a number of carbohydrate sugars. These compounds are basic building blocks in the construction of such natural structural materials as cellulose and starch. The determination of their structure was no mere academic exercise, for such basic chemical knowledge was a prerequisite to the biochemical understanding of how these materials act when ingested. Although much of his work was in the field of carbohydrate chemistry, one of Haworth's outstanding achievements was the development of a synthetic route to ascorbic acid – more commonly known as Vitamin C. This made possible the production of this anti-scurvy vitamin more cheaply than it could be obtained from natural sources. It was partly due to the painstaking work of chemists such as Haworth in unravelling the way in which organic molecules a.e put together that the modern science of molecular biology was made possible. **M. A. S.**

'NOBEL PRIZEWINNERS IN CHEMISTRY', BY EDUARD FARBER (ABELARD-SCHUMAN, 1963); 'NOBEL LECTURES, CHEMISTRY 1922-41' (ELSEVIER, 1966).

William Randolph Hearst (U.S., 1863–1951): newspaper proprietor. Hearst did not invent the techniques of the yellow Press, but he gave jaundice to journalism by his acts and example. His pioneering lay in using every possible mechanical reporting device to reduce a popular crusade to the level of a travelling circus. By lowering public taste, he raised circulation. "What we're after is the 'gee-whizz' emotion," one of his staff said. On this formula Hearst founded what became the world's biggest publishing empire by the 1930s. Notorious as an instigator of the Spanish-American War of 1898, a failed politician in the Progressive Era, an Anglophobe until 1917, a pro-Nazi in the 1930s, an anti-Red in the 1940s, Hearst championed populist reforms in his early days and changed

most of the world's newspapers. For better or worse, he was the first great Press lord who rose on the irresistible combination of patriotism, populism and pap. His tragic life of conspicuous waste inspired one masterpiece – Orson Welles's *Citizen Kane*. **A. A. S.**

'HEARST, LORD OF SAN SIMEON', BY OLIVER CARLSON AND ERNEST SUTHERLAND BATES (VIKING PRESS, 1936); 'THE PRESS AND AMERICA', BY EDWIN EMERY AND HENRY SMITH (PRENTICE-HALL, NEW YORK, 1954); 'IMPERIAL HEARST' BY FERDINAND LUNDBERG (EQUINOX, NEW YORK, 1936).

John Heartfield (German, 1891–1968): artist. Born Helmut Herzfeld, Heartfield anglicised his name in 1913 in protest against German militarism. With George Grosz he invented the technique of photomontage (which Grosz said they "discovered at five-o'clock one May morning"), whereby pieces of photographs are combined to make a point. The practice of bringing together unrelated images in an unexpected context is related to Dada and Surrealist art, and Heartfield's first photomontages were of Dada 'nonsense' subjects. Political subjects for newspapers and book-jackets followed. Heartfield's anti-Nazi broadsides forced him into exile; first to Czechoslovakia in 1933 and then in 1937 to Britain where he designed covers for Penguins and worked on and off for *Reynolds News, Picture Post* and *Lilliput*. He returned to East Berlin in 1950, where his photomontages were not at first appreciated. Through Brecht (q.v.) he got commissions for stage designs, an area in which he made important innovations. Later he gained full State approval, became an adviser on propaganda and Professor at the Art Academy. Photomontage is one of the most important techniques in 20th-century art, combining the objectivity of the lens with the subjectivity of the artist. As a user of photomontage as a political weapon, Heartfield has no equal. **F. P. W.**

'JOHN HEARTFIELD', BY WIELAND HERZEFELDE (VED VERLAG DER KUNST, 1962).

Photomontage (above) by John Heartfield. The cow represents depression-struck Germany forced to eat its own flesh to survive

Hugh Hefner (U.S., b. 1926): publisher. With the first number of *Playboy* magazine in December 1953, Hefner struck an answering chord in the young urban American male. His fantasies became their fantasies. Circulation and advertising revenue rocketed. His readers, mostly college-educated, were the best defined and well-heeled group that advertisers had

found for many a long day. Hefner established headquarters in The Mansion, a 40-roomed house in Chicago. Observing no regular working or sleeping hours, he pads around in a dressing gown, his work centre being the circular Playbed, surrounded by electronic devices and Bunny girls, who serve drinks to the constant hordes of visitors. *Playboy*, ac-

cording to Hefner, is a "total package", in that both advertising and editorial matter – busty cartoons, girlie features, the nude 'Playmate' in the magazine's centre-page gatefold, and some of the best of modern writing – combine to convey the good life, a combination of status and sex. But sex at one remove: when in 1960 Hefner brought girls off the pages and into the first of the Playboy Clubs, the bunnies, in their provocative costumes, were declared untouchable. In 1962 Hefner began to publish The Playboy Philosophy, a somewhat turgid and interminable argument for permissiveness. His enterprises, in which he has an overwhelming controlling interest, now gross close to $100 million every year. **G. P. G. N.**

'BIG BUNNY', BY JOE GOLDBERG (BALLANTINE BOOKS, NEW YORK, 1967).

Martin Heidegger (German, b. 1889): philosopher. Heidegger is the most systematic of existentialists. His most important book, *Being and Time* (1927), is a study of the special peculiarities of human existence (*Dasein*). For most European philosophers man is essentially a rational animal, a spectator of the world that is set over against him and in pursuit of knowledge about it. For Heidegger man is pre-eminently an active being, the possessor of a will, immersed in the world which is given a form

only by his active preoccupations. It is man's special fate to create himself by decisions which select from the possibilities open to him. He may try to escape from this by 'inauthenticity', the strategy of living in accordance with routine or habit, the attempt to imitate a mere thing. For authentic living what is necessary is the resolute confrontation of death, the annihilation that inspires metaphysical anxiety. Heidegger extracts a large dramatic potential from his initially abstract subject-matter. Latterly he has turned from human existence to the mystery of being in general, a nebulous topic which he pursues in poetic meditations and by means of fanciful excursions into etymology. Well-disposed towards Hitler, Heidegger has often expressed his hatred of technological civilisation. **A. Q.**

'BEING AND TIME', BY MARTIN HEIDEGGER (S.C.M., 1962); 'IRRATIONAL MAN', BY W. BARRETT (HEINEMANN, 1968).

Jascha Heifetz (U.S., ex-Russian, b. 1901): violinist. Of all the Jewish violin virtuosos who have emerged from Eastern Europe in this century, Heifetz and Huberman (q.v.) have perhaps made the strongest impact. At the age of nine, Heifetz became the youngest member of Leopold Auer's famous class at the Imperial Conservatory in St Petersburg, and by the time he was 12 his technique was so outstanding, so flawless, that he toured Russia, Germany and Scandinavia with sensational success – perhaps the greatest miracle since Paganini, unlike whom he has always shown strong emotional reserve. While Paganini had to play

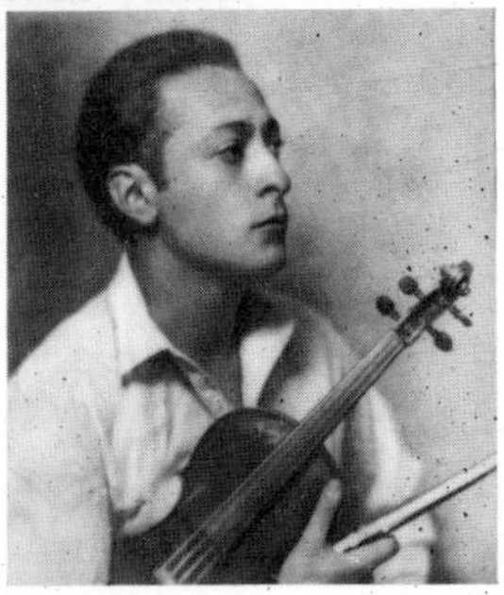

himself into a frenzy, Heifetz, in Carl Flesch's (q.v.) words, "can always start playing without any preliminary practice; his fingers and bow function like a machine which runs at its maximal capacity as soon as you press a button". His influence has been great – if not always favourable: exaggerated tempi sound exaggerated indeed in the hands of lesser men. "There has probably never been a violinist," writes Flesch, "who has approached the summit of perfection more closely." **H. K.**

'THE MEMOIRS OF CARL FLESCH', TRANS. AND ED. HANS KELLER (ROCKLIFF, 1957).

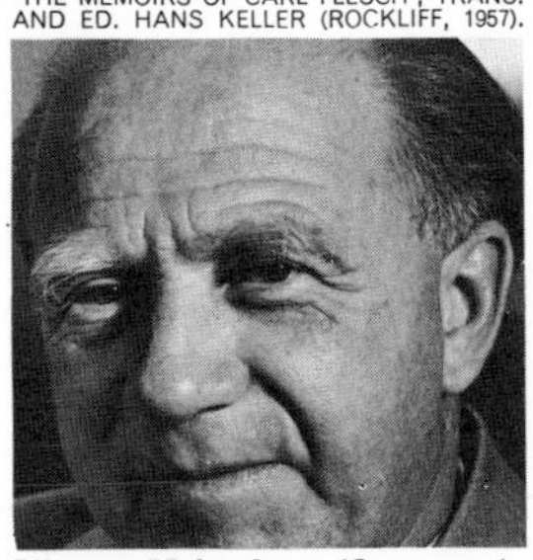

Werner Heisenberg (German, b. 1901): physicist. Heisenberg, at the age of 23, staggered the scientific world with his theory of quantum mechanics, which earned him a Nobel Prize in 1932. His controversial theory was based on the idea that it is impossible to say where an electron is at any instant, or to try to follow it through its orbit round the atomic nucleus. He therefore rejected the well-established planetary orbit concept put forward by Niels Bohr (q.v.) and formulated instead a theory which defined the electron's position and speed in terms of abstract mathematical structures called 'matrices'. From this he successfully predicted that hydrogen must exist in two forms. Heisenberg's other major contribution to theoretical physics – his 'Uncertainty Principle' – laid down that when calculating the position and momentum of atomic particles there is always an error involved, which, although negligible on the human scale, cannot be ignored in studies of the atom. He gave physicists a powerful tool – quantum mechanics – for interpreting the secrets of radiation phenomena. **N. V.**

'SOURCE OF QUANTUM MECHANICS', ED. B. L. VAN DER WAERDEN (CONSTABLE, 1968).

Ernest Hemingway (U.S., 1899–1961): writer. Currently, Hemingway's work is out of fashion, but he may come to seem the Christ-figure for an age of violence, enacting in his own encounters, tensions, and dicta the deepest stresses of a civilisation as blood-sick as the Aztecs'. He was wounded in Italy as an ambulance driver in 1918, then worked as a journalist in France and Spain in the 1920s. He studied violence in the bull-ring, as a war correspondent, and as a big-game hunter. He died, shot by his own gun, in 1961. He has had a huge influence on pulp magazine fiction, journalism, and

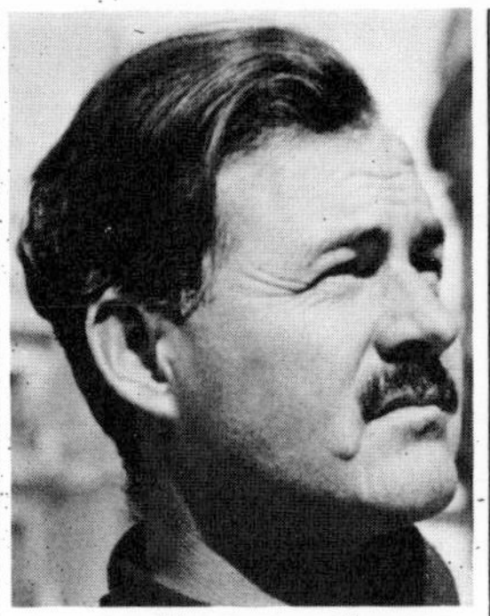

screen-writing, as well as on the novel and the short story. His philosophy of courage as "grace under pressure" illustrates his attempt to link morality with aesthetics. His best books were *The First Forty Nine Stories, Across The River And Into The Trees* (despite the critics) and *A Farewell To Arms*. But *all* should be read, including the treatise on bull-fighting, *Death In The Afternoon*, and the account of big-game hunting, *Green Hills of Africa*. At his worst, Hemingway's standards of finish are very high, and, at its best, his prose is the purest poetry of our time, with power to move the susceptible like passages from the New Testament. The myth of the Hemingway hero remains a touchstone for how to behave in the extreme situation. **G. M. MacB.**

'THE APPRENTICESHIP OF ERNEST HEMINGWAY', BY CHARLES A. FENTON (MENTOR BOOKS, 1954); 'ERNEST HEMINGWAY', BY PHILIP YOUNG (RINEHART, 1952); 'ERNEST HEMINGWAY', BY CARLOS BAKER (SCRIBNERS, 1969); 'PAPA HEMINGWAY', BY A. E. HOTCHNER (WEIDENFELD AND NICOLSON, 1966).

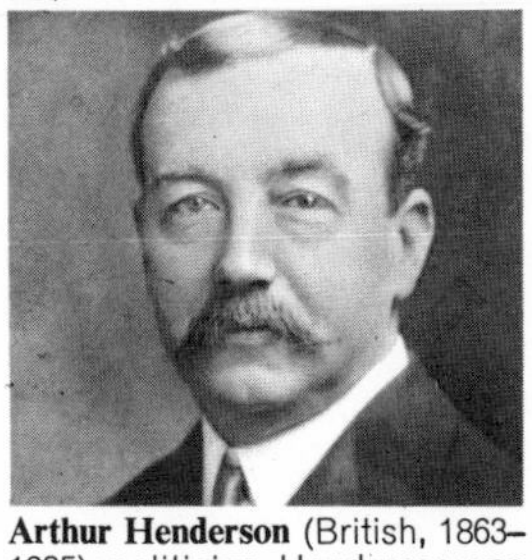

Arthur Henderson (British, 1863–1935): politician. Henderson was the chief organiser of the Labour Party throughout its formative years. Born in Glasgow and reared in Newcastle, he played a leading role from the time of his election as Labour's fifth independent Member of Parliament. He was the first Labour man to achieve cabinet office in the 1915 coalition and, as a member of the War Cabinet in 1916, his elevation symbolised the new power of Labour in time of war. As Secretary of the Party, he carried through the reforms of 1918 which established Labour as a centralised mass party, and helped to draw up a new programme of moderate Socialism: Labour was now able to cash in on the transformations of war and to replace the Liberals as the major progressive party. He was Home Secretary in 1924 and Foreign Secretary in 1929–31, striving nobly to preserve international harmony in a time of economic collapse. He led the opposition to MacDonald in the 1931 crisis (when MacDonald took close supporters into a National Government), and thus helped to preserve the self-respect of the Labour Party. Henderson did more than any other to build the Labour Party as a modern electoral machine with a moderate reformist appeal. **A. M.**

'ARTHUR HENDERSON', BY MARY AGNES HAMILTON (HEINEMANN, 1938); 'ARTHUR HENDERSON', BY HENRY R. WINKLER IN 'THE DIPLOMATS', ED. GORDON CRAIG AND FELIX GILBERT (PRINCETON U.P., 1953); 'THE BRITISH LABOUR PARTY', BY CARL F. BRAND (STANFORD U.P., 1964).

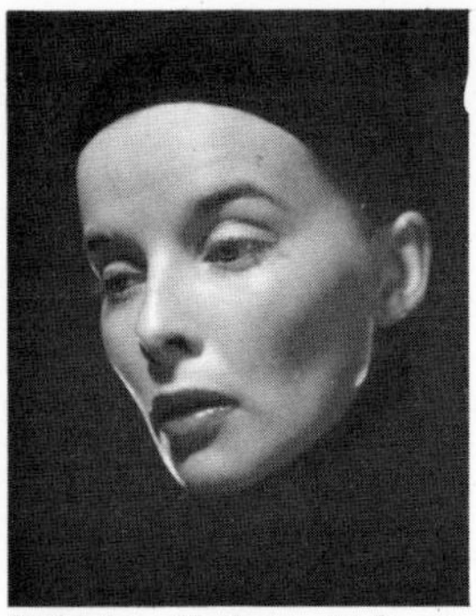

Katharine Hepburn (U.S., b. 1909): film actress. Katharine Hepburn is an actress who might have been born to play the great independent-minded Shavian heroines: the Major Barbara of the American cinema. She began her stage career more or less rampageously, first attracting Hollywood's attention while playing an Amazon warrior on Broadway. She achieved instant screen stardom in *A Bill of Divorcement* (1932), simultaneously startling a conformist movie industry by such unstarry habits as sitting on pavements to read her mail. James Agate wrote of her, admiringly, as having "a cheek-bone like a death's head allied to a manner as sinister and aggressive as crossbones". Dorothy Parker made the celebrated crack (of a stage performance) about "running the gamut from A to B". She mellowed by way of the imperious but vulnerable Tracy Lord in Philip Barry's tailor-written *The Philadelphia Story*, into the string of films with Spencer Tracy, one of the screen's most cheerful and civilising partnerships. Academy Awards in both 1968 and 1969 (the latter for her blazing, burnished Eleanor of Aquitaine in *The Lion in Winter*) testify to Hepburn's unique position as surviving star and original anti-star, Hollywood's glitteringly mannered voice of reasoned independence. She perennially suggests a Louisa May Alcott heroine rewritten by Shaw as an embodiment of the Life Force, or a games-playing Emily Dickinson. **P. H.**

Helenio Herrera (French, ex-Argentine, b. 1916): football manager. The most flamboyant and controversial of the managers of his time, Herrera is reputed to have earned £50,000 a year during his latter years with Internazionale of Milan; he was guaranteed 100 million lire (over £70,000) for one season, when he left them to join Roma in 1968. He grew up in the slums of Casablanca, played professional football in France at full-back, was naturalised French and fought in the Ardennes. In 1947 he became manager of Stade Français, leaving two years later for Spain where – but for a season with Belenenses, Portugal, 1957/8 – he remained

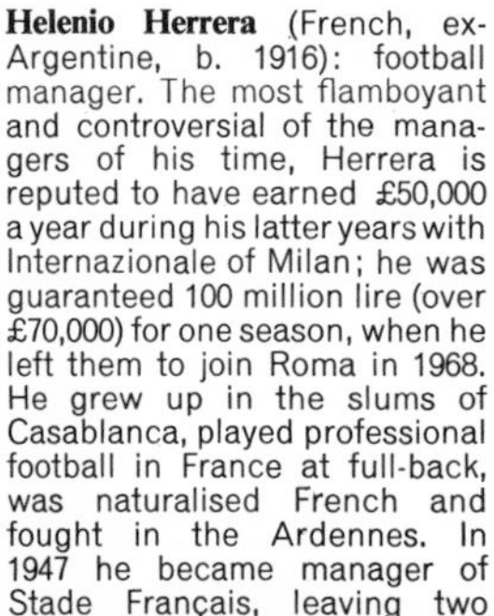

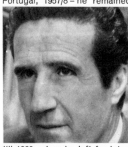

till 1960, when he left for Internazionale and Italy. In the previous two years he had achieved great success with Barcelona, establishing a reputation for ruthless, paternalist discipline, reinforced by quasi-'magical' dressing-room ceremony. In Milan, initial failure moved him towards an ultra-defensive concept of football which in ensuing years brought the club two European, two world clubs' and three Italian Championships. In Italy, the habit of taking his team away to *ritiro* in the country, three days before a match, was an essential and symptomatic feature of his policy. He is the embodiment and promoter of the tendency of 20th-century sport towards commercialism and ferocious pragmatism. **B. G.**

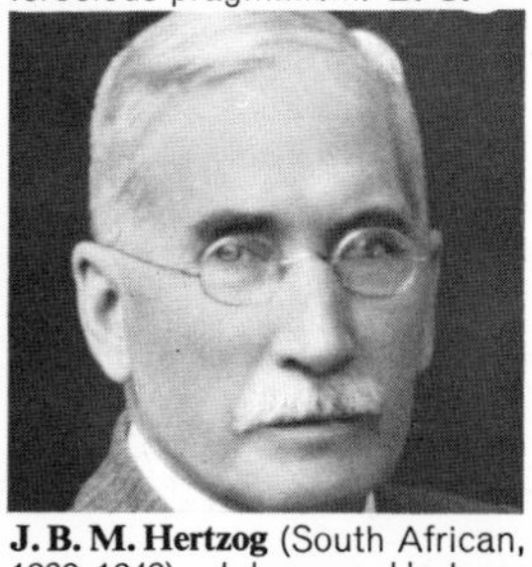

J. B. M. Hertzog (South African, 1866–1942): statesman. Hertzog, Smuts' (q.v.) principal rival, was the founder of modern Afrikaner nationalism. Malan, Strijdom (qq.v.) and Verwoerd were his immediate successors. An Orange Free State judge, he, like Smuts, became a leading Boer general, a participant in drafting the Union constitution, and a minister in Botha's first Cabinet in 1910. He soon broke from Botha, favouring a 'two-stream' policy and opposing involvement in "Britain's wars". After the 1924 electoral triumph over Smuts he gave constitutional recognition to Afrikaans in place of Dutch, introduced the new flag and helped shape Balfour's definition of Dominion Status and the 1931 Statute of Westminster. Head of the post-Depression coalition, with Smuts as deputy, he enacted the Hertzog racial segregation laws of 1936. Despite his defeat by Smuts in opposition to war against Germany in September 1939, he remained faithful to his acceptance of British-Boer equality within South Africa. He died lonely and neglected by extreme Nationalists. The Republic of South Africa, the survival and strength of the Afrikaans language and culture and the power of Afrikaner nationalism owe much to the Boer judge turned general who rejected Boer-British conciliation. **K. K.**

'GENERAL J. B. M. HERTZOG,' BY C. M. VAN DEN HEEVER, (A.P.B. BOOKSTORE, JOHANNESBURG, 1946).

Theodor Herzl (Hungarian, 1860–1904): statesman. Theodor Herzl was the patriarch of Zionism. Spending most of his life on the precipice of the old century, the degradation of the Dreyfus case took him into the abyss of the new. Impelled by a bitter anger to desert the fleshpots of journalism in Vienna, the struggle for Jewish national existence ate up his fortune and strength but produced his master work, *Der Judenstaat* (The Jewish State). Herzl made Zionism a mass organisation with funds and programme. But his pursuit of territory and protection from a Great Patron was less fruitful. Disappointed in turn by the Kaiser in Jerusalem, the Sultan in Constantinople, and Lansdowne in London, the appalling augury of the Kishinneff pogrom persuaded him to accept Chamberlain's offer of a homeland in Uganda. Put before the sixth Zionist Congress in 1903 as an "emergency measure" Herzl was

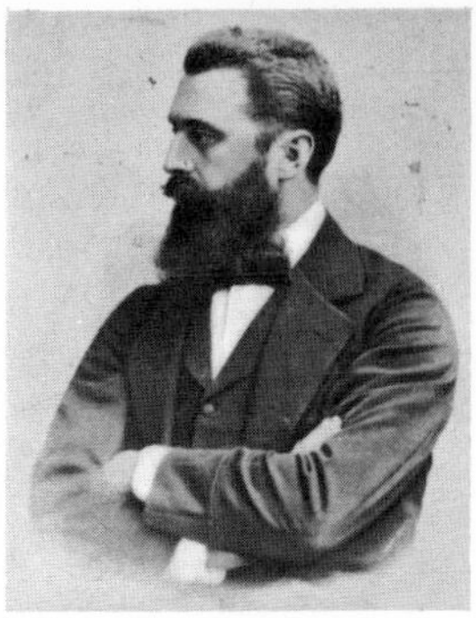

faced with revolt and accusations of betraying the Palestine dream. Like Moses, whose stature he matched, he died amid quarrel and pessimism, never to know that his remains would rest on a hill overlooking Jerusalem beside the motto his life embodied: "If You Will It, It Is No Legend". **S. S.**

'THE JEWISH STATE', BY THEODOR HERZL (REVISED EDITION, PORDES, 1967); 'THEODOR HERZL, FOUNDER OF ZIONISM', BY ALEX BEIN (MERIDIAN BOOKS, 1962).

Victor Hess (U.S., ex-Austrian, 1883–1964): physicist. Hess was the discoverer of the streams of highly energetic particles, constantly bombarding the Earth, which we know as cosmic rays. He researched on the natural radioactivity of the Earth at the Physical Institute in Vienna. He found that the gamma-rays emitted from terrestrial radioactive sources did not decrease in strength with increasing altitude quite as expected. Hess proposed that extra gamma-rays came from space. He proved his point by making a series of seven historic balloon flights in 1911 and 1912, when his ioni-

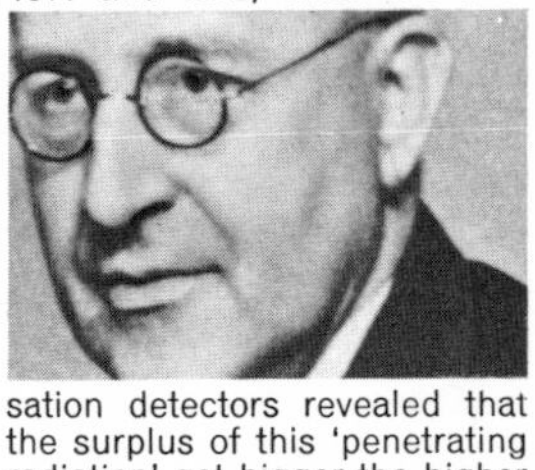

sation detectors revealed that the surplus of this 'penetrating radiation' got bigger the higher he went. He also showed that the radiation did not vary from daytime to nighttime, thus establishing that it did not originate in the Sun but must come from farther away in space. Hess shared the Nobel Prize with Carl Anderson in 1936. Because cosmic rays – since found to consist of several kinds of particle – have such high energies they were studied extensively in the days before big particle-accelerating machines. A number of new elementary particles was discovered from their interactions in cloud chambers. Nowadays the unsolved problem of their origin continues to interest physicists. **P. H. S. S.**

'COSMIC RAYS', BY A. W. WOLFENDALE (NEWNES, 1963); 'COSMIC RAYS', BY BRUNO ROSSI (ALLEN AND UNWIN, 1966).

Thor Heyerdahl (Norwegian, b. 1914): anthropologist. Heyerdahl is the chief exponent of the value of practical experiment in solving archaeological problems. He has recreated the techniques of prehistory to demonstrate the plausibility of ancient man's seemingly incredible enterprise. In 1948 he sailed, with five companions, across the Pacific in a raft, Kon-Tiki, to show that the Polynesian Islands could have been peopled by Indians drifting from South America. In 1956 he led an expedition to the Easter Islands and not only established an archaeological sequence but proved that ancient man could have transported and erected, with primitive techniques, the

mysterious giant statues that throng the islands. In 1969 Heyerdahl attempted to show a link between the ancient cultures of Egypt and Mexico, by establishing that the Egyptians could have reached South America in a papyrus boat borne by the Atlantic currents. Many archaeological theories seem soluble on paper, many seem too far-fetched to be acceptable, given the limited knowledge of pre-historic man. Any scientist who, like Thor Heyerdahl, is prepared to recreate the past by simulating precisely the conditions under which man evolved his society can contribute greatly to knowledge. **P. G. St. B. C.**

'THE KON-TIKI EXPEDITION', BY THOR HEYERDAHL (ALLEN AND UNWIN, 1950); 'AMERICAN INDIANS IN THE PACIFIC', BY THOR HEYERDAHL (ALLEN AND UNWIN, 1952); 'AKU-AKU', BY THOR HEYERDAHL (ALLEN AND UNWIN, 1958).

Sir Edmund Hillary (New Zealander, b. 1919): explorer. Hillary aimed high – at the rooftop of the world. Born in Auckland, New Zealand, a bee-keeper by profession, he turned climber, scientist and explorer. He was the first man to conquer – a rope's length ahead of the Sherpa Tenzing – the summit of Mount Everest, on May 29, 1953, and he was knighted in the same year. Then he aimed at the South Pole. In 1958, at the head of the New Zealand section of the British Commonwealth Transantarctic Expedition led by Sir Vivian Fuchs, he was the first to reach the Pole overland after Amundsen and Capt. R. F. Scott (qq.v.). From 1960 till 1965 Hillary undertook various expeditions to Nepal – including an abortive search for the 'Abominable Snowman'. In gratitude for the Sherpas' services to mountaineering he built near Mount Everest the first Sherpa hospital and six schools in whose running, now that his climbing days are over, he takes an active interest. **J. A.**

BOOKS BY HILLARY: 'HIGH ADVENTURE' (HODDER AND STOUGHTON, 1955); 'THE CROSSING OF ANTARCTICA' (WITH SIR VIVIAN FUCHS, CASSELL, 1958); 'HIGH IN THE THIN COLD AIR' (HODDER AND STOUGHTON, 1963); 'SCHOOL HOUSE IN THE CLOUDS' (HODDER AND STOUGHTON, 1965).

James Hillier (Canadian, b. 1915): research physicist and engineer. Hillier made the electron microscope into a flexible and powerful research tool. Its principle is a simple one; during the 19th century it was realised that the resolution of any microscope was inversely proportional to the wavelength of the radiation it used. Electrons, with their very short wavelength, therefore offered a means of producing better resolution than light, but it was

not until 1934 that it proved possible even to equal the resolution of the light microscope. In Germany, the pioneers of the electron microscope gave up and worked on something else. But James Hillier and Albert Prebus at the University of Toronto started work in 1937 on improving it. Two years later Hillier was recruited (very wisely) by the Radio Corporation of

America, and by the end of the next year had completed the Model B electron microscope, with which so many electron microscopists began their careers. Hillier made many

important improvements to the microscope; perhaps the most important was his method for compensating field asymmetries (1945–46). Without this, any further improvement of resolution would have been impossible. In 1944 Hillier developed the first electron probe microanalyser, which has become an important laboratory tool. **N. J. M. H.**

Conrad Hilton (U.S., b. 1887): hotelier. The son of a successful merchant in San Antonio, New Mexico, Conrad Hilton bought his first hotel, the Mobley in the booming Texas oil town of Cisco,

in 1919. He is now chairman of Hilton Hotels Corporation, which owns or franchises over 100 hotels in the U.S.; he is also chairman of Hilton International, an overseas chain of 55 hotels from England to Egypt (this company is now controlled by TWA). Conrad Hilton was the first man to realise that hotels were not simply homes-away-from-home for holidaymakers, but sleeping-quarters-cum-offices for America's vast armies of peripatetic salesmen and businessmen. From Albuquerque, New Mexico, to Clearwater, Florida, Hiltons offer standardised, efficient and relatively luxurious quarters at a time when older hotels are dying from the competition of cut-price motels. The same principle has been applied to the overseas hotels, but with different results. The very standardisation of the service means that Hiltons are temples to American efficiency abroad. Visitors to the Hilton in Istanbul could well imagine themselves to be in Miami. **A. L. C.**

'BE MY GUEST', BY CONRAD HILTON (PRENTICE-HALL, N.Y., 1957).

RAYMOND GABBOTT

Heinrich Himmler (German, 1900–1945): policeman. Himmler was Hitler's chief of police concerned both to maintain discipline in the Nazis' "years of struggle" and to impose the New Order on Europe during the Third Reich's apogee. It is doubtful whether Hitler could have seized or held power without Himmler's personal devotion and bureaucratic zeal. He was the son of a devoutly Catholic Bavarian schoolmaster. A veteran of the Right-wing irregular Free Corps units and of Hitler's 1923 *putsch*, he joined the black-uniformed 'protective squad' (S.S.), becoming its *Reichsführer* in 1929. He welded this into a semi-military, racially pure élite, using it in 1934 to crush the rival lower-class, rowdy Storm Troopers (S.A.). As police chief in Munich he created the Dachau concentration camp. He became successively head of the Secret Police (Gestapo), the Security Service (S.D.) and Ministry of the Interior. His organisations were independent of the regular Civil Service and the courts. He was no mere super-cop. He believed in his mission with a Grand Inquisitor's and crusader's fire: to free Germans from the 'evils of civilisation', settle the East with Teutonic soldier-farmers, and above all to see through the extermination of Europe's Jews of which he had overall charge – "a page of glory in our history" (he told his lieutenants) "which has never been written and will never be written". He took poison at Lüneberg after being captured. **P. G. J. P.**

'HEINRICH HIMMLER', BY ROGER MANVELL AND HEINRICH FRAENKEL (HEINEMANN, 1965); 'THE KERSTEN MEMOIRS', BY FELIX KERSTEN (HUTCHINSON, 1956); 'THE FINAL SOLUTION', BY GERALD REITLINGER (VALENTINE MITCHELL, 1968).

Paul Hindemith (German, 1895–1963): musician. A persuasive exponent of free chromaticism underpinned by strong tonality and a reactionary from the excesses of German romanticism, Hindemith was the lifelong apostle of music as a readily intelligible yet uplifting communal art. An able instrumentalist and conductor, he was for many years a renowned violist. A key-figure in the early years of the Donaueschingen Festival, Hindemith was regarded in the 1920s as decidedly advanced and difficult. Leaving Germany under Nazi pressure (he had taught at the Berlin Conservatoire with great distinction from 1927), his later life alternated between Switzerland (Zürich University) and the U.S. (Yale and Harvard), in academic positions which prompted his important theoretical writings. Typical of the man and brilliantly organised, these are aimed at the stimulation of disciplined and dedicated musicianship – and their renown is still growing. Yet his very numerous and never less than supremely accomplished compositions now find less favour than 20 years ago. And certainly, if permissiveness and self-expression are the hallmarks of today's artistic ethos, Hindemith's logical, objective and morally-conscious works do not seem destined for an overwhelming following just now. **S. C. V. D.**

'A COMPOSER'S WORLD', BY PAUL HINDEMITH (OUP, 1953).

Paul von Hindenburg (German, 1847–1934): statesman. After being the figurehead of Germany's First World War effort Hindenburg became, as President of the Republic, the man who largely let the Nazis get power. After an orthodox army career he was retired in 1908 for criticising the Kaiser's handling of manoeuvres. In August 1914 he was brought back to act as nominal chief to Ludendorff (q.v.) in defeating the Russians in East Prussia. Thenceforward Ludendorff did the work and provided the ideas but Hindenburg, besides taking the responsibility and credit, provided psychological ballast when Ludendorff got nerves. He was made Supreme Commander in 1916. After Ludendorff's dis-

missal, Hindenburg in November 1918 insisted on the Kaiser fleeing to Holland to escape from his mutinous troops. He then led the army home and retired. But in 1924 he was induced to become President and remained loyal to the Republic until in March 1930 he was persuaded (by his son Oscar, General von Schleicher [q.v.] and others) to introduce rule by emergency decree, under Brüning as Chancellor. Two years later the same influences persuaded the old gentleman to replace Brüning by the less democratic Papen (q.v.). Papen proved a failure. He was ousted by Schleicher (q.v.), but revenged himself by overcoming Hindenburg's distaste for Hitler, who was thus made Chancellor in January 1933. This attempt to replace the democratic Weimar Republic with a restoration of authoritarian Prussian ideals ended in the destruction of the Germany he valued. **M. L. G. B.**

'HINDENBURG: THE WOODEN TITAN', BY J. WHEELER-BENNETT (MACMILLAN, 1967); 'HINDENBURG AND THE WEIMAR REPUBLIC', BY A. DORPALEN (PRINCETON U.P., 1964).

Alfred Hinds (British, b. 1917): escapologist. One of Hinds's contributions to the 20th century was his demonstration that stone walls do not a prison make. He was sentenced in 1953 for 12 years and began escaping. He had been convicted of the £30,000 Maples haul, but protested his innocence with a persistence that convinced everyone except the police and an Old Bailey jury. He conducted a series of foredoomed legal actions (31 court appearances) against the authorities; and in the course of one he locked his jailers in a High Court lavatory and went AWOL to Bristol by air. Finally in a libel action against a policeman who said in a book that he was "guilty" (instead of merely convicted) of the Maples job, he got a civil jury to say he was innocent. The Criminal Appeal Court refused to quash his conviction. The Home Office agreed. On these facts Hinds has established personal injustice as an industry. **C. H. R.**

'CONTEMPT OF COURT', BY ALFRED HINDS (BODLEY HEAD, 1966).

Earl Hines (U.S., b. 1905): jazz musician. From a musical family – his father played trumpet and his mother was an organist – 'Fatha' Hines has been acclaimed as one of the great jazz pianists since the late Twenties when he was a member of Louis Armstrong's Hot Five. In the Forties he led a big band which included Charlie Parker, Dizzy Gillespie (qq.v.), Sarah Vaughan and Billy Eckstine. Thus he was a seminal figure in the post-Second World War 'bebop revolution as an employer – but this is insignificant compared with the influence of his piano style upon modern players. In the Twenties his harmonic concept was well

ahead of his contemporaries, and his percussive right-hand single-note melodic style became known as 'trumpet style'. He is the founder of the school of modern jazz piano which leads through Teddy Wilson, Bud Powell, Oscar Peterson and virtually every player of the instrument in jazz during the 1950s and 1960s. In the 1950s he was a forgotten figure, but recently there has been renewed interest in him. He has appeared regularly in Europe during the 1960s with great success. **R. S.**

'BLUES IN THIRDS' (FONTANA FJL.902); 'SWINGING IN CHICAGO' (ACE OF HEARTS AH.159); 'ONCE UPON A TIME' (HMV CLP. 3560).

Sir Cyril Hinshelwood (British, 1897–1967): chemist. Hinshelwood was a living denial of the two cultures argument: he was simultaneously the President of the Royal Society and of the Classical Association (1955–60). A scientist of world reputation, he spoke six languages, Latin and Russian among them; at the centenary celebrations of The Chemical Society in 1946, he greeted each foreign visitor in his own tongue. Hinshelwood's greatest scientific work concerned the reactions of gases – the manner and speed with which combinations between molecules take place. The im-

portance of this work stretches across the whole domain of chemistry and its insights have been of major importance for both pure knowledge and industrial application. Hinshelwood also worked on the growth of bacteria where he propounded, based on his kinetic understanding, the principle of total integration. A Nobel Prize winner in 1956, jointly with Semenov, Hinshelwood worked most of his life in Oxford. His achievements brought understanding to the problems of chemical behaviour of gases. **P. J. F.**

'NOBEL PRIZEWINNERS IN CHEMISTRY', BY EDUARD FARBER (ABELARD SCHUMAN, REVISED 1963).

Sir Christopher Hinton, later Lord Hinton (British, b. 1901): engineer. The man who made the peaceful harnessing of nuclear energy a practical proposition started as an apprentice at Swindon railway works. After winning a scholarship to Cambridge, he worked as an engineer until the Second World War. After the war when the department of Atomic Energy was set up he was offered the charge of the production side. As managing director of the industrial group he was responsible for the design, construction and operation of the atomic energy plants throughout Britain. Besides Calder Hall, the world's first nuclear power station, Wellsian establishments at Springfields, Windscale, Capenhurst, Dounreay and Chapel Cross bear powerful witness to the vigour of Hinton's little more than ten years in atomic energy. While chairman of the Central Electricity Generating Board (1957–64) he pioneered the use of nuclear power and oil as alternatives to coal as fuel for the British power supply industry. **P. O. W.**

'ATOMIC ENERGY', BY R. R. NIMMO (CHAPMAN AND HALL, 1949); 'ALL ABOUT NUCLEAR POWER', BY DAVID LE ROI (A. WHEATON, 1965).

Hirohito (Japanese, b. 1901): head of state. A liberal, with scholarly scientific interests, Hirohito succeeded to the Japanese throne on Christmas Day 1926, and suffered great anguish during the 1930s when the Japanese Army became increasingly powerful and aggressive at home and abroad. In theory the Emperor was all-powerful. Regarded by millions as the semi-divine descendant of the Sun Goddess, in reality he was politically impotent. But in August 1945 when Japan faced the prospect not only of utter defeat but also of near-obliteration Hirohito made his voice heard. Even after the atomic bombing of Hiroshima and Nagasaki the Japanese Supreme War Council was evenly divided as to whether to surrender or fight on. The Emperor, with the casting vote, made it plain that Japan must surrender. Without this unprecedented intervention the Japanese would have fought on desperately not only in the homeland but also in many theatres of war throughout East and South East Asia. **G. R. S.**

'HIROHITO', BY LEONARD MOSLEY (WEIDENFELD AND NICOLSON, 1966); 'JAPAN'S DECISION TO SURRENDER', BY ROBERT J. C. BUTOW (STANFORD UNIVERSITY PRESS, 1964).

Alfred Hitchcock (British, b. 1899): film director. London-born and Jesuit-educated, Hitchcock has arguably the most guileful intelligence that has ever applied itself consistently to film-making. He entered films in 1920 by way of the title department at Islington; directed some relatively unHitchcockian silents ("Does this mean I won't be able to play for the Old Boys, sir?" asks Ivor Novello, the expelled public schoolboy in his *Downhill*) before settling into his lifelong relationship with suspense. He creates an unmistakable, unerring Hitchcock situation, from the glimpse of a nun in high heels in *The Lady Vanishes* to the murder in the shower in *Psycho*: the predictable staged in the unpredictable way. He is the great exponent of 'pure film' ("I don't care about the subject matter; I don't care about the acting; but I do care about the pieces of film . . . all the technical ingredients that make the audience scream") with unmatched power to manipulate, tantalise and control the reactions of an audience. Hitchcock may conceivably be as subtle a builder of moral complexities as some critics have found him; in any case he is the artist-showman who has played most blandly and teasingly with the nerves of this century. **P. H.**

'HITCHCOCK', BY FRANCOIS TRUFFAUT (SECKER AND WARBURG, 1968); 'HITCHCOCK'S FILMS', BY ROBIN WOOD (ZWEMMER, 1965); 'THE FILMS OF ALFRED HITCHCOCK', BY G. PERRY (STUDIO VISTA 1965).

ADOLF – DER ÜBERMENSCH

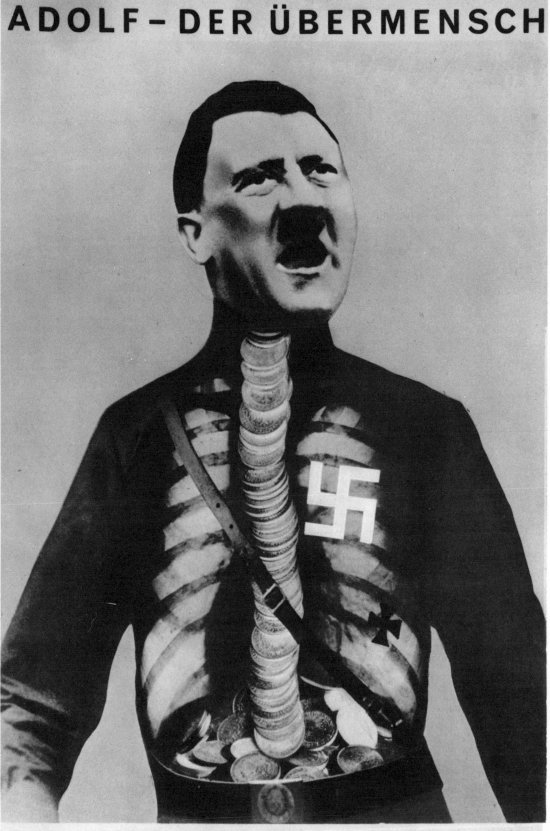

SCHLUCKT GOLD UND REDET BLECH

Adolf Hitler (German, ex-Austrian, 1889–1945): head of state. The most effective and successful demagogue of all time rose, in 12 years, from street-corner agitator to military master of Europe. Hitler was the son of an Austrian customs official. A failure at school, he drifted to Vienna. He was disgusted by the capital's cosmopolitanism, smug Liberal Press, alien-looking Jewish community, and impressed by the lower middle-class mass movement built up

by the anti-semitic Mayor, Karl Lueger, and the emotional impact of the Social Democrats' mass parades. After First World War service with the German army, he joined the National Socialist (Nazi) Party, soon gaining autocratic control. But the failure of the 1923 *putsch* convinced him he needed armed forces, property owners and legality on his side. Opportunity came with the Great Depression. Sweeping electoral gains made him Chancellor (1933)

with dictatorial powers. Playing on the victor Powers' bad consciences and pacifism, he reversed the military and territorial terms of Versailles. But his invasion of Poland provoked the Second World War. Spectacular early victories provided a cloak for establishing the long-cherished 'Thousand Year Empire', characterised by supremacy of the leader's will, terror at home, expansion in the East, slavery for the racially inferior and extermination of

'enemy races' (Jews, gypsies). But first El Alamein, then Stalingrad and finally D-Day spelt the end of his Empire. Nine days before VE-Day, with Russian tanks a few hundred yards from the Berlin *Führerbunker*, he married his mistress Eva Braun. Next day (April 30, 1945) she took poison while he – almost certainly – shot himself. **P. G. J. P.**

'HITLER, A STUDY IN TYRANNY', BY ALAN BULLOCK (ODHAMS, 1952); 'MEIN KAMPF', BY ADOLF HITLER, TRANS. JAMES MURPHY (HURST AND BLACKETT, 1939); 'THE LAST DAYS OF HITLER', BY H. R. TREVOR-ROPER (MACMILLAN, 1947).

Ho Chi Minh (Vietnamese, 1890–1969): politician. A legendary figure of international Communism, Ho Chi Minh was present at the foundation of the French Communist Party in 1920. In September 1945, he proclaimed the Democratic Republic of Vietnam in Hanoi. He remained its President during the long struggle to secure the unification of Vietnam under Communist leadership, first against France and then against the government of the Republic of (South) Vietnam backed by the United States. Although an enigmatic personage because of incomplete biographical data, he was undoubtedly the most outstanding Vietnamese of the age. He brought together in his person an attachment to Marxist ethics and nationalist sentiments, with the latter taking priority. A firm advocate of revolution, he was essentially a practitioner rather than a grand theoretician. In later years, as an old man, he was represented as the ascetic but benign father figure of the Vietnamese people. He symbolised for many, especially youthful dissenters in the Western world, the heroic stoicism of revolutionary dedication to a just cause. His main contribution to revolutionary practice was to demonstrate the vital role of organisation and genuine nationalist appeal. **M. L.**

'HO CHI MINH', BY JEAN LACOUTURE (ALLEN LANE, THE PENGUIN PRESS, 1958).

Sir Jack Hobbs (British, 1882–1963): cricketer. If W. G. Grace was the Champion of cricket and Donald Bradman (q.v.) the prolific run-machine, John Berry Hobbs could aptly be called the Master. With easy grace and a freedom of stroke play that was delightful to watch, his batting technique was as near perfect as there ever will be. Lithe, short of stature, fleet of foot, with a lightning throw, he also became the first great cover-point fieldsman. He broke through to the top in the era of the amateur, and for many years reigned supreme. He played his first match for Surrey in 1905, winning his England cap two years later. The First World War deprived cricket of four of his best years, but he was still playing for England in 1930, retiring in 1934. In this period he amassed 61,237

runs at an average of 50, with 197 centuries, the best record of all time. Amazingly enough, 98 of these hundreds were made after his fortieth birthday. In 61 Tests he scored 5410 runs at an average of 56. His highest score, 316 not out in 1926, remains the highest score ever made at Lord's. Blessed with a serene temperament and a lively sense of humour, he was quiet and unassuming and quite unspoilt by success. **M. C. C.**

'JACK HOBBS', BY RONALD MASON (HOLLIS AND CARTER, 1960).

Alan Hodgkin (British, b. 1914): biophysicist. Crabs and squids: horrendous creatures to provide the working material for a Nobel Prize winner. Alan Hodgkin was using single nerve fibres from the shore crab – to test a theory of nervous conduction – and switched to squid, which has giant single nerve fibres as much as a millimetre in diameter, when he went to the U.S. in 1938. His work was interrupted by the Second World War, but in the late 1940s Hodgkin and A. F. Huxley continued their neurophysiological research. They devised a system of mathematical equations describing the nerve impulse, showed that the classical – Bernstein – theory was wrong, and presented evidence for the sodium theory, which says that the nervous impulse is a function of the nerve membrane's selective permeability to sodium ions. Our understanding of the brain – and the nerves that supply it – is still primitive, but Hodgkin and Huxley's work provided basic information which may lead to increased understanding of, for instance, heart and kidney, and to the investigation of diseases of the nervous system. **P. G. R.**

Billie Holiday (U.S., 1915–1959): singer. Billie Holliday (below) is almost every jazz musician's favourite singer. She began singing in Harlem clubs at 16 and made her first record with Benny Goodman (q.v.) in 1933. In the late Thirties she made a series of classic records with a group led by Teddy Wilson and which also included the great tenor saxophonist Lester Young (q.v.), with whom she formed a close association which was to last all her life. Her voice had a bittersweet quality and coupled with her unique, strangely moving phrasing she was able to convey great emotion, which was always in the jazz tradition. 'Lady Day', as she was affectionately known, unlike most girl singers sounded like a woman. She died of narcotic addiction after a tragic personal life. **R. S.**

'LADY SINGS THE BLUES', BY BILLIE HOLIDAY WITH WILLIAM DUFFY (BARRIE BOOKS, 1958). RECORDS: 'THE GOLDEN YEARS', VOLS 1 & 2 (CBS BPG. 62037-8) (BOX SET: 66301); 'BILLIE HOLIDAY' (WING, LL. 1212).

John Holland (U.S., ex-Irish, 1841–1914): engineer. The Polaris submarine is the most powerful single instrument of war today. The inevitable outcome of three weapon technologies – submarine, nuclear warhead and missile – it springs from the original genius of John Philip Holland, an Irish-American schoolmaster. The Holland, his first successful craft, was accepted experimentally by the U.S. Navy in 1900. Vickers in Britain acquired the patent rights, subsequently rescued the Holland's insolvent entrepreneurs, the Electric Boat Company, and launched their improved version in 1901. Fifteen years later in the Great War the German U-boat, sprung

HIT-HON

from these remote and inauspicious beginnings, brought Britain to the edge of defeat. The early generations were submersibles; true submarines came in 1955 with the nuclear-powered Nautilus. In 1960 with the triumphant development of the Polaris submarine, built appropriately by the Electric Boat Company, the concept reached the ultimate limit of power. In half a century Holland's crude invention had changed the nature of sea warfare. **D. D.**

'VICKERS: A HISTORY', BY J. D. SCOTT (WEIDENFELD AND NICOLSON, 1962); 'SEA POWER', ED. ELMER B. POTTER AND C. W. NIMITZ (PRENTICE-HALL, NEW YORK, 1960).

Gustav Holst (British, 1874–1934): composer. A composer of marked individuality, Holst, after studying with Stanford, shunned conventional posts and played in theatre orchestras as a trombonist. In later life, notably as director of music at St Paul's

Girls' School and Morley College, he showed rare gifts as a teacher. Holst combined a deep-seated mysticism with a severely practical approach to music as a craft. His suite *The Planets* (1918) demonstrated brilliant understanding of bold orchestration for large forces, and has reached a wide audience. His mysticism is more pronounced, his diction more austere, in his highly regarded *Hymn of Jesus*, and both works contain striking instances of Holst's frequent exploration of irregular metres. He taught himself Sanskrit, with musical results in the *Hymns from the Rig Veda* and other works. Holst's melodic clarity and rhythmic inventiveness acted as a corrective in the prevailing twilight influence of Delius (q.v.). **S. C. V. D.**

'GUSTAV HOLST', BY IMOGEN HOLST (O.U.P., 1938); 'THE MUSIC OF GUSTAV HOLST', BY IMOGEN HOLST (O.U.P., 1968).

Soichiro Honda (Japanese, b. 1906): tycoon. Honda, the motor engineer, built up the biggest motor-cycle business ever known, selling elegant machines to a public which had previously thought of them purely as noisy machines for enthusiasts. He is the symbol of the Japanese miracle. He started after the Second World War using re-

conditioned army surplus power units and then went on to conquer the world of orthodox motor cycles by getting more reliable power out of faster-running units than anyone thought possible. He is a non-manager, who prefers to work in his company's research institute; who never visits his company's Tokyo headquarters, never goes even to directors' meetings and leaves all management matters to a young, able band of executives. Honda turned to cars only six years ago, and is now the fourth biggest maker in Japan. **A. N. F.**

William Henry Hoover (U.S., 1849–1932): manufacturer. 'Hoovering' is synonymous with vacuum-cleaning. Hoover developed his machines in North Canton, Ohio, at about the time that he became its first mayor in 1905. He was originally a manufacturer of leather goods (particularly accessories for horse-drawn vehicles), who recognised that the motor-car would put him out of business. When a fellow-citizen brought him a crude prototype of a cleaner, an electric motor driving a tufted roller, blowing air into a pillow case, Hoover had several made, and sold them to households in the town. In August 1908, over a pitcher of lemonade on his

front porch, Hoover and four partners drew up plans for the Electric Suction Sweeper Company, and soon issued stock. In that year, 372 sweepers were produced. After the First World War, the company became worldwide, as did its slogan: "It Sweeps as it Beats as it Cleans." **G. P. G. N.**

Herbert Hoover (U.S., 1874–1964): statesman. From his birth to his inauguration as President in March 1929, Herbert Hoover's career embodied the American success story. An orphan at 11, he worked his way up from a clerkship to renown as the "great engineer". In the 1914 war he undertook the administration of relief that brought him worldwide acclaim. He entered American public life as

Secretary of Commerce in the Republican Administrations of the 1920s. Although never previously a candidate for office, his pre-1921 professional and humanitarian achievements and his post-1921 record as the promoter of business prosperity made him the natural successor to Calvin Coolidge. But during the four years of his Presidency, America suffered economic catastrophe: Hoover himself went from being the most admired to being the most despised man in America. He brought idealism, expertise and great administrative skill to the Presidency but they proved tragically inadequate because his administrative skills were no substitute for the political talents he entirely lacked. His failure during the Depression left bankrupt for a time one of the main strands in the American past – the pragmatic idealism of the humanitarian who 'get things done'. But, by discrediting the laissez-faire attitude which Hoover himself opposed, it also cleared the way for Franklin Roosevelt's (q.v.) improvisatory genius. **W. H. J.**

MEMOIRS', BY HERBERT HOOVER (3 VOLS., MACMILLAN, NEW YORK, 1951–52); 'REPUBLICAN ASCENDANCY', BY JOHN D. HICKS (HARPER AND ROW, NEW YORK, 1963); 'HERBERT HOOVER AND THE GREAT DEPRESSION', BY HARRIS GAYLORD WARREN (O.U.P., NEW YORK, 1959)

J. Edgar Hoover (U.S., b. 1895): detective. John Edgar Hoover has been even more closely identified with America's Federal Bureau of Investigation than was Franklin D. Roosevelt (q.v.) with the New Deal. In 1921 he became Assistant Director and in 1924 Director of the FBI, itself only founded 16 years earlier. The FBI, which he reformed on assuming control, has grown with him for nearly 50 years. Its jurisdiction is limited to Federal crimes, but this has been greatly extended to include such offences as bank robbery, kidnapping, espionage and sabotage. It has established a national finger-print system, improved the collection of crime statistics, and encouraged higher standards of police investigation. In a report on Communism which he wrote in 1919, Hoover struck, perhaps for the first time, the most significant keynote of his life: "These doctrines threaten the happiness of the community, the safety of every individual, and the continuance of every home and fireside. They would destroy the peace of the country and thrust it into a condition of anarchy and lawlessness and immorality that passes imagination." In 1958 he wrote: "My conclusions of 1919 remain the same. Communism is the major menace of our time." **H. C. A.**

'THE HAUNTED FIFTIES', BY I. F. STONE (MERLIN PRESS, 1964); 'THE F.B.I. NOBODY KNOWS', BY FRED J. COOK (JONATHAN CAPE, 1965); 'THE F.B.I. STORY', BY DON WHITEHEAD, WITH A FOREWORD BY J. EDGAR HOOVER (FREDERICK MULLER, 1967).

Miklós Horthy (Hungarian, 1868–1957): statesman. Admiral Horthy, Fleet Commander during the War, set himself up as ruler of Hungary at the end of 1919. He tried to restore the monarchy, but was forbidden to do so by the Powers; hence he could only appoint himself Regent. Horthy's rule was conservative and nationalist; he aimed to recover the lands lost in 1918. Consequently he worked with Hitler (q.v.), who offered Hungary some land, and went to war on

Hitler's side in 1941 (his Prime Minister shot himself in protest). But Horthy was not a Nazi; he protected the Hungarian Jews, and imprisoned the local Nazis. In October 1944 he tried to get Hungary out of the war, but was kidnapped, on Hitler's orders, and imprisoned (above, his German reference card) while a puppet regime was installed by the Germans. He was again imprisoned by the Allies, but was finally allowed in 1948 to go into exile in Portugal, where he died. **N. S.**

'MEMOIRS', BY MIKLOS HORTHY (HUTCHINSON, 1956); 'OCTOBER 15TH', BY C. A. MACARTNEY, 2 VOLS (EDINBURGH UNIVERSITY PRESS, 1961).

Sir Frederick Gowland Hopkins (British, 1861–1947): biochemist. Renowned for his discovery in the field of the growth stimulating vitamins, Hopkins revolutionised biochemical thought in two other fundamental fields – the energy mechanisms in cells and the processes underlying muscular contraction. His early discovery that the amino-acid called tryptophan was essential for growth led to the novel concept that diseases could be produced by the *absence* of a factor as well as in other ways. Six years later, in 1912, he showed that rats would not grow on a diet of pure carbohydrate, fat and protein alone – but that a trace of another, unknown substance was necessary as well. He made a further discovery which explained some of the biochemical processes taking part in every cell of the body. He isolated the sulphur-containing substance glutathione, which

plays a key part in tissue respiration. This led naturally to his appreciating the importance of the enzymes inside the cells – protein substances which catalyse every biochemical process in the body. Well over 1000 of these have now been described. **R. A. P.**

'THE BIOCHEMICAL APPROACH TO LIFE', BY F. R. JEVONS (ALLEN AND UNWIN, 1964); 'THE STRUCTURE AND FUNCTION OF ANIMAL CELL COMPONENTS', BY P. N. CAMPBELL (PERGAMON, 1966); 'DYNAMIC ASPECTS OF BIOCHEMISTRY', BY E. BALDWIN (CAMBRIDGE UNIVERSITY PRESS, 1967).

Harry Houdini (U.S., 1874–1926): escapologist. Born Erich Weiss, the century's definitive illusionist derived his stage name from the French magician Robert Houdin. At 17 he decided to go into show business, and became apprentice to a rope-escape artist in a museum. His first big break came when he was hired by Martin Beck, a famous impresario, in 1899; Beck advised him to concentrate on escaping from handcuffs, chains, locked cabinets, and so on. And it was probably Beck who suggested a new way of getting publicity – publicly challenging the police department of any town where he intended to perform to try to lock him up or otherwise confine him. He also had a trick of leaping into rivers from a bridge, loaded with chains and handcuffs, and he knew more about locks than any locksmith. This enabled him to do such spectacular feats as escaping from a locked safe, or from a water-filled cabinet in which he was suspended upside down. He made highly successful cliff-hanger films in the early 1920s, and also set out on a crusade to unmask fraudulent spirit mediums. In 1926, he invited a youth to hit him before his muscles were 'set' for it; he died of peritonitis. **C. W.**

'HOUDINI', BY WILLIAM LINDSAY GRESHAM (HENRY HOLT, N.Y., 1959); 'HOUDINI ON MAGIC', ED. W. GIBSON AND M. YOUNG (DOVER, 1953, DISTRIB. CONSTABLE).

Ebenezer Howard (British, 1850–1928): town planner. The Garden City, as a strategic cure for the 20th-century 'urban explosion', was invented single-handed by Ebenezer Howard, a London shorthand reporter. With its land held in a single municipal ownership, the Garden City is a typically British compound of moderate co-operative socialism (the heir to Robert Owen's New Lanark and New Harmony) with a middle-class insistence on the individuality of each home (in

contrast to Continental flats or charitable tenements). The Garden Cities founded by Howard – Letchworth (1903) and Welwyn (1919) – conceal beneath their mild suburban architecture the originality of his main idea: that urban growth in future should be split up incrementally into compact communities of 30,000 people, each surrounded by its own green belt of agricultural land and supported by its own industries. Howard was no scientist like Geddes (q.v.), but he had an instinctive understanding of the need to combat artificiality and rootlessness with abundant landscape and close-knit community life. As a 30,000 population proved insufficient to attract urban amenities, the British New Towns, by far the most extensive implementation of Howard's idea, started (1946) with targets of 60–80,000 population; the latest are aiming for over 200,000. Howard's American disciples include Lewis Mumford, author of *The Culture of Cities*, and Clarence Stein, inventor of the Radburn system of traffic planning. **N. J. W. T.**

'GARDEN CITIES OF TOMORROW', BY EBENEZER HOWARD WITH INTRODUCTIONS BY SIR F. OSBORN AND LEWIS MUMFORD (FABER AND FABER, 1946); 'THE BUILDING OF SATELLITE TOWNS', BY C. B. PURDOM (DENT, 1925); 'THE SEARCH FOR ENVIRONMENT: THE GARDEN CITY, BEFORE AND AFTER', BY WALTER L. CREESE (YALE UNIVERSITY PRESS, 1966).

Fred Hoyle (British, b. 1915): astronomer. Hoyle is best known as one of the three originators of the so-called 'steady-state' theory, which postulates that the universe, instead of starting in some catastrophic fashion, has always looked the same with no historical beginning or foreseeable end. However, his contributions to cosmology and astrophysics are much wider than just this, and he is one of the most important influences upon present-day astronomical thinking. A graduate of Cambridge University, and Smith's Prizeman in 1938, he is now Plumian Professor of Astronomy and Experimental Philosophy there, and Director of Cambridge's new Institute of Theoretical Astronomy. In 1948 Hoyle published his version of the 'steady-state' theory independently of Bondi (q.v.) and Gold, who are also associated with the idea. Because the universe is expanding, and 'holes' would otherwise be left in it, it was necessary to postulate at the same time that matter is continuously and spontaneously created within it – possibly, Hoyle now thinks, in objects where the density is extremely high. He has also made important contributions

to our understanding of how the heavier elements are synthesised from hydrogen atoms by nucleosynthesis in stars, a subject which forms the core of the study of stellar evolution. In 1964 he presented a theory by which the local mass of an object was regarded as a result of all the rest of the matter in the universe. The laws governing microphysical processes are, he believes, a reflection of the collective effect of the universe as a whole. His theorising could turn out to have far-reaching consequences for the whole of physics. **P. H. S. S.**

'OF MEN AND GALAXIES', BY FRED HOYLE (HEINEMANN, 1965); 'GALAXIES, NUCLEI AND QUASARS', BY FRED HOYLE (HEINEMANN, 1966).

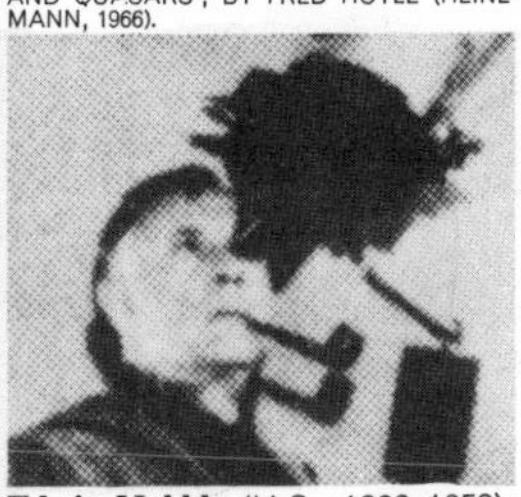

Edwin Hubble (U.S., 1889–1953): astronomer. Our modern picture of the universe is largely due to Edwin Hubble who first conclusively proved the existence of large systems of stars outside our own Galaxy. At Mount Wilson Observatory in 1919 he carried out difficult photographic studies of faint nebulae in the sky. Careful observation led him to establish in 1924 that extragalactic objects, like the Andromeda Nebula, were in fact large systems like the Milky Way, each composed of hundreds of thousands of millions of stars. In 1926 Hubble published a classification system of them which is still used today. His earlier work led on to one of the most important concepts in cosmology, that of the expanding universe. The light from very distant objects is shifted towards the red end of the spectrum, an effect that had already been interpreted as a change in pitch, like that of a receding train whistle, caused by the enormous speed at which these objects are moving away from us. From studies of variable stars in other galaxies, Hubble was able to gauge their distance at ranges up to 150 million light years. Comparing distances and red shifts, he showed that the farther off a galaxy lay, the faster it was moving away from us – an effect which means that, whatever its origin, the universe must be expanding. Thus Hubble set the stage for the present exciting cosmological debate. **P. H. S. S.**

'THE RIDDLE OF THE UNIVERSE', BY W. M. SMART (LONGMANS, 1968); 'GALAXIES', BY H. SHAPLEY (HARVARD U. P., 1961); 'THE EVOLUTION OF STARS AND GALAXIES', BY W. BAADE (HARVARD U. P., 1963); 'THE REALM OF NEBULAE', BY E. P. HUBBLE (O. U. P., 1930).

Bronislaw Huberman (Austrian, ex-Polish, 1882–1947): violinist. Huberman is best described as the Furtwängler (q.v.) of the violin: deeply contemptuous of mere technique and routine, he depended on spontaneous inspiration. When it failed him, his performance flagged; but when he was inspired, unique interpretations – full-blooded

and spiritual at the same time – were the result which, almost incidentally, reached the heights of virtuosity. A pupil of Joachim, he played the Brahms Concerto in Vienna at the age of 14 in the presence of the composer (who much admired him). Brahms reacted by bursting into tears and promised to write a Fantasy for him, but died before he could do so. With short interruptions, Huberman toured the world from 1902 until he died. He founded the Palestine Orchestra (now the Israel Philharmonic) in 1936: the road outside the new Concert Hall in Tel Aviv is named after him. In this country he never made quite the same overwhelming impression as elsewhere – possibly because of the intensity of his approach. He was very active as a writer, too, both on aesthetic subjects and on 'Pan-Europe', his lifelong passion. Half gypsy and half saint, he looked like a Jewish Beethoven and was no doubt the age's most characteristic violinist; in fact, in view of his gramophone records, he still is. No fiddler who has heard them has remained unaffected. **H. K.**

Trevor Huddleston (British, b. 1913): cleric. When Father Trevor Huddleston set sail for South Africa in July 1943 there was no hint that he was to play a decisive role in awakening the conscience of the world to what was happening to the black African in South Africa. After a few years as a curate in Swin-

don he joined the Community of the Resurrection at Mirfield. In 1943 they sent him to run their mission in Sophiatown, a shanty-like slum on the outskirts of Johannesburg. In his book *Naught For Your Comfort*, he describes how he finally became committed to militant action. He saw black friends continually humiliated by the indignities of apartheid. Finally, at the African National Congress in 1952 that launched the Defiance Campaign, he crystallised his ideas in these words: "It has been the teaching of the Church throughout the centuries that when government degenerates into tyranny, laws cease to be binding on its subjects." It was a declaration of war, and he carried on unceasingly until he was recalled in 1955. He is now Bishop of Stepney. **L. v. d. P.**

'NAUGHT FOR YOUR COMFORT', BY FATHER TREVOR HUDDLESTON (COLLINS, 1956).

Alfred Hugenberg (German, 1865–1951): politician. Hugenberg's chief claim to fame is that he helped Hitler (q.v.) to power in 1933. He was an extremely rich businessman with highly nationalist, anti-socialist views. Although not himself a Nazi, he felt he could capture Hitler for

his own conservative programme; he was himself captured by Hitler. Before 1933 Hugenberg was one of the biggest businessmen in Germany – he made money in the Great War as a director of Krupps, and later almost monopolised films and advertising in Weimar Germany. He was the founder of the Pan-German League and the Nationalist Party. In 1928 he became leader of this Party, but his highly conservative social programme had no appeal to the masses. Hugenberg thought he could get mass support by capturing Hitler for his cause; he made an alliance with Hitler, and received a ministerial seat in his first cabinet in January 1933. But Hitler set up a dictatorship, and abolished all other parties. Hugenberg was forced to resign. Thereafter he lost all power, living only to see in 1945 the utter ruin of everything he had stood for. His assets were taken over by East Germany, and he died a broken man. **N. S.**

'HITLER: A STUDY IN TYRANNY', BY ALAN BULLOCK (ODHAMS, 1952); 'A HISTORY OF THE WEIMAR REPUBLIC', BY ERICH EYCK, 2 VOLS (WILEY, 1968).

Charles Huggins (U.S., ex-Canadian, b. 1901): surgeon. By his work on the hormonal control of cancer, by his shining example of scientific probity and by his inspiration, Charles Huggins has profoundly influenced the 20th-century treatment of advanced cancer. After graduating from Harvard University, Huggins came to the National Institute of Medical Research, London, to acquire knowledge of research methods. Appointed Professor of Surgery in the University of Chicago, his work on urological problems and research into the treatment of cancer led, after the discovery of stilboestrol by Sir Charles Dodds in 1938, to the treatment of prostatic cancer by oestrogens, the first time that cancer had been controlled by giving a hormone by mouth. Later, Huggins pioneered the operation for total removal of both adrenals in the treatment of human breast cancer. With the induction of breast cancer in animals by the injection of identifiable hydrocarbons, it was possible for Huggins and his co-workers to investigate the use of hormonal substances to combat these induced cancers; by the time he was awarded the Nobel Prize for Physiology and Medicine in 1966, Huggins had already investigated eight hormone-induced cancers in man and animals which could be cured or alleviated by hormone interference. **H. J. B. A.**

'ON CANCER AND HORMONES: ESSAYS IN EXPERIMENTAL BIOLOGY', BY A. HADDOW ET AL. (CHICAGO ACADEMIC PRESS, 1961); 'CANCER', ED. R. W. RAVEN, VOL. 6, PART X, CHEMOTHERAPY (BUTTERWORTH, 1959); 'CURRENT CONCEPTS IN BREAST CANCER', BY A. SEGALOFF, K. K. MEYER AND S. DEBAKEY (WILLIAMS AND WILKINS, BALTIMORE, 1967); 'FRONTIERS OF MAMMARY CANCER', BY C. HUGGINS (GLASGOW U. P., JACKSON SON AND CO., GLASGOW, 1961).

Howard Hughes (U.S., b. 1905): Aviator, film-maker and tycoon. For some 25 years he has hidden himself from the public eye. For over four years he lived in a penthouse over the Desert Inn, Las Vegas, guarded by gun-toting thugs and complex electronic alarm systems. His film star wife Jean Peters (*Three Coins in the Fountain*) was rarely seen publicly until her divorce in 1971. He inherited his first million from his father and at 19 bought out the Hughes Tool Company, makers of oil drilling bits. He went to Hollywood, lost a fortune on a film too bad to be released, then spent another on a First World War flying picture, *Hell's Angels*. Its flying sequences have never been equalled. Three pilots died. A blonde playing cameos in Laurel and Hardy (q.v.) shorts was his star – Jean Harlow (q.v.). In the Thirties he set up an aircraft factory, and broke many air records in planes he designed himself. He bought an airline, TWA. In the Forties he made *The Outlaw*, discovered Jane Russell and designed a special cantilevered bra for her heaving bosom, earning condemnation from the decency societies. He designed the Lockheed Constellation and a huge flying boat that flew no more than a mile. He bought the ailing RKO film company and witnessed its doom. In 1966, after bitter legal battles, he sold TWA for over 500m. dollars and has since bought a domestic airline. He left Las Vegas in 1970, allegedly for the Bahamas. There were those who believed him dead for years. **G. C. P.**

'THE BASHFUL BILLIONAIRE', BY ALBERT B. GERBER (SOUVENIR PRESS, 1968); 'HOWARD HUGHES', BY JOHN KEATS (MACGIBBON AND KEE, 1967).

Edmund Husserl (German, 1859–1938): philosopher. Husserl's significance lies firstly in the elaboration of phenomenology as a philosophical method and

secondly in his use of that method in relation to the analysis of pure consciousness. Phenomenology is concerned with describing subjective experience. It differs from psychology in not concerning itself with the casual aspects of the events described. Husserl was concerned with the intuition of essences. He considered that geometry involves the intuition of ideal essentials, i.e. points and straight lines are not found in the factual world but in an ideal conceptual world and we understand intuitively the various relationships. Philosophy is similar, but includes the intuitive analysis and description of all essences. Husserl was not a system-building philosopher but sought ever deeper analyses of experience, going on to attempt to explore the structure of consciousness itself. The Existential philosophers – especially Heidegger, Merleau-Ponty and Jean-Paul Sartre (qq.v.) – on whom Husserl's influence has been profound, have adapted and used the methodology he developed. **B. R. O.**

'THE PHENOMENOLOGY OF INTERNAL TIME-CONSCIOUSNESS', BY EDMUND HUSSERL (INDIANA U.P., 1964).

Sir Kenneth Hutchison (British, b. 1903): engineer. London's last ditch defence against Hitler's flying bombs was a 2000 strong forest of steel cables supported by barrage balloons full of hydrogen. Life-giving oxygen was simultaneously required in vast quantities for high flying aircraft.

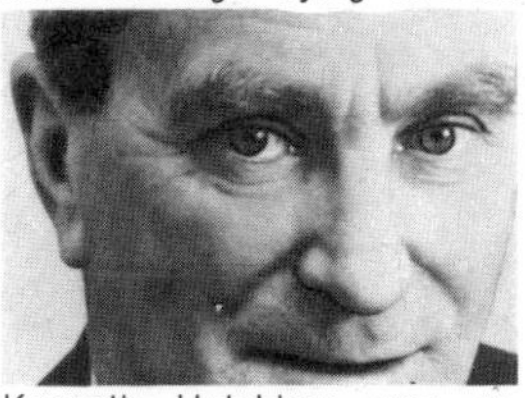

Kenneth Hutchison was responsible for producing these vital elements at this time. Following chemistry research at Oxford he started work at the Gas Light and Coke Company in the mid-Twenties, becoming a director after the war. When the gas industry was nationalised he was appointed chairman of the South Eastern Gas Board, and has been President of both the Institutions of Gas and Chemical Engineers. Gas from the North Sea is one of many schemes with which he has been actively engaged. He has also been responsible for developing cheaper methods of gas production and distribution, including pioneering work on obtaining gas from oil rather than coal, and the development of methods of transporting liquefied natural gas. Hutchison's research into new ways of satisfying the hungry demand for gas and of utilising the by-products of the industry have made a significant contribution to living standards over the past few decades. **P. O. W.**

'FORTUNE IN THE NORTH SEA', BY PETER HINDE (G.T. FOULIS, 1966); 'NATURAL GAS', BY E. N. TIRATSOO (SCIENTIFIC PRESS, 1967).

Aldous Huxley (British, 1894–1963): writer. Aldous Huxley once said: "There is no virtue in not knowing what can be known," and he deployed a uniquely wide range of knowledge in a series of books intended to show the way to a life free from the horrors he saw ahead. He was born into a brilliant family – his brother was Julian Huxley (overleaf). In his earliest novels he satirised the lively society of the 1920s that he so much enjoyed. His feeling that modern man was separating himself from his true nature was elegantly expressed in *Point Counter Point*, but it was in *Brave New World* (1932) that he most clearly showed how little one could trust in progress. He moved to California where he recovered from near-blindness and came into contact with the mysticism and mind-affecting drugs that featured in, for example, *The Perennial Philosophy*. His belief that mankind could be saved by the pursuit of a spiritual, perhaps drug-produced, happiness makes him the almost certainly unwilling father of the hippies. **W. A. O.**

'THE HUXLEYS', BY RONALD W. CLARK (HEINEMANN, 1968).

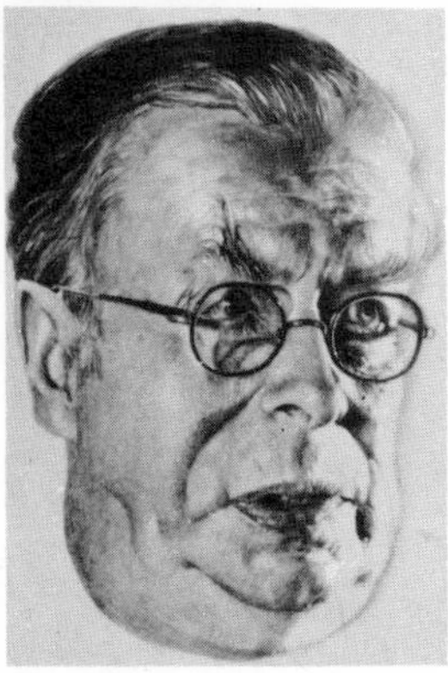

Sir Julian Huxley (British, b. 1887): biologist. Julian Huxley has been an important intellectual force in 20th-century biology, especially as an evolutionist. In his research, and even more in his writings, he tried to bring together the Darwinian theory of Natural Selection and the developing science of Mendelian genetics. This fusion came about, and he could rightly, in 1942, call his important book *Evolution: the Modern Synthesis* – a synthesis to which he had contributed enormously. A biologist with a very wide range of interests, he promoted such practical ventures as wild-life conservation, and in films, broadcasts, essays and books, he drew attention to the world of animals and its relevance to man. **J. B. M.**

'EVOLUTION: THE MODERN SYNTHESIS', BY JULIAN HUXLEY (HARPER AND G. ALLEN, 1942); 'ESSAYS OF A BIOLOGIST', BY JULIAN HUXLEY (PENGUIN, 1939).

I

Mihaly Igloi (U.S., b. Hungary 1908): athletics coach. Mihaly Igloi used to spot champion runners in their embryo state by perching himself in a tree at junior cross-country competitions. His country's 1500-metre champion in 1939, he was a prisoner of the Russians during the war when he evolved the tough methods of training which made him supreme. His three most famous Hungarian protégés were Sandor Iharos, Istvan Rozsavolgyi and Laszlo Tabori, whom he handled as a 'state trainer' with the Honved Army Club. In 1955, these three were responsible for the most remarkable pageant of record-breaking in athletics history, equalling or beating the world records for the 1000, 1500, 2000, 3000, 5000 metres, the 6000 metres relay (with Ferenc Mikes), and the 2 and 3 miles. In the same year, Tabori ran a 3 min. 59 sec. mile, only a second outside Landy's world record. After the Hungarian uprising in 1956, Igloi, an often inscrutable man, went from the Melbourne Olympics to live in America. There he became the catalyst responsible for America's present success in middle distance running, an area in which Americans had never previously done well. A stickler for conditioning (Iharos used to have 700 training sessions a year), Igloi goaded them to work. He had his first notable success in the USA with Jim Beatty, who was not exceptional until he met Igloi. Thus, when Beatty started breaking U.S. records and turned magically into one of the world's finest milers, nobody was prepared to doubt Igloi's proud boast: "Any country I can make good runner." **Jo. L.**

Sir Christopher Ingold (British, b. 1893): chemist. Professor of Chemistry at University College London from 1930 and now Professor Emeritus, Sir Christopher Ingold is one of a small band who laid the foundations of our knowledge of how chemical substances react. A large part of chemistry consists of making new materials. Intelligent selection of what to make and how to make it – considerations important both in academic research and in industry – can be arrived at only through an understanding of what happens in a chemical reaction. Ingold's main achievement was to develop a set of logical explanations for the ways in which chemical reactions happen. He rationalised these ideas in a number of general predictive concepts. Although most of his contributions were in organic chemistry – the part of chemistry where

carbon plays a predominant part – his ideas are today applied across the board and have immense influence on topics as diverse as biochemistry and the production of petrochemicals. Modern researches into chemical reactions have a seminal influence on our knowledge of the behaviour of matter and, technologically, on the emergence of the contemporary chemical industry. **P. J. F.**

Alick Isaacs (British, 1921–1967): virologist. For most of his working life Isaacs was concerned in the study of the influenza viruses. A particular interest was the well-known phenomenon whereby one virus could interfere with the growth of another, not necessarily related to it (q.v. Sir MacFarlane Burnet), and he made great efforts to discover the underlying mechanism. In 1957, working with a Swiss visitor, J. Lindenmann, at the National Institute for Medical Research, Mill Hill, he discovered that cells treated with virus, particularly dead or damaged virus, would release a protein which prevented virus growth; this they christened interferon. A period of intensive work followed and Isaacs was concerned in writing more than 50 papers on the subject in the nine years before his tragic death at the age of 45. It was at first hoped that a practically useful natural chemotherapeutic agent against virus

diseases had been discovered. Moreover, Isaacs' work led to a revolution in our ideas by showing that the body has a rapidly effective means of defence against viruses, independent of the familiar mechanism of antibody production. **C. H. A.**

'INTERFERON', BY ALICK ISAACS IN 'ADVANCES OF VIRUS RESEARCH', VOL. 10 (ACADEMIC PRESS, 1964); 'INTERFERON, A CIBA FOUNDATION SYMPOSIUM', ED. G. E. W. WOLSTENHOLME AND M. O'CONNOR (CHURCHILL, 1968).

Sir Alec Issigonis (British, b. 1905): engineer. Issigonis, the creator of the BMC Mini car, has an outstanding ability to interpret his thoughts by free-hand sketches which enable draughtsmen and others to understand exactly what is required. He was 42 when the first car with which he was connected, the Morris Minor, came off the

production line in 1948; over $1\frac{1}{4}$ million of these cars have been marketed to date. Small car design has occupied much of his thought, so when BMC wanted a new small car in 1957 Issigonis immediately applied himself to producing a truly small high-performance car with proper accommodation for four people and standards of stability previously unknown. On August 18, 1959, the first Mini was unveiled and the English language had acquired a new word. Today more than 2 million Minis have left the production line. In 1962 Issigonis's next car appeared, the 1100, which incorporated hydrolastic suspension, the creation of Alexander Moulton (another British engineer, whose bicycles are a common sight today). The 1100 strengthened Issigonis's right to be considered as the developer of a new era of popular motoring. **P. H. E. B.**

Koyota Iwasaki (Japanese, 1879–1945): tycoon. Grandson of the middle-grade Samurai Yataro Iwasaki, who founded Japan's Mitsubishi Company in the 1870s just after the opening to the West and the Meiji revolution, Koyota Iwasaki forged the giant 20th-century banking, commercial and industrial group which built Japan's Zero fighters and the battleships that nearly won the Battle of Midway. His father sent him to Cambridge in 1900; and there is still plenty of British flavour, particularly about Mitsubishi's shipping and shipbuilding side. But back in Tokyo, first as vice-president in 1906 and then unquestioned company head from 1916 to 1945, he ran the group like an iron-handed emperor, and drove it to a point where its ships, planes, lorries, chemicals, and heavy electrical goods represented well over 10 per cent. of Japan's whole national income. After the U.S. victory in 1945, almost the first act of the MacArthur (q.v.) military Government was to implement laws which effectively broke up Mitsubishi, biggest of all the *zaibatsu* companies, which had come, even more than Krupp in Germany, to represent Japanese armed might. **P. W.**

J

François Jacob (French, b. 1920): geneticist. The genes carry the instructions that tell organisms what substances to make to carry on life. Jacob's most distinguished research helped to show how the genes themselves are controlled. Jacob and Monod (q.v.), working with micro-organisms, found that there were at least three classes of genes: ordinary 'structural' genes, and '*regulator*' and '*operator*' genes that controlled them. The structural genes can make proteins only if instructed to do so by operator genes – themselves held in check by regulator genes, unless these are prevented from so doing by specific substances. Thus the control of protein synthesis proceeds by the inhibition of an inhibition, a type of control mechanism found also in the nervous system. That the genes themselves are controlled by others was an enormously important discovery. **J. B. M.**

Karl Jansky (U.S., 1905–1950): radio engineer. Jansky is the man to whom radioastronomy owes its beginning. During the years 1931 and 1932 he was employed by Bell Telephone Laboratories to look into the question of possible sources of radio interference that might upset long-distance radio communications. Working at Holmdel, New Jersey, with only a primitive aerial array he picked up 'atmospherics' which he proved came from the Milky Way itself, particularly from its denser parts. The radio signals varied with a period of 23 hours 56 minutes – that of a sidereal day, the period of the Earth's rotation relative to the stars. Hence, he reasoned, they must be coming from outside the solar system. Little notice was taken of Jansky's important discovery till 1942 when Reber (q.v.), another U.S. radio engineer, built a 30ft. radio dish and produced the first rough radio map of the Milky Way. Even so the subject was neglected until its explosion following the Second World War. But Karl Jansky's experiment was the spearhead of radioastronomy. **P. H. S. S.**

'OUR PRESENT KNOWLEDGE OF THE UNIVERSE', BY A. C. B. LOVELL (MANCHESTER U.P., 1967); 'INTRODUCTION TO RADIO-ASTRONOMY', BY R. C. JENNISON (PHILOSOPHICAL LIBRARY, NEW YORK, 1967).

Jean Jaurès (French, 1859–1914): politician and philosopher. Jaurès was the father of French parliamentary Socialism. From a poor family, he won scholarships and was academically very successful. Then the brilliant philosopher of the Ecole Normale Supérieure became attracted to Socialism. But not as an academic exercise. Socialism for Jaurès stood for everything that was best in humanity; it was all the ideas of justice and democracy put in a philosophical and historical background. Jaurès was an orator who travelled around France, a volatile, generous man who fought two pistol duels and let his daughter go to Communion while he attacked the Church in public. An outstanding figure in the Chamber of Deputies, he committed French Socialism to parliamentary democracy in 1905 by creating the unified

SFIO (French Section of the Workers' International) from myriad groups of Marxists, Trade Unionists and Anarchists. Winning 54 seats, its influence as an Opposition was crucial before the First World War, and Jaurès' prestige as a leader colossal. Even when his colleagues clung to his coat-tails he insisted upon speaking about Dreyfus, because justice was not a matter of political calculation. Similarly, he was always patriotic. But the belief that he was willing to sacrifice the national interest to some working-class vision caused him to be assassinated on the eve of war. He was a generous and sincere man, and it is these qualities which probably explain the myth that still persists among some French people: had Jaurès lived there would have been no war. **D. W. J. J.**

'LIFE OF JEAN JAURES', BY HARVEY GOLDBERG (UNIVERSITY OF WISCONSIN PRESS, 1962).

Gertrude Jekyll (British, 1843–1932): artist, gardener, craftswoman. These were the words carved on her monument by the famous architect Sir Edwin Lutyens (q.v.) her friend and working partner for many years. She had a marked influence in her own lifetime – and ever since. Much that has been popular and in fashion in gardening since the First World War was directly inspired by Miss Jekyll: silver-leaved plants, the one-colour border, the woodland garden,

the importance of foliage, fragrance and the climbing rose, hostas, ferns, yuccas, even London Pride. With her friend William Robinson (author of *The*

English Flower Garden) she set her face against the formal bedding-out horticultural style of the Victorians; she had as much respect for wild ferns, primroses and bluebells as for sophisticated plants. She was an artist as well as a gardener, and was cultured, travelled and well-read, with a wide circle of friends which included Ruskin, Barbara Bodichon (co-founder of Girton) and Ellen Willmott, author of *The Genus Rosa.* The creation of her own garden at Munstead Wood, in Surrey, was her joy, and, rising above myopia and the threat of blindness, she worked with Lutyens on many others – including the Deanery at Sonning, The Salutation at Sandwich, and Great Dixter, at Northiam. At the latter, and at Sissinghurst in Kent (both open to the public), her great tradition lives on. **L. R.**

BOOKS BY GERTRUDE JEKYLL: 'WOOD AND GARDEN', (LONGMANS GREEN, 1899); 'HOME AND GARDENS', (LONGMANS GREEN, 1900); 'COLOUR IN THE FLOWER GARDEN', (COUNTRY LIFE, 1908). 'MISS JEKYLL', BY BETTY MASSINGHAM (COUNTRY LIFE, 1966).

Mohammed Ali Jinnah (Pakistani, 1876–1948): statesman. For most of his early career a moderate and secular Indian nationalist, Jinnah from 1934 presided over the reorganised All-India Muslim League which came to demand a separate state – Pakistan – in which religion was to be the sole determinant of nationality. He was by no means the unquestioned leader of Indian Muslims, but after 1934 the prospect of devolution and the fears of Muslim minority provinces which had done badly out of the 1932 Communal Award gave Jinnah the opportunity to revitalise the Muslim League. By an uncharacteristic, but politically expedient, policy of mass contact, by stressing Islam and by the demand for Pakistan, Jinnah at last succeeded in capturing the Muslim majority provinces of Punjab and Bengal and in making the League speak for all Muslims. Yet, paradoxically, after Partition and the creation of the new state of Pakistan, this anglicised Muslim (who married a Parsi) tried, as first Governor-General, to return Pakistan to a policy of secular nationalism and to make overtures to India for a subcontinental co-operation. **A. S.**

'JINNAH: CREATOR OF PAKISTAN', BY H. BOLITHO (JOHN MURRAY, 1954); 'QUAID-E-AZAM JINNAH AS I KNEW HIM', BY M. A. H. ISPAHANI (FORWERD PUBLICATIONS TRUST, KARACHI, 1966).

John XXIII (Italian, 1881–1963): Pope Angelo Roncalli – the most human pope in history – was proud of his peasant ancestry and of his own priesthood in North Italy. Traditionally devout, he was more sympathetic to social and intellectual stirrings than were most of his seniors in the Church. After a brief spell in the central administration, he was enlisted in the Papal diplomatic service and packed off, in 1925, to Bulgaria. When they moved him, it was only to Istanbul. A bigger job came 20 years later, as the Papacy's ambassador to the confusions of Church and State in post-war France. One reward for his genial diplomacy was his appointment as Patriarch of Venice; another when he was elected Pope in 1958 at 77. His Encyclicals allied the Church with social progressives. To renew his Church for the modern

world, he summoned its bishops and non-Catholic observers to the Second Vatican Council. His addresses were the Council's chief ornaments, and during this Council he died. He made the Vatican a target of love. **D. L. E.**

'POPE JOHN', BY MERIOL TREVOR (MACMILLAN, 1967); 'JOURNAL OF A SOUL', BY POPE JOHN XXIII (GEOFFREY CHAPMAN, 1965); 'PACEM IN TERRIS', BY POPE JOHN XXIII (CATHOLIC TRUTH SOCIETY, 1964).

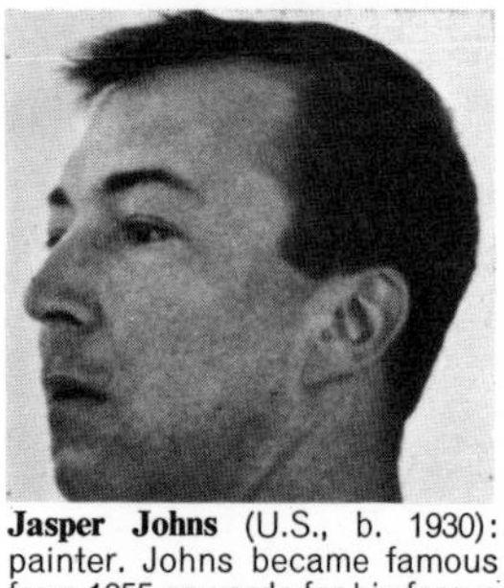

Jasper Johns (U.S., b. 1930): painter. Johns became famous from 1955 onwards for his forays into the ambiguous middle-ground between 'life' and 'art'. With his paintings of common objects (targets, flags, numbers, the map of the USA) and his painted sculptures of beer cans and paint brushes he gave a new turn to the central discussion of post-war art. Where the previous generation of Americans had staked everything on making an image that had not existed before and was entirely of their own invention, Johns took images which were so familiar as not to qualify at all for 'art' in the traditional sense. In all the flags, the given subject was necessarily the same; but each flag was completely unlike the others and had, against all the odds, its own identity. Similarly the beer cans turn out to differ as much from 'the real thing' as a dress painted by Velazquez differs from a fashion-plate. At a critical time for the relationship between art and life, Johns brought the two together and got them to swap identities: both were the better for it, and for the aristocratic disdain for convention with which the swap was effected. **J. R.**

'JASPER JOHNS', BY LEO STEINBERG (WITTENBORN, NEW YORK, 1963).

Amy Johnson (British, 1903–1941): aviator. Amy Johnson made her first flight on a five-shilling flip when she was 23, hung around aerodromes and learned to fly. In May 1930, only 10 months after getting her pilot's licence, she flew a second-hand Gypsy Moth solo from Croydon to Australia in 20 days, earning £10,000 from the *Daily Mail*, and a CBE. She flew across Russia to Tokyo, and to the Cape and back; her courage was fanatical, but she never learned to land well. Her

highly publicised marriage to Jim Mollison, playboy-aviator, broke up. Then in 1941 the RAF plane she was ferrying ran out of fuel; she parachuted into the Thames Estuary, and drowned. When a skeleton was found on the Essex coast in 1962 the coroner said it was the fortieth time Amy Johnson's body had been recovered. As a girl she had an unhappy affair with a Swiss, and Francis Chichester has said that this made her look on flying as "a genteel method of suicide after she had been jilted". She was a romantic heroine of the 1930s – in the words of the song, "Wonderful Amy the Aeroplane Girl". **T. F. C.**

'AMY JOHNSON', BY CONSTANCE BABINGTON SMITH (COLLINS, 1967).

Howard Johnson (U.S., b. 1898): restaurateur. Twenty-eight delicious flavours of ice cream from Apple Strudel to Vanilla are the basis of the Howard Johnson success story. Bankrupted by his father's debts, he started a modest ice cream parlour in Wollaston, Massachusetts, in 1925. Today the empire consists of 850 restaurants, the largest chain of its kind in the world, and 450 motor lodges, and is run by his

40-year-old son. Johnson pioneered the franchised highway restaurant, supplying standard menus and materials to those willing to pay to work under his trademark, a vivid orange roof visible like a beacon for hungry drivers. The growth of the automobile has been the spur, and new sites are plotted with changing traffic patterns in mind. Food is wholesome and appetising with agreeable gimmicks such as the Big Chicken Fry every Monday coast to coast – all you can eat with French Fries and Cole Slaw. Hygienic and familiar, the Howard Johnson's is a reassuring emblem of the American scene wherever you are, from Florence, Alabama to Oshkosh, Wisconsin. **G. C. P.**

Jack Johnson (U.S., 1878–1946): boxer. Johnson was the first Negro to win the world heavyweight championship – now virtually a preserve of the coloured fighter – and one of the few boxers thoroughly to master the fighting art. He had a superb left jab and an uncanny ability for avoiding blows, and like Muhammad Ali (q.v.) held his hands low, though he was not so fast on his feet. His career encompassed 109 major fights and exhibitions, and in 1908 he won the world title by beating Tommy Burns in Sydney, Australia. He lost it in Havana in 1915 to Jess Willard when he was 'knocked out' in the 26th round, seeming to shield his eyes from the sun as he was counted out; years later he signed a statement admitting he had "taken a dive". Johnson was the victim of both the brash arrogance he displayed as champion and the period in which he lived: in 1913 he was convicted under the Mann 'White Slave' Act for transporting a woman from one State to another for immoral purposes and he fled to Europe, only to be imprisoned upon his return to the U.S. in 1920. Nothing, however, can ever detract from the standard of skill he set for every champion, black or white, who followed him, a skill rarely, if ever, equalled since. His record clearly shows that he was usually content to win on points (a good way for a black boxer to ensure he kept getting fights); but once he was hurt Johnson soon finished with his opponents. He died, from a car crash, in 1946 and any promoter today would settle for just one pup off him. **J. S.**

'JACK JOHNSON AND HIS TIMES', BY DENZIL BATCHELOR (PHOENIX, 1956).

Lyndon Baines Johnson (U.S., b. 1908): statesman. LBJ will be remembered for his initials (which he inflicted on his wife, daughters, ranch and cattle) and for the sorrows that befell the United States during his Presidency. This harsh but unavoidable verdict results from the greatest American political tragedy since the fall of Woodrow Wilson (q.v.). Johnson came to the highest office trailing a record of brilliant success as Congressman, Senator and campaigner (without him Jack Kennedy [q.v.] would not have been elected President). At first it seemed that as President Johnson would eclipse his former achievements: he pushed through, with extraordinary skill and speed, a vast reforming legislative programme. But foreign affairs (which he never properly understood) proved his bane. He got bogged down inextricably in the cruel, foolish and hated Vietnamese War, and, against his election pledges, intensified it. The political and economic costs of the war stopped him tackling the Siamese twin problems of poverty and racism, with which he was otherwise superbly equipped to deal. Riot became endemic in America. Johnson was forced to renounce all hope of re-election, and saw his chosen successor repudiated by the people in favour of Richard Nixon (q.v.). The monument to his great talents is inscribed with the names of the dead in the war abroad and the insurrections at home. **D. H. V. B.**

'LYNDON B. JOHNSON: THE EXERCISE OF POWER', BY ROWLAND EVANS AND ROBERT NOVAK (ALLEN AND UNWIN, 1967); 'AN AMERICAN MELODRAMA: THE PRESIDENTIAL CAMPAIGN OF 1968', BY LEWIS CHESTER, GODFREY HODGSON, AND BRUCE PAGE (ANDRE DEUTSCH, 1969); 'DIVIDED THEY STAND', BY DAVID ENGLISH (MICHAEL JOSEPH, 1969); 'THE TRAGEDY OF LYNDON JOHNSON', BY ERIC F. GOLDMAN (MACDONALD, 1969).

Philip Johnson (U.S., b. 1906): architect. Wealthy, intellectual and glamorous, Johnson has helped to lead American architecture away from the austerities of the Thirties. He first made his name as the co-author of the book which gave the white-walled, flat-roofed International Style its name. After a belated architectural training at Harvard under Gropius and Breuer (qq.v.), he designed as his own home (1949) the Glass House at New Canaan, Connecticut. In it he subtly revealed the historical roots of the transparent boxes of Mies van der Rohe (q.v.): the German classicism of Schinkel, the Beaux Arts view of the Acropolis and Suprematist abstractions of Malevich (q.v.). Johnson invests his stylistic pilferings from the European inheritance with the gaiety of the 'camp': the glittering portico and ceiling of the New York State Theatre (1961–4); the marble peristyle of the Sheldon Art Gallery, University of Nebraska (1963–4) and the desert fort of the Negev nuclear reactor, Israel (1960–1); the castellated ductwork of the Kline Science Center at Yale (1964–7). **N. J. W. T.**

'THE INTERNATIONAL STYLE', BY PHILIP JOHNSON AND H. R. HITCHCOCK (MUSEUM OF MODERN ART, 1932; REPRINTED, 1966); 'ARCHITECTURE,' BY PHILIP JOHNSON (THAMES AND HUDSON, 1966).

Al Jolson (U.S., 1886–1950): singer. Trail-blazer of this century's pop singers, Jolson (born Asa Yoelson, son of a synagogue cantor) was the first to become a major star singing songs influenced by Negro jazz. He also made the first talking picture (*The Jazz Singer*, 1927) and left the biggest theatrical fortune then recorded despite losing around £1m. in the 1929 crash. During the 1920s he was the best-known singer in the world, earning £5000 a week. *Sonny Boy*, from his second film (*The Singing Fool*), was the first million-seller record of the talkie era. Other crooners overtook him in the 1930s, but he had an astonishing revival in the

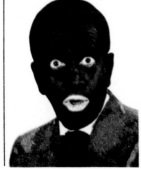

mid-1940s when Larry Parks played him, with Jolson's voice on the sound-track, in two movies, *The Jolson Story* and *Jolson Sings Again*. Bizarrely, all his old hits became million-sellers again. He'd just returned from entertaining U.S. troops in Korea when he died in a San Francisco hotel. There were 25,000 people at his funeral. **D. J.**

RECORDS: 'SAY IT WITH SONGS' (AH 87); 'LET ME SING AND I'M HAPPY' (AH 33)

Bobby Jones (U.S., b. 1902): golfer. Robert Tyre Jones is now no longer able to attend the annual playing of his brainchild, the Masters Tournament at Augusta, Georgia; he is too ill. Since the war, he has had an arthritic condition of the spine that has made him a wheelchair invalid. Only his great spirit, which enabled him to conquer completely the world of golf in eight short years between 1923 and 1930, culminating in the

Grand Slam (winning in one year the British and American amateur and open championships), has kept him an active physical force. As well as having as perfect a natural swing as will ever be seen, he was a great golfer. During his decade of dominance, he was four times open champion, and five times amateur champion, of America; British open champion three times, and amateur titleholder once. His contribution to golf can be expressed thus: dedication, ruthlessness, perfection of stroke, will-to-win, and – the final accolade – retirement when he had achieved all he set out to do. **J. B.**

'GOLF IS MY GAME', BY BOBBY JONES (CHATTO AND WINDUS, 1961).

James Joyce (Irish, 1882–1941): novelist. Author of *Ulysses* (1922), masterpiece. Praising it, T. S. Eliot (q.v.) said that by using "the mythical method" rather than "narrative method" Joyce had taken an important step toward "making the modern world possible for art". Preparatory muscular exercises were performed in the short stories of *Dubliners* (1914) and the lyric-confessional prose of *A Portrait of the Artist as*

a Young Man (1916). An expatriate, Joyce lived at various times in Trieste, Rome, Paris, and Zürich, but he kept his memory of Dublin green. His life is one of the great modern instances of artistic independence, a devotion to art maintained in "silence, exile, and cunning". The step taken in *Ulysses* involves a critical relation between past and present. The past, so far as the structure of the book goes, is Homeric, story and characters invoking counterparts in the *Odyssey*. The present includes the sights, sounds, and smells of Dublin on June 16, 1904, and the sundry activities of such characters as Stephen Dedalus, Leopold Bloom, Molly Bloom, Gerty MacDowell, Blazes Boylan and "stately plump Buck Mulligan". Certain verbal possibilities discovered in *Ulysses* were fully released in *Finnegans Wake* (1939), an anthologist's joy, but unlikely to be selected as the 4000th Penguin. **D. Do.**

'JAMES JOYCE: A CRITICAL INTRODUCTION', BY HARRY LEVIN (FABER AND FABER, 1960); 'JAMES JOYCE', BY RICHARD ELLMANN (O.U.P., 1959).

England, began to broadcast the news from Berlin and soon graduated to propaganda: his fake upper-class accent led to the Haw Haw nickname, originally coined for Norman Baillie-Stewart. He became a naturalised German in 1940, and as before this he was an American by nationality, he was not, technically, a traitor; but he did hold a British passport, and was hanged for treason in 1946. **C. W.**

'THE MEANING OF TREASON', BY REBECCA WEST (MACMILLAN, 1949).

Carl Jung (Swiss, 1875–1961): psychiatrist. Jung's reputation as a pioneer in modern psychiatry was established by the publication in 1906 of *The Psychology of Dementia Praecox* (now called schizophrenia). He was then a physician at the Burghölzli, a teaching hospital of Zürich University. In 1907 Freud (q.v.) invited him to visit Vienna. The welcome was warm,

Hugo Junkers (German, 1859–1935): engineer. Professor Junkers, a pioneer of aircraft design, gave his name to the German aircraft company which produced a series of important bombers in the Second World War. In 1910 he designed his all-wing aeroplane, and in 1915 the first all-metal aircraft. His ideas were too advanced for his time, and his aeroplanes were not built in any quantities in the First World War. It was in the early Twenties that Junkers's name first found prominence, when his cantilever monoplanes with corrugated duralumin construction first began to show their advantages. Even greater

for Jung was his first Gentile follower, and this relieved Freud's fear that psychoanalysis might become a Jewish national affair. The six-year collaboration was not always harmonious – Freud the extravert and Jung the introvert were almost destined to clash. Jung's chief aim in research was to show that the body and mind functioned as a unit. He was the first to demonstrate objectively that emotion has physical accompaniments – known today as psychosomatic phenomena. Laying special emphasis on the neuroses he studied the structure and content of the mind in health and in sickness. In *Psychological Types* he introduced 'extraversion' and 'introversion', terms now in everyday use. Experimental investigations showed the autonomous nature of the unconscious and the grouping therein of 'complexes' – another Jungian term. In addition to individual distinctiveness, Jung believed the mind had collective qualities identical in all men, a common substrata, similar to the instincts – 'The Collective Unconscious'. His system of thought, *Analytical Psychology*, gives a prominent place to dream-analysis in psychological treatment. **E. A. B.**

'ANALYTICAL PSYCHOLOGY', BY C. G. JUNG (ROUTLEDGE AND KEGAN PAUL, 1968); 'MAN AND HIS SYMBOLS', EDITED BY CARL G. JUNG (ALDUS BOOKS, 1964); 'WHAT JUNG REALLY SAID', BY E. A. BENNET (MACDONALD, 1966); 'AN INTRODUCTION TO JUNG'S PSYCHOLOGY', BY F. FORDHAM WEST (MACMILLAN, 1949).

success was achieved by the series of larger and more efficient airliners which followed, and which were used either by the airline which Junkers formed in 1921 (later called Lufthansa) or as wartime troop transports. During the last years of Junkers' life the company he had formed abandoned corrugated duralumin for more conventional stressed skin construction, and developed the Ju87 dive-bomber and the Ju88 series. The Ju87 achieved a considerable reputation in the early years of the war, but was much less effective in the Battle of Britain, when it lacked effective fighter cover. **N. J. M. H.**

Franz Kafka (Czech, 1883–1924): novelist. Kafka frustrates interpretation, as his life was frustrated: cut off from Czechs as a German-speaker, from Germans as a Jew, from Jews as an unbeliever, he presses deeper into dereliction, comfortless. "No 'and yet' " is almost the last entry in his diary. Rarely did he allow himself the sense that evil passively endured would turn to good. A quietist, Kafka knew nothing but his own torment of guilt, and waited for it to shape itself in art. *The Trial* (1925) and *The Castle* (1926) attract by their mystery – perhaps about a religious quest, perhaps more about Kafka's relationship with his father: he had read Freud (q.v.), but also Kierkegaard. His besetting fault – the spinning of neurotic spirals of self-doubt – harms both these novels, which remained incomplete. His most achieved work is *The Metamorphosis* (1915), about a man transformed into an insect – a clearheaded account of a condition like his own. Its classic form may owe something to his view of writing as a form of prayer, as though for once wholeness came even to his desolation. Since he yields completely, in all his work there is the possibility of total loss; when he does make a whole, it seems a victory inherent in his admission of defeat. **R. D. G.**

'THE DIARIES OF FRANZ KAFKA, 1910–1923', (PENGUIN, 1964); 'FRANZ KAFKA TODAY', EDITED BY A. FLORES AND H. SWANDER (WISCONSIN U.P., 1958); 'KAFKA, A COLLECTION OF CRITICAL ESSAYS', ED. RONALD GRAY (PRENTICE-HALL, NEW YORK, 1962); 'FRANZ KAFKA', BY KLAUS WAGENBACH (ROWOHLT, HAMBURG, 1964).

Heike Kamerlingh Onnes (Dutch, 1853–1926): physicist. Kamerlingh Onnes was the first man to succeed in liquefying the gas helium and is thus the founder of very-low-temperature research (cryogenics). Helium had been found on Earth in 1905 and he succeeded in liquefying it in 1908. The gas liquefies at 4.2° above Absolute zero; in fact Kamerlingh Onnes reached 0.7° Absolute on the same day as his successful liquefaction. He immediately began to use liquid helium as a tool for low-temperature research and, in 1913, was awarded the Nobel Prize for his studies on the optical, magnetic, and magneto-optical properties of substances in these very cold regions. In the year 1911 he discovered, in mercury, the phenomenon known as superconductivity, in which metals at a very low temperature lose virtually all their electrical resistance. Today, at least 22 elements and hundreds of alloys are known to be superconducting at very low temperatures. Kamerlingh Onnes also suggested, and recognised the advantages of, large superconducting magnets, able to produce powerful magnetic fields with low currents without the problem of excess heat. **P. H. S. S.**

'THE QUEST FOR ABSOLUTE ZERO', BY K. MENDELSSOHN (WEIDENFELD AND NICOLSON, 1966).

Wassily Kandinsky (Russian, 1866–1944): painter. Just before 1914 Munich was, after Paris, the second capital of European art. A dominant personality

William Joyce (German, ex-U.S., 1906–1946): propagandist. 'Lord Haw Haw's' broadcasts were intended to undermine British morale in the Second World War. The ridicule they inspired in fact stiffened the nation's will to fight. Joyce had joined Sir Oswald Mosley's (q.v.) British Union of Fascists in 1933. He was a brilliant speaker and organiser, and after Mosley 'purged' him in 1937, he formed the National Socialist League whose figurehead was Hitler (q.v.) himself: unlike Mosley, Joyce was passionately anti-semitic. After two years of cheap lodgings and street-corner oratory, he slipped out of

Louis Kahn (U.S., b. 1901): architect. Like Philip Johnson (q.v.) a late developer, Kahn also emerged as a disciple of Mies van der Rohe (q.v.) in the Yale Art Gallery (1952–4); but its ceiling of chunky concrete tetrahedrons already indicated a more earthily realistic attitude. Given the difficulty of tidying away elaborate mechanical devices within the Miesian box, Kahn divided his spaces into 'served' and 'servant', i.e. big open spaces served by towers of lifts, stairs and ducts. Kahn achieved his personal synthesis in the Richards Medical Research Building at the University of Pennsylvania (1958–60) – the towers of the services standing round the perimeter and giving the whole complex a grandly evocative San Gimignano silhouette. Kahn has developed this romantic classicism, with increasingly wilful details, in the Salk Laboratories at La Jolla, California (1962–5); the Government Buildings at Dacca, East Pakistan (1966–); and the Palace of Congresses, Venice (designed 1969). **N. J. W. T.**

there was Kandinsky, a Russian intellectual with mystical inclinations who had turned from law to painting. A natural leader, he headed the 'Blue Rider' group, which included in its orbit Paul Klee, the Russian painter Malevich, the composer Arnold Schoenberg (qq.v.) and the Douanier Rousseau. In 1912 he published *Concerning the Spiritual in Art*, a plea for the dematerialisation of painting which led logically to a mystical conception of abstract art. This he put into practice in two series of large paintings, the *Compositions* and the *Improvisations*, which argued the case for a purely abstract art in terms of an appropriately tumultuous helter-skelter of form and colour. After trying to work with the Soviets in Russia, Kandinsky returned to the West in 1921 and taught (1922–33) at the Bauhaus before moving to Paris. After 1922 his work lost its uproarious, overtly dynamic character and took on a look of exact calculation and analytical balance. **J. R.**

'KANDINSKY', BY WILL GROHMANN (THAMES AND HUDSON, 1959); 'KANDINSKY', BY FRANK WHITFORD (HAMLYN, 1967).

Paul Karrer (Swiss, 1889–1971): biological chemist. Vitamin A, an essential growth factor which also effects vision in dim light, was postulated in 1906, but its existence was known only from its biological effects. It was not until 1931 that Karrer isolated the pure substance from cod liver oil. He then worked out how the atoms of which it is composed are arranged and showed that the vitamin was similar to the coloured material from carrots, carotene. (So there *is* a link between eating carrots and being able to see in the dark.) Karrer's subsequent work helped to solve many problems associated with the chemistry of other vitamins – B₂, C, E and K – as well as with many other plant and animal products. In addition to this, his great general contribution to the science of chemistry is the world-renowned *Textbook of Organic Chemistry*, which must have passed, at some time, through the hands of virtually every organic chemist practising today. The biological chemistry of Karrer is one of the foundations of the giant pharmaceutical industry of today. **M. A. S.**

'ORGANIC CHEMISTRY', BY PAUL KARRER (FOURTH EDITION, ELSEVIER, 1950); 'NOBEL PRIZEWINNERS IN CHEMISTRY', BY EDUARD FARBER (ABELARD- SCHUMAN, 1963); 'NOBEL LECTURES, CHEMISTRY 1922-41' (ELSEVIER, 1966).

wing 'revisionism' (Eduard Bernstein) and Left-wing radicalism (Rosa Luxemburg [q.v.]), and so became the leading exponent of Marxist orthodoxy, a kind of Marxist 'Pope'. A pacifist in the First World War; a member of the Independent Socialist Party at its foundation, he opposed both imperialist annexations and Lenin's proletarian dictatorship. He remained always a staunch adherent of democratic and radical socialism. After the German revolution he briefly became Under-Secretary in the German Foreign Office, using the opportunity to publish the German documents relating to the outbreak of war. When his party withdrew from the Government Kautsky left Berlin and settled in Vienna where he continued to influence the Austrian Socialists. Driven from Vienna by the Nazis he fled to Prague and thence to Amsterdam, a fugitive from countries which seemed to have rejected both freedom and socialism. **F. L. C.**

'THE SECOND INTERNATIONAL, 1899-1914'. BY JAMES JOLL (EYRE AND SPOTTISWOODE, 1955); 'MARXISM', BY GEORGE LICHTHEIM (ROUTLEDGE AND KEGAN PAUL, 1961).

Buster Keaton (U.S., 1895–1966): film actor. At once the simplest and the subtlest, the most lucid and the most profoundly silent of the silent cinema's great comedians, the incomparable Buster will remain in legend as the Great Stone Face, the mechanical man whose limbs pedalled and semaphored ferociously, while the face above them remained grave, unsmiling and beautifully imperturbable. In fact, the flick of the features expressed everything: his was the only face on the silent screen, apart from Garbo's (q.v.), to register every process of thought. Keaton was born into vaudeville, being literally hurled about the stage in infancy as part of the family act (Harry Houdini [q.v.] first called him Buster: his real names were Joseph Francis). He entered films, rather casually, in 1917; his partial fade-out at the end of the 1920s was brought about less by the talkies or by alcohol than by problems of adjusting his working methods to new big-studio regimes. A splendid solitary, alone with a Civil War locomotive (*The General*), an ocean liner (*The Navigator*), or in maddened flight from herds of wild cattle or wilder wives, Keaton had a feeling for accuracy, scale and the authenticity of appearances which made him one of the great instinctive filmmakers, as well as one of the most irresistibly and thoughtfully funny men ever to walk in front of a camera. **P. H.**

'BUSTER KEATON', BY DAVID ROBINSON (SECKER AND WARBURG, 1969) 'MY WONDERFUL WORLD OF SLAPSTICK', BY BUSTER KEATON (ALLEN AND UNWIN, 1967).

McKnight Kauffer (U.S., 1890–1954): poster designer. Edward McKnight Kauffer had greater influence over British graphic art than any other artist between the wars. He settled in Britain in 1914 after studying art in Chicago, Munich and Paris and stayed 26 years. Borrowing from Futurism and Cubism in the 1920s he pioneered geometric design and clear lettering, and in the 1930s developed a formula for simplifying landscape similar to that of the painter André Derain. His 1920 poster for the *Daily Herald*, *The Early Bird*, a dynamic triangular flight of birds, has considerable impact and from then on he had over 100 commissions from London Transport and many from Shell. Among his best-known posters were London Transport's *London Museum*, *Winter Sales* (reproduced above), *Buckingham Palace from St. James's Park*, and *Landscape 1938*; his cockerel design for Eno's, the *To Cornwall* poster for the G.W.R., and for Shell *B.P. Ethyl*, a brilliant combination of lettering and a photograph of a horse from the Elgin Marbles. His main exhibitions were in 1926 at the Ashmolean, in 1937 at the New York Museum of Modern Art, and a posthumous exhibition in 1955 at the V. and A. His posters on London Transport hoardings and Shell tankers and lorries spread to the four corners of Britain the modern version of poster art. **Ph. G.**

Karl Kautsky (Austrian and German, 1854–1938): Marxist theoretician. Kautsky was perhaps the most influential pupil of Marx and the chief interpreter of his theories for the parties of the Socialist International. As editor of the theoretical organ of the German Social Democrats, *Neue Zeit*, and through prolific Marxist writing, he influenced generations of socialist leaders. Within the party, he occupied a 'centrist' position, fighting Right-

Sir Frank Kearton (British, b. 1911): industrialist. Probably the supreme British example of a technologist turned manager, Lord Kearton first exploded into public notice during the 1961 bid by ICI to take over Courtaulds (q.v. Paul Chambers). Kearton, an ex-ICI man himself, mounted a furious, and successful, opposition to the bid, which led directly not only to his becoming chairman in 1964, but to a massive injection of new life into the long-declining Lancashire textile trade. In an unprecedented series of mergers and amalgamations, Kearton has extended Courtaulds' grip all the way from nylon fibre to high street boutiques, and the outcome of his strategy will determine the fate of a substantial slice of Britain's economy over the next two decades. His influence and ideas will be felt over a much wider field than textiles: as the architect and first Chairman of the Government's Industrial Reorganisation Corporation (1966–8) he was largely instrumental in forcing through such giant mergers as GEC-AEI and the British Leyland Motor Corporation. **P. W.**

Edward Kendall (U.S., b. 1886): chemist. One of Kendall's greatest achievements was to synthesise the hormone cortisone, believed to be produced by the adrenal gland. He did so in 1948 by a process starting with a constituent of ox bile, which crowned 15 years' intense efforts to isolate and identify steroid hormones. This led to several major advances, starting with the discovery by his colleague, Philip Hench, that cortisone dramatically relieved the symptoms of arthritis. (They shared a Nobel Prize with the Polish chemist Reichstein in 1950.) Early hopes of a cure for rheumatism were not realised by Kendall's discovery. But the research it provoked led to the synthesis of hormones of greater therapeutic value. Some are important in controlling inflammation and allergic conditions, such as asthma. Others prolong life in the so-called autoimmune and collagen diseases. Man-made steroids can replace the hormones missing in Addison's disease of the adrenals, and new synthetic substances related to sex hormones form the basis of the contraceptive pill. **C. H. G.**

John Cowdery Kendrew (British, b. 1917): molecular biologist. Proteins are important naturally occurring substances with a complex structure. Kendrew first determined the structure of one – in general outline in 1957, in atomic detail in 1959. For this work he shared the 1962 Nobel Prize for Chemistry with Max Perutz (q.v.). Perutz was working on haemoglobin when Kendrew joined him and started on myoglobin – relatively a smaller molecule about one quarter the size of haemoglobin with only 2500 atoms. The technique Kendrew used involved replac-

ing parts of the molecule with a heavy metal atom and using X-ray crystallography to plot the changes that occurred when the metal was in different positions. Many thousands of X-ray spots had to be measured, but in the end Kendrew demonstrated that the basic chain of a protein molecule is spiral. His solution also revealed the general nature of the forces binding the component parts of the protein molecule together, and it defined the environment of the iron atom to which oxygen becomes attached in myoglobin. The work has led to knowledge of the structure of haemoglobin, and to an understanding of the way that oxygen is carried by the blood. **P. G. R.**

John Fitzgerald Kennedy (U.S., 1917–1963): statesman. The historical Jack Kennedy was killed before he had, as President, achieved very much. He is to be remembered as the most glittering success so far in the most daring experiment in dynastic politics yet attempted in the American Republic. The chief items on his Presidential balance-sheet will be reckoned his election in 1960, which defeated a long tradition of bigotry and showed that a Catholic could make it; his acceptance of the military chiefs' disastrous plan to invade Cuba at the Bay of Pigs; his facing down of Khrushchev in the 1962 Cuban missiles affair, which led to a welcome, if temporary, improvement in Russo-American relations; his launching of a rational and high-minded reform programme within the United States; the nuclear test-ban treaty; and (the biggest debit item by far) his intensification of the fatal American commitment in Vietnam, which showed that the Cold War resonances of his Inaugural Address were not mere window-dressing. There was also a mythical Jack Kennedy, deriving from the real man's charm, good looks, gaiety, vigour and intelligence. This Kennedy, according to true believers, would certainly have repented and repaired his mistakes. No-one can really say how true this is. But a legend will survive: young hope cut down by an assassin's bullets. This too must be reckoned in the balance. **D. H. V. B.**

'A THOUSAND DAYS', BY ARTHUR SCHLE-SINGER JR. (ANDRÉ DEUTSCH, 1965); 'KENNEDY', BY THEODORE SORENSEN (HODDER AND STOUGHTON, 1965); 'THE POLITICS OF JOHN F. KENNEDY', BY EDMUND IONS (ROUTLEDGE AND KEGAN PAUL, 1967).

Robert Francis Kennedy (U.S., 1925–1968): politician. In 1968 the Democratic Party wanted as a candidate for the presidency someone who would be acceptable to every major section of the party, who was not identified with the disastrous policies of the Johnson Administration, who was identified with the greater, happier days of FDR or Jack Kennedy (qq.v.), and whose record suggested that he had the character and principles successfully to bear the burdens of a Presidential campaign and the Presidential office. Robert Kennedy had all these qualifications. He had been his elder brother's most trusted adviser, and played a leading part both in electing him and as his Attorney-General. More than any other white politician he had made the causes of the poor and the black his own, and he possessed great appeal to the young and to the opponents of the Vietnamese War. As Senator for New York since 1964 he had built up an efficient personal political machine, and maintained friendly contacts with other professionals throughout the country. But the man and the hour were not to meet. A demented alien youth had indulged his fantasies by murdering Kennedy in Los Angeles, and Bobby had become, like his brother Jack, merely a symbol of hope destroyed. The future of the United States would be shaped by other, less compassionate and courageous spirits. **D. H. V. B.**

'THE PURSUIT OF JUSTICE', BY ROBERT F. KENNEDY (HAMISH HAMILTON, 1965); 'THIRTEEN DAYS', BY ROBERT F. KENNEDY (MACMILLAN, 1969); 'A THOUSAND DAYS', BY ARTHUR SCHLESINGER, JR. (ANDRÉ DEUTSCH, 1965); 'AN AMERICAN MELO-DRAMA: THE PRESIDENTIAL CAMPAIGN OF 1968', BY LEWIS CHESTER, GODFREY HODG-SON AND BRUCE PAGE (DEUTSCH, 1969).

Jomo Kenyatta (Kenyan, born c. 1893): politician. It is hard to who has presided for a decade who has presided for six years over one of the least revolutionary governments in Africa, was once the symbolic figure of violent resistance to colonial rule. Kenyatta, more than most nationalist leaders, drew his inspiration from the past. He came to prominence defending Kikuyu initiation customs from missionary attacks, and during his long stay in England from 1931 till 1946 he studied anthropology and wrote a book glorifying Kikuyu life in pre-colonial times. Nationalism in Kenya, however, faced not merely a colonial administration but sixty thousand European settlers. Under Kenyatta's leadership, the Kikuyu were the first to offer serious opposition. Mau Mau began in 1950 with

a few spectacular murders of Europeans on outlying farms. It developed into a bloody civil war among the Kikuyu themselves, between the militant freedom fighters and those who for the time being acquiesced in colonial rule. In 1953 Kenyatta was convicted of managing the movement, and he remained in prison and detention for nine years, during which time he became the hero not only of Kenya Africans but of struggling nationalists all over the continent. He emerged, a charismatic figure, on the eve of independence. **R. O.**

'FACING MOUNT KENYA', BY JOMO KENYATTA (SECKER AND WARBURG, 1953); 'THE MYTH OF MAU MAU', BY CARL ROSBERG AND JOHN NOTTINGHAM (PRAEGER, NEW YORK, 1966).

Alexander Kerensky (Russian, 1881–1971): politician. Kerensky was the man who might have prevented the Bolshevik Revolution. Like Lenin (q.v.), he was born in Simbírsk and trained as a lawyer. Unlike Lenin, he was attracted by Populism rather than Marxism, and entered the Duma in 1912 as leader of the moderate Trudovik group. The February Revolution of 1917 thrust him into prominence. The only leading member of both the Provisional Government and the Petrograd (St Petersburg) Soviet, he had great energy and oratorical ability, which initially won him enormous popularity. Yet the resulting sense of Napoleonic destiny was not completed by much political shrewdness. Prime Minister from July 1917, he concentrated on reviving the war effort when peace, land reform and a Constituent Assembly were called for. Increasingly isolated from Left and Right, he negotiated in August with General Kornilov to suppress the Bolsheviks, but when Kornilov attempted a coup Kerensky had to call on Bolshevik support. Kerensky then assumed supreme military command, but from September his fall was only a matter of time. Late in October Lenin took power and Kerensky fled from Petrograd. The Commander-in-Chief of the Russian army, however, could find only 700 Cossacks with which to reconquer Petrograd, and his attempt was easily crushed. After several months in hiding, Kerensky left Russia for the West where, half a century after leaving the stage of history which he so briefly occupied, he still lived. **J. D. B.**

'TEN DAYS THAT SHOOK THE WORLD', BY JOHN REED (REPRINT, PENGUIN, 1966); 'THE RUSSIAN REVOLUTION 1917: A PERSONAL RECORD' BY N. N. SUKHANOV; ED. AND TRANS. BY J. CARMICHAEL (O.U.P., 1955).

Jerome Kern (U.S., 1885–1945): composer. Jerome Kern was the first U.S.-born composer to give classical form and style to American popular music. His first big hit came in 1914 when *They Didn't Believe Me* sold two million sheet music copies. The song had an important influence on George Gershwin (q.v.) who said that it made him realise that a popular tune could have dignity. Kern's musical *Showboat* also influenced Gershwin who, after hearing the score, was inspired with the idea for his Negro folk opera, *Porgy and Bess*. Every song that Kern wrote, save one, was for either a show or a film. The exception was *The Last Time I Saw Paris*, written to the lyric of Oscar Hammerstein, also an exception in that it is the only Kern song

written after the words: in every other case the music came first. In 1945 Kern returned to New York to begin work on a musical about the famous woman sharpshooter, Annie Oakley. But on December 12 he suffered a fatal heart attack. The project was taken up by Irving Berlin (q.v.) who wrote perhaps his liveliest score for *Annie Get Your Gun*. Deems Taylor's epitaph for Kern was just: "The man who invented the show tune." **L. A.**

RECORD: ORIGINAL SOUNDTRACK OF 'SHOWBOAT' (MFP 1244).

John Maynard Keynes (British, 1883–1946): economist. Certainly the most creative and influential economic thinker of the century so far. Between the wars J. M. Keynes fought a running battle against the orthodox experts who sought to dispel the Great Depression by the ritual re-creation of the vanished Edwardian economy. The Keynesian 'revolution', brought to a pitch in the 'General Theory' of 1936, rejected the official nostalgia. In Keynes's estimation, the old *laissez-faire* remedies – especially the instruction that the country must *save* its way out of trouble – merely aggravated the

terrifying unemployment problem. The crux of the new Keynesian canon was that the people were *not* to save; instead, the State was to spend. It would organise investment, sponsor public works – and so create employment. In the depths of the slump, Keynes concluded that capitalism contained a pronounced trend towards stagnation. And while other economists sought conventional answers to the problems of recovery, Keynes decided that only massive State action could solve them. Before the Second World War, Britain, traditionally hostile to government intervention, resisted the Keynesian remedies. But after 1945, most free-enterprise democracies – Britain included – accepted a striking redefinition of government's economic role. The modern State, with its heavy public expenditure and its active interest in employment and investment levels, is a Keynesian product. **R. C. T.**

'THE LIFE OF JOHN MAYNARD KEYNES', BY R. F. HARROD (MACMILLAN, 1952); 'ESSAYS IN PERSUASION', BY J. M. KEYNES (MACMILLAN, 1931); 'THE BRITISH ECONOMY 1920-57', BY A. J. YOUNGSON (ALLEN AND UNWIN, 1960).

Nikita Khrushchev (Russian 1894–1971): statesman. Born a miner's son, Khrushchev's early years in the Russo-Ukrainian borderland were hard. First a shepherd boy, later a mining technician, his education was rudimentary. A Party member from 1918, he began full-time political work only in 1931, but his rise was meteoric: on the Party's Central Committee from 1934, head of the Moscow Party machine in 1935, a full member of the Politburo in 1939. After the Second World War he earned a considerable reputation for rebuilding the devastated Ukraine. Though head of the Party from 1953, it was three years before he achieved political supremacy. At the Twentieth Party Congress in 1956, he attacked Stalin's (q.v.) unjust repressions and personality cult. Liberalisation followed in intellectual life, in the economy and in foreign affairs. Breaking with precedent,

and to emphasise his commitment to peaceful coexistence, he embarked on many foreign tours. But opposition within the leadership to his policies of economic decentralisation and reduction in conventional forces, to his violent polemics with China, to his handling of the Cuban crisis, to his extensive de-Stalinisation, and to his flamboyant conduct, led to his fall in October 1964. Yet its very manner (compulsory retirement rather than elimination) sufficiently indicates the change in Soviet life since his predecessor's death. **A. Q. D.**

'KHRUSHCHEV'S RUSSIA', BY EDWARD CRANKSHAW (PENGUIN, 1959); 'KHRUSHCHEV', BY EDWARD CRANKSHAW (COLLINS, 1966); 'KHRUSHCHEV', BY MARK FRANKLAND (PENGUIN, 1966); 'POWER IN THE KREMLIN', BY MICHEL TATU (COLLINS, 1969).

Jean-Claude Killy (French, b. 1943): skier.'Customs Official' is now in his passport, but he is known as a skier – with enough confidence in his abilities to have seen the 13 top men in downhill ski racing go down the Olympic course and know he could beat them; and beat them he did by one hundredth of a second. Killy's great skiing ability earned him eight World Championship titles, two World Cups and three Olympic Gold Medals, but a skier – an athlete – a man who sparkles on the snow is not expected to sparkle elsewhere. Killy is at home racing cars at Monza, meeting the President or coping with his numerous admirers. After

the Grenoble Winter Olympics (1968) he signed $2 million worth of commercial contracts, including modelling ski clothes for *Ladies' Home Journal,* writing a syndicated column, working as a ski-design consultant and granting the right for his name to be used on a skin conditioner product for men. In taking advantage of his amateur achievements, Killy is the archetype of the successful mid-20th-century sportsman. **D. H. T.**

'SKI AVEC KILLY', BY JEAN-CLAUDE KILLY (DENOEL, PARIS, 1969); 'HOW TO SKI THE NEW FRENCH WAY', BY GEORGE JOUBERT AND JEAN JAURNET (KAYE AND WARD, 1967).

Mackenzie King (Canadian, 1874–1950): statesman. The grandson of Mackenzie, the leader of the 1837 rebellion, Mackenzie King was very much a Canadian. As Prime Minister for more than 20 years – 1921–6, 1926–30, 1935–48 – King was the Walpole of Ottawa. The memory of his row with Governor-General Byng in 1926 makes it

unlikely that the British Crown will ever refuse to dissolve a Commonwealth parliament again, even if asked to do so by a minority premier. Mackenzie King, perhaps unwittingly, made a double contribution to Commonwealth constitutional development, for the recognition of Dominion independence in the Statute of Westminster in 1931 was a by-product of that clash. King deftly handled the issue of conscription, adopting it in 1942 but delaying its full operation until late 1944, and Canada made a sizeable contribution to the Normandy landings without sacrificing her national unity. Canada shares a continent with the Americans, and Commonwealth membership with Britain; that she is friendly with both but subservient to neither is the legacy of the Mackenzie King era. **G. W. M.**

'WILLIAM LYON MACKENZIE KING', VOL I, BY R. MACGREGOR DAWSON, VOL 2, BY H. BLAIR NEATBY (TORONTO U.P., 1958–62).

Martin Luther King (U.S. 1929–1968): minister and Civil Rights pioneer. Lincoln freed the slaves, Luther King gave them their self-respect. His Civil Rights successes were numerous – beginning in 1957 when he led the Negroes of Montgomery, Alabama, in a boycott of the buses which ended segregation on buses in practically every city in the South. His sit-ins in 1960 enabled Negroes to share lunch counters, libraries and parks with whites. His 1961 'freedom-rides' ended segregation in inter-state travel. These and his poignant confrontation with 'Bull' Connor's brutal Birmingham police in 1963 and the climactic march on Washington, which forced through Congress the most powerful Civil Rights legislation in the century, were all steps forward but were more successful against legislated prejudice in the South than the subtler variety in the North. By the end of his life Luther

King was being outflanked by more aggressive leaders of the Negro revolution. What sets Luther King apart is the ethic which provided his energy, peaceful non-violence fuelled with the Christian ideals of love, truth, and goodness. He gave the Negroes of the South a moral superiority over the racists and shattered the racial doctrines by which discrimination had been justified. His life was threatened, his home was bombed, he had many premonitions of death, and he was still preaching non-violence when he was shot dead on a Memphis hotel balcony on April 4, 1968. **H. M. E.**

BOOKS BY KING: 'STRIDE TOWARDS FREEDOM' (GOLLANCZ, 1959); 'WHY WE CAN'T WAIT' (HARPER AND ROW,1965).

Alfred Kinsey (U.S., 1894–1956): sexologist. Kinsey was a professor of zoology who turned from studying wasps to studying sex. Twelve thousand volunteers answered questionnaires which yielded complicated sociological statistics. *Sexual Behaviour in the Human Male* (1948) and *Sexual Behaviour in the Human Female* (1953) now form the baseline for all sociological studies of sex. Experts criticised the sampling and statistics and thought the conclusions overgeneralised and exaggerated. Yet Kinsey revealed the prevalence in the community of a range of sexual practices hitherto thought immoral or illegal – pre-marital and extra-marital intercourse, oral-genital contacts and homosexuality. This, together with his findings on masturbation, impotence and frigidity, challenged moralistic concepts of 'normal' sex, and extolled a purely biological viewpoint. Yet Kinsey undervalued the importance of our inner emotional lives, thus partly contributing to today's fragmentation between sexual, loving and moral values. Kinsey exposed sexual ignorance among doctors, law-makers and laymen, and increased our tolerance of all forms of sexual behaviour. **I. R.**

'THE ENCYCLOPAEDIA OF SEXUAL BEHAVIOUR', EDITED BY ALBERT ELLIS AND ALBERT ABARBANEL (HEINEMANN, 1961); KINSEY'S BOOKS WERE PUBLISHED HERE BY W. B. SAUNDERS.

Rudyard Kipling (British, 1865–1936): writer. Kipling was a genius. He was the greatest of all short story writers. He invented a new type of story: it was more real than real life, the people in the stories were more real than real people in real life, and yet everything was suffused with a rich patina of sentiment, romance, love, hatred and sentimentality. Thus he lured everyone into his own peculiar world with a siren voice and he recreated real people in the image of his imaginary characters. He wrote about India in the heyday of the British Empire. But it was he who created the Anglo-Indian – the Indian Civil Servant, Strickland of the Indian Police, the Brushwood Boy Subaltern, the Privates and the Drummer Boy of the Indian Army, Mrs Hauksbee the memsahib. After *Plain Tales from the Hills* it was impossible for Britons in India (or in the Colonial Empire generally) not to act like these creations of Kipling – and this led on to General Dyer and Amritsar, the revolt of "the silent, sullen peoples", the "lesser breeds", Gandhi, Nehru (qq.v.), and finally the break-up of empire. Thus Kipling by his genius created a major portion of imperialism and so played a major part in the destruction of the Empire. **L. W.**

'KIPLING AND THE CRITICS', ED. E. GILBERT (PETER OWEN, 1966); 'KIPLING IN INDIA', BY LOUIS L. CORNELL (MACMILLAN, 1966); 'RUDYARD KIPLING', BY J. I. M. STEWART (GOLLANCZ, 1966); 'RUDYARD KIPLING, REALIST AND FABULIST', BY BONAMY DOBREE (O.U.P., 1967).

News from the Outside World.

Rollin Kirby (U.S., 1876–1951): cartoonist. Kirby, a former painter who had studied under James McNeil Whistler, did not begin cartooning until 1913 when he was nearing 40. He became the first editorial cartoonist to win a Pulitzer Prize. During the Prohibition era his pen was one of the fiercest of forces in the war against this unpopular restriction. His snooper-reformer caricature, the Bluenose, was a catalyst for the opponents of Volstead and the puritans who tried to enforce abstinence with legal sanctions. Equally telling were his prods at the incumbent Republicans of the Twenties. Although he thought and drew as a New Yorker, his work was so widely syndicated throughout the United States that his liberal voice was a national rallying sign. Following the scandals of President Harding's administration he was unrelenting in his lampooning of the holier-than-thou pose of the Republicans. His day-to-day thrusts were instrumental in the eventual election of Franklin D. Roosevelt (q.v.) and the repeal of the Prohibition amendment. Many newspaper cartoonists after Kirby were influenced by his approach to his targets. **M. C.**

'COMIC ART IN AMERICA', BY STEPHEN BECKER (SIMON AND SCHUSTER, NEW YORK, 1959).

Raphaël Kirchner (Austrian, 1876–1917): painter. Creator of the first pin-up girl in Western popular art to win international fame, Kirchner grew up in Paris, became a painter, and lived on contributions to illustrated papers. His work appeared regularly in *La Vie*

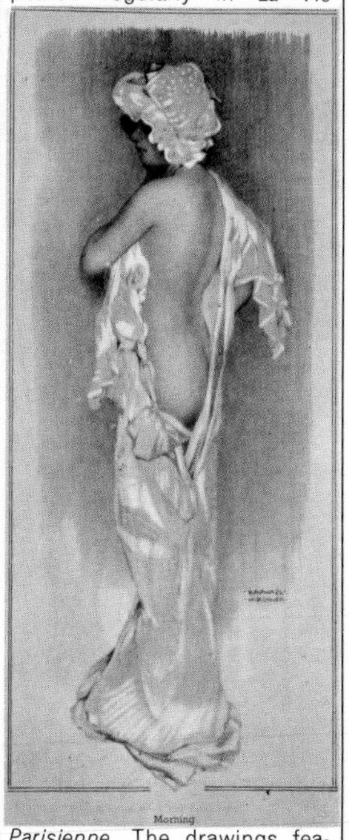

Parisienne. The drawings feature a slender, immature girl, partly undressed, quite unlike the fashionable bosomy figure of the 1900s, and have a tender, frank, erotic quality with origins in Viennese rather than French graphic art. The Allied armies in France in 1914–18 proved an insatiable market for Kirchner girls in albums, postcards and single sheets; and in 1916 a Kirchner exhibition in London was a sell-out. He went on to the U.S. with his wife (reputed to be the model for all his work) and Ziegfeld (q.v.) commissioned him to decorate the Amsterdam Theatre, New York. A set of panels, each of a Kirchner girl, established him and he began contributing to American magazines and painting portraits. He was in reach of wealth and success when in August 1917 he contracted appendicitis and died during an emergency operation. His wife survived till 1925 when she died in a mental hospital, calling, "*Raphie, où es-tu?*" **J. E. B.**

'THE GIRLS FROM LA VIE PARISIENNE' (NEVILLE SPEARMAN, LONDON, 1961).

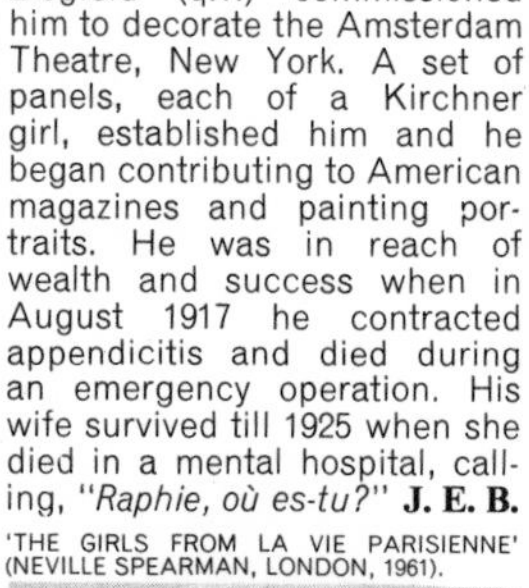

Lord Kitchener (British, 1850–1916): soldier. If he was not a great man, he was at least a great poster, said Margot Asquith – unfairly: but it is true to say that Kitchener's image was almost as important as his actions. As the strong right arm of British imperialism in the 1890s and 1900s, he conquered then governed the Sudan, subdued South Africa, built up the Indian Army, and ruled Egypt – dourly, efficiently and thoroughly. His Sudan campaign of 1896–8 was a ruthless revenge for General Gordon's death, and fertilised by the sun and the sand and the blood some of that romantic hero's charisma seemed to rub off on the very unromantic Kitchener. Popular idolatry made him indispensable as War Secretary in 1914. He hypnotised almost a whole generation into volunteering for his army, but then directed their efforts hesitantly and ineptly. Fifty years after his death by drowning in June 1916 his material achievements have all been reversed by events. But his legend remains to reflect the mood of the British people at their most aggressive at the turn of the century – when national revenge was still considered a virtue. **B. J. P.**

'KITCHENER, PORTRAIT OF AN IMPERIALIST', BY PHILIP MAGNUS (MURRAY, 1958); 'THE RIVER WAR', BY WINSTON CHURCHILL (EYRE AND SPOTTISWOODE, 1933).

Paul Klee (Swiss, 1879–1940): artist. One of the most intelligent artists who ever lived, Klee was born Swiss, moved to Munich to study in 1898, was a founder-member of the 'Blue Rider' group with Kandinsky (q.v.) and others, fought in the German Army in 1914–18, taught at the Bauhaus from 1921 to 1931, and returned to Switzerland in 1933 when his work was stigmatised as "degenerate" by the Nazis. He was many things in one: poet and pedagogue, seer and grammarian, musician and mystic. A practised educator and the author of a massive treatise on the structure of pictorial form, he relied in his work primarily on intimations of the kind that cannot be learned. ("I want to be as though newborn," he wrote in 1902, "knowing nothing about Europe, ignoring facts and

fashions, reverting almost to the primitive.") Though a part of 'the modern movement' from 1911 onwards and a particularly discerning analyst of what other men had done, he owed his characteristic wry, darting, fugitive and often ironical poetry to the astute and continuous investigation of his own inmost nature. In his many hundreds of small pictures, most of them numbered and titled in a handwriting like benevolent barbed wire, there are ideas enough for a dozen ordinary lifetimes. His work is, in fact, a one-man inventory of European preoccupations during a time of supreme commotion in every department of life. **J. R.**

'THE THINKING EYE', BY PAUL KLEE (LUND HUMPHRIES, 1964); 'THE MIND AND WORK OF PAUL KLEE', BY W. HAFTMANN (FABER, 1954); 'PAUL KLEE', BY W. GROHMANN (THAMES AND HUDSON, 1967).

Zoltán Kodály (Hungarian, 1882–1967): composer. Kodály may be described as the Hungarian Vaughan Williams (q.v.). His association with Bartók (q.v.) yielded unique results: for once there were two outstanding

1000
KIL-KRE

creative personalities engaged in a scientific investigation into (Magyar) folk music, with the result that the musicologically valuable was married to the aesthetically important. Considering that one of the century's basic problems is the chronic latent conflict between the scholar and the artist, the fruits of this collaboration can hardly be overestimated; while the fact that such a harmonious union of interests and personalities proved at all possible has stimulated, and will continue to stimulate, a *rapprochement* between intellectual areas whose separation was not foreseen at the birth of art and science. In Hungary itself, Kodály's influence as a powerful public figure was revolutionary: he well-nigh abolished musical illiteracy. The list of his compositions – stage works, church music, choral works, orchestral, chamber, and educational music, 57 folk song arrangements – is enormous; quite a few have established themselves in our midstream repertory. He was a prolific writer and critic too, as well as a born teacher, whose best-known pupil – at any rate in this country – was Mátyás Seiber. In Hungary today, most outstanding musicians are his ex-pupils and continue to teach what he taught. **H. K.**

'ZOLTAN KODALY: HIS LIFE AND WORK', BY LASZLO EOSZE, TRANSLATED BY ISTVAN FARKAS AND GYULA GULYAS (COLLET'S, 1962); KODALY ISSUE OF 'THE NEW HUNGARIAN QUARTERLY' (CORVINA PRESS, BUDAPEST, OCT.–DEC., 1962).

Wolfgang Kohler (U.S., ex-German, 1887–1967): psychologist. Kohler was one of the prime movers in the Gestalt school of psychology, which recognised that learning involves the appreciation of patterns – *Gestalten* – rather than of artificially isolated single objects. He was led to this belief by watching chimpanzees solve problems. Confronted with a banana out of reach, the animal would try some tentative solutions before suddenly getting an insight into the patterns of elements involved. This suddenness was different from the behaviour that psychologists had assumed to happen, in which learning occurs only by a slow strengthening of habits, following the pattern that Pavlov (q.v.) had described. In the study of perception the Gestalt School derived principles by which stimuli were thought to be integrated into patterns and by which patterns were directed towards 'good figures'. These principles were given physiological backing drawn from Pavlov's concepts of electrical wave forces in the brain. Kohler's own work attempted to use these principles to account for figural after-effects – changes in perception after prolonged fixation of a patterned stimulus. His importance in the 20th-century is that, as part of the Gestalt school, he forced theorists' attention on to the integrative aspects of experience. **B. R. O.**

'MENTALITY OF THE APES', BY WOLFGANG KOHLER (KEGAN PAUL, 1925); 'PRINCIPLES OF GESTALT PSYCHOLOGY', BY K. KOFFKA (ROUTLEDGE, 1966).

Willem Kolff (U.S., ex-Dutch, b. 1911): physician. The frontispiece to Willem J. Kolff's book *New Ways of Treating Uraemia* shows an array of four artificial kidneys. The caption tells us they were "ready September 1944"; since they were constructed in Kampen, in occupied Holland, the date and place together spell out the difficulties met and overcome by Kolff, for at the same time he was playing an active role in the Dutch Resistance. After the war Kolff moved to Cleveland, Ohio, where he made use of American technology to construct a much smaller, and disposable, version of his original coil-kidney. He also used American mass media to overcome doubt and delay in the application of his invention. The temporary substitution of the artificial for the natural kidney, disabled by disease, has now become established practice. In acute renal failure, artificial kidneys gain time for the patient's own kidneys to recover from reversible damage; in chronic renal failure, the Scribner arteriovenous shunt allows life to be maintained by intermittent haemodialysis for months, stretching into years; and transplantation programmes depend on the ability to maintain life until the transplanted kidney regains adequate function after its unusual journey from donor to recipient. **D. A. K. B.**

'NEW WAYS OF TREATING URAEMIA', BY WILLEM KOLFF (J. AND A. CHURCHILL, 1947); 'RENAL DISEASE', ED. D. A. K. BLACK (BLACKWELL, 1967).

Willem de Kooning (U.S., ex-Dutch, b. 1904): painter. De Kooning was born in Rotterdam and lived there till he was 22. He went to work at the age of 12 with a firm of commercial artists. Eight years of evening classes at the Rotterdam Academy equipped him to earn a living as carpenter, house-painter, and all-purpose craftsman (he later designed his own house). In 1926 he entered the U.S. as a naturalised immigrant and has lived there ever since. He has painted full-time, when possible, since 1934, but had his first substantial success in 1955. A founder-member of the First New York School, he rejected the 'European aesthetic' in the early 1940s but retained something of classic expressionism in his use of paint, and something of the remade anatomies of Picasso (q.v.) and the Surrealists in his treatment of the human form. Against the tide of abstract painting, he persisted in painting the human figure: "It was absurd to do it, but even

more absurd not to . . ." In the *Women* series (1950 onwards) he combined freedom and spontaneity of action painting with an attempt to give Michelangelesque grandeur to the contemporary American idea of womanhood: hilarious, high-rouged, full-fleshed, all-devouring. (Of later *Women*, T. B. Hess wrote: "You could name a hurricane after any one of them. But like hurricanes they are an intimate part of our climate.") **J. R.**

'WILLEM DE KOONING', BY T. B. HESS (ARTS COUNCIL, 1969).

Sir Alexander Korda (British, ex-Hungarian, 1893–1956): film director and producer. Unquestionably one of the creators of the British cinema, Korda was a well-known film director in Budapest during the First World War and worked in Vienna, Berlin, Hollywood and Paris before coming to England in 1930. His brothers Zoltan and Vincent (his designer) followed; he founded a company, London Films; as director of *The Private Life of Henry VIII* (1933) he made American audiences for the first time recognise the British cinema; and success encouraged him to build Denham Studios. During the Thirties he produced an adventurous list: *The Scarlet Pimpernel, Things To Come, The Four Feathers* and, with such directors as Clair, Flaherty (qq.v.) and Sternberg, *The Ghost Goes West, Elephant Boy* and the unfinished *I, Claudius*; while he himself directed the elegantly composed *Rembrandt*. After the war he was concerned in the production of many distinguished films: *The Fallen Idol, The Third Man, The Sound Barrier, Richard III*. His struggle to make the British cinema international resulted several times in financial crisis. Nevertheless, with his Continental panache he raised the standards of the British screen and was a pioneer in its transformation from provincialism to sophistication. **D. P.**

'ALEXANDER KORDA', BY PAUL TABORI (OLDBOURNE BOOK CO., 1959).

Alexei Kosygin (Russian, b. 1904): politician. Of all Soviet leaders since Stalin (q.v.), Kosygin has had the least purely political experience. After graduating from the Leningrad Textile Institute in 1935, he went into textile plant administration and by 1939 was Minister of the USSR Textile Industry. Important governmental posts followed, with a corresponding rise in the Party to full membership of the Politburo in 1948. Demoted after Stalin's death, his fortunes revived under Khrushchev (q.v.). From 1960 he directed the state economic machine, and in 1964 succeeded Khrushchev as Chairman of the Council of Ministers (Prime Minister). At first Kosygin appeared to play the leading role in foreign as well as economic affairs – he visited China in 1965 and mediated between India and Pakistan in 1966. But recently Brezhnev (q.v.) has assumed a more directing role. Economically, Kosygin clearly ranks with the progressives. In 1965 he introduced important re-

forms in production based on a profit criterion, although conservative opposition modified their effect. For Kosygin himself, this liberalism may not extend to other issues, but, as Czechoslovakia showed, economic reform can have far-reaching political and social consequences. **A. Q. D.**

'POWER IN THE KREMLIN', BY MICHAEL TATU (COLLINS, 1969); 'RUSSIA: HOPES AND FEARS', BY ALEXANDER WERTH (BARRIE AND ROCKLIFF, AND PENGUIN, 1969).

Jack Kramer (U.S., b. 1921): impresario. But for Jack Kramer professional tennis would have remained chaotic, and open play between amateurs and professionals would still be in the future. After a distinguished amateur career (U.S. Boys Champion 1936, youngest ever player in a Davis Cup Challenge Round 1939, American and Wimbledon Singles Champion 1947) he turned professional. His immense personal integrity as player, entrepreneur, administrator and negotiator has transformed professional tennis from a money-grabbing, irresponsible circus into a well-respected group of highly paid exponents of sport-cum-show-business. He repeatedly made world headlines by signing Wimbledon champions on professional contracts that bled amateur tennis of its top stars. Then, in 1962, he made contact with the All-England Club at Wimbledon to suggest a professional tournament at this temple of amateurism. So impressed

was chairman Herman David that David intensified his campaign for open tennis. This finally overcame world opposition and became fact in March 1968 and that summer Wimbledon became an open tournament. Kramer is among the top four all-time great tennis players and pre-eminent in the general history of tennis. **C. M. J.**

Sir Hans Krebs (British, ex-German, b. 1900): biochemist. Krebs is famous for the light he has thrown on the way that living creatures get energy from food. His first research interest was the breakdown of amino-acids for energy; in many cases the first step in this process is the removal of a nitrogen atom (de-amination), and it was Krebs who first observed this. Later he studied the way nitrogen was eliminated from the body in the

urine. After he came to England, Krebs began his study of carbohydrate metabolism (for which he won a Nobel Prize with Lipmann). His interest began with the problem of how lactic acid can be broken down to yield carbon dioxide and water, taking up oxygen in the process. Krebs found that a chain of biochemical reactions was involved in which acid is repeatedly regenerated to react with products of lactic acid. During these changes carbon dioxide is lost, and hydrogen atoms are given up which combine with free oxygen atoms to produce water. This Krebs cycle turned out to be the most important energy producer in living organisms. **N. J. M. H.**

Fritz Kreisler (U.S., ex-Austrian, 1875–1962): violinist, composer. When Kreisler was 24 "a career began which in respect of its intensity, duration and material results remains unique in the

history of violin playing" (Carl Flesch [q.v.]). He had been a virtuoso at the age of 12, but turned into a café crawler (a time-honoured Viennese occupation) and, almost, an orchestral fiddler. As he grew into the age's most popular violin virtuoso (to whom the Elgar violin concerto was dedicated), the influence of his seductive, sweet tone on violinists' sound-ideals became overwhelming. He is the father of the *sempre vibrato*. Like Huberman (q.v.), and unlike everybody else, he thought practice a "bad habit"; hence his freshness. His playing of his own small pieces made them sound like great music, while his compositions of 'old music' ("arrangements", as he called them) made it sound like other composers'. It was only in 1935 that he owned up to having written such things as the *Praeludium and Allegro* 'by Pugnani'; Pugnani probably never wrote anything as good. **H. K.**

'FRITZ KREISLER', BY LOUIS P. LOCHNER (ROCKLIFF, 1951).

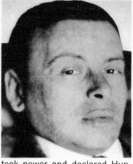

Alfried Krupp (German, 1907–1967): tycoon. The son of Gustav, who armed Hitler, and descendant of three centuries of the Krupps whose Essen factories had supplied the battlefields of the world, Alfried took over the firm in 1942. Three years later he was given a 12-year jail sentence at Nuremberg for using slave labour, and the Allies determined to break up Krupp in such a way that it could never rise again. They failed totally – the vast iron, coal, steel and engineering interests proved impossible to sell – and in 1951, when Alfried was released, the factories were still virtually intact. Even though Krupp in 1953 was theoretically stripped of its coal and steel assets, the truck, locomotive and ship-building sectors remained, and Alfried, once again among the five richest individuals in the world, set about defining Krupp's new role. This was to be supplying capital and consumer goods to the newly emergent nations, and for some years the company blossomed as never before. But by 1967 the huge accompanying burden of debts, long-term credits and elastic order books had stretched even the Krupp fortune beyond its limits. The bankers moved in, Krupp became just another publicly-quoted company and, by the summer, Alfried (whose son renounced any claim to the company) was dead. **P. W.**

'THE ARMS OF KRUPP', BY WILLIAM MANCHESTER (MICHAEL JOSEPH, 1969).

Stanley Kubrick (U.S., b. 1928): film director. A Napoleonic and solitary film-maker, Kubrick has directed in *Lolita, Dr. Strangelove* and *2001: A Space Odyssey* three consecutive films combining cold wit, intellectual bravura and sheer film-maker's nerve in formidable proportions. He is perhaps the most consistently brilliant of the post-war generation of American film-makers; yet he is probably critically under-valued, as a lone wolf conforming to none of the more identifiable trends and making infrequent films to his own grand designs. He started his career as a magazine photographer and first attracted critical attention with a blue-print crime and catastrophe picture, *The Killing,* in 1956; *Paths of Glory* (1958) consolidated his reputation. He is fascinated by destiny, human error, and the working out of human and inhuman traps, from Humbert Humbert's fatal entanglement to the dying gasps of a berserk computer aboard a spacecraft. Stylistically, Kubrick remains Orson Welles's closest heir in the American cinema; but he is probably more concerned with themes of power and the future than power and the past. In the diamond-cutting, ferociously logical four-minute warning of *Dr Strangelove* and the mind-stretching space-show of *2001* he has made two of the cinema's most compelling and apprehensive gestures towards the 21st century. **P. H.**

Richard Kuhn (Austrian, 1900–1967): biological chemist. Kuhn was one of a school of chemists who, between the wars, identified and synthesised many of the complex biological molecules that play an essential role in maintaining life. It was this work that largely made modern biochemistry possible. With Szent-Györgyi (q.v.) and Wagner-Jauregg, Kuhn was the first to isolate the important vitamin riboflavin; to obtain one gram of this substance, it was necessary to treat chemically over 5000 litres of skimmed milk. Where compounds exist in natural materials in such minute concentrations, it is necessary to develop highly sophisticated experimental techniques for separating them out and one of Kuhn's major contributions was the application of chromatography – a method which depends on the differential absorption of substances on an inert material – to such separations. In this way, he was able to show that carotene, a precursor of Vitamin A, consisted of three different molecules. For his work on carotenoids and vitamins, Kuhn was awarded the 1938 Nobel Prize in chemistry, but was forced by the Nazi Government to decline the honour. **M. A. S.**

'NOBEL LECTURES IN CHEMISTRY 1922–1941' (ELSEVIER, 1966); 'LABORATORY TECHNIQUES IN CHEMISTRY AND BIOCHEMISTRY', BY P. S. DIAMOND AND R. F. DENMAN (BUTTERWORTH, 1966).

Béla Kun (Hungarian, 1886–1939): statesman. An enigmatic figure who began as an office clerk in Transylvania and ended as a Comintern leader and merciless purger, Béla Kun was himself purged and shot for 'espionage' in Russia. He became leader of the Hungarian Bolsheviks in Russia where he was prisoner of war from 1916. In November 1918 Lenin and Bukharin (qq.v.) sent him to Budapest where Kun soon engineered a split within the Socialists and established the Communist Party. Then, in March 1919, his party merged with the Socialists on a Bolshevik programme, took power and declared Hungary a Soviet Republic, allied to Lenin's Russia. It survived 133 days. Kun combined Leninism with nationalism: although a Bolshevik, he hurtled to power on a wave of national feeling; he won over the middle classes by waging war against the "bourgeois Little Entente" – the Czechs and the Rumanians; and he managed to establish the first Communist Government in a country not adjacent to Russia, thus lending credibility to the belief that Lenin's revolution would sweep westwards. **L. F. P.**

'BELA KUN AND THE HUNGARIAN SOVIET REPUBLIC', BY R. L. TOKES (PRAEGER, NEW YORK, 1967).

Akira Kurosawa (Japanese, b. 1910): film director. Until 1951, the Japanese film industry was the submerged part of the international iceberg, producing twice as many films per year as Hollywood in its heyday, none of them known in the West. The film that made the breakthrough was Kurosawa's *Rashomon,*

which won the Golden Lion at the 1951 Venice Film Festival with its bizarre, exultantly passionate tale of a murder told from three different points of view with the full range of hieratic gestures and stylised vocal acrobatics one has come to recognise as peculiarly Japanese. Since then, with his adaptations of Dostoievsky's *The Idiot,* Shakespeare's *Macbeth* (as *Throne of Blood*), Gorki's *The Lower Depths,* and more particularly his joyously action-packed Samurai Westerns such as *The Seven Samurai* and *The Hidden Fortress* which earned him the title of the John Ford of Japan, Kurosawa has become the one internationally-known Japanese director. Kurosawa's work is brilliant, but for all its Japanese trimmings his outlook and his style are essentially Western, so much so that two of his films have been revamped by Hollywood – *Rashomon* as *The Outrage,* and *The Seven Samurai* as *The Magnificent Seven* – while a third, *Yojimbo,* was liberally drawn upon by the Italians to make *A Fistful Of Dollars.* For the real Japanese flavour, one must turn to Kenji Mizoguchi (1898–1956), a poet where Kurosawa is merely a writer, whose hauntingly beautiful, steel-sprung films – *Ugetsu Monogatari, The Life of O'Haru, Sansho Dayu* – contain some of the greatest cinema in the medium. **T. M.**

'THE FILMS OF AKIRA KUROSAWA', BY DONALD RICHIE (CALIFORNIA U.P., 1965).

Fiorello La Guardia (U.S., 1882–1947): Mayor of New York City. If the 'Little Flower' had not actually existed, no novelist or librettist would have dared to invent so improbable a hero. He was an Admirable Crichton of ethnic politics: Italian immigrant father; Jewish mother; boyhood in Arizona (his father was stationed there as an army bandsman) which left him with a taste for Western headgear; endearingly tiny physique (5ft. 2in.: he once hailed a man even shorter than himself as "Shorty"); loquacity in six languages, including Yiddish; glamorous First World War service as an aviator; 10 crusading years in Congress, wrestling with the torpor of Washington D.C. in the Coolidge-Hoover (q.v.) era. Then 12 crowded, constructive, cocky, virtuously virtuoso years as Mayor of New York. La Guardia threw out the slack old Irish bosses, brought in lowlier minorities and generally cleaned the place up. He handled his appalling task

imperiously and lovingly, as if it were a small town and he the burgomaster. For almost the first and quite possibly the last time in its history, La Guardia by a miracle made New York seem manageable. **M. F. C.**

'THE MAKING OF AN INSURGENT: AN AUTOBIOGRAPHY', BY FIORELLO LA GUARDIA (PUTNAM, NEW YORK, 1961); 'LA GUARDIA COMES TO POWER, 1933', BY ARTHUR MANN (LIPPINCOTT, PHILADELPHIA, 1965); 'THE POLITICS OF UPHEAVAL', BY ARTHUR M. SCHLESINGER JR. (HEINEMANN, 1961).

Robert La Follette (U.S., 1855–1925): politician. 'Fighting Bob' La Follette, the contemporary and rival of Teddy Roosevelt (q.v.), was to millions of Americans – especially the plain people of the Middle West – a hero who articulated their angers and aspirations. Born in a log cabin, he carved a place for himself, first as a Wisconsin lawyer, then as Congressman, Governor (1900–1905) and Senator (1906–1925). He made Wisconsin a model progressive

State. In Washington he was a relentless Mr Deeds, under no illusion as to the corruptions of machine politics. He could not, would not, compromise: his strength was his defect. The moralistic energy that brought him glory helped to deny him the ultimate triumphs. Roosevelt snatched the leadership of the new Progressive party – La Follette's own creation – in 1912. Mid-Western parochialism-cum-idealism impelled him to vote against America's declaration of war in 1917. His last fight in 1924 was again on the losing side: his five million votes as Progressive candidate for President were dwarfed by the ballots for Coolidge Republicanism. La Follette was a crusader. He pioneered a mode of participatory politics that has come very much alive again, even if today's practitioners have forgotten him. **M. F. C.**

'LA FOLLETTE'S AUTOBIOGRAPHY' (WISCONSIN U.P., 1963); 'ROBERT LA FOLLETTE', BY R. S. MAXWELL (SPECTRUM, 1969).

Problems of the Soviet Academy of Sciences. Between 1941 and 1947 he successfully applied quantum theory to the whole liquid, rather than to individual atoms of helium as others had done. Later, between 1956 and 1958, he provided a theory for the behaviour of the much rarer isotope of helium, helium-3 (the common isotope is helium-4). This theory also proved to be correct and has led, among other things, to the development of an ingenious very-low-temperature refrigerator based on the two isotopes. Landau was awarded the Nobel Prize in 1962. His studies of liquid helium represent a highly important aspect of cryogenics (the science of extremely low temperatures). **P. H. S. S.**

'THE QUEST FOR ABSOLUTE ZERO', BY K. MENDELSSOHN (WEIDENFELD AND NICOLSON, 1966).

Sir Allen Lane (British, 1902–1970): publisher. The most influential book publisher in the English-speaking world this century, Lane started work at 16 at his uncle's firm The Bodley Head. In 1935, against the advice of book-trade pundits, he started his own firm, Penguin Books, with an initial list of 10 paperback reprints of established titles bought from other publishers' backlists; the paperbacks retailed at 6d each, the price of a packet of cigarettes. He went on to develop an extensive list of non-fiction paperbacks, many of them original, of good design and the highest educational and cultural merit. He was not the first publisher of paperbacks – there were prede-

established cinematic classics by the Thirties; except for *Fury* and *You Live Only Once* (1937), his inevitably uneven American work has only recently begun to receive its due. Directly and indirectly, Lang's bleak vision and taut, 'semi-expressionist' style have made him a potent influence on two generations of film makers ranging from Hitchcock and Welles to Kubrick (qq.v.), Frankenheimer and French New-Wave directors like Rivette and Godard (q.v.) (in whose *Le Mépris* he appeared playing himself). **P. N. F.**

'TOWER OF BABEL', BY ERIC RHODE (WEIDENFELD AND NICOLSON, 1966); 'FROM CALIGARI TO HITLER', BY SIEGFRIED KRACAUER (O.U.P., 1966); 'FRITZ LANG IN AMERICA', BY PETER BOGDANOVITCH (STUDIO VISTA, 1968).

Paul Langevin (French, 1872–1946): physicist. Professor Paul Langevin was a brilliant fundamental physicist who nevertheless insisted on the close connection between pure science and technology. He demonstrated this when he invented what is now called sonar for submarine detection during the First World War. He used a piezo-electric crystal to generate and detect ultrasonic waves, a method that led to all modern ultrasonic devices. Lord Rutherford (q.v.), who also engaged in submarine work in the First World War, acknowledged Langevin's priority and visited him several times for consultation; and in 1928 Langevin was elected as a Foreign Member of the Royal Society, which also awarded him its Hughes Medal.

Ronald D. Laing (British, b. 1927): psychiatrist. The work of Laing and that of D. G. Cooper has led the movement to reinstate the dignity of psychiatric patients. Laing enters the psychotic's world from the inside – an adaption of Husserl's (q.v.) phenomenological method – and from this viewpoint refuses to demote the patient to an inferior status. The very label 'patient' is seen as part of this demoting process and is rejected. The search to understand those phenomena we call mental illness is redirected from looking inside the patient for, say, a metabolic fault which will 'explain' his illness, to looking out at the people in the 'patient's' world, especially his family. Laing argues that the patient-to-be is put in a position where his true self has to be denied (cf. Gregory Bateson [q.v.] and the Double Bind) and a false, protective self created. The better established the false self, the less integrated can the real self be. Laing calls for a respectful awe of these experiences; and of drug and mystical experiences. Paradoxically, Laing's success as a therapist indicates his theoretical weakness. If there is no illness, there ought to be no cure. **B. R. O.**

'REASON AND VIOLENCE', BY R. D. LAING AND D. G. COOPER (TAVISTOCK, 1964); 'THE POLITICS OF EXPERIENCE AND THE BIRD OF PARADISE', BY R. D. LAING (PENGUIN, 1967).

cessors like Tauchnitz – or of low-priced scholarly books for the general reader, but he was the first to publish such books on a large scale and so realise fully the needs of the new reading public brought into being by the Education Acts of 1870 and later of 1944. His great strength lay in maintaining standards while increasing production – the current output is 400 titles a year – in contrast to many of his rivals. **C. B. H.**

Langevin investigated the peculiar random dancing of tiny particles in liquids, the so-called Brownian movement, used the newly-developed electron theory to establish the basis of magnetism, and he derived the famous equation connecting mass and energy independently of Einstein (q.v.). He criticised and modified profoundly the fundamental notions of time, space, mechanics, the structure of matter and radiation. **C. L. B.**

Edwin Land (U.S., b. 1909): physicist. A Harvard student who did not complete his degree course, he now has countless honorary doctorates. Land was fascinated by the need for a useful polarising device. In the 1930s he invented sheet Polaroid, which revolutionised the use of polarised light, previously obtainable only in very small beams. Polarised light is light in which the waves vibrate only in one plane, and reflected light is partially plane-polarised. This fact has enabled Polaroid to be used for sunglasses to cut down glare from reflected sunlight. Land went into business in 1935, when he was 26. The Polaroid Corporation was formed in 1937, Land thus showing himself an astute businessman as well as a scientist. He has been chairman and director of research ever since. To the general public he is better known for his invention of 'instant photography', now in use throughout the world for pleasure and scientific research. The successful development of a colour version of the Land Polaroid Camera, in collaboration with leading university scientists, is one of the more striking developments in applied physical chemistry of this century. **C. L. B.**

Lev Landau (Russian, 1908–1968): physicist. Lev Landau's researches covered a wide range of theoretical problems in fields ranging from fluid mechanics to quantum theory,

but his main contribution was in fluid mechanics. Many substances behave unusually at very low temperatures – helium, for example, at – 271°C. becomes 'superfluid' and flows through fine tubes and slits as though it were frictionless. Landau's particularly brilliant work was to explain the behaviour of 'superfluid' liquid helium. A graduate of Leningrad University, in 1937 Landau became head of the theoretical department of the Institute for Physical

Fritz Lang (German, b. 1890): film director. Trained as an architect in Vienna, Lang entered the German film industry immediately after the First World War and with such pictures as *Metropolis*, *M* and the *Dr Mabuse* series created a fantastic, highly stylised, doom-laden cinema whose protagonists were the victims or manipulators of urban tensions and historical forces. Admired by Hitler and offered the head job of the Nazi film industry by Goebbels (qq.v.), Lang fled to France in 1933 and then to Hollywood where he began the second half of his career with the lynch law film *Fury* (1936). Though never accorded there the freedom and rarely the respect he had in Germany, Lang pursued his chosen theme of man as the victim of inescapable fate, his own nature and the pressures of city life, in a succession of spy movies, thrillers and psychological melodramas. His best German movies were

Irving Langmuir (U.S., 1889–1957): engineer. Irving Langmuir's research on heated wires and the gases round them led to the introduction of the gas-filled electric lamp used everywhere today in place of the old vacuum lamp. His further work on the emission of electrons from heated filaments led to the standard thoriated-tungsten cathodes of all thermionic valves. He was the inventor of cloud-seeding as a way of producing rain from clouds, and he made

many other contributions to science and technology. His real scientific activity began when he joined the laboratories of the U.S. General Electric Company in 1909, where he stayed all his life. After the gasfilled lamp came more fundamental studies of surface phenomena in liquids, gases and solids, for which he was awarded a Nobel Prize in 1932. One incidental outcome of his work was the theoretical foundation for detergents. He originated the idea of molecular monolayers, so fruitful in subsequent fundamental research. He invented a theory of valency. He invented the condensation pump for producing high vacuums, developed sonar for submarine detection in the First World War, and improved smoke screens in the Second. He was still youthfully investigating with simple techniques – science was fun, he said – when he died. **C. L. B.**

'COLLECTED WORKS OF IRVING LANGMUIR' (PERGAMON PRESS, 1962); 'BIOGRAPHICAL MEMOIRS OF FELLOWS OF THE ROYAL SOCIETY, VOL. 4' (THE ROYAL SOCIETY, 1958).

George Lansbury (British, 1859–1940): politician. A perpetual sponsor of good causes, Lansbury was Labour's most popular leader. He contributed with the Webbs (q.v.) to the famous Minority Poor Law Report (1909) which foreshadowed later developments in the Welfare State. The man who "let his bleeding heart run away with his bloody head", he supported the suffragettes and launched the *Daily Herald* in 1912 – the first really successful Socialist daily newspaper. As Labour Mayor of Poplar he went to prison (1920) in protest against the harsh administration of unemployment benefits. He represented the Left in the second Labour Government (1929–31) as First Commissioner of Works. One of the few front-bench survivors in Labour's 1931 electoral disaster, he provided surprisingly able leadership for the Labour remnant and did much to restore confidence to the party. However, his absolute pacifism contributed to confusion in Labour foreign policy in the 1930s; he was forced to resign his leadership when attacked by Ernest Bevin for "hawking his conscience". The prototype of the humanitarian conscience in the Labour Movement, George Lansbury left his mark on many facets of 20th-century British life, from the lido in Hyde Park to reform in local taxation and unemployment administration. **A. M.**

'THE LIFE OF GEORGE LANSBURY', BY RAYMOND POSTGATE (LONGMANS, 1951); 'BRITAIN BETWEEN THE WARS', BY C. L. MOWAT (METHUEN, 1955); 'A HISTORY OF THE LABOUR PARTY FROM 1914', BY G. D. H. COLE (ROUTLEDGE, 1948).

Karl Landsteiner (U.S., ex-Austrian, 1868–1943): pathologist. Thousands owe their lives to this Viennese pathologist who, in 1900, discovered the ABO blood groups, and made transfusion safe. Landsteiner demonstrated that when red blood cells from one person are mixed with serum from another, agglutination (clumping) sometimes results. This is because human blood contains naturally-occurring antibodies which react against antigens on the red cells of some, but not all, other people's blood. Transfusion is safe with blood of one's own group or of group O. Landsteiner's second triumph, the discovery of the rhesus blood groups, came 10 years later. He and Wiener discovered that the blood of 85 per cent. of humans contained a factor also present in the blood of rhesus monkeys – and therefore called the rhesus factor. If a woman whose blood does not contain this factor (a woman with rhesus-negative blood) has a child by a man whose blood is 'rhesus-positive', there is a chance that rhesus-positive blood from the child will get into the mother's bloodstream. Here it will produce antibodies that can attack the blood of any subsequent rhesus-positive children, producing 'rhesus babies' that are anaemic for this reason. These antibodies were first recognised, but not named, by Levine and Stetson. Karl Landsteiner's work foreshadowed modern preventive medicine which seeks to identify high-risk individuals and take steps for their protection. **C. A. C.**

Nick La Rocca (U.S., 1889–1961): bandleader. The hard-hitting cornetist Dominick James 'Nick' La· Rocca formed the Original Dixieland Jazz Band in Chicago in 1916 with four other white musicians from New Orleans – Larry Shields, Eddie Edwards, Henry Ragas and Tony Spargo. The Original Dixieland Jazz Band went on to achieve an impressive list of firsts: they were the first jazz band to incorporate the word 'jazz' in their publicity; the first to issue a record (*Darktown Strutters Ball*, at Indiana in 1917); the first to sell a million records of the same number (*Livery Stable Blues*); and at Reisenwebers in New York they were voted 'First Sensational Amusement Novelty of 1917. They were also the first jazz band to visit London (in 1919). By 1923 their rackety

ragtime had fallen out of fashion. Paul Whiteman (q.v.), the new jazz idol, opened his 1924 concert of 'symphonic jazz' with a note-for-note version of *Livery Stable Blues*, a burlesque of what he called "crude jazz of the past". The Orginal Dixieland Jazz Band broke up, and though a revival was attempted in 1936 it failed. In the late Thirties historical research debunked their claim as originators of jazz, placing them as a lightweight advance guard to the heavier guns from New Orleans. However, they had made their impact by introducing the world to jazz; and their large repertoire of tunes – *Jazz Band Ball*, *Tiger.Rag*, etc. – is still solid material for Dixieland bands everywhere. **H. R. A. L.**

RECORDS: 'THE ORIGINAL DIXIELAND JAZZ BAND', MUSIC FOR PLEASURE (MFP1106).

became mayor of Aubervilliers (which he ably defended against the Communists till 1944), then deputy in the 1924 Chamber, soon shifting to the Right. By charm and wiliness he kept former supporters and gained new adherents. Prime Minister in two, Foreign Minister in three inter-war governments, he was a partisan of understanding with Germany and Italy, particularly the latter, as shown in such ventures as the Hoare-Laval pact. After the fall of France in 1940, he engineered the voluntary dissolution of the Third Republic and the setting up of the Vichy State under Pétain (q.v.). He was appointed Pétain's official successor, and as Premier followed a policy of Franco-German co-operation. Dismissed by Pétain in December 1940, he returned, on German insistence, in April 1942, and remained in power until the Liberation of France. He perpetually defended French interests against German encroachments, while still continuing a policy of bargaining. He was condemned to death in 1945, after a parody of a trial, amid general vilification. He did his best for France according to his lights, but was unable to see beyond the bargains he could conclude with his country's enemy. **R. M. G.**

'TWO FRENCHMEN: PIERRE LAVAL AND CHARLES DE GAULLE', BY DAVID THOMSON (CRESSET PRESS, 1951); 'PIERRE LAVAL AND THE ECLIPSE OF FRANCE', BY GEOFFREY WARNER (EYRE AND SPOTTISWOODE, 1968).

David Herbert Lawrence (British, 1885–1930): writer. D. H. Lawrence, one of our greatest and most controversial novelists, describes his early life and the struggles of his Nottinghamshire mining family in his autobiographical novel *Sons and Lovers* (1913). Many of his best stories and novels are set in this area, although in his later life he travelled in Europe,

legal decision that *Lady Chatterley's Lover* (1928) was not obscene has enabled us to write more freely about sex. Lawrence himself, however, must stand chiefly as a novelist who can be superbly convincing about what life actually feels like in the intimate and ordinary relationships of human beings and the natural world. **K. McL.**

'THE DARK SUN', BY G. HOUGH (DUCKWORTH, 1956); 'THE DEED OF LIFE', BY J. MOYNAHAN (OXFORD U.P., 1966); 'D. H. LAWRENCE - NOVELIST', BY F. R. LEAVIS (CHATTO AND WINDUS, 1955); 'D. H. LAWRENCE. A PERSONAL RECORD', BY JESSIE CHAMBERS (CASSELL, 1965).

Thomas Edward Lawrence (British, 1888–1935): writer. T. E. Lawrence was the archaeologist who became British liaison officer with the Arab revolt against the Turks, and who helped to form and lead the Arab force operating on the flank of Allenby's advance into Syria; then played a part in the Peace Conference and in the Colonial Office under Churchill (q.v.), trying for a Middle Eastern settlement. He left public life, joined the RAF, and was killed in a motorbike accident. He is a perplexing figure. Was the Arab revolt as important as he claimed in *Seven Pillars of Wisdom*? Probably not, but not as trivial as others have maintained. Was his role in it as important as he and his friends suggested? Again,

probably not: his stories of his own exploits were exaggerated and scarcely fair to other officers, Arab or British. Another puzzle: why did he enter the RAF – because "the Arabs had been cheated", or because of some sense of alienation? His complex character projected by his writing may always attract interest. **A, H. H.**

'SELECTED LETTERS OF T. E. LAWRENCE', EDITED BY D. GARNETT (JONATHAN CAPE, 1938); 'LAWRENCE OF ARABIA', BY R. ALDINGTON (COLLINS, 1955).

Max von Laue (German, 1879–1960): physicist. It was von Laue who discovered the only technique for determining the structure of protein and DNA molecules as well as others. He connected two half-formed ideas; one of them was the wave nature of X-rays, which was still not entirely accepted when he was working at Munich University from 1909–1912; the other was the lattice structure of crystals, which, though accepted, was not thought very important. Von Laue realised that the relation between the lattice constant of crystals and the supposed wavelength of X-rays was such that the crystals ought to diffract the X-rays. Von Laue predicted that if a pencil of X-rays were passed through a crystal, then, on the other side, the photographic film would register a strong central spot, plus other spots symmetrically arranged around it from the diffracted rays. From this pattern can be deduced the arrangement of atoms in the molecule. This discovery led the way to development by the two Braggs (qq.v.) of X-ray diffraction. **N. J. M. H.**

Sir Wilfrid Laurier (Canadian, 1841–1919): statesman. Laurier, who was Prime Minister of Canada from 1896–1911, did much to make Canada feel independent. He bridged the 19th and 20th centuries. He wanted to fulfil his own prediction that 1900 would mark the beginning of "Canada's century"; but he belonged to the last generation of Canadian politicians who accepted British knighthoods. The national policy had its spectacular failures; Laurier's railway programme led to financial chaos and his trade treaty with the United States was rejected by the anti-American electorate. Laurier believed that

the Empire could only survive as a commonwealth of free states, and insisted that Canada should have her own navy, rather than contributing ships to Britain. This pleased neither the loyalist English nor the isolationist French, and in the 1911 election he was simultaneously branded as anti-British and a jingoist. "I am neither," he replied, "I am a Canadian." His campaign against conscription in 1917 shattered the harmony between French and English Canadians, and the unity of his party, and his career ended in tragedy. Laurier was an attractive personality: his wife insisted on marrying him the day he proposed, although she was engaged to someone else. **G. W. M.**

'LAURIER, THE FIRST CANADIAN', BY JOSEPH SCHULL (MACMILLAN, TORONTO, 1965); 'LIFE AND LETTERS OF SIR WILFRID LAURIER', BY O. D. SKELTON, 2 VOLS. (S. B. GUNDY, TORONTO, 1921).

Pierre Laval (French, 1883–1945): politician. Laval moved from pacifism in the First World War to collaboration in the Second. He was Socialist deputy for the working-class district of Aubervilliers throughout the First World War, but after electoral defeat in 1919 he left the Socialist Party. As an Independent, he

Australia and Mexico, and wrote extensively about all of them. After *Sons and Lovers* Lawrence tried out new ways of writing about close relationships as they exist below the level of conscious thought, most successfully in *The Rainbow* (1915) and *Women In Love* (1921). His hatred of the calculating and fear-ridden materialism that he considered characteristic of the 20th century led him to put great value on instinctive spontaneous emotion, particularly sexual passion and a delight in animals, flowers and children. During his lifetime these beliefs brought him notoriety and misunderstanding, but since then the

Stan Laurel (British, 1890–1965) and **Oliver Hardy** (U.S., 1892–1957): film actors. Oliver Hardy was the fat one who twiddled his tie. Stan Laurel was the thin one who got slapped. Their theme tune was *The Dance of the Cuckoos*, and for 21 years it piped blithely through 90 of the sweetest, most inventive screen comedies ever made. Their humour was wholly without malice; they wore their innocence like armour. Hardy was a Southerner, whose courtliness imposed a ban on the telling of blue jokes in mixed company. He was immensely proud of having descended from Nelson's *aide-de-camp*. Laurel was the son of a Lancashire showman, who joined Fred Karno's music-hall troupe, became Chaplin's (q.v.) understudy on a tour of America, and drifted into movies. The Stan

and Ollie partnership began in 1926 with a picture called *Putting Pants on Philip*, was consolidated with *The Battle of the Century* (in which four thousand pies were flung into assorted faces), and continued amicably until their last film in 1952. Their roles were immovably fixed – silly Stan bringing down disaster on pompous Ollie – but the comic permutations, especially in the films of Hal Roach, were endless. Few comedies, whatever their vintage, could improve on the moment in *Swiss Miss* when bowler-hatted Stan and Ollie meet a gorilla half-way across an Alpine gorge with an upright piano. No-one has deepened the anguish of Ollie's *cri de coeur* when embroiled in one of Stan's catastrophes: "This is *another* fine mess you've got me into." **P. O.**

Louis Seymour Bazett Leakey (Kenyan, b. 1903): anthropologist. L. S. B. Leakey is best known for his excavation of the rich fossil remains in the Olduvai Gorge in Tanzania. He has worked on this site with his wife Mary since the early Thirties, finding over 100 extinct animals and primitive chipped stone tools ('Oldowan'). The first big discovery was that of a 'robust' hominid in 1959. Believing the 1¾ million-year-old skull to be different from both South African hominids, Leakey named it *Zinjanthropus boisei*. Because of his huge molars Zinjanthropus earned the nickname of 'Nutcracker man'. In 1961 examples of a 'gracile' hominid, later called *Homo habilis* (handy man), were found. Hand and foot bones were similar to *Homo sapiens,* and evidence revealed a small-brained, lightly built creature, under 4 ft. 6 ins. tall, who walked much as we do, hunting in small bands, probably staying for several days in one place, and making tools for killing and preparing game and digging up roots. Although the exact evolutionary positions of *Zinjanthropus* and *Homo habilis* are still hotly debated there is no doubt that they are important in man's development. **J. H.**

'AFRICAN GENESIS', BY ROBERT ARDREY (COLLINS, 1961); 'MAN, TIME AND FOSSILS', BY RUTH MOORE (CAPE, 1962).

Frank Raymond Leavis (British, b. 1895): critic. F. R. Leavis is the major literary critic of our time. From 1932–1953, in addition to teaching English at Cambridge, he edited *Scrutiny*, a review which sustained itself through the most challenging and imaginative criticism of literature and culture to be found in any magazine of this century. Much of the criticism was written by Leavis: its main achievements are the demonstration, always through example, comment and qualification, of significant continuities in English literature and criticism; the line of wit in major poets from Donne to T. S. Eliot (q.v.); the great tradition of moral realism in the novel from Jane Austen to D. H. Lawrence (q.v.); the presence of a literary-critical tradition in Dr Johnson, Coleridge, Arnold and Eliot; the heritage of Shakespeare. In the work of these and other writers Leavis finds qualities he has devoted his life to honouring and that his own best work strongly exemplifies: an 'exploratory-creative' attitude toward experience that reveals itself through sequential realisations of words on the page, in the presence of which the reader must become correspondingly alive. His career

provides a unique sense of what sincerity can mean in this century and of how the literary critic's judgments are judgments about life. **W. H. P.**

'NEW BEARINGS IN ENGLISH POETRY', BY F. R. LEAVIS (CHATTO AND WINDUS, 1950); 'REVALUATION', BY F. R. LEAVIS (CHATTO, 1936); 'THE GREAT TRADITION', BY F. R. LEAVIS (CHATTO, 1948); 'THE COMMON PURSUIT', BY F. R. LEAVIS (CHATTO, 1952).

Joshua Lederberg (U.S., b. 1925): geneticist. Lederberg's demonstration that bacteria enjoy a simplified form of sexual activity won him a share in the 1958 Nobel Prize. In the late Forties and early Fifties he produced by X-ray treatment mutant bac-

teria unable to make certain specific natural substances – the bacteria could survive only

if they were fed with, for instance, thiamine. When cultures with different deficiencies were mixed it was found that some nutritionally independent bacteria grew and it occurred thousands of times more often than the normal – very low – mutation rate would account for. The only satisfactory explanation was that a sexual mating process must have taken place, followed by a reassortment of genetic material. Over the years Lederberg and his colleagues were able to confirm the reality and validity of this conclusion and set the scene for the new understanding of the nature of genetic materials. Lederberg also discovered another method of altering genetic constitution in bacteria called genetic transduction, in which only fragments were transferred. This was the first manipulation of any genetic material and opens up the possibility of controlling genetic structure. It could have very broad significance in biology, particularly in the differentiation of, for instance, tumour cells. **P. G. R.**

Gypsy Rose Lee (U.S., 1914–1970): striptease artist. Gypsy Rose Lee was the first famous American strip-tease artist. At the age of four when she was still Rose Louise Hovick, nicknamed Plug, she made her stage debut in West Seattle at a Club Celebration following the installation of the Knights of Pythias. She supported her two and a half year old sister June, and sang '*I'm a Hard-boiled Rose*'. Divorced and poor, their mother went on tour with 'Dainty June and her Newsboy Songsters'. They travelled with six little boys, guinea-pigs, white mice, a turtle and a monkey. Rose Louise was 10 when they made the Orpheum Circuit playing the big towns. After five

years, following the elopement of her sister, then 13, the act became 'Rose Louise and her Hollywood Blondes'. To save money they lived in a tent. At Toledo the leading lady, who 'stripped', was jailed for assault. So Rose got the part, and changed her name to 'Gypsy Rose Lee'. When she was 17, the racketeer Waxey Gordon had her teeth capped, and got her into a Ziegfeld show. Billed as the Queen of Burlesque, Gypsy Rose Lee played in Minsky's, was elected Queen of Columbia College by the students, starred in the Ziegfeld Follies on Broadway, and had a film made of her life. **B. C.**

'GYPSY—A MEMOIR', BY GYPSY ROSE LEE (ANDRE DEUTSCH, 1957).

Fernand Léger (French, 1881–1955): painter. Machines and the men who look after them were the prime subjects of Léger's art. He was way ahead of his time in his understanding of what technology and the mass media would do to the texture of ordinary life. Born in Normandy of peasant stock, Léger was a prominent figure in the Parisian art world before 1914 and, with Picasso, Braque (qq.v.) and Juan Gris, one of the founding-fathers of Cubism. War service headed him away, however, from any tendency towards a hermetic art: "The sight of the breech of a 75mm. gun was enough to make me forget it." Likewise the slangy, understated courage of his comrades in the trenches made a deep impression upon him: "Once I had my teeth into that sort of reality I never let go of objects again." After demobilisation Léger began on the robust, affirmative, highly-energised symphonic studies of industrial life which occupied him till his death. Where his work before 1914 had been formalised to the point almost of de-humanisation, he later made a supreme effort to speak directly to his public, "to mark a return to simplicity with an art that is unsubtle and intelligible to all". This resulted in his last decade in a series of monumental canvases, natural heirs to Seurat's *Bathing Party* in the National Gallery, on the theme of working-class leisure and outdoor enjoyments. Léger intended his art as the most potent of remedies for alienation, and he meant it to be as effective in the U.S., where he lived from 1940–5, as in his native Europe. **J. R.**

'LEGER'S THE GREAT PARADE', BY PETER DE FRANCIA (CASSELL, 1969); 'FERNAND LEGER', BY DOUGLAS COOPER (LUND HUMPHRIES, 1950).

Suzanne Lenglen (French, 1899–1938): tennis player. Lenglen was the greatest woman tennis player the world has seen. In the early 1920s Wimbledon was a spill-over of Edwardian England; a clique of the game's

aristocrats where players might even refrain from practising for fear of seeming 'unsporting' to those less privileged. Lenglen's impact was electric and immediate; its essence a subtle compound of French logic, French daring and unbounded technical ability. Before Lenglen women played tennis in insteplength dresses worn over corsets and starched petticoats; fashion never previously revealed a woman's leg. Lenglen's insistence on supremacy tolerated no handicaps, so she tossed aside all current concepts of 'decency' and revolutionised the whole field of women's dress. In an essentially amateur setting she was already the complete professional; for six years she dominated the game. Today one can recognise in the Lenglen concept of 50 years ago an audacious blueprint of tennis patterns still likely to be contemporary in the year 2000. **T. Ti.**

'WIMBLEDON STORY', BY NORAH GORDON CLEATHER (SPORTING HANDBOOKS, 1947); 'FIFTY YEARS OF WIMBLEDON', BY A. WALLIS MYERS ('THE FIELD', 1926).

Vladimir Ilyich Lenin (Russian, 1870–1924): statesman. Lenin was probably the greatest revolutionary genius of modern times. He was a Marxist by the age of 22, and after being exiled to Siberia by the Tsarist authorities he emigrated to the West. He lived for a time in London, where he rapidly became known for his concept of a small disciplined party of professional revolutionaries leading the working-class struggle for Socialism. He first systematically presented this theory in *What Is To Be Done?* (1902), and his faction of Russian Marxists became known as the Bolsheviks. In February 1917 the Tsar fell, and Lenin returned to Russia. Alone among revolutionary leaders, he called for an uncompromising fight with the bourgeois Provisional Government. By September 1917 his Bolsheviks dominated the workers', peasants' and soldiers' councils (or soviets). Convinced – rightly – that the chances of a Left-wing revolution would never again be so favourable, and – wrongly – that a Bolshevik revolution would precipitate revolution in the advanced West, which would then come to backward Russia's aid, Lenin seized power at the end of October 1917. For three years Russia was torn by a civil war of immense brutality which left the Bolsheviks victorious but the country devastated: and in 1921 Lenin was compelled partially to restore the capitalist market economy, to ban opposition parties, and to introduce stricter discipline within the Communist Party itself. In May 1922 he suffered a stroke and from then on was largely incapacitated, yet in his last writings he was able to warn against increasing bureaucracy and the accumulation of power by the Party's General Secretary, Stalin (q.v.). **J. D. B.**

'THE BOLSHEVIK REVOLUTION 1917–1923', BY E. H. CARR, 3 VOLS. (MACMILLAN, 1950–1953); 'THE STATE AND REVOLUTION', BY V. I. ULIANOV (LENIN) (ALLEN AND UNWIN, 1919); 'WHAT IS TO BE DONE?', BY LENIN (MARTIN LAWRENCE, 1934); 'LENIN AND THE BOLSHEVIKS', BY ADAM B. ULAM (SECKER AND WARBURG, 1966).

Michel Leiris (French, b. 1901): poet and anthropologist. Leiris is one of the poets who made anthropology attractive to the layman, and an anthropologist who found in this subject the myths from which to create poetry; he understood the importance of communication between the science of man and the art of literature. A Surrealist from 1924 to 1929, he gained from Surrealism and Existentialism a permanent

revolutionary belief in the need for psychological and social emancipation from the bourgeois condition. Leiris joined the Dakar-Djibouti anthropological expedition in 1931 to 1933; in later years he travelled widely – to Egypt, Martinique, China, Japan and Cuba. His journal *L'Afrique Fantôme* (1934) began both his anthropological career and a series of major autobiographical writings. In *L'Age d'Homme* (1939) he considered literature as a bullfight, the child becoming man and poet through searing personal (erotic) exposure to the bull, Truth. In *Biffures* (1948), *Fourbis* (1955) and *Fibrilles* (1966) Leiris pursued his themes – the relation of words and myths to reality, the taming of death, the breaking of one's own limits; in short, the welding of ethics and poetics. His obsessional desire never to cheat in word or deed made him a sober, unrhetorical, classical pioneer of contemporary confessional literature. He demonstrates, according to Lévi-Strauss (q.v.), that every attempt to understand others must be founded in an even more passionate attempt to understand oneself. **N. T.**

'MANHOOD (L'AGE D'HOMME)', BY MICHEL LEIRIS (JONATHAN CAPE, 1968).

William Lever (British, 1851–1925): tycoon. The quintessential Lancashire grocer (his first shop was in Wigan), Lever went into soap (Sunlight) in 1880, founded Port Sunlight and entered the 20th century standing for Parliament (Wirral), putting together a massive soap empire by means of take-over and merger (S. F. Pears. Joseph Crosfield, John Knight, Prices, R. S. Hudson) and fighting a prolonged battle with the *Daily Mail*, which set out to destroy the 'soap trust'. By now Lever Brothers (which became Unilever after his death, when it linked up with the massive Dutch margarine interests of Van den Bergh) was already becoming a major international company, with powerful offshoots in Germany, Belgium, the U.S., Canada and Australia. Worried by his dependence on raw material fluctuations, Lever set off on a series of forays into Africa which ultimately became the huge trading complex of the United Africa Company. After his wife's death, Lever embarked on his major failure – his paternalistic attempt to 'colonise' the Hebridean island of Lewis (hence his title, Lord Leverhulme of the Western Isles, which infuriated the Gaelic Society of Inverness). The main relic of this now is the MacFisheries chain, set up to sell the island products which never came. **P. W.**

'THE HISTORY OF UNILEVER', BY CHARLES WILSON, 2 VOLS. (CASSELL, 1968); 'LORD OF THE ISLES', BY NIGEL NICOLSON (WEIDENFELD AND NICOLSON, 1960).

Claude Lévi-Strauss (French, b. 1908): anthropologist and philosopher. Levi-Strauss's analysis of the structure of primitive thought has found relevance in modern society. His work brought him into brilliant dialogue with Jean-Paul Sartre (q.v.) about the nature of history and the "inspiration of the savage mind", which he claims science has re-established in its rightful place. From 1935-36, while teaching in Brazil, he studied the Indians of the Amazon and Mato Grosso, with particular reference to kinship systems. His *Elementary Structures of Kinship*, published in 1949, turned on its head the then current view of marriage between kinship groups—which saw marriage as a means of recruiting new members and ensuring the continuation of the kinship group. Lévi-Strauss, however, argued that kinship groups were merely units in a system of alliances made by marriage, and attempted to show the general significance of these bonds in the total structure of simple societies. His analysis of the savage mind led him to dispute conventional theories of history, and to view human knowledge as a complete system into which the philosophies of primitive man fit as happily as those of modern society. **J. H.**

BY CLAUDE LEVI-STRAUSS: 'THE SAVAGE MIND' (WEIDENFELD AND NICOLSON, 1966); 'STRUCTURAL ANTHROPOLOGY' (ALLEN LANE, 1968); 'ELEMENTARY STRUCTURES OF KINSHIP' (EYRE AND SPOTTISWOODE, 1969).

John L. Lewis (U.S., 1880–1969): labour leader. Hearing that the Governor of Michigan might intervene in a sit-down strike at a Detroit automobile plant, Lewis

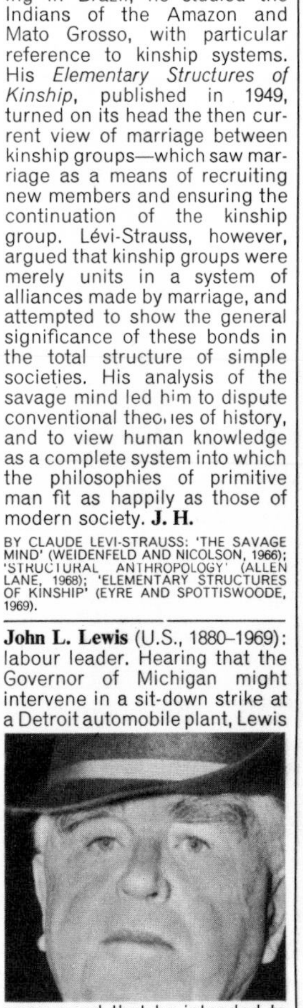

announced that he intended to arrive in person, "walk up to the largest window, . . . divest myself of my outer raiment, . . . and bare my bosom. Then, when you order your troops to fire, mine will be the first breast that those bullets will strike." The courage and the wordiness were characteristic. Lewis, son of a Welsh immigrant miner, was President for 40 years of the United Mine Workers, and led them like a truculent impresario. During the Depression he broke with the conventional-minded American Federation of Labor to help found the Congress of Industrial Organizations and win unionisation for millions of voiceless workers. But his ego was as immense as his spirit; 'Old Blood and Thunder', quarrelling with Roosevelt (q.v.), alienating associates, lost the leadership of the CIO. Though he battled on, especially for his beloved miners, his combative genius did not again reach the heights of the 1930s. Lewis in that decade proved himself probably the greatest and certainly the most spectacular labour spokesman the U.S. has ever known. **M. F. C.**

'THE CIO CHALLENGE TO THE AFL', BY WALTER GALENSON (HARVARD U.P., 1960); 'THE A.F. OF L. FROM THE DEATH OF GOMPERS TO THE MERGER', BY PHILIP TAFT (HARPER, 1959); 'THE AMERICAN LABOR MOVEMENT', ED. LEON LITWACK (PRENTICE HALL, 1962); 'AMERICAN LABOR', BY HENRY PELLING (CHICAGO U.P., 1960).

Sinclair Lewis (U.S., 1885–1951): writer. The master caricaturist of America's Main Street, Sinclair Lewis had a social, not literary, influence. He was no

craftsman; his recipe for a good book was wit, vocabulary and endurance. Among his acknowledged literary derivations were Dickens (comic portraiture), Wells (q.v.) (reformism), Hamlin Garland (Mid-West locale) and Mencken (burlesque and iconoclasm). His instinct for the timely is seen in his panorama of newsworthy types – technicians, businessmen, scientists, clergymen, social reformers, philanthropists, actors; and in his subjects – revivalism, Fascism, racism. Lewis was born in Minnesota, won a Yale B.A. in 1907, then became a hack writer – he concocted plots for Jack London's (q.v.) fiction factory. His first success was *Main Street;* his best or most controversial works were *Babbitt, Elmer Gantry*, and *Kingsblood Royal.* In 1930 he became the first American writer to win the Nobel Prize. He showed a persistent ambivalence toward the middle class, whose cowardice and fatuity he mocked, but whose cynicism, romanticism, irreverence and philistinism he embodied. Europe mistook his message; Lewis was not scornful of bathrooms and cars, only angry when his beloved bourgeoisie betrayed their virtues. Never a literary innovator (he suspected the *avant-garde*), he was rather a moralist who incarnated national archetypes, poeticised the humdrum, and demonstrated how the America reviled by fastidious expatriates was as fabulous as Cathay. **D. A.**

'SINCLAIR LEWIS: AN AMERICAN LIFE', BY MARK SCHORER (HEINEMANN, 1961).

Willard Libby (U.S., b. 1908): geochemist. Radiocarbon dating – a technique first suggested by Libby – has provided geologists and archaeologists with a genuinely scientific method for accurately dating ancient materials of biological origin. Much of the chronology of the ancient Egyptian dynasties has been confirmed by applying this technique to materials from the period – pieces of wood from tombs, for example. Atoms of the

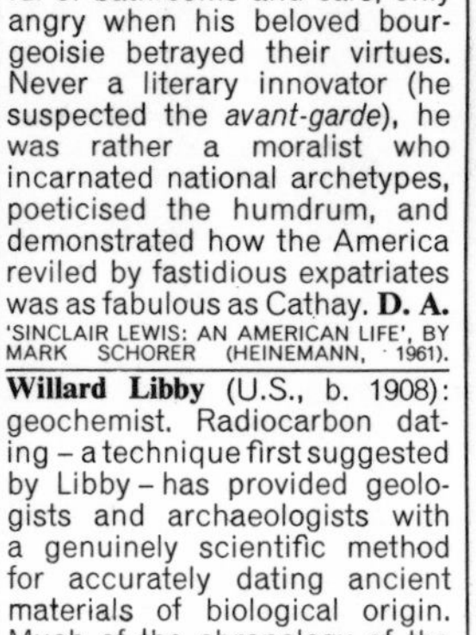

element carbon exist in several forms, the differences between them being in the number of sub-atomic particles from which they are made up. One such form, carbon-14, occurs in nature at one-billionth the concentration of common carbon (carbon-12). While a plant or animal is alive, carbon-14 is present in its cells in the same ratio; but when it dies, the carbon-14 gradually decreases by radioactive decay, while ordinary carbon does not. In 1947, Libby proposed that one could estimate the age of dead organic matter by the extent of depletion of its carbon-14, since it was known that half the carbon-14 would have disappeared after 5600 years. For developing the technique, which has since been expanded to include other radio-active atoms which allow dating of materials that were never alive, Libby was awarded the 1960 Nobel Prize in Chemistry. **M. A. S.**

'NOBEL LECTURES, CHEMISTRY 1942-62' (ELSEVIER, 1964); 'RADIOCARBON DATING', BY W. F. LIBBY (CHICAGO U.P., 1955); 'ARCHAIC EGYPT', BY W. B. EMERY (PENGUIN, 1961).

Sir Basil Liddell Hart (British, 1895–1970): military theorist. Liddell Hart was the military writer to pioneer the theory of armoured warfare. Soon after the First World War he foresaw the potentialities of mechanised armies based on tanks, and with General J. F. C. Fuller became the leading advocate of mechanisation. But his views were less extreme than Fuller's, and it was his ideas on combining tanks with other armoured troops into new type mobile formations that set a pattern for the armoured forces created in Germany and elsewhere. These forces revolutionised warfare during the Second World War and have been the principal component of armies ever since. Liddell Hart also attacked the prevailing doctrines of total war and unconditional surrender, advancing alternative concepts of con-

fined military action which have now become an accepted part of strategic thought. His prolific and creative writings on war have influenced military and political leaders and have made him the foremost military writer of the age. **R. M. O.**

'THE MEMOIRS OF CAPTAIN LIDDELL HART', BY BASIL LIDDELL HART (CASSELL, 1965); 'STRATEGY – THE INDIRECT APPROACH', BY BASIL LIDDELL HART (FABER, 1967).

Trygve Lie (Norwegian, 1896–1968): statesman. Though Foreign Minister of Norway from 1941 to 1946, Lie's main achievement was in establishing the executive role of the Secretary General of the United Nations. Under the League of Nations a Secretary General had been a discreet civil servant, unwilling to take open personal initiatives.

Lie came to office in 1946 with only indefinite Charter powers. He built on these and wrote later of "the series of precedents by which I had carefully sought . . . to build up the influence and prestige of the Secretary General". His period of office saw the U.N. dominated by Great Power rivalries. Lie attempted to intervene in these but reconciliation proved impossible. After America dragged her heels in early 1950 over the admission of Communist China, Russia largely boycotted the U.N. Hence she was not present when the decision was taken that June, on Lie's recommendation, to send a force to South Korea. This ostensibly U.N. force was largely an American operation and the Soviets blamed Lie for its success and tried, but failed, to remove him in 1950. However, they kept up the pressure until he resigned in 1952. After the Korean War Russia paid more attention to the U.N. Hammarskjöld (q.v.) deliberately avoided involving himself in Great Power disputes. As first holder of the post Trygve Lie established the executive role of the Secretary General. Inability to reconcile the Great Powers was inevitable; to have attempted courageously was achievement enough. **H. J. B.**

'IN THE CAUSE OF PEACE', BY TRYGVE LIE (MACMILLAN, 1954); 'THE SECRETARY GENERAL OF THE U.N.', BY S. M. SCHWEBEL (HARVARD U.P., OXFORD, 1952).

Charles Lindbergh (American, b. 1902): aviator. Lindbergh has been the man to have made the single most famous flight of the century. The son of a Congressman, he spent a year at an army flying school, and later worked as an airmail pilot, flying from St. Louis to Chicago. Raymond Orteig had put up a 25,000 dollar prize for the first non-stop solo flight across the Atlantic. Lindbergh, backed by a group of St. Louis businessmen, took off in his Ryan monoplane *Spirit of St. Louis* on May 20, 1927. The next day he landed in

Paris, to be greeted by enormous crowds. The flight had taken him $33\frac{1}{2}$ hours. Five years after his exploit, Lindbergh became the centre of the most famous crime of the decade. His 21-month-old son Charles Augustus was kidnapped and murdered, and four years later Bruno Hauptmann was executed for these crimes. Lindbergh went to Europe to escape the immense publicity and toured extensively. For statements about the pre-war political situation he was criticised by Roosevelt (q.v.) and resigned his Air Corps Reserve Commission, yet he was later actively involved in the war. His book *The Spirit of St. Louis* won the Pulitzer prize in 1954. In retrospect, possibly only the abdication excited as much publicity in those years as the flight performed and the crime endured by Lindbergh. **A. C. C.**

'THE SPIRIT OF ST. LOUIS', BY CHARLES A. LINDBERGH (J. MURRAY, 1953).

Walter Lippmann (U.S., b. 1889): journalist. The most eminent of American journalists was distinguished in his trade by the age of 25, and has been renowned ever since. His sincerity, industry and intelligence cannot seriously be questioned. But his judgment has been as often wrong as right, and the efforts of some of his admirers to set him up as a political thinker on the same level as Hobbes and Rousseau – or even on that of Herbert Croly (q.v.), his early associate – only

provoke amazement. His greatest contribution has been that in his ceaseless journalistic flow – as one of the founders of the *New Republic*, as editor of the *New York World*, and above all as a syndicated columnist – he has done much to provoke serious thought and argument about the problems of the day, seldom or never sinking to the cheap or the sensational. **D. H. V. B.**

'ESSAYS IN THE PUBLIC PHILOSOPHY', BY WALTER LIPPMANN (HAMISH HAMILTON, 1955); 'THE CROSSROADS OF LIBERALISM', BY CHARLES FORCEY (O.U.P., 1961); 'WALTER LIPPMANN AND HIS TIMES', BY MARQUIS CHILDS AND JAMES RESTON (HARCOURT BRACE, NEW YORK, 1959).

David Lloyd George (British, 1863–1945): politician. Britain's most dynamic 20th-century Liberal politician will always be associated with Wales, although he was born in Manchester. He entered Parliament in 1890, "an incarnation of the Celtic spirit", and the Cabinet in 1905. By 1914 he had gone through what for many politicians would have been a whole political career; he had also aroused more enemies in society than any minister before him as a result of his tactics, policies, and fierce and gripping political rhetoric. His famous budget of 1909 was

designed as a 'War Budget' to raise money to wage "implacable war against poverty and squalidness"; his National Insurance Act of 1911 was a landmark in the making of the Welfare State. During the First World War he emerged as the great national leader, pushing Asquith (q.v.) to one side and creating a triumphant coalition which included many who had been his most bitter enemies before 1914. He had charm as well as power, and he revelled in his own intuitions. At the end of the War he was a member of 'the big three' who made the Peace, which he subsequently criticised as if it had been the work of others. His power collapsed with his intuitions in 1922. It was never recovered. **A. B.**

'LLOYD GEORGE', BY THOMAS JONES (O.U.P., 1951); 'LLOYD GEORGE, RISE AND FALL', BY A. J. P. TAYLOR (CAMBRIDGE U.P., 1961).

Raymond Loewy (U.S., ex-French, b. 1893): industrial designer. Loewy was the man who put 'streamlining' into the design of everyday life. He transformed popular taste in both industry and commerce by linking quality, efficiency, and safety with a new concept of environmental beauty. He engulfed the entire functional world – from decorated dugouts in the First World War to railway engines, motorcars and toothbrushes. His lines gave the Studebaker car – and its imitators – a new speed image. His Schick double-headed razor showed that the most mundane object could claim an elegance of its own. He designed whole suburbs as well as furniture and ladies' underwear. He devised new methods of sales promotion and lay-outs for big stores (like Lord and Taylor's White Plains branch), meticulously supervising every detail – from the erection of the outer walls to the wrapping of each single product to be sold. "The great packager", they called him. He was born in Paris, where he studied engineering, and in 1919 emigrated to America. There he started as a fashion designer, then branched out into advertising and, finally, into the field of industrial design. His services were even sought by a builder of tombstones. But Loewy politely declined. "I cannot improve on death," he replied. **J. A.**

'NEVER LEAVE WELL ENOUGH ALONE', BY R. LOEWY (SIMON & SCHUSTER, N.Y., 1951).

Jack London (U.S., 1876–1916): writer. Factoryhand, oyster-pirate, road-kid, sailor, hobo, gold-prospector, Marxist revolutionary, war-correspondent, best-seller, would-be circumnavigator, alchoholic and experimental farmer, London wrote 51 books in 16 years. He began as a tough action writer with stories of the Yukon Gold Rush of '98, then won international fame with *The Call of the Wild* (translated into 36 languages, including Esperanto), appealing to those preferring simple struggles against Nature to the complexities of Civilisation, whether capitalist or Communist. *The People of the Abyss* (1903) about London slums showed him as social reporter, *The Sea Wolf* (1904) as 'the American Conrad'. *The Iron Heel* (1907) was an uncanny prevision of Fascism. *Martin Eden* (1909) became the archetype of U.S. portraits of the artist as a young man. *John Barleycorn* (1913) did harm in promoting prohibition, but is the first serious study of alcoholism. London embodied the longing for the frontiersman's simplicities of life and death, like Hemingway (q.v.). Unlike Hemingway in his careless style and width of scope, he is now seen as seminal to many strains of American literature. **A. C.-M.**

'THE BODLEY HEAD JACK LONDON', 4 VOLUMES EDITED BY A. CALDER-MARSHALL (BODLEY HEAD, 1963–66); 'JACK LONDON', BY RICHARD O'CONNOR (GOLLANCZ, 1965); 'JACK LONDON AND THE KLONDIKE', BY FRANKLIN WALDER (BODLEY HEAD, 1966); 'JACK LONDON AND HIS TIMES', BY JOAN LONDON (WASHINGTON U.P., 1969).

Huey Long (U.S., 1893–1935): politician. Racketeer-radical, with a manner that blended fundamentalist preacher and travelling salesman, Huey Long barnstormed his way into the governorship of Louisiana in the 1920s. It was a corrupt state, dominated by New Orleans and by big business. With his victory it was just as corrupt. The difference was that the 'Kingfish' ran it from the State capital, Baton Rouge, on behalf of the rednecks from whom he had sprung – "Every Man a King", with Huey as emperor. He soaked the rich to pay for roads, hospitals, schools, bribes, extravagances. He turned the legislature into a bunch of frightened yes-men. Soon Louisiana seemed too small.

He became a U.S. Senator (1932), founder of a nationwide Share Our Wealth movement that claimed seven million members, self-proclaimed next President (*My First Days in the White House*, 1935). Emperor-like, he was assassinated in the marble halls of his capitol. Clown, rabblerouser, bullyboy, Long

was a populist turned megalomaniac, the nearest thing in the Depression years to an American-style dictator. **M. F. C.**

'HUEY LONG'S LOUISIANA', BY ALLAN SINDLER (JOHNS HOPKINS PRESS, BALTIMORE, 1956); 'THE POLITICS OF UPHEAVAL', BY ARTHUR M. SCHLESINGER, JR. (HEINEMANN, 1961); 'THE NEW DEAL', BY JOHN MAJOR (LONGMANS, 1968).

Stefan Lorant (U.S., ex-Hungarian, b. 1901): editor. Lorant was one of those chiefly responsible for the development of modern photo-journalism. He left Budapest for Berlin in his twenties. Combining acute journalistic sense with expert knowledge of photography, he was already Berlin editor of *Münchner Illustrierte* in 1928. Two years later he became editor-in-chief. His axiom was that the camera should follow and record events as they happen, not stop to compose them into formal shots. He had an unfailing eye for the strongest picture in a series and a natural sense for effective layout. Strongly political, he used photographs as cartoons, to assert viewpoints and arouse emotions. Imprisoned under the Nazis, he was released through the efforts of Hungarian journalists. He came to Britain in 1934, founded *Weekly Illustrated* for Odhams Press, but quickly left. Then he launched *Lilliput* in 1937, on a tiny amount of borrowed capital, sold it to Hulton Press, and started *Picture Post*, becoming its first editor. He left England for America in 1940. Since then he has worked mainly on photographic books. His original book on Abraham Lincoln (1941) included every known photograph, with a number he had himself unearthed. Lorant helped to create modern picture journalism, the forerunner of today's television news and also, of course, of the newspaper colour magazines. **T. H.**

'I WAS HITLER'S PRISONER', BY STEFAN LORANT (PENGUIN BOOKS, 1939); 'THE NEW WORLD', ED. STEFAN LORANT (DUELL, SLOAN AND PEARCE, NEW YORK, 1946); 'THE PRESIDENCY', BY STEFAN LORANT (MACMILLAN, NEW YORK, 1951); 'LINCOLN: A PICTURE STORY OF HIS LIFE', BY STEFAN LORANT (HARPER AND BROTHERS, NEW YORK, 1954).

Konrad Lorenz (Austrian, b.1903): naturalist. Lorenz talks to animals in their own language: he has been able to understand and reproduce the signal code of many different species of social animal, and though he is best known for books describing in delightful terms his experiences with all sorts of animals – jackdaws, geese, monkeys, cockatoos, as well as cats and dogs – and including a wealth of behavioural insight (treating animals more kindly than humans), he played an important part in behavioural psychology by describing the 'imprint' and 'releaser' mechanisms. The 'imprint' mechanism orientates an animal towards the beings with which it spent certain critical parts of its youth: it does not necessarily know which species it belongs to if it grows up out of contact with that species. The 'releaser' mechanism unlocks innate perceptory patterns: dogs respond predictably to specific attitudes in other dogs. Lorenz has, perhaps, too much affection for his animals for the classic scientific approach, but his tolerance of aberrant behaviour could well be mimicked by many investigators of human activity. **P. G. R.**

'KING SOLOMON'S RING', BY KONRAD LORENZ (METHUEN, 1952); 'MAN MEETS DOG', BY KONRAD LORENZ (METHUEN, 1954); 'ON AGGRESSION', BY KONRAD LORENZ (METHUEN, 1966).

Joe Louis (U.S., b. 1914): boxer. Joe Louis made the black man acceptable in sport. That may sound patronising, but before Louis, boxing – and most other sports – happily spat in the Negro's face. No black man had been allowed to fight for the World heavyweight title for 22 years. Once Louis got there, in 1937, no white man was to win it for another 15 years, and nobody bitched. Louis was the 20th-century's great catalyst in sport's black-white relationships. Jesse Owens (q.v.), the American sprinter, was another, but not to the same degree. Louis cleared the way for Jackie Robinson in baseball, Charlie Sifford in golf. Too bad Muhammad Ali (q.v.) has undone some of the good work. Today Louis, who never curled his lip at a white man or anyone else, would be derided by militant Negroes. Hatred is in fashion. Louis made his point – his race's point – with dignity. He said: "I never hated any man, not even in the ring. You don't hate that easy. Hating is something that comes deep. It's something only bad people do." OK, so he was naive. Who cares? Joe Louis happened to be the greatest heavyweight there ever was – and never told you so. **H. C.**

'MASTERS OF BOXING', BY HARRY CARPENTER (HEINEMANN, 1964); 'THE SWEET SCIENCE', BY A. J. LIEBLING (GOLLANCZ, 1956); 'THE HEAVYWEIGHT CHAMPIONS', BY JOHN DURANT (ARCO, NEW YORK, 1961).

Sir Bernard Lovell (British, b. 1913): radioastronomer. Though he is well known as a broadcaster, writer and populariser of science, Lovell will be remembered primarily as the man who had the vision and enterprise to build the great 250 ft. radio telescope at Jodrell Bank. Born in Gloucester and educated at Bristol University, he has been on the staff of Manchester University since 1936, apart from the war years which he spent helping to develop radar at the Telecommunications Research Establishment at Malvern (now the Royal Radar Establishment). By his persistence and organising ability he constructed what was still, 13 years after its completion, the world's largest steerable radio dish. This instrument, backed by a top-class laboratory, gave the then rather new science of radioastronomy a tremendous boost, and revealed that it had immensely important things to contribute to our knowledge of the universe. Currently radioastronomy is making the most exciting discoveries in the sky and plays a key role in the debate raging around the origin of the universe. Sir Bernard thus promoted a vital step forward in astrophysics. **P. H. S. S.**

'OUR PRESENT KNOWLEDGE OF THE UNIVERSE', BY A. C. B. LOVELL (MANCHESTER U.P., 1967); 'THE STORY OF JODRELL BANK', BY A. C. B. LOVELL (O.U.P., 1968).

Sir David Low (New Zealander, 1891–1963): cartoonist. Low came to England at the age of 28 and immediately created the cartoon of a two-headed horse to represent Lloyd George's (q.v.) coalition party. In a long cartooning life Low drew for the *Guardian*, *Daily Herald*, and *New Statesman*, but his best work was, oddly enough, reserved for Lord Beaverbrook (q.v.) who persuaded him to join the *Evening Standard*. Left-wing and sporting a bohemian beard, Low frequently satirised his master and featured him in Blimp cartoons, which usually began; "Gad Sir, Lord Beaverbrook is right . . ." The TUC carthorse and Colonel Blimp were his most successful creations – he insisted that Blimp was real, and that he'd overheard him in a Turkish bath "in his birthday suit saying what Japan did was no concern of Britain". Low owed more to Continental artists, like Daumier, than to English political cartoonists. He quickly dropped the pen for a flowing brush, which he handled with the ease of a Chinese master. The war years gave him most scope for his broad simplifications, and his propaganda effort earned him a knighthood. His most famous drawing showed Hitler and Stalin (qq.v.) viewing each other across the corpse of Poland in 1939, Hitler saying, "The scum of the earth, I presume?" and Stalin grinning back, "The bloody assassin of the workers, I presume?" One of England's greatest cartoonists, he was certainly the most patriotic. **M. B.**

'YEARS OF WRATH', BY DAVID LOW (GOLLANCZ, 1949).

Ernst Lubitsch (U.S., ex-German, 1892–1947): director. Lubitsch made his name in the German film industry. He went to the United States in 1922, and stayed to make films like *The Marriage Circle*, *Forbidden Paradise* and *Kiss Me Again*. In the Thirties people began to talk of 'the Lubitsch touch' with international successes like *The Love Parade*, *Bluebeard's Eigth Wife* and *Ninotchka*; *To Be or Not To Be* and *Heaven Can Wait* are other examples from the Forties. The 'touch' was his ability to combine in a single line of dialogue, a facial expression, a gesture or a coincidence a mixture of comedy and tragedy, laughter and tears. He was not interested in film structure so much as its ability to capture moments of ironic truth within the human comedy. To describe Lubitsch as a comedy director is totally inadequate. He was German, also Viennese, also Hellenic, also Jewish, also Parisian, also American, and also Lubitsch. He was a master film-maker. D. W. Griffith (q.v.) was his spiritual father; Billy Wilder is his spiritual son. Every film-maker worth a damn is a relation of Lubitsch. He used to say: "Is this the best we can do? Does it ring the bell? When it's right it rings the bell." **P. Ma.**

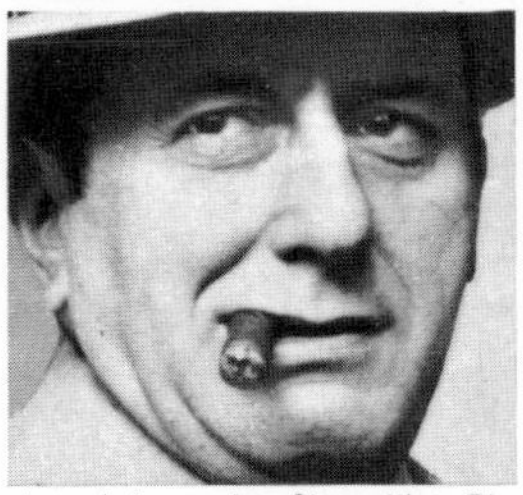

Henry Luce (U.S., 1898–1967): publisher. Henry Robinson Luce was born in Tengchow, China, the son of American Presbyterian missionaries. After Yale and Oxford he worked briefly as a newspaper reporter, then, in 1923, with his friend Briton Hadden, he launched *Time*, The Weekly Newsmagazine, on $86,000 subscribed by their Yale friends. It now has a world-wide audience of 20 million. After Hadden's death in 1929, Luce became sole publisher. His business magazine, *Fortune*, followed and, in 1936, came *Life*, a picture weekly whose format has been widely imitated. Time Inc. expanded into book publishing, films (*The March of Time*), radio, TV, and paper manufacturing. Luce devoted most of his time to editing, bringing contributions to a processed uniformity ('Timestyle'), hitherto unequalled. In *Time*, and behind the political scene, he was a fierce upholder of American patriotism, and a devoted anti-Communist. His wife, Clare Boothe Luce, became a U.S. ambassador. He believed himself a true progressive, and supported Negro Civil Rights, freedom as he saw it everywhere, and, at the beginning of the War, American intervention on Britain's behalf. At his death, LBJ said: "His magazines are an authentic part of the life of America." **R. T. E.**

'TIME, INC', BY ROBERT T. ELSON (ATHENEUM, NEW YORK, 1968).

Erich Ludendorff (German, 1865–1937): general. Without Ludendorff Germany might well have collapsed before 1918. But he wrecked the chance of a moderate peace by obstinately pressing for unattainable complete victory. Although he was not an aristocrat and had married a divorcee, his ability and industry got him key army jobs before the First World War. His – exaggerated – share in taking Liège in August 1914 led to his being picked, with Hindenburg (q.v.) as a figurehead, to save the situation in East Prussia. Using plans already drawn up, he beat the Russians at Tannenberg and the Masurian Lakes. For two years he nagged Supreme Headquarters to give the Eastern front more emphasis; then in July 1916 he was put in charge of SHQ, though still with Hindenburg as his chief. Ludendorff strove to get Germany fully mobilised – and was soon running the entire Government. In 1917 he insisted on all-out submarine warfare and the dismissal of Bethmann Hollweg (q.v.). When Lenin (q.v.), whom Ludendorff had allowed to pass through Germany on his way back from Switzerland to Russia to lead the October Revolution, asked for an armistice, he insisted on the harsh Treaty of Brest-Litovsk. After his 1918 Western offensive failed, his nerve collapsed and he told Hindenburg an Armistice was essential. He soon recovered but was dismissed for denouncing the terms demanded by Wilson (q.v.). In 1923 he took part in Hitler's (q.v.) unsuccessful *putsch* in Munich; thereafter he became increasingly cranky. **M. L. G. B.**

'LUDENDORFF', BY D. J. GOODSPEED (HART-DAVIS, 1966); 'THE SWORDBEARERS', BY C. BARNETT (EYRE AND SPOTTISWOODE, 1963); 'GERMANY'S AIMS IN THE FIRST WORLD WAR', BY FRITZ FISCHER (CHATTO AND WINDUS, 1967); 'THE POLITICS OF THE PRUSSIAN ARMY 1640–1945', BY G. CRAIG (O.U.P., 1955).

Frederick Lugard (British, 1858–1945): empire builder. Lugard stood for all that was decent in British imperialism in Africa – swift, humane conquest; a light form of overrule, working through native institutions and modernising them slowly; tolerance for the beliefs and customs of other peoples; and a clear vision of African self-government following the period of tutelage. A soldier by training, Lugard first went to Africa in 1887 (he had been crossed in love). For 12 years he served the private enterprise imperialism of chartered companies in East, South and West Africa before becoming the first Governor of Northern Nigeria from 1900 till 1906. Then for six years he governed Hong Kong, returning to Africa as the first Governor-General of all Nigeria from 1912 until 1918. Nigeria had a fifth of the population of Africa. In pre-colonial times a loose Fulani empire had stretched over perhaps a quarter of it. The rest had been divided into some hundreds of political and ethnic groups. In 20 interrupted years Lugard laid the foundations of unity. He certainly did not envisage an independent Nigeria emerging 40 years on from then. He had pointed it in that direction, but on a slower schedule. **R. O.**

'LUGARD', BY MARGERY PERHAM, 2 VOLS. (COLLINS, 1956, 1960); 'THE STORY OF NIGERIA', BY MICHAEL CROWDER (FABER, 1962).

Georg Lukacs (Hungarian, 1885–1971). Lukacs was among the most celebrated of the Marxist critics. The example of his writing has been a potent factor in the revival of interest in Marxist criticism and in the renewed authority of Marxism itself. Before 1914 he opposed the popular Marxism of the Second International but greeted the Russian Revolution as a reinstatement of Marxism in practical politics. *History and Class Consciousness* (1923) emphasised the role of consciousness and initiated the concept of 'reification'. He was Commissar for Education under Béla Kun (q.v.) before being exiled. In 1956, Lukacs became Nagy's (q.v.) Minister of Culture. His later criticism, essentially an aesthetic version of the Popular Front, emphasised the continuity between Socialism and high bourgeois culture. His 'great tradition' becomes the realist novel, which constitutes for Lukács a new genre, the modern epic: for him, Tolstoy replaces Dostoievsky. Great writers reflect the essence of social reality; and so implicitly demonstrate its intelligibility. Modernism, by contrast, is subjective, and thus debilitating. These premises underlie his later work, like *The Historical Novel*. He remained guardedly critical of Socialist Realism. The early Lukács influenced the existentialist Marxism of critics like the French Lucien Goldman. Here he is known mostly by his later writing, which seems culturally conservative. **G. P.**

'THE HISTORICAL NOVEL', BY GEORG LUKACS (MERLIN PRESS, 1962).

Sir Arnold Lunn (British, b. 1888): skier. Lunn – mountaineer, author (he has published more than 50 books on many different subjects), editor, controversialist, lecturer, after-dinner speaker and wit – is best known as a founding father of organised winter sports not only for Britons but for skiers all over the world. He founded the Alpine Ski Club in 1908 and the Kandahar Ski Club in 1924. He started the Anglo-Swiss race in 1925 and the Arlberg-Kandahar in 1928. He drafted the International Rules for Downhill and Slalom competitions in 1930 and organised the first world championship in these races in 1931 at Mürren, his winter home. He was knighted for services to skiing and Anglo-Swiss relations in 1952. Awarded an honorary D. Phil. by Zürich University in 1954, he delivered the Lowell lectures in the U.S. and has had an unparalleled international influence by editing the British Ski Year Book for a continuous 50 years. He first skied in 1898 in Chamonix and has skied ever since – in spite of a serious climbing accident in 1909 which left a lifelong handicap. He made the first ski ascents of the Dom (1917) and the Eiger (1924). His love of God, mountains and fair play has made him great – and his devotion to skiing and skiers has brought him countless friends. **W. J. R.**

'THE STORY OF SKI-ING', BY SIR ARNOLD LUNN (EYRE AND SPOTTISWOODE, 1952).

Albert Luthuli (South African, 1898–1967): chief. This impressive Zulu Christian leader devoted his early life to school-teaching. Later he was the able holder of a Natal chieftaincy until his deposition by the Pretoria Government following his election, in 1952, as President-General of the African National Congress. His stature grew rapidly following firstly his criticisms of inadequacies of the Natives Representative Council, and second, from 1948 onwards, his complete rejection of *apartheid*, which outraged his every conviction. A genuine non-racialist, he worked co-operatively with Indians, Coloureds and Europeans for the establishment of a true democracy and true union of all communities. His personal participation in the defiance of unjust laws, his uncompromising condemnation of the Sharpeville shootings and his superbly dignified indifference to repeated police restrictions helped to preserve the morale of all opponents of *apartheid*. Luthuli's unflinching magnanimity aroused universal admiration and deepened the world's appreciation of the worth of Africans and the legitimacy of their aspirations everywhere, especially in the Republic of South Africa. He won the Nobel Peace Prize in 1960. **K. K.**

'ALBERT JOHN LUTHULI AND THE SOUTH AFRICAN RACE CONFLICT', BY EDWARD CALLAN (WESTERN MICHIGAN UNIVERSITY INSTITUTE OF INTERNATIONAL AND AREA STUDIES, 1965); 'LET MY PEOPLE GO', BY A. J. LUTHULI (COLLINS, 1962).

Sir Edwin Lutyens (British, 1869–1944): architect. Lutyens was the most inventive of the domestic architects who made Britain pre-eminent in the 'transitional years' (1890–1910) before the emergence of modern architecture. Less puritanically minded than Voysey or Mackintosh, Lutyens nonetheless had a more profound influence in the way he integrated his buildings with the surrounding environment of the 'natural garden' which had been brought to maturity in his native Surrey by his patron and colleague, Miss Gertrude Jekyll (q.v.). Lutyens' early houses (Munstead Wood, for Miss Jekyll, 1896–7; Orchards, Godalming, 1897–1900; Grey Walls, Gullane, 1899–1901;

The Deanery, Sonning, 1899–1901; Little Thakeham, 1902–4; Marsh Court, Stockbridge, 1901–5) showed a masterly handling of the external spaces appropriate to the lavish weekend parties of those days – courtyards, loggias, terraces, pergolas – these spaces proving equally appropriate, as Lutyens himself showed at Hampstead Garden Suburb Central Square (1908–11), to the achievement of modern town planning. In his later days Lutyens turned increasingly to the Grand Manner (Heathcote, Ilkley, 1906; the Viceroy's House, New Delhi, 1912–30); but more important was his obsession with the spiritual significance of geometry, as in his memorials (Cenotaph, Whitehall, 1919–20; Memorial to the Missing of the Somme, Thiepval, 1925–32). **N. J. W. T.**

'THE LIFE OF SIR EDWIN LUTYENS', BY CHRISTOPHER HUSSEY (COUNTRY LIFE, 1950); 'THE ARCHITECTURE OF SIR EDWIN LUTYENS', BY A. S. G. BUTLER ET AL. (COUNTRY LIFE, 1950); 'HOUSES AND GARDENS BY E. L. LUTYENS' BY SIR LAWRENCE WEAVER (COUNTRY LIFE, 1913).

Rosa Luxemburg (German, ex-Polish, 1871–1919): writer and politician. The heroine of Polish and German revolutionary Socialism and the martyr of the German defeat of 1919 was born of Polish-Jewish parents in Russian Poland. At the age of 16 she joined the revolutionary Socialist

movement. Later she became co-founder of the Social Democratic Party of the kingdom of Poland, opposing Poland's independence and co-operating closely with Russian revolutionaries. After studying at Zürich University she made ner home in Berlin, where she participated passionately in Socialist activities, wrote on economics and politics for Socialist papers and journals, taught at the Central Party school and became theoretical leader of its Left wing. Outstanding in her opposition to all injustice and especially to Prussian militarism, she vehemently rejected the First World War and her Party's pro-war policy, combining with other extreme left-wingers to form the Spartacus group. From prison she wrote her famous indictment of Social Democracy and the war, the Junius pamphlet, and later a critique of tne Bolshevik Revolution

Released by the revolution of November, 1918, she was co-founder of the German Communist Party in late December. Victim of repeated and vicious attacks on 'Red Rosa', she was murdered two weeks later by White troops after an abortive Communist uprising. She was and remained a symbol of uncompromising Socialist principles. **F. L. C.**

'ROSA LUXEMBURG', BY J. P. NETTL (O.U.P., 1966).

Louis Lyautey (French, 1854–1934): colonial soldier. Lyautey was a man who at one time seemed to symbolise France for the world beyond France. Yet in reality he expressed one of the fundamental ideas of European colonialism: that it was a holding operation, not one of transformation. His experience was in Indo-China and Madagascar, and he became Resident-General in Morocco in 1912. A reflective soldier, he wanted the military to play a social role in the conquered territory, and he sought to preserve and to utilise the traditional structures of indigenous society, to govern with the mandarin rather thar against him. Thus he believed in association, indirect rule, control rather than administration. He was successful in that he was able to hold Morocco with very few men in the First World War. But when France was expected to do more than just preserve law and order, and actively to promote economic change, then it was no longer possible to preserve the old Morocco. It could be said that a colonialist such as Lyautey set his sights low; or simply that he did not set out to destroy indigenous civilisation. **D. W. J. J.**

'LYAUTEY', BY ANDRE MAUROIS (JOHN LANE, THE BODLEY HEAD, 1931).

Douglas MacArthur (U.S., 1880–1964): soldier. MacArthur was a unique American pro-consul and perhaps the greatest general in the history of the U.S. He became Chief of Staff in Washington from 1930-5, the youngest and one of the most politically controversial ever to hold the post. From 1936 till their capture by the Japanese in 1942 he was effective military commander in the Philippines. Beginning from Australia, to

which he retreated, he directed with his habitual flamboyance the superb combined-operations strategy against Imperial Japan which had ensureɑ Allied victory even before the atomic bomb ended the war in August 1945. Under his autocratic rule, Japan was then demilitarised and 'democratised'. From Tokyo he directed the almost miraculous American counter-offensive in the early days of the Korean War, but *hubris* overtook

him when he promised victory "by Christmas" (1950) but instead was hurled back by the military intervention of Red China. When he then appealed to the American public against President Truman's (q.v.) prohibition on attacking Chinese territory, he was dismissed. As he himself prophesied, thereafter the old soldier merely faded away. **H. C. A.**

'REMINISCENCES', BY DOUGLAS MACARTHUR (HEINEMANN, 1965); 'MACARTHUR: THE LIFE OF A GENERAL', BY A. P. JULIAN (DUELL, SLOAN AND PEARCE, N.Y., 1963).

Joseph McCarthy (U.S., 1908–1957): politician. In 1950, Joe McCarthy, an unimpressive junior Senator from Wisconsin, by no means sure of re-election, jumped on to the anti-Communist bandwaggon and for four years rode it at top speed. In retrospect his career appears one continuous pseudo-event. Nothing he did or said rings true, not even the imaginary wound he claimed from war service. Even his indignation at the "twenty years of treason" seems simulated – a mere device to grab and retain the headlines. In this, at least, he succeeded. Lies, threats, innuendo, promises of shattering disclosures, all gave him a

frightening notoriety. At last he over-reached himself in the climactic half-sinister half-clownish hearings of 1954, televised on the screens of the nation. His fellow-Senators decided that he had gone too far, and had failed to prove his case. They voted to 'condemn' him. McCarthy subsided into alcoholic obscurity; America recovered as from a bad dream. His effect has been compared to that of Marat in revolutionary Paris. But McCarthy was no ideologue; rather he was a con man masquerading as grand inquisitor. **M. F. C.**

'SENATOR JOE MCCARTHY', BY RICHARD H. ROVERE (MERIDIAN BOOKS, N. Y., 1964); 'MCCARTHY AND THE INTELLECTUALS', BY MICHAEL ROGIN (M.I.T. PRESS, 1967).

Ramsay MacDonald (British, 1866–1937): statesman. There seem to be two appropriate styles of ambiguity in the Labour Party. The first consists of talking too little: the second of talking too much. The first was Attlee's (q.v.) method: the second that of Ramsay Mac Donald. The illegitimate son of a Scottish farm labourer and a servant girl, MacDonald was the chief architect of the Labour Party, as leader 1911–14 and 1922–31, and as Prime Minister in 1924 and 1929–1931 (from 1931–5 he headed the National Government). He possessed to a remarkable degree the gift, as Churchill (q.v.) put it, "of compressing the largest number of words into the smallest amount of thought". But what in old age became senile waffle ("on and on and on, and up and up and up") started out as an indispensable technique of holding the party together. His magnificent baritone voice seemed to dissolve all differences; a sombre tribute to the sacrifice of thought to beauty – and necessity. The full price was paid only in 1931 when he emerged as the 'saviour' of the City of London. The whole edifice of vague theorising collapsed before the brutal logic of the bankers; and MacDonald and the party he had largely created paid for their incoherence. **R. Sk.**

'A PATTERN OF RULERS', BY LORD FRANCIS WILLIAMS (LONGMANS, 1965); 'J. RAMSAY MACDONALD', BY MRS. M. A. HAMILTON (CAPE, 1929).

Edwin McMillan (U.S., b. 1907): nuclear physicist. McMillan discovered the synthetic element called neptunium. He embarked in 1940 on the now famous series of nuclear experiments which eventually tracked down a beta-particle reaction with a peculiar half-life of only 2.3 days. In the experiments uranium (atomic number 92) was bombarded with neutrons, care being taken to prevent nuclear fission from taking place; the result was a minute quantity of this entirely new element. With its atomic number of 93, neptunium was heavier still than uranium in the league table of elements, and the first of the so-called trans-uranium elements. After working during the war on the U.S. Manhattan atomic bomb programme, McMillan turned his attention back to an earlier task of trying to build ever bigger atom-smashing machines, called cyclotrons. He successfully devised a means for keeping the beam of particles 'in step' as it accelerated round its circular path inside the cyclotron. Prior to his invention (which was also developed independently in Britain and in the Soviet Union) the accelerating particles, which became heavier as they approached the speed of light, got out of step. McMillan provided the needed synchronisation and his apparatus – the precursor of today's mighty particle accelerators – was called a synchrotron. In 1951 he shared the Nobel Prize in Chemistry with Glenn Seaborg (q.v.). **N. V.**

RAMSAY MACDONALD: PHOTOMONTAGE BY JOHN HEARTFIELD

Harold Macmillan (British, b. 1894): statesman. Macmillan, who was Prime Minister from 1957 to 1963, was an adventurer, though his nature was mild; a father-figure, though fundamentally boyish. He really hated war and poverty, having seen both at first hand. The First World War, however, gave him patriotism; the Second revealed his flair for diplomacy; while Stockton's slums rendered his patrician character paternal. A rebel, too. He burnt Chamberlain (q.v.) in effigy, introduced the Premium Bonds gamble, sacked half his Cabinet overnight, and stood, as Prime Minister, for the Oxford Chancellorship which a tamer man would have funked. Though his main policies broke in his hands (Common Market, disarmament Summit Conference, financial stability), he was right in all of them, and superbly right about Africa. He had a great gift for political in-fighting, and the stages by which he advanced to Downing Street were finely calculated. He once said that the art of politics was to make angles into curves. He said the British must act like Greeks, now that Americans are Romans. He was excellent with Presidents, Mayors and backbenchers. Though proud, he had little arrogance. The chief influences on him were Churchill (magnificence), de Gaulle (political tenacity), and Alexander (calm) (qq.v.). His chief influence was to make the Conservative Party cleverer and more humane. **N. N.**

'MEMOIRS', BY HAROLD MACMILLAN, 3 VOLUMES, (MACMILLAN, 1966, 1967, 1969); 'MEMOIRS 1940–1945', BY FIELD MARSHAL EARL ALEXANDER OF TUNIS (CASSELL, 1962); 'A THOUSAND DAYS', BY ARTHUR SCHLESINGER (ANDRE DEUTSCH, 1965).

Robert McNamara (U.S., b. 1916): statesman. Robert McNamara, greatest of United States Secretaries of Defense, personified the application of America's supreme technological capabilities to her military needs in the mid-20th century. A precocious child and an exceptional student, he entered business and later taught in the Harvard Business School. In 1946 he successfully advised the Ford motor company on its serious managerial problems. He stayed on with Ford until in 1960 he became President of the company, the first non-member of the Ford family to do so. In 1961 President Kennedy (q.v.) made him Secretary of Defense, and he continued to serve in the same capacity under President Johnson (q.v.). He had a greater impact on the Pentagon than any of his predecessors. He streamlined administration, increased cost-effectiveness, improved logistical systems, and above all did his utmost to impose real unity on the defence forces. He became closely associated with the onset and conduct of the Vietnam war, but is reputed to have had earlier doubts about its wisdom than some of his colleagues. In April 1968 he characteristically began a new career as President of the World Bank by instituting a fundamental review of its purpose and activities. **H. C. A.**

'THE ESSENCE OF SECURITY: REFLECTIONS IN OFFICE', BY ROBERT MCNAMARA (HARPER AND ROW, NEW YORK, 1968); 'THE PENTAGON', BY C. R. MOLLENHOFF (PUTMAN, NEW YORK, 1967); 'THE MCNAMARA STRATEGY', BY W. W. KAUFMAN (HARPER AND ROW, NEW YORK, 1964).

René Magritte (Belgian, 1898–1967): painter. In his work, as in life, Magritte had a look of extreme circumspection. Where the other Surrealists created scandal wherever they went, Magritte was outwardly inconspicuous: 'news' could not be made of his villa in a side-street in Brussels, his ideal

marriage, his easel in a small upper room, his close-knit circle of writer-friends, his unvarying Pomeranian dog. Believing with Breton (q.v.) that "Beauty must be convulsive", the other Surrealists went all out for nightmare in their work, piling strangeness on strangeness in search of a total dislocation of 'reality'. Magritte left things as they were, with just one pointful exception: a stone bird aloft in a fleecy sky, a tuba haloed with flame on the seashore, a cloud couchant on the grass. Like his favourite, Edgar Allan Poe, he was a master of mystery and the unexpected. But he was also a philosopher who gave the key to his work as early as 1929 when he wrote that "An object never fulfils the same function as its name or its image". Out of this proposition came some of the most haunting images which painting has lately had to show. **J. R.**

'MAGRITTE', BY DAVID SYLVESTER (ARTS COUNCIL CATALOGUE, 1969).

Gustav Mahler (Austrian, 1860–1911): composer, conductor. "The future's contemporary", Kurt Blankopf calls him in a recent biography – a happy phrase, since Mahler's influence stretches right across the 20th-century scene. Shostakovich and Britten acknowledge their indebtedness to him, as did Schoenberg, Berg, and Webern – and as indeed does Stockhausen (qq.v.). Mahler was a truth-seeker rather than a beauty-seeker, preferring the sharp contrasts of quasi-chamber-musical textures, even in a large orchestra, to merely mellifluous orchestral blends; and intense thematicism to mere atmosphere. He was a seer, a hearer: what he heard was what Schoenberg came to call "the emancipation of the disson-

ance". With *The Song of the Earth* and Deryck Cooke's magnificent 'performing edition' of the sketched-out *Tenth Symphony*, there are 11 large-scale symphonies, in addition to song-cycles, songs, and an early cantata. During his decade at the Vienna Court Opera (1897–1907), he revolutionised opera production; passionately anti-routine, his conducting was an inspiration to those who could take it – i.e. to all outstanding musicians. He would do one thing at rehearsal, another in performance: "I don't rehearse in order to fix," he told the Vienna Philharmonic, "but in order to familiarise you with my conducting." **H. K.**

'GUSTAV MAHLER: THE EARLY YEARS', BY DONALD MITCHELL (ROCKLIFF, 1958); 'GUSTAV MAHLER', BY BRUNO WALTER, TRANSLATED BY LOTTE WALTER LINDT (HAMISH HAMILTON, 1958); 'GUSTAV MAHLER: MEMORIES AND LETTERS', BY ALMA MAHLER, ED. D. MITCHELL, TRANS. B. CREIGHTON (JOHN MURRAY, 1968).

Archbishop Makarios (Cypriot, b. 1913): statesman. His Beatitude Archbishop Makarios is the spiritual head of the Cypriot Church, and President Makarios is the first elected head of State of the Republic of Cyprus. As the church is the richest body in Cyprus, Makarios also controls personally the finances of the island. Thus Michael, a poor farmer's son, is now nearer to

absolute monarchy than most of this world's kings or dictators. Makarios wears priest's robes at all times, but lives more like a politician and a businessman, receiving visitors from early morning till late at night, always available to simple people and important personalities alike. This combination of churchman, politician, diplomat, financier, and guerrilla fighter has produced an enigmatic figure, and Makarios' black robes and black beard remind most people more of a demoniac image than of a Christian one. Makarios was the key figure during Cyprus's recent tormented years. But the highlight of his career remains the plebiscite – held at his suggestion – of January 1950, when 97 per cent. of the Greek population voted in favour of Union with Greece and his dream of 'Enosis' electrified the island. Since then the realisation of 'Enosis' has not progressed, but it has taken root, and is bound to influence the future of this essentially Greek island. **H. V.**

Bernard Malamud (U.S., b. 1914): novelist. The characters in Malamud's novels range from a baseball player to a Jew accused of ritual murder in Tsarist Russia, but they all have to endure a similar crisis of the spirit. They all think they can deny history, avoid involvement with other people, and seek out a 'new life' based on the wishes of the self. Their desire for a historical freedom is a very American one, but in every case they run into obstacles and find themselves imprisoned in unexpected ways. What they have to learn is that to be born is to be born into history, and they can only find a 'new life' when they recognise their involvement with, and responsibility for, other people. Through suffering they learn the need to transcend their earlier self-preoccupation. Malamud's beautifully wrought novels are all subtly shaped to illuminate this basic pattern. In his most famous, *The Fixer* (1966), he took the infamous facts of the Mendel Beilis case (Russia 1913) and transformed them into a positive parable about the painful coming to maturity of a man. In providing a series of authoritative fables about the necessary ordeals of maturity Malamud has contributed a new dimension of moral relevance to the American novel. **T. T.**

'CONTEMPORARY AMERICAN NOVELISTS', EDITED BY HARRY T. MOORE (SOUTHERN ILLINOIS U.P., 1964); 'AFTER ALIENATION', BY MARCUS KLEIN (MERIDIAN BOOKS, 1965).

Daniel Malan (South African, 1874–1959): politician. South Africa's first Predikant Prime Minister, Dr Malan graduated as a Doctor of Divinity from Utrecht, Holland, in 1905 and served as a Dutch Reformed Church minister in the Cape. He was appointed editor of *Die Burger* in 1915 when it became the first official newspaper of the Nationalist Party. He was a capable Minister of the Interior in the 1924 Hertzog (q.v.) Ministry, but broke with Hertzog when the latter joined a coalition with Smuts (q.v.), and went into political wilderness as leader of the 'purified' Nationalists. He came into his own in the 1940s, and as leader and principal spokesman for the *apartheid* policy narrowly defeated Smuts and Hofmeyr in the 1948 election – a victory he heralded by declaring that South Africa once more belonged to the Afrikaners. Dr Malan embodied Calvinist-theological dedication together with intense political fanaticism of a kind unique to Afrikaner-nationalism. **K. K.**

Kasimir Malevich (Russian, 1878–1935): artist. As painter, pedagogue, and polemicist Malevich was the most brilliant of the youngish men who from 1910 onwards made Moscow the artistic capital of Russia. He was convinced that a "pure, living art" would have to begin with the abolition of traditional art. A new life demanded a new art: Malevich was 40 years ahead of his time in seeing "I-beams and electricity" as important elements in that new art, and there is a ring of today about his reproach to parents who "drive their children into the pasture of what is old, and brand their young souls, as in a passport-office, with the stamp of reliability". At the same time, Malevich was a devout Christian mystic: and in his own work, after a period during which he adapted Western European idioms to old Russian folk-subjects, he turned in 1915 towards the use of the simplest possible geometrical elements in an art from which all referential matter had been removed. The purity and intensity of the paintings which resulted have still not been surpassed by later painters. **J. R.**

'ESSAYS ON ART', BY KASIMIR MALEVICH (RAPP AND WHITING, 1969); 'THE GREAT EXPERIMENT: RUSSIAN ART 1863–1922', BY C. GRAY (THAMES AND HUDSON, 1962).

Bronislaw Malinowski (British, ex-Polish, 1884–1942): anthropologist. Malinowski set new standards in field study with his

intensive and comprehensive observations of the people of the Trobriand Islands and north-west Melanesia. These studies, together with those of A. R. Radcliffe-Brown on the Andaman Islanders, formed the core of Functional Anthropology which, by looking at the institutions of a society, attempts to see what functions those institutions fulfil in the society: e.g., a myth is seen not as a rather poor and inaccurate history of past culture but as fulfilling a definite function in a present culture by, say, perpetuating and exemplifying its traditional morality and social structure. The two men differed: Radcliffe-Brown's approach was more sociological – seeking the interrelations of institutions within and between cultures; Malinowski's kept nearer to the individual viewpoint, looking at the ways in which institutions modified and satisfied individual needs. **B. R. O.**

BOOKS BY BRONISLAW MALINOWSKI: 'CRIME AND CUSTOM IN SAVAGE SOCIETY' (ROUTLEDGE AND KEGAN PAUL, 1926); 'SEX AND REPRESSION IN SAVAGE SOCIETY' (ROUTLEDGE AND KEGAN PAUL, 1927).

André Malraux (French, b. 1901): writer and politician. It is typical of Malraux that there should have been confusion over his date of birth: the year 1895 was once mentioned. Presumably such confusion could have been cleared up by Malraux himself, but perhaps he wants to be something of a myth and a legend. His many accomplishments: archaeologist and explorer; something of an adventurer (he fought on the Republi-can side during the Spanish Civil War); colonel in the French Resistance movement; author of many famous novels. His principal preoccupation since 1945 has been with the philosophy of art and with Gaullist politics – from 1958 to 1969 he was de Gaulle's (q.v.) Minister of State, with a special responsibility for cultural affairs. More recently he has been writing his memoirs. All these elements can be seen as facets of his major preoccupation: man must be made to recognise his own qualities. Through the adventure and aspiration of action he will come to know himself, through art and myth he will be able to situate himself amidst the great cultural structures. Malraux stands for a flamboyant intensity of feeling and vision: he allies the contemporary and political to the metaphysical. He moves easily from the magnificent to the ridiculous. **D. W. J. J.**

'ANTIMEMOIRS', BY ANDRE MALRAUX (HAMISH HAMILTON, 1968).

Nelson Mandela (South African, b. 1918): freedom fighter. Mandela personifies the passionate, self-sacrificing defiance of a younger generation of Africans in South Africa. A member of the African National Congress since 1944, it was in 1951, three years after the official adoption of *apartheid* by the new Afrikaner-Nationalist Government, that he became Nationalist President of the African National Congress Youth League, an organisation which he led as National Volunteer-in-Chief of the Defiance Campaign. He courted and suffered arrest for challenging racial laws and in 1962 was sentenced to five years imprisonment. Brought from Pretoria Prison to be the first accused at the Rivonia trial he has since been confined to Robben Island. From the dock Mandela launched an uncompromising attack on both white and black domination. "I have cherished the idea of a democratic and free society in which all persons live together in harmony and with equal opportunities. It is an ideal which I hope to live for and achieve. But if needs be, it is an ideal for which I am prepared to die." **K. K.**

'NO EASY WALK TO FREEDOM', BY NELSON MANDELA (HEINEMANN, LONDON, 1965).

Iuliu Maniu (Rumanian, 1873–1952): statesman. Maniu was a national leader who, once national unity was complete, found himself awkwardly cast as leader of a peasant political movement in a rapidly changing society. His political experience began in Austria-Hungary where, as a Transylvanian, he participated in the Rumanian national movement. When Austria-Hungary fell to pieces Transylvania, under Maniu's leadership, united with Rumania to form an integral national state. Maniu's nationalism grew from his belief in political liberty and social progress, and he joined his National Party with the Peasant Party to champion reform in the new state. On the advent of the Depression the National-Peasants took power, but hopes for change were soon dashed by economic blight, political extremism and diplomatic uncertainty. Maniu resigned over an affair involving the royal mistress, Madame Lupescu, and watched helplessly as Rumania drifted into dictatorship and was dismembered by foreign predators. He supported war against the Soviet Union in 1941, but three years later turned on the dictatorship and helped to bring it down. He rallied his forces to prevent the Communists from seizing power. After a brave but vain resistance he was tried and imprisoned in 1947. He was never heard from again. More bourgeois than peasant, more a patriot than a reformer, Maniu shrank from radicalism as time fast lost patience with Rumania. **J. M. K.**

'RUMANIA: POLITICAL PROBLEMS OF AN AGRARIAN STATE', BY HENRY L. ROBERTS (YALE U.P., 1951).

Thomas Mann (German, 1875–1955): novelist. Born of a patrician-middle-class Lübeck family Thomas Mann experienced the conflict between a bourgeois and an artistic temperament which became his major theme in *Buddenbrooks* (1901) – a German *Forsyte Saga* which celebrates the decadence of a solid bourgeois culture and views artistic exploration as a truancy. Yet Mann's work remains an oblique and ironic defence of basic bourgeois humanist values. Before 1914 he was conservative, inheriting the German romantic hostility to liberal democracy. But *Death in Venice* (1912) already perceives the complicity between artistic self-sufficiency and social barbarism. *The Magic Mountain* (1925) embodies Mann's post-war liberalism and develops a powerful critique of pre-war German culture as diseased. In *Joseph and his Brethren* (1933–44), Joseph, artist and dreamer, becomes a humane, Rooseveltian administrator, resolving the

artist-bourgeois dilemma – but only mythically. A Nobel Prize winner, Mann finally abandoned Germany in 1933. His last major work, *Doctor Faustus* (1947), returns to the Faustian myth and the Goethean standards implicit throughout his work. Its hero is the modern artist as a Faustian figure doomed to isolation and madness. Mann reveals Fascism through this work as the final stage of the disease of German culture. His insight into the contradictions of that culture redeems his intellectual preciosity which is its product. He now has classic status and no influence. **G. P.**

'ESSAYS ON THOMAS MANN', BY GEORG LUKACS (MERLIN PRESS, 1964); 'THE DIS-INHERITED MIND', BY ERICH HELLER (BOWES AND BOWES, 1959).

Manolete (Spanish, 1917–1947): bullfighter. Manuel Rodriguez Sanchez the man became Mano-

lete the legend within 10 years. He was born in Córdoba where his proud fellow citizens have erected a statue to his memory. His special claim to fame was the elaborate and dangerous pass now known as the *manoletina*, itself a development of the *orteguina* created by his famous forerunner Ortega. But, although he was a great favourite of the crowds, his reputation is now in doubt. Manolete came to maturity during the Civil War when finely-bred bulls were scarce. By 1939, when he was at the peak of his career, many of the great herds had been slaughtered – for food or for partisan revenge. It was easy, his critics now say, to be brave and graceful before such lightweight bulls: but how would he have performed before the most powerful toros? Manolete died a bullfighter's death at Linares in 1947 before his critics could know the answer. **A. B. R.**

'MANOLETE', BY FRANCISCO NARBONA (EDICIONES ESPEJO, MADRID, 1948); 'BULL FEVER', BY KENNETH TYNAN (LONGMANS, 1955); 'THE BULLS OF IBERIA', BY ANGUS MACNAB (HEINEMANN, 1957).

Sicco Mansholt (Dutch, b. 1908): administrator. As first European Minister of Agriculture, Sicco Mansholt has been one of the boldest and most intelligent Eurocrats. His earthy vitality and inspired administration have endowed the EEC Commission with both political force and intellectual authority. A farmer and a Socialist, Mansholt was Dutch Minister of Agriculture in successive governments. Playing a central role in the establishment of the Benelux customs union in the Fifties, he was an early partisan of a

federal Europe and Walter Hallstein's champion in his quarrel with de Gaulle (qq.v.) over the authority of the Community. As Vice-President of the EEC Commission since 1958 Mansholt has continuously pressed for the adoption of a common agricultural policy as devised in a price-regulation plan drawn up by himself. After great wrangling a modified form of his plan came into force in 1967 and has been the source of much bad feeling among small producers in France ever since. Mansholt's self-confessed aim is to encourage the larger farm with fewer workers and to reduce prices to accelerate the already marked drift from the land. A farmer who has never lost touch with his roots, Mansholt is not only committed to making the Common Market live up to its name but to presiding over the extinction of the European peasant. **S. S.**

'THE NEW EUROPEANS', BY ANTHONY SAMPSON (HODDER, 1968); 'EUROPEAN UNIFICATION IN THE SIXTIES', BY MIRIAM CAMPS (O.U.P., 1967).

PAINTING OF MAO TSE-TUNG BY BURTON SILVERMAN

Mao Tse-tung (Chinese, b. 1893): statesman. No other man in history has led two great revolutions and triumphed in both. No Communist has waged an inner-party struggle outside the party and won. A personality cult has grown up around Mao, the like of which the world has not known since the Christianisation of Europe. His little red book has reached the fantastic circulation of over 800 million copies, outstripping even the Bible. Mao's first revolution from 1927 to 1949 was a grim struggle against the Nationalist Party, which in his eyes represented the imperialist and feudal domination of China. Again from 1949 to 1966, during China's transition from new democracy to Socialism, he found himself in opposition to other party leaders. But he had his way in 1955 by successfully launching the agrarian socialisation and in 1958 the Great Leap Forward. The culmination of this was the Cultural Revolution. In both revolutions Mao depended on the armed forces and the masses. He substituted the peasantry for the proletariat as the popular basis of his revolution, thus replacing an almost fictitious class by a real one. So instead of urban uprisings towards the seizure of power, the revolutionaries now fought from the countryside to the cities. Such a process proved to be protracted: hence the need to arouse and sustain the zeal of the masses. Relying more on China's inexhaustible manpower than on technology, he has to work through political indoctrination rather than improving the mode of production in classical Marxian terms. As soon as this work slackens his scheme is to start the revolutionary process all over again. These waves of revolution, he hopes, will lead China to a better life. **J..C.**

'MAO TSE-TUNG', BY S. R. SCHRAM (REVISED EDITION, ALLEN LANE AND PENGUIN, 1967); 'MAO AND THE CHINESE REVOLUTION' BY JEROME CH'EN (O.U.P., 1967); 'MAO', BY J. CH'EN (PRENTICE-HALL, 1969).

Guglielmo Marconi (Italian, 1874–1937): engineer. If there is one name synonymous with wireless it is Marconi. Following some early work in his native Bologna Marconi came to England in 1896, and in 1901 made history. On a beach at Poldhu in Cornwall a team of Marconi's men operated a crude wireless transmitter sending the letter S in code. On the other side of the Atlantic, at Signal Hill, St John's, in Newfoundland, Marconi and his assistants sat round an equally crude receiver, using an aerial flown by a kite. The signal came through – and again, and again. The Atlantic had been bridged by wireless – and this was before the days of valves and amplification. The experts who knew that radio waves travelled in straight lines were confounded. (The various layers of charged particles that girdle the earth and 'bend' the waves by reflection round it were soon postulated, but it was more than 20 years before they yielded up their secrets.) Ship-to-shore communication now became operational and in 1907 a public service for wireless messages was opened between England and Canada. World fame and honours from both Britain and Italy were showered upon Marconi, who continued with his experiments until just before his death. **P. O. W.**

'MY FATHER MARCONI', BY D. MARCONI (FREDERICK MULLER, 1962); 'FROM MARCONI TO TELSTAR', BY N. WYMER (LONGMANS, 1966); 'RADIO COMMUNICATION: HISTORY AND DEVELOPMENT', A SCIENCE MUSEUM HANDBOOK (HMSO, 1934).

Filippo Marinetti (Italian, 1876–1944): writer. The first Futurist Manifesto (February 20, 1909) sums up the essentials of Marinetti's doctrine. It asserts that "a racing automobile is more beautiful than the Victory of Samothrace", and that war is "the only cure for the world". It mixes stock Italian nationalism with the doctrines of Nietzsche. But there remain a number of important insights, which were elaborated in further tracts. For example, Marinetti's obsession with 'dynamism' and 'simultaneity' led him to recognise the possibility of multi-media art-forms, though often neither the talent nor the technical means were available to put his theories into practice. Futurist painting seems less remarkable than the ideas which prompted it. Even more disappointing are Marinetti's own literary experiments, the "*parole in libertà*", or "words set at liberty". A tireless self-publicist, and a strangely fascinating mixture of prophet and charlatan, Marinetti became world-famous between 1909 and 1914. The war snuffed out his influence on the arts, and he moved into the orbit of Mussolini (q.v.). He died forgotten in 1944, still stubbornly faithful to Fascism. Strangely enough, today's avant-garde now seems intent on carrying out the programme Marinetti outlined, and current modernism proclaims Futurist ideas, without, apparently, knowing their source. **E. L.-S.**

'INTELLECTUALS IN POLITICS', BY J. JOLL (WEIDENFELD AND NICOLSON, 1960); 'FUTURIST ART AND THEORY', BY M. W. MARTIN (O.U.P., 1968).

Jacques Maritain (French, b. 1882): philosopher. Maritain is felt by some, especially Roman Catholics, to be the greatest philosopher in Christendom. Yet others tend to see him as occupying a philosophical backwater and feel that, at best, his influence is as a source of irritation which arises from his failure to consider alternative viewpoints seriously. Maritain was unsatisfied with natural science lectures at the Sorbonne, so he and his future wife attended lectures by Bergson (q.v.), whose Vitalistic philosophy "liberated their sense of the absolute". Bergson postulated an original life-force, *élan vital,* that is above individuals and passes from one genera-

tion to another. This reality above individuals was to be for Maritain the way from the natural sciences to scholastic realism; this is the theory that abstract terms have greater objective reality than physical particulars, e.g. the concept 'circle' is more 'real' than a real penny. Maritain was married in 1904 and he and his wife were converted to Catholicism in 1906. He has become perhaps the best known apologist for the philosophy of Thomas Aquinas whose theories he advocates with forcefulness and clarity. By those who do not share his views he is sometimes seen as a dogmatist refurbishing Thomistic doctrine. He has however been a source of consolation to many Catholics. **B. R. O.**

'DISTINGUISH TO UNITE OR THE DEGREES OF KNOWLEDGE', BY JACQUES MARITAIN (BLES, 1959).

Lord Marks (British, 1888–1964): retailer. Simon Marks transformed a small business that started out as a penny bazaar in the market at Leeds ("Don't ask the price, it's a penny") into one of Britain's largest and most profitable retail chains. But by concentrating on quality, which he achieved by a rigid and detailed control of his suppliers, he revolutionised the

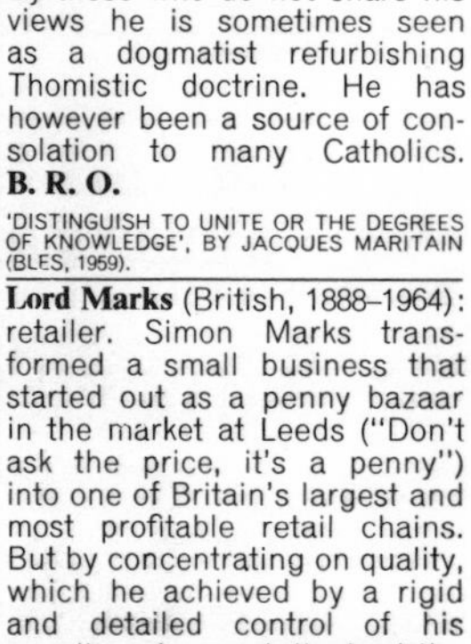

cheaper end of the clothing business and with it much of the textile industry. He offered goods that were so universally acceptable that Marks and Spencer has come to be regarded as much an agent of social change as it is a business. Much of Lord Marks's success stemmed from the extraordinarily close relationship he built up over some 60 years with his brother-in-law, Lord Sieff. The two men, who grew up together in Manchester, went to the same school and married each other's sisters, developed together many of the firm's most admired innovations; one such was Operation Simplification, a cost-saving exercise which resulted in the abolition of some 26 million pieces of paper a year. **S. P. A.**

'ST. MICHAEL, A HISTORY OF MARKS AND SPENCER', BY GORONWY REES (WEIDENFELD AND NICOLSON, 1969).

George C. Marshall (U.S., 1880–1959): soldier, administrator. On September 1, 1939, Marshall became Chief-of-Staff of the U.S. army and air corps. The forces in his domain amounted to fewer than 200,000 men. He himself was almost unknown in the world at large. Yet six years later his American army numbered over eight million. As chairman of the joint chiefs of staff he had earned the respect of everyone with whom he laboured at the arduous task of organising global coalition war. During the next decade, as President Truman's (q.v.) Secretary of State (1947–1949) and Secretary of Defense (1950–51), he became world-famous as architect of the Marshall Plan – the means by which American dollars were transfused into a battered post-war Europe. Marshall had fought for victory; now he fought for economic and social reconstruction, but he remained as austerely enigmatic as ever. Unlike other Service chiefs he declined to write his memoirs or engage in controversy: his integrity was as rare as George Washington's. Marshall did almost as much to shape our world as a Churchill or a Roosevelt – yet he went about his work with a supreme talent for anonymity. **M. F. C.**

'GEORGE C. MARSHALL', BY FORREST C. POGUE, 2 VOLS., (VIKING, NEW YORK, 1963 AND 1965); 'MEMOIRS', BY HARRY S. TRUMAN, 2 VOLS. (DOUBLEDAY, N. Y., 1958).

Sir Leslie Martin (British, b. 1908); **Sir Robert Matthew** (British, b. 1906): architects. The postwar Architects to the London County Council (Matthew 1946–53; Martin [below] 1953–6, after being Deputy Architect 1948–53), built up an architectural organisation without parallel in the world for both quantity and quality. It was in effect the culmination of Gropius's (q.v.)

Bauhaus teaching: vast housing estates (Alton East at Roehampton, begun 1952) and comprehensive schools (their best is Tulse Hill, 1955) were designed anonymously by inter-professional teams, committed to humane social ideals. The department also gave Europe the first major public building in the modern manner, the Royal Festival Hall (1949–51). Changes in taste gradually made necessary a more personal architecture and this the LCC was also able to foster, for Martin attracted bright assistants for the Alton West estate, Roehampton (1955–9). The succeeding Greater London Council's Architect's Department, under Hubert Bennett, remained an international leader in town planning (Thamesmead, begun 1967), just as the associated Inner London Education Authority has pioneered primary schools (Vittoria, Islington, 1966–8). Matthew, former Professor of Architecture at Edinburgh, now runs a firm with a similar sense of teamwork (University of York, begun 1963; University of Bath, begun 1966; Central Lancashire New City, planned 1966–9); while Martin, Professor of Architecture at Cambridge, reflects his stronger individuality in Harvey Court, Cambridge (1961–3), and St Cross Building, Oxford (1962–4). **N. J. W. T.**

The Marx Brothers (U.S.): film actors. The sons of German-Jewish immigrant parents, Chico (1891–1961), Harpo (1893–1964), Groucho (b. 1895) and Zeppo (b. 1901) developed their comic craft from childhood, first in the hard school of vaudeville, then on Broadway, from which they entered movies as established stage stars with the coming of sound. Individually immensely gifted, the Marx Brothers were always at their best as a team, though they failed miserably in their two post-war team efforts. Their five films for Paramount (1929–33), after which Zeppo departed, were cruder and more abandoned than their five smoother, somewhat over-produced pictures for M.G.M. (1935–41); but these highlights of their career all revealed a unique ability to combine the rough knockabout slapstick of vaudeville with a sophisticated wisecracking and a near-surrealist verbal and visual sense. Thus they produced a sustained anarchic comic vision directed against all forms of social and intellectual pretension, Cinematically their influential movies provided a bridge between silent comedy and more recent developments; socially their pictures, from *The Cocoanuts* (1929) to *The Big Store* (1941), are a permanent part of the cultural history of the Thirties. **P. N. F.**

'THE MARX BROTHERS AT THE MOVIES', BY PAUL D. ZIMMERMAN AND BURT GOLDBLATT (PUTNAM, N.Y., 1969); 'THE MARX BROTHERS: THEIR WORLD OF COMEDY', BY ALLEN EYLES (ZWEMMER, 1966); 'GROUCHO AND ME', BY GROUCHO MARX (GOLLANCZ, 1959); 'HARPO SPEAKS', BY HARPO MARX (GOLLANCZ, 1961).

Thomas Masaryk (Czech, 1850–1937): statesman. Masaryk is remembered as the founder of Czech and Slovak independence and as an outstanding political and social theorist. The son of a Moravian coachman,

he became a professor at Prague University, and was known before the First World War as a philosopher and sociologist, a Czech political leader, a member of the Austrian Parliament and a spokesman of the South Slav cause in the Habsburg Monarchy. He won a reputation as a fearless defender of the truth by his public exposure of forged historical documents used by extreme Czech nationalists, by his defence of a Jew falsely accused of ritual murder, and by his support of Serbs and Croats accused of treason by the

Austrian authorities on the basis of false evidence. In 1915 Masaryk left Austria to lead the political movement for the independence of Bohemia and the unification of Czechs and Slovaks in one state. This action took him in turn to Italy, France, Britain, Russia and the United States, before returning to his liberated country as the first President of Czechoslovakia at the end of 1918. He remained President until his retirement in 1935, one of those rare people who successfully combine an academic and a political career. **H. S.-W.**

'THE MAKING OF A STATE', BY THOMAS MASARYK (ALLEN AND UNWIN, 1927); 'PRESIDENT MASARYK TELLS HIS STORY', RECOUNTED BY KAREL CAPEK (ALLEN AND UNWIN, 1934); 'HISTORY OF THE CZECHS AND SLOVAKS', BY R. W. SETON-WATSON (HUTCHINSON, 1943).

Mata Hari (Dutch, 1876–1917): dancer, stripper, whore and incompetent beautiful spy (overleaf). Born Margaretha Geertruida Zelle, a Dutch merchant's daughter, she married, at 18, a Dutch army officer of Scots descent. She abandoned him, changed her name to Mata Hari (Eye of the Day) and grew famous as a courtesan and exotic dancer; she claimed Oriental birth and education by Buddhist monks. In France in the First World War she was in the pay of both French and German Intelligence: little evidence exists that either side profited much by her services although her admirers claim she caused the deaths of 70,000 Allied troops and prolonged the war by six months. In 1917 the French tried her on eight spying charges and, in a tide of anti-espionage hysteria, she was shot. She became the 20th-century prototype for dangerous women: a model for all *femmes fatales* in silent films. **P. N.**

'BEWITCHING WOMEN', BY BARBARA CARTLAND (FREDERICK MULLER, 1955); 'MATA HARI', BY MAJOR THOMAS COULSON (HUTCHINSON, 1930); 'THE STORY OF THE SECRET SERVICE', BY R. W. ROWAN (MILES, 1938).

Henri Matisse (French, 1869–1954): painter. Matisse for much of his life was regarded as the poet laureate of bourgeois fulfilment. People knew him primarily for the work of the Twenties and Thirties in which beautiful women lay around half-dressed in rooms shuttered against the Southern sun. They were delicious paintings: monuments to the insouciance of the Third Republic. But they typed Matisse, quite unfairly, as the Boucher or Fragonard of his day. Matisse was, on the contrary, as radical an artist as any in this century, Picasso (q.v.) not excepted. Starting with an initial gift apparently no more

than modest, he was a late and slow developer; but any estimate of him must come to terms with Matisse the revolutionary colourist (1905), Matisse the master of a spare, monumental art (1909–10), Matisse the re-inventor of the human form (1916–1917), Matisse the wall-decorator on the scale of Veronese, Matisse the sculptor, Matisse the creator (in the Vence chapel) of an ideal space permeated by immaterial colour and, finally, Matisse the bed-ridden ancient of the early 1950s who carried the whole art of painting into a new era of its existence by cutting with shears into huge sheets of coloured paper. (For this, see *L'Escargot* in the Tate Gallery.) No man in this century has contributed more to the renewal of painting. **J. R.**

'MATISSE, HIS ART AND HIS PUBLIC', BY A. H. BARR (F. CASS, 1966); 'MATISSE', BY A. BOWNESS (FONTANA, 1968); 'MATISSE', BY F. BRILL (HAMLYN, 1967).

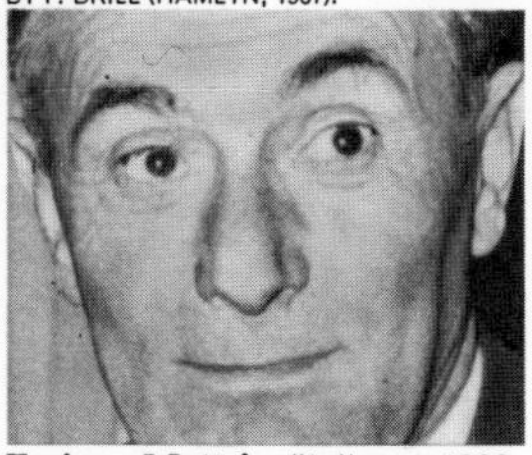

Enrico Mattei (Italian, 1906–1962): tycoon. Mattei was one of the most potent of the post-war economic myth-makers; the dedicated State executive beating Big Business at its own game; the anti-bureaucrat who gets things done and the patriot who challenged the international oil companies. He ended the war organising the North Italian partisans; then became Commissar to the ex-Fascist Azienda Nazionale Italiana Petroli (AGIP, whose six-legged dog sign now surmounts one in four Italian petrol stations). Vaguely ordered to run the thing down, he pressed on instead with the search for natural gas in the Po Valley, bulldozed through a major pipelaying programme, garnered massive publicity, and in 1949 found oil at a village called Cortemaggiore. There wasn't much of it – most of what is sold as "*Cortemaggiore la potente benzina Italiana*" was and is refined from imported crude oil – but it was enough. Mattei wheeled and dealed to keep control of the Po Valley gas, persuaded the Government to make him head of the ENI organisation set up to run the whole Italian oil industry, and set off on the chain of overseas moves – Iran, Egypt, Morocco, and Central Europe – which made him the main thorn in the flesh of the Big Seven international oil companies. He died, in a private plane crash, at the height of his career. **P. W.**

'MATTEI: OIL AND POWER POLITICS', BY P. H. FRANKEL (FABER, 1966).

Stanley Matthews (British, b. 1915): footballer. The idol of soccer fans everywhere for more than a quarter of a century, holder of 56 caps for England – no other player of his day created an atmosphere like Matthews. For the crowd on the terraces it was his ball control, his unique body swerve, his sudden acceleration and his accurate passes. For his opponents it was how to stop Stan. To the public, whether soccer fan or no, Stan's Cup Winner's medal (with Blackpool) in 1953, like Gordon Richards's (q.v.) Derby, satisfied a national aspiration. But to the Potteries, the skinny barber's son was simply 'Our Stan'. So alarmed were they by rumours in 1938 that he was leaving Stoke City that they packed the Town Hall to urge him to stay. He beat Billy Meredith's record for longevity on the field by turning out for Stoke after his fiftieth birthday – the result of total dedication to fitness. But in these days of soccer rowdies, Matthews will be remembered for his sportsmanship. Not one caution did he receive during his 33 years as a player; not once did he demur at the referee's decision. So it was fitting that he should be soccer's first, and so far only, player-knight. **E. M. V. R.**

'THE STANLEY MATTHEWS STORY', BY STANLEY MATTHEWS (OLDBOURNE PRESS, 1960); 'MASTERS OF SOCCER', BY T. DELANEY AND M. EDELSTON (NALDRETT PRESS, 1960); 'SOCCER: THE GREAT ONES', ED. BY JOHN ARLOTT (PELHAM BOOKS, 1968).

Charles Maurras (French, 1868–1952): writer. The revolutionary tradition in France upholds the belief that government can change things for the better. Since the beginning of the century Maurras' name has stood for counter-revolution. In 1898 it was discovered that some of the documents produced to help convict Dreyfus, a Jewish officer, at his trial for treason four years earlier had been forged. Maurras said it did not matter. The safety and unity of France could not be imperilled in the name of justice; justice could not exist without the State;

those who committed the forgeries were patriots. From this time onwards Maurras was a prolific, lucid and violent writer. He attacked those whom he saw as France's enemies: Protestants, Jews, Freemasons, Republicans, Socialists. He fiercely championed tradition, monarchy, religion, the old civilisation and the old stability. His prime concern was to analyse and denounce the decadence of France. In 1940, the defeat of the Republic seemed the opportunity for his counter-revolution. Yet in 1945 he was convicted of collaboration with the Germans and he was in prison until shortly before his death. He demonstrated the fragility of liberalism and his spectacular prose gave new force to traditional conservatism. **D. W. J. J.**

'THREE FACES OF FASCISM', BY ERNST NOLTE (WEIDENFELD AND NICOLSON, 1965); 'FRANCE AND THE DREYFUS AFFAIR', BY DOUGLAS JOHNSON (BLANDFORD PRESS, 1966).

Vladimir Mayakovsky (Russian, 1893–1930): poet and playwright. From his poetic debut in 1913 as a member of the Russian Futurist group, Mayakovsky startled the public with the novelty of his verse and the flamboyance of his appearance. His early poems – *A Cloud in Trousers* and *Backbone-Flute* – combine personal anguish with a violent protest against contemporary life. A revolutionary – several times imprisoned since youth – he saw

in the events of 1917 a solution to his own problems and to those of society. In post-revolutionary work he attempted to create a new art – "an art that will pull the republic out of the mud" – to correspond to the new political order. An optimistic view of the new life – in the poems *150,000,000* and *Okay!* – is tempered by satire in the dramas *The Bed-bug* and *The Bath-house*. In 1930, harassed by literary opponents and beset by personal anxieties, he shot himself. Possibly the greatest revolutionary poet of the 20th century, Mayakovsky wrote in a completely new idiom: his verse is demotic and declamatory, dazzlingly brilliant in technique, and juxtaposes farce and tragedy, realism and fantasy. It had a profound influence on contemporaries, such as Pasternak (q.v.) and Aseev. His style has been taken up in recent years by poets such as Yevtushenko and Voznesensky. **T. J. B.**

'MAYAKOVSKY', BY HERBERT MARSHALL (DOBSON, 1965); 'FROM GORKY TO PASTERNAK', BY HELEN MUCHNIC (METHUEN, 1963); 'THE CREATIVE EXPERIMENT', BY C. M. BOWRA (MACMILLAN, 1949).

Louis B. Mayer (U.S., 1885–1957): film producer. Mayer's career and personality make him the virtual archetype of the Hollywood mogul. Born in Russia, he came to North America in the 1890s with his poor Jewish parents and worked as a scrap-dealer until opening his first cinema in 1907. He entered film-making during The First World War and in 1924 became production head of Metro-Goldwyn-Mayer on the merger of his company with the Metro and Goldwyn concerns. From then until 1951 the short, plump, capricious Mayer ruled the M.G.M. lot as if it were his personal kingdom, and became the highest salaried individual in America. Much of the company's enormous success was established by his chief lieutenant, Irving Thalberg, but Mayer had a considerable eye for star material (he brought Garbo [q.v.], Greer Garson and Hedy Lamarr to America) and an instinct for what would appeal to a mass world-wide audience. His extreme Right-wing views, philistinism, arbitrary behaviour, vicious temper, lecherous conduct and vengeful nature made the deeply insecure Mayer both hated and feared, though many people managed to form a satisfactory working relationship with him. Like Columbia's Harry Cohn and the Warner Brothers, Mayer was essentially a product of his thrusting immigrant generation: and he belonged to the 'big studio' era of American film production that had more or less vanished by the time of his death. **P. N. F.**

'HOLLYWOOD RAJAH', BY BOSLEY CROWTHER (HOLT, RINEHART AND WINSTON, N.Y., 1960); 'PICTURE', BY LILLIAN ROSS (GOLLANCZ, 1952); 'THE MOVIE MOGULS', BY PHILIP FRENCH (WEIDENFELD AND NICOLSON, 1969).

Margaret Mead (U.S., b. 1901): anthropologist. Margaret Mead has managed to popularise what is still, to many, an obscure discipline – her early study, *Coming of Age in Samoa*, was a best-seller. A central theme in her work is that the modern

world can learn much from other societies. By emphasising comparative techniques she is at the same time stressing the need for a common base-line for making comparisons. She has used psychoanalytical models, patterns of physical maturation and other biological norms for this base-line. Her approach is thus multi-disciplinary – e.g. her looking to psychology to help unravel facts about a culture is shown in her photographic study, with Gregory Bateson (q.v.), of Balinese children. Her work during and after the war gave a more central position to advanced societies and the way they change. More recently, her emphasis on the uniformity of modern society and the need to capitalise on any of its natural differences (see *Male and Female*) has led back to an interest in the fundamental biological base-lines, especially patterns determined by evolution, and predictably to the application of these findings to contemporary living. Her importance to the 20th century is that she makes us aware of the cost of progress in terms of losses to culture. **B. R. O.**

BOOKS BY MARGARET MEAD: 'COMING OF AGE IN SAMOA' (PENGUIN, 1944); 'MALE AND FEMALE' (GOLLANCZ, 1949); 'ANTHROPOLOGY: A HUMAN SCIENCE' (VAN NOSTRAND, PRINCETON, N. J., 1964).

Sir Peter Medawar (British, b. 1915): biologist and medical scientist. Whatever the ethics involved, safely transplanting hearts, kidneys and other organs depends on a much deeper understanding of the immunological reactions concerned. Peter Medawar shared the 1960 Nobel prize in medicine with F. M. Burnet (q.v.) for his proof of Burnet's theory that the body can be made – under certain conditions – to accept a transplant of foreign tissue. Immunological tolerance exists when the body allows foreign cells to live.

Medawar showed that the immune mechanism is not hereditary but develops slowly through foetal life, and that foreign cells introduced into the organism early enough in development would be accepted just as the body's own cells are. Later on, when more foreign cells from

the same source were introduced, the body would treat them as 'self components' and not reject them. The concept of actively acquired tolerance was formulated: its discovery meant that the problem of using homografts (grafts from the same species) was soluble in principle. **P. G. R.**

'THE UNIQUENESS OF THE INDIVIDUAL', BY P. B. MEDAWAR (METHUEN, 1957); 'THE FUTURE OF MAN', BY P. B. MEDAWAR (METHUEN, 1960).

Golda Meir (Israeli, ex-Russian, b. 1898): head of state. By the time she was eight Golda Mabowehz, as she was born, had moved first from the Ukraine to White Russia and thence to the U.S. She arrived in Palestine in 1921, three years after her marriage; from then on her life was one of total service to the Jewish community there. She raised poultry at a *kibbutz*, became a delegate to the Histadrut

Labour Federation, was a founding member of Mapai, the Israel Labour Party, worked for and ran Jewish women's organisations and played a major role in the Zionist struggle to secure the independent State of Israel in 1948. She was Israel's Minister of Labour from 1949 to 1956, and Minister for Foreign Affairs from 1956 to 1965. Then she became Secretary-General of Mapai and the right-hand of Prime Minister Eshkol, retiring in 1968 because of ill-health. She came back as Prime Minister, as compromise candidate, in March 1969, after Eshkol's death, rallying to her the two political young lions, Defence Minister Moshe Dayan

and Deputy Prime Minister Yigal Allon. Mrs Meir is both mother figure and iron disciplinarian, warm-hearted but level-headed and supremely efficient. Israel's Grand Old Man, Ben Gurion (q.v.), called her "the only man in my Cabinet". In 1947–48 she held secret talks with King Abdullah of Jordan (q.v.) to try to maintain

peace with him; she says she would talk with any Arab leader now, to break the deadlock. Mrs Meir is always formidable, but always human. **T. C. F. P.**

Lise Meitner (Swedish, ex-Austrian, 1878–1968): physicist. With her nephew Otto Frisch she was one of the first to give the correct explanation of the experiments of Otto Hahn (q.v.) and Fritz Strassmann when they discovered nuclear fission. Lise Meitner took her doctorate in Vienna, but subsequently went to work with Max Planck (q.v.) in Berlin and collaborated with Hahn in studies of radioactive decay. In 1917 she became head of the physics department of

the Kaiser Wilhelm Institute for Chemistry, but in 1938 fled to Stockholm. The following year Otto Hahn wrote to her of his experiments in bombarding uranium with neutrons. He had found the element barium among the products. Meitner and Frisch immediately realised that a new kind of nuclear reaction was taking place in which the uranium atoms were split into two approximatley equal parts. This discovery, nuclear fission, came at a crucial moment, just before the Second World War. It was quickly seized upon by Enrico Fermi (q.v.) who appreciated that a chain reaction was possible, so leading directly to atomic energy and the atom bomb. Lise Meitner thus played one of the chief roles in the birth of the nuclear age. **P. H. S. S.**

'THE WORLD OF THE ATOM', ED. H. A. BOORSE AND L. MOTZ (BASIC BOOKS, 1966).

Nellie Melba (Australian, 1861–1931): soprano. Immortalised in pêche Melba and Melba toast, the real Melba reigned at Covent Garden from her début there in 1888 until after the First World War. In an age of brilliant singers trained to a high pitch of technical skill, her powers were everywhere recognised as supreme. Her attack was amazing. ("she

opened her mouth", it was said, "and a tone was in existence"); her trills and staccato notes were as accurate as if played on a keyboard; her sustained singing as pure and smooth over more than two octaves as the line of a great violinist. Though an undistinguished actress and linguist, she made herself into an excellent musician. She made her name in such brilliant roles as Gilda, Lucia di Lammermoor and Ophélie in Thomas's *Hamlet*, and in the transitional parts of Violetta, Juliette and Marguerite; her later triumphs were mainly in the more lyrical music of Desdemona and Mimi. The pure tone and brilliant finish of her singing are evident in the many gramophone records which she made between 1904 and 1926, when live recordings from her Covent Garden farewell performance displayed the lasting freshness and purity of the voice at 65. In private life she was an able, amusing, downright, free-spoken woman, who made some professional enemies but was welcomed in the highest society. **D. S.-T.**

'MELBA', BY JOHN HETHERINGTON (FABER, 1967).

Georges Méliès (French, 1861–1938): film director. Director of the Théâtre Robert-Houdin and one of the great stage musicians, Méliès saw the Lumière Cinématographe in 1895, recognised it as a valuable addition to his theatre, and at once invented his own movie camera and began to make films. The earliest film-maker to perceive clearly that the cinema was a theatrical and spectacular form and not simply a scientific novelty, Méliès built the world's first studio and was the first artist consistently to stage his films with scenarios, decors, costumes, actors. He applied the apparatus of a resourceful stage magician to the problems of the cinema, and thus rapidly developed the whole range of camera techniques. No-one has ever deployed trick techniques such as superimposition, substitution and stop action with

greater ingenuity or accomplishment. An able graphic artist, Méliès gave his films, such as *Voyage to the Moon* (1902), *20,000 Leagues under the Sea* (1907) and *Conquest of the Pole* (1912), a personal and unique decorative style that derived from, yet metamorphosed, the stagings of 19th-century spectacle theatres – at once primitive, sophisticated, childlike and surreal. Ultimately ruined by inability to keep up with fashions, by competition and piracy and by his refusal to make economies that would compromise his own work, Méliès had ceased to produce by the time of the First World War. He was the cinema's first conscious artist and is certainly the earliest film-maker whose work survives today on its own terms. **D. R.**

Pierre Mendès-France (French, b. 1907): statesman. A political whiz-kid before the War and the youngest minister in Blum's (q.v.) Popular Front Government,

Mendès-France began a career committed to reconciling Socialist idealism with practical administration in dashing style. During the War, he joined the Free French forces in London and was summoned to Algiers by General de Gaulle (q.v.) in 1943 to join the provisional government. He became Economics Minister in 1944, and began a sweeping nationalisation of the leading sectors of French industry, but resigned in April 1945 when his austerity plans were rejected by General de Gaulle. In limbo as the Director of the International Monetary Fund for 11 years, Mendès-France remained the one great politician untarnished by the machinations of the Fourth Republic and on June 18, 1954, after the French defeat at Dien Bien Phu, he was elected Prime Minister of France. At the Geneva Conference he wound up the Indo-China War but was overthrown by a parliamentary coalition which disagreed with his opposition to the European Defence Project. Returning to power in 1956 in Guy Mollet's Government, he resigned when he saw that Mollet was bent on intensifying the Algerian War. He was opposed to the return of de Gaulle (1958) and lost his parliamentary seat the same year. Mendès-France found himself once more on the political sidelines where, except for a brief interlude in 1967–8, he has remained, lonely, incorruptible, impotent – in the grandeur of his isolation the Socialist twin of de Gaulle's eminence. **M. U.**

Sir Robert Menzies (Australian, b. 1894): statesman. Menzies was Prime Minister of Australia from 1939–41, when he led his country into the Second World War on the Allied side (although in 1938 he had strongly backed Chamberlain's (q.v.) appeasement policy); then again for a marathon term from 1949 to 1966, as head of his own creation, the Australian Liberal Party (Australian Liberal = British Conservative). On the international stage the causes he fought for were generally lost ones – Eden's (q.v.) policy over Suez, South Africa's membership of the Commonwealth. His British-oriented conception of the Commonwealth lost favour in his own

time. So keen on the British connection as to arouse suspicions in Australia of Anglophilia, he was soon (in the 1950s and 1960s) forced by circumstances and his own rabid anti-Communism towards a closer alignment with the U.S. in South-East Asia. Under Menzies, Australia became affluent, independent of Britain, diplomatically enmeshed in world affairs – and perhaps lost some of her youthful innocence in the process. **B. J. P.**

'AFTERNOON LIGHT', BY SIR ROBERT MENZIES (CASSELL, 1967); 'AUSTRALIA IN THE TWENTIETH CENTURY', BY TREVOR R. REESE (PALL MALL, 1964).

Josef von Mering (German, 1849–1908): physician. Sadly, it is not Mering's fine research into sugar diabetes that has most affected the 20th century, but his introduction, with his colleague Fischer in 1903, of the first barbiturate sleeping pill. While students at Strasburg, he and Fischer shared an interest in chemistry. Subsequently he studied the chemistry of cartilage, practised hypnotism (with Krafft-Ebing), worked under Ludwig at Leipzig on gout, mineral waters, quicksilver,

brain physiology and the cause of typhus, and set up practice in a nose and throat clinic. His tireless, arrogant, impulsive personality was soothed by his wife Maria. Having shown that a drug, phloridzin, would cause diabetes in dogs, Mering went on to demonstrate, with Minkowski in 1890, that removal of the pancreas caused diabetes in dogs. He became Professor of Pharmacology at Halle University, joining his old friend Emil Fischer to work on sedatives. While there, Mering visited, and was entranced by, Verona; so their eventual discovery, barbitone, was named Veronal. About 25 barbiturate pills per adult per annum are now taken in Britain. They are the commonest method in the West for suicide and escaping from tension. **I. O.**

'THE PHARMACOLOGICAL BASIS OF THERAPEUTICS', BY L. S. GOODMAN AND A. GILMAN (MACMILLAN, NEW YORK, 1965).

Maurice Merleau-Ponty (French, 1908–1961): philosopher. Merleau-Ponty was closely associated with Sartre (q.v.), until their breach in the 1950s, when Sartre was moving ever closer to the Communist Party. With Simone de Beauvoir, they had founded the influential review *Les Temps Modernes* in 1945 and they were both strongly influenced by the philosophies of Husserl and Heidegger (qq.v.). But Merleau-Ponty was utterly opposed to the kind of dualism to which these influences led Sartre, one which insists on a profound distinction between man, as a pure consciousness with unlimited freedom, and an inert world of objects set over

against him. For Merleau-Ponty man is a 'being-in-the-world', an embodied perceiver of a world with which he is actively involved and which is to be conceived neither as the order of his own sensations nor as a scientific abstraction inferred from them, but as something endowed with meaning for him by his social and linguistic inheritance. Man conceived as a 'body-subject' is involved in the world in a way that implies that his freedom is limited. Of recent French philosophers Merleau-Ponty has proved the most accessible to Anglo-Saxon thinkers. **A. Q.**

BOOKS BY MERLEAU-PONTY: 'THE STRUCTURE OF BEHAVIOUR' (METHUEN, 1965); 'THE PHENOMENOLOGY OF PERCEPTION' (ROUTLEDGE, 1962).

Olivier Messiaen (French, b. 1908): composer. A pupil of Paul Dukas, and the teacher of, among others, Boulez and Stockhausen (qq.v.), Olivier Messiaen is the most original voice in French music since Debussy (q.v.), and a seminal force in the music of our time. A native of Avignon, he is by origin half-Flemish and half-Provençal. Trained at the Paris Conservatoire, he has been organist at the Sainte-Trinité since 1931, and first became known in France and abroad as a composer of organ music. A devout Catholic, he has never been reticent either about the religious inspiration of his work or the techniques by which he has accomplished it. In technical writings expounding his music

he has admitted many influences: among the purely musical are plainsong, Greek and Hindu rhythms, and birdsong. This last has been the almost exclusive source of his melodic material in recent years. Landmarks in his output are *La Nativité du Seigneur* (organ) 1935, *Vingt Regards sur l'Enfant-Jésus* (piano) 1944, *Turangalîla-Symphonie* (orchestra) 1948, *Catalogue d'Oiseaux* (piano) 1958, *Chronochromie* (orchestra) 1960, *Transfiguration* (choir and orchestra) 1969. **F. A.**

Ioannis Metaxas (Greek, 1871–1941): soldier and politician. General Metaxas secured a place in history at 3 a.m. on October 28, 1940, when Ambassador Grazzi woke him up with the 'request' that Italian troops should be allowed to enter Greece. In his dressing-gown, the 69-year-old Premier gave Greece's curt answer to the ultimatum: "It is war . . ." The same day Metaxas's four-year-old dictatorship disintegrated; and, as a general, Metaxas led the Greek army in the heroic Albanian campaign. His recent

past was forgotten if not forgiven, and when he died suddenly of a heart attack at the height of the war effort he was sincerely mourned as an invaluable military leader. Metaxas, a short plump man, was reared in the German military tradition and was nicknamed 'Little Moltke' in Berlin's Kriegsakademie. Accepted as a distinguished soldier and an able administrator, he was never popular either in the army or in political life. Extremely ambitious, he failed in his attempts to create a 'monarchist' party, and he became Prime Minister after the death of Demertzis, in whose Government he was Minister of Defence. Five months later he dissolved Parliament and established himself as dictator. Violently resented by the liberal-minded Greeks – he had Pericles's funeral oration excised from school textbooks – he had to his credit his military foresight which led to the preparedness of the Greek Army. **H. V.**

'THE STORY OF MODERN GREECE', BY C. M. WOODHOUSE (FABER, 1969); 'MODERN GREECE', BY JOHN CAMPBELL AND PHILIP SHERRARD (BENN, 1968).

CECIL B. DE MILLE BY BRIAN LOVE; PHOTOGRAPH BY PETER CAMPION

Thomas Midgley (U.S., 1889–1944): chemist. Midgley, the discoverer of the anti-knock compound used in petrol, typifies the industrial inventor-scientist whose discoveries arise from, and have a profound effect on, the world we live in. If the fuel in the cylinder of a petrol engine does not burn smoothly and its last portion explodes, then knocking is produced. The tendency to knock shown by a particular petrol is measured by its octane number: the higher the number the less the knocking. Midgley found that addition of tetraethyl lead to petrol reduced its tendency to knock and thus greatly encouraged the use of petrol as an energy source. In practice the anti-knock compound also contains ethylene bromide, which forms a volatile compound with lead and can be carried away with the exhaust gases, to mingle harmlessly (as far as present evidence goes) with the atmosphere. Also taking part in the development of refrigerants and synthetic rubbers, Midgley was vice-president of Ethyl Gasoline Corporation and Kinetic Chemicals Corporation. The development of all modern high-efficiency petrol engines depends on the use of anti-knock components. **P. J. F.**

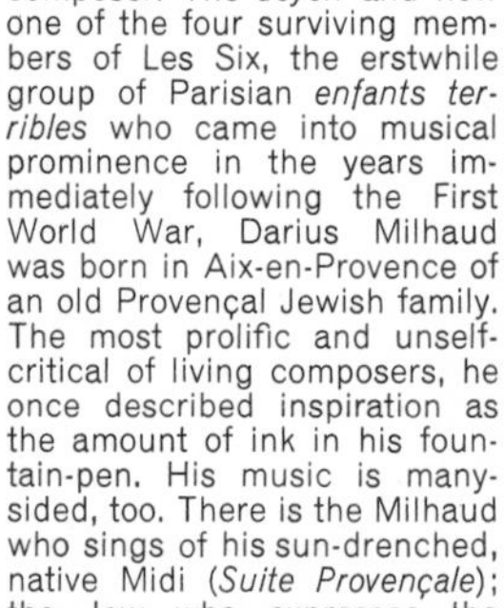

Darius Milhaud (French, b. 1892): composer. The *doyen* and now one of the four surviving members of Les Six, the erstwhile group of Parisian *enfants terribles* who came into musical prominence in the years immediately following the First World War, Darius Milhaud was born in Aix-en-Provence of an old Provençal Jewish family. The most prolific and unself-critical of living composers, he once described inspiration as the amount of ink in his fountain-pen. His music is many-sided, too. There is the Milhaud who sings of his sun-drenched, native Midi (*Suite Provençale*); the Jew who expresses the aspirations of his race (*Poèmes Juifs*); the attaché in Claudel's French Embassy returning from Rio haunted by South American rhythms (*Saudades do Brasil*); the young composer who successfully fused fugal instruction acquired at the Paris Conservatoire with jazz heard in New York and London (*La Création du Monde*). He could enter into the fun of Les Six by setting catalogues to music (*Machines agricoles, Catalogue de Fleurs*), but revealed a more serious nature in vast musical canvases (*Oresteia, Christophe Colomb*). There is also the speculative writer whose polytonality sometimes verges on atonality. Milhaud went to America in 1940, and, after the Liberation of Paris, divided his time between France and the U.S., where he had become a teacher in California. **F. A.**

Cecil B. De Mille (U.S., 1881–1959): film director. De Mille was the founding father of Hollywood. Seeking an outdoor location for his first film, *The Squaw Man* (1913), he headed south-west by train, rejecting Flagstaff, Arizona (his first choice), because it was raining, and continued to the end of the line, Los Angeles, where the sun shone and the scenery was perfect. Hollywood was the name of the nearby village where he set up his camera. He produced and directed over 70 films, concentrating early in his career on historical and biblical epics which combined a fundamentalist view of religion with sex, sadism, and a genuine flair for spectacle. His screen trademark was the bath scene. In *The Sign of the Cross* (1932), Claudette Colbert, playing Poppaea, made her toilet in a bath of asses' milk. In *Unconquered* (1947), frontierswoman Paulette Goddard was dunked in a wooden barrel. De Mille's brother observed: "He [Cecil] made of the bathroom a delightful resort which undoubtedly had its effect upon bathrooms of the entire nation." As he became an elder statesman of the film industry, De Mille saw himself not only as people's entertainer, but also as their missionary. His film *The Ten Commandments* (1923, remade in 1956), he insisted, was written, literally, by God. The writers whose names featured in the screen credits were merely executives who quarried the scenario from Holy Writ. Primarily, he was a superb story-teller whose imagination was still lit by a theatrical and Victorian upbringing. He remained faithful to his own fashion, and his films faltered only when he allowed them to become over-burdened by facts supplied by his army of researchers: "Cecil B. De Mille/Rather against his will/Was persuaded to leave Moses/Out of the Wars of the Roses" (Nicolas Bentley). He had a child's-eye view of history: when he died some three billion, two hundred and fourteen million customers had paid to share it. **P. O.**

'I BLOW MY OWN HORN', BY JESSE L. LASKY (GOLLANCZ, 1957).

Glenn Miller (U.S., 1904–1944): bandleader. Miller was the most influential figure of all in the 'sweet' band field of modern popular music. Scores of orchestras and orchestrators imitate his style today; a 'Glenn Miller Orchestra', officially endorsed by his estate, has played carbon-copy Miller since his death; and his memory is perpetuated by devoted fan-clubs, many of whose members refuse to believe he is dead. (A plane carrying him from England to France vanished without trace on December 16, 1944.) Born in Iowa, he began as a jazz trombonist in his teens, but by 1930 was a top studio man for jazz-based popular music. A strict disciplinarian, he drilled his band meticulously to produce the idiosyncratic sound he wanted – and when he launched it in 1938 swiftly built a following which outstripped even Benny Goodman's (q.v.). His distinctive innovation was the smooth sound created by a clarinet playing one octave above four saxophones, balanced by silky trombones and mellow trumpets. With a dash of 'commercial' swing added, the formula was irresistible. Record after record was a million-seller – *In The Mood, American Patrol, Moonlight Serenade, Kalamazoo* et al. – and Miller became the world's most popular danceband leader, earning almost £1 million a year. In 1942, with two successful movies completed (*Sun Valley Serenade* and *Orchestra Wives*) he enlisted, and his A.E.F. orchestra became the rave of the late war years. His disc sales probably exceed 50 million, and in 1954 a movie, *The Glenn Miller Story*, with James Stewart playing the lead, enshrined the legend further. **D. J.**

'THE BIG BANDS', BY GEORGE T. SIMON (COLLIER-MACMILLAN, 1968). RECORDS: 'THE CHESTERFIELD BROADCAST' (RCA-VICTOR, VOL. 1 RD. 7932 OR S.F 7932; VOL. II RD. 7982 OR SF. 7982); 'GLENN MILLER–SELECTIONS FROM THE GLENN MILLER STORY' (RCA RD. 27068).

Henry Miller (U.S., b. 1891): writer. Born in New York, Miller spent the Thirties in Paris. After a trip to Greece, he returned to the U.S. in 1940. He settled in California, where he has exhibited paintings; but it is his travel books and novels (including a trilogy, *The Rosy Crucifixion*) which have been widely influential. Set in America and its Parisian outpost, written in the first person and described by Miller as "about myself", his novels, beginning with *Tropic of Cancer* (1931), were published in English in Paris. The taboo words, which Miller confusingly employs both in their true sense and as mere curse-words, frightened off American and British publishers until the Sixties. His work has been emphatically praised by critics and authors, notably Lawrence Durrell and Miller himself – but not by this author-critic, for whom it illustrates the imbecility of obscenity taboos: only persecution could cause the admirable forthrightness of Miller's literary personality to be mistaken for talent and could attract acclaim to his formless mixture of clichés with quasi-biblical avuncularness. **Br. Br.**

'TROPIC OF CANCER', BY HENRY MILLER (CALDER, 1963); 'DON'T NEVER FORGET', BY BRIGID BROPHY (CAPE, 1966).

Robert Millikan (U.S., 1868–1953): physicist. Famous for measuring the charge on an electron, Millikan started this incredibly difficult work in 1906. He struck on the brilliantly ingenious idea of following the course of a tiny droplet of electrically-charged water falling by gravity through air while being resisted by the upward pull of a charged plate above. For five years he experimented in vain. However, switching to oil droplets in 1911 to overcome evaporation effects, the expected results gradually began to take place. Occasionally a droplet would attach itself to an injected ion (an atom stripped of its electrons) and would then fall more slowly, or even move upwards. Millikan argued that the minimum change in motion was due to the additional presence or absence of a single electron. By balancing the effects of the electromagnetic attraction upwards and the gravitational pull downwards, he was not only able to calculate the charge on an electron but also to prove categorically that any electric charge could exist only as the sum of a number of unit charges – the final proof for the particle-like nature of electricity first suggested a century earlier by Faraday. **N. V.**

George Minot (U.S., 1885–1950): physician. Until 1926 it was estimated that, in the U.S. alone, 10,000 people died of pernicious anaemia every year. Now the disease is easily controlled by vitamin B_{12} injections and life expectancy is normal. The story of this therapeutic revolution is a complex one, but a key figure was George Richards Minot of Boston. Whipple had found that dogs made anaemic by bleeding recovered more rapidly if fed with liver. Thereafter Minot and William P. Murphy tried, with vigour, a liver diet in treating humans suffering from pernicious anaemia. Others had given special diets, but Minot persisted and had remarkable success. Within a short time liver extracts were being given by injection and soon William B. Castle, also of Boston, showed that a secretion of the stomach (intrinsic factor) interacted in some way with a food factor to give the antianaemic factor of liver. The food factor is vitamin B_{12}, and intrinsic factor enables it to be absorbed through the small bowel, from where it goes to the liver. Pernicious anaemia patients lack intrinsic factor, but, strangely, liver also contains another vitamin, folic acid, that temporarily will control the anaemia (but not other features) of pernicious anaemia and can be absorbed in that disease. Possibly Minot's liver treatment was effective largely because of the wrong vitamin, but his persistence gave the first life-saving step in treatment. **R. H. G.**

'BLOOD', 1948, PP. 1–128 (GRUNE AND STRATTON, NEW YORK); 'TREATMENT OF PERNICIOUS ANEMIA: HISTORICAL ASPECTS', BY W. B. CASTLE (CLINICAL PHARMACOLOGY AND THERAPEUTICS, VOL. 7, PP. 147–161, 1966).

Joan Miró (Spanish, b. 1893): painter. Brought up largely at Montroig, in the baked earth of the Catalan countryside, Miró came to Paris in 1919 and became known (partly through Picasso [q.v.], a family friend) for the minutely-detailed farmscapes in which Montroig was seen with dreamlike clarity. (One of these belonged to Ernest Hemingway [q.v.], and paralleled Hemingway's own attempts to see the world clearly, simply and as if for the first time.) Miró then turned to Surrealism, developing a picture-language all his own in which conventional narrative was abandoned and sign and symbol, sometimes recognisable and sometimes not, joined in a gnat-like dance. Miró possessed, to a supreme degree, the Surrealist's gift of metamorphosis and remained loyal to the hallucinatory principle, with all that it involved in the way of multilateral free association, after most of his colleagues had foundered in routine. When painting turned in another direction in the 1950s and 60s Miró went with it, relying more on his seductive colour-sense and less on his undiminished ability to go on inventing meaningful signs. With his grown-up schoolboy's sense of fun, his delight in steeplechasing across the barriers of 'style' and 'content' and his readiness to prick the bubble of self-importance, Miró has been invaluable to 20th-century art. **J. R.**

'MIRO', BY J. DUPIN (THAMES AND HUDSON, 1962).

Mistinguett (French, 1875–1956): music hall entertainer. Jeanne Bourgeois, known as Mistinguett, is the most famous star in the entire history of the French music hall. In the brilliant cavalcades of glittering, half-dressed chorus girls at the Folies Bergère and the Casino de Paris in the years immediately before and after the First World War, Mistinguett shone with a lurid lustre because of her talent as a low comedienne and the fabulous beauty of her legs, which were the most heavily insured in the world. She had as her partner Maurice Chevalier, who has remained touchingly faithful to her memory. Wearing an enormous weight of feathers on her head, her body flashing with innumerable spangles, Mistinguett would descend the famous staircase of the Casino de Paris with a panache unrivalled either before or since. She made known without equivocation the full splendour of the human body, adorned or unadorned. Unfortunately she did not appear in England until 1947, when she was over 70 and her memory was beginning to fail. She appeared fragile and timid, but even then, when she lifted her skirts, her legs seemed unbelievably beautiful. **H. H.**

'MISTINGUETT: QUEEN OF THE PARIS NIGHT', BY MISTINGUETT, TRANSLATED BY LUCIENNE HILL (ELEK, 1954).

Reginald Joseph Mitchell (British, 1895–1937): engineer. The designer of the Spitfire fighter was apprenticed to a locomotive firm at 16. In 1916 he joined Supermarine Aviation works and within three years became Chief Engineer and Designer. He designed float seaplanes between 1922 and 1931; and from these and a land plane

development he evolved the Spitfire. The prototype, powered by a Rolls-Royce Merlin engine, flew on March 5, 1936. (The Hurricane prototype designed by Sydney Camm had flown on November 6, 1934.) Deliveries of Spitfires to Fighter Command began in 1938, and by August 1940 Fighter Command had 19 Spitfire squadrons operational (355 mph at 19,000 ft.) and 30 squadrons equipped with Hurricanes (317 mph at 17,500 ft.). Together they played a decisive role in the Battle of Britain: without Spitfires to deal with the best German fighters, the Hurricanes would not have prevailed. Altogether, 22,759 Spitfires and Seafires (the naval version) were produced in 32 types. They remained in the front line for 15½ years, during which time the engine power was nearly doubled by Rolls-Royce, and the maximum speed raised from 362 to 452 mph without radical departure from R. J. Mitchell's original design. It was among the most remarkable military aircraft ever built. **N. F.**

'R. J. MITCHELL', BY COLSTON SHEPHERD (DICTIONARY OF NATIONAL BIOGRAPHY, 1931–1940).

Laszlo Moholy-Nagy (U.S., ex-Hungarian, 1895–1946): designer. His was the probing spirit of the creative artist forging ahead of his time. Moholy-Nagy's vision of non-representational art con-

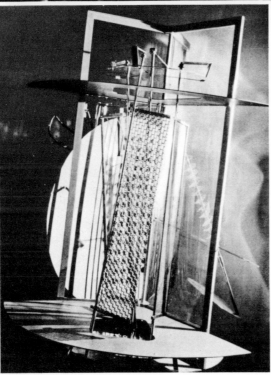

MOHOLY-NAGY: LIGHT-SPACE MODULATOR (1921-1930).

sisting of pure visual components – colour, light, texture and equilibrium of shapes, his 'photograms' (compositions on film), his 'light modulators' (paintings on transparent materials based on metals with mobile light effects), his employment of motion picture projection in his constructivist stage designs – pointed the way to new forms of art communication. Born in Hungary he settled after the First World War in Germany where, in the progressive atmosphere of the Bauhaus art movement, he taught painting and metal work, furthering the development of inborn visual gifts, maintaining that "everybody is talented". In 1935 he came to London, and went two years later to Chicago where, in his Institute of Design, he attempted to revive the spirit of the Bauhaus. **J. A.**

'THE NEW VISION', BY L. MOHOLY-NAGY (WITTENBORN, N.Y., 4TH ED. 1947).

Guy Mollet (French, b. 1905): statesman. Party-machine man par excellence, for nearly 25 years Guy Mollet has been the master of the Socialist establishment in France – although he helped de Gaulle (q.v.) to power in 1958. An unknown teachers' union worker, he became a captain in the Maquis in the Second World War and in 1945 was elected Mayor of Arras, a Socialist fief in Northern France. After serving as Minister in

1946 and Deputy Prime Minister in 1951, in 1956 he was appointed head of the Government. After the victory of the 'Republican Front', Mendès-France (q.v.) and Mollet promised peace in Algeria, but when he visited Algiers Mollet was greeted by a mass demonstration of the French Algerians and a shower of tomatoes. Struck by this indication of the popular will, Mollet became a defender of French Algeria, and after Mendès-France's resignation took the responsibility for Suez. It was the incapacity of the Fourth Republic to deal with Algeria which led him to support de Gaulle in 1958; but his socialism soon alienated him from the one-man show of the Fifth. In his special way Mollet has stayed a Romantic Socialist, a leader of schoolteachers and civil servants. **M. U.**

'THE SUEZ AFFAIR', BY HUGH THOMAS (WEIDENFELD AND NICOLSON, 1967).

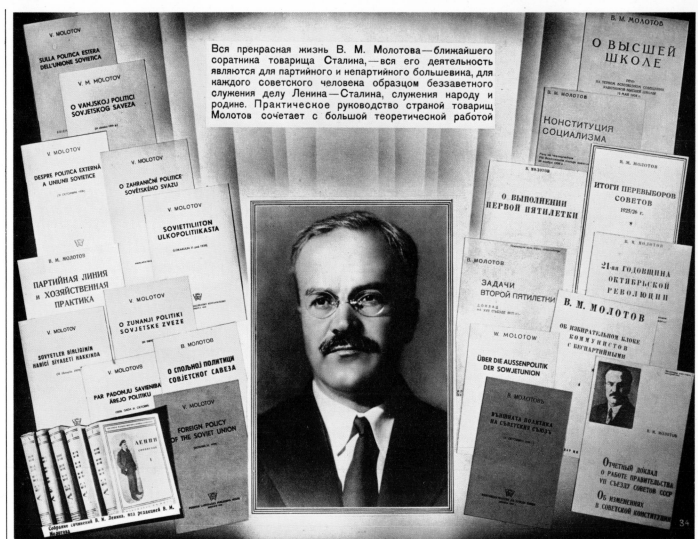

Вся прекрасная жизнь В. М. Молотова—ближайшего соратника товарища Сталина,—вся его деятельность являются для партийного и непартийного большевика, для каждого советского человека образцом беззаветного служения делу Ленина—Сталина, служения народу и родине. Практическое руководство страной товарищ Молотов сочетает с большой теоретической работой

Vyecheslav Molotov (Russian, b. 1890): politician. For 35 years Stalin's (q.v.) right-hand man, Molotov was on the losing side in the battle for the succession after Stalin's death. In 1957 Khrushchev (q.v.) removed him from all his offices, sending him first as Ambassador to Mongolia, then as Soviet representative to the international Atomic Energy Authority in Vienna. In 1962 he was expelled from the Communist Party to live in retirement in Moscow. He had been Secretary of the All-Russian Communist Party from 1921–1936, Chairman of the Council of People's Commissars from 1930–1941, Commiscor (Minister) for Foreign Affairs from 1939–1949, and again from 1953–1956. Molotov was safe, secure, imperturbable, and above all loyal to Stalin. The Nazi-Soviet pack in August 1939 was his first major achievement. The German invasion in 1941 came as almost as traumatic a shock to him as it did to Stalin. Desperately suspicious, it was only very gradually that he learnt to see more than one move ahead or to sacrifice short-term advantage to long-term gain. He played a central role in the Soviet negotiations with the West from 1942 to 1949, earning the nickname of the 'abominable No-man' for the number of times he exercised the Soviet veto at the U.N. He was possibly one of the stupidest foreign ministers of the century, and his removal from office in 1949 marked the first sign of a lull in the Stalinist phase of the Cold War. **D. C. W.**

'KHRUSHCHEV'S RUSSIA', BY EDWARD CRANKSHAW (PENGUIN, 1959); 'STALIN' BY ISAAC DEUTSCHER (O.U.P., 1949)' 'THE GREAT TERROR', BY ROBERT CONQUEST (MACMILLAN, 1968).

Helmuth J. L. von Moltke (German, 1848–1916): chief of staff. As Commander of the German Armies in 1914, von Moltke might have altered the course of history if he had been able to carry through the plan of his predecessor Schlieffen for knocking out France in six weeks. For Germany would then have won the war in the West before Britain was deployed, and Russia, left alone, would probably have made peace. But Moltke, who had got his post

largely because he was the nephew of the Field-Marshal responsible for Germany's lightning victories in 1864, 1866 and 1870, lacked self-confidence and was a sick man. He altered Schlieffen's plan by weakening the right wing on whose sweep through Belgium everything depended. At a crucial moment he sent four divisions off to hold the Russian advance in East Prussia and let seven more get tied up round fortresses. Consequently his line grew thin and a gap developed in it. When the French pushed into this across the Marne, Moltke was too far away to handle the situation and the commanders on the spot decided to retreat. Moltke told the Kaiser the war was lost and was promptly replaced. But the Schlieffen Plan, besides being mismanaged, was itself overbold. **M. L. G. B.**

AUGUST 1914' (ALSO CALLED 'THE GUNS OF AUGUST'), BY B. TUCHMAN (CONSTABLE, 1961); 'THE SWORDBEARERS', BY C. BARNETT (EYRE AND SPOTTISWOODE, 1963); 'THE SCHLIEFFEN PLAN', BY G. RITTER (OSWALD WOLFF, 1958); 'THE POLITICS OF THE RUSSIAN ARMY', BY G. CRAIG (O.U.P., 1955).

Piet Mondrian (Dutch, 1872–1944): painter. Mondrian was a natural evangelist who saw himself not as 'a painter', a man who ministered to the pleasures of the passing moment, but as a redeemer, a man who would save mankind by revealing a universal order. He was a dedicated student of landscape-painting from his sixteenth year onwards. Lengthy experiment convinced him that existing methods of breaking down appearances were insufficiently radical for his purpose and that he would have to break through to a form of expression that was wholly his own. In this he was joined by his friends of the De Stijl group who were seeking, from 1917 onwards, to downgrade traditional art and to demonstrate the superiority of abstraction, simplification and mathematical structure. In 1919 Mondrian found his own style: a grid-structure in which heavy black lines moved vertically and horizontally through rectangular areas of pure primary colour: the two elements in the picture were independent, yet indispensable to one another, and Mondrian believed that Nature

in all her variety and versatility could be epitomised in terms of this structure. For the remaining 25 years of his life Mondrian proved that what he had invented was, in effect, an inexhaustible successor to painting of a more orthodox sort. It has been much debased since; but a great deal of what is worth preserving in the art and architecture of the past 25 years is owed to Mondrian's example. **J. R.**

'PIET MONDRIAN', BY MICHEL SEUPHOR (THAMES AND HUDSON, 1957)

Egas Moniz (Portuguese, 1874–1955): neurophysiologist. Moniz was moved by the sadness and pain of disease, especially that of the mentally ill. The breadth and wisdom of this doctor of medicine, even at an early age, made his countrymen seek his help in many ways – as Member of Parliament, Ambassador to Madrid and Portugal's Minister for External Affairs. At 47 he turned back to medicine and his great scientific contributions began. Even so, at 77 he was invited to stand for the Presidency (he declined). Moniz was the first to promote the concept that brain and mind are

inseparable. With Lima, his colleague in surgical neurology, he was the pioneer in 1927 of intracranial angiography. By injecting radio-opaque dyes into the blood vessels of the neck which supply the brain they showed for the first time in a living person all the anatomical details of the cerebral blood vessels. This single contribution now saves thousands of lives. In 1935 Moniz and Lima performed the first leucotomy on a patient with intractable

depression. This was an entirely new physical approach to mental disorder and the earliest attempt at stereotactic surgery. Unfortunately, it was followed by over-enthusiastic and sometimes clumsy surgery with disturbing side-effects, and it was replaced by the developing chemotherapeutic methods. But currently there is a move back to his method in suitable cases, as stereotactic surgery has become remarkably precise. **F. J. G.**

ARCHIVES OF NEUROLOGY, VOL. 75, 1959, P. 329; BRITISH MEDICAL JOURNAL, VOL. 2, 1965, P. 1566; LANCET, VOL. II, 1955, P. 1345 AND P. 1397; AMERICAN JOURNAL OF PSYCHIATRY, VOL. 112, 1956, P. 769.

Jean Monnet (French, b. 1888): statesman. Throughout his life Jean Monnet has been a man of one idea and one method. The idea – that unity makes strength; the method – the resolution of problems through an institution which can act independently of its component parts. In 1914 Monnet managed to persuade the Prime Minister of France, René Viviani, of the importance of pooled raw materials and transports; and when in 1916 the idea became fact, he was the mainspring of the Allied Executive Committees for the distribution of common resources. So successful was he that, in 1919, at 31, he was offered the post of Deputy Secretary-General of the League of Nations. In 1940, following the defeat of the French armies, he was behind Churchill's (q.v.) offer of union between the United Kingdom and France. Soon after, armed with a British passport, he left London for Washington to negotiate Lend-Lease. In 1945, he was entrusted by General de Gaulle (q.v.) with the direction of the National Plan. Determined to set out the priorities for reconstruction, Monnet saw his own role as that of a co-ordinator, producing a single will from differing sectional interests. In 1950 he produced the Schuman Plan for the first common market, limited to coal and steel, and since then his single goal has been a Europe capable of transcending national interests. In 1956 he resigned all official posts to create an 'Action Committee for the United States of Europe'. **M. U.**

'EUROPEAN UNIFICATION IN THE SIXTIES', BY MIRIAM CAMPS (O.U.P., 1967); 'EUROPE AGAINST DE GAULLE', BY JOHN PINDER (PALL MALL, 1963); 'AS FRANCE GOES', BY DAVID SCHOENBRUN (GOLLANCZ, 1957).

Jacques Monod (French, b. 1910): biologist. The regulation of protein synthesis is one basic

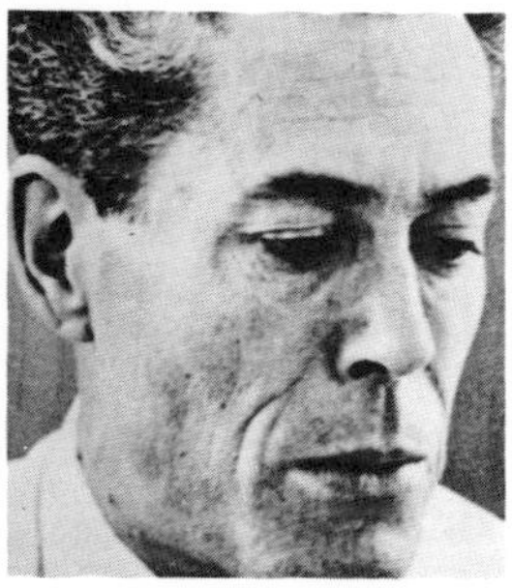

activity of living cells. It determines how and when they grow and what their characteristics are. Jacques Monod and F. Jacob (q.v.) discovered a class of genes – hitherto unknown – whose job it is to regulate other genes. Their concept of messenger RNA and the operon helped to provide a unified theory of the molecular mechanics of the genetic apparatus. The operon is a cluster of neighbouring genes that controls a particular sequence of reactions; it includes the operator gene whose message to the structural genes instructs them to 'go ahead and make enzymes'. But the operator gene can do this only if it is released from the inhibition exerted by a repressor substance continually produced under the influence of another regulatory gene further along the chromosome from the operon. The point is that the mechanism of control in all these systems is negative: they operate by inhibition rather than by activation. While the theory poses as many questions as it answers, this topic, the control of the activity of the cell, is now of absorbing interest to research workers including those studying cancer – an uncontrolled multiplication of particular cells. **P. G. R.**

Marilyn Monroe (U.S., 1926–62): film actress (page 29). The last, and among the greatest, of the studio-launched Hollywood stars who combined personal charisma with contemporary sexual ideals – in Monroe's case those of the early Fifties when the Cold War, briefly turning hot in Korea, needed an updated, infinitely more subtle version of Betty Grable, whom the same studio (20th Century-Fox) had provided for the Second World War. Product of a disturbed working-class Los Angeles childhood, Marilyn (née Norma Jean Mortenson or Baker) first made good as a teenage pin-up model, then as a starlet. She initially attracted critical attention for her acting ability in small roles in *The Asphalt Jungle, All About Eve* and *Clash By Night* but achieved star status as a result of calculated, often lubricious publicity and her own extraordinary physical appeal in her eighteenth movie *Niagara* (1953). *Gentlemen Prefer Blondes* and *How to Marry a Millionaire* played up a dumb blonde persona, but it was Billy Wilder who patiently brought out her comic skill, first in *The Seven Year Itch* (1955). Two of her last three films, Wilder's *Some Like It Hot* (1959) and John Huston's *The Misfits* (1961), clinched her reputation as an outstanding comedienne and a genuinely impressive dramatic actress. Her second and third marriages to contrasting national and ethnic heroes (the Italian-American baseball star Joe DiMaggio and the Jewish playwright Arthur Miller), coupled with her often unfairly ridiculed professional aspirations, made her the centre of discussion and controversy. Following her death (from an overdose of sleeping pills) her brief, complex, unhappy career continued to be the subject of endless speculation, from the pens of sentimental hacks as well as those of intellectuals like her ex-husband Arthur Miller in his play *After the Fall* (1964). A victim of herself, a self-immolating celluloid sex goddess, a personal American tragedy? But she is most suitably celebrated through the enjoyment of her best films. **P. N. F.**

'THE FILMS OF MARILYN MONROE', BY MICHAEL CONWAY AND MARK RICCI (BONANZA BOOKS, NEW YORK, 1964); 'THE DEATH OF MARILYN MONROE', FROM DIANA TRILLING'S 'CLAREMONT ESSAYS' (SECKER AND WARBURG, 1965).

Viscount Montgomery of Alamein (British, b. 1887): soldier. A bishop's son, Bernard Law Montgomery dedicated himself to study high command. He took over the Eighth Army in the Egyptian desert in August 1942 when Rommel was almost at Cairo. His defensive battle at Alam Halfa and his victory at Alamein in October was a turning point for the British after three years of depressing defeats, and led to the destruction of German and Italian forces in North Africa and in Sicily. Montgomery then commanded

the Allied Armies' landing in Normandy. His strategy enabled the Americans to right wheel and break out in one of the most rapid armoured advances yet. Supreme Commander Eisenhower (q.v.), assuming control of the land forces, then preferred a broad front strategy to Montgomery's concentrated left hook, resulting subsequently in endless controversy as to whether the Germans could have been totally defeated that winter. During the German Ardennes offensive, he brilliantly commanded the Allied northern flank, but his tactless cockiness irritated the Americans. Montgomery's military thinking combined simplicity with force and clarity – no-one could write more clearly or concisely – and he was intensely thorough in the preparation and administration of all his battles. His great quality, besides this intellectual mastery of his profession, was the self-confidence which infected his troops. He used publicity methods, particularly in dress, to produce high morale in a short time. After the war he became CIGS and Deputy Supreme Commander of NATO. Since retirement he has written best-selling memoirs and books on the history of warfare and (his favourite subject) leadership. Some historians rank him as probably the greatest British soldier since Wellington. He never lost a battle. **C. D. H.**

'THE MEMOIRS OF FIELD-MARSHAL THE VISCOUNT MONTGOMERY OF ALAMEIN', (COLLINS, 1958); 'MONTGOMERY', BY A. MOOREHEAD (HAMISH HAMILTON, 1946).

Henry de Montherlant (French, b. 1896): novelist and playwright. What pleased him about Montherlant, wrote André Gide (q.v.), was "the accent of undeniable authenticity" that he detected

in the younger novelist's style. Gide, with his strongly puritan background, felt that he had a duty to the world at large. Montherlant, on the other hand, though a savage critic of society, has never sought to preach or proselytise. His deepest loyalty has always been to himself; and in a long series of novels, dramas and essays he has provided, from 1922 onwards, a wonderfully vivid impression of the varying aspects of his personality – the adventurer, the traveller, the lover and, most important, the uncommitted artist. Henry de Montherlant, above all else, is an extraordinarily gifted wordmaster, but, unlike many stylists, both prolific and astonishingly versatile. His first novel, *Le Songe*, was published in 1922; his latest, *Un Assassin et mon Maître*, in 1971; and he has had time to revivify the modern French theatre. At the age of 73, he remains one of the fieriest particles still circulating in the world of letters. **P. Q.**

'MONTHERLANT LE SEPARE', BY PHILIPPE DE SAINT ROBERT (FLAMMARION, 1969); 'MONTHERLANT, L'HOMME ENCOMBRE DE DIEU', BY JEAN DE BEER (FLAMMARION, 1963); 'MONTHERLANT', BY HENRI PERRUCHOT (GALLIMARD, 1959); 'MONTHERLANT PAR LUI-MEME', AN ANTHOLOGY, ED. PIERRE SIPRIOT (ED. DU SEUIL, 1953).

Maria Montessori (Italian, 1870–1952): physician. Maria Montessori was the first woman in Italy to qualify as a doctor. Her interests drew her towards psychiatry, and especially the situation of young children confined in mental hospitals. Before she was 30 she was head of a special school for such children, and to do the job she invented a whole array of toys that taught. There were jig-saws, moveable alphabets, lacing puzzles and many varieties of colour-matching and shape-pairing. She insisted on the link between children's sensory knowledge and their cognitive development: so a characteristic Montessori invention would be a sandpaper alphabet – the child

not only saw and heard the letters, but traced them with his finger-tips. She achieved sensational results: her mentally retarded children fared as well in reading and writing as many children in ordinary schools. In 1907 she linked up with a housing developer who built rooms for her on his working-class estates. Here she opened her first *Casa dei Bambini* and attracted international attention with her programme for pre-school children. Like all great educators, she extended our sense of educability. She showed that even deprived children could be given freedom and play – *and* be reading and counting by the age of four. Her almost unnoticed bequest was to change the toy culture of Western Europe, so as to make it relevant not only to children's fantasy needs but to their manipulative and perceptual growth as well. **B. J.**

'THE MONTESSORI METHOD', BY MARIA MONTESSORI (SCHOCKEN, NEW YORK, 1964).

Sir Robert Morant (British, 1863–1920): civil servant. Robert Morant was an astonishing administrative genius who shaped, in the first 20 years of this century, the fundamental principles of the Welfare State. At 32 he came late to the Civil Service, but he had shown an early aptitude for administration when he organised a system of education in Thailand (then Siam). Administration was a great adventure for him and his

volcanic energy was never inhibited by a life in the Civil Service. He knew what was right and lobbied away behind the scenes until he got it. Morant was largely instrumental in the passing of the important Education Act of 1902 and as Permanent Secretary of the Board of Education he set about shaping a national system of education. His genius for organisation was demonstrated again with the passing of the National Insurance Act in 1911. Detested by half the country, with a large number of doctors in open revolt, Morant guided the medical profession through the difficult stages of interpretation. Since 1907, however, he had been nursing his great idea – a Ministry of Health, which was eventually set up in 1919 with him as First Secretary. He was a man for whom no idea was too big, no detail too small. **G. P. G .N.**

George Edward Moore (British, 1873–1958): philosopher. A contemporary of Bertrand Russell's (q.v.) at Cambridge in the 1890s, Moore played a large part in their joint escape from the prevailing idealism, an escape which led in due course to their becoming the founders of modern analytic philosophy. The Idealists maintained that philosophy alone, by employing a method of reasoning peculiar to it, could arrive at the real truth about the world: science and common knowledge concerned only the appearances of things and although practically useful were not really true. Moore took up a stolidly common-sensical posture in the face of such idealist paradoxes as that time is unreal; and with the utmost patience and lucidity unravelled the arguments by which such exciting-looking conclusions were supported. His careful exposures of the misuses of words which made these arguments look plausible soon became standard philosophical practice, under the name of 'analysis', this being conceived as an exact account of the meaning of a word in the most elementary terms. Moore never wholly gave up his original view of analysis as merely a preliminary to the positive task of giving a general

account of the nature of the world. But analysis is what he exclusively practised. His moral philosophy was doubly influential: on philosophers through its firm rejection of 'naturalism', i.e. any attempt to define moral ideas in non-moral terms such as happiness or evolutionary survival; and on a generation of intellectuals by way of his emphasis on the supreme value of personal relations and the contemplation of beauty. **A. Q.**

'PRINCIPIA ETHICA', BY G. E. MOORE (CAMBRIDGE, 1903); 'PHILOSOPHICAL STUDIES', BY G. E. MOORE (BLACKWELL, OXFORD, 1922); 'G. E. MOORE', BY A. R. WHITE (O.U.P., 1958); 'THE PHILOSOPHY OF G. E. MOORE', EDITED BY P. SCHILPP (EVANSTON, ILL., 1942, C.U.P., 1943).

Henry Moore (British, b. 1898): sculptor. Henry Moore was the seventh child of a family the members of which worked hard and expected no favours from life. Before he got to Leeds Art School (in 1919) he had fought in France and been gassed. At the Royal College in London he showed a robust and independent interest in extra-curricular art: above all, the archaic and primitive art in the British Museum. In 1925 he spent six months in Italy. Thereafter his feeling for the

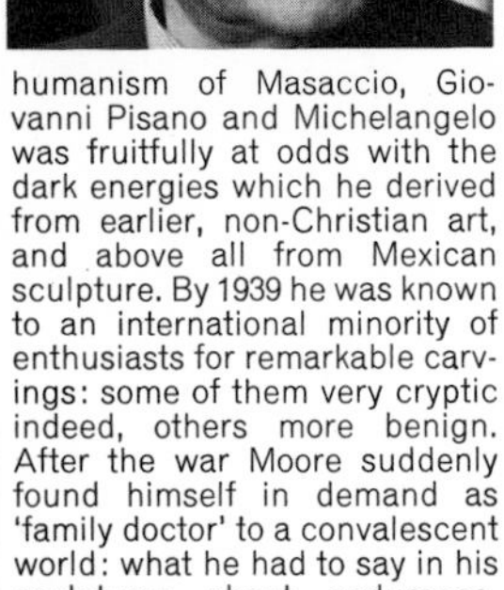

humanism of Masaccio, Giovanni Pisano and Michelangelo was fruitfully at odds with the dark energies which he derived from earlier, non-Christian art, and above all from Mexican sculpture. By 1939 he was known to an international minority of enthusiasts for remarkable carvings: some of them very cryptic indeed, others more benign. After the war Moore suddenly found himself in demand as 'family doctor' to a convalescent world: what he had to say in his sculptures about endurance, about survival, about the family, and about the heroic energies of womanhood was found to be irresistible, and the international status of British art was transformed decisively and beyond recognition. It is a tribute to Moore's capacity for self-renewal that he did not at any time suppress the darker and more enigmatic forces within his own nature, but went on with the production of tough-minded and difficult pieces: a private diary, in short, that runs parallel with his career as public orator. **J. R.**

'HENRY MOORE', BY H. READ (THAMES AND HUDSON, 1965); 'HENRY MOORE', BY D. SYLVESTER (ARTS COUNCIL CATALOGUE, 1968); 'HENRY MOORE', BY J. RUSSELL (ALLEN LANE PENGUIN PRESS, 1968).

John Moores (British, b. 1896): businessman. Britons owe one of their latterday national institutions, football pools, to John Moores. He 'kicked off' from his Liverpool base in 1923 with a top dividend of £150, distributing 4000 coupons by hand to homegoing football fans. Once he got his profit margins right, he and his brother Cecil began to make money. Yet the pools now form only a fifth of the business of his Littlewoods' empire, still a private concern whose turnover probably exceeds £200m. a year. Of equal social importance, and greater in financial terms, was his decision to pioneer the

mail-order business in Britain in 1932, following a visit to America; then he entered the chain-store game in 1937, competing with Woolworths and Marks and Spencer. Now there are around 100 stores, 20,000 employees in the chain-store and mail order business, as well as over 100,000 part-time organisers for his Littlewoods mail-order clubs. Moores, born in Eccles, began as a post-office messenger in Manchester at the age of 14, and attributes his business success simply to energy ("Work seven days a week and nothing can stop you"). He quit his pools chairmanship in 1960 to lead the revival of Everton F.C., lending the club almost £200,000 to buy star players. (He resigned in 1965.) He began sponsoring a highly successful *biennale* of British art in Liverpool in 1957, which helps living painters. **D. J.**

Thomas Morgan (American, 1866–1945): geneticist. If Mendel was the grandfather of genetics, Thomas Morgan was the father. Mendel's work was virtually ignored for 30 years after publication: shortly after its rediscovery in 1900, Morgan, sceptical about the validity of Mendel's laws, started to check them – inventing a new bio-

logical tool to do so. His use of Drosophila – the very fast-breeding fruit fly – meant that many generations could be studied in a short time (36 a year). And as *Drosophila* has only four chromosomes, it provides valuable material for the study of Mendelian segregation. To Morgan's surprise his work confirmed Mendel's laws, but he discovered deviations that led to the 'crossing-over' theory concerning segments of chromosomes and confirmed that the chromosome was the carrier of the gene. By 1911 the first chromosome maps had been drawn: these were based on the theory that the frequency with which genes stayed together after crossing over and recombination was a measure of their spatial separation. Morgan and his co-workers were able to interpret the whole range of Mendelian phenomena in terms of this theory during years of patient and comprehensive work. The concept has proved to be of the greatest practical importance not only in medicine and biology but also in agriculture and stock breeding. **P. G. R.**

'THEORY OF THE GENE', BY T. H. MORGAN (YALE U.P., 1926); 'A HISTORY OF GENETICS,' BY A. H. STURTEVANT (HARPER AND ROW, 1965).

Henry Mosely (British, 1887–1915): chemist. Mosely's life story is one of the most tragic of all the great scientists of the 20th century. At 27, he had contributed more to science than most can expect in a lifetime; but he volunteered for service early in the First World War, and within a few weeks he was killed in the Dardanelles. His first work had involved a study of the beta-emission from radium, but he moved to examine the bright X-ray spectra of the elements. He found that all elements gave similar spectra, and that the frequency of the line was proportional to the square of a number which varied by one on moving from one element to the next. From this he drew

conclusions of far-reaching importance. He decided that the nuclear charge in fundamental units was equal to the atomic number – the ordinal number of the element in the Periodic Tables – and went from 1 in hydrogen to 92 in uranium. The atomic number, not the atomic weight, was the fundamental 'signature' of the element; it was Mosely who first realised this. According to Rutherford (q.v.) this finding "ranks in importance with the discoveries of the periodic law of the elements and of spectrum analysis, and is in many respects more fundamental than either". **N. J. M. H.**

Sir Oswald Mosley (British, b. 1896): politician. Mosley is the most tragic British public figure of this century. In the 1920s he was undoubtedly the coming man in British politics. He was young, handsome, a powerful orator and a dynamic personality. Invalided out of the war, he had entered Parliament, aged 22, in 1918. After joining the Labour Party in 1924 he had become the leading advocate within the party of Keynesian economics. Chancellor of the Duchy of Lancaster in 1929, he resigned a year later over the Government's failure to deal with unemployment (the only Labour Minister to do so), delivering a classic parliamentary speech to mark the occasion. From that point his decline was precipitous. As founder and leader of the British Union of Fascists (1932) he became associated with violence, anti-semitism, and, worst of all, pro-Germanism. The Government had to pass a Public Order Act (1936) to disband his 'private army'. In-

terned under Regulation 18b in 1940, he has lived mainly in Ireland and France since the war. Perhaps he has after all got his just deserts; but his originality and courage, if rightly directed, could have been of immense service to his country. **R. Sk.**

'MY LIFE', BY SIR OSWALD MOSLEY (NELSON, 1968); 'THE FASCISTS IN BRITAIN', BY COLIN CROSS (BARRIE AND ROCKLIFF, 1961); 'ANTI-SEMITISM AND THE BRITISH UNION OF FASCISTS', BY W. F. MANDLE (LONGMANS, 1968); 'POLITICAL VIOLENCE AND PUBLIC ORDER', BY R. BENEWICK (ALLEN LANE, 1969).

Stirling Moss (British, b. 1929): racing driver. After Haileybury, Moss took a tentative stab at the hotel business, but there was never much doubt that he would emulate his father, a London dentist, who raced at Indianapolis in 1924/5. In his first electrifying season, 1948, he entered

14 races in his 497cc Cooper and won ten. In the fifteen years of his racing career he won every Grand Prix worth winning and became a national folk hero. He was probably not quite such a master of Formula One as Fangio (q.v.) or Clark, but in sports car racing he was supreme; and if there had been a motor-racing decathlon Moss would have carried it off. In the public mind, though, his best drive was the 1955 Mille Miglia, which he won (the first Englishman ever to do so) in 10 hours 7 minutes at an average speed of 98 mph. Short (5 ft. 8 in.), muscular, ascetic, manic in his energy, ambition, and drive, Moss was an intense patriot who would often elect to risk losing in a British car rather than win in a foreign one. When one M.P. accused him of dodging military service, he sent all 625 a copy of his RAF medical test, which failed him because of a kidney condition. He nearly died in a crash at Goodwood on Easter Monday, 1962, and was unconscious for 28 days. He finally pulled through but decided, after thorough circuit tests, that if he could no longer excel, he would not race again. He remains an aficionado and patron of the sport. **G. S.**

'ALL BUT MY LIFE', BY STIRLING MOSS WITH KEN PURDY (KIMBER, 1963); 'WITH MOSS IN THE MILLE MIGLIA, 1955, 1956, 1957', BY DENIS JENKINSON (REPRINTED FROM MOTOR SPORT, 1968); 'LE MANS 1959', BY STIRLING MOSS (CASSELL, 1959); 'DESIGN AND BEHAVIOUR OF THE RACING CAR', BY STIRLING MOSS AND LAURENCE POMEROY (KIMBER 1963).

Lord Louis Mountbatten, later Earl Mountbatten of Burma (British, b. 1900): sailor and administrator. The granting of self-government to India and Pakistan in 1947 heralded the demise of Britain's empire. It was Attlee's (q.v.) Government

which pronounced the death sentence. But Mountbatten, the last Viceroy, was deputed to administer a gentle euthanasia. His enlightened and liberal achievement was the high point of a diverse career that had never been far from the centre of events. His vigour and adaptability had been proved during the war as an inspirational destroyer commander and a resourceful head of Combined Operations; as one of the great supremos of the war he had been architect of the reconquest of South East Asia. In India he had a personal style which captivated Nehru and mollified Jinnah (qq.v.) and he was able within five months to transfer power into the hands of two successor States, who remained friendly to their ex-masters. Mountbatten has been criticised for partiality to the Hindus, for sacrificing Moslem interests in Kashmir to India's adhesion to the Commonwealth, and for too much haste. But in an India still only half-digested after 150 years of British rule, simmering with violence, and with the machinery of government rapidly breaking down, it is difficult to see how any other solution was practicable. He triumphantly achieved an amazing transformation: easing a proud nation down from her imperial perch, and making it appear a victory. **B. J. P.**

'THE TRANSFER OF POWER IN INDIA', BY E. W. R. LUMBY (ALLEN AND UNWIN, 1954); 'THE LAST YEARS OF BRITISH INDIA', BY MICHAEL EDWARDES (CASSELL, 1963); 'THE LIFE AND TIMES OF LORD MOUNTBATTEN', BY JOHN TERRAINE (HUTCHINSON, 1968).

Erwin Mueller (U.S., ex-German, b. 1911): physicist. With the invention of the field ion microscope in 1936, Mueller made it possible for man to see the atoms which had first been postulated 23 centuries before by Democritus. The microscope consists of a very fine needle tip maintained at high temperature in a high vacuum.

The tip is made to emit ions or electrons, which fly off in straight lines radial to the curvature of the tip, and hit a fluorescent screen. Because the screen is many thousands of times bigger than the tip, the result is a magnified image of the tip of the specimen, in which it is possible to see the individual atoms. Magnifications of up to one million times are possible, and the microscope is easily the most powerful ever built. It is mainly useful for high melting alloys or metals, but some organic molecules, like phthalocyanine, have been seen. The latest development of the microscope, also carried out by

Mueller, is to attach to it a time-of-flight mass spectrometer. Then individual atoms can be extracted from the tip and identified. This is done by having a small hole in the screen which is moved around until it coincides with the atom. A sharp increase in voltage strips the atom from the tip and it flies through the hole into the spectrometer. The time it takes to travel along the tube enables the atom to be identified. **N. J. M. H.**

George Mueller (U.S., b. 1918): engineer. Mueller is an expert in electronics and communications, and played a leading role in the development of the communications system for the first successful American space probe, Pioneer One, which followed the first Sputnik into space in 1957. Later he took overall responsibility for design, development, and testing of components for the first American intercontinental ballistic missiles, and was responsible for the Atlas, Titan, Minuteman and Thor programmes. He succeeded to his present job as controller of manned space flight when morale was low, taking over control of 300,000 employees and a budget running to 10 million dollars a day. The great success of the Apollo programme since then is due in large part to his efforts. In 1969 he was in charge of the largest systems operation ever undertaken, the project which put the Americans on to the Moon. **N. J. M. H.**

Hermann Muller (U.S., 1890–1967): geneticist. One of the century's outstanding geneticists, he was the first person to experiment with artificial gene mutations produced in fruit flies by irradiation with X-rays. In 1915, while a student of the famous geneticist Thomas Morgan (q.v.) of Columbia University, he was a member of a team which first mapped statistically the linear pattern of genes along the chromosomes of a fruit fly. In 1927, at the University of Texas, Muller carried out the work which revealed that X-rays were 'mutagenic'. He showed that new characters induced in fruit flies by this means could sometimes be passed on to future generations, though most were lethal. The special significance of this research, for which Muller received the Nobel Prize for Physiology or Medicine in 1946, is that an increase in mutation rate can be extremely dangerous to life. In 1934, with A. A. Prokofyeva, he first measured the size of a single

gene and later took a prominent part in the debate which centred round the precise definition of a gene. Muller's work was thus fundamental to our whole understanding of the hereditary process – without it, for one thing, we should be far less able to assess the potential genetic hazard from radioactive fallout, or from other kinds of radiation. **P. H. S. S.**

'THE MESSAGE OF THE GENES', BY NAVIN SULLIVAN (ROUTLEDGE AND KEGAN PAUL, 1968).

Paul Müller (Swiss, 1899–1965): chemist. In the hotter regions of the world most of the serious diseases are insect-borne. They include malaria, yellow fever, plague, typhus, relapsing fevers, and various filariases. Today, by spraying the walls of dwellings with residual insecticides, at a cost of a few shillings per head annually, people can be protected from diseases spread by house-haunting insects. Indeed, some of these diseases have been entirely eradicated from vast areas by these means. It all began with Müller's discovery of DDT, the first, and still in some ways the best, of new synthetic contact insecticides. When in 1925 he joined the firm of J. R. Geigy as a research chemist, his work was at first concerned with dyestuffs and tanning materials, but in 1935 he switched to seeking new pesticides for agriculture. He became convinced of the need for an insecticide which would act on contact with the insect without having to be swallowed. The ideal compound would be toxic to insects, harmless to warm-blooded animals and plants; it would be non-irritant and odourless, long-lasting and relatively cheap. After the trial of many thousands of substances, he discovered in 1939 the DDT group. Further research perfected the insecticide which became known to the Allies during the war, when its first important use was to quell a typhus epidemic in Naples. Müller was awarded the Nobel Prize for his discovery in 1948. Since then, DDT has been so widely used that it has become a household word as well as a tool in Public Health and a valuable aid in agriculture. **J. R. B.**

Ed Murrow (U.S., 1908–1965): broadcaster. Ed Murrow was the most famous, the most influential, and in many ways the finest reporter of our time. He never worked for a newspaper, but used his cool, dry voice, his debonair dark-suited presence, his air of dedication and authority, and his talent for the occasional purple passage, to record events on radio and television with devastating effect. Born the son of an itinerant farmer at Pole Cat Creek, North Carolina, Murrow worked his way through college to become a studious organiser of cultural programmes for CBS. Chance allowed him to make the first on-the-spot radio report of the Nazi *Anschluss* in Austria in 1938, and from that time he dedicated himself to reporting European affairs to America. He

made his name, and forged his style, while reporting the Blitz in England, when his American view of Londoners under fire did much to build the mythology of that time, and to bring America into the war on our side. Subsequently he moved into television, where the same cool, authoritative style virtually created the still-dominant traditions of TV interviewing and documentary. The last few years before his obsessive chain smoking killed him with lung cancer were spent as the Director of United States Information Services. Murrow was outstanding proof that the general idea of a 'reporter' as a merchant of facts dedicated only to the dispassionate search for truth is totally misleading. His greatest and most influential achievements, reporting the Blitz and devastating Senator Joe McCarthy (q.v.) in 1954, were in no way dispassionate, but bravely prejudiced expressions of his own Anglophile, liberal,

and sceptical beliefs. **N. O. T.**

'DUE TO CIRCUMSTANCES BEYOND OUR CONTROL', BY F. W. FRIENDLY (MACGIBBON AND KEE, 1967).

Robert [von] Musil (Austrian, 1880–1942): writer. A man's qualities are determined by his job, his social status, his childhood experiences; the opinions of his friends and his evaluations of their opinions; his ambitions and fears. But when you have peeled off all these layers of the human onion, shedding a discreet ironical tear in the process, what is left? This is the riddle that Robert Musil set out to solve in *The Man Without Qualities*, the strange, obsessive, shapeless novel-cum-philosophical tract placed in the Vienna of 1913, the last year of Europe's 'golden peace'. Here every job turns out to be a farce, social status is nothing but graft, a particular opinion or conviction is no better than its alternative. Every event, and history itself, is dissolved in the diversity of

interpretations. What if a man's consciousness recognises this state of affairs for what it is, yet cannot transcend it and, seeking to get beyond the *functions*, fails to find the *substance* to which to relate them? The mammoth book which Musil left unfinished, dying, pen in hand, after more than 20 years of frantic labour, offers no answer: but the questions it asks are our questions. **J. P. S.**

'THE MAN WITHOUT QUALITIES', BY ROBERT MUSIL, TRANS. BY EITHNE WILKINS AND E. KAISER, 3 VOLS. (SECKER AND WARBURG, 1953, 1954, 1960).

Benito Mussolini (Italian, 1883–1945): dictator. *Il Duce*, the leader of the Italian Fascist movement, was dictator of Italy for 20 years. By turns schoolmaster, journalist, revolutionary agitator and Socialist leader, he was expelled by the Socialists in 1914 because he wanted Italy to join the fight against Germany. He therefore invented Fascism in 1919 as a blend of Socialism and nationalism. After twice failing to enter Parliament, he succeeded in 1921 when the liberals wanted a counterweight to Socialism. Right-wing elements helped organise the March on Rome in 1922 – a minor insurrection which persuaded the King to appoint him Prime Minister, after which Parliament accorded him full powers. Skilful propaganda rather than ruthlessness allowed him to develop a police state – totalitarian and, in the end, mildly racialist. A few useful reforms were accomplished, but at enormous cost. One achievement survived him, a concordat with the Vatican. Most of all Mussolini wanted to make Italy strong and feared. So in 1935–6 he appropriated Abyssinia, and later Albania. Prudently, he remained neutral when the Second World War broke out; but the collapse of France, and hope of conquering Greece and North Africa, drove him to join Hitler (q.v.) in June 1940. Defeat led to his removal in 1943 by the Fascist Grand Council; and, trying to establish a north-Italian republic under German patronage, he was killed by partisans, acting on orders from Milan, in 1945. **D. M. S.**

'MUSSOLINI', BY LAURA FERMI (UNIVERSITY OF CHICAGO PRESS, 1961); 'MUSSOLINI AND ITALIAN FASCISM', BY S. WILLIAM HALPERIN (VAN NOSTRAND, 1963); 'ITALY: A MODERN HISTORY', BY DENIS MACK SMITH (UNIVERSITY OF MICHIGAN PRESS, REVISED EDITION 1969).

N

Vladimir Nabokov (U.S., ex-Russian, b. 1899): novelist. Born in St Petersburg in 1899, Nabokov emigrated from Russia in 1919, and spent 1919–1923 at Trinity College, Cambridge, studying French and Russian literature. Since then he has lived in Berlin, Paris, the U.S. and Switzerland. He is not, however, a man of the world; he lives exclusively, translates Pushkin, studies butterflies, despises Freud (q.v.) ("the Viennese witch-doctor") and deploys a coloratura style in formidable novels, including *The Gift, Lolita, Pnin, The Real Life of Sebastian Knight, Despair*, and, his latest, *Ada*. Supremely blest in his gifts, he can do anything, apparently, which can be done with words alone. Many of his novels are more fruitfully read as dreams than as reality. What he pursues is aesthetic bliss, often to be won by the knowing use of multiple perspectives, mirror-images, double identities, oblique analogies. The countenance offered by his style is rarely inviting, but the pleasures of intimacy, as in *Lolita*, are great. Ostensibly a decadent, he reveals considerable tenderness for unregarded things, distaste for objects commonly visited with smiles. Some of his most resplendent books are located

with great precision half-way between a despised banality and its corrective parody: they are thrillers, romances, detective stories, each with a difference to indicate how an artist might handle the genre. About his finest work, as in *Ada* and some pages of *Pale Fire,* there hangs "the savour of anciency", affectionately recalled: the author's attitude to modern things is correspondingly astringent. If he did not exist, it would be extraordinarily difficult to invent such a rare bird. **D. Do.**

'NABOKOV, HIS LIFE IN ART', BY ANDREW FIELD (HODDER AND STOUGHTON, 1967); 'ESCAPE INTO AESTHETICS', BY PAGE STEGNER (DIAL PRESS, NEW YORK, 1966); 'SPEAK, MEMORY', BY VLADIMIR NABOKOV (GOLLANCZ, 1951).

Imre Nagy (Hungarian, 1896–*c.* 1958): politician. Nagy was the first Communist leader in power to give up the principle of one-party rule in favour of multi-party democracy. A Moscow-trained Communist leader whose 1945 land reform benefited many peasants, he had no important role under Rákosi's autocracy, but after Stalin's (q.v.) death in 1953 the Soviet leaders made him Premier. He launched the New Course, introducing economic reforms and political liberalisation. Later he was ousted from

office by Rákosi, who had remained Party boss. Rákosi fell after Khrushchev's (q.v.) denunciation of Stalin in 1956 and Nagy expected to take over. Events outran him, however. On October 23 a popular revolt broke out in Budapest. Nagy was now reappointed Premier and, after some hesitation, accepted popular demands to combine Socialism with democracy and national independence. The Government transformed itself into a coalition of four parties, and the Russians promised to withdraw troops from Hungary. But more arrived and Nagy, having no better option, abrogated the Warsaw Treaty, declared Hungary's neutrality and asked for help from the U.N. Forcibly removed by Soviet troops, Nagy was tried in secret and executed. He courageously refused to admit guilt, though this would have saved his life. He chose death and became a national hero. **L. F. P.**

'IMRE NAGY ON COMMUNISM: IN DEFENCE OF THE NEW COURSE', (THAMES AND HUDSON, 1957); 'RIFT AND REVOLT IN HUNGARY', BY F. A. VALI (HARVARD/OXFORD U.P., 1961); 'REVOLUTION IN HUNGARY', BY P. E. ZINNER (COLUMBIA U.P., 1962).

James Naismith (U.S., ex-Canadian, 1861–1939): teacher. Naismith was one of the few men in history who can claim to have invented a major sport. His peach baskets, nailed to a gymnasium balcony, were the beginning of basketball, the only sport devised in the U.S. with no roots in another country. Conceived at the turn of the century the game spread like wildfire and now, played in 124 countries, it is the world's most popular indoor team sport. Naismith was educated at

McGill University in Canada where he first felt the longing for an indoor winter game. And later he devised one while teaching at the YMCA Training School at Springfield, Mass., to offset his pupils' flagging interest in non-competitive gymnastics. The sport never looked back and Naismith went quietly on, earning degrees in medicine and theology and a reputation as a home-spun idealist: "The hands and feet, as parts of the soul, can be taught goodness, too." He was a chaplain in the First World War and, for the last four decades of his life, a beloved Professor of Education at the University of Kansas. **D. A. D.**

'CAVALCADE OF BASKETBALL', BY A. M WEYAND (MACMILLAN, NEW YORK, 1960)

Sir Lewis Namier (British, ex-Polish, 1888–1960): historian. However one looked at L. B. Namier, there seemed always to be two of him. Jewish aristocrat and English Tory, businessman and man of learning, the public curmudgeon and the private charmer. Even as an historian he divided into two. The man best known to fellow scholars spent his life collecting biographical details on 18th-century M.P.s in order to discover the realities of their politics. The man known to a wide readership wrote scintillating analytical essays about the European revolutions of the 19th and 20th centuries. Namier the essayist destroyed insularity and widened the horizons of debate. Namier the research scholar narrowed down the excitements of politics to family relationships and the sordid particulars of patronage. What united the two Namiers was his passionate and unrelenting scholarship. Namier possessed

a mind of exceptional power which always saw afresh; whatever he produced came out of him and no-one else. This made him a revolutionary. Where Namier had walked, the ground might be scorched, but it lay ready to be tilled again. English historians can never be quite as they were before this apple from the tree of knowledge landed in their midst. **G. R. E.**

'PERSONALITIES AND POWERS', BY SIR LEWIS NAMIER (HAMISH HAMILTON, 1955); 'L. B. NAMIER: A PERSONAL IMPRESSION', BY ISAIAH BERLIN (ENCOUNTER, NOVEMBER, 1966).

Gamal Abdel Nasser (Egyptian, 1918–1971): statesman. After serving in the Palestine war (1948), Nasser led the officers' revolution of 1952 against King Farouk (q.v.) and his regime. Power, at first exercised collectively with Neguib as figurehead, gradually concentrated in Nasser's hands; he became President of the Egyptian Republic in 1956. In the first years the monarchy was abolished, political parties dissolved, landownership reformed, and agriculture and industry expanded to cope with an increasing population; the High Dam at Aswan, built with Russian aid, provides electric power as well as water for irrigation. After 1961 he pursued a Socialist trend: more land-reform, nationalisation of industry, trade, the Press; more schools and social welfare. But there was a certain lack of contact between the Government and people, in spite of the official party (the 'Socialist Union'), and a growing alienation of

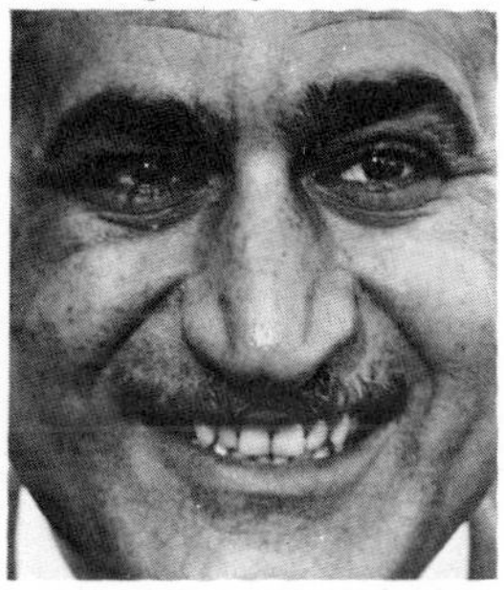

much of the educated class. In foreign affairs, Nasser ended the British occupation (1954) and adopted neutralism, not joining either Power-bloc but making Egypt the leader of the Arab states. This produced periods of conflict with France (over Algeria), Britain (Arabian Peninsula) and with the USA; and also dependence on the USSR for arms and aid. His appeal to Arab peoples in the name of Arab nationalism created difficulties with other governments – tension with Iraq until 1958, failure of the union with Syria (United Arab Republic 1958–61), involvement in the Yemeni civil war – and two confrontations with Israel: the Suez crisis (1956) when Israeli and Anglo-French attacks were stopped by American and Russian pressure, and major defeat in the Six Day War of June, 1967. His prestige and economic policy never fully recovered, but at least Egyptians will always regard him as an important figure, the first fully Egyptian ruler after centuries of domination by Mamlukes, Turks and British. **A. H. H.**

'MODERN EGYPT,' BY T. LITTLE (BENN, 1967); 'NASSER', BY P. MANSFIELD (METHUEN, 1969); 'THE MODERN HISTORY OF EGYPT', BY P. J. VATIKIOTIS (WEIDENFELD AND NICOLSON, 1969).

Giulio Natta (Italian, b. 1903): chemist. Professor of industrial chemistry at Milan Polytechnic, Natta is a key figure in the development of modern plastics. Through his work on polymers, carried out with the help of Montecatini, the Italian chemical firm, he proved in a European context that co-operation between industry and universities is not only possible but profitable. Natta developed a number of industrially important processes but his most significant achievement was to clarify the structures of a range of plastics, of which polythene and polypropylene are members. This knowlege enabled us to increase our control over final properties. Plastics derive their characteristics not only from the sum of their components, but also from the order in which their building blocks are arranged. The pattern of primary constituents can be altered at will through the use of specific catalysts and variations in pro-

duction conditions, so materials can be tailor-made. Concepts developed by Natta are being used to develop further materials of increased usefulness. **P. J. F.**

'INTRODUCTION TO PLASTICS,' BY J. H. BRISTON AND C. C. GOSSELIN (NEWNES, 1968).

Jawaharlal Nehru (Indian, 1889–1964): statesman. Nehru owed much to his father, Pandit Motilal Nehru, a prominent advocate and later President of the Indian National Congress. He was educated at Harrow and Trinity College, Cambridge, and then became a barrister at the Inner Temple. Soon after his return to India Nehru started on his long and intensive campaign against the British Raj in India. By 1920 he had linked up with Gandhi (q.v.), whose views on non-violence and non-cooperation he shared. He became General Secretary of the All India Congress Committee in 1929, and was President altogether five times, on the last occasion for three years (1951–1954). Nehru consistently opposed any British attempt to lead towards greater independence for India. He was in prison for over nine years and wrote *The Unity of India* (1936), *Discovery of India* (1946) and his autobiography. On the occasion of Indian Independence, in 1947, it was natural

that Nehru should be chosen as Prime Minister since he had enshrined so many of the ideals and hopes of the new Indian Nation. His premiership was clouded at the end by the Chinese War and the occupation of Goa and Hyderabad, which seemed to go against Gandhi's doctrine of non-violence. Nehru will nevertheless be remembered statesmen in India's history: statesman in India's history: one who always advocated close relations with Britain and who bore no bitterness after his long struggle. **R. A. B.**

'TOWARD FREEDOM – AN AUTOBIOGRAPHY', BY JAWAHARLAL NEHRU (ASIA PUBLISHING HOUSE, 1936).

A. S. Neill (British, b. 1883): teacher. Neill decided that most formal learning was meaningless ritual and that teachers were the prisoners of their classrooms. He abandoned the strap and his children chomped sweets instead. Neill published his first big book *A Dominie's Log* in 1915 and spent 10 years picking up psychoanalysis at the feet of the fading Homer Lane in London, and then taught in free schools on the

Continent. But no school was free enough for Neill, and in 1924, with five children, he founded Summerhill, a tiny school in nondescript buildings, starved of money, and far off the beaten track, near Leiston in Suffolk. And yet it is world-famous because it puts the child absolutely at the centre and gives him the maximum freedoms – including the freedoms never to attend a lesson and to dispense with unpopular teachers. Neill's books have helped create the finest school in the world – the English primary school – because Neill insisted that the good teacher is first and last "on the side of the child". **B. J.**

'SUMMERHILL', BY A. S. NEILL (PENGUIN, 1968).

George Nepia (New Zealander, b. 1905): Rugby footballer. There was never another Rugby player quite like George Nepia. He came to England, an unknown Maori boy, with the 1924–5 All Blacks – the Invincibles. They won every one of their 30 matches in Britain and France – and Nepia played in them all. It would have been a remarkable feat by anyone. By a boy of 19 it was superhuman. Nepia was a full-back, tough as teak, a fearsome tackler, master of the long 'spiral' kick to touch. By the end of the tour his fame

had rocketed round the world. Crowds flocked to see him wherever he played. Scribes reached for their superlatives. Denzil Batchelor, in a striking tribute, wrote: "He was between short and tall, and his thighs were like young tree trunks. His head was fit for a prow of a Viking longship, with its passionless sculpted bronze features and plume of blue-black hair. Behind the game, he slunk from side to side like a black panther behind bars, like a lord of the jungle on the prowl for a kill." Later, under the financial pressures of the Thirties, Nepia turned to Rugby League; but he had done enough, in the Union game, to become one of its immortals. **V. G. J. J.**

'I, GEORGE NEPIA', BY GEORGE NEPIA AND TERRY McLEAN (HERBERT JENKINS, 1963).

Pier Luigi Nervi (Italian, b. 1891): architect. As Brunel used iron and Eiffel steel, so Nervi exploits reinforced concrete superbly for those megastructures of the modern world where the urban mob has become a disciplined crowd: railway stations, sports stadia, exhibition halls, warehouses. He refined his *Ferrocimento* to unprecedented thinness and strength in the municipal stadium at Florence (1929–32) and in a series of hangars for the Italian air force (1935–41, destroyed). He has developed his own system of precasting concrete in complex ribbed and panelled profiles, creating vaults and domes of breathtaking grace; the exhibi-

tion hall at Turin (1948–9), the circular concourses at Rome Lido and at the spa of Chianciano (1950–2), two sports halls and the Flaminio Stadium for the Rome Olympics and the Palazzo del Lavoro at Turin (1959–61). Two English commissions remain unbuilt for lack of funds: the new nave of Portsmouth Cathedral (designed 1966) and the Pitt-Rivers Museum at Oxford (designed 1967). Though responsible for some of the most beautiful structures of the century, Nervi has little interest in everyday building; the appendages of his exhibition structures, designed by collaborating architects, often lack distinction. **N. J. W. T.**

'THE WORKS OF PIER LUIGI NERVI', BY JURGEN JOEDICKE (ARCHITECTURAL PRESS, 1957); 'PIER-LUIGI NERVI', BY ADA LOUISE HUXTABLE (MAYFLOWER, 1960).

John von Neumann (U.S., ex-Hungarian, 1903–1957): mathematician. A brilliant scholar with an enormous range of interests, Neumann was especially important for his contribu-

tion to the social sciences. In 1928 he proposed a mathematical technique for analysing conflict. This was the beginning of Game Theory, which von Neumann later developed with Oskar Morgenstern in an important book, *The Theory of Games and Economic Behaviour*. In this they rigorously analysed the rules governing the selection of optimal strategies by players, rules applicable to such other 'games' as politics, business, war, even the game that animals play against the environment – evolution. Von Neumann's concepts formed the basis for a new area of research that has been exploited with great profit by innumerable workers. He also studied the logic of electronic computers and developed new computer techniques. He became interested in computer-brain analogies shortly before his premature death. **J. B. M.**

'THEORY OF GAMES AND ECONOMIC BEHAVIOUR', BY J. VON NEUMANN AND O. MORGENSTERN (PRINCETON U.P., 1944); 'THE COMPUTER AND THE BRAIN', BY J. VON NEUMANN (YALE U.P., 1963).

Barnett Newman (U.S., 1905–1970): painter. Born in Manhattan of Russian-Jewish origin, Newman was a founder-member of the first New York School. Not only did he, with the others, talk of "an art that could challenge all history": he created it. The new art was not to correspond to an idea of beauty preserved in other men's paintings: it was to be something quite different – something, as he said in 1947, "that cannot be described within the present framework of established notions of plasticity". Newman at that time had just emerged from nearly 20 years' enforced putting-aside of his ambitions as a painter. (He had had to help his father during the Depression in the family clothing business: "Women's clothes are painting," he once said, "and men's clothes are sculpture.") He was into his fifties before his painting had any kind of practical success, and his shows in 1950 and 1951 antagonised even his closest

friends and colleagues by the assurance and conviction with which, as he said later, "I busted geometry". But his grand, plain, vertical images made their way, and Newman was proved to have been right when he foretold that the transcendental experience on offer would be understood "by anyone who will look at it without the nostalgic glasses of history". **J. R.**

'BARNETT NEWMAN', BY T. B. HESS (WALKER AND CO., NEW YORK, 1969).

Stavros Niarchos (Greek, b. 1909): shipowner. Niarchos lacks much of the panache and extroversion that characterises the other Greek shipowning titan, Aristotle Onassis (q.v.). Though he may capture a smaller share of the world's headlines, he is probably richer than his rival and certainly controls a larger fleet. His surname means 'master of ships' but, despite the omen, Niarchos was brought up in bourgeois surroundings. His first connection with the sea was in 1935 when he persuaded his uncles to buy six freighters to

carry grain for the mill. Within a year the young Niarchos had quadrupled profits. The second man to build a 100,000 tonner (the Manhattan in 1962), Niarchos exercises an iron-fisted control over his empire from his twin bases in Gstaad in Switzerland and Spetsopoula, his Aegean island. He has said: "Our kind of business must be controlled by one individual because you need very fast thinking. I can make a decision on anything in minutes. If I had to spend my time convincing my colleagues I wouldn't have time to fight competitors." **S. P. A.**

Ben Nicholson (British, b. 1894): painter. As the son of William Nicholson and the nephew of James Pryde, Ben Nicholson grew up in a painter's environment and among people who took it for granted that certain established ways of painting, stylish within their chosen limits, would continue for ever. He broke away from all this, retaining only a lifelong pride in his father's mastery of tonal values and poetic feeling for still life, and chose for himself quite a different set of heroes. At one extreme were Braque, Picasso and, later, Mondrian (qq.v.): masters, all of them, whom Nicholson alone, among the English painters of his generation, was able to assimilate without losing his own identity. At the other extreme were people unknown to the world of galleries and critics and collectors: the men who laid the stones at Car-

nac, for instance, and untutored painters like Alfred Wallis of St Ives, and ball-game giants like Cochet and Lacoste. In the end it was Ben Nicholson, long derided as a crank, who turned out to have contributed most, among English painters, to the 'modern movement' in its heroic phase. **J. R.**

'BEN NICHOLSON' (STUDIO INTERNATIONAL SPECIAL, 1969); 'BEN NICHOLSON' (TATE GALLERY CATALOGUE, 1969); 'BEN NICHOLSON', INTRODUCED BY JOHN RUSSELL (THAMES AND HUDSON, 1969).

Vaslav Nijinsky (Russian, 1890–1950): dancer/choreographer. Born in Kiev of itinerant dancers, Nijinsky joined the Imperial Ballet School where he was hailed as a prodigy before graduation. He studied under Legat and Cecchetti, and danced at the Maryinsky as the Favourite Slave in Fokine's (q.v.) *Le Pavillon d'Armide*. He regularly partnered Kchessinskaya and Karsavina. In 1908 he met Diaghilev (q.v.) who became his lover. In the first season of the Ballets Russes the following year, Paris was amazed by the standard of male dancing, and of Nijinsky in particular, with his incomparable technical and expressive qualities. In 1911 he became *premier danseur* of Diaghilev's own company: his roles included *Le Spectre de la Rose* and *Petrouchka*. Diaghilev encouraged him in choreography: his first ballet, *L'Après-midi d'un Faune*, originally a *succès de scandale*, was soon recognised as a masterpiece. Nijinsky replaced Fokine as *maître de ballet* and composed the first primitive ballet, *Le Sacre du Printemps* – which caused a riot and was soon abandoned – and *Jeux*, the first ballet on a modern sporting theme. The company lacked confidence in his novel choreography, but he was a pioneer, way ahead of his time. In South America Nijinsky married, and was dismissed by Diaghilev.

After internment during part of the First World War, he rejoined the Ballets Russes in North America and produced his last ballet, *Till Eulenspiegel*. He developed persecution mania, and after his last performance in Buenos Aires settled in Switzerland, where he went out of his mind. He lived on for 30 years (he died in England), cared for by his wife. **R. B.**

'NIJINSKY', BY ROMOLA NIJINSKY (GOLLANCZ, 1933); 'NIJINSKY', ED. PAUL MAGRIEL (HENRY HOLT, NEW YORK, 1946).

Chester Nimitz (U.S., 1885–1966): admiral. On Christmas Day, 1942, Nimitz landed in the devastation of Pearl Harbour. His record (it included court-martial for stranding his ship) was unspectacular. Twenty-ninth on the Admirals List, his selection to revitalise the Pacific Fleet was criticised. Brilliant appraisals of the situation, instant recognition of the possibilities of superseding the lost slow battleships by fast carriers, established his authority. His vital partnership with Admiral 'Bull' Halsey opened in raids from the Marshall Islands to New Guinea. In April, 1943, U.S. morale was restored by the Tokyo raid. In May the Coral Sea battle held the southern Japanese advance. In June he broke Yamamoto (q.v.) at Midway, where Admiral Spruance ended the era of battleships. Sweeping carrier actions thereafter carried America by way of the Philippine Sea, Leyte Gulf and Okinawa to Japan. Remorseless submarine campaigns and fantastic air attacks shattered Japan's resistance even before the Hiroshima bomb. Nimitz's place with the greatest Admirals is secure. Yet he exercised control from Pearl Harbour, and signed the Surrender for the U.S. without ever having heard a shot fired in anger. **D. D.**

'SEA POWER', BY E. B. POTTER AND CHESTER W. NIMITZ (PRENTICE-HALL, 1960); 'CHESTER WILLIAM NIMITZ', BY E. B. POTTER (U.S. NAVAL INSTITUTE PROCEEDINGS, JULY, 1966); 'HISTORY OF THE UNITED STATES NAVAL OPERATIONS IN WORLD WAR II', BY SAMUEL ELIOT MORISON (O.U.P., 15 VOLS., 1947–1962).

Richard Nixon (U.S., b. 1913): head of state. Nixon entered the House of Representatives in 1946 after fighting in the Second World War and achieved fame in 1948 for exposing Alger Hiss, a distinguished civil servant, as a Communist and perjurer. This success helped get him elected Senator from California in 1950, and he was chosen to be Eisenhower's running-mate in 1952. Solid work for the party earned him the Republican nomination for President in 1960, but he was narrowly defeated by Jack Kennedy. In 1962 he was defeated in an attempt at becoming Governor of California. His political career seemed to be over, and he settled in New York as a practising lawyer, with great success. But he continued to work hard for the Republican Party, and was never entirely lost to sight. The result was an unprecedented comeback in 1968: he won his party's Presidential nomination for the second time, and also the election. But he remains an enigma to the world. Secretive, cautious, conservative, decent, limited, he is a professional politician to his fingertips. His place among the makers of the 20th century will be incontrovertible if he ends the Vietnamese War and calms the Negro revolution. **D. H. V. B.**

'SIX CRISES', BY RICHARD M. NIXON (DOUBLEDAY, N.Y., 1962); 'THE MAKING OF THE PRESIDENT, 1960', BY THEODORE H. WHITE (CAPE, 1962); 'DIVIDED THEY STAND', BY DAVID ENGLISH (MICHAEL JOSEPH, 1969).

Kwame Nkrumah (Ghanaian, born *c.* 1909): politician. Nkrumah, though now in exile, will be remembered as the first and most significant of all the leaders of independent Africa. He spent 10 years in higher education in the U.S., acquiring a strong sense of Negro solidarity and a burning vision of a free and independent United States of Africa. He returned to the Gold Coast in 1947 and immediately set about organising a mass party with which to challenge British rule, using strikes and civil disobedience to force confrontation. Imprisoned for sedi-

tion in 1950, his party won an overwhelming electoral victory in 1951, and he was released to head the Government. Thereafter he co-operated with the last British governor, Sir Charles Arden-Clarke, in a completely peaceful transfer of power, achieving independence for Ghana in 1957. From 1951 until 1961 Nkrumah was the undisputed leader of the African revolution, stimulating independence movements in other colonies and always preaching the pan-African ideal. Yet decline came quickly. Once firmly in power, he persecuted and then abolished the parliamentary opposition. His own party, given the monopoly, lost touch with the electorate and became increasingly corrupt. Nkrumah himself became a feared and hated dictator. He was overthrown by a military coup in 1966. **R. O.**

'GHANA; THE AUTOBIOGRAPHY OF KWAME NKRUMAH' (NELSON, 1957).

Lord Northcliffe (British, 1865–1922): newspaper publisher. Alfred Harmsworth was the creator of present-day popular journalism and the most successful publisher of the 20th century. He achieved this through understanding the tastes, prejudices, and limitations of the vast new reading public created by the Education Act of 1870. After leaving school at 16 he freelanced, and at 20 became editor of *Bicycling News*. One year later he launched his first weekly, *Answers*, on a capital of £1000. In all his activities his own journalistic acumen was supported by the financial skill of his brother Harold, later Lord Rothermere. In 1894 he moved into the field of daily journalism, buying the near-defunct *London Evening News* for £23,000 and making £25,000 from it in the first year. He followed this by launching a new-style morning paper, the *Daily Mail* – "The Penny Newspaper for One Half-Penny" – in 1896, establishing an immediate world circulation record which was maintained throughout his lifetime. Next he bought up a Sunday, the *Weekly Dispatch*, launched the *Daily Mirror* (1903), rescued *The Observer* (1905) and took over control of *The Times* (1908). This marked the peak of his prestige. Though doing valuable national work in the First World War, Northcliffe had little political grasp. Towards the end of his life, he lost judgment, balance, and finally sanity. **T. H.**

'NORTHCLIFFE: AN INTIMATE BIOGRAPHY', BY HAMILTON FYFE (ALLEN AND UNWIN, 1930); 'STRICTLY PERSONAL', BY CECIL KING (WEIDENFELD AND NICOLSON, 1969).

Montagu Norman (British, 1871–1950): banker. Lord Norman, a strange, depressive, lonely, arrogant figure, dominated the financial world of the Twenties as no central banker, either before or since, has done. Entering the Bank of England as a part-time dogsbody during the First World War, by 1918 he was Deputy Governor, and by 1920 Governor – the job he filled for an unprecedented 24-year term. Through his central role in the handling of German reparations, post-war reconstruction, the restructuring of Britain's steel and shipbuilding industries, and above all the 1925 restoration of the Gold Standard at the pre-war sterling-dollar parity, he played a crucial part in the drama of slump, depression and mass unemployment which filled those years. In 1931, while he was recovering from a nervous

breakdown, his policies finally foundered, as Britain went off gold once more; and for his remaining years he was seen less as an independent arbiter of nations, more as Britain's most skilful technocrat in a world of managed currencies. But after his retirement in 1944, the Government made certain, first by law, and then by nationalising the Bank, that no governor should ever hold such independent power again. **P. W.**

'MONTAGU NORMAN', BY ANDREW BOYLE (CASSELL, 1967).

John Northrop (U.S., b. 1891): biochemist. When J. B. Sumner (q.v.) produced in 1926 his startling conclusion that enzymes were basically protein, he was ignored, to say the least, by his colleagues. But John Northrop considered Sumner might well be right and extended Sumner's work with much more elaborate techniques. By 1930 he had isolated and crystallised pepsin, the protein-splitting digestive enzyme in gastric secretions, and proved it to be a protein. In the next five years trypsin and chymotrypsin were isolated and purified, as well as ribonuclease and desoxyribonuclease: all were protein. The last two have been indispensable tools in the recent extraordinary advances in the knowledge of nucleic acids – the master molecule of the living cell. With the work of Sumner and Northrop enzymes ceased to be mysterious substances and came to possess a known chemical nature. The next problem to attract Northrop's attention was the completely un-

known nature of viruses. W. M. Stanley (q.v.) had been using the Sumner and Northrop techniques to isolate the tobacco mosaic virus and in 1938 Northrop isolated the first bacterial virus, which was also, as he had suspected, a protein. In fact, a bacterial virus had been reported by Max Schlesinger in 1933, but this work had attracted little attention. **P. G. R.**

'CRYSTALLINE ENZYMES', BY J. H. NORTHROP, M. KUNITZ AND R. M. HERRIOT (COLUMBIA U.P., 1948).

Lord Nuffield (British, 1877–1963): manufacturer. Nuffield was to Britain what Ford was to the U.S; the Morris Oxford was the answer to the Model T Ford. This was the first of a stream of cars to pour from Nuffield's vigorous enterprise. William Richard Morris, a farmer's son, enjoyed amateur cycle racing and began work in a cycle repairer's shop in Oxford. It was not long before he set up a similar business of his

own and soon he turned to manufacturing bicycles in works set up in buildings of the Military College and old Grammar School at Cowley, near Oxford. Motor cycles followed, and late in 1912 came the first Morris Oxford car to give firm foundation to the fame and fortune to follow. Nuffield's success in the British car manufacturing industry was immense. A merger between Morris and Austin (1952) created a vast organisation incorporating many famous brands of cars. One of the biggest philanthropists of his time, Lord Nuffield's prodigious bequests totalled some £25,000,000 in his lifetime, the Nuffield Foundation alone being endowed to the tune of £10,000,000. But for many his name will always be associated with cars like the famous Hotchkiss-engined 'Bullnose' Morris and the M.G. (Morris Garage) sports cars of the Twenties and Thirties. **P. O. W.**

'THE LIFE OF LORD NUFFIELD', BY E. BRUNNER AND P. W. S. ANDREWS (BLACKWELL, OXFORD, 1955).

Paavo Nurmi (Finnish, b. 1897): athlete. "Nurmi, Nurmi," the cry that echoed round the Olympic stadiums of the 1920s, hailed the inexorable success of the Flying Finn. Nurmi won nine gold and three silver Olympic medals and amassed an unrivalled total of 31 world records between 1920 and 1932. At the Antwerp Games in 1920 he retained for Finland the 10,000 metres title won in Stockholm in 1912 by his boyhood idol Hannes Kolehmainen. Four years later in Paris he won all four of his races, including the 1500 metres and the 5000 metres in the space of 90 minutes. But

for his disqualification for professionalism just prior to the Los Angeles games of 1932, he might have crowned his career with a tenth gold medal in the marathon. Nurmi has a stiffly erect gait and poker-faced expression. Occasionally he used to glance at his right palm wherein nestled some inspiration, believed by the crowds to be a portrait of his mother but known to his lapped opponents to be a stop-watch. In July, 1952, when the Olympic Games were staged in his nation's capital, Helsinki, the great stadium erupted when a balding but still trim figure in the familiar blue and white national colours glided on to the track carrying the torch on its last lap from Greece. Officialdom had forgiven and not forgotten. **N. McW.**

'A WORLD HISTORY OF TRACK AND FIELD ATHLETICS 1864-1964', BY R. L. QUERCETANI (O.U.P., 1964).

Tazio Nuvolari (Italian, 1892–1953): racing driver. Still held by many to have been the greatest motor racing driver of all time, despite the later claims of Fangio, Moss (qq.v.) and Clark, Nuvolari reached his zenith in the 1930s with Alfa Romeo and Auto Union. Apparently fearless, always a thin, wiry figure (he was only five feet tall) with wizened features and yet great muscular strength, Nuvolari soon got the reputation of being a David who could conquer any Goliath of the circuits. He graduated to four wheels after a distinguished early career on two, but a certain Italian recklessness kept him out of a full works team until he joined Alfa Romeo in 1930. Thereafter, for seven years, he scored victory after victory, often in inferior cars against apparently insuperable odds, often inflicting defeat on the otherwise invincible Germans. His greatest race was probably the 1935 German Grand Prix when, in a four-year-old Alfa Romeo, he beat five brand-new Mercedes-Benz and four Auto Unions. In 1937 Auto Union hired Nuvolari to drive their huge, 600 bhp rear-engined car. Dwarfed by the machine, he won the Italian and British Grands Prix the following year. Nuvolari drove his last race in the French Grand Prix of 1948, at the age of 56. He died in his home town of Mantua five years later, after a long illness, leaving behind him a still-continuing argument as to whether his exploits have ever been surpassed. **J. M. B.**

'NUVOLARI', BY COUNT GIOVANNI LURANI (CASSELL, 1959); 'GRAND PRIX RACING: FACTS AND FIGURES', BY GEORGE MONKHOUSE AND ROLAND KING-FARLOW (FOULIS, 1964).

Julius Nyerere (Tanzanian, b. 1922): head of state. Nyerere's 96 per cent. poll when re-elected in 1965 as President of Tanzania reflected genuine support for this unusual leader of independent Africa whose interpretation of African Socialism has aroused admiration and exasperation among his allies in both the political East and West. Christian teacher, Edinburgh graduate, Nyerere was a founder-member of the Tanganyika African National Union in 1954. He is an opponent of racism and the cult of personality; the Arusha Declaration of 1967 expressed his principal objective of "universal human dignity and social equality". An exponent of a democratic one-party system as the best means of achieving social and economic advancement in a poor, predominantly agricultural nation, Nyerere has given priority to self-help and nationalisation, though external aid and private enterprise are not excluded. His implementation of non-alignment in foreign relations, as over Communist Chinese aid, has sometimes aroused alarm, but his skill in effecting union with Zanzibar and in handling other local and domestic crises has won praise. His success in insisting on self-reliance as a foremost principle of national policy could make him one of Africa's, and the Third World's, most significant men of the century. **K. K.**

'FREEDOM AND UNITY', BY JULIUS K. NYERERE (O.U.P., 1967).

O

Hermann Oberth (German, b. 1894): engineer. Oberth, with Robert H. Goddard and Konstantin Tsiolkovsky (qq.v.), laid the theoretical foundation of space travel. He was inspired by Jules Verne, but soon rejected Verne's idea of being fired into space from a giant cannon. Rockets were the only possibility, he decided, though he was well aware of their

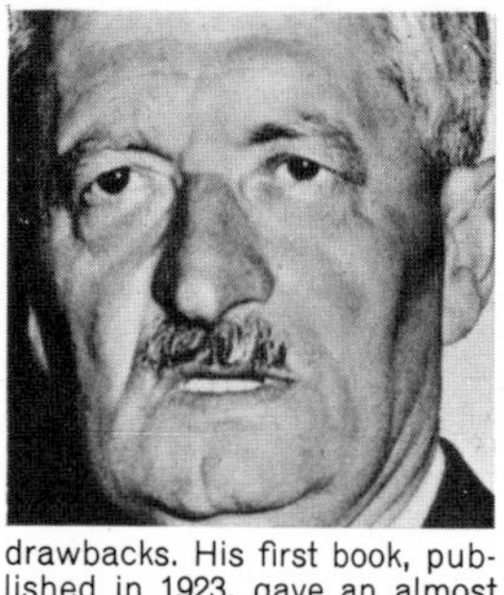

drawbacks. His first book, published in 1923, gave an almost complete discussion of all aspects of space travel, from observation satellites to manned space stations. Oberth showed that rockets could travel through a void, and that they could move faster than their exhaust velocities, two points of contention among early space pioneers. In practical matters Oberth was less successful than Goddard; one early experiment was partly financed by film director Fritz Lang (q.v.), who was making a film called *Girl in the Moon*, but it was not a success. However, Oberth's failure to get to grips with the nuts and bolts of space travel was far outweighed by the brilliance and originality of his ideas, which are astonishingly close to those of today. One proposal was for a giant mirror to be erected in space to reflect the Sun and keep shipping lanes clear of ice. **N. J. M. H.**

'ROCKETS, MISSILES AND SPACE TRAVEL', BY W. LEY (CHAPMAN AND HALL, REVISED ED., 1958); 'HISTORY OF ROCKETRY AND SPACE TRAVEL' BY WERNHER VON BRAUN AND F. I. ORDWAY (NELSON, 1966).

Sean O'Casey (Irish, 1880–1964): dramatist. For 30 years, up to the Wesker-Behan-Littlewood mood of the 1950s, O'Casey was a Marxist exile in southern England, mistrusted by the West End in a drab phase of drama. His offence: taking working-class characters seriously. At home in Dublin his Easter Rising play had stirred up riots. His offence: exposing patriotism. Then the Abbey Theatre had turned down *The Silver Tassie*. His offence: anti-war propaganda. There is no doubt that O'Casey was a dramatist on the side of life, but debate centres on his output after 1926; on extravaganzas written in old age like *The Bishop's Bonfire* (burnt out? refuelled?). Academics respect his formal experiments; detractors fault his autobiographies for overblown rhetoric. He's rightly admired for his do-it-yourself education, though it may have proved a handicap in exile where intellect feeds on itself. But he had energy, humanity and courage. And about *The Plough and the Stars* and *Juno and the Paycock* no reservations need be made.

They reflect war in perhaps its most intimately terrible form, and all too relevant: violence in the streets. To have experienced it, to have dramatised it incomparably and to have condemned it, blaming everyone and no-one, is O'Casey's noble gift to a violent century. **L. K.**

'SEAN O'CASEY, MODERN JUDGMENTS', BY R. F. AYLING (MACMILLAN, 1969); 'SEAN O'CASEY', BY D. KRAUSE (MACGIBBON AND KEE, 1960).

David Ogilvy (British, b. 1911): advertising executive. Once described as "the most sought after wizard of the advertising world", Ogilvy's main achievement was to add the miracle ingredient commonsense to the adjective-saturated Fifties. He didn't enter advertising in America until the age of 39 (his previous roles included that of chef in the Hotel Majestic, Paris), but he quickly – and volubly – took Madison Avenue by storm. Information, rather than emotional pap, formed the basis of much of his advertising, although, as a vigorous exponent of brand imagery, he was careful to include both visual richness and continuity of selling claim. His most celebrated advertisements were probably for Rolls-Royce ("At 60 mph the loudest noise in this new Rolls-Royce comes from the tick of the electric clock") and for the eye-patched 'Man in the Hathaway shirt'. He rapidly built up a formidable list of blue-chip accounts for his agency. Today David Ogilvy's approach – though not entirely supplanted – has been taken a stage further by admen who believe that greater subtlety and wit is needed to master the consumer. At 60, Ogilvy is still a figure in advertising, though he now describes himself as "an extinct volcano". **R. W.**

'CONFESSIONS OF AN ADVERTISING MAN', BY DAVID OGILVY (LONGMANS, 1964).

Claes Oldenburg (U.S., b. 1929): artist (above, with 'multiple' wedding cake). Born in Stockholm, Oldenburg grew up mostly in the U.S. (his father was in the Swedish diplomatic service). After graduating from Yale he worked as a journalist in Chicago. Employed from 1956–59 in the Cooper Museum Library in New York, he gradually came to terms with the city as a self-generating spectacle, an open stage on which the qualities normally set apart for 'art' or 'theatre' were in lavish and perpetual supply. By taking everyday objects and releasing their inner natures he got people to look again at their environment until they could say, with Constable, "I never saw an ugly thing in my life". (He once wrote in praise of "the majestic art of dogturds, rising like cathedrals".) "All the fun," he said, "is in locking horns with impossibilities – for example: combining our notions of sculpture with our notions of a simple, 'vulgar' object: hamburger or bedroom." Gifted with an innate theatrical sense (he was a pioneer of the happening in New York) he knows just how much a given idea will bear; and when he gives a cigarette-butt or a ballcock the treatment that Bernini reserved for nymph and triton we simply wonder why we had been so blind to the baroque extravagance of the one and the serene roundness of the other. Oldenburg is many things in one, but above all he is a poet whose work is a charm against alienation. **J. R.**

'CLAES OLDENBURG', BY B. ROSE (MUSEUM OF MODERN ART, NEW YORK, AUTUMN 1969); CATALOGUE OF OLDENBURG. EXHIBITION (MODERNA MUSEET, STOCKHOLM, 1966).

Joe 'King' Oliver (U.S., 1885–1938): cornetist, bandleader. King Oliver was third in the 'royal' line of New Orleans cornetists, after Buddy 'King' Bolden and Freddy 'King' Keppard. He was playing with top New Orleans bands in his teens,

and went north to Chicago in 1918 where he led King Oliver's Creole Jazz Band with Johnny and Baby Dodds and, from 1922 to 1924, Louis Armstrong (q.v.). During this period Oliver made a superlative batch of recordings – *Dippermouth Blues*, *Mabel's Dream*, *Chattanooga Stomp*. He was resident at Royal (afterwards Lincoln) Gardens, the focal point for young white Chicagoans like Bix Beiderbecke, Benny Goodman (qq.v.), Eddie Condon and Gene Krupa, and for touring musicians in transit. The change of fashion in the Twenties led to the Oliver band putting on instrumental weight (saxophones, etc.) with consequent loss of agility, and he declined steadily into poverty. His early records show Oliver to be a commanding player, perhaps the first New Orleans cornetist to sense the dramatic possibilities of the jazz solo, and he pioneered the 'wa-wa' muted effect imitated to the present day. He was the leader of the first great jazz ensemble, a 'university' for young musicians. It was Louis Armstrong who said: "Things that five-part brass sections play today, he played first." **H. R. A. L.**

'KINGS OF JAZZ', SERIES 8, BY MARTIN WILLIAMS (CASSELL, 1960); 'KING JOE OLIVER', BY W. C. ALLEN and B. L. RUST (SIDGWICK AND JACKSON, 1956).

Lord Olivier (British, b. 1907): actor and director. Laurence Olivier is the last great *monstre sacré* of the British theatre. Though he is not in the least a selfish or indulgent actor (he is as ready to take small parts as large) he is the only British player whose mere presence will fill theatres in London, the regions, and abroad, where he is almost as famous as he is in Britain. A romantic actor, able, as in his Richard III, to accomplish the most flamboyant effects, he is also immensely appreciative of detail, and can from a single phrase (like his famous "troops of friends" in *Macbeth*) distil the greatest and quietest beauty and pathos. His versatility is celebrated; on one night he has played Oedipus and Mr Puff. His interests range from Shakespeare, through the naturalistic drama, to the new theatre of social protest established by John Osborne, in whose *The Entertainer* he achieved one of his highest successes. In 1961 he was appointed director of the Chichester Festival Theatre, and soon afterwards became director of the National Theatre, which, with the creatively discordant collaboration of Lord Chandos and Kenneth Tynan, he has made into one of the world's foremost playhouses. Olivier is the only contemporary English actor who has played Othello successfully. In even the stoniest part he can discover traces of humanity, as when he found humour in the misogynistic hero of Strindberg's *The Dance of Death*. He has had a distinguished film career, appearing on the screen with his second wife Vivien Leigh, from whom he was divorced in 1960, and also with his present wife, Joan Plowright. **H. H.**

'THE OLIVIERS', BY FELIX BARKER (HAMISH HAMILTON, 1953); 'CRY GOD FOR LARRY', BY VIRGINIA FAIRWEATHER (CALDER AND BOYARS, 1969). 'OLIVIER: SHAKESPEARE', ED. P. WHITEHEAD AND R. BEAN (LORRIMER, 1966).

J. Robert Oppenheimer (U.S., 1904–1967): theoretical physicist. Oppenheimer is famous as the leader of the wartime Manhattan Project carried out at Los Alamos to make the atom bomb. Born in New York, he graduated at Harvard and then worked with Max Born in Göttingen, one of the centres at that time associated with the growth of new mathematical techniques. In 1929 he returned to California University. As Professor there from 1936 he established the first important American school of theoretical physics – later augmented by the influx of many famous European refugees from Hitler. Oppenheimer himself made many important contributions to the theory of the electron, cosmic rays, nuclear physics, and the physics of fundamental particles. After the end of the Second World War he took over as head of Los Alamos but was unfairly arraigned before the House Un-American Activities Committee, charged with tolerating Communist sympathies in certain of his colleagues. He left the laboratory in 1947 to direct the Princeton Institute of Advanced Studies which he developed into the world's most outstanding centre of theoretical physics. His name, however, will be permanently linked with his leadership of the atom bomb project. **P. H. S. S.**

'BRIGHTER THAN A THOUSAND SUNS', BY ROBERT JUNGK (GOLLANCZ, 1968).

John Boyd Orr (British, 1880–1971): administrator. Even movements that now seem obviously sound once needed a prophet and Lord Boyd Orr was the inspiration behind the drive after the Second World War to improve agriculture to feed the world's increasing millions. His own interest started much earlier. He qualified as a doctor in Scotland and studied animal nutrition, particularly at the Rowett Institute in Aberdeen which he converted from a small research station to one of international importance. His interest moved from animal nutrition to that of humans during the period between the two wars and he drew attention to the malnutrition that existed even in developed countries and was widespread in the underdeveloped ones. It was clear to him that hunger could be fought only by developing agriculture, and that crop surpluses should be used as food and not destroyed to maintain prices. After the Second World War he became the first Secretary-General of the Food and Agriculture Organisation of the United Nations, and his energetic and continuing interest in food production, world government and trade between East and West made him a major influence in the movement towards One World. **W. A. O.**

'AS I RECALL', BY LORD BOYD ORR (MACGIBBON AND KEE, 1966); 'FOOD, HEALTH AND INCOME', BY JOHN BOYD ORR (MACMILLAN, 1936).

Aristotle Onassis (Greek, b. 1906): shipowner. Like his former brother-in-law and life-long rival Stavros Niarchos (q.v.), Onassis is an outsider in the tight, traditional world of Greek shipping, where the families run back at least five generations. Son of a Smyrna tobacco merchant, he began his career as a 16-year-old telephone clerk in Buenos Aires but soon moved into his father's trade. The profits from this business enabled him to become a shipowner – buying half a dozen derelict ships from the Canadians during a shipping slump in 1930. After he had kept them mothballed for two years, the market recovered and the Onassis ships put to sea. From this base Onassis has over the last 40 years built up one of the world's largest individually-owned merchant fleets. In the process he has made a fortune of at least 500 million dollars and has pioneered many of the financial techniques now commonly used in the shipping industry. He has always been a bold and unconventional operator, fond of making all major decisions himself. Perhaps his biggest achievement was in being the first to spot the oil companies' growing need for massive tankers; he launched his first, a 15,000 tonner, as early as 1938. Well known as a socialite (Sir Winston Churchill [q.v.] was a frequent guest aboard his yacht, Onassis captured the headlines in 1968 by marrying Jacqueline Kennedy, the widow of the late President. **S. P. A.**

'ONASSIS', BY WILLI FRISCHAUER (BODLEY HEAD, 1968).

Eugene O'Neill (U.S., 1888–1953): dramatist. Poet of misfits and dreamers; an escape-artist, born in New York, son of an old-school actor. His early life was spent backstage and on the road. He ran away to sea, wandering for two years, then studied Ibsen, Chekhov and Strindberg at Harvard, and tried his own hand with the aid of the Provincetown Players and the New York Theatre Guild. Between 1914 and 1934 he wrote many plays, tackling anything once: expressionism in *The Hairy Ape* (1922), stream of consciousness in *Strange Interlude* (1928), Freud (q.v.) and Aeschylus in *Mourning Becomes Electra* (1931), Africana in *The Emperor Jones* (1920). Typical atmospheres are bleakly deterministic, in keeping with his sense of "the Force behind"; malicious chance, doomed heredity, evil in the scene rather than in the character. When *Days without End* failed in 1934, he went into the desert, pondering life and art. The great result was *Long Day's Journey into Night* (1940), his "play of old sorrow, written in tears and blood": an old-

fashioned play, but a masterpiece in its genre. No symbolism, beyond a touch of fog and a glimpse of sea; instead, a remarkable sense of character, feeling, the friction of people. His literary talent, like his invention, is not impressive: it has been said of him that he has a writing problem, as other victims have money problems or drink problems. But his theatrical flair, often erratic, is powerful, especially when propelled by a commitment to the rhythm of his own experience. In his last years he saw the theatre moving in alien directions; but he remains, in his own dogged way, a heavy-weight. **D. Do.**

'O'NEILL', BY ARTHUR AND BARBARA GELB, (CAPE, 1962); 'EUGENE O'NEILL', BY CLIFFORD LEECH (OLIVER AND BOYD, 1963); 'THE ORDINARY UNIVERSE', BY DENIS DONOGHUE (FABER AND FABER, 1968).

Sir Ernest Oppenheimer (British, ex-German, 1880–1957): diamond and mining magnate. 'King of Diamonds' became a journalistic cliché for the man who took over and extended the mantle of Cecil John Rhodes in both South and Central Africa. Oppenheimer acquired the German South West African diamond concessions after the First World War. From this base he moved into a power struggle with the old Diamond Syndicate, which ended in his gaining control of De Beers and the diamond market. During the Depression he laid out £13 million to buy up diamonds and prevent the collapse of the market. The risk

paid off. When boom times followed Britain's going off the gold standard in 1931, the stones sold for £40 million. Reinvested, this capital provided the cornerstone for economic development in South Africa and particularly Zambia (then Northern Rhodesia) where Oppenheimer developed the copper, lead and zinc mines. The Oppenheimer empire, ruled and expanded by his son Harry, now stretches across the world. **J. J. H. C.**

'ERNEST OPPENHEIMER AND THE ECONOMIC DEVELOPMENT OF SOUTHERN AFRICA', BY SIR THEODORE GREGORY (O.U.P., 1962).

George Orwell (British, 1903–1950): novelist and writer. Orwell would have said that centuries are shaped by political adventurers, faceless administrators and persons clever at exploiting the latest techniques. He would not have cared to be named among those responsible for the 20th, which appeared to him to be distinguished by elite mendacity and mob credulousness. He rendered this vision disturbingly in *Animal Farm* (1945), despairingly in *Nineteen Eighty-Four* (1949). That was his literary achievement, but there is also something mind-capturing about his personality, some quality of boyish and Quixotic courage. First typed as the Etonian who frequented dosshouses and espoused the cause of the underdog, he is better remembered for the straightforwardness with which he transcribed lived experience – with the police in Burma and fighting in the Spanish Civil War – in his essays and in *Homage to Catalonia* (1938). **R. H.**

'COLLECTED ESSAYS, JOURNALISM AND LETTERS OF GEORGE ORWELL' (SECKER, 1968); 'A STUDY OF GEORGE ORWELL', BY C. HOLLIS (HOLLIS AND CARTER, 1956); 'FOUR ABSENTEES', BY R. HEPPENSTALL (BARRIE AND ROCKLIFF, 1960).

John Osborne (British, b. 1929): dramatist. Osborne's greatest fame, and his greatest liability, too, has been the label 'Angry Young Man'. His origin is 'impoverished middle-class', boarding-school educated. His early career as a journalist and actor in rep. included three plays produced out of London before *Look Back in Anger* (1956) launched him as Britain's most exciting new dramatist since Noël Coward (q.v.). The play's central character, Jimmy Porter, gave a generation its cult hero, compelling with his stormy rhetoric even those who wondered plaintively what he was angry about. Later plays have shown Osborne experimenting with non-realistic staging devices to put over a gloomy allegory of England in decline (*The Entertainer*), turning to history in search of a hero to his taste (*Luther*), tangling with the Lord Chamberlain over his representation of a Vienna all too gay (*A Patriot for Me*) and being consecrated with a commission from the National Theatre (*A Bond Honoured*). *Inadmissible Evidence* (1964), perhaps his best play, reaffirmed his edgy instinct for contemporary neurosis; *The Hotel in Amsterdam* showed it bubbling even in the Jet Set. Deep distress still shows little sign of humanising his soul, but his tirades continue to appeal to a more genuinely popular audience than any of his contemporaries can command. **J. R. T.**

'ANGER AND AFTER', BY JOHN RUSSELL TAYLOR (METHUEN, 1962–69); 'THE PLAYS OF JOHN OSBORNE', BY SIMON TRUSSLER (GOLLANCZ, 1969).

Wilhelm Ostwald (German, ex-Latvian, 1853–1932): chemist. Viruses, man and the chemical industry would come to a stop without the existence of catalysts – although a hundred years ago the very idea of catalysts was faintly ridiculous. The man who established them as a potent chemical idea and subsequently both as a research and as an industrial tool was Wilhelm Ostwald, citizen of Riga and subsequently Professor of Chemistry at Leipzig. Catalysts are substances that alter the speed of a chemical reaction: sometimes they make it go slower, but usually their effect is to make it go appreciably faster. Catalysts generally emerge unscathed, so that, in an industrial context, they can be recovered and used again.

Their importance cannot be overestimated. Virtually any chemical process of importance, from the manufacture of sulphuric acid to the vast complexes of the petrochemical industry, is based on the use of catalysts. So is the body chemistry of all living creatures. A special class of catalysts, the enzymes, allows the thousands of chemical transformations necessary for life. Ostwald received the Nobel Prize in 1909, but the line of researches he started on the nature of catalysts is still going on. **P. J. F.**

'NOBEL LECTURES IN CHEMISTRY 1921–42', (ELSEVIER, 1966); 'BASIC PRINCIPLES OF CHEMISTRY', BY HARRY B. GRAY AND G. P. HAIGHT (BENJAMIN, NEW YORK, 1967).

Lee Harvey Oswald (U.S., 1939–1963): assassin. Oswald entered history when he assassinated John F. Kennedy (q.v.) in Dealey Plaza, Dallas, Texas, on November 22, 1963. His short life of failure and frustration ended two days later, when he himself was murdered before a global television audience in the Dallas County Jail by Jack Ruby. Oswald's father died before he was born; his family moved from New Orleans to Dallas to New York and back to New Orleans before he was 15. At 17 Oswald followed an older brother into the Marines; at 20, a civilian again, he defected to the Soviet Union; shocked by the lack of welcome and appreciation, he attempted suicide within a month of his arrival. In June 1962 he returned to Texas with his Russian wife. An abortive attempt on the life of General Walker, a Right-wing extremist, was followed by a move to New Orleans where he established himself as a one-man Fair Play for Cuba Committment. He returned to Dallas in October 1963, and got a job at the Texas School Book Depository which overlooks the route followed by President Kennedy's motorcade. Despite widespread suspicions, the efforts of numerous investigators and well-founded dissatisfaction with the methods of the Warren Commission which investigated the assassination, it has not been demonstrated either that Oswald was the agent of a conspiracy or an innocent fall guy. The act associated with his name marked the explosion into American public life of the violence expressive of that rootless America where the dream is not fulfilled. **W. H. J.**

THE WARREN COMMISSION REPORT (U.S. GOVT. PRINTING OFFICE, WASHINGTON, 1964); 'INQUEST: THE WARREN COMMISSION AND THE ESTABLISHMENT OF TRUTH', BY EDWARD JAY EPSTEIN (HUTCHINSON, 1966); 'RUSH TO JUDGMENT', BY MARK LANE (BODLEY HEAD, 1966); 'A MOTHER IN HISTORY', BY JEAN STAFFORD (CHATTO AND WINDUS, 1966).

Jesse Owens (U.S., b. 1913): athlete. All heroes depend on *Zeitgeist*, but the immortals must have that and more. James Cleveland Owens is such an immortal. Owens's first imprint on the history of athletics was made at Ann Arbor, Michigan, in 1935. "He had a very bad back injury," said coach Larry Snyder. "We almost had to carry him from the bus. I told him to try it out in the 100 yards, but to withdraw if he felt any pain." Owens 'tried out' with a 100-yard run of 9.4 seconds, equalling the world record. Within an hour he had broken another four world records (220 yards, 200 metres, 220-yard hurdles, 200-metre hurdles) and was facing a crisp specially-prepared grass long jump runway. He took only one leap, cutting sand at 26ft 8¼in., a record that was to stand for over 20 years. Owens's greatest days were still to come. These were August 2–9, 1936, in Hitler's (q.v.) grey, Wagnerian Olympic stadium. He made 12 appearances in the Berlin Games and was 12 times victorious, taking four gold medals. The immediate post-Olympic period was a dismal one, involving an abortive series of professional appearances. Owens reappeared in 1956 as President Eisenhower's (q.v.) special envoy to the Melbourne Olympics and he is being used by the Munich Olympic Committee to publicise the 1972 Games. It is, however, Leni Riefenstahl's magnificent 1936 Olympic film that has captured forever the most lasting impressions of Owens. Crouching like a pan-ther before his record long jump, gulping nervously at the start of the 100 metres, his legs a black blur as he passes Mariani in the sprint relay, he is speed, he is grace, he is beauty. It is thus that he will be remembered. **T. McN.**

'A WORLD HISTORY OF TRACK AND FIELD ATHLETICS 1864–1964', BY R. L. QUERCETANI (O.U.P., 1964).

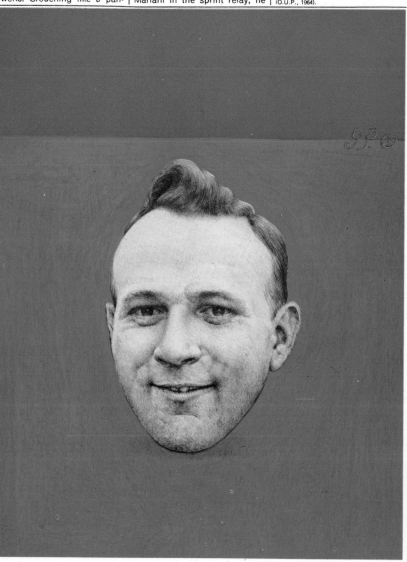

P

Arnold Palmer (U.S., b. 1929): golfer. Palmer has done more than any other one man to popularise golf, both by the magnificence of his own achievements in world professional golf and by the compulsive magnetism of his personality. Revered in America (and practically everywhere else), where he is constantly followed by thousands of fans known as 'Arnie's Army', Palmer's ability to come from behind to win caused the word 'charge' to be added to golfing jargon. Where others earn success with elegant, controlled swinging Palmer pioneered a smash-bash technique. While rivals play conservatively, he boldly goes for everything. In the 1966 U.S. Open, for example, when he was leading Casper by seven shots with nine holes to play, he went for the Open aggregate record and lost both lead and championship. He saved the status of the British Open by playing in it from 1960, winning the title in the two following years; and he won the American Amateur in 1954, the Open in 1960, and the Masters four times – 1958, 1960, 1962, 1964. The first golfer to be made use of commercially – by Cleveland attorney Mark McCormack – Palmer has become a multi-millionaire, with golf driving ranges, dry-cleaning stores, and everything down to Arnold Palmer lawn mowers marketed in his name the world over. He is now recognised, by everyone except Palmer, to be on the wane. **B. W.**

Friedrich Paneth (Austrian, 1887–1958): chemist. Paneth was a member of the invisible college of scientists which made the

study of radiations a potent force of our time. Educated in Vienna, Munich and Glasgow, he became Professor of Chemistry at Durham and during the Second World War led the chemistry division of the British-Canadian atomic energy team at Montreal. His most significant contributions are in the peaceful uses of radioactivity. Together with Hevesy, he developed the use of radioactive tracers which one can visualise as marked or tagged atoms whose paths can be followed through various transformations. These techniques found uses in fields ranging from plant growth to the treatment of tumours. Examining some important chemical transformations, he introduced the concept of free radicals – highly active chemical species of exceedingly short life that play an important part in many chemical systems, some of great industrial utility. **P. J. F.**

'A BIOGRAPHICAL DICTIONARY OF SCIENTISTS', ED. T. I. WILLIAMS (A. AND C. BLACK, 1960).

Emmeline Pankhurst (British, 1858–1928): campaigner. Emmeline Goulden, eldest of the 10 children of a Manchester cotton printer, married Richard Pankhurst, a left-wing barrister, in 1879, and had four children within six years. Pankhurst died in 1898 before Emmeline and her almost equally famous daughters Christabel and Sylvia began to make history. In 1903 Mrs Pankhurst founded the Women's

Social and Political Union with the simplest possible slogan, 'Votes for Women'. Between then and the outbreak of war in 1914 her name was seldom out of the newspapers. An eloquent and passionate speaker, she was prepared also to experiment with almost all forms of direct action, including what she called "the argument of the stone". Not surprisingly she turned the women's suffrage movement from a joke into a threat to the established order. She was given several gaol sentences. She also became the terror not only of reactionaries but of respectable liberal politicians. Yet in 1914 she transferred her efforts to recruiting platforms and ended her days as a Conservative candidate for Parliament. In the month of her death women finally got the vote on the same terms as men. **A. B.**

'MY OWN STORY', BY E. PANKHURST (NASH, 1914); 'VOTES FOR WOMEN', BY R. FULFORD (FABER, 1957).

Erwin Panofsky (U.S., ex-German, 1892–1968): art historian. The most intellectually glamorous art historian of his generation, Panofsky became the dominant influence on the growth of art historical studies in the U.S. He went there as a refugee from the Nazis. His ideal and technique as a historian (subtly combining several lines of thought well-

established in Germany) was to transform the fragments of past art and related activity into a scheme of systematic knowledge: systematic in that it fitted a painting or a piece of sculpture into the culture in which it was produced, finding what it shared with the attitudes of other aspects of that culture, like its religion and philosophy. The search for a common attitude underlying different aspects of mental life at any one time was closely connected with his absorption with the problems of mediaeval and Renaissance symbolism – an absorption charged with rare visual sensitivity. Individual aspects of works were treated by Panofsky, where possible, as parts of a visual theme or argument developing through history: for instance, he assumed that an underlying tension existed between mediaeval modes of symbolisation and naturalism, and he saw van Eyck resolving the tension between them. He achieved greatest conviction where artists were themselves theoretically and historically self-conscious, most brilliantly in his monograph on Dürer. **M. I. P.**

BOOKS BY PANOFSKY: 'MEANING IN THE VISUAL ARTS' (DOUBLEDAY, NEW YORK, 1955); 'A. DURER' (PRINCETON U.P., 1943); 'EARLY NETHERLANDISH PAINTING' (HARVARD U.P., 1953); 'STUDIES IN ICONOLOGY' (OXFORD UNIVERSITY PRESS, NEW YORK, 1939).

George Papanicolaou (U.S., ex-Greek, 1883–1962): cytologist. As a medical officer in the Balkan War (1912–13), Papanicolaou met Americans who inspired him to visit the U.S. He arrived in New York with his wife and

life-long assistant Mary in 1913, and worked as a salesman until his appointment as Anatomical Assistant, and later as Professor, at Cornell University. There he used vaginal smears to study the reproductive cycle in guinea pigs and humans. In 1927 he observed cancer cells in a vaginal smear for the first time. Abandoning endocrine studies for good, he devoted the rest of his life to detecting curable cancer in the uterus, bladder, stomach, bowel and lung. Pathologists, who imagined that he was invading their territory, and surgeons, who denied the existence of invisible cancer, opposed him persistently; but community tests in British Columbia proved the value of the 'Pap Test'. Dr Pap, as his friends called him, was the first to see that this technique could eliminate many cancers as causes of death. **S. W.**

Vilfredo Pareto (Italian, 1848–1923): economist and sociologist. Pareto was trained as an engineer and spent his early life in industry; but dismayed by the low quality of everyday economic argument and policy making, he sought to apply to economics the methods of the physical sciences. He eventually established himself at the University of Lausanne and became one of the great pioneers of mathematical economics. Certain of his theoretical contributions – e.g. on economic equilibrium or the distribution of incomes – remain of importance. Resistance to his ideas on the part of businessmen and politicians then led Pareto to an interest in sociology which he regarded as being specifically concerned with the sources and social functions of non-rational thought and action. Here, perhaps his major contribution was in drawing attention to basic regularities in human conduct which persist

across societies and cultures, although *rationalised* by a great variety of doctrines and ideologies. As against theories of progressive social evolution or revolution, Vilfredo Pareto emphasised those processes which, he believed, were found in all human societies and were reflected in recurrent *cycles* of change. **J. H. G.**

'PARETO AND MOSCA', ED. JAMES H. MEISEL (PRENTICE-HALL, 1965); 'SOCIOLOGICAL WRITINGS', BY VILFREDO PARETO, ED. S. E. FINER (PALL MALL PRESS, 1966).

Charlie Parker (U.S., 1920–1955): jazz musician. Parker was the first post-war jazzman to join the ranks of King Oliver, Bix Beiderbecke (qq.v.) and a handful of others as a legendary figure. Parker emerged from the rather tired jazz sounds of the Forties to produce a terse, angular style which rocked the jazz boat and injected new life into the music. In 1941 he met trumpet-player Dizzy Gillespie (q.v.), and by 1945 they had

evolved a sort of anti-melodic style of playing together which had become the talk of musicians and enthusiasts alike in the eastern U.S. Critics were harsh in judgment of the new music, and the disheartened Parker had a continual fight against lack of acceptance and an increased involvement in drugs. Moreover he was unable, unlike Gillespie, to turn his new discoveries in music into a commercial asset. From 1946 onwards his playing activities were interspersed with periods of total physical breakdown, and his deteriorating mental state made him virtually unemployable. But during this final period (1950–55) he was able to make a considerable number of recordings, some of which show him still at the height of his powers. **J. P. W. D.**

'BIRD: THE LEGEND OF CHARLIE PARKER', ED. R. G. REISNER (MACGIBBON AND KEE, 1963). RECORD: 'CHARLIE PARKER', VOLS. 1–6 (EROS SAGA 8005/6/7, 8031, 8035, 8052).

Dorothy Parker (U.S., 1893–1967): wit, poet. She was born of a Jewish father and a Scottish mother, went to convent school, and became a Manhattan Madame de Sévigné. She wrote fashion captions for *Vogue* at ten dollars a week and said brevity was the soul of lingerie. She became dramatic critic of *Vanity Fair* and the *New Yorker* and said in a one-line review that *The House Beautiful* was the play lousy. In New York in the 1920s Dorothy Parker was surrounded by a court of James Thurber (q.v.), E. B. White, Ogden Nash, and Ring Lardner. She said men seldom made passes at girls who wore glasses, claimed that if all the girls at the Yale prom. were laid end to end

she wouldn't be at all surprised. She reported on the Spanish Civil War, wrote short stories and Hollywood film scripts, and was married three times, twice to the same man. She bequeathed most of her estate to Martin Luther King. She will live for her sad, sharp poems of love and death. Edmund Wilson said she was not Emily Brontë or Jane Austen, but had put into what she wrote a voice, a few moments of human experience, that nobody else had conveyed. **T. F. C.**

'THE BEST OF DOROTHY PARKER' (METHUEN, 1952); 'NOT SO DEEP AS A WELL', COLLECTED POEMS OF DOROTHY PARKER' (HAMISH HAMILTON, 1937).

Talcott Parsons (U.S., b. 1902): sociologist. Parsons must be rated as the most notable of modern sociological theorists. His major objective has been to specify the analytical elements out of which a general theory of human society might be built. Initially, under the influence of Max Weber (q.v.), Talcott Parsons concentrated on the elements of a theory of social *action* – seeking to identify the fundamental dilemmas by which all such action is patterned. More recently, his attention has shifted towards the theory of social *systems*; the attempt here being to specify the exigencies with

which all viable societies must cope, and to relate these to the range of variation in their structural features. Probably his major substantive contribution has been in developing the insights of Durkheim (q.v.) into the integrative functions of cultural values – these being, Parsons emphasises, both *institutionalised* in social structures and *internalised* in individual personalities. **J. H. G.**

'THE SOCIAL THEORIES OF TALCOTT PARSONS', ED. MAX BLACK (PRENTICE-HALL, 1961).

Nikola Pašić (Serbian, 1845–1926): statesman. Pašić was the outstanding political figure in Serbia in the first quarter of the century and one of the founders of the much larger state of Yugoslavia. In his youth a revolutionary, he was for a time associated in Switzerland with Michael Bakunin. The Radical

Party which he founded at first stood for the interests of the small peasants. In 1883 it was involved in an armed rising in the Timok valley. In 1889 Pasic returned from exile and in 1891 he became Prime Minister for the first time. Under King Peter (1903–1921) Pasic dominated civil affairs and grew steadily more conservative, while his Radical Party grew into a powerful interest group of newly rich businessmen and senior bureaucrats. Pasic's leadership of Serbia in the First World War was a major contributing factor in the creation of Yugoslavia. However, he thought in terms of extending the territory of the Serbian state rather than of forming a fraternal union of Serbs, Croats and Slovenes. He therefore only half-heartedly resisted Italian claims on Croatian territory, and he imposed a centralist constitution on the new kingdom against Croatian wishes. A great patriot but a narrow nationalist, Pasic deserves credit for Serbia's glories, but he has much responsibility for the national hatreds which brought Yugoslavia to disaster 15 years after his death. **H. S.-W.**

'A SHORT HISTORY OF YUGOSLAVIA', ED. S. CLISSOLD (C.U.P., 1966); 'SERBIA BETWEEN EAST AND WEST', BY WAYNE VUCINICH (STANFORD U.P./OXFORD, 1954).

La Pasionaria (Spanish, b. 1895): Communist leader. Dolores Ibarruri ('La Pasionaria') achieved fame by a speech on the Republican Madrid Radio at the outbreak of the Spanish Civil War. "It is better to die on our feet than live on our knees. They shall not pass." Born to poverty in the Basque mining country she 'sought liberation' from domestic service by marrying a miner who was frequently imprisoned for Socialist activities. Elected to the Central Committee of the Spanish Communist Party in 1930, she became an editor of the Party daily and was arrested by the Republican Government in 1931. She went to Moscow in November 1933. Arrested again in January 1936, she was released on her election as Deputy upon the victory of the Popular Front in 1936. At rallies she castigated non-Communist generals as "revelling in brothels" and supported the hard line against the "charlatan Trotskyites" who resented Communist domination of the governmental and military apparatus. Her early poverty, her severe black dress and her tremendous gifts as a popular orator gave her a moral and romantic appeal to Left wing intellectuals and direct contact with the masses. She went into exile in Russia in 1939. **R. Ca.**

'THEY SHALL NOT PASS', BY DOLORES IBARRURI (LAWRENCE AND WISHART, 1967).

Boris Pasternak (Russian, 1890–1960); writer. The leading Russian poet – many would say the leading world poet – of the century. In his great novel *Doctor Zhivago* the lyric quality breaks through, uniquely, to the level of high tragedy. Its publication in the West in 1958 and the award to its author of the Nobel Prize for Literature drew on him – and not for

the first time – the whole animus of the Soviet state. Pasternak did not hate the Revolution. When many of Russia's greatest were emigrating, it did not occur to him to leave: his strength had always arisen from a special feeling for the Russian countryside and the Russian character. What he rejected was the primacy of politics and the exaltation of the temporary against the enduring. What he loathed in Stalinist and post-Stalinist Russia was "the inhuman power of the lie". At present he stands above all for the resistance of a courageous and crea-

tive mind to the vast and ignorant power of the machinery of despotism. All the same, he was essentially a lyric poet, of shattering brilliance and depth; and for the new generation in Russia it is his poetry which represents all that is still rich and vivid, and so promising, in the life and language of their country. **G. R. A. C.**

BOOKS BY BORIS PASTERNAK: 'DOCTOR ZHIVAGO', TR. M. HAYWARD AND M, HARARI (HARVILL, 1958); 'POEMS 1955–1959', TR. M. HARARI (HARVILL/COLLINS, 1960); 'SELECTED POEMS', TR. J. M. COHEN (LINDSAY DRUMMOND, 1946); 'THE CREATIVE EXPERIMENT', BY C. M. BOWRA (MACMILLAN, 1949).

Paul VI (Italian, b. 1897): Pope. His shrewd predecessor, Pope John (q.v.), nicknamed him Hamlet. Paul's decrees against contraceptives and against rebels or legendary saints in the Catholic Church have won him another reputation: of being too decisive. But he still seems to be a tragic figure, as since 1963 he has tried to cope with problems which John uncovered but did

not face. His policy has attempted to combine the preservation of piety and discipline in the Church with intelligent leadership of the world's social hopes. The piety is in his own inner nature because he has never lived away from Catholic discipline. Going to Rome after ordination in 1920, he was based almost entirely on the Eternal City until he became Archbishop of Milan in 1954. In the Vatican's Civil Service he became one of the two chief assistants to Pius XII (q.v.). The intelligence is lifelong, too. His father was a prominent politician

in the Popular Party, a Catholic laymen's movement which the Vatican (not unwillingly) sacrificed to Mussolini (q.v.). Giovanni Battista may have carried on some of this father's lively independence; at least, his master Pope Pius did not trust him enough to make him a cardinal. As a clever young theologian he was the chaplain of intellectuals; as an archbishop he was the unconventionally active pastor of the industrial workers. Nothing less heavy than his sense of responsibility as the Vicar of Christ has outweighed his sympathy with modern men. **D. L. E.**

'POPE PAUL VI', BY ROY MACGREGORHASTIE (FREDERICK MULLER, 1964); 'HUMANAE VITAE', BY POPE PAUL VI (ENCYCLICAL FORBIDDING ARTIFICIAL BIRTH CONTROL, CLARK AND CRAWFURD, 1968).

Wolfgang Pauli (U.S.,ex-Austrian, 1900–1958): theoretical physicist. A giant of 20th-century theoretical physics, Pauli was responsible for a theory of enormous significance – the so-called exclusion principle.

After graduating in Vienna where he was born, he went in 1918 to Munich University to work under Sommerfeld. After starting to study relativity he switched to thinking about the quantum theory of the atom, then just at the start of a major period of growth. Atomic spectra, although largely explained on the basis of electrons confined to 'quantised' orbits around the atom's nucleus, revealed several features that remained unaccounted for. The quantum theory stipulates that these electrons can exist only in certain specified energy states; with great insight Pauli realised also that it was impossible for more than one electron to lie in any one of these energy states. Once an energy level was filled with an electron it was effectively 'closed' to any other. The exclusion principle explained the 'shell structure' of the atom in which electrons form concentric shells around the nucleus; it explained why some elements are chemically more reactive

than others; and it explained atomic spectra in complete detail. Further, it had wide implications for the theory of the nucleus itself and the symmetry laws of nature. Pauli became Professor of Theoretical Physics at the Federal Institute of Technology, Zurich, in 1928. He received the Nobel Prize in 1945, for work which has formed a cornerstone of modern physics. **P. H. S. S.**

'THE WORLD OF THE ATOM', ED. H. A. BOORSE AND L. MOTZ (BASIC BOOKS, 1966).

Linus Pauling (U.S., b. 1901): chemist. The genius of Pauling cannot be in doubt. Double Nobel laureate, for Chemistry in 1954 and again for Peace in 1962, he has the supreme gift of scientific intuition that arranges facts into patterns having the truth of simplicity in place of random disorder. All who are working today in chemistry and related sciences have been brought up on his books about the chemical bond in which the most fundamental ideas of chemistry have been used to illuminate the manifold arrangements of substances and their reactions. These same ideas have been brought to bear on the chemistry of the living organism, especially on the constitution of proteins and nucleic acids. As if scientific contributions were not enough, Pauling's name is also associated with ideas concerning the involvement of scientists in modern society. Although his views are by no means universally accepted, they at least

forced a serious debate on these topics to the benefit of all. But for generations of scientists he is by far the most important figure in bringing home the underlying reality of the materials they work with and in acting as a seed for crystallising the thoughts and ideas that ensure the continued development of science. **P. J. F.**

'THE NATURE OF THE CHEMICAL BOND', BY LINUS PAULING (CORNELL U.P., 1939, O.U.P., 1960); 'THE DOUBLE HELIX', BY J. D. WATSON (WEIDENFELD AND NICOLSON, 1968).

Ivan Petrovitch Pavlov (Russian, 1849–1936): physiologist. Pavlov's work on the digestive system won him a Nobel prize in 1904 but he is most famous for his work on the conditioned reflex. An ordinary reflex action of salivation will occur if dry food is placed in a dog's mouth, but Pavlov observed that sometimes salivation occurred at the sight of food or at other stimuli associated with it. He reproduced this effect in an experimental situation where the presentation of food was always preceded by another stimulus (a buzzer, for example). After a number of such paired presentations the buzzer alone was sufficient to elicit salivation. This reaction to the buzzer alone is called the conditioned reflex and the process of establishing it is called conditioning. Pavlov saw himself as a physiologist studying the brain, but his model of brain function has since been invalidated. His greatest impact in the West has been in psychology. J. B. Watson (q.v.) incorporated the concept into behaviourism, which gave great impetus to experimental psychology, especially in the study of learning. This led, among other things, to the development of teaching machines and to behaviour therapy where neurotic behaviour is seen as a bad habit to be unlearned. Aldous Huxley's (q.v.) novel *Brave New World* contains a vision of the misuse of conditioning techniques. **B. R. O.**

'CONDITIONED REFLEXES', BY I. P. PAVLOV (DOVER BOOKS, N.Y., CONSTABLE, 1960).

Anna Pavlova (Russian, *c.* 1885–1931): dancer. A frail child born in poverty in St Petersburg, Pavlova joined the Imperial Theatre School at 10 and became so outstanding a student that she danced with the company before her graduation. She was promoted to prima ballerina in 1906 and danced major roles for 10 years at the Maryinsky. In 1907 she began her famous tours in Europe, partnered by Bolm, Legat, Mordkin, etc. She appeared in *Les Sylphides* in Diaghilev's (q.v.) first season, and as a guest artist in London in 1910. Two years later she left Russia for good to form her own company. Her most famous dance was *The Dying Swan* arranged for her in 1905 to Saint-Saëns' music by Fokine (q.v.). She was an early follower of Fokine, but reverted to a more old-fashioned and conventional style, in which she knew how to exploit her marvellous qualities. The music, decor and choreography of her ballets were undistinguished. Most were dances specially arranged for her, expressing mood or period,

or characterising flowers or creatures: *Autumn Leaves, Christmas, Oriental Impressions, Dragonfly, Californian Poppy.* Whatever she danced was transmuted. She inspired a generation and spread the love of ballet through the world. **R. B.**

'ANNA PAVLOVA', BY V. DANDRE (CASSELL, 1932). 'PAVLOVA', BY WALFORD HYDEN (CONSTABLE, 1931).

Pelé (Brazilian, b. 1940): footballer. The finest footballer of his era, and possibly the most effective of all time, was a compound of strength, courage, speed, technique and elastic agility. He had scored over 1000 goals in first-class football before he was 29. Born Edson

Arantes do Nascimento into a poor Negro family, he was discovered by Brito, a former international, who brought him to the Santos club when he was 16. At 16 he was an international, at 17 he scored two astonishing goals in the World Cup Final of 1958 against Sweden in Stockholm. He was less fortunate in the 1962 and 1966 World Cups, dropping out after a couple of matches in 1962 with a pulled muscle, and suffering painful injury, at the hands of brutal defenders, in 1966. This caused him to swear he'd never play in another World Cup; but he changed his mind, and proved a crucial force in Brazil's triumphant 1970 win. His success as a striking, goal-scoring inside-left was the more remarkable in that it coincided with the era of packed, ruthless defences. Pelé himself believed, perhaps to his ultimate cost, in a policy of retaliation. **B. G.**

'THE BRAZIL BOOK OF FOOTBALL', ED. STRATTON SMITH (SOUVENIR PRESS, 1963); 'SOCCER: A PANORAMA', BY BRIAN GLANVILLE (EYRE AND SPOTTISWOODE, 1969).

Juan Perón (Argentinian, b. 1895): head of state. A typical middle-class Argentine army officer – more able and ambitious than most – Perón entered active politics in 1943 with the Group of United Officers. Argentina was, at that time, in political and social upheaval and the military offered stability, hegemony over South America and a break with 'capitalist imperialists' (meaning the United States and Great Britain). Up to 1945 Perón worked to win the loyalty of the common people from his position in the Department of Social Security. He replaced established union leaders with his own supporters and won the underdogs' devotion by lavish (occasionally implemented) promises. His wife, Eva Duarte, an adept demagogue, helped to bring him to the front rank of politics. In October 1946, in surprisingly clean elections, he was voted President of the Republic. He soon brought in some of his

own schemes: he tried to industrialise the country, he purged the Supreme Court, and gagged the opposition. He appeared to be set as Argentina's dictator for life. He was re-elected 1951, but lost support as he devastated the economy and alienated the military and others. Perón was ousted in September 1955, and now lives in Spain – still hoping that his party will recall him. **J. S.**

'THE PERON ERA', BY R. J. ALEXANDER (COLUMBIA UNIVERSITY PRESS, 1951); 'PERON'S ARGENTINA', BY G. I. BLANKSTEN (UNIVERSITY OF CHICAGO PRESS, 1953).

Max Perutz (British, ex-Austrian, b. 1914): crystallographer and molecular biologist. Best known for his work on the structure of haemoglobin, he introduced a technique in which heavy metal atoms replace side chains on the molecule and produce a measurable and meaningful change in X-ray diffraction patterns. The work of Sumner and Northrop (qq.v.) had shown that enzymes were proteinaceous, but gave no clue to their structure. Sanger (q.v.) had developed chemical methods for determining molecular structure, and Perutz decided that a combination of physical and chemical methods would be necessary. He took the first X-ray diffraction pictures of haemoglobin and chymotrypsin in 1937. The next 15 years were spent in the development of crystallography and in 1953 Perutz introduced his new technique. His colleague Kendrew (q.v.) used it to determine the structure of the simpler myoglobin molecule in 1957 and in 1959 Perutz got his three-dimensional picture of haemoglobin. The function of haemoglobin is to transport

oxygen from lungs to tissues, and in 1962 Perutz described the change in structure that occurs when oxygen is carried. This discovery suggested the way in which enzymes might change when combining with their substrate. **P. G. R.**

'PROTEINS AND NUCLEIC ACIDS', BY MAX PERUTZ (ELSEVIER, 1965).

Marshal Philippe Pétain (French, 1856–1951): soldier and head of state. At the outbreak of the First World War Pétain was 58, a colonel, and two years from retirement. By 1918 he was a Marshal of France. By his defence of Verdun, and his quelling of the 1917 army mutinies, he had become a national hero. In the inter-war period, in various roles, he took much responsibility for military policy, particularly that faith in the defensive which produced the Maginot Line. In 1939 he was France's first ambassador to Franco's Spain. Recalled during the Fall of France to join Reynaud's Government he negotiated the Armistice with Germany, and at 84 he was made head of the new Vichy State. In its internal affairs, he pursued a policy of regeneration of the nation by the National Revolution: a return to the traditional values of

work, the family, patriotism and the land. Externally, he attempted to find a *modus vivendi* with the Germans, which failed at every step owing to their continually heightened demands. In 1940, his attitude seemed to many the correct one; he had saved his defeated nation from destruction, the war seemed at an end. But by 1942 his position had become indefensible, and in 1945 a bitter liberated nation convicted him of treason. **R. M. G.**

'THE SWORDBEARERS', BY CORRELLI BARNETT (EYRE AND SPOTTISWOODE, 1963); 'TWO MEN WHO SAVED FRANCE, PETAIN AND DE GAULLE', BY MAJOR-GENERAL SIR EDWARD SPEARS (EYRE AND SPOTTISWOODE, 1966).

William Earl Petersen (U.S., 1892–1971): dairy scientist. Petersen was brought up on a Minnesota dairy farm and studied agriculture at the University of Minnesota. He joined the department of Dairy Husbandry there in 1921, retiring in 1960 as Professor. Petersen produced the first experimental case of milk fever in cattle in 1929, demonstrating the role of calcium deficiency. Effective treatment could then be developed. He constructed a 'mechanical cow' to keep the udders of freshly slaughtered cows functioning long enough to permit research into the physiology of milk secretion – until then a mystery. He discovered that a hormone, oxy-

tocin, controls milk 'let down', and proposed the first rational theory of milk ejection, thus interesting scientists for the first time in milking and milking machines. He saw the practical implications of his discoveries, and devised a cow-handling technique to stimulate hormone production and aid milking. With his vivid personality, he drew vast audiences to hear him. Most milking routines are now based on his findings. **S. L.**

'PRINCIPLES OF DAIRY FARMING', BY K. RUSSELL (FARMING PRESS, 1967).

Sir Flinders Petrie (British, 1853–1942): archaeologist. Petrie was one of the founders of modern scientific archaeology. He worked mostly in Egypt, and his practice of minute observation revolutionised Egyptology. In his own words he "weaved history out of scattered evidence". In the course of an enormously long active life – he was working in Jerusalem at the age of 89 – he approached excavation in a completely professional spirit. He was assiduous in preventing his diggers from selling objects secretly to dealers: in order to secure good relations with them, he paid workmen himself.

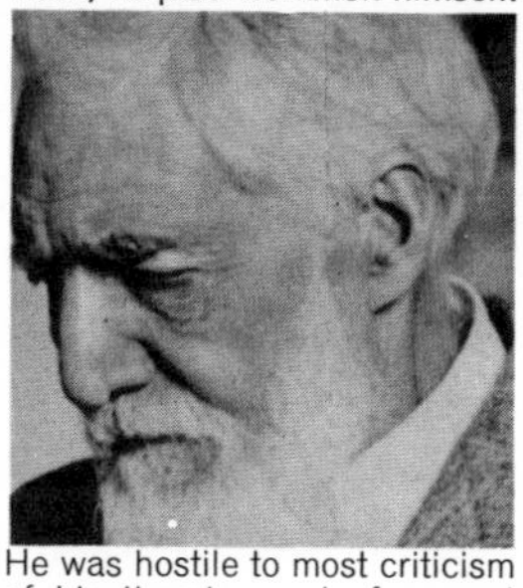

He was hostile to most criticism of his theories and of a most independent turn of mind. But he had the happy facility of making inspired deductions. He dated the middle Minoan period before Sir Arthur Evans discovered it, and did much pioneering work on the Egyptian bases of Greek history. **A. C. C.**

Sir Nikolaus Pevsner (British, ex-German, b. 1902): art historian. Among the refugee scholars with whom the Nazis endowed this country, Pevsner was outstanding both for the agility with which he adapted to English ways and for the enthusiastic discernment with which he sought out aspects of English art, architecture and design that had previously found few to praise them. Born in Leipzig, he arrived in England in 1935 and soon made a name for him-

self as teacher, editor and free-minded historian. His *Pioneers of the Modern Movement* (1936, later enlarged as *Pioneers of Modern Design*) and *An Outline of European Architecture* remain classics of their kind, and in his role as general editor he made a consistent success of the many-volumed *The Pelican History of Art.* But Pevsner is known above all for the unique contribution to our knowledge of ourselves which he made with his *Buildings of England* series. Backed by Penguin Books, he set out in 1945 to survey at first hand every single building in England that was worthy of commemoration. This vast adventure was memorable for the easy informality of the approach, the often caustic wit, the scholarship so lightly worn, and the insight into the humane resources of his adopted country. **J. R.**

BOOKS BY PEVSNER: 'PIONEERS OF MODERN DESIGN – FROM WILLIAM MORRIS TO WALTER GROPIUS' (MUSEUM OF MODERN ART, NEW YORK, 1948); AN OUTLINE OF EUROPEAN ARCHITECTURE' (PENGUIN, 1943); 'STUDIES IN ART, ARCHITECTURE AND DESIGN', 2 VOLS. (THAMES AND HUDSON, 1968).

Kim Philby (Soviet, ex-British, b. 1912): spy. About as successful a spy as we know of, Philby lived a double life for 30 years, gave his masters a series of particular coups and an invaluable general disclosure of Western intelligence operations, and at the end made a successful, if somewhat squeaky, getaway. He entered the Soviet service in 1933 after a conven-

tional upper-middle-class youth at Westminster and Trinity College, Cambridge. Via journalism, he penetrated the British Secret Intelligence Service and used that as a springboard to penetrate the American CIA. He actually set up Britain's counter-Soviet intelligence system in 1944, thus achieving the remarkable professional coup of being appointed to catch himself. Philby was able to make almost complete disclosure to the Russians of Western counter-espionage operations, thus protecting and making more useful many other spies – particularly Donald Maclean. Western plans to subvert European Communist governments in the Cold War years were largely defused by Philby. In joint command of one Anglo-American 'pilot plan' in Albania, he was able to betray it bloodily to the Russians. The defection of Burgess and Maclean in 1951 brought him under suspicion, and lost him his executive role in SIS. But he hung around the fringes of espionage until he fled to Russia in January 1963. He now lives in Moscow with his fourth wife Melinda, divorced wife of Donald Maclean. Apart from his espionage achievements, Philby shattered for ever the comfortable English belief that the traditional badges of school, club and university guaranteed the ideological reliability of the man within. **B. P.**

'PHILBY – THE SPY WHO BETRAYED A GENERATION', BY B. PAGE, D. LEITCH AND P. KNIGHTLY (REVISED ED., PENGUIN, 1969); 'MY SILENT WAR', BY KIM PHILBY (MACGIBBON AND KEE, 1968).

Anton Philips (Dutch, 1874–1951): industrialist. Although the Philips company was actually founded by his brother Gerard, it was Anton Philips who built it up from a struggling lightbulb manufacturing firm into a great international electrical combine. He did it primarily by sheer salesmanship. While Gerard worked at the Eindhoven factory on the technical problems of making better lamps, Anton travelled all over Europe – but particularly in Germany and Russia – to open up the big markets which were essential for economic production. Strong, energetic, competitive, his normal good humour occasionally swept aside by short fits of uncontrollable anger, he undertook an endless series of exhausting selling trips in the years before the First World War. Then, when he finally took over as head of the company from his brother in 1921, he maintained the pace of expansion by setting up a worldwide network of selling and manufacturing companies and established Philips's dominance in consumer goods once and for all by going into the mass-production of one of the world's first small, cheap radio sets. He did more to put modern electrical appliances into European homes than any other man, and as a result Philips is today the biggest electrical company in the world outside American ownership. **C. T. J.**

'ANTON PHILIPS OF EINDHOVEN', BY P. J. BOUMAN (WEIDENFELD AND NICOLSON, 1958).

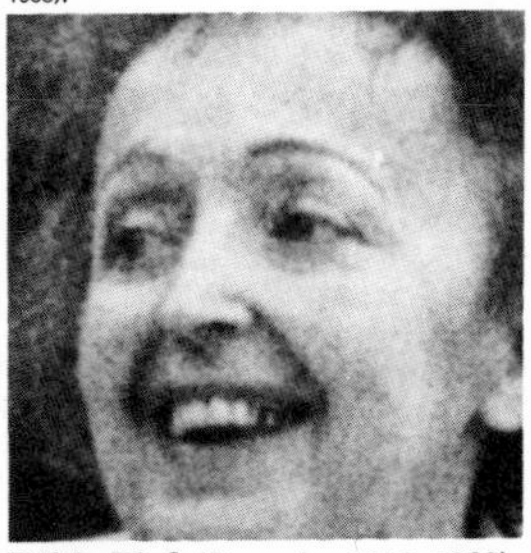

Edith Piaf (French, 1915–1963): singer. One of her songs was *Je ne Regrette Rien*, and that was how she was. Directly yet subtly, voice brimming with emotion, she sang of the tormented past. Words and music were nostalgic, aching, sometimes bitter, yet always tinged with the defiant optimism of *I Regret Nothing*. She became the darling of intellectual critics and an international symbol during the world-weary 1950s; through experiencing her artistry of distress, audiences deflected their own despair. A Parisian, illegitimate daughter of an acrobat, she was a street-singer when a night-club owner put her on stage. With her tattered clothes, bird-like face and diminutive (4 ft. 10 in.) frame, they naturally called her 'Piaf', argot for 'sparrow'. The legend was already being born, and the life of pain, tragedy and illness which followed nurtured it. One lover was murdered; another, boxer Marcel Cerdan, died in an air crash. She had a child who died of meningitis; she was divorced; she became very rich. In 1961 she collapsed during the run of her come-back show after a severe illness. She appeared in several movies, including Renoir's *French Can-Can*, and Cocteau wrote a play for her. Maurice Chevalier lauded her greatness. She was always making 'discoveries', among them Les Compagnons de la Chanson. Another of them, Theo Sarapo, she married a year before she died. Some of her songs (e.g. *La Vie en Rose*) will survive for ever. Piaf, Dietrich (q.v.) and the tragically similar Garland were perhaps the only women entertainers in mid-century able to unhinge an audience with emotion. **D. J.**

'THE WHEEL OF FORTUNE: THE AUTOBIOGRAPHY OF EDITH PIAF' (PETER OWEN, 1965). RECORDS: 'THE WORLD OF PIAF', 'SINCERELY EDITH PIAF' (COLUMBIA SCX 6317, SX 1276).

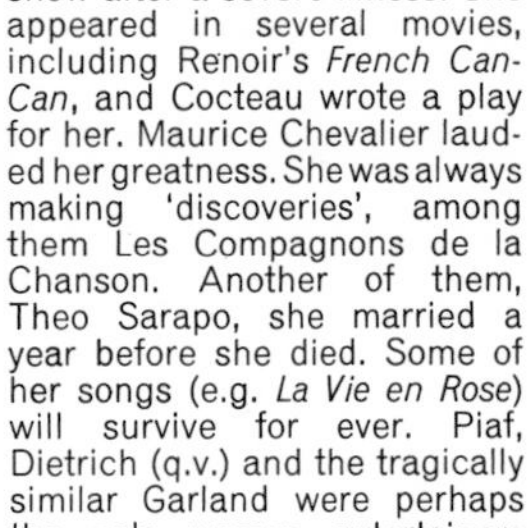

Jean Piaget (Swiss, b. 1896): psychologist. The significance of Piaget – cut off by his Swiss nationality, his lack of English or interest in travelling, his often elliptical prose style and reticent personality – has only been generally realised in his old age. Yet he made the critical breakthrough as a young father – by doing infinitely well what most young fathers do transiently. He studied his own three children – Laurent, Lucienne and Jacqueline. He kept a remarkable log book, recording and speculating on their every action. "Observation 126. Jacqueline at 1.11 can point back at the house on the way home; though she begins by pointing behind her, she changes her mind when she realises they are on the return trip". In other words, she's mastered an important concept about the shifting spatial relationship between her and the house. Not only does Piaget track delicately how the human child diverges from the rest of the animal kingdom, but he shows – often to disbelieving teachers – that a child's concepts are so different at each stage as to make much teaching completely irrelevant. Famous examples are the child's belief that there is more biscuit if a whole biscuit is broken into several pieces; or that a pint of milk in a tall thin jar is more than a pint in a low flat dish – even if it is repeatedly poured back and forth under his eyes. Piaget not only described this, but he was the first to explain how and why. Because of him, it is theoretically possible to teach more children to think more logically and with more pleasure. **B. J.**

BOOKS BY PIAGET: 'THE LANGUAGE AND THOUGHT OF THE CHILD' (ROUTLEDGE, 3RD ED., 1959); 'PLAY, DREAMS AND IMITATION IN CHILDHOOD' (HEINEMANN, 1951).

Pablo Picasso (Spanish, b. 1881): artist. For a great part of this century Western art was dominated as much by the personality as by the production of Pablo Picasso. That personality was as magnetic as any in the history of art; and that production continually re-drew the map of art, marking out one new continent after another, some of them accessible to later artists, others a bailiwick over which Picasso had sole control. Few artists have been so much written about or so laboriously placed in 'history'; but Picasso's is an instinctive and an intuitive genius, powered by the demands of an exceptionally imperious and acquisitive nature and a uniquely sharp eye for what will 'tell' in any given situation. As much performer as painter or sculptor, he had an unrivalled ability to project whatever he chose to do: public attention was his for the asking, and he had the born performer's incapacity to disappoint. He also had the European's belief, elsewhere now somewhat in disrepute, that the artist's business is to create a masterpiece; and he proved himself able to do just this in the long series of large-scale paintings which included *La Vie* (1903), *Les Demoiselles d'Avignon* (1907), *The Accordionist* (1911), *The Three Musicians* (1921), *The Three Dancers* (1925),

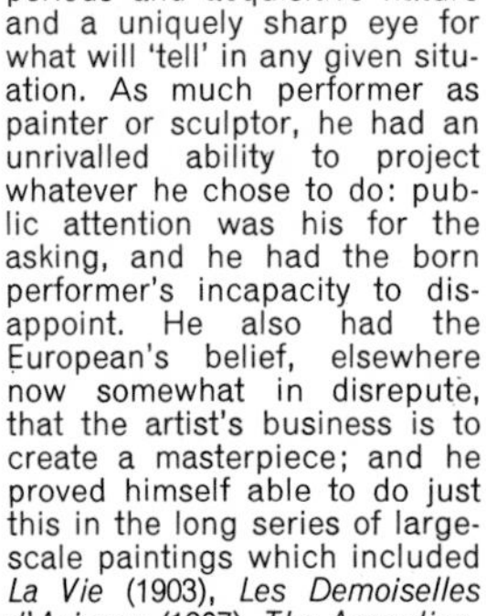

Guernica (1937), and *Night-Fishing at Antibes* (1939). Sideway moves into the domains of stage-design, book-illustration, ceramics, and playwriting had characteristically arresting results; and Picasso had also a parallel and no less individual activity as a sculptor in media as various as bronze, cut-out metal, wood, string, wire, torn paper and found objects. At 70, he was in the position of the long-distance runner who has lapped the rest of the field so often that it became meaningless to speak of him being 'out in front'; it was clear that even if the general direction of art passed into other and younger hands, Picasso would retain the status of Perpetual President of modern art for as long as he chose. **J. R.**

'PICASSO', BY R. PENROSE (GOLLANCZ, 1958); 'PICASSO', BY BOECK AND SABARTES (THAMES AND HUDSON, 1955).

Auguste Piccard (Swiss, 1884–1962): physicist and explorer. Piccard's early interest in cosmic rays and the high altitude, ion-filled layers of rarefied air drove him to develop a special balloon and sealed aluminium gondola so that he could observe the upper atmosphere at first hand. In 1931 he and a colleague ascended from Augsburg in Germany to a height of 51,775 ft. during an 18-hour flight – half again as high as anyone had been before – and became the first men to penetrate the stratosphere. The following year Piccard took his balloon to America and, with his twin brother, Jean Félix, made an even higher flight. After some 27 balloon ascents in all, Piccard directed his talent in the opposite direction. By the late 1930s he had completed the design for a 'bathyscaphe' – a submersible vessel for charting the ocean depths. The Second World War intervened but by 1948 the vessel was finally ready. It used a ballast of iron pellets (which could be jettisoned in an emergency) for descending and a 'balloon' of petrol for buoyancy and stability. After a full six years of trials the bathyscaphe clinched the manned depth record with an amazing dive to 13,287 ft. Meanwhile, however, Piccard had built a second vessel, called Trieste, which he later sold to the U.S. Navy. In 1960, with two men on board (one his son, Jacques), the Trieste descended to the bottom of the deepest known trench in the world – the 35,800 ft. deep Mariana Trench off Guam in the Pacific Ocean. **N. V.**

'IN BALLOON AND BATHYSCAPHE', BY AUGUSTE PICCARD (CASSELL, 1956); 'SEVEN MILES DOWN: THE STORY OF THE BATHYSCAPHE TRIESTE', BY JACQUES PICCARD AND R. S. DIETZ (LONGMANS, 1962).

Mary Pickford (Canadian, b. 1893); film actress. Mary Pickford shines inextinguishably in the generation which transformed the cinema from a primitive joke into an international force. Born Gladys Mary Smith, she spent the greater part of her youth supporting her widowed mother and impoverished family as a child actor on the stage. In 1909, with 11 years' acting behind her, she began her screen career with D. W. Griffith (q.v.) and played her first leading role a year later in *The Violin Maker of Cremona*. With her golden ringlets, her unaffected comedy and pathos and her spitfire vitality she became one of the best-loved figures in the rapidly-growing star system. *Poor Little Rich Girl, Rebecca of Sunnybrook Farm, Daddy Long Legs, Pollyanna* – popular demand insisted on child-roles. By the time she appeared in *Little Lord Fauntleroy* she was already 27 and, together with Chaplin (q.v.), Griffith and her husband Douglas Fairbanks (q.v.), had founded United Artists, an independent outlet for their productions. The childish image grew irksome, but the public rejected her efforts, in *Rosita* and *Dorothy Vernon of Haddon Hall*, to change it. Finally, with her first talking film, *Coquette*, which won her an Oscar in 1929, she was allowed to grow up. The same year she appeared with Fairbanks in *The Taming of the Shrew;* her last film, *Secrets* (with Leslie Howard), was released in 1933. Four decades after her retirement from acting, she is still remembered as 'The World's Sweetheart'; but the saccharine phrase belies the formidable talents of this hawk in dove's feathers. **D. P.**

'SUNSHINE AND SHADOW', AUTOBIOGRAPHY BY MARY PICKFORD (HEINEMANN, 1956); 'THE PARADE'S GQNE BY', BY KEVIN BROWNLOW (SECKER AND WARBURG, 1968).

Lester Piggott (British, b. 1935): jockey. In the summer of 1951, racing was moving towards the close of a great jockey era, peopled by the likes of Sir Gordon Richards, Charlie Smirke, Harry Wragg and Charlie Elliott; and Piggott, aged 15, was already being hailed as racing's new Messiah. He was impetuous, impatient and sometimes a little rough. He won races he should have lost and he also lost races he should have won. But already there were some horses that ran for him the way they ran for no-one else. He matured his skills on Never Say Die, Crepello, Petite Etoile and St Paddy. He mastered the savage Zucchero,

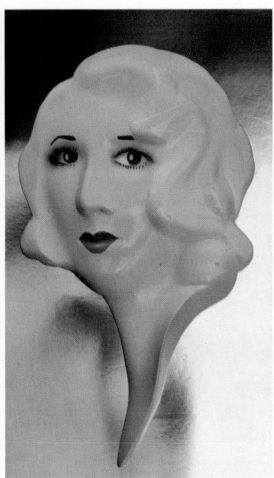

Hormone Conference and the Worcester Foundation for Experimental Biology, both of which have played a large part in the development of endocrinology and reproductive biology since the war. Of his own researches, the main lines were extensive studies on the ova and spermatozoa of animals, including the experimental production of 'virgin birth' and investigation into the chemistry and biological action of the sex hormones. From the latter arose his study with M. C. Chang of the inhibition of ovulation by orally active progesterone-like substances, and thence, under his dynamic influence, the development with John Rock of oral contraception. He was thus able to lift the shadow of conjugal anxiety and

frustration from millions of men and women, consequently making a tremendous contribution towards human happiness. **A. S. P.**
'THE CONTROL OF FERTILITY', BY GREGORY PINCUS (ACADEMIC PRESS, 1965).

PHI-PIR

Luigi Pirandello (Italian, 1867–1936): novelist and playwright. To Pirandello belongs the credit of having dramatised, more potently and passionately than any other writer, the 20th-century obsession *par excellence* – man's despairing search for an identity that forever eludes him. Starting as a writer of naturalistic fiction in the manner of his fellow Sicilian Giovanni Verga, and under the pressure of his own tormented existence with a lunatic wife, Pirandello used the stage to display the anguish of the fractured personality, the break-up of the self under the onslaughts of time and circumstance. Ibsen's plays had shown the inexorable continuity be-

until by the close of the Fifties he was accepted as the greatest whip rider of the day, the strongest finisher of our time. Today, with the shortest stirrups and the longest legs in the business, he is more than that – a past master at riding every sort of race, every sort of horse. Lifting Pieces of Eight across the line in the Champion Stakes at the end of one of the strongest finishing bursts in memory; poised along the neck of the exhausted Ribero, wise enough to know that the lightest touch of a whip would have lost him the St Leger; above all the victories in the 2000 Guineas, Derby and Washington International on Sir Ivor, each the ultimate in the timing of the late, late run – in those three races, he came as close to riding perfection as any man can ever come. With Piggott, superlatives are unavoidable: he is the greatest all-round jockey in the world. **W. H. C.**

Jozef Pilsudski (Polish, ex-Russian, 1867–1935): statesman. Pilsudski was the principal founder of modern Poland. Born a Russian subject, of a Polish landowning family from Lithuania, he studied at Kharkov University, became a revolutionary, and experienced

prison, Siberian banishment, underground conspiracy and emigration. For nearly 20 years a Socialist, he was always a nationalist. In 1914 he was convinced that the Central Powers would defeat Russia and be defeated by France and Britain. He led Polish armed forces on the Austrian side but was then interned by the Germans in Magdeburg. When his prophecy was fulfilled in 1918, he emerged from captivity to set up the new Polish state. In 1920, in agreement with Ukrainian nationalists, he invaded Russia, hoping to create a great Polish-Ukrainian federal union. The Soviet Red Army defeated him and invaded Poland, but it was Pilsudski who launched the decisive counter-offensive south of Warsaw which drove the Russians out of Poland. Pilsudski believed in strong government, and could find no place in the parliamentary system established in 1921. Five years later he seized power by armed rebellion. In his old age he became an embittered despot, stifling criticism and persecuting political opponents. In his prime he was an original thinker and a fine writer as well as a great leader. While firmly resisting Russians and Germans, he showed a more generous understanding of the weaker neighbours of the Poles – Ukrainians, Lithuanians and Jews – than any other Polish statesman. **H. S.-W.**
'THE MEMOIRS OF A POLISH REVOLUTIONARY AND SOLDIER', BY J. PILSUDSKI, (TR. AND ED. D. R. GILLIE (FABER, 1931); 'A HISTORY OF MODERN POLAND', BY HANS ROOS (EYRE AND SPOTTISWOODE, 1966), 'PILSUDSKI'S COUP D'ETAT', BY JOSEPH ROTHSCHILD (COLUMBIA U.P., 1966).

Gregory Pincus (U.S., 1903–1967): biologist. Pincus made many contributions to biological science, by his researches on the physiology of reproduction, by his stimulation of others and by his inspired initiative in organising the Laurentian

LESTER PIGGOTT BY BRIAN LOVE

tween the past and the present. Pirandello's show the even more frightening *discontinuity*, the failure of the human personality to sustain itself through time. His most famous play, *Six Characters in Search of an Author* (1921), expounds the paradox that fictional characters are more real than live people precisely because they *cannot* change and disintegrate, but must remain eternally themselves. *Henry IV* (1922) explores the flickering borderline between sanity and madness, and the use of madness as a consoling illusion against an intolerable reality. Even when, as at this moment, his plays do not seem to be holding the stage, Pirandello's methods and insights remain broodingly present, a legacy of the pioneer who broke through some of the most deeply entrenched conventions of the theatre in order to challenge some of the most tenaciously held beliefs concerning human life. **J. A. B.**

BOOKS BY PIRANDELLO: 'RIGHT YOU ARE! (IF YOU THINK SO)', (PLAYS) (PENGUIN, 1962); SHORT STORIES, TR. F. MAY (O.U.P., 1965); 'QUATTRO NOVELLE', (HARRAP, 1939). 'THE DRAMA OF LUIGI PIRANDELLO', BY DOMENICO VITTORINI (UNIVERSITY OF PENNSYLVANIA PRESS, 1935).

Norman Pirie (British, b. 1907): biochemist. Early in his long career at Rothamsted Pirie isolated, with Bawden (q.v.), a virus in crystalline form for the first time (tobacco mosaic virus), an achievement that paved the way for the study of macromolecules and molecular genetics. As a measure of the success with which this aspect of biology has developed over the last 30 years, witness the number of biologists in this series whose work lies in this area – Crick, Wilkins, Jacob, Monod (qq.v.), etc. The discovery that a virus could be crystallised like a chemical compound posed again the old question on the distinction between 'living' and 'non-living'; and Pirie, in his extensive writings on the origin of life, has repeatedly stressed the impossibility of defining life. Recently his has been an extremely powerful and lucid voice on the problems of over-population, food productivity and population control. **J. B. M.**

'FOOD RESOURCES, CONVENTIONAL AND NOVEL', BY NORMAN PIRIE (PENGUIN, 1969).

Erwin Piscator (German, 1893–1966): theatrical director. Piscator was responsible for many of the innovations that characterise the modern theatre. He was the first to make use of documentary films, cartoons and posters – and the first to introduce a conveyor-belt stage (in *The Adventures of the Good Soldier Schweik* in 1928). He coined the term 'total theatre'. He was one of the principal Teutonic exponents of the connection between drama and politics. He is said to have anticipated Brecht (q.v.) in the invention of 'epic' drama. What is certain is that he impregnated the German theatre with advanced politics. He is one of the many directors who have lessened the role of the author in the theatre, and frequently manipulated texts to suit his theories. He combined Max Reinhardt's (q.v.) management of spectacle with Brecht's social commitment and the shock tactics of Expressionism. He left Germany in 1933, went to America, and returned to Germany in 1951, when he took over the new Freie Volksbühne theatre in West Berlin in 1962. Among his discoveries at the New York

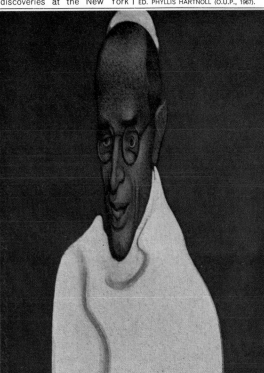

Pius XII (Italian, 1876–1958): Pope. Any strong Pope ruling between 1939 and 1958 would have strengthened the faith of many of the world's 400 million Roman Catholics and have commanded the rest of the world's grudging respect, as once again the Papacy outlasted secular tyrants. At the time, Pius XII seemed to gain from his inflexibility. His Church applauded when in 1950 he proclaimed that the Virgin Mary had been assumed 'body and soul' into the heavenly glory. The world admired his relief work and his pleas for peace. But was not Eugenio Pacelli too hostile to Communism, or to new thought in Western Europe? Did he not speak to international pilgrimages more than to his own bishops? And had he not compromised at precisely the wrong place, by doing a deal with Adolf Hitler in order to protect German Catholics, not the Jews? Such questions have undermined his reputation. **D. L. E.**

'PORTRAIT OF PIUS XII', BY P. C. NAZARENO (DENT, 1956); 'THE POLITICS OF THE VATICAN', BY P. NICHOLS (PALL MALL, 1968).

Max Planck (German, 1858–1947): theoretical physicist. The whole of the past 75 years of physics has been built up from the discovery that energy, at a microscopic level, exists in indivisible packets, or quanta, just as matter exists as particles. The man responsible for bringing about this great revolution was Planck. He must be classed with the Galileos, Newtons, and

Theatre Workshop which he founded before returning to Germany were Marlon Brando (q.v.) and the directors of the 'Living Theatre', Judith Malina and Julian Beck. **H. H.**

'OXFORD COMPANION TO THE THEATRE', ED. PHYLLIS HARTNOLL (O.U.P., 1967).

Faradays of the world. Born in Kiel, he studied at Munich University and, later, Berlin. His early work was on thermodynamics and in 1896 his attention became focused upon the difficult problem of explaining the spectrum of radiation emitted by a so-called 'black body' – a body that radiates perfectly. These studies culminated in the concept of the 'elementary quantum of action', or Planck's constant, which defined the 'atomistic' nature of energy. His subsequent collaboration with Einstein (q.v.) made Berlin the world's most important

centre for theoretical physics before and after the First World War. Planck's theoretical contributions ranged far and wide but his great genius is reflected primarily in the intellectual breakthrough in understanding the very nature of radiation, and of the atom and its interactions. **P. H. S. S.**

'THE WORLD OF THE ATOM', ED. HENRY A. BOORSE AND LLOYD MOTZ (BASIC BOOKS, 1966).

Raymond Poincaré (French, 1860–1934): statesman. Poincaré's hallmark was success, but his successes were always short-lived. He was a statesman who made a point of being competent and of solving each problem as it came before him. A clever but uncomplicated lawyer from Lorraine, he became President of the Republic in 1913 and a spokesman of French nationalism. Believing that war was inevitable, he prepared for it (*Poincaré-la-guerre*). Returning to more active politics, he was Prime Minister from 1922 to 1924, and occupied the Ruhr in an unsuccessful attempt to make Germany pay for the war (*Poincaré-la-Ruhr*). Prime Minister again from 1926 to 1929, he applied a rigidly orthodox policy to stabilise the franc (*Poincaré-le-bien-aimé*). Thus for some he was a symbol of everything that was best in France: honest, patriotic, simple, straightforward. But for others he was narrow-minded in his hostility to the Germans (and in his anti-clericalism), and his emphasis on financial stability was disastrous to French economic development. Poincaré embodied the virtues and the failings of conservative France. His anti-clericalism was a matter of rational and social principle; it was also an unthinking prejudice. **D. W. J. J.**

'RAYMOND POINCARE AND THE FRENCH PRESIDENCY', BY GORDON WRIGHT (STANFORD U.P., 1942).

Jackson Pollock (U.S., 1912–1956): painter. Pollock personified the all-American qualities of energy. daring, ambition and an open-minded confidence in the future. Steeped in Americana. he painted seascapes after Albert Pinkham Ryder, was a student of Thomas Hart Benton, studied American Indian painting. In New York in the early Forties he took up the Surrealist notion of automatic painting and began to give a more direct outlet to the emotional drive of an exceptionally powerful nature. In 1947, in the big drip paintings, Pollock laid down the basic principle – that American painting could challenge the painting of any other country, and do it with methods and with ambitions, that were all its own. Painting on the scale of epic, with the canvas laid flat on the floor, the focus distributed evenly all over the picture, and the mazy, lariat-line of the paint keeping up a labyrinthine activity that the eye can never quite un-riddle, Pollock changed our idea of what painting can be. At an earlier stage he had had European influences, but what Pollock gave to painting in the end was his own: an irresistible direct seduction and what has been called "the first significant change in pictorial space since Cubism". **J. R.**

'JACKSON POLLOCK', BY B. ROBERTSON (THAMES AND HUDSON, 1960).

Paul Poiret (French, 1879–1949): couturier and designer. First employed by an umbrella manufacturer, Poiret began to filch little bits of silk that were left over when the umbrellas were cut and dress little dolls with the remnants. He also made sketches of fantastic ensembles, and taking these one day to Madame Cheruit, he received such encouragement that he was emboldened to show them to other couturiers. Doucet gave him his chance, and a cloak for Réjane made his reputation. Later he worked for Worth and was so successful that he was soon able to set up on his own. Raoul Dufy and Matisse (q.v.) both designed fabrics for him, and his designs had an exciting theatricality; but he was also an innovator: he introduced a walking skirt called *le trotteur* and created the sort of garments that didn't need the tightly-laced corsets that were so popular in the 19th century. "I waged war upon the corset," he said. Poiret is mostly known for the brilliant way that he westernised oriental fashion, and his success was partly due to the enthusiasm aroused at that time by Diaghilev's *Schéhérazade*. The First World War put an end to his activities. **J. L.**

'MY FIRST FIFTY YEARS', BY PAUL POIRET (GOLLANCZ, 1931).

Sir Karl Popper (British, ex-Austrian, b. 1902): philosopher. When Popper's important first book, *The Logic of Scientific Discovery,* was published in 1935 he was loosely associated with the positivists of the Vienna Circle, especially Carnap (q.v.). But although he philosophised in their style and shared their problems, his particular concern being the nature of scientific knowledge, he was deeply critical of many of their fundamental assumptions. He rejected the view they shared with most empiricists that scientific knowledge is derived by a mechanical procedure of scientific generalisation from indubitable certainties about sense-experience. His contention is that science begins with the imaginative conjecturing of theories which become acceptable, although never more than provisionally, to the extent that they survive determined attempts to falsify them by observation of the material world. In New Zealand, from 1938 to 1945, he applied this theory of knowledge critically, in his massive *The Open Society and its Enemies,* to the large theories about the inevitable course of history which are the metaphysical foundation of Communist and Fascist totalitarianism, emphasising the parallel between dogmatic ideas about knowledge and political authoritarianism. From 1945 to 1969 he was a Professor at the London School of Economics. Although he firmly distinguishes science from metaphysics he does not reject the latter as the positivists did: indeed, he is prepared to assert the freedom of the human will while admitting that this belief lies beyond the reach of scientific testing. **A. Q.**

BOOKS BY POPPER: 'THE LOGIC OF SCIENTIFIC DISCOVERY' (HUTCHINSON, 1959); 'THE OPEN SOCIETY AND ITS ENEMIES' (ROUTLEDGE, 1945); 'THE POVERTY OF HISTORICISM' (ROUTLEDGE, 1957); 'CONJECTURES AND REFUTATIONS' (ROUTLEDGE, 1963); 'THE CRITICAL APPROACH TO SCIENCE AND PHILOSOPHY', ED. M. BUNGE (COLLIER MACMILLAN, 1964).

Ferdinand Porsche (German, ex-Czech, ex-Austrian, 1875–1951): engineer. Porsche put Europe on wheels. During the years before the Depression, when most car makers were concentrating on the safe, exclusive market of cars for the wealthy, he lost job after job by insisting on the need for cars which ordinary people could afford. He designed and built small-car prototypes for Zundapp and NSU, but neither company could afford to market them at a saleable price – only Hitler, with the backing of the Nazi Government, had the resources to set such a programme in motion, and the result was the Porsche-designed Volkswagen, Europe's answer to the Model T Ford as a means of motorising a con-

tinent. In the event the first VWs for private sale only emerged after the war, from a bomb-shattered factory no-one wanted, starting a rise to international success which is a striking tribute to the soundness of Porsche's original design, now 40 years old. Porsche himself, after refusing Stalin's offer to name his own salary as head of the Russian state motor industry, was involved in wartime vehicle production. Afterwards he was held to ransom by the French on war-crime charges and although he was later released and acquitted his health was broken, and he died in 1951. Already the VW was well on its way to fulfilling his dream, and the cars bearing his own name (his own design company started producing sports cars to raise the ransom money) made Porsche a household word in the world of motor sport. **D. O.**

Cole Porter (U.S., 1892–1964): composer. Porter broke most of the success-story rules. He was born rich and married richer. His first Broadway hit, *Hitchy-Koo of 1919,* also contained his first big selling song, *An Old*

Fashioned Garden, but he then returned to Paris and wrote only for amusement while studying music – not until 1928 did he write *Let's Do It.* He repeated the success in 1929 with the show *50 Million Frenchmen* which had *You Do Something To Me* as its hit song. His *Kiss Me Kate,* which is considered the perfect musical, and one of Porter's greatest scores, if not *the* greatest, nearly didn't get produced at all. It took months to raise the necessary $180,000 to put it on. But when it opened the *New York Mirror's* Robert Garland wrote: "If this isn't the best musical comedy I ever saw,

I don't remember what the best musical comedy I ever saw was called." His biggest selling song was *Don't Fence Me In,* written in 1934 but not used until 1944 when it was sung by Roy Rogers in the film *Hollywood Canteen.* An invalid since a horse riding accident in 1937, Cole Porter suffered 30 operations. He was proud that in the era of teams like Rodgers and Hart, Kern and Hammerstein, George and Ira Gershwin, he worked alone. When asked once who wrote *Some Enchanted Evening,* he replied: "Rodgers and Hammerstein. If you can imagine it taking *two* men to write one song." **L. A.**

'THE LIFE THAT LATE HE LED', BY GEORGE GELLS (W. H. ALLEN, 1967).

Beatrix Potter (British, 1866–1943): writer and illustrator. The creator of Peter Rabbit was the daughter of wealthy and oppressive parents. She had an isolated and lonely childhood in London, in which country holidays were memorable interludes. She developed an enthusiasm for natural history and for making minutely detailed drawings from the rabbits, mice, frogs, hedgehogs and other

small animals smuggled into her nursery and affectionately cherished. *Peter Rabbit,* begun as a series of letters written to amuse a convalescent child, was privately printed in 1900 and was followed by *The Tailor of Gloucester* in 1902. Throughout her writing career she was associated with the firm of Frederick Warne, who by 1913 had published 24 of her animal stories. From her earnings she bought a small farm in Sawrey in the Lake District, and broke partially from the domination of her parents. The break became complete in 1913, when she married William Heelis, and abandoned writing for farming. Her tales have a robust and totally unsentimental humour and the exquisite accompanying watercolour illustrations combine fantasy and exact observation in a style that is unique. She is one of the rare writers equally acceptable to children and adults, and her animal characters, many of which were drawn from her own pets and the animals at Sawrey, have entered the national nursery mythology. **G. E. A.**

'THE TALE OF BEATRIX POTTER', BY MARGARET LANE (WARNE, REVISED, 1968); 'THE JOURNAL OF BEATRIX POTTER', ED. LESLIE LINDER (WARNE, 1966); 'THE ART OF BEATRIX POTTER', BY L. LINDER AND W. A. HERRING (WARNE, 1955).

Francis Poulenc (French, 1899–1963): composer. Parisian-born, Poulenc was the youngest of Les Six and with his friend Auric the closest to the collective ideals – propounded by Jean Cocteau (q.v.) – of that heterogeneous and short-lived group of French composers which became prominent soon after the First World War. His music never lost the spontaneous gaiety of his early works, but the passage of years revealed a romantic quality formerly held in check or masked by gentle irony. Few composers have had his knowledge and enthusiasm for the music of his contemporaries and yet, apart from some Stravinskyan touches, remained so little influenced by it. Impatient with formal processes, his music came more from his heart and his pianist's fingers than from his brain. His oft-repeated claim in the last 20 years of his life that he was primarily a composer of religious music only made sense when his opera *Dialogue des Carmelites* (1956) was revealed at La Scala. He composed a great deal for his own instrument, the piano, but was essentially a melodist and first and foremost a composer of songs – the incomparable setter of Apollinaire (q.v.), Aragon, Eluard and Jacob. Since his own musical style was aphoristic, he succeeded best in this field. **F. A.**

'FRANCIS POULENC', BY HENRI HELL (CALDER AND BOYARS, 1959).

Valdemar Poulsen (Danish, 1869–1942): engineer. Although the idea of recording sounds magnetically was mooted by one Oberlin Smith in 1888, Poulsen was the first to achieve it. His 'Telegraphone', demonstrated at the Paris Exposition of 1900, was the forerunner of the now ubiquitous tape recorder. It used a moving steel tape which was magnetised in sympathy with electric currents from a microphone to store and reproduce messages. The inventor was with the telephone company in Copenhagen and conceived it as a message-taking device for telephones. He also had the idea of using a length of wire or a strip of flexible material covered with magnetised powder in place of the steel tape. The familiar reddish brown plastic recording tape is the modern equivalent. In 1903, Poulsen and some U.S. associates formed the American Telegraphone Company to exploit the device, but success for this type of recording was years

off and the company failed. Poulsen's other contributions included notable pioneering work in the use of the high frequency currents from electric arcs in wireless transmitters. Tape recording has revolutionised the recording of sound in broadcasting, films and the gramophone industry and videotape recorders are now in common use. **P. O. W.**

'THE TAPE RECORDER BOOK' (FOCAL PRESS, 1967); 'MAGNETIC RECORDING HANDBOOK', BY G. R. HICKMAN (NEWNES, 1963).

Ezra Pound (U.S., b. 1885): poet and critic (previous page). Pound's first masterpieces were

translations – *The Seafarer* from Anglo-Saxon, the Chinese versions of *Cathay*, and *Homage to Sextus Propertius*, where he used off-key renderings of the Latin to bring out parallels between Propertius versus the Roman Empire and Pound versus the British. Pound's translations 'make it new', extending our sense of viable traditions as well as our sense of the mingling of cultures. One poet has described Pound's growth as "a movement from unnecessarily simplified statement to unnecessarily complicated ellipsis"; *Hugh Selwyn Mauberley*, *Sextus Propertius* and the early Cantos coming at a point of equilibrium. The Cantos attempt to range through many cultures and to register their gists; their 'failure' is perhaps more important to us than many a more easily compounded success. At his finest Pound recaptures for poetry a hint of "that radiant world where one thought cuts through another

with clean edge", which he found in Dante and Cavalcanti. **C. T.**

'EZRA POUND, POET AS SCULPTOR', BY D. DAVIE (ROUTLEDGE, 1964): 'SAILING AFTER KNOWLEDGE: THE CANTOS OF EZRA POUND', BY GEORGE DEKKER (ROUTLEDGE, 1963); 'THE TRIAL OF EZRA POUND', BY JULIAN CORNELL (FABER, 1967); 'POET IN EXILE', BY NOEL STOCK (MANCHESTER U.P. 1964).

Cecil Frank Powell (British, 1903–1969): physicist. Powell was the co-discoverer, with G. P. S. Occhialini, of the elementary particle known as the pi-meson (or pion) which acts as the carrier of the force between the

protons and neutrons that make up an atomic nucleus. In 1935 the Japanese physicist Yukawa had predicted the existence of a very short-lived particle, some 200 times the mass of the electron, which is 'tossed' between the protons and neutrons in atomic nuclei and binds them together. In 1936 the mu-meson (or muon) had been discovered by Anderson and others but did not fit Yukawa's theory. Powell then developed a photographic emulsion technique which enabled continuous detection and permitted very short-lived particles to be spotted. In 1947 he and Occhialini discovered Yukawa's particle in cosmic rays using emulsions exposed at the top of the Pic du Midi in the Pyrenees. Powell's contribution extends beyond the discovery of the pi-meson. He also did much in the field of cosmic-ray research. **P. H. S. S.**

'COSMIC RAYS', BY BRUNO ROSSI (ALLEN AND UNWIN, 1966); 'COSMIC RAYS', BY A. W. WOLFENDALE (GEORGE NEWNES, 1963).

Elvis Presley (U.S., b. 1935): singer. Before Presley, 20th-century popular music spanned from jazz (the 'art' end) to the soft, romantic slush of 'moon-June' crooner ballads (the commercial end). Then, in the mid-1950s, came rock 'n' roll, which mixed crooning with the hard, raucous noise of black rhythm 'n' blues. Bill Haley first hit the mass-market, but Presley was the hero figure who gave the nascent teenage movement a leader. From him a whole generation took its life-style: from the obsession with clothes (hear his song, *Blue Suede Shoes*) right through to mid-century youth's obsession with itself, for Presley was a teenage-only idol, cut off from the adult world. Born in Mississippi, nurtured on blues, country music and gospel sounds, he was 21 when his first hit record (*Heartbreak Hotel*) smashed into the charts in 1956. Almost immediately he began turning over £8m. annually. Gone was the romanticism of the old popular music; now it was 'pop', the sharp explosive sound symbolising the aggressive thunder of electric guitars and harsh-voiced singing. Presley's grinding hips, proclaiming raw and overt sexuality, set the swaggering tone of teenage independence. He made movies (e.g. *Jailhouse Rock*) and then, suddenly, came a change. In 1958 he was drafted, was a model soldier, and soon softened into a sentimental ballad singer. In this schmaltzy mould his songs and movies have remained during the 1960s, despite occasional hit-parade exceptions (e.g. *U.S. Male*) and a smash-hit season at Las Vegas in 1970. His record sales, thrusting towards 300 million, have been exceeded only by Crosby and, perhaps, the Beatles. **D. J.**

'POP FROM THE BEGINNING', BY NIK COHN (WEIDENFELD AND NICOLSON, 1969); RECORDS: 'ELVIS'S GOLDEN RECORDS', 'ELVIS IS BACK', 'ELVIS': ORIGINAL SOUNDTRACK RECORDING FROM HIS NBC TV SPECIAL (ALL ON RCA/VICTOR).

John Boynton Priestley (British, b. 1894): writer. J. B. Priestley is perhaps the last of the great literary all-rounders. His prodigious output of novels, plays, essays *et alia* represents the central tradition of English literature – that of the craftsmen who simultaneously entertain and criticise their own time. Born in Yorkshire, he is an essentially English writer who was given a fiercely humanitarian concern for society by the abrupt end of the glowing Camelot years of his Edwardian youth. His early best-seller, *The Good Companions*, is less typical of his major works than more complex novels like *Bright Day* and *Lost Empires*, or the reflective curiosity of *Man and Time* and *Margin Released*, and though his world-wide popular reputation has alienated some critics he has always been a lively experimentalist with an uncompromising literary integrity. The English radical conscience which led him to attack Depression politics before the

Second World War, and to spark off the Campaign for Nuclear Disarmament after it, also illuminated the wartime broadcasts which made him a national hero during the London Blitz: his fundamental concern has always been the condition of man. This, and the life enhancing quality of his work, have made him a symbol of permanence in our shifting century. **S. M. C.**

'J. B. PRIESTLEY: AN INFORMAL STUDY OF HIS WORK', BY DAVID HUGHES (HART-DAVIS, 1958); 'J. B. PRIESTLEY – THE DRAMATIST', BY GARETH LLOYD EVANS (HEINE-MANN, 1964).

Miguel Primo de Rivera (Spanish, 1870–1930): military ruler. In September, 1923, in the tradition of his uncle (an Andalusian aristocrat and military politician), Primo de Rivera staged the last of the 19th-century style *pronunciamientos* against what he considered a decadent parliamentary regime. By a bout of military rule he intended to purge Spain of corrupt, 'professional' politicians, and then to restore constitutional govern-

ment to 'clean hands'. A relatively mild dictator with a homemade anti-liberal ideology, he worked in bouts of tremendous energy followed by fits of depression. His regime lasted till January, 1930, because he was favoured by a mild boom which allowed an adventurous policy of public works, because he came to terms with the Socialists and because he ended the Moroccan war. The difficulties of finding a successor regime were insuperable; he could find no substitute for the professional politicians he had insulted. In 1929, with the peseta falling, the students went into the streets against him at a time when both King Alfonso XIII and the army were unwilling to support him. He withdrew to Paris and died. His dictatorship brought down the King, condemned for his early support of an unconstitutional regime. **R. Ca.**

'SPAIN 1808–1939,' BY RAYMOND CARR (O.U.P., 1966).

Sergey Prokofiev (Russian, 1891–1953): composer. Prokofiev is a widely performed and admired composer who perhaps never realised his full potentialities because his career was twice interrupted. A pupil of Rimsky-Korsakov, he began life as an *enfant terrible* of Russian music, but went to live abroad in 1918 (for artistic rather than political reasons). His hopes that the Western European and American climates would prove more hospitable to his talent were not fully realised; although he won

a limited success in the orchestral and instrumental field, notably with the *Classical Symphony*, the *First Violin Concerto* and the *Third Piano Concerto* (he was himself an excellent pianist), his dramatic powers ran largely to waste. Returning to Russia in 1934, he found himself under suspicion as a Westernised 'formalist', and skilfully adapted his style to more openly tuneful and even heroic requirements in his later symphonies, e.g. such delightful ballets as *Cinderella* and *Romeo and Juliet,* and in several operas. Among these *The Duenna* (after Sheridan) and *War and Peace* (after Tolstoy) hold the stage but lack the genius and zest of the two that he wrote abroad: the fantastic *Love of The Three Oranges* and the tragic *Fiery Angel*. In Prokofiev's temperament a romantic impulse co-existed with a marked love of parody and caricature. His highly individual style has left a strong mark on that of Shostakovich (q.v.). **D. S.-T.**

'PROKOFIEV', BY I. S. NESTYEV (O.U.P., 1961).

Marcel Proust (French, 1871–1922): novelist. When the First World War came to an end, the greatest living novelist was Proust, and his work has dominated fiction for nearly half a century. No more revealing document exists for the first 50 years of the Third Republic than *A la Recherche du Temps Perdu*. That is not, however, all; for his investigations reach depths of con-

sciousness not yet plumbed in the novel and greatly enlarge its psychological possibilities. Our real self, he claimed, is hidden from us, and his symbolism is an effort to recapture the lost past – or rather mislaid past, for nothing is ever lost

and sensations are like radioactive material which nothing can destroy. He did not, however, believe that it could be recaptured at will, but only through unconscious effort, by an unforeseen 'illumination', when a vivid memory suddenly flashes across the inner screen of vision. His work is dominated by the distinction between voluntary and involuntary memory. For Proust two worlds exist, one in time and the other in eternity, where everything is preserved, which can be reached only when occasional flashes of perception reveal it. It is the function of the artist to seize on these rare moments and to use them to illuminate the life of time. **E. M. S.**

'MARCEL PROUST', BY GEORGE PAINTER, 2 VOLS. (CHATTO AND WINDUS, 1961–65); 'PROUST', BY J. M. COCKING (BOWES AND BOWES, 1956); 'THE TWO WORLDS OF PROUST', BY H. MARSH (O.U.P., 1948).

Giacomo Puccini (Italian, 1858–1924): composer. Puccini is the only operatic composer since Wagner and Verdi to make a large and effective contribution to the regular international repertory: without *La Bohème*, *Tosca* and *Madama Butterfly* the balance-sheets of most opera-houses would look dismal indeed. His aims are not exalted; his world is the world of strong theatre, violent melodrama, easy pathos – of Victorien Sardou and

David Belasco. To such theatrical material he brought an unfailing sense of theatre, and a power, unique among his contemporaries and successors, of expressing dramatic emotion in melodic terms. He was ingenious in his use of exotic material for effects of local colour, and in turning the innovations of others (*e.g.,* of Debussy and Stravinsky [qq.v.]) to his own dramatic purposes. But what have captivated singers and audiences are the ardent, spontaneous vocal line and quick musical response to each fresh scene, situation or character. Puccini is sometimes cheap, but never dull. Besides the three great successes mentioned above, he wrote *Manon Lescaut, La Fanciulla del West,* the not-quite-completed *Turandot* and a trilogy of one-acters among which the comedy, *Gianni Schicchi*, is regarded by many musicians as his masterpiece. **D. S.-T.**

'PUCCINI', BY MOSCO CARNER (DUCKWORTH, 1958); 'THE OPERAS OF PUCCINI' BY WILLIAM ASHBROOK (CASSELL, 1969).

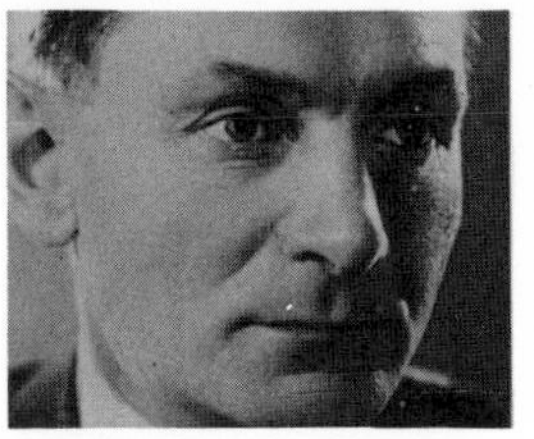

Vsevolod Pudovkin (Russian, 1893–1953): film director. With Eisenstein, Dovzhenko (qq.v.) and Vertov, Pudovkin was one of the four cornerstones of the heroic days of the Soviet cinema. He was trained as a chemist, spent 1915–1918 as a PoW, then in 1920 saw D. W. Griffith's (q.v.) *Intolerance*. The experience stirred him to enter the State Film School and later Kuleshov's workshop. After working as actor, writer and assistant, his first full-length film was *Mechanism of the Brain* (1926), an exposition of Pavlovian theory. *Mother* (1926) came a year after Eisenstein's *Potemkin*: the two films together were a staggering revelation of the full intellectual and emotional potential of the cinema. Succeeding silent films (*The End of St. Petersburg, Storm over Asia*) showed the same ability to depict the individual against the background of vast political and social events. Pudovkin's profoundest influence has been his theoretical writings, most specifically his pronouncement in 1926 that "the foundation of film art is editing. The film is not *shot*, but *built*". The much-publicised conflict between Pudovkin's idea of editing as *linkage* and Eisenstein's idea of the dynamism of *collision*, though its practical application may have been limited, was of primary importance in focusing attention upon a theoretical and philosophical approach to film method and theory. **D. R.**

'KINO: A HISTORY OF THE RUSSIAN AND SOVIET FILM', BY JAY LEYDA (ALLEN AND UNWIN, 1960).

Q

Mary Quant (British, b. 1934): fashion designer. Her impact on the mid 20th-century appearance of women was due to an originality of appeal which might almost be called anarchy. She made clothes generally practical but with what seemed a zany look for people just between the conformist spirit of schooldays and not old

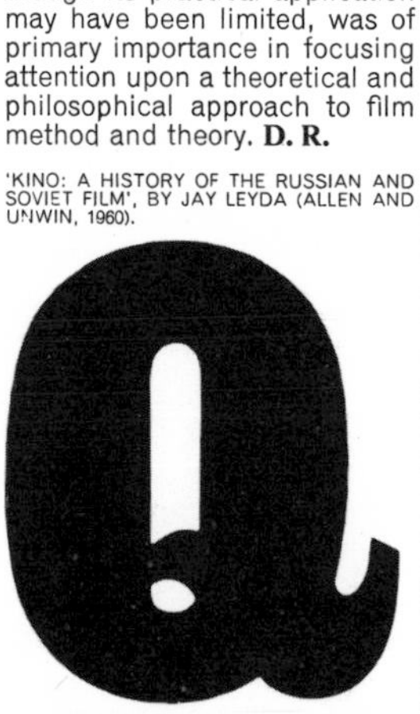

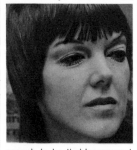

enough to be tied by responsibilities. Quant opened her first boutique in Chelsea in 1955 in one room with one machine and a clear disregard for what was being done by any designer in Paris. Youth was feeling even more revolutionary than usual, and was not in the mood, even it if had had the means, for the well-established haute couture. She herself was only 21 and had never had lessons in fashion design though she had studied art at Goldsmith's College. Fortunately she had two partners who understood business, Alexander Plunkett-Greene, whom she later married, and Archie McLeish. The policy of her shop, Bazaar, was to please the generation which had hitherto, economically and physically, been ignored by creative dressmakers. She often used anti-traditional materials (denim for parties, lace for suits), introduced the 'sack' before Paris and, though her models were fairly expensive, soon won a large clientele. Her influence contributed much to the Swinging London movement. **D. L. M.**

'QUANT BY QUANT' (CASSELL, 1966).

Vidkun Quisling (Norwegian, 1887–1945): traitor. Quisling, as his name came to denote, was a traitor who collaborated with the Germans when his country was *de jure* at war with them. He had a brilliant career in the Norwegian military academy and graduated with the highest honours ever awarded. In the early Twenties he was often in the Soviet Union working with Nansen in connection with famine relief in the Ukraine. He returned to Norway, started a political career as a fanatical anti-Communist, and in 1931

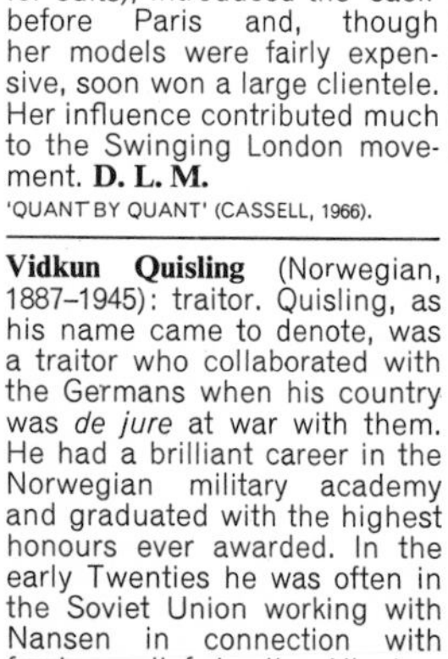

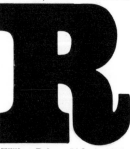

joined the Agrarian Government as Minister of Defence. After its fall he started his own party, the National Union, which performed disastrously at the polls. He was in touch with the Nazi leaders before the invasion of Norway and after it proclaimed himself Prime Minister. At this stage he lacked support from the Germans in occupation and was ejected. He retained the support of Hitler (q.v.), however; the National Union was declared the official party, and in 1942 Quisling was appointed Minister-President. In 1943 he declared that Norway was Germany's ally and at war with her enemies. In 1945 he surrendered himself voluntarily, was tried as a traitor and shot. There have been attempts to exculpate Quisling, as a man with the interests of his country at heart. In fact he seems to have been an ordinary authoritarian of Fascist predilections. **A. C. C.**

R

William Raborn (U.S., b. 1905): naval strategist. The shock of Russia's premature achievement of the H-bomb jolted the Pentagon into ordering Army/

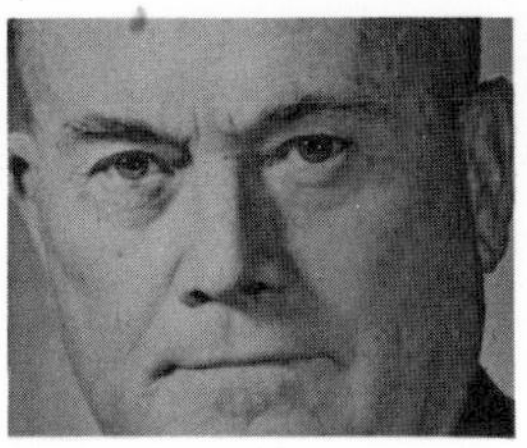

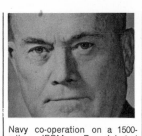

Navy co-operation on a 1500-mile IRBM. Rear-Admiral Raborn, wartime airman turned staff officer, was given 10 years and the famous 'blank cheque'. Army pressures forced development towards the giant 60-ft. liquid-fuel Jupiter missile, which was feasible only for large surface ships; so 'Red' Raborn, sacrificing two years, ruthlessly pulled out. With consummate technical daring, he opted for solid-fuel missiles dependent on yet unachieved technologies capable of launching from submerged submarines. In January 1957, Polaris was approved as a six-year programme. In October, Russia's Sputnik rocked the Pentagon. Raborn, fighting unimagined problems of solid fuel, inertial navigation, submerged firing, and accuracy, was asked to cut project time. With staggering effrontery, he promised to halve it. A specialised submarine could not be built in time. One of Rickover's (q.v.) nuclears was taken on the building slip, halved, separated, and a 130-ft. missile section, with its inconceivably advanced equipment, was inserted. In April 1959 the sixth Polaris missile prototype fired successfully. In December U.S.S. George Washington was commissioned and eight months later fired her first missile submerged – incomparably the most powerful weapon ever devised by man. **D. D.**

'ATOMIC SUBMARINES', BY NORMAN POLMAR (VAN NOSTRAND, N.Y., 1960): 'THE FAR AND THE DEEP' BY EDWARD P. STAFFORD (ARTHUR BARKER, 1968): 'POLARIS!', BY J. BAAR AND W.E. HOWARD (HARCOURT, BRACE, 1960).

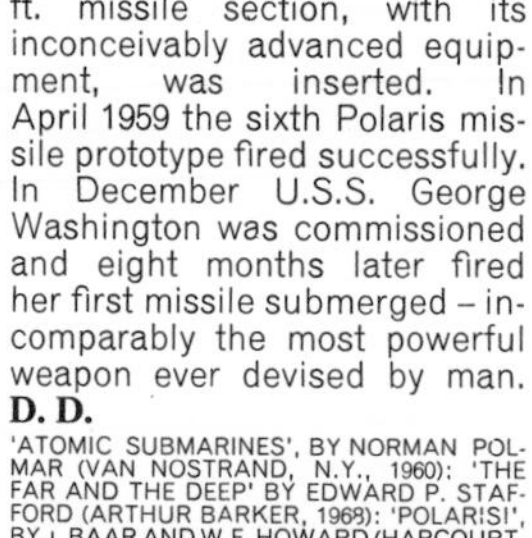

Sergey Rachmaninov (Russian, 1873–1943): composer. One of the greatest pianists of the century, Rachmaninov left his native Russia at the time of the Revolution, settling eventually in Paris and then in America. Russian expatriates tend to be the most homesick of all, and it is probable that the Tchaikovsky-like yearning sadness which was from the first his most characteristic mood as a composer was intensified by the nostalgia of exile. Although much of his music became widely popular (in the case of the juvenile C sharp minor Prelude, embarrassingly so), and although his vogue in Soviet Russia was as great as in the West, Rachmaninov grew increasingly taciturn and unproductive during his later years. The Second and Third Piano Concertos remain the best known of his larger works; but the *Paganini Rhapsody* is still finer. Renewed interest has lately been shown in all three of his symphonies. **D. S.-T.**

'SERGEI RACHMANINOFF', BY SERGEI BERTENSSON AND JAY LEYDA (ALLEN AND UNWIN, 1965).

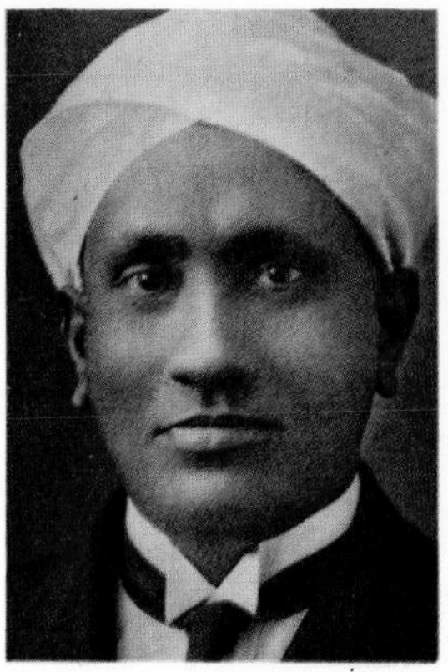

Sir Venkata Raman (Indian, 1888–1970): spectroscopist. Spectroscopy can sound forbidding with its implications of computers and mathematical calculations. Yet it not only allows the scientist to find out about the constitution of matter but also provides a fingerprinting device to establish the identity of materials. Depending on what he is looking for, the chemist or physicist can use various spectroscopic techniques, some relying on the motion of atoms, some on the tug-of-war of atoms in a molecule. Professor Raman, 1930 Nobel Prize winner in physics, was educated at various Indian universities and became Director of the Research Institute bearing his name. He discovered a whole new field of spectroscopy, referred to as Raman spectra, that essentially relies on the interaction between light and the motions of atoms in a molecule. It is a relatively easy technique and can be used for substances where other spectroscopic methods are not available and has proved extremely useful in large areas of physical science. **P. J. F.**

TEXTBOOK OF PHYSICAL CHEMISTRY', BY S. GLASSTONE (2ND ED. MACMILLAN, 1951).

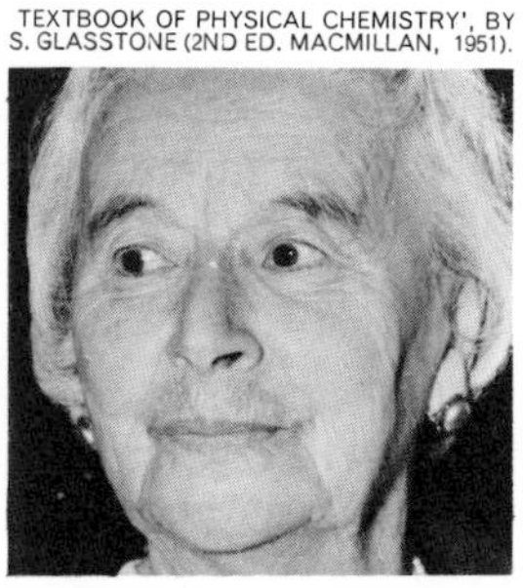

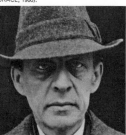

Marie Rambert (British, ex-Polish, b. 1888): ballet teacher. Dame Marie Rambert, who was to found the Ballet Rambert, was born in Warsaw, studied medicine in Paris, then eurhythmics with Dalcroze, from whom Diaghilev (q.v.) engaged her in 1912 to assist Nijinsky (q.v.) with the score of *Le Sacre du Printemps*. In 1920 she founded her own school in London from which was to emerge the Ballet Club (1931) at the Mercury Theatre, and later Ballet Rambert. Karsavina, Woizikowski, Markova, Pearl Argyle, Maude Lloyd, Harold Turner and William Chappell danced for Rambert. The choreographers Frederick Ashton, Antony Tudor, Andrée Howard, Walter Gore and John Cranko did their first work for her. Ballet Rambert performed mainly new works by young choreographers, but after the war reappeared as a larger company mounting the classics as well. It was recently reformed on a smaller basis with a modern repertory under the artistic direction of Norman Morrice: again new young choreographers are emerging, and ballets are composed to electronic and pop music. Rambert's teaching has always combined technical excellence with the importance of the individual dancer and his understanding of his role. **R. B.**

'SIXTEEN YEARS OF BALLET RAMBERT', BY LIONEL BRADLEY (HINRICHSEN EDITION, 1946); 'DANCERS OF MERCURY,' BY MARY CLARKE (A. AND C. BLACK, 1962).

J. Arthur Rank (British, b. 1888): film magnate. Lord Rank, more than any man, determined the shape of today's British film industry. From buying projectors for Methodist churches and dabbling in religious films (1933), this middle-aged flour tycoon progressed to control a £50 million empire including 539 Odeon and Gaumont cinemas,

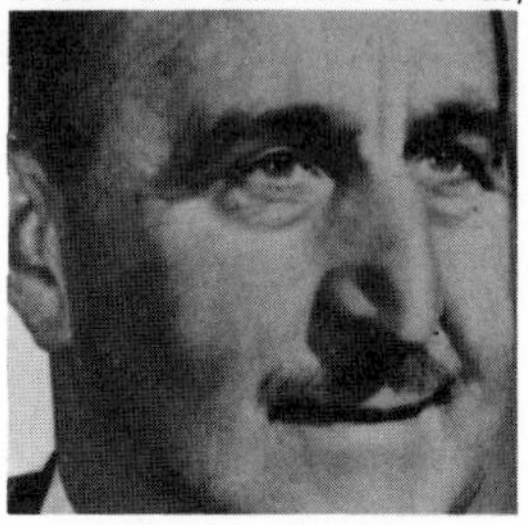

General Film Distributors and Pinewood and Denham studios. He financed great directors (Lean, Reed) and films (*Henry V*, the Ealing comedies); saved film production from collapsing in the Second World War as it had done in the First; prevented U.S. take-over of British cinemas and, temporarily, of British production; gave British works a better chance against Hollywood on his own screens; and put them on screens world-wide through his distribution network. Behind his success were business brilliance, private wealth, Wardour Street's goading and tempting, lucky breaks and, he might say, divine inspiration. But indulgence of spendthrift producers, abortive assaults on the U.S. market, Entertainments Tax and government muddling brought disaster, with over-production and a £16 million overdraft in 1949. Television later decimated his circuits. His most lasting legacy: monopolistic domination of film exhibition by giant circuits (Rank and its rival ABC) and a generation of ageing stars (Mason, Lockwood, Granger). **T. P. K.**

'A COMPETITIVE CINEMA', BY TERENCE KELLY, GRAHAM NORTON AND GEORGE PERRY (INSTITUTE OF ECONOMIC AFFAIRS, 1966). 'MR. RANK', BY ALAN WOOD (HODDER AND STOUGHTON, 1952).

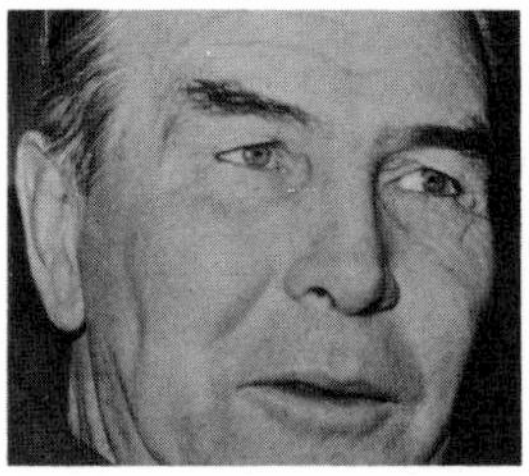

Adam Rapacki (Polish, 1909–70): politician. Poland's foreign minister from 1956–68 joined the Socialist Party in 1936, rising within a year, at the age of 27, to its central executive committee. In December 1948 Rapacki supported the merger of the Socialists with the Communists, and was rewarded with membership of the Politburo of the new combined party. Six years later, he was demoted from full membership, but returned with the defeat of the Polish Stalinists in 1956, becoming Foreign Minister the same year. He established himself as the spokesman for a major disengagement of the American and Soviet military forces con-

ROBERT RAUSCHENBERG: PHOTOGRAPH BY DAVID MONTGOMERY

fronting one another in Central Europe. In October 1957, he proposed the establishment of a zone, covering all Central Europe, free of nuclear weapons. The Rapacki Plan, as these proposals were called, was immediately embraced by the Soviet Union, despite suggestions that his proposal was really intended to decrease Soviet military pressure on his country. Although the proposal was rejected by the U.S., he has raised it at regular intervals since, the last serious occasion being in 1964. His gentlemanly manner and sympathetic mien won his country a good deal of support in the West which the cruder behaviour of his colleagues might have jeopardised. **D. C. W.**

Gregori Efimovich Rasputin (Russian, c. 1871–1916): mystic. With no education but great shrewdness and magnetic presence, Rasputin preached redemption through sin. By encouraging physical contact with the incarnation of the Deity, he gratified his uncontrollable sexual appetite and gulled St Petersburg into cultivating him as a Holy Man. Introduced in 1907 to the Tsar and Tsarina he won the latter's slavish infatuation by appearing to save her haemo-

philiac son Alexis from death on two occasions. When Nicholas II took command of the Front in 1915 Rasputin came to exercise absolute control at home through the Empress. Replacing able ministers with incompetent toadies, he interfered with food supplies and transports, urging the Tsar to crush all attempts to modify his autocracy. On the night of December 30–31, 1916, a trio of a Grand Duke, a Prince and a conservative politician assassinated him, but not before he had munched his way through cakes and wine drenched in potassium cyanide and survived shooting to succumb finally under the ice of the Neva. **S. S.**

'RASPUTIN AND THE FALL OF THE ROMANOVS', BY C. WILSON (A. BARKER, 1964).

Walther Rathenau (German, 1867–1922): industrialist and statesman. Rathenau made economic planning acceptable to non-Socialists. His qualifications for the job were distinctly odd: as head of the vast electrical engineering concern, AEG, he was one of the biggest Capitalists in pre-1914 Germany. Yet he found Capitalism lacking in promise, devoid of satisfaction for the workers. His intention was to change the system, not by revolution, but by pressure from within. His opportunity came early in the First World War when he was asked by the Prussian War Office to stabilise the hard-pressed economy. Two important reforms followed.

First, in a considerable extension of State powers, an Economic General Staff was formed with full control over the supply of vital war materials. Second, a new business organisation was created in which State and private ownership were *combined*. This was Rathenau's most radical innovation. It was literally a half-way house between private enterprise and State Socialism, and reflected precisely Rathenau's intention to modify Capitalism from the inside; it remained the basis of German planning until 1945. Germany never forgave Rathenau for his Jewish origin. After his reforms of the wartime economy, he was forced to leave the War Ministry, and after a post-war phase of diplomatic activity he was assassinated. Yet, in a few brief months, he demonstrated decisively that Capitalism and economic planning could co-exist. **R. C. T.**

'INTELLECTUALS IN POLITICS', BY J. B. JOLL (WEIDENFELD AND NICOLSON, 1960); 'IN DAYS TO COME', BY W. RATHENAU, TR. EDEN AND CEDAR PAUL (ALLEN AND UNWIN, 1921).

Robert Rauschenberg (U.S., b. 1925): artist. Rauschenberg is a natural genius. He is one of the rare people who, anywhere and at any time, can make something memorable out of any image and any material (his own bed, for instance, or a stuffed goat and a motor-car tyre) that lies to hand. He grew up in Texas – his grandfather, a doctor from Berlin, had married a pure-blooded Cherokee Indian – and he knew almost nothing of 'art' when he went to study with Josef Albers in 1948. But from 1952 he pioneered idea after idea that was fundamental to the art of the future: minimal art, in the all-white paintings of 1952; earthwork-art, in the dirt-paintings of the same date; mixed-media art, in painting that had light and movement and sound built into them; and

above all the attempt to break down the barriers between one art and another (his own dance-performances, and his work with Merce Cunningham) and between the artist and the art-consumer. His combine-paintings of 1954–59 are among the supreme achievements of modern art, and after winning First Prize at the Venice Biennale in 1964 he could have coasted along in the top league of self-duplicating international artists. Characteristically he dismissed that possibility and began a long series of major works, each entirely unlike the others, in which audience-participation is fundamental and the role of the artist as superior being is put aside. **J. R.**

'ROBERT RAUSCHENBERG', BY A. SOLOMON (JEWISH MUSEUM, NEW YORK, 1963).

Maurice Ravel (French, 1875–1937): composer. Ravel was a perfectionist, no less fastidious than his contemporary, Debussy (q.v.). He does not currently enjoy Debussy's posthumous fame as a *chef d'école* or father-figure though in more than one musical respect he anticipated him. Ravel forged a very personal style early in his career: the world success of his *Pavane pour une Infante défunte* (1899) anticipated that of his *Boléro* (1928) 30 years later. Compatriots as well as contemporaries, Ravel and Debussy have often been bracketed together, but for convenience rather than with justification, for their musical think-

ing is often poles apart. Whereas Debussy uses harmony empirically, with Ravel the same chords may be points of colour arrived at more logically as the result of the movement of lines of melody. The harmonic vocabulary of both composers is identical, but their way of using it in musical language is very different. Ravel contributed masterpieces to every form he essayed: piano music: *Jeux d'eau* (1901), *Miroirs* and *Sonatine* (1905), *Gaspard de la Nuit* (1908), *Le Tombeau de Couperin* (1917); ballet: *Daphnis et Chloë* (1912) for Diaghilev (q.v.); one-act operas: *L'Heure espagnole* (1907) and *L'Enfant et les Sortilèges* (1925); songs with orchestra: *Shéhérazade* (1903); piano concertos: two, of which one is for left hand (1931); songs with piano: *Histoires naturelles* (1906). In 1905, with a few of these works already acclaimed, Ravel was not allowed to enter for the *Prix de Rome*. He revenged himself on officialdom in 1920 when he refused the ribbon of the *Légion d'Honneur*, but he accepted an honorary Doctorate of Music at Oxford in 1928. **F. A.**

'RAVEL', BY NORMAN DEMUTH (DENT, 1947); 'RAVEL: LIFE AND WORKS', BY ROLLO H. MYERS (DUCKWORTH, 1960); 'THE LIFE OF MAURICE RAVEL', BY MADELEINE GOSS (TUDOR, N.Y., 1945).

Grote Reber (U.S., b. 1911): radio engineer. An enthusiastic radio ham, Reber was still at school when he was fired by Karl Jansky's (q.v.) discovery of radio waves coming from the Milky Way. As a young student at Illinois Institute of Technology he tried to bounce radio waves off the Moon (years later the U.S. Army finally succeeded). In 1937 this lone apostle of radio astronomy built the first true radio telescope in his back garden. Using this 31-ft. diameter 'dish' Reber discovered points in the sky which emitted radio waves that were stronger

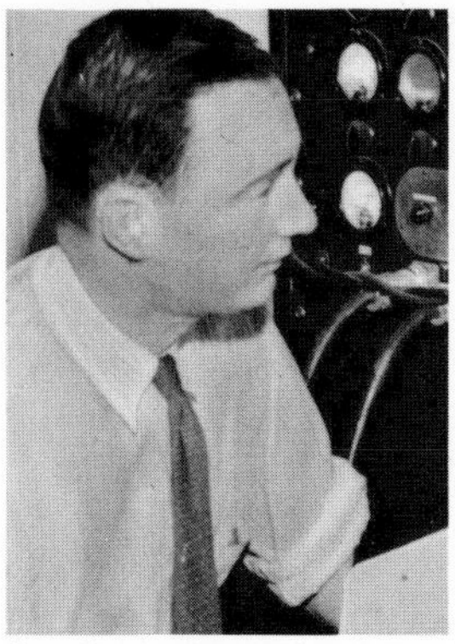

than the background radiation. Such 'radio stars' did not coincide with any stars seen by the optical telescopes of the day; a decade later Baade (q.v.) discovered one to be a distant pair of colliding galaxies. After the Second World War, Reber presented his original telescope to the U.S. National Bureau of Standards. It is said that, if it was Jansky who gave birth to radio astronomy, Reber wet-nursed it through its infancy. **N. V.**

'THE EXPLORATION OF SPACE BY RADIO', BY R. H. BROWN AND A. C. B. LOVELL (CHAPMAN, 1957); 'THE EXPLOSION OF SCIENCE: THE PHYSICAL UNIVERSE', BY SIR BERNARD LOVELL AND T. MARGERISON (THAMES AND HUDSON, 1967).

Otis Redding (U.S., 1941–1967): singer. This century's popular music has always had its fashions, from ragtime to rock, and in the 1960s the vogue word was 'soul'. Soul music was a yearning for the 'real thing' after the vulgarised mutation of the blues called rock 'n' roll. It was also associated with black militancy in America. Once, urban American blacks toned down their pop music, trying to be white; in the 1960s they beefed up traditional rhythm and blues with a transfusion of highly emotional, old-time gospel music, now no longer a part of their past they wanted to forget. In soul you scream, shake, feel and sweat; and Otis Redding became, for hip whites at least, the king of soul, much imitated. When he died in a plane crash at Madison, Wisconsin, his hero status was assured. Born in Georgia, he had a not uncommon black American singer's background – father a preacher, sang in church choir, joined a band called Johnny Jenkins and the Pinetroopers, inspired by blues man Little Richard. His first disc, *These Arms of Mine*, sold 750,000 and he roared out *Satisfaction* (as did the Stones). His singing was tricky, full of blues feeling and sock-it-to-'em guts. He was perhaps not as good as, say, James Brown, Aretha Franklin, even Ray Charles, but the dice fell right for him. He had just been voted World's Top Male Singer in the British *Melody Maker* Pop Poll when he was killed. **D. J.**

RECORDS: 'OTIS BLUE – OTIS REDDING SINGS SOUL' (ATL.587036); 'HISTORY OF OTIS REDDING' (ATL. 228001).

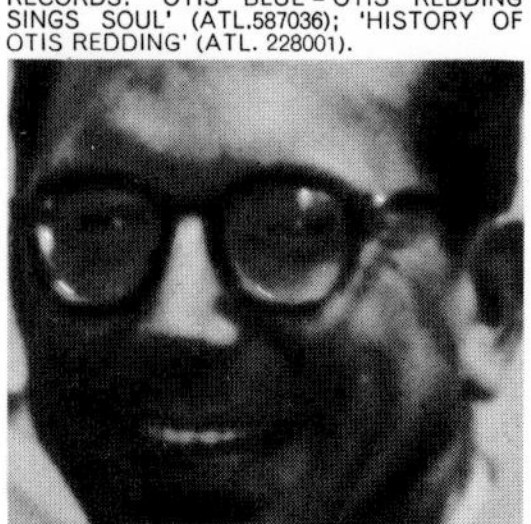

Rosser Reeves (U.S., b. 1910): advertising pioneer. Long-time dean of Madison Avenue theorists, Reeves invented the doctrine of the Unique Selling Proposition (USP) and used it to help build the Ted Bates advertising agency to an annual billing rate of nearly 300 million dollars by the time he relinquished the chairmanship in 1966. Reeves's USP for Colgate Dental Cream – "it cleans your breath while it cleans your teeth" – kept it at the top of the U.S. toothpaste market for almost a quarter of a century, although in fact, as Reeves admitted, every dentifrice cleans your breath. He was the arch-adept at solving the problem which he most neatly expressed in the story of the client who came into his office, threw two newly-minted half-dollars on the desk and said: "Mine is the one on the left. You prove it's better." His efforts at differentiating and building brand-loyalty for otherwise identical products made the fortune of a whole range of items, from Viceroy cigarettes ("20,000 filters") to Carter's Little Liver Pills ("Helps you break the laxative habit"). But possibly his most significant job was the 1.5 million dollar TV-spot campaign which he wrote for Eisenhower (q.v.) in 1952. Students of democracy are still arguing about the ethical significance of selling presidents like soap. **P. W.**

'MADISON AVENUE U.S.A.', BY MARTIN MAYER (BODLEY HEAD, 1958); 'REALITY IN ADVERTISING', BY ROSSER REEVES (MACGIBBON AND KEE, 1961).

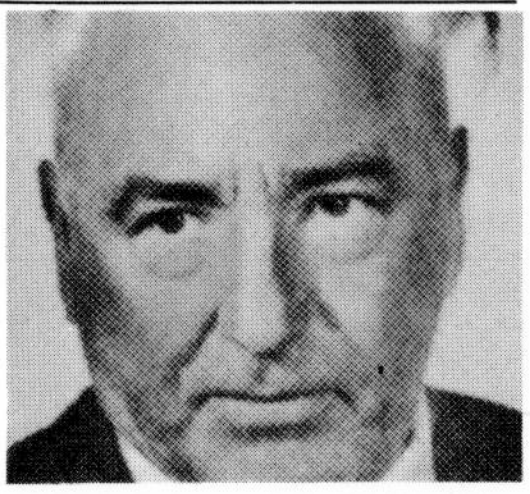

Wilhelm Reich (Austrian, 1897–1957): psychiatrist. Reich was expelled from Freud's (q.v.) International Psychoanalytic Association in 1934. His early work on character analysis had led to important developments in analytic technique. He later identified libido (roughly – sexual energy) with bio-electrical forces recorded from electrodes placed on the body. This energy called Orgone was said also to be found in sand, soil and the atmosphere. It has not been validated subsequently. For Reich, psychic health is the product of Orgastic Potency – the total discharge of sexual excitation in the orgasm. He held that Malinowski (q.v.) had shown that sexual repression was socially determined and alterable rather than biologically fixed – Freud's view. Reich argued that the authoritarian family represses infantile and adolescent sexuality, generates the Oedipal complex, leads to the abdication of initiative and to a population tolerant of repression and dictatorship. He fled to America in 1939, where he was persecuted there by some members of the medical profession, and he died in prison where he had been committed for contempt of court. It is, perhaps, easy to dismiss Reich as a crank, but what he has to tell the 20th century about sexuality and society is important, and has parallels to D. H. Lawrence's (q.v.) thinking. A. S. Neill (q.v.) incorporated some of Reich's ideas into Summerhill School. **B. R. O.**

'THE FUNCTION OF THE ORGASM', BY W. REICH (PANTHER, 1968).

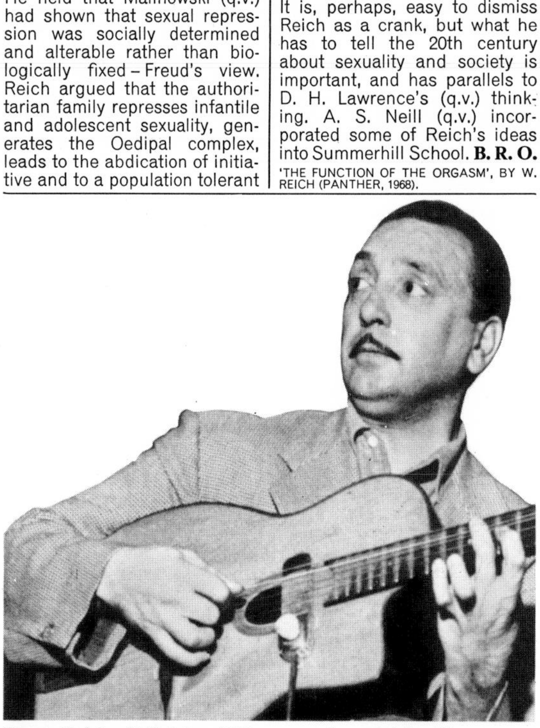

Django Reinhardt (Belgian, 1910–1953): jazz musician. Jean-Baptiste Reinhardt, as a gypsy boy, roamed through France and Belgium and taught himself the banjo, the violin, and the guitar, his great instrument. When he was 18 he was badly burned in a caravan fire, lost the use of two fingers of his left hand, and had to develop a style of fingering that was virtually a new guitar technique. He wandered round Parisian cafés, made his first reputation with André Ekyan's band, but is best known for his playing from 1934 onwards with the quartet of the Hot Club of France, in which he and Stéphane Grappelly on violin were the soloists. Django wandered off every now and again, but they stayed together until 1939. Reinhardt made only one trip to America, with Duke Ellington in 1946, but the tour was not a success and he returned to France and retired. He died of cerebral congestion at Fontainebleau just before a reunion of French gypsies at which his Gypsy Mass was to be performed. Reinhardt's rhapsodic style shone through everything he did, but he cannot be called simply a gypsy player: he was one of the few European jazzmen to influence American contemporaries. **T. F. C.**

'DJANGO AND HIS AMERICAN FRIENDS' (VOL. 1. HMV CLP 1890, VOL. 2. HMV CLP 1907).

Max Reinhardt (U.S., ex-Austrian, 1873–1943): theatrical director. Reinhardt was one of the most grandiose spectacular directors of the century; his management of crowds became legendary, he was the D. W. Griffith (q.v.) of the stage. Until 1903 he was an actor specialising in playing old men; thereafter he directed only. In 1920 he founded the Salzburg Festival. In 1933 he directed *A Midsummer Night's Dream* in the open air

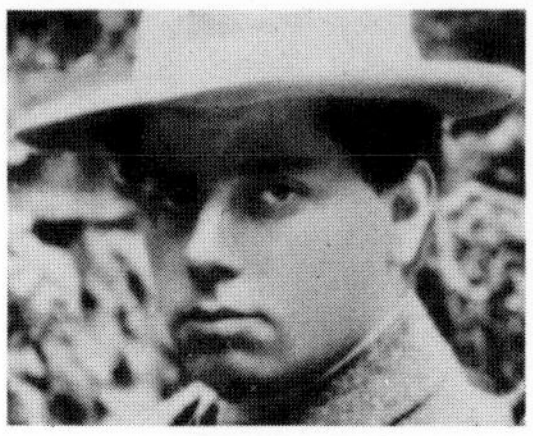

in wet weather for Oxford University Dramatic Society at ruinous expense; he later filmed the same play in Hollywood, after fleeing to the United States following the rise of Hitler (q.v.). He also worked in small theatres, but it is on his vast spectaculars, such as *Oedipus Rex* and *The Miracle* (which he directed for C. B. Cochran [q.v.] at Olympia in 1911), that his fame rests. *The Miracle* was revived in later years, with Lady Diana Cooper as the Madonna. This marked the apotheosis of the theatre as a social and class phenomenon. Part of Reinhardt's intention was to reduce the importance of both the author and the star actor, and in this he was in harmony with the spirit of his time. His insistence on new mechanical devices has had considerable influence on the structure of modern playhouses, especially in American academic institutions. **H. H.**

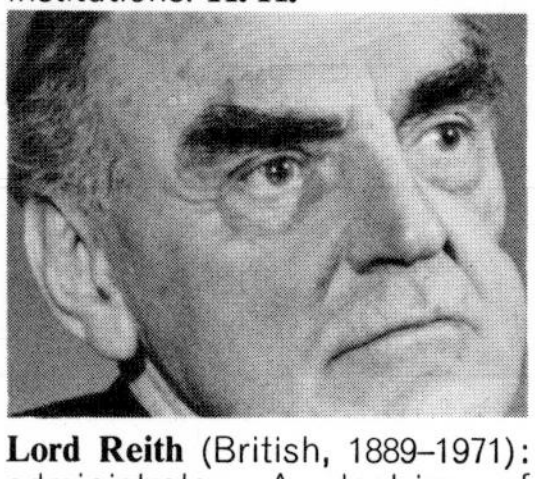

Lord Reith (British, 1889–1971): administrator. A doctrine of broadcasting providing an alternative to either outright commercialism or government control formed in John Reith's mind almost from his appointment as first – and last – general manager of the British Broadcasting Company in 1922. From his strange and complex temperament came the idea of a public corporation, supported by licence revenue, and charged with a duty to inform, educate and entertain. He demanded such standards from broadcasters as his Presbyterian conscience set for himself: consequently, when the BBC was set up in 1927, with Reith, knighted, as Director-General, it often seemed as if the Corporation was controlled by a high-minded mandarinate, with little interest in or appreciation of popular tastes. Against this, the BBC, undoubtedly due to Reithian policies, raised the whole level of national interest in the arts, especially music, and, in its news broadcasts, particularly to overseas, gained a deserved reputation for reliability. Reith left the Corporation in 1938. A spell as a Minister in wartime Governments was followed by relatively humble work as a serving officer at the Admiralty; after 1945, he chaired various Government commissions. **G. P. G. N.**

BOOKS BY LORD REITH: 'INTO THE WIND' (HODDER AND STOUGHTON, 1949); 'WEARING SPURS' (HUTCHINSON, 1966).

Jean Renoir (French, b. 1894): film director. Younger son of the Impressionist painter Auguste Renoir, Jean Renoir fell in love with the cinema after seeing Chaplin's (q.v.) early comedies while serving as cavalry officer and pilot in the First World War. The tone of his own career was set by *Nana*, made in 1926 under the influence of Stroheim's (q.v.) acid dissection of social follies

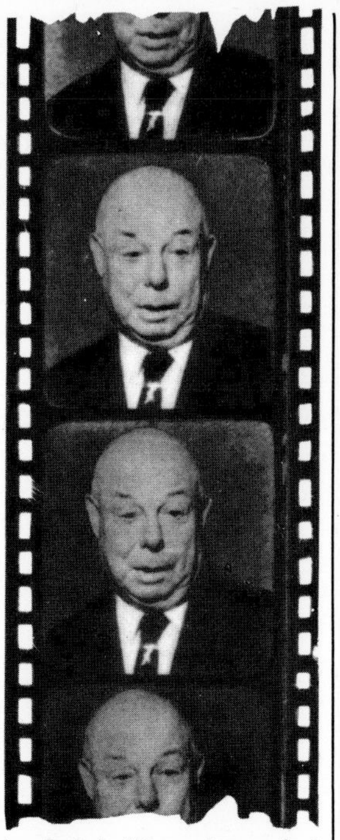

in *Foolish Wives*. Less of a moralist than Stroheim, Renoir refused to see people as good or bad, wicked or deserving; instead, encouraging his actors to cast off preconceived ideas, and delighting in improvisation so that his films have the joyous freedom of the *Commedia dell' Arte*, he simply watched and waited, observing the complex relationship between character and milieu. "Everyone has his reasons," he says, playing the role of Octave in his own masterpiece, *La Règle du Jeu*; and it is this sympathetic acceptance of humanity, allied to his father's uncanny instinct for the quality of light and the feel and touch of things, which gives his films their unique combination of realism, open-endedness and sensuous grace. It was years before the cinema caught up with the improvisational liberties of his masterpieces from the Thirties, *La Chienne, Bondu Sauve des Eaux, Toni, Le Règle du Jeu*; it may be years yet before it catches up with the Mozartian serenity of later films like *French Cancan* and *Eléna et les Hommes*. **T. M.**

'RENOIR, MY FATHER', BY JEAN RENOIR (COLLINS, 1962; FONTANA, 1966).

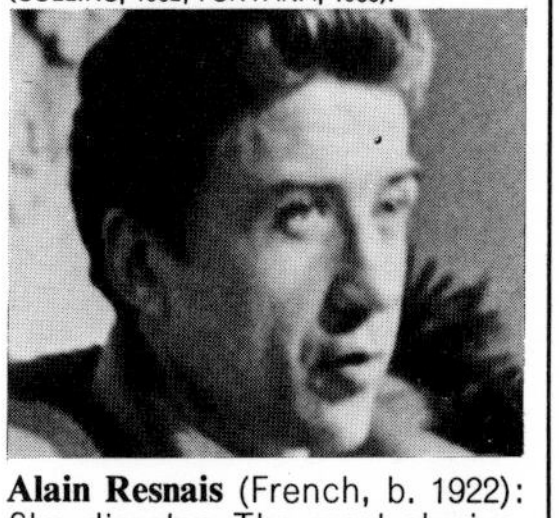

Alain Resnais (French, b. 1922): film director. The most elusive, diffident and subtle of the big names of the modern French cinema, Alain Resnais has been called the cinema's Proust, because of the obsessive concern with memory and recollection that runs through his work, from the baroque corridors of *L'Année Dernière à Marienbad* to war-shattered and rebuilt Boulogne in *Muriel*, the most intricate and involving of his films. He grew up in Brittany, and at the age of 14 was trying to film a *Fantômas* adventure with schoolchildren; moving the camera up close, he has recorded, with the optimistic notion that this would make his actors look larger and more imposing. His short films range from a series about modern painters ("because I wanted to meet them") to *Nuit et Brouillard*, the infinitely restrained and painful evocation of the ghosts of Auschwitz. His first feature, *Hiroshima mon Amour* (1959), remains one of the catalystic influences on modern international film style, through its dazzling use of fragmented time. Resnais has a chameleon gift for taking on colouring from his novelist script-writers (Marguerite Duras, Alain Robbe-Grillet, Jean Cayrol), while at the same time the form, structure and fluency of his films are clearly determined by his own complex fascination with themes of time lost, remembered and regained. **P. H.**

'ALAIN RESNAIS OR THE THEME OF TIME', BY JOHN WARD (SECKER AND WARBURG, 1968); 'THE CINEMA OF ALAIN RESNAIS', BY ROY ARMES (ZWEMMER, 1968).

Joachim von Ribbentrop (German, 1893–1946): diplomat. A relentless frequenter of Hitler's (q.v.) ante-chamber and an incessant sycophant, he soon worked his way up the Nazi Party (which he joined only when its success was assured in 1932), from being adviser on foreign affairs to Hitler's deputy, Rudolf Hess, through successive appointments as special envoy on disarmament questions (1934–1936) and ambassador to London (1936–38), to that of Hitler's Foreign Minister. Greatly disliked by most of the original Nazi leadership, he won Hitler's respect by the ease of his social manners, the apparent range of his cosmopolitan contacts (he was an incurable name-dropper) and the way in which he echoed Hitler's own extreme ideas. His attitude to diplomacy, that it was a matter of overwhelming opposition by a series of headline grabbing coups – his main successes were the Anglo-German naval agreement (1935), the anti-Comintern Pact with Japan (1936), and the Pact of Steel with Italy and the Nazi-Soviet Non-aggression Pact (1939) – paralleled Hitler's own approach to foreign policy. His constant reassurances that Britain would not implement the guarantees she gave to Poland in March 1939 did much to play a major part in the process by which Hitler's plans for a limited war against Poland involved Europe in the Second World War six months later. By 1943 he had become a mere cypher among the Nazi leaders. He was tried at Nuremberg on war crime charges and hanged on October 16, 1946. **D. C. W.**

Frank Richards (British, 1875–1961): writer. Richards (real name Charles Hamilton) created Billy Bunter, Harry Wharton and Co., Bob Cherry, Hurree Jamset Ram Singh, Quelch, and the other immortals of Greyfriars School. At 17 he sold his first story for five guineas. He wrote more than 10,000 of them, mostly for the *Gem* and *Magnet*

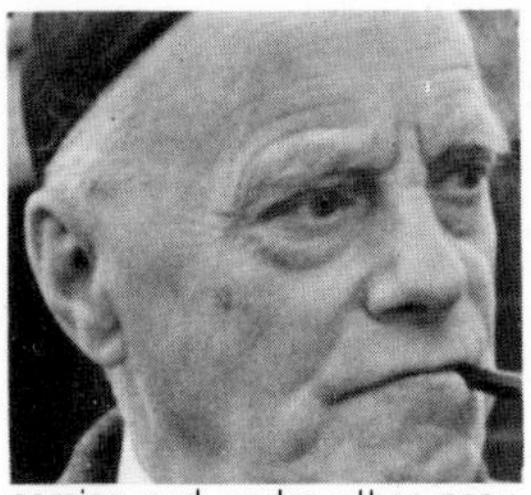

comics and under other pseudonyms. When he was 84 he said he must have written 60 million words – the equivalent of 800 novels. He was a bit of a recluse, and reticent about his private life – one of his pleasures was reciting the Odes of Horace aloud. He translated popular songs into Latin, *Waltzing Matilda* becoming *"Veni ut saltemus, Matilda, veni"*. Bunter appeared in a television series and in pantomime, but the yells of "Yarooh", "Leggo", and "Yah, rot", seemed less authentic than in the *Magnet*. Richards lost £50,000 gambling on the Stock Exchange; one of his loves was playing the tables at Monte Carlo, and he left only £11,317 in his will. He was a story-teller of genius, who more than anyone upheld the fictional but gallant ethos of the public school. Greyfriars was familiar to thousands who never heard of Eton, and Bunter the guzzling rotter was an English gentleman. **T. F. C.**

'FRANK RICHARDS: AN AUTOBIOGRAPHY' (CHARLES SKILTON, 1952).

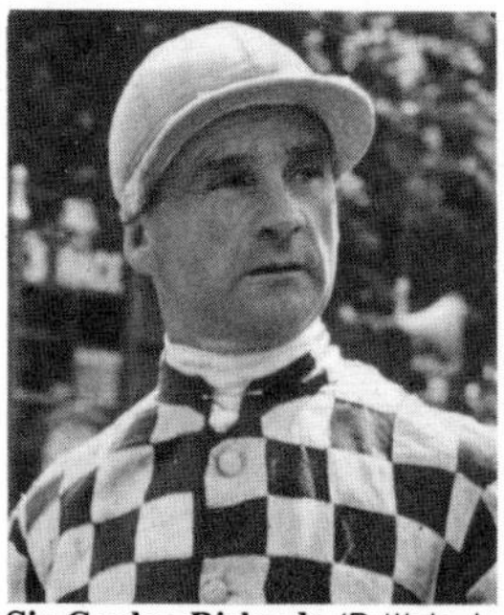

Sir Gordon Richards (British, b. 1904): jockey. Born in Shropshire of working-class parents, Richards rode his first winner in 1921 and was champion jockey by 1925. The following year he fell gravely ill and his career looked in jeopardy, but happily he recovered and by 1927 he was champion again. From that point he never looked back; when he retired in 1954 he had been champion jockey 26 times. Altogether he rode 4870 winners, a total unapproached by any other British rider, while his 269 winners in 1947 form another record. For years the Derby eluded him but at last he won in 1953 on Pinza. Since his retirement as a jockey in 1954, he has had conspicuous success as a trainer. Small, sturdy and short in the leg, he has always walked with a jaunty, confident, semi-nautical gait that offers no clue to a tendency to worry. His style was unorthodox, a risky one for lesser men to copy. In a tight finish he rode rather upright, sometimes distinctly sideways, with a loose rein, nevertheless retaining perfect control. Uncannily good at the start, he was usually ideally placed at the critical stage of the race. He employed his whip to encourage, rarely to chastise. To his skill was added a most ardent determination to win. No great jockey has ever lost fewer races he ought to have won, and punters have never had a better friend. **R. F. M.**

'MY STORY', BY SIR GORDON RICHARDS (HODDER AND STOUGHTON, 1955).

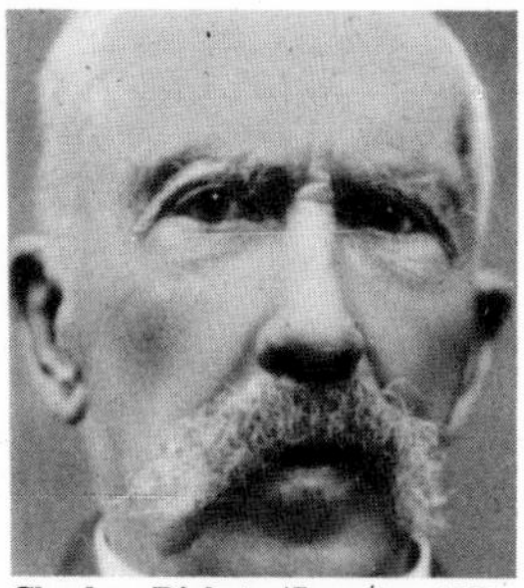

Charles Richet (French, 1850–1935): physiologist. Richet was awarded the Nobel Prize in Medicine and Physiology in 1913, in recognition of his work on *anaphylaxis,* a word he coined to describe a striking and entirely unexpected increase of toxicity which he found when he repeated an injection of the poisonous stings of jelly fish or the tentacles of sea anemones into dogs. It was afterwards shown that this phenomenon of anaphylactic shock could develop not only to toxic substances, but also to quite harmless ones like pollens and danders and even certain foods, as people who suffer from hay fever and other allergies will know. Recently, the subject has assumed increased importance with the development of allergies to widely used drugs like penicillin. Minute doses of this drug, which is usually non-toxic, can produce a variety of unpleasant and even dangerous manifestations in people who have the misfortune to develop anaphylactic antibodies to the drug. So Richet's discovery of anaphylaxis, which he modestly claimed was not at all the result of deep thinking but of a simple, almost accidental observation, started research which is of vital importance to an understanding and control of the multitude of allergies from which at least 10 per cent. of us suffer in one form or another. **J. L. M.**

Hyman George Rickover (U.S., b. 1900): naval strategist. In 1946 Captain Rickover, moth-balling ships in California, discovered that the U.S. Navy proposed to appoint officers to Oak Ridge Atomic Research Centre. On applying, he was sidetracked; he insisted, and was assigned. Washington files yielded studies for nuclear ship propulsion by Ross Gunn and Philip Abelson: reading them, Rickover became obsessed by submarine possibilities. Leading Oak Ridge's naval group by force of personality, he secured Edward Teller's (q.v.) backing for a naval reactor project. But despite Teller it was dropped, the group dissolved, and Rickover appointed a 'document declassification officer'. However, reorganising himself as special assistant to Admiral

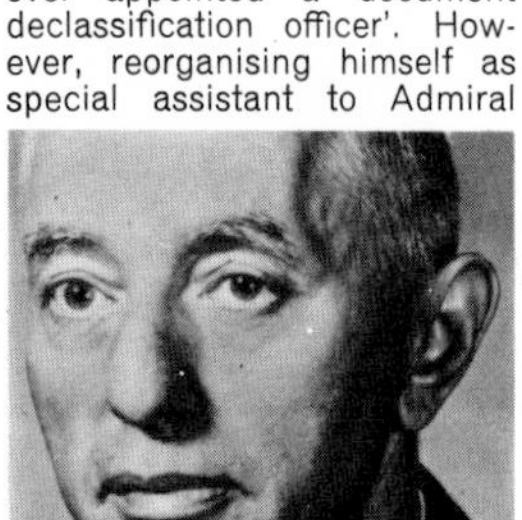

Mills, who headed the Bureau of Ships, Rickover took a memorandum urging its development to Admiral Nimitz. Nimitz signed it; the Atomic Energy Commission co-operated and Rickover promoted his group as Nuclear Branch of the Bureau. Pressurising, intriguing, blasting, he won, in 1950, Presidential authorisation for U.S.S. Nautilus. In 1951 the Electric Boat Company (q.v. Holland) started work, and President Truman (q.v.) laid her keel in 1952. Rickover was passed over and slated for retirement. Extraordinary expedients saved him, and he was made a Rear Admiral. Stubborn and daemonically energetic, he forced the nuclear submarine upon the world. **D. D.**

'ATOMIC SUBMARINES', BY NORMAN POLMAR (VAN NOSTRAND, N.Y., 1963).

Gerrit Rietveld (Dutch, 1888–1964): architect. Twice in his youth, in a chair (1917) and a

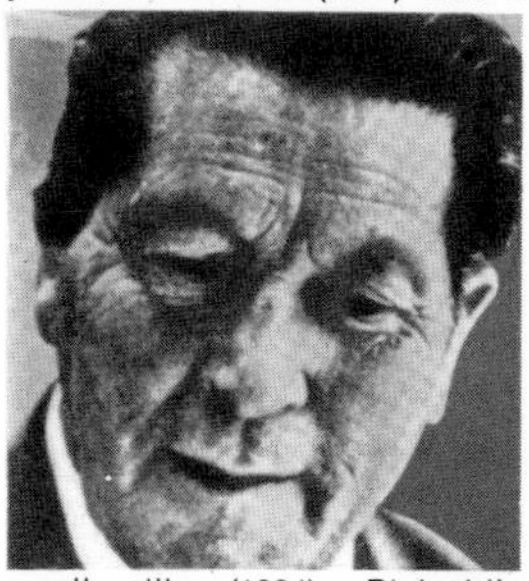

small villa (1924), Rietveld's modest talent acted as a catalyst for modern design, when he was a member of De Stijl, the group of artists led by Mondrian (q.v.) and van Doesburg. The chair, though gawky in its elementarist nakedness, fundamentally influenced the Bauhaus prototypes of Breuer (q.v.). In the villa, the Schroeder House at Utrecht, while summing up manifold postwar influences – the Russian Suprematists and Constructivists, the French Cubists, the traditional architecture of Japan, the Prairie Houses of Wright (q.v.) – Rietveld discovered a wholly new fluidity and transparency of space, which was taken up immediately by Le Corbusier (q.v.). Eventually, in the late Fifties, he was given some larger jobs (Technical College at Arnhem), but he is still remembered chiefly for his furniture designs, with cabinets articulated like Brutalist blocks of flats. **N. J. W. T.**

'THE WORK OF G. RIETVELD, ARCHITECT', BY THEODORE M. BROWN (UTRECHT, 1958).

Rainer Maria Rilke (Austrian, 1875–1926): poet. Rilke was one of the century's most international poets. He considered the European capitals his spiritual home and travelled to France where he fell under the spell of Valéry, Gide (qq.v.) and Rodin. A foolish upbringing overshadowed his youth; for years his mother dressed him as a girl, and his father then plunged the long-haired son into a military academy. A number of female hagiographers distorted Rilke's personal image. But as an artist he was formidable. Art absorbed his total being. Art, he said, was something too great and too difficult for one life. Acceptance of our earthly task and transformation are the keynotes in his later poems. After his *Stundenbuch* (inspired by Russian fairy tales about God), the *Buch der Bilder* and *Neue Gedichte* appeared. In his *Ding-Gedichte* he endeavoured, under Rodin's influence, to condense his poetic vision into objective images. He also wrote short stories: tales about God – *Geschichten vom lieben Gott*; and the notebooks – *Die Aufzeichnungen des Malte Laurids Brigge,* a modern 'burnt-out Werther'; and the popular lay of love and death – *Die Weise von Liebe und Tod des Cornets Christoph Rilke*. But his most compelling works are the *Duineser Elegien* and the *Sonette an Orpheus*. **A. C.**

'TWENTIETH CENTURY GERMAN LITERATURE', IV VOL. OF 'INTRODUCTIONS', BY A. CLOSS (THE CRESSET PRESS, 1969); 'RILKE: POEMS 1906-1926', BY J. B. LEISHMAN (HOGARTH PRESS, 1957).

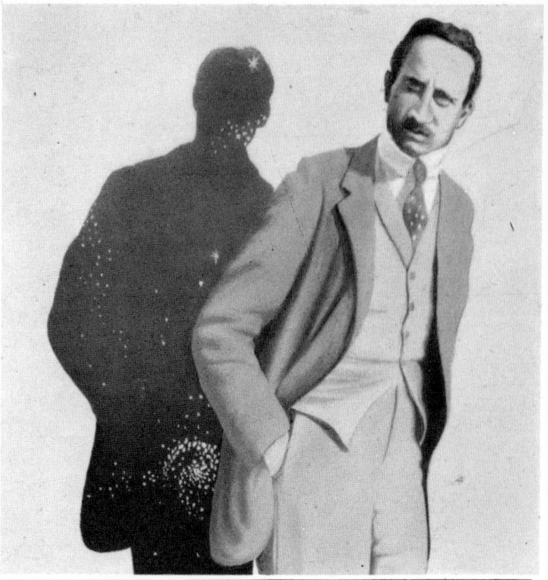

ILLUSTRATION OF RILKE BY MICHAEL McINNERNEY

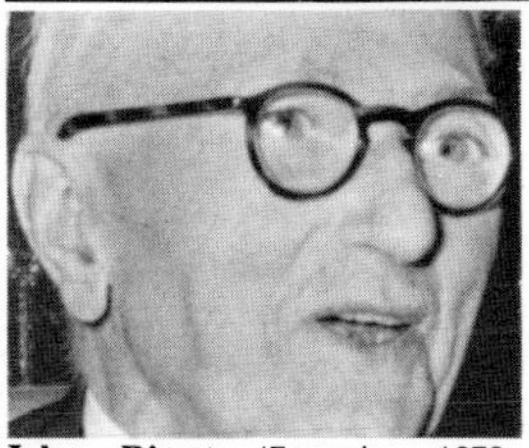

Jules Rimet (French, 1873–1956): football administrator. There hangs in the offices of FIFA in Zürich a plaque on which is simply inscribed: *"La FIFA: En mémoire de son regretté Président et Président d'Honneur Jules Rimet 1919–1956."* Coming to Paris from Theuley-les-Lavancourt as a young man in 1885, Jules Rimet founded the Red Star Club of Paris. He was its first President and in 1910 became the President of the French Football League. When the French Football Federation was created in 1919, he became its President, a post he occupied until 1949. He was also the President of the French National Sports Committee from 1932 to 1947. Together with representatives of Holland, Switzerland, Belgium, Spain and Italy he formed FIFA (Fédération Internationale de Football Association), and was elected its President in 1921. During his 35 years' service in that capacity he became the best known administrator in world football. Jules Rimet was the promoter of the World Cup Competition and when, after the Second World War, it was decided to restart it with countries competing from all over the world, Rimet's name was incorporated in the title of the Competition: for in that same year he had served FIFA for 25 years. **S. F. R.**

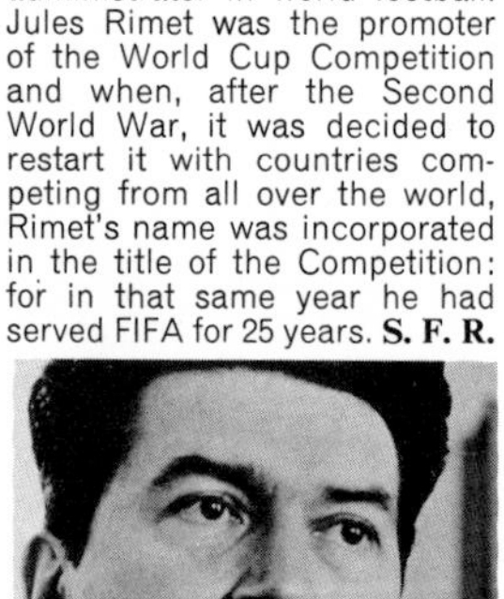

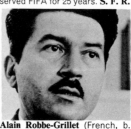

Alain Robbe-Grillet (French, b. 1922): novelist and film director. The most famous practitioner and theoretician of the French 'New Novel': as he explains in *Pour un nouveau roman* (1963), his aim is to bring about in the novel an aesthetic revolution comparable to those that have occurred in painting and music. He sees himself as a contemporary realist, eliminating what he considers to be the outworn conventions of plot, character and psychological analysis. These are replaced by elaborate and precise patterns of description, which are meant to convey directly the truth of a modern sensibility, equally indifferent to both religious belief and the philosophy of the Absurd, although definitely nearer to the latter. All his works, from *Les Gommes* (1953) to *La Maison de Rendez-vous* (1965), are in the nature of detective stories with a deliberately distorted and indecipherable time-sequence, which present life as an open mystery impervious to interpretation. In 1961 he published the *ciné-roman* (detailed scenario) of *L'Année Dernière à Marienbad,* which had been made into a film by Alain Resnais (q.v.). Since then he has written and directed several more films, including *L'Immortelle, Trans-Europe Express* and *L'homme que ment*. **J. G. W.**

'ALAIN ROBBE-GRILLET', BY J. G. WEIGHTMAN, IN 'THE NOVELIST AS PHILOSOPHER', ED. JOHN CRUICKSHANK (O.U.P., 1962).

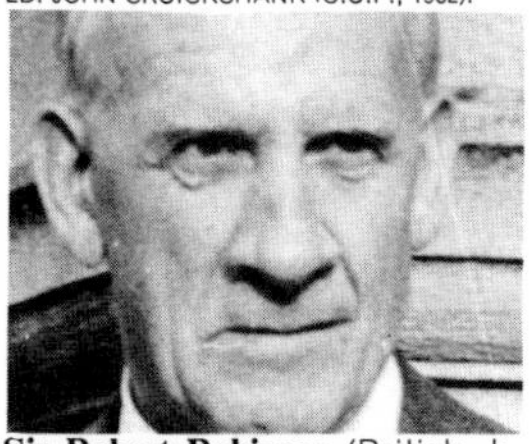

Sir Robert Robinson (British, b. 1886): chemist. Plants and their constituents have always offered a major challenge to chemists. Robert Robinson achieved his greatest distinction in the elucidation of structures of important classes of compounds occurring in nature. Among these are the alkaloids, both medicines and poisons: cocaine, strychnine, atropine and morphine among them. The extraction of natural products from plants was mainly a 19th-century achievement. Their synthesis, which in turn allowed modifications for medicinal and other uses, is taking place in the 20th, when the British school of synthetic chemistry has been both active and successful. In addition to his work on natural products, Robinson also took a leading part in the study of the ways chemical transformations take place and it is perhaps characteristic that not only has he been president of the Royal Society (1945–50) and of the Chemical Society (1939–41) but also of the British Chess Federation (1950–53). **P. J. F.**

'NOBEL LECTURES IN CHEMISTRY 1942–62' (ELSEVIER, 1964).

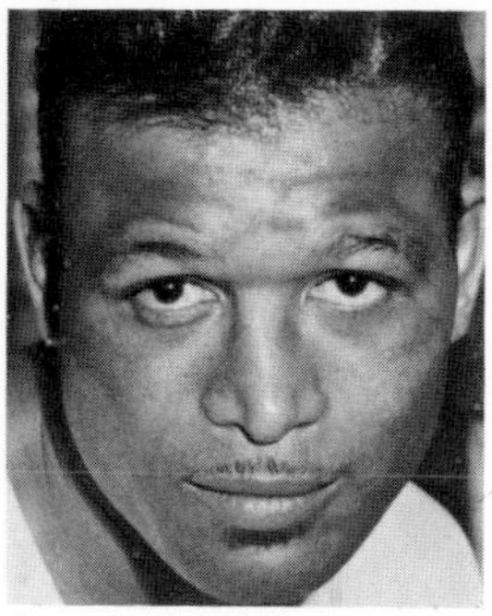

Sugar Ray Robinson (U.S., b. 1920): boxer. The date was October 4, 1940. The place New York City. The name Walker Smith. Small-time hall, unknown opponent, hard-bitten, tough audience. Then bang – the lights went out in two rounds for the opponent and on for 'Smithy'. A new star was born, a star that was to shine brightly for 25 years in the toughest, roughest sport in the world, a star whose every action, snazzy dress, flashy speech were copied by every kid in the world. Sugar Ray Robinson, alias Smith, alias every superlative ever invented by man, graced the ring and took his place at the top of a division that gave the world names like Ketchel, Greb, Walker. A man whose every movement and every action screamed out Prince. A man who was hated, loved and for many years misunderstood. A man who won the world welterweight title in 1946, won and lost the world middleweight title five times. A man who in 1952 boxed for the world light-heavyweight title and was beaten, not by his opponent but by heat exhaustion. After 13 rounds of brilliant boxing, winning by the proverbial mile, Sugar Ray couldn't find enough strength in his legs to lift himself off the stool for the next round. The spirit screamed out "Let's go, baby", but the legs cried enough. He travelled Europe with a huge entourage, his hairdresser, his masseur, his trainer, comedian, manager, wife. He took Paris, Berlin and London by storm. His pink Cadillac was his sign of success. His boxing style has been copied by thousands of youngsters, but they were all poor imitations. There was only one 'Smithy'. **B. N.**

'THE ENCYCLOPAEDIA OF BOXING', 3RD. ED. COMP. BY M. GOLESWORTHY (HALE, 1965).

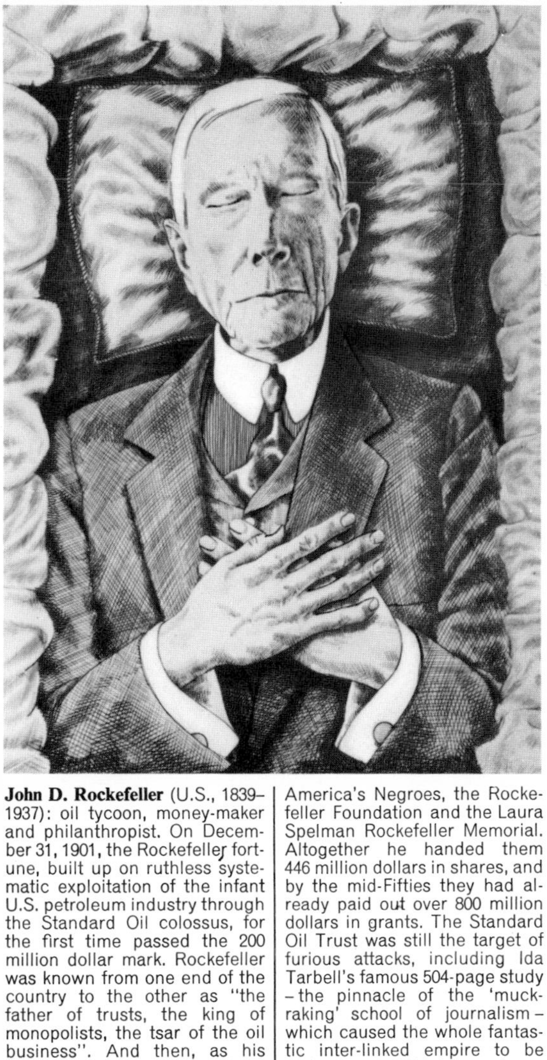

John D. Rockefeller (U.S., 1839–1937): oil tycoon, money-maker and philanthropist. On December 31, 1901, the Rockefeller fortune, built up on ruthless systematic exploitation of the infant U.S. petroleum industry through the Standard Oil colossus, for the first time passed the 200 million dollar mark. Rockefeller was known from one end of the country to the other as "the father of trusts, the king of monopolists, the tsar of the oil business". And then, as his fortune surged ever upwards in the wake of the new-fangled motor-car to its 1913 peak of 900 million dollars, he started to give the money away. He founded the University of Chicago, followed it with the Rockefeller Institute for Medical Research (which rid the South of hookworm and led the world crusade against epidemic meningitis and yellow fever), the General Education Board, to build up schooling among America's Negroes, the Rockefeller Foundation and the Laura Spelman Rockefeller Memorial. Altogether he handed them 446 million dollars in shares, and by the mid-Fifties they had already paid out over 800 million dollars in grants. The Standard Oil Trust was still the target of furious attacks, including Ida Tarbell's famous 504-page study – the pinnacle of the 'muckraking' school of journalism – which caused the whole fantastic inter-linked empire to be broken up, in 1911, into no fewer than 38 separate parts, including today's Esso. The result, as even Teddy Roosevelt (q.v.), the leading trust-buster, admitted, was virtually nothing – all that happened was that Rockefeller's shares doubled as the full value of his empire was realised. And the most hated American gradually became a synonym for 20th-century philanthropy. **T.**

'A STUDY IN POWER: JOHN D. ROCKEFELLER', BY ALLAN NEVINS (SCRIBNER, N. Y., 1953).

Richard Rodgers (U.S., b. 1902): composer. Rodgers met Lorenz Hart at Columbia University, and "in one afternoon", said Rodgers later, "I acquired a career, a partner, a best friend – and a source of permanent irritation." Not every musical they wrote was a hit, but most of the songs were, including *Blue Room* for *The Girl Friend*, *My Heart Stood Still* for *A Connecticut Yankee*, *Mountain Greenery* for *Garrick Gaieties of 1926*, *With a Song in My Heart*, and the title song, for *Spring is Here*, and a tune that started life as *Oh Lord, Please Won't You Send Me a Man*, ended as *Blue Moon* and sold over a million sheet-music copies, their biggest hit to date. American musical comedy grew up with

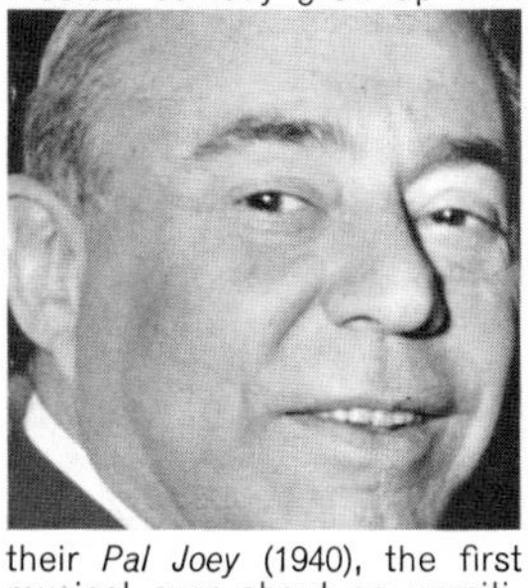

their *Pal Joey* (1940), the first musical ever about an unmitigated louse (played with superb perception by Gene Kelly). After Hart's tragic death in 1943 Rodgers started work with Oscar Hammerstein II. Their *Oklahoma!* became even more of a trailblazer than *Pal Joey*. It ran five years and 2248 performances, a new Broadway record for a musical, and made a profit of seven million dollars. With Hammerstein Rodgers was quite literally a different composer. His tunes and rhythms had matched the wit, acid and sentiment that only Hart could write. Hammerstein had a more folksy quality and Rodgers's musical personality seemed to change completely to accommodate this different style. Musicians are apt to prefer the Rodgers of Rodgers and Hart, but the public has made its own decision, opting hugely for *South Pacific*, *The King and I*, *Flower Drum Song* and *The Sound of Music*. **L. A.**

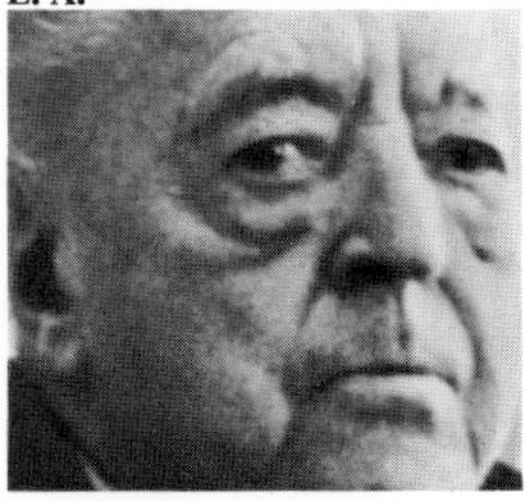

Ludwig Mies van der Rohe (U.S., ex-German, 1886–1969): architect. The perfectionist of modern architecture in its purest rectilinear forms of glass and steel, Mies van der Rohe learnt from Behrens (q.v.) the disciplines of industrial production and of Prussian classicism. As a leader of the Berlin School, he prophesied the glass skyscraper (1920–1) and the strip-windowed concrete office block (1922), besides building brick houses with long bare walls penetrating the landscape. The continuity of structure (steel and marble) and exquisite transparency of space in his German Pavilion at Barcelona (1929) were translated into practical terms in his Weissenhof flats at Stuttgart (1929) and Tugendhat House at Brno (1930). Moving to Chicago in 1937, he rediscovered that city's skyscraper tradition in his glass boxes ("less is more"), such as 860 Lake Shore Drive (1949–52) and the Seagram Building in New York (1955–8). He revived the horizontal temple ideal in the Farnsworth House (1946–50), in the Illinois Institute of Technology (1942–), where he himself taught, and in the Museum of the Twentieth Century, back in Berlin (1966–8). Younger architects criticise the Miesian box as an absolutist straitjacket, remote from social problems. **N. J. W. T.**

'MIES VAN DER ROHE', BY PHILIP JOHNSON (MUSEUM OF MODERN ART, N.Y., 1953); 'MIES VAN DER ROHE', BY ARTHUR DREXLER (MAYFLOWER, 1960); 'MIES VAN DER ROHE', BY PETER BLAKE (PENGUIN, 1963).

Charles Stewart Rolls (British, 1877–1910) and **Sir Henry Royce** (British, 1863–1933): engineers. The two names are now inseparable, though Royce was nearly

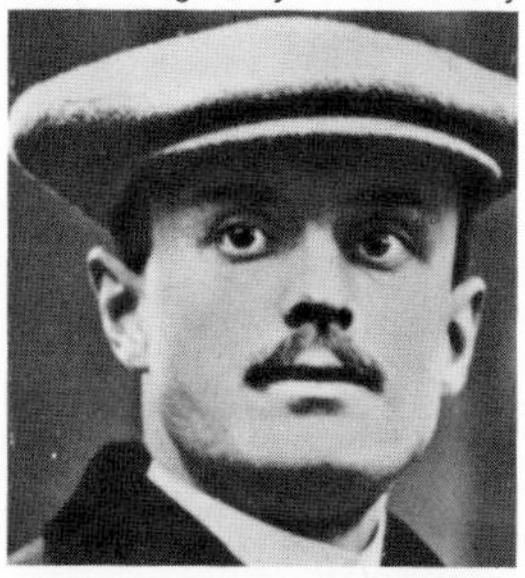

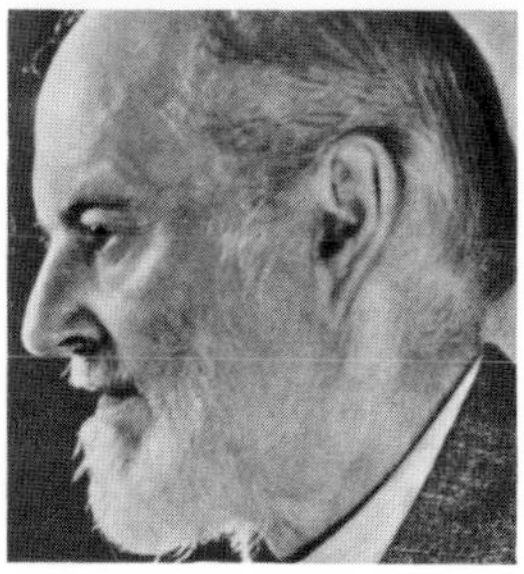

40 when he met Rolls, who was to die in a flying accident only a few years later. Rolls, third son of Baron Llangattock, graduated in engineering at Cambridge in 1898. His $3\frac{1}{2}$hp Peugeot car, obtained two years earlier, had already established him as a pioneer motorist. He took part successfully in many motor trials and represented Great Britain in the Gordon Bennett motor race in 1905. He became a lively agent for the Royce car built by an electrical and mechanical engineering firm founded by Royce in 1884 near Trafford Park, Manchester. In 1904 Rolls and Royce made an agreement for these cars to be known as Rolls-Royce cars. They were first advertised as such in *The Autocar* in December 1904. Rolls-Royce Ltd. was founded in 1906 to build motor cars and aero-engines. Rolls was a keen balloonist and became equally intrigued with aeroplanes. He flew the Channel both ways in 1910, no mean feat for the time. Regrettably, this interest gained him the unenviable distinction of being the first British national to be killed in a flying accident. Royce, who had been an apprentice in the G.N.R. locomotive works, and was also a pioneer in electric street lighting, went on to build up the company whose name was to become a synonym for just simply 'the best'. The Rolls-Royce car has been an international prestige symbol for half a century and shows little sign of losing its enviable position. Car manufacture has for some time been a relatively minor activity of the company, which is now prominent in several fields, particularly aero-engines. **P. O. W.**

'A HISTORY OF ROLLS-ROYCE MOTOR CARS', BY C. W. MORTON (G. T. FOULIS AND CO., 1964); 'THE ROLLS-ROYCE MOTOR CAR', BY A. BIRD AND I. HALLOWS (BATSFORD, 1964).

Franklin Delano Roosevelt (U.S., 1882–1945): statesman. Roosevelt's reputation may now have gone into a decline (like that of his wartime partner Churchill).

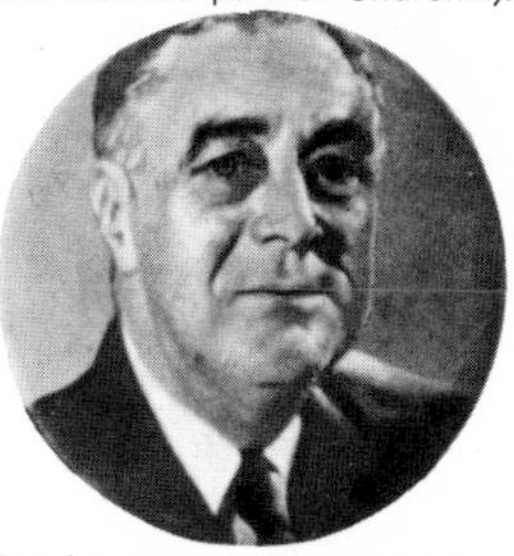

But for anyone alive during the years 1933–1945, when FDR was Democratic President of the U.S., he still looms large. True, millions of American Republicans detested "that man in the White House" and believed he was ruining the country. But even they knew that he was the leader. At first the point was less clear. In his early political career FDR seemed a commonplace, though personable, product of upper-class society. Marriage to the redoubtable Eleanor Roosevelt (his cousin), a crippling attack of polio and the trauma of the Depression all had a galvanising effect. Taking office at a moment of national collapse, he restored to his countrymen (and other Western nations) the priceless gift of hope. Ubiquitous, shrewd, gay in spirit, he won the trust of immense numbers. They returned him to the White House in 1936, again in 1940 (the first President to secure a third term) and yet again in 1944. No less resilient in wartime, though ageing rapidly under its burdens, he directed operations from the initial disaster of Pearl Harbour (which his enemies accused him of arranging) until his death on the eve of victory over Germany. FDR, like any man, had his weaknesses; yet he compares extraordinarily well with the other men of destiny, allies or adversaries, of his era. **M. F. C.**

'THE AGE OF ROOSEVELT', BY ARTHUR SCHLESINGER, JR. (HEINEMANN, 1957–61); 'ROOSEVELT: THE LION AND THE FOX', BY JAMES M. BURNS (HARCOURT, BRACE, N. Y., 1956); 'ROOSEVELT AND MODERN AMERICA', BY JOHN A WOODS (ENGLISH UNIVERSITIES PRESS, 1959); 'FRANKLIN D. ROOSEVELT: A PROFILE', ED. WILLIAM E. LEUCHTENBURG (HILL AND WANG, 1967).

Theodore Roosevelt (U.S., 1858–1919): head of state. An intellectual posing as a cowboy, a conservative posing as a reformer, a neurotic posing as the embodiment of muscular, masculine sanity, Roosevelt was a master politician. He was one of the jingo circle that largely pushed the United States into the

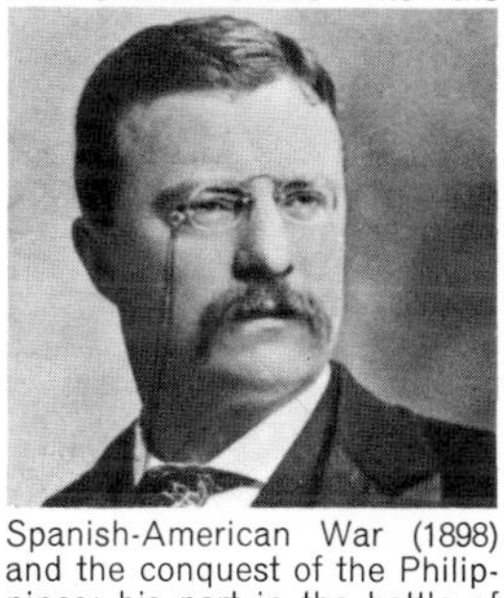

Spanish-American War (1898) and the conquest of the Philippines; his part in the battle of San Juan Hill made him successively a national hero, Vice President, and, on the assassination of William McKinley (1901), President of the United States at the uniquely early age of 42. In foreign affairs he continued to show himself a bully, a jingo, and a fidget, and appreciably worsened relations with Germany, Japan and Latin America;

but his basic caution prevented him from doing much harm. Domestically his mission (in which he was entirely successful) was to satisfy his personal craving for power by rescuing the Presidency from subservience to any other institution whatever, whether Congress, party or big business. He did this by flamboyant courting of public favour, and incessantly playing off reformers against reactionaries, usually to the advantage of the latter. He retired in 1909, and shot big game. He ran again for the Presidency in 1912, on an independent ticket, thus ensuring the election of Woodrow Wilson (q.v.). His last years were spent in an agitation to take America into the Great War, and in bitterness at not being allowed to fight in the struggle. **D. H. V. B.**

'THEODORE ROOSEVELT: AN AUTOBIOGRAPHY' (MACMILLAN, 1913); 'THE REPUBLICAN ROOSEVELT', BY J. M. BLUM (HARVARD U.P., 1954); 'THE TRIUMPH OF CONSERVATISM', BY GABRIEL KOLKO (QUADRANGLE, CHICAGO, 1967).

Hermann Rorschach (Swiss, 1884–1922): psychiatrist. Rorschach has given psychology a humane and meaningful diagnostic technique. He was born in Zürich where his father was an art teacher. He studied medicine both in Switzerland and in Germany. In 1921 he published *Psychodiagnostics,* an account of a diagnostic psychological test based on perception. It is very different from the Binet (q.v.) type of test, where the testee has to find the correct answers to a series of questions. In the Rorschach test the testee is given a series of symmetrical inkblots and is asked about them. Different people give different answers. For example some people concentrate on details whereas others concentrate on the overall shape. Rorschach developed a way of systematically scoring and analysing the replies. It incorporates in part Jung's (q.v.) concepts on neurosis and psychosis. In 1952 the International Rorschach Society was founded in Berne. The Rorschach test is now very widely used in clinical and educational psychology. It has been greatly disparaged by some experimental psychologists who have questioned its objectivity. These criticisms have some validity, but as yet the alternative tests offered greatly underestimate the complexity of human personality. **B. R. O.**

Harold Ross (U.S., 1892–1951): editor. Ross founded *The New Yorker* in 1925 and edited it until his death. He created the *New Yorker* formula, metropolitan, urbane, "a reflection in words and pictures" of New York life, and after a shaky start the magazine became a winner. Perspicacious and perverse, Ross was a vicious goad and a kind persuader. The *New Yorker* style seemed effortlessly casual, yet compelling. Ross had a passion for accuracy and clarity. "Who he?" he would scrawl in the margin of a manuscript when he encountered an unfamiliar name. His contri-

butors were his colleagues on the Algonquin Round Table – the wits Dorothy Parker (q.v.), Robert Benchley, Wolcott Gibbs; later the humour of James Thurber (q.v.), Ogden Nash, Peter Arno and Charles Addams became inseparable from the magazine. But *The New Yorker* could be serious. In 1946 Ross ran in one issue John Hersey's entire 40,000 word reportage of Hiroshima. Fat and sleek, today's magazine still has the Ross look, a reminder in the age of mini-skirts of the silk stockings of yesteryear. **G. P. G. N.**

'THE YEARS WITH ROSS', BY JAMES THURBER (HAMISH HAMILTON, 1959).

Roberto Rossellini (Italian, b. 1906): film director. Wartime expediency forged a film style for Roberto Rossellini, whose *Open City* marked the beginning of the Italian cinema's neo-realist movement. Previously, his pictures ranged from 'white telephone' comedies (so-called

because the phone was a standard prop) to brackish propaganda. But late in 1944, with the Germans still holding Rome, Rossellini recruited a team of actors and technicians – many of them non-professional – to make a film which re-created as accurately as possible the tensions, the terrors, and the resistance of anti-Fascists during the Nazi occupation. It was technically ragged. Rossellini was forced to use whatever scraps of film stock he could find. Shooting was often abandoned when funds ran out. But its raw veracity overcame all technical deficiencies. His principal actress was the then unknown Anna Magnani. Their partnership continued with *The Human Voice* (taken from a Cocteau [q.v.] play) and *The Miracle,* in which Magnani played a feeble-minded peasant made pregnant by a passing stranger whom she believed to be St Joseph. It foundered when Rossellini became involved professionally and personally with Ingrid Bergman. When Bergman and Rossellini made *Stromboli* (the location was a volcanic island), Magnani countered with *Volcano,* a similar story which was shot just across the bay. Neither film made any impact on the critics or the box-office. Rossellini's career has apparently become bogged down in indifferent pictures, marital feuds, and money troubles. Most recently he has become interested in making educational films for television. His new slogan – "Truth can be exciting" – sounds like neo-realism wearing a grey flannel suit. **P. O.**

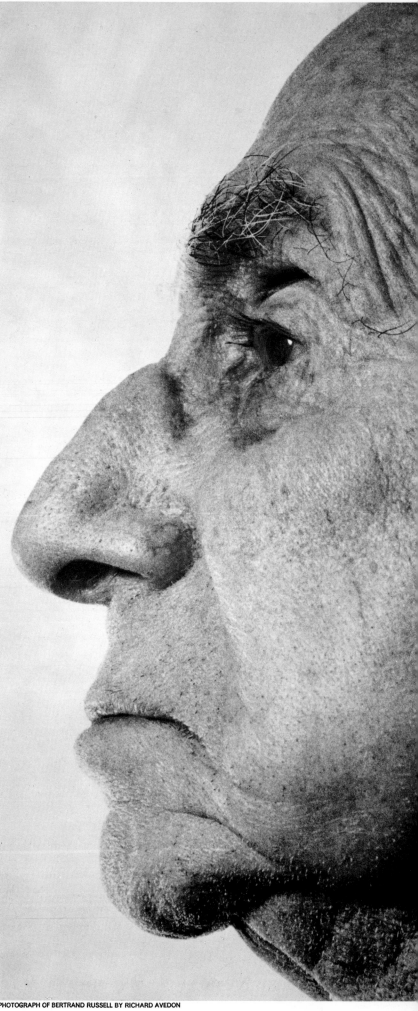

PHOTOGRAPH OF BERTRAND RUSSELL BY RICHARD AVEDON

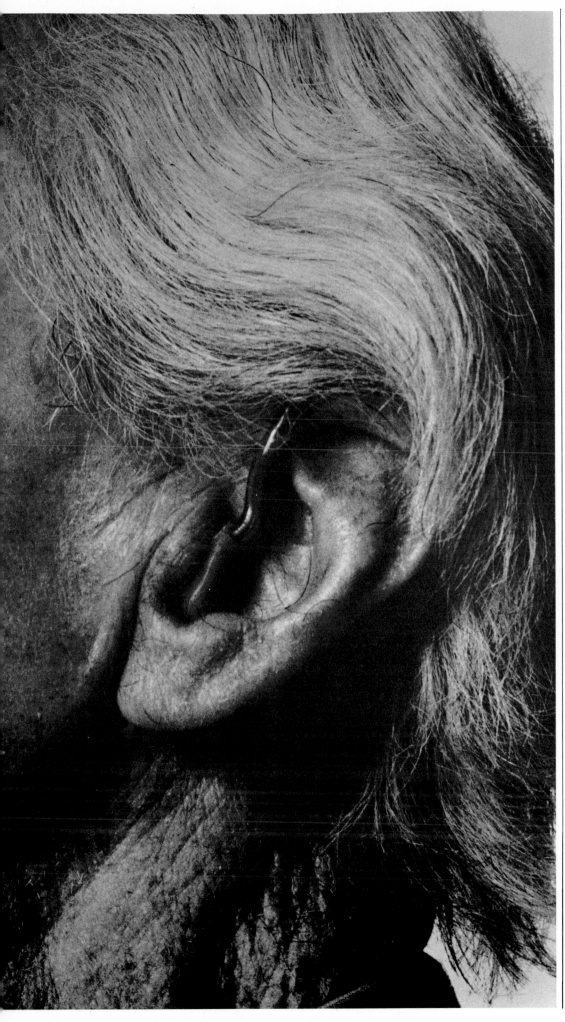

Max Rostal (British, ex-Austrian, b. 1905): violinist. The true heir to Carl Flesch (q.v.), whose teaching methods he has modernised, Rostal may be the greatest violin teacher alive. Even more successfully than Flesch, he has, throughout his career, pursued a double life, with little conflict between the virtuoso and the teacher; as a viola player, too, he is outstanding. Pupil of Arnold Rosé in Vienna and of Flesch in Berlin,

he became the latter's assistant in 1928 and Professor at the Berlin State Academy in 1930. With the advent of Hitler (q.v.), he emigrated to London; in 1944, he was appointed professor at the Guildhall School of Music. Since 1958 he has lived in Berne, where he is professor at the Conservatory, and he constantly commutes between there and Cologne, where he is professor at the State Academy: it is unfortunate that this country has lost his teaching genius. His pupils, like Flesch's, show the stature of the teacher; they include Erich Gruenberg and, of course, three-quarters of the Amadeus Quartet. A more active exponent of contemporary music than Flesch, he has given many a first performance, including that of Benjamin Frankel's Violin Concerto. **H. K.**
'THE MEMOIRS OF CARL FLESCH', ED. AND TRANS. HANS KELLER (ROCKLIFF, 1957).

Samuel Rothapfel (U.S., 1882–1936): showman. 'Roxy' was the father of the super-cinema. In the golden age of the picture palace his nickname was synonymous with entertainment in surroundings of unbelievable luxury. Beginning his career with Nickelodeons, coin operated peepshow machines in converted shops, he lived to open the world's largest cinema, New York's Radio City Music Hall. Roxy pioneered 'atmospheric' auditoriums, with cloud effects and permanent settings reminiscent of the Alhambra at Granada, the Louvre, the Parthenon and St Peter's. The Cathedral of the Motion Picture was the Roxy on 7th Avenue at 50th Street, New York, opened in 1927. The foyers were so spacious that 2500 people could wait for the show to begin, the ushers were drilled like guardsmen and all round in gilded niches were costly statues and paintings. Its auditorium seated 6214 people, plus a 110-piece orchestra, and 42 Roxyettes could span the stage in a single line. Its era was brief; in 1960 it was demolished to make room for an office block. **G. C. P.**
'THE BEST REMAINING SEATS', BY BEN M. HALL (BRAMHALL HOUSE, NEW YORK, 1961).

Mark Rothko (U.S., ex-Russian, 1903–1970): painter. Born of Jewish parents, and threatened therefore by the pogroms of the early 20th century, Rothko was taken to the U.S. when he was 10 and lived there until his death. He began to paint in 1925 and first exhibited in 1929. He went on to explore a vein of Surrealist fancy midway between Miró (q.v.) and Arshile Gorky; by 1950 he was painting very large canvases in which rectangular soft-edged areas of pure colour floated side by side in a space-continuum. These were conceived not as decorations but as objects of contemplation: Rothko's feeling for "the spiritual in art" links him to other great Russian-born artists – above all Kandinsky and Malevich (qq.v.) – who see the work of art not as a superior plaything or a growth-stock with exceptional potential but as a sanctuary for fundamental truth. (He once joined with his colleagues Newman [q.v.] and Gottlieb in saying that "elemental truth" demanded "the simple expression of the complex thought".) The mystical side of Rothko's nature found a natural outlet in the decoration of a chapel at St Thomas University, Houston; but many prize his work above all for its revelation of what can be done with pure, saturated, enveloping colour. **J. R.**

'AMERICAN ART SINCE 1900', BY B. ROSE (THAMES AND HUDSON, 1967); 'ROTHKO', BY P. SELZ (MUSEUM OF MODERN ART, NEW YORK, 1961).

Artur Rubinstein (U.S., ex-Polish, b. 1886): pianist. Artur Rubinstein's position now seems unassailable, but it didn't always. Born in Łódź in 1886 (the official date – Rubinstein himself claims he is three years younger), he was noticed at an early age by Joachim and sent to Berlin. There study under Bartsch (piano) and Max Bruch (composition) launched him on the first flamboyant stage of his career. For the next 20 years, Rubinstein undertook enormous concert tours; the public fell for his Polish temperament, and the critics praised everything but his Chopin. It wasn't enough, though. "When I was young, I was lazy. I had talent, but there were many things in life more important than practising. Good food, good cigars, great wines, women . . .". Rubinstein the great natural, the *bon vivant* who also played the piano – superbly: five years of intensive study in the early Thirties shattered that reputation and founded today's: the instinctive scholar, passionate but controlled, and the king of Chopin players. **C. G. T.**

'THE GREAT PIANISTS', BY HAROLD C. SCHONBERG (GOLLANCZ, 1964).

Helena Rubinstein (U.S., ex-Polish, c. 1872-1965): cosmetics magnate. Born in Cracow, she emigrated to Australia, where she opened her first salon in Melbourne at the turn of the century. She had great success, thanks particularly to one product – Crème Valaze, made from the herbal recipe of a Hungarian cosmetic friend of her family; it had a soothing, whitening effect on sun-dried Australian skins. (It's still in her range, now called Skin Clearing Cream.) A few years later she opened a London salon in Grafton Street, Mayfair, "to attract the carriage trade". From there her empire spread to Paris, New York and all over the world. As she moved on to each new venture, sisters were installed as 'caretakers', in charge of each of her salons. She is said to have given the English business as a present to her sister Ceska, and it turned out to be one of the most successful of all her companies, introducing the use of pure silk in cosmetics. A great innovator, indefatigable worker, self-confessed matriarch and very much the *grande dame*, she pioneered coloured face powder and foundation, and introduced the health farm concept of beauty; later she launched one of the first men's cosmetic ranges. **J. P.**

'MY LIFE FOR BEAUTY', BY HELENA RUBINSTEIN (BODLEY HEAD, 1965).

Stanley Keith Runcorn (British, b. 1922): geophysicist. Professor of Physics at the University of Newcastle upon Tyne since 1956, Runcorn has a substantial finger in many pies, but his chief contribution has been to establish with his co-workers the once highly controversial theory of continental drift on a

much firmer basis. Runcorn, who worked from 1943 to 1946 at the Radar Research and Development Establishment, did research on terrestrial magnetism under Professor P. M. S. Blackett at Manchester University and became director of the research department of geodesy and geophysics at Cambridge in 1950. Here he built up a research team studying the natural fossil magnetism preserved in rocks. Together with researchers elsewhere they showed that the directions of this magnetism could only reasonably be explained if the landmasses containing the rocks had formerly occupied other positions on the globe. Maps of earlier geological periods reconstructed on this basis fitted many of the suppositions of earlier proponents of continental drift. Professor Runcorn, who is still continuing his work, among other important studies, has thus helped to confirm one of the most fundamental hypotheses of the earth sciences. **P. H. S. S.**

'CONTINENTAL DRIFT', ED. P. S. K. RUNCORN (ACADEMIC PRESS, 1962); 'PRINCIPLES OF PHYSICAL GEOLOGY', BY A. HOLMES (NELSON, REVISED ED., 1965).

Bertrand Russell, later 3rd Earl Russell (British, 1872–1970): philosopher. Russell, although best known to the public for his radical social doctrines about marriage, education, religion and, above all, war and peace, remains the most productive, influential and important British philosopher of the century. Trained at Cambridge as a mathematician he was led to philosophy by his desire to justify the unargued assumptions upon which mathematics depends. In the period from 1900 to 1912 he was occupied with his former tutor A. N. Whitehead (q.v.) in writing the three densely argued volumes of *Principia Mathematica* (1910–13). In it they sought to prove that all mathematics can be rigorously deduced from self-evident truths of formal logic, a discipline which they developed far beyond its traditional Aristotelian nucleus. In the succeeding years he turned mainly to theory of knowledge, using the conceptual instruments of the new logic to expound a sceptical kind of empiricism with affinities to Hume's. With his brilliant pupil Wittgenstein (q.v.) he elaborated the doctrine of 'logical atomism', for which the task of philosophy is the analysis of knowledge into its basic and least dubitable elements. During the 1914 war he gave up academic pursuits for pacifist agitation, for which he was imprisoned in 1918. During the inter-war years he ran a progressive school with his second wife and supported himself by scientific popularisation and journalism on social and political issues. He spent the war years in America with his third wife and while there wrote his very successful *History of Western Philosophy* (1945). In the 1950s he became embattled again in vigorous, sometimes extra-legal and occasionally frantic opposition to nuclear weapons and was once again imprisoned. Even in his nineties, although he became less directly involved in public affairs, his peace foundation operated on a broad front in what many felt to be a one-sidedly anti-American way. During his last years he published three fascinating autobiographical volumes. The vast mass of his written work is brilliantly clear and consistently witty and mocking. A spiritual as well as a literal aristocrat, he constantly combined moral passion with magnanimity and selflessness of purpose. **A. Q.**

BOOKS BY BERTRAND RUSSELL: 'THE PROBLEMS OF PHILOSOPHY' (WILLIAMS AND NORGATE, 1912); 'OUR KNOWLEDGE OF THE EXTERNAL WORLD' (OPEN COURT, CHICAGO, 1914); 'PRINCIPLES OF SOCIAL RECONSTRUCTION' (ALLEN AND UNWIN, 1916); 'HISTORY OF WESTERN PHILOSOPHY' (ALLEN AND UNWIN, 1946); 'MY PHILOSOPHICAL DEVELOPMENT' (ALLEN AND UNWIN, 1959); 'AUTOBIOGRAPHY', 3 VOLS. (ALLEN AND UNWIN, 1967-69); 'THE PHILOSOPHY OF BERTRAND RUSSELL', ED. P. A. SCHILPP (C.U.P., 1944).

Babe Ruth (U.S., c. 1895–1948): baseball player. Raised in a Baltimore, Maryland, orphanage, George Herman Ruth was baseball's greatest home run hitter and perhaps the game's most dynamic player. A long-time New York Yankee player, the 'Sultan of Swat' hit 714 homers for an unequalled lifetime record. In each of 11 seasons he hit more than 40, in four of them he hit at least 50 home runs. His 1927 record of 60 lasted 34 years. Even in his farewell game in 1935 he slammed three homers, one of them among the longest ever hit. Potato-nosed and moon-faced, Ruth's 15-stone-plus bulk atop spindly legs gave him a mincing gait. Yet he played with gusto (as he ate and drank) and performed with effortless ease. He struck out as dramatically as he hit home runs and was worth 85,000 dollars annual pay even in Depression years like 1930, so great was his drawing power. Along with Dempsey, Tilden, Bobby Jones and Hagen, he ruled America's Golden Age of Sport, the Twenties, and he was among the first five elected to Baseball's Hall of Fame. Although a much deader baseball was used in his heyday compared to today's lively ball, Ruth reigned supreme. More than anyone else he shaped baseball into a crowd-rousing home run spectacle. **D. B.**

Lord Rutherford (British, ex-New Zealand, 1871–1937): physicist. Ernest Rutherford came to Cambridge University in 1895. An early observation was that

there were two main types of ray given off by radioactive materials – positively charged 'alpha rays' and negatively charged 'beta rays'. In 1900, he discovered that some of the radiation was not affected by a magnetic field, and realised that these rays were ultra high frequency electromagnetic waves – gamma rays. Two years afterwards, Rutherford and Soddy (q.v.) showed that uranium and thorium broke down radioactively into a series of intermediate elements, each of which broke down at a given rate – with half of any quantity disappearing in a fixed time. Rutherford termed this fixed period the 'half-life'. Rutherford's interest in alpha particles later led to one of the most profound discoveries of the 20th century. If the positive alphas were fired at a sheet of gold foil, most passed through unaffected; but a few were deflected sharply as if by a massive positively charged region within the atom. From this experiment came Rutherford's theory of the atom – a tiny nucleus containing all the positively charged protons (which he had discovered the year before) surrounded in planet-like orbits by the light negatively charged electrons. Although he was a man of genius, he could be 'ivory towerish', and he believed quite strongly that the vast energy trapped in the atomic nucleus would never find practical application. **N. V.**

'RUTHERFORD AND THE NATURE OF THE ATOM', BY E. N. DA C. ANDRADE (HEINEMANN, 1965).

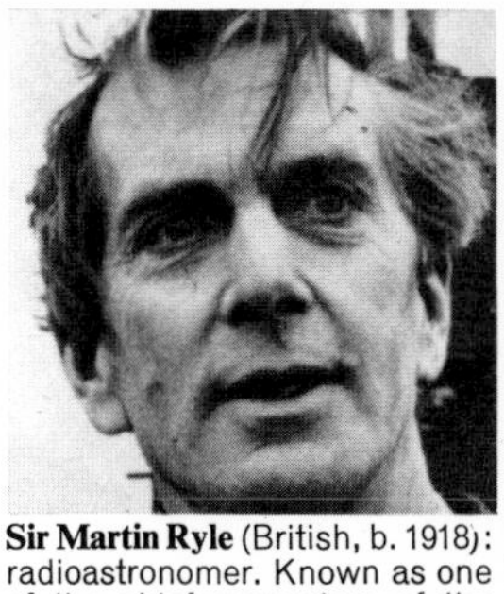

Sir Martin Ryle (British, b. 1918): radioastronomer. Known as one of the chief supporters of the Big Bang theory of the origin of the universe, Ryle has done more towards testing the ideas of cosmologists experimentally than any other astronomer. Educated at Oxford University, he spent the war years, like many contemporary scientists, helping to develop radar at the Telecommunications Research Establishment, Malvern. Afterwards he went to Cambridge where he is now professor of radioastronomy and director of the Mullard Radioastronomy Observatory at Lord's Bridge nearby. Ryle was responsible for building up this laboratory and developing techniques there for accurate mapping of the sky at radio wavelengths. In particular, he has been responsible for cataloguing the known radio sources. Because work on radio sources has extended our picture of the universe to much greater distances than before, it provides a crucial cosmological test. If the universe began as a Big Bang from which the fragments are still receding – as Sir Martin Ryle and most other astronomers now believe – one would expect its appearance at great distances to differ from that nearer to us. The latest Cambridge catalogue of radio sources indicates strongly that such is indeed the case, contrary to the Steady State theory of Hoyle, Bondi (qq.v.) and Gold. **P. H. S. S.**

'RADIOASTRONOMY', BY F. GRAHAM SMITH (PENGUIN, 1966).

S

Eero Saarinen (U.S., ex-Finnish, 1910–1961): architect. Saarinen flouted the hitherto supreme ambition of international modern architecture to achieve consistency. His much-criticised eclecticism was in fact a prophetic response to the 'pluralism' of an affluent society, at a time when Mies van der Rohe and Skidmore's (qq.v.) were forcing American architecture into the elegant straitjacket of the glass box. That style Saarinen thought appropriate only to big business, and he used it accordingly for his first major work, the General Motors Technical Centre (1949–55), and his last, the Deere Company Headquarters (1961–5). In between, he spawned an amazing variety of plastic forms; a three-point concrete dome and a heavy brick cylinder for (respectively) the auditorium and the chapel at Massachusetts Institute of Technology (1953–5); then a

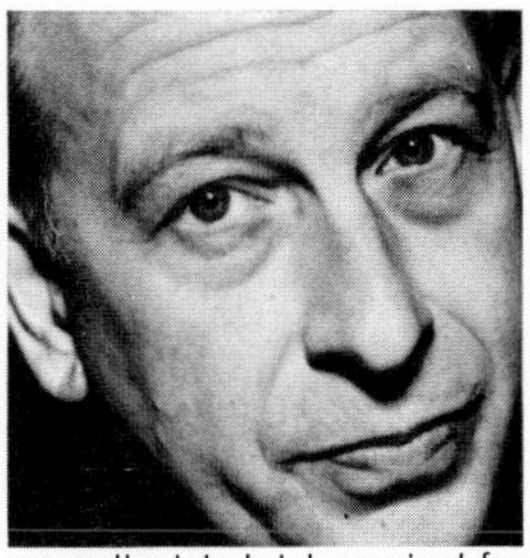

neo-collegiate brick precinct for Morse and Stiles Colleges, Yale (1960–3); Expressionist vaults for the Yale Ice Hockey Rink (1956–8) and the TWA Terminal, New York (1959–62). **N. J. W. T.**

'EERO SAARINEN ON HIS WORK', EDITED BY ALINE B. SAARINEN (YALE U.P., 1962).

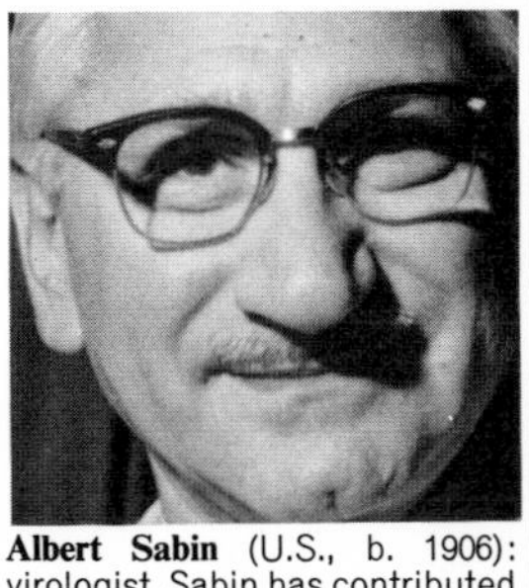

Albert Sabin (U.S., b. 1906): virologist. Sabin has contributed to the knowledge of many viruses and other infectious agents. During the war he contributed to medical knowledge of sand-fly fever and dengue but he is best known because of the 'Sabin poliomyelitis vaccine'. The virtual conquest of poliomyelitis in temperate countries began with the discovery of J. F. Enders (q.v.) and his colleagues on cultivation of the virus, and there soon followed the knowledge that killed vaccines containing three virus types would produce immunity. Jonas Salk produced such a vaccine which achieved great success. There were indications, however, that a living attenuated vaccine would be cheaper, easier to administer, and likely to give longer immunity. Koprowski made the first such vaccine, and was followed by Cox and Sabin. Sabin, by very careful selection of vaccine strains, obtained the safest and most effective vaccine. This can be given to children in sweets and was first used on a huge scale in the USSR, with excellent results. Sabin has thus played a major role in the conquest of a terrible disease. **C. H. A.**

'A HISTORY OF IMMUNIZATION', BY H. J. PARISH (E.& S. LIVINGSTONE, 1965); 'VICTORY WITH VACCINES', BY H. J. PARISH (E. & S. LIVINGSTONE, 1968).

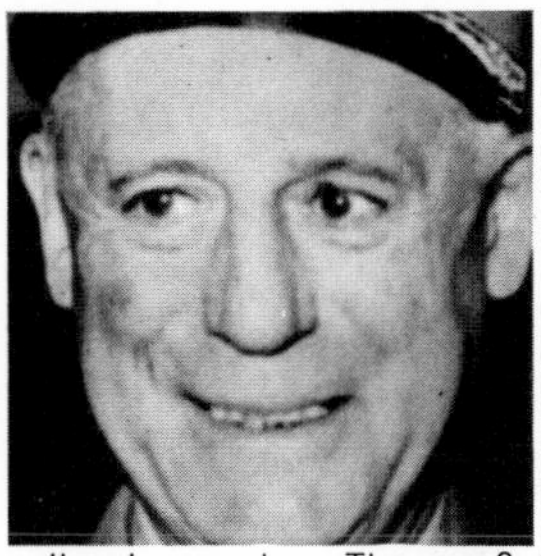

Raoul Salan (French, b. 1899): soldier. General Salan was the last and saddest captain of the French empire. His attachment to the colonies, his global vision and his driving personal ambition led him to betray the Fourth Republic in 1958 and the Fifth in 1961. After liberating Toulon in 1944, he took command of the Far Eastern forces three years later and with his reflective demeanour and wide knowledge of oriental customs earned the nickname of 'the mandarin'. Sent to Algeria in 1956, Salan was thought of as a republican, even a leftist officer, but the Indo-China war and a reading of Mao had persuaded him to apply revolutionary methods in defence of the empire. While taking no direct part in initiating the revolt of May 1958 he took advantage of its apparent success to launch an appeal for the formation of a Government of Public Safety in France under the arbitration of General de Gaulle, whom he believed the only man capable of galvanising national energies. The confidence was not reciprocated. Salan was recalled to France in 1959 and given the honorific post of Military Governor of Paris. Chafing to return to Algeria he denounced the regime for "uncertainty" from there in 1960; and in 1961, together with three other generals, attempted a putsch. When this failed Salan went underground, trying to give a popular veneer to his resistance. Finally arrested and given a life sentence he was released in June 1968, to live out his days forgotten, like the ideals he so obstinately defended. **M. U.**

'NORTH AFRICA'S FRENCH LEGACY', BY DAVID GORDON (HARVARD, 1962); 'THE STRUGGLE FOR ALGERIA', BY JOSEPH KRAFT (DOUBLEDAY, TORONTO, 1961).

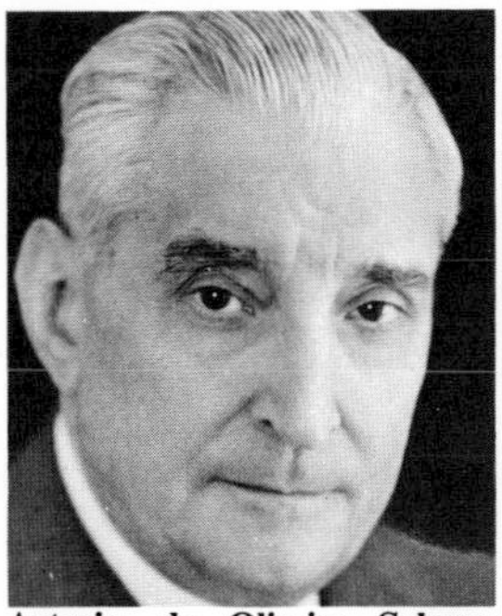

Antonio de Oliveira Salazar Portuguese, 1889–1970): head of state. Dictator of Portugal and in power from 1928 until his death, Salazar's unrivalled record for 20th-century staying power was firmly based on a kid-glove absolutism. He mastered his country by administering economic and political sedatives so strong that she may never recover enough energy to shake off the lethargy of peasant poverty and ignorance. Professor of Economics at Coimbra University, Dr Salazar resigned a parliamentary seat to show his distaste for the corrupt and anarchic Republic. When the leaders of a successful army coup in 1926 offered him the Portfolio of Finance he declined to rescue the tottering escudo unless given complete freedom of action. Two years later he got it and promptly performed the authentically Portuguese miracle of balancing the budget, a feat since repeated annually. He hitched Portugal to an uncompromising defence of empire, a corporate Fascist state which he institutionalised in 1933, and a delicate navigation between the ancient British alliance and the Axis, securing with Franco 'juridical neutrality' during the War. By the late Fifties the 'new State' was showing its age in economic strain. Dissent at home expressed itself in Delgado's presidential campaign in 1958 and the seizure of the Santa Maria in 1961. Wedded to the past and nervous of the future, the gentlest tyranny of the century, the accomplishment of sustained inertia, has probably, like Salazar himself, died. **S. S.**

'A NEW HISTORY OF PORTUGAL', BY H. V. LIVERMORE (C.U.P., 1966); 'DOCTRINE AND ACTION', BY DR. ANTONIO SALAZAR (FABER, 1939); 'THE MEMOIRS OF GENERAL DELGADO' (CASSELL, 1964).

Jerome David Salinger (U.S., b. 1919): writer. Salinger became a significant artist and a popular favourite during the Fifties. The Forties and the Sixties were periods of violence, and they called forth strenuousness and combativeness in their writers. But the Fifties were angel food-cake years, bland and spongy and gaudy. They encouraged an evasive alienation in their artists, and J. D. Salinger was their laureate as Mailer is ours. He is an artist of extraordinary

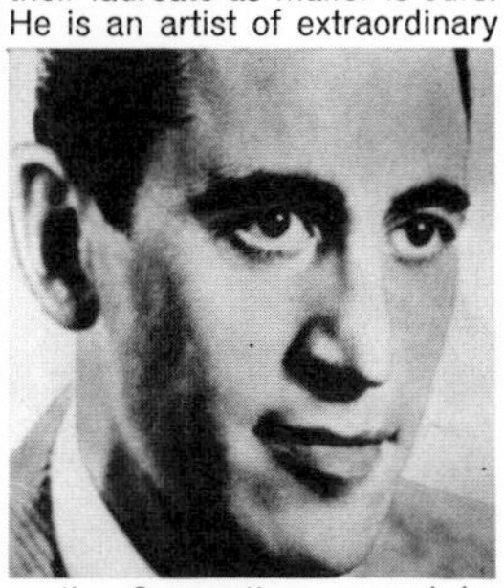

purity. Our writers cannot be compared with him in exactness of word-choice, rightness of sentence-rhythm, evocativeness of detail. But in the later Glass family stories he made himself a prophet too. In that role he never had real authority, though as baroque extravaganzas (compare Jean-Paul Richter's) those stories are full of fascinating things. His great achievement remains *The Catcher in the Rye*, where the limitations of his temperament, his bias towards an artificial and whimsical charm, are counterbalanced by the form. Formally it is one of the most perfect of all novels, and yet packed tight with realistic detail. And it contains one of the most vivid of all fictional characters, Holden Caulfield. Holden's elegant naiveté of the heart is Salinger's finest achievement so far, and the loveliest symbol of a whole decade. **M. G.**

'SALINGER: A CRITICAL AND PERSONAL PORTRAIT', ED. H. A. GRUNWALD (HARPER AND ROW, N.Y., 1962); 'J. D. SALINGER', BY JAMES E. MILLER JR. (UNIVERSITY OF MINNEAPOLIS PRESS, 1965).

Erich Salomon (German, 1886–1944): photographer. First of the great 'candid cameramen', Salomon flourished in the mid-war period of important European conferences. Photographers then had the status of electricians – they were obliged to work with heavy cameras and magnesium flash-powder, and their presence was resented. Salomon was the son of a wealthy German-Jewish banker. Inflation immediately after the First World War dissolved the family fortune and he joined the Ullstein publishing house, working in publicity. He had long wanted to take natural photo-

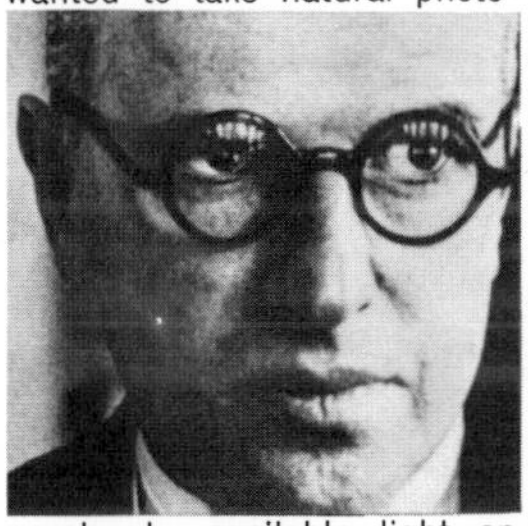

graphs by available light on privileged occasions, and a development of the Ermanox camera made this possible. In 1928, he photographed a murderer in court for *Berliner Illustrierte Zeitung*, hiding his camera in a briefcase, and later he photographed international conferences and banquets, using the utmost ingenuity to get inside, and taking unconventional and revealing pictures. Aristide Briand (q.v.), the French Premier, admiringly dubbed him "le roi des indiscrets". He fled to Holland from the Nazis in the Thirties, but was later betrayed by a Dutch Nazi; he went with his wife to the Auschwitz death-chambers. His lively, irreverent pictures aroused a new interest in photographic journalism. **T. H.**

'ERICH SALOMON: PORTRAIT OF AN AGE', BY PETER HUNTER-SALOMON (COLLIER-MACMILLAN, 1967); 'A CONCISE HISTORY OF PHOTOGRAPHY', BY H. AND A. GERNSHEIM (THAMES AND HUDSON, 1965).

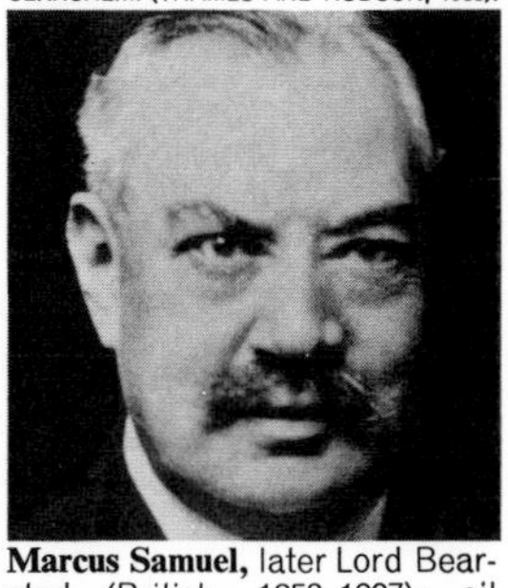

Marcus Samuel, later Lord Bearsted (British, 1853–1927): oil magnate and banker. Practically single-handed, this tenth child of a Jewish East End dealer in ornamental seashells built up Shell (named after his father's business) into one of the world's largest oil companies. Shell was the first commercial company to see and exploit the potential of long-range tankers. Marcus and his brother Sam extended their father's trading business in the Far East and built up a chain of inter-connected trading posts throughout the Orient. This chain enabled them to supply the hungry Far Eastern markets with Rothschild-owned Russian oil and kerosene at prices that even Rockefeller could not match. But Samuel was not a good administrator – a weakness accentuated by social ambitions. In 1907 Shell was merged with Sir Henri Deterding's Royal Dutch. **S. P. A.**

'MARCUS SAMUEL', BY ROBERT HENRIQUES (BARRIE AND ROCKLIFF, 1960).

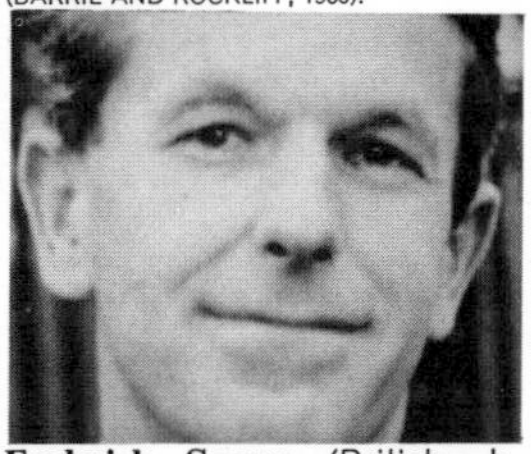

Frederick Sanger (British, b. 1918): chemist. Proteins are complex molecules built up from the same 20 or so amino-acids into thousands of different arrangements: enzymes, viruses, antibodies, toxins, and some hormones such as insulin. Sanger's interest lay in determining the exact order of amino-acids – essential for an understanding of the protein's activity in a life process. He succeeded with insulin, and was the first to establish a protein amino-acid sequence. For this he won the Nobel Prize for Chemistry in 1958. Paper chromatography techniques had been developed by the mid-1940s, but they told only which amino-acids were in the protein, and not their order. Sanger and his colleagues developed techniques to solve the structure of insulin – isolated a quarter of a century before by Banting (q.v.) – and produced their formula in 1955. They went on to show that there were differences in the insulin structures found in different species. Sanger's work paved the way for the molecular and immunological work of, for instance, Kendrew, Perutz and Medawar (qq.v.). **P. G. R.**

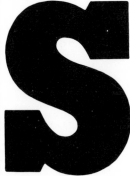

nated intellectual life in Paris, and created a multitude of not always discerning devotees, during the late 1940s and the 1950s. Much influenced by German philosophy, he wrote *L'Etre et le néant* (1943) which presents man as abandoned in a godless universe in which he must exercise his consequent freedom and responsibility in order to create values. The more recent *Critique de la raison dialectique* (1960) attempts to reconcile a subjective, individualistic existentialism with the historical, collectivist emphases of Marxism. With these two works Sartre moves from a predominantly psychological account of human relationships to one which underlines man's struggle against economic scarcity. In keeping with this development he defends terror and violence as the means necessary to create human fraternity. Here, as in several other respects, Sartre and Camus (q.v.) represent significant intellectual polarities in post-war Europe. Sartre played a prominent part in French denunciations of colonialism in Algeria; more recently he has accused the USA of genocide in Vietnam. Such attitudes follow from his belief in the writer's duty to 'commit' himself, and his own plays and novels illuminate many current dilemmas. **J. Cr.**

'SARTRE', BY M. CRANSTON (OLIVER AND BOYD, 1962); 'SARTRE: ROMANTIC RATIONALIST', BY I. MURDOCH (BOWES AND BOWES, CAMBRIDGE, 1953; FONTANA, 1967).

Vidal Sassoon (British, b. 1928): hairdresser. Sassoon grew up in Petticoat Lane, and started hairdressing at 14 in Whitechapel. He worked his way up through suburban salons, ending up in Mayfair where for a time he worked for 'Teazy Weazy' Raymond. Eventually he opened his own salon – two small rooms on a third floor in Bond Street – and although he had many celebrities as clients it was nearly 10 years before

his breakthrough; this came when in 1963 he caught the mood of the new clothes with a revolutionary geometric cut, short at the back and long at the sides, which he created for a Mary Quant (q.v.) press show. He described it as cutting hair like cloth to "shape the head and give a clean, swinging line". This was followed by the Asymmetric, the V-shaped Cut, the Five Point Cut, the One Eyed

Margaret Sanger (U.S., 1883–1966): birth control pioneer. The phrase 'birth control' was coined in 1914 – fairly certainly by Margaret Sanger. Then 30, she was a former nurse who had been fighting for women's rights since girlhood and whose work among the urban poor of New York had convinced her that contraceptive knowledge was one of them. Half a century ago Comstock's law of 1873, which forbade the dissemination of birth control information through the mails, represented the views of the American medical profession, who almost to a man believed, and declared, that attempts to prevent conception were injurious and wicked. Mrs Sanger was the most energetic of the courageous handful of people who disputed this, not only in her writings both for other newspapers and for her own *Woman Rebel* (several numbers of which were suppressed), but in action. She opened the first birth control clinic in America in 1916, in Brooklyn; she and her sister were soon in prison. Undaunted, she issued *Birth Control Review* and continued to lecture, and by the mid-Twenties her persistence had won a hearing in the U.S. for advocates of birth control – and, soon after, the co-operation of the medical profession. By 1932 there were 80 clinics. From 1922 she had extended her mission abroad, pioneering birth control in Japan and China, and helped form the committee which became (in 1952) the International Planned Parenthood Federation. **S. M. R.**

'THE BIRTH CONTROLLERS', BY PETER FRYER (SECKER AND WARBURG, 1965); 'AN AUTOBIOGRAPHY', BY MARGARET SANGER (GOLLANCZ, 1939).

David Sarnoff (U.S., ex-Russian, b. 1891): communications pioneer. 'The General', as Sarnoff is known (he was made a U.S. Army Brigadier-General in 1944 after a long association with Army communications), got into wireless as an office boy in 1906. As a Marconi operator, he was

the first to pick up the Titanic's distress signals, and thereafter stuck to his post for 72 hours. He rose rapidly in Marconi, and in 1915 proposed the making of millions of popular 'radio music boxes'. At the instigation of the Government, the Radio Corporation of America was formed in 1919. Sarnoff became General Manager in 1921, and henceforth dominated RCA, over which he still presides as honorary chairman. He developed the company both commercially and as an inventive force. At once he set about investigating the possibilities of television, and set up the NBC radio network as a service of RCA. He secured Toscanini to conduct the NBC Symphony Orchestra, acquired gramophone record interests, and built the RCA building in the Rockefeller Center. In 1939, he launched the first television service in the U.S. at the World's Fair. It was NBC which developed the all-electronic compatible colour TV system we use today, spurred on by Sarnoff. **G. P. G. N.**

'DAVID SARNOFF: A BIOGRAPHY', BY EUGENE LYONS (HARPER AND ROW, 1966).

Jean-Paul Sartre (French, b. 1905): philosopher. Sartre's atheistic existentialism domi-

Look and the Greek Goddess. Sassoon now has three salons in London and several abroad His achievement has been his no-nonsense approach and his rejection of the chi-chi and mystique that used to surround hairdressing. There are a string of successful ex-Sassoon stylists, thanks mainly to his sensible attitude to personal publicity; he was the first to allow his hairdressers to get credits for their work in magazines and newspapers. This has now become general practice, and has done much to encourage competition and improve standards. **J. P.**

'SORRY I KEPT YOU WAITING MADAM', BY VIDAL SASSOON (CASSELL, 1968).

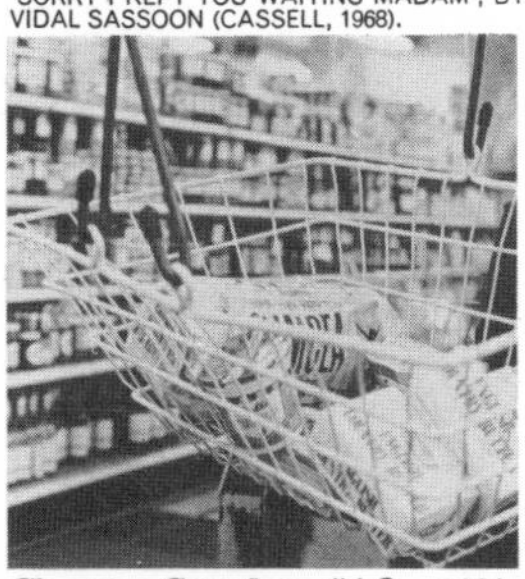

Clarence Saunders (U.S., 1881–1953): retailing pioneer. In 1919 America saw the world's first supermarket. Conceived by Saunders, a poor boy whose first job in a grocery store brought him four dollars a week, the idea of self-service was pioneered in Memphis, Tennessee. He rapidly established a chain, 1200 of which were owned outright by his company, Piggly-Wiggly, Inc. A bitter clash with the New York Stock Exchange forced Saunders into bankruptcy in 1924. Undaunted, in 1928 he created a new supermarket chain, 'Clarence Saunders, Sole Owner of my Name Stores, Inc.' But the depression hit Sole Owner stores and they went bankrupt in 1930. He then organised the Keedoozle store, an electrically operated grocery in which customers selected goods by inserting a key in glass display cases, the purchases then being wrapped and delivered to the cashier's desk by conveyor belt. He was experimenting with Food Electric, which featured automated bill-addition, when he died in 1953. Few have applied such an inventive mind to retailing. **M. T.**

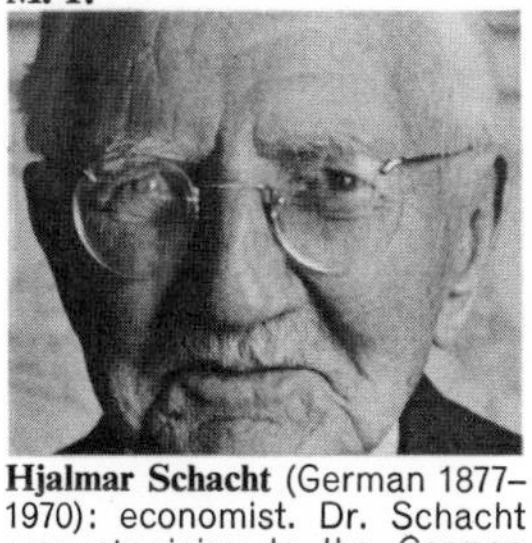

Hjalmar Schacht (German 1877–1970): economist. Dr. Schacht was physician to the German economy in the inter-war period. He was remarkably gifted at reviving his patient from coma. As head of Reichsbank, Schacht attempted, throughout the Twenties, to rescue Germany from the rigours of an incomparably vicious inflation. His methods were audacious – brand new currencies were *created* as need arose – and did provide some respite. But in the Great Crash of 1929–31 the economy was cracked apart and Schacht's work undone. By 1933, Germany contained six million unemployed and acquired Hitler (q.v.) as Chancellor. Under the new regime, Schacht became Minister for Economics and set about solving the unemployment problem with characteristic inventiveness. He exercised control over the economy through a sophisticated planning system which effectively combined State and private enterprise, and he used State loans to create jobs. But his biggest innovation was to discover that economic recovery could be quickly secured by investing in rearmament. Employment, the first priority, was successfully created – but with it came an economy geared to war. Ironically, Schacht's rescue operation laid the economic basis for *Blitzkreig* and pointed out to the rest of the world a short, if perilous, road to economic resurgence. **R. C. T.**

'MY FIRST 76 YEARS', BY H. SCHACHT (WINGATE, 1955); 'SCHACHT: HITLER'S MAGICIAN', BY N. MUEHLEN (ROUTLEDGE, 1938); 'SOCIAL AND ECONOMIC HISTORY OF GERMANY 1888–1938', BY F. W. BRUCK (RUSSELL AND RUSSELL, N.Y., 1962).

Elsa Schiaparelli (Italian, b. 1890): couturier. Schiaparelli rivalled Chanel as the most influential dress designer of the 1930s, with couture houses in Paris and London. She created a new kind of hard, aggressive chic, and made ugliness elegant. Her built-up shoulder line, launched in 1931, dominated the silhouette until Dior's New Look of 1947. Schiaparelli began by designing 'amusing' sweaters, and in 1927 opened a top-floor salon in the Rue de la Paix, originating 'separates' and 'spectator sportswear'. Later her couture house in the Place Vendôme was the first to have a boutique (1935), its décor by Salvador Dali (q.v.). Cocteau (q.v.), Bérard and Vertes designed prints for her and she encouraged fabric manufacturers to produce daring materials. She was the first couture designer to use man-made fibres or zips. She brought a sense of fun to fashion with outrageous hats, coloured wigs,

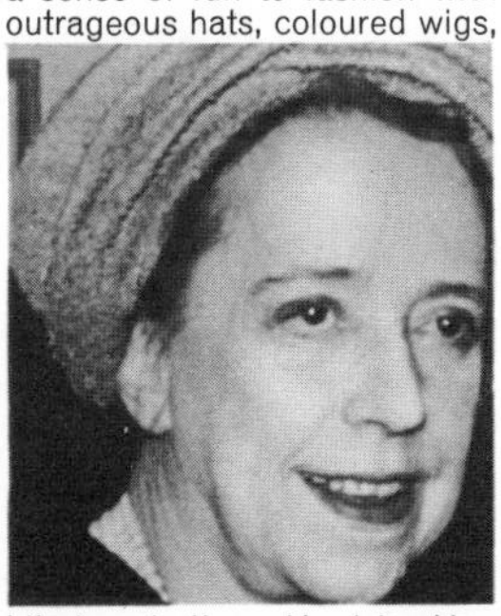

hilarious buttons. Her 'shocking pink' has now passed into the vocabulary of colour. She introduced tweeds for town, trouser suits, evening sweaters. She was in America through the war, and re-opened her Paris couture house in 1945. But the fashion climate was very different from the calculated frivolity of pre-war Paris, and she retired in the early 1950s. **A. A.**

'MY SHOCKING LIFE', BY ELSA SCHIAPARELLI (DENT, 1964); 'IN MY FASHION', BY BETTINA BALLARD (SECKER AND WARBURG, 1960); 'PARIS A LA MODE', BY CELIA BERTIN (GOLLANCZ, 1966).

Kurt von Schleicher (German, 1882–1934): soldier. Von Schleicher made a mockery of the tradition that Prussian Generals were above politics. A master of intrigue, he used his friendship

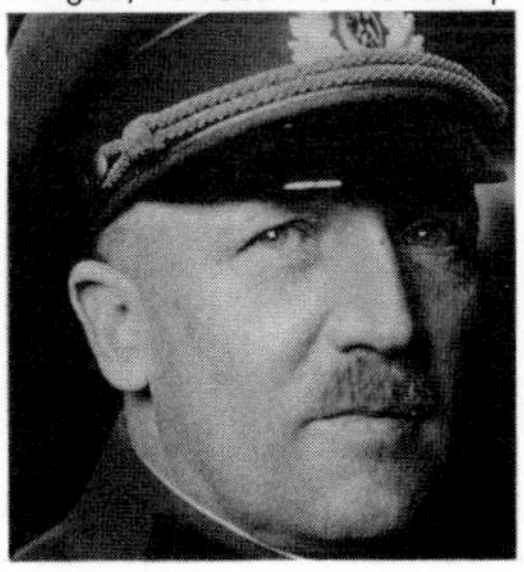

with the son of the aged President of the German Republic, Field Marshal von Hindenburg (q.v.), to gain influence in the President's Palace, and his close association with General Groener, Minister of Defence from 1928 to 1932, to gain political control of the Army. In the deepening crisis of the Weimar Republic from 1929 to 1933, as unemployment mounted and the Nazi vote grew, Schleicher saw authoritarian executive government without parliament as the last hope of the Republic. In June 1932 he became Minister of Defence in the 'Cabinet of Barons', headed by von Papen. Von Papen's incompetence and the worsening of the economic and political crises forced Schleicher's hand. After a complex series of manoeuvres, he succeeded von Papen as Chancellor of the Reich in December 1932. As Chancellor, Schleicher failed to win the Nazi Party's Left Wing or to gain support elsewhere. Hitler (q.v.) and Papen combined forces against him, and by frightening the 84-year-old President with Schleicher's alleged radicalism Papen forced the General's resignation on January 28, 1933. Hitler became Chancellor two days later, and on June 30, 1934, paid Schleicher back – the General was murdered by the S.S. **J. St.**

'THE RISE AND FALL OF THE THIRD REICH', BY W. L. SHIRER (SECKER AND WARBURG, 1960); 'HITLER, A STUDY IN TYRANNY', BY ALAN BULLOCK (ODHAMS, REVISED ED., 1964). 'GERMAN HISTORY, 1933–45', BY H. KRAUSNICK AND H. MAU (WOLFF, 1959).

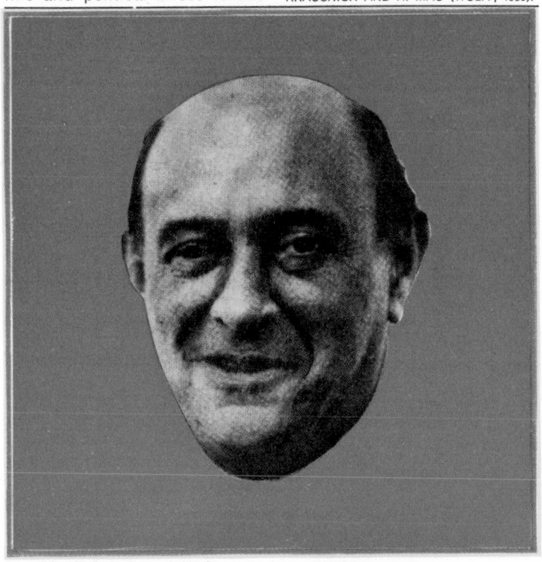

Arnold Schoenberg (U.S., ex-Austrian, 1874–1951): composer. Demonstrably the most decisive single influence in the history of music, the self-taught Schoenberg was long thought an amateur, but eventually recognised as a great composer. In the circumstances, it was not easy to gauge the depth of certain paranoid elements in his character: "You haven't got a persecution complex," *The New Yorker*'s psychoanalyst might have said, "you're just being persecuted." He thought about music like a theorist, but invariably composed in a fever of inspiration, finishing a gigantic score like the 'monodrama' *Erwartung* in 16 days: theories always came after the creative event. His period of 'free atonality' (from 1908 until the early Twenties) marked the musical revolution of the century; his subsequent 'method of composing with twelve tones' became its chief constructive innovation, even though he never taught it: he called it his "private affair". As a teacher, he used the classical and romantic masters as models of mastery. But he was himself a masters' master: Berg and Webern (qq.v.) were among his pupils and life-long disciples. *Moses and Aron* (1930–32), which preceded his re-conversion to Judaism prompted by the advent of the Nazis, has now entered the operatic repertory despite its enormous performing difficulties. Works like the fiddle concerto or the Orchestral Variations are also floating towards the midstream of our musical life. **H. K.**

'STYLE AND IDEA', BY ARNOLD SCHOENBERG, ED. DIKA NEWLIN (PHILOSOPHICAL LIBRARY, N.Y., 1950); 'ARNOLD SCHOENBERG LETTERS', ED. ERWIN STEIN, TRANS. EITHNE WILKINS AND ERNST KAISER (FABER, 1964); 'ARNOLD SCHOENBERG', BY HANS HEINZ STUCKENSCHMIDT, TRANS. EDITH TEMPLE ROBERTS AND HUMPHREY SEARLE (CALDER, 1959); 'SCHOENBERG AND HIS SCHOOL', BY RENÉ LEIBOWITZ (PHILOSOPHICAL LIBRARY, N.Y., 1949).

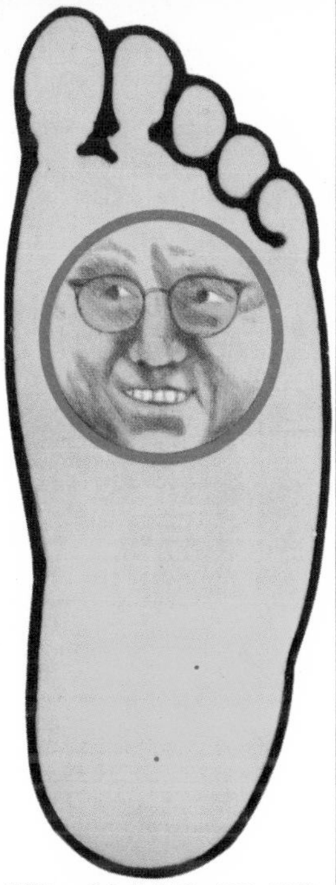

William Scholl (U.S., 1882–1968): doctor. At an early age, Scholl saw his career ahead as the "foot doctor to the world". He became apprenticed to an Indiana shoemaker at 16, and a year later moved to a shoe store in Chicago, and established himself as a salesman and a craftsman. By 22, he had put himself through medical college in Illinois, invented and patented his first arch support, and begun manufacturing. The company he founded in 1904 now holds more than 200 patents in his name. Scholl's brother Frank established a branch in London in 1910, and branches across Europe followed. The company now has branches in 57 countries. Scholl trained his salesmen in "practicpedics", wrote a *Dictionary of the Foot*, and put shoe fitting on a scientific basis. He was largely responsible for the introduction by the shoe trade of a much greater variety of lasts and sizes. From the world-famous 'Foot Eazer' onwards, Scholl's mechanical and medical aids made it possible to keep the feet healthy and comfortable. **A. H. S.**

Gerhard Schrader (German, b. 1903): chemist. Schrader joined I. G. Farben's Elberfeld factory as a research chemist in 1928, and is still with its successor company, Bayer, directing the Crop Protection Laboratory at Wuppertal. His talent for original research was soon evident and he now has 350 patents to his credit, chiefly insecticidal chemicals. In the 1930s, with the biologist Dr H. Kukenthal, he began his search for biologically active chemicals. His first success (1935) was in organofluorine insecticide, but this proved impracticably poisonous. He then detected insecticidal activity in phosphorus compounds used in rubber research: his subsequent research, initially single-handed, led to production of many new potent synthetic insecticides, all members of the prolific organophosphorus family. Some of them work by contact, others systemically, being absorbed into treated plants which they make lethal to attacking pests. Though the earliest ones were unpleasantly toxic, later pro-

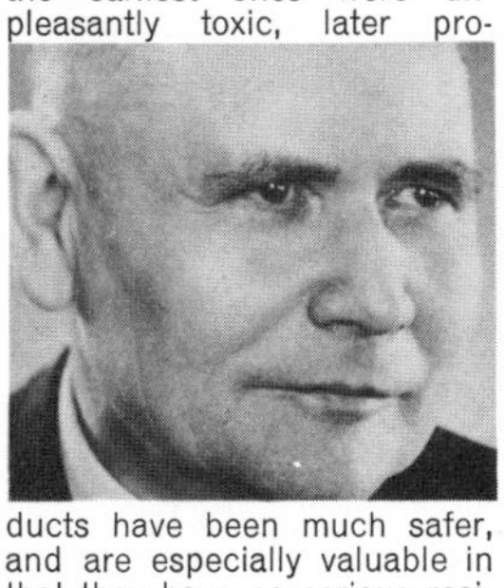

ducts have been much safer, and are especially valuable in that they have no serious residue problems. His first commercial product, Bladen, was available in Germany in 1943, and Schrader's wartime work stimulated worldwide advance in the production and use of organo-phosphorus insecticides, among the most important aids to crop protection so far developed. **S. L.**

'THE SCIENCE AND PRINCIPLES OF CROP PROTECTION', BY H. MARTIN (ARNOLD, 1964); 'INSECT CONTROL BY CHEMICALS', BY A. W. A. BROWN (CHAPMAN AND HALL, 1951).

Erwin Schrödinger (Austrian, 1887–1961): physicist. Absorbing himself in quantum mechanics in the early 1920s after hearing about de Broglie's (q.v.) proposed matter waves, Schrödinger argued that the picture of the atom, as interpreted by the great Danish physicist Niels Bohr (q.v.), could be modified to take matter waves into account. The concept put forward by Schrödinger consisted of an electron in orbit, around which its matter waves extended only in an exact number of wavelengths, so setting up a standing wave front. This, reasoned Schrödinger, would result in an electric charge which was not accelerating and therefore, as long as it stayed in its orbit, the electron need not radiate light. A corollary was that it was impossible to have an orbit

between two permissible ones because less than a whole number of wavelengths would be required to set up the standing wave. This neatly accounted for the existence of discrete orbits of electrons round the nucleus of the atom with nothing in between. Along with Dirac (q.v.) and Max Born, Schrödinger worked out the theoretical details of modern wave mechanics and so Max Planck's 25-year-old quantum theory was finally placed on a sound mathematical basis. **N. V.**

'MY VIEW OF THE WORLD', BY E. SCHRODINGER (C.U.P., 1964); 'ERWIN SCHRODINGER: AN INTRODUCTION TO HIS WRITINGS', BY W. T. SCOTT (U. OF MASSACHUSETTS PRESS, AMHERST, 1967).

Albert Schweitzer (Alsatian, 1875–1965): philosopher and missionary. Schweitzer was an impressive figure, with his mane and magnificent sculptured head. He gained three doctorates (philosophy, theology, medicine); was awarded the Nobel Peace Prize (1952) and Order of Merit. At 38, he renounced glittering academic prospects and went, "a poor negro doctor", to the hot humidity of Lambaréné in Equatorial Africa. Difficult to appraise, impossible to categorise, Schweitzer evoked and will always evoke irreconcilable pronunciamentos from extremist partisans. Enigmatic, eccentric, contradictory, controversial; idolised and denigrated, revered as saint or dismissed as crank. A Christian repudiated by shocked orthodoxy; anti-establishment and anti-atom-bomb protester, strangely conservative and resistant to change; anti-colonialist conscience-stricken by the Western world's awful debt to Africa, yet himself unconsciously perpetuating some pre-wind-of-change attitudes; simple country doctor who somehow inspired devotion from surgeons, nurses and hero-worshippers; first-class musician, Bach-lover and organ-builder who played hymns on a decrepit piano in Lambaréné's communal refectory. His hospital – shrine or cesspool, beacon or anachronism – is a monument to his idealism and shrewd peasant insights into rural Africa's real needs. *Le grand Docteur* revered all life, treating with Christian charity the sick and leprous. Better philosopher than doctor, not a great scientist, perhaps not a great 'conventional' missionary – but a great and good man. **S. G. B.**

'ON THE EDGE OF THE PRIMEVAL FOREST', AND 'MORE FROM THE PRIMEVAL FOREST', BY A. SCHWEITZER (A. AND C. BLACK, 1953 AND 1956); 'ALBERT SCHWEITZER: THE MAN AND HIS MIND', BY G. SEAVER (A. AND C. BLACK, 1969).

Kurt Schwitters (German, 1887–1948): artist. For purity and independence of character, Schwitters had few rivals among the artists of his time. Born in Hanover, he studied for five years in Dresden before returning in 1915 to his native city and setting up as a professional portraitist. The almost total collapse of the German social structure after 1918 prompted him to scavenge among the ruins of civilisation and to re-build art from scratch in collages made out of the debris of bourgeois society: buttons, bits of wire, bus and theatre tickets, postage stamps, cigarette paper, steel rulers, letter-heads, corks, combs. Disdaining politics, he said, "I aim only at art. No-one can serve two masters. I am the enemy of kitsch, even if it calls itself Dada." For this the Berlin Dadaists excommunicated him, not surprisingly. He was also a poet who pioneered the wordless 'phonetic poem' and could perform it to hallucinatory effect. He died in England in poverty and near isolation, sustained by the devotion of a very few English friends. The case of Schwitters was one in which our national genius for non-recognition found its apotheosis. **J. R.**

'KURT SCHWITTERS IN ENGLAND', BY S. THEMERSON (GABERBOCCHUS PRESS, 1958).

Robert Falcon Scott (British, 1868–1912): explorer. "Had we lived," Scott wrote, dying in the ice of Antarctica, "I should have had a tale to tell of the hardihood, endurance and courage of my companions which would have stirred the heart of every Englishman." Born near Devonport he entered the Navy and in 1900 was appointed to the command of the National Antarctic Expedition which left on board the Discovery in August 1901. He returned in 1904, having penetrated deeper into the polar regions, south or north, than any man before him. In June 1910 he boarded the

Terra Nova at the head of a second Antarctic Expedition, this time with the aim to be the first man to reach the South pole. He got to the pole on January 18, 1912, only to find that Amundsen (q.v.) had been there one month before him, leaving his tent and a Norwegian flag behind. On the return journey, only a few miles from their base, Scott and his party perished from starvation and exposure. On the last page of his diary he wrote: "We shall stick it out to the end . . . but we are getting weaker and the end cannot be far . . ." And the last entry: "For God's sake, look after our people." **J. A.**

'SCOTT OF THE ANTARCTIC', BY R. POUND (CASSELL, 1966); 'CAPTAIN SCOTT: THE FULL STORY', BY H. LUDLAM (FOULSHAM, 1965); 'THE EPIC OF CAPTAIN SCOTT', BY M. LINDSAY (HEINEMANN, 1962).

Glenn Seaborg (U.S., b. 1912): physicist. Seaborg's greatest achievement in atomic physics was the discovery of a whole new range of elements and the explanation of how these fit into the known, overall pattern, the Periodic Table. In this he was the leader of a group of scientists using increasingly complex experimental techniques, and for his work on the so-called transuranium elements he received the Nobel Prize in 1951, jointly with E. M. McMillan. During the war he was head of

plutonium research on the Manhattan Project – which led to the atomic bomb – in Chicago, becoming in 1954 Director of Nuclear Chemistry Research at the Lawrence Radiation Laboratories and in 1961 head of the U.S. Atomic Energy Commission. Seaborg has also taken an eminent part in the reformation of American science education and the development of U.S. atomic energy policy. The scientific discoveries exemplified by Seaborg's work have extended our knowledge of the nature of matter and may have significant consequences in the future. **P. J. F.**

'NOBEL LECTURES IN CHEMISTRY, 1942-62' (ELSEVIER, 1964); 'BRIGHTER THAN A THOUSAND SUNS', BY R. JUNGK (PENGUIN, 1966).

Hans von Seeckt (German, 1866–1936): soldier. As Chief of the Army Command from 1920 to 1926, General von Seeckt did more than any other man to preserve the spirit and structure of the old Prussian Army in the aftermath of the defeat in the First World War. Ironically the Allies helped him to do this by enforcing a reduction of Germany's Army to 100,000 professional soldiers. Seeckt and the regimental commanders used the exclusiveness of this tiny force to weed out officers and

men suspected of sympathy with the Weimar Republic. The Army under Seeckt became a bastion of monarchical sentiment in a Republican regime, a state within the state. Seeckt believed that the Army must be above politics, serving the greater good; in practice things looked rather different. The Army was not available to control risings by the Right Wing but only too eager to fire on Republicans, workers, Socialists or Communists. In foreign affairs Seeckt pursued one goal only: the restoration of Germany's military position in Europe. He was prepared to violate the Versailles Treaty and to make deals with Soviet Russia if his ends were served. The victories of 1939 and 1940 belong in part at least to this most Prussian of generals. **J. St.**

'THE REICHSWEHR AND POLITICS, 1918-1933', BY F. L. CARSTEN (O.U.P., 1966); 'THE POLITICS OF THE PRUSSIAN ARMY, 1640-1945', BY G. A. CRAIG (O.U.P., 1965).

Andrés Segovia (Spanish, b. 1893): guitarist. Guitar history does not, of course, start with Segovia. In western Europe the guitar was fashionable as a non-folk instrument as early as the 16th century; Weber wrote for it, Berlioz and Paganini played it, and many outstanding virtuosi, including Sor and Giuliani, devoted their lives to it. The greatest of them was probably Francisco Tárrega (1852–1909). But Tárrega rarely travelled outside Spain; Segovia's achievement has been to internationalise the Spanish guitar, both by playing it all over the world and also by inspiring and adapting non-Spanish music for it. The repertoire has extended in all directions: Bellini, Brahms and Mendelssohn, as well as the more expected Albéniz and Scarlatti; and, controversial though Segovia's Bach transcriptions may be in actual technique, at least they have shown that the guitar is a serious medium for great music. Segovia's world is a classic one, and no Britten or Stravinsky (qq.v.) has yet written for him, though his superb artistry has been acknowledged by composers as good as Roussel and Villa-Lobos. Like Landowska on the harpsichord, Segovia has created informed acceptance of his instrument; without him, we should probably have had no Williams or Bream. **C. G. T.**

ARTICLES: 'GUITAR' AND 'SEGOVIA' IN GROVE'S DICTIONARY, FIFTH EDITION, 1954.

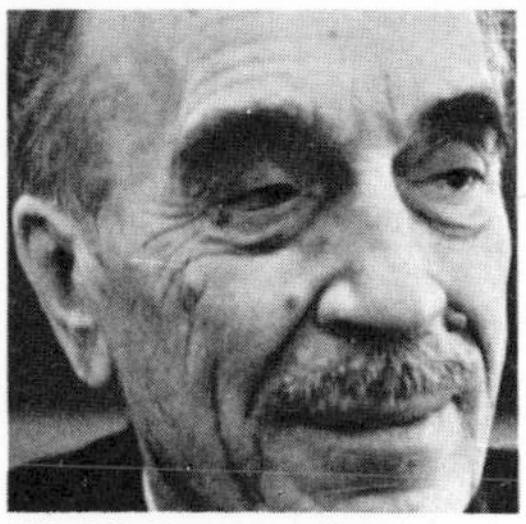

Nikolai Semenov (Russian, b. 1896): chemist. The burning of a flame seems a simple process. Yet reactions of this kind have provided new insights into the behaviour of chemical substances and in particular into the transformations called chain reactions. In these, what happens to a particular compound is consequent on the reactions along a chain of chemical transformations. Such studies have far more than purely theoretical interest: a number of important plastics, for example, are produced through careful arrangement of such reactions. But there are also numerous other scientific developments where the concept of chain reactions has allowed the emergence of new fields of knowledge and technology – aspects of the manufacture of petrochemicals are important examples. Semenov, Nobel laureate in 1956 jointly with Sir Cyril Hinshelwood (q.v.), has been one of the most fertile workers in this field. The discovery and subsequent development of chain reactions have proved to be of lasting importance in both chemical knowledge and industrial technology. **P. J. F.**

'NOBEL LECTURES IN CHEMISTRY 1942–62' (ELSEVIER, 1964).

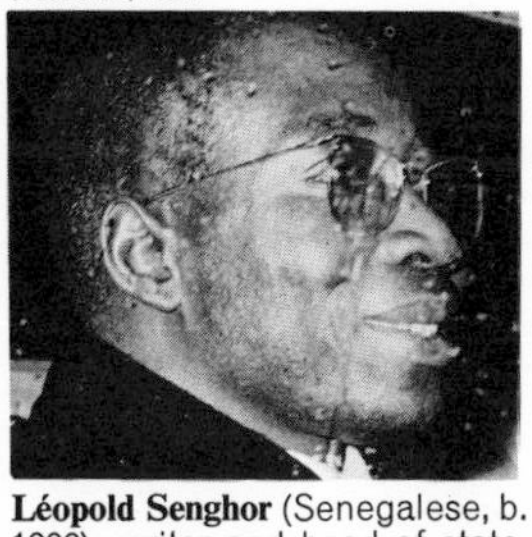

Léopold Senghor (Senegalese, b. 1906): writer and head of state. As President of Senegal, Senghor rules over three-and-a-half million people. But his historical importance rests on other grounds. He is the first African to be recognised as a French man of letters. A poet, philosopher and political thinker, he has used his gifts to glorify things African, but always within the context of a wide Christian humanism. Though the inventor and apostle of *négritude,* he has always stressed that African genius and the European are complementary. *Négritude* is the contribution of the black man to humanity as a whole. Senghor's thought has a quality very different from the strident pragmatism of nearly all English-speaking African writers and political leaders. In his lofty and utterly genuine universalism he likewise towers above the lesser men among his own disciples who have turned *négritude* into a noisy doctrine of racialist self-assertion. Senghor is the foremost intellectual of Africa. This has not prevented him from organising the first effective mass party in French-speaking Africa, a party under which Senegal has enjoyed a relatively stable independence since 1958. **R. O.**

'ON AFRICAN SOCIALISM', BY L. S. SENGHOR (PALL MALL, 1964); 'THE ORIGINS OF MODERN AFRICAN THOUGHT', BY ROBERT W. JULY (FABER, 1968); 'POLITICAL PARTIES IN FRENCH-SPEAKING WEST AFRICA', BY RUTH S. MORGENTHAU (O.U.P., 1964).

Sir Ernest Shackleton (British, 1874–1922): explorer. Sub-lieut. Shackleton joined Scott's (q.v.) National Antarctic Expedition in the Discovery in 1901. They returned on foot, Shackleton stricken with scurvy but with an unquenchable zest for adventure, Antarctic research, and public acclaim. For four years he planned a daring expedition to explore the Barrier and to reach the south pole, and sailed in the Nimrod in 1907. In 1909 he

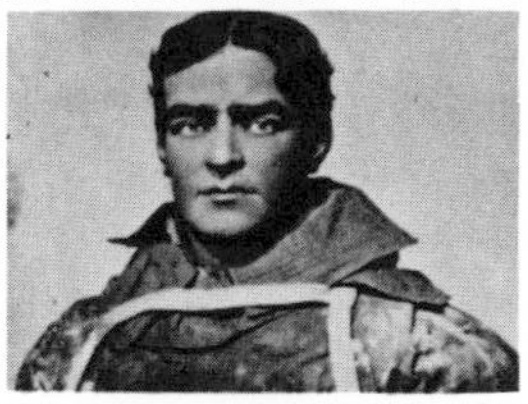

returned, a national hero. He had reached 88° 23′ S., and had sent parties to the south magnetic pole and the top of Mount Erebus. He was knighted, Parliament gave him £20,000, and he met the rest of the cost with an extensive lecture tour, being lionised everywhere. While dabbling in business, he planned to cross the Antarctic with the Endurance and the Aurora. In 1915 the Endurance was crushed in ice 200 miles from land, after drifting for nine months. Shackleton reached Elephant Island after six months, and then led five of his team 800 miles in a 22-ft. boat, crossed South Georgia and reached a Norwegian whaling station. After several attempts he returned to rescue his party, and the Aurora party in the Ross Sea. Shackleton died at South Georgia on an expedition to explore Enderby Island. As well as his discoveries and their important scientific results, he had established many new techniques, and set a bold and unconventional style for explorers. **A. H. S.**

'SHACKLETON'S VALIANT VOYAGE', BY A. LANSING (UNIVERSITY OF LONDON, 1964); 'SIR ERNEST SHACKLETON', BY B. W. SMITH (BLACKIE, 1960).

George Bernard Shaw (Irish 1856–1950): dramatist, critic, propagandist. Shaw was born in Dublin and his early background was slapdash bohemian; later he reacted sharply against this by being austere and methodical, a teetotaller and vegetarian. At 20 he went to London and wrote several unsuccessful novels. In 1884 he joined the Fabian Society and became the chief public advocate of its cool gradualist Socialism. Taking every opportunity to speak anywhere, he turned himself into an expert, attractive performer. After some years of music criticism, he was brilliantly successful as drama critic of the *Saturday Review.* In 1898 he married Charlotte Payne-Townshend, and as she had a comfortable income he retired from journalism to concentrate on playwriting. He had already written several plays, none of them properly produced, though at least two, *Arms and the Man* and *You Never Can Tell,* are among his best. He was indeed a born dramatist, creating a new comedy of debate, almost always theatrically adroit. During the Vedrenne-Barker seasons, 1905–1907, no fewer than 11 of his plays were successfully presented, establishing him as a dramatist. From then onwards his reputation grew and spread until he was seen to be a leading figure of world theatre. He refused all national honours but accepted the 1925 Nobel Prize for Literature. As a challenger of accepted ideas, a witty iconoclast, Shaw was more at home in late Victorian and Edwardian times than after the First War, growing old in a world he did not always quite understand. He was a very effective but not a profoundly original thinker, borrowing ideas from Lamarck, Marx, Samuel Butler and Ibsen, and the Socialism he advocated, especially later, tended to be too authoritarian and illiberal. The best of his plays will easily outlast his polemical writing. In private, Shaw was quite different from the gadfly *persona* he delighted to display in public, being sensible, kind and generous, a friendly great man. **J. B. P.**

'SIXTEEN SELF-SKETCHES', BY G. B. SHAW (CONSTABLE, 1949); 'BERNARD SHAW', BY H. PEARSON (FOUR SQUARE, 1964).

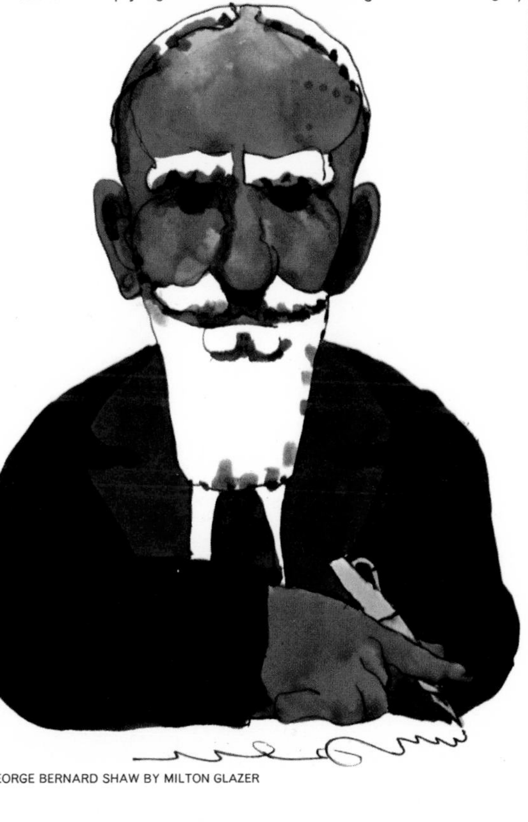

GEORGE BERNARD SHAW BY MILTON GLAZER

John Shea (U.S., b. 1924): otologist. There is often an element of chance about great medical discoveries – or rediscoveries. There must also be knowledge and foresight,

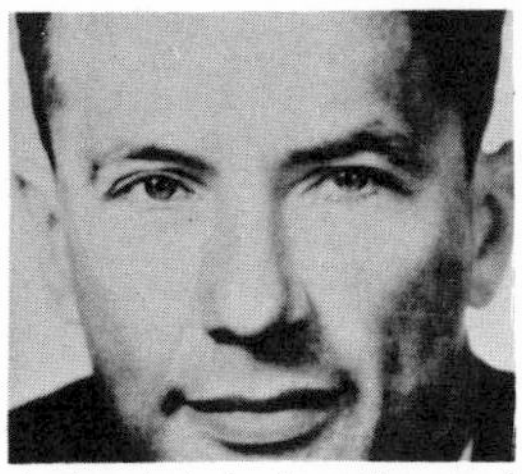

single-minded tenacity and nowadays time and finance to develop a project. These criteria apply to John Shea of Memphis, Tennessee, one of the pioneers of the surgery of deafness. Otosclerosis, a common hereditary disorder, causes progressive hearing loss due to fixation of the stapes, one of the three bones in the middle ear. Before the beginning of this century attempts had been made to mobilise and even remove this bone but they were abandoned and soon forgotten – no antibiotics, no operating microscopes and no prosthetics in those days. For half a century the best otological opinion advised against surgery. This prejudice was partly overcome by the moderately successful fenestration operation designed to by-pass the obstruction to sound waves entering the inner ear. In 1952 Dr Sam Rosen of New York, during a fenestration operation, palpated and accidentally freed the stapes, and restored hearing. The effect was short-lived. In 1956 John Shea, with courage and imagination, removed the diseased bone and replaced it by a polythene prosthesis. The results were spectacular, the inertia was overcome and the modern surgery of deafness was born. This stimulus led to advances in the past decade which have revolutionised surgical otology and brought relief and hearing to thousands. **A. W. M.**

Sir Charles Sherrington (British, 1857–1952): neurophysiologist. Sherrington's contributions to the study of the nervous system – like those of the Spanish anatomist Ramon y Cajal – were so extensive and so fundamental that they form the basis of present-day neurology. His

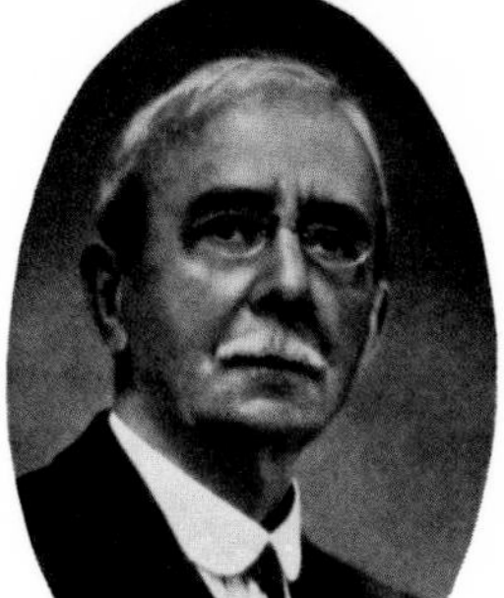

early work on the destination and origin of motor and sensory nerve roots led him to the discovery that muscles contain large numbers of sensory nerve fibres. From this arose his interest in the system that maintains posture and controls fine movement, a system that he termed *proprioceptive* because of its dependence on information from within the animal's own body. This work had far-reaching clinical applications, but it was perhaps even more important theoretically, for it involved precise investigation of the reflex arcs, an understanding of the reciprocal innervation of antagonistic muscles and the realisation that integration and co-ordination occurred in the central nervous system at the junctions between neurons that Sherrington had himself named *synapses.* (It was a study of these that recently earned Eccles [q.v.] a share in a Nobel Prize.) Sherrington's famous *The Integrative Action of the Nervous System,* published over 60 years ago, reads remarkably freshly today and emphasises how much current physiological thinking rests upon his concepts. **J. B. M.**

'THE INTEGRATIVE ACTION OF THE NERVOUS SYSTEM', BY C. S. SHERRINGTON (YALE U.P., 1906, O.U.P., 1961).

William Shockley (U.S., ex-British, b. 1910): physicist. Dr Shockley's name and those of his colleagues at the Bell Telephone

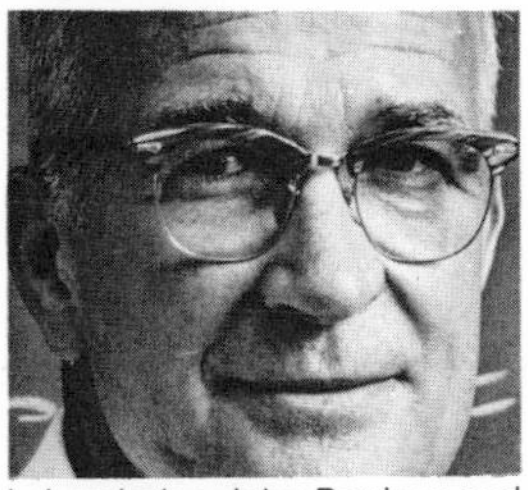

Laboratories, John Bardeen and Walter H. Brattain (qq.v.), will go down in history for the invention of the transistor. This is a tiny crystal arrangement which has replaced the thermionic valve in radio receivers and all electronic devices from small instruments to radar gear and computers. Bardeen and Brattain were the actual inventors of the transistor as such, which, as described in the *U.S. Physical Review* in June 1948, had point contacts – more robust versions of the old cat's whisker. A year later Shockley, who led the three-man team, published a theoretical account of how to produce the same amplifying effect by means of a junction between two dissimilarly-treated parts of one crystal of germanium (later replaced largely by silicon). This junction transistor, more reproducible, reliable and rugged than the point-contact transistor, led to all modern methods of manufacture of solid state devices, including integrated circuits, and founded a revolutionary multi-million-dollar industry. Besides inventing the junction transistor, Dr Shockley has made original contributions to several branches of physics, including ferromagnetism, the properties of metals and the theory of solids. **C. L. B.**

'THE FIRST FIVE YEARS OF THE TRANSISTOR', BY MERVIN KELLY (BELL TELEPHONE MAGAZINE, MURRAY HILL, NEW JERSEY, SUMMER 1953).

Willie Shoemaker (U.S., b. 1931): jockey. Great jockeys are made, not born, but it helps to be born small. William Lee 'Wee Willie' Shoemaker was a premature baby and weighed two-and-a-half pounds at birth. He is now 4 ft. 11 ins. and weighs about

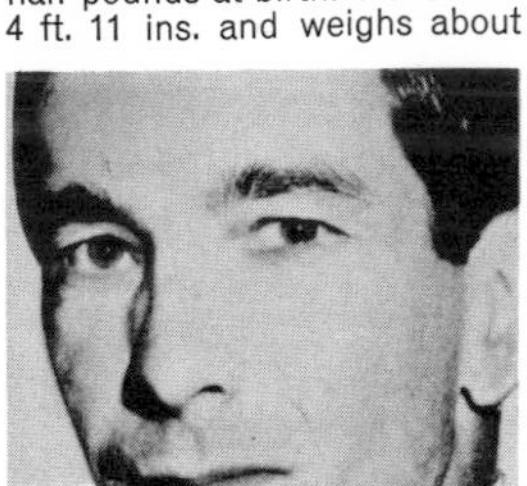

seven stone. In his 18 years of riding, he has won more than 40 million dollars in purses – a world record – and had 5812 winners up to April 30, 1969, the day a horse fell on him and injured his pelvis and bladder. On January 23, 1968, a horse fell on him and broke his femur, putting him out of action for more than a year. He came back to the races the following February, rode three horses on his first day and won on all of them. And only three months after the second accident he was back in the saddle again, to overhaul, by September 1970, Johnny Longden's all-time world record of 6032 winners. Shoemaker has been American national champion jockey (with most winners) five times; in most money won he has been champion 10 times. He is known among horsemen for his sensitive hands, cool judge of pace, and amiability – even his fellow jockeys and losing punters like him. He is quiet, co-operative with trainers, Press and public, and though a millionaire, never shows it. He admires English and French racing, deplores the American custom of over-racing young horses, and favours Sunday racing and off-track betting, both banned in the U.S. His remaining ambition, before finally retiring, is to ride a season in France. **M. R. W.**

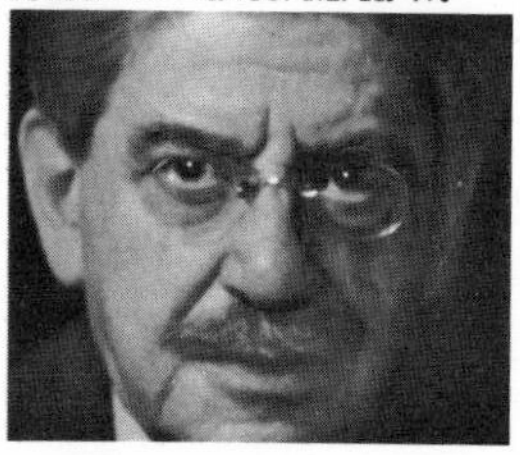

Sir Isaac Shoenberg (British, ex-Russian, 1880–1963): radio engineer. Three weeks before the outbreak of the First World War Shoenberg came to England to study mathematics, but the war cut off his grant from the Tsar and he joined the Patents Department of the Marconi Company. In eight years he was Joint General Manager. He later became a director of research at EMI (formed by a merger of HMV and Columbia) and decided to challenge the Baird TV system which was already transmitting a flickering 30-line picture. He recruited a powerful team of scientists and engineers, including Alan Blumlein, who developed stereophonic recording before the Second World War. The team's work was based on the ideas put forward by an English scientist, A. A. Campbell-Swinton. In 1908, in an incredibly farsighted letter to *Nature*, he had outlined the blueprint for today's electronic TV system. In six years Shoenberg's team, inspired by his leadership, developed an all-electronic 405-line TV system which was standard for BBC1 and ITV programmes until 1969. Today, 625 and higher line standards make 405 seem a modest figure, but at the time it was an enormous advance, and called for a decision of immense courage. **P. O. W.**

'TELEVISION'S STORY AND CHALLENGE', BY DEREK HORTON (HARRAP, 1951); 'ADVENTURE IN VISION', BY JOHN SWIFT (JOHN LEHMANN, 1950); 'HOW TELEVISION WORKS', BY W. A. HOLM (PHILIPS TECHNICAL LIBRARY, 1958).

Dmitri Shostakovich (Russian, b. 1906): composer and pianist. Conservatism, at the level of genius, is as difficult as innovation – more so at times, especially ours. Shostakovich and Britten (q.v.) are, perhaps, the only two mid-century geniuses who are able to address themselves to their audiences without addressing themselves to the problem of contemporary music: no wonder they are close friends. For Schoenberg (q.v.), key was

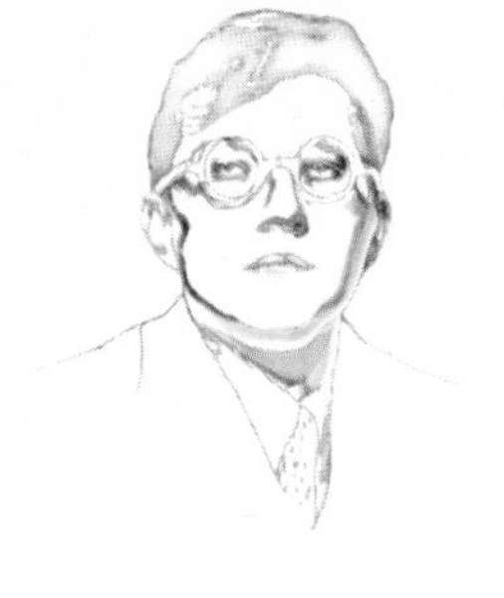

dead by 1909, or dead-and-alive anyway; for Shostakovich and Britten, it is violently alive 60 years after the atonal event – which is the time-span separating, say, *Lohengrin* from *Don Giovanni*. Another common character trait is their anti-specialism: their output covers all fields. But while Britten has written 15 operas, Shostakovich has written 14 symphonies (including one he has just finished for Britten), not to speak of his 11 string quartets: he is no doubt the profoundest of the few symphonic thinkers alive. In intermittent conflict with Soviet authority, he nevertheless received the Stalin Prize for his piano quintet and has established himself as the grand old man of Russian music; how far his undeniable loyalty to the world-view in which he has grown up has helped and/or hindered his creativity is difficult to judge from this side of the curtain. **H. K.**

'DMITRI SHOSTAKOVICH', BY ROBERT LAYTON, IN 'THE SYMPHONY', ED. ROBERT SIMPSON, VOL. II (PENGUIN, 1967); 'SHOSTAKOVICH'S EIGHTH SYMPHONY', BY JULIAN HERBAGE (MUSICAL TIMES, JULY 1944).

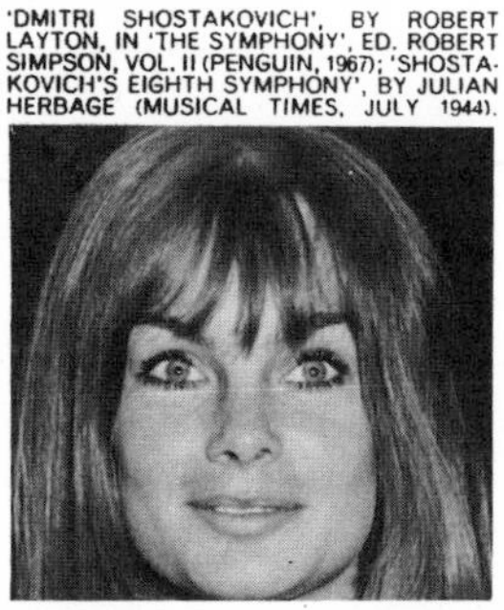

Jean Shrimpton (British, b. 1942): fashion model. Shrimpton changed the face of England in the Sixties. She invented a new look, a new beauty, and changed the whole fashion of modelling. She first appeared as a fashion model, in *Vogue*, in 1961 when she was 18, photographed by a young East Ender – David Bailey. Almost overnight, older models became obsolete. Before Shrimpton models were cool, remote and elegant, women with classically beautiful features who were proud to look artificial and were paid to look sophisticated (perhaps the most famous was the dazzling Suzy Parker). Jean Shrimpton's beauty was fresh, friendly, free and, it appeared, easy. "I was as I was," she said, "and Bailey photographed me like that – a young girl slightly petulant, slightly innocent, very wide-eyed." Her looks cut across the classes and appealed to every level. "I had an acceptable type of beauty, not too remote, not too grand. I was *like people*." 'People' longed to be like her and female faces all over the world suddenly became framed in long casual hair, make-up became softer and simpler, faces looked younger (in fact, the logical result of her influence was Twiggy). But only Shrimpton looks like Shrimpton. "When I see someone who has copied her *idea* of me, I am amused. I couldn't copy anyone. That's the whole point." **P. D.**

'MY OWN STORY: THE TRUTH ABOUT MODELLING', BY JEAN SHRIMPTON (ALLEN AND UNWIN, 1964).

Jean Sibelius (Finnish, 1865–1957): composer. Probably the most original and powerful musical talent yet in Scandinavia, and the acknowledged giant of Finnish music, Sibelius travelled widely in his youth, studying in Berlin and Vienna as well as in Helsinki. He absorbed himself early in the *Kalevala* (the epic of Finnish mythology) and this, coupled with an inbred nature-mysticism, led to the cycle of symphonic poems (from *En Saga*, 1892, to *Tapiola*, 1925) on which,

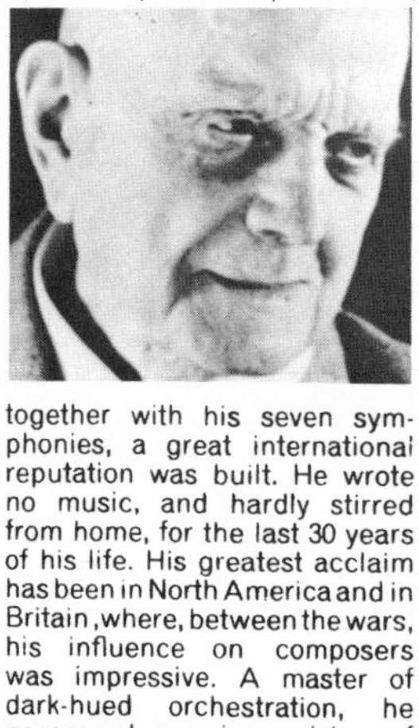

together with his seven symphonies, a great international reputation was built. He wrote no music, and hardly stirred from home, for the last 30 years of his life. His greatest acclaim has been in North America and in Britain, where, between the wars, his influence on composers was impressive. A master of dark-hued orchestration, he possessed a unique vision of musical form by which initially vague ideas gradually grew into distinct shapes of an austere emotional intensity. The over-zealous enthusiasm, claiming Sibelius as the one true symphonic successor to Beethoven and Brahms, has been tempered since his death by an equally exaggerated belittling of his stature. **S. C. V. D.**

'SIBELIUS', BY R. LAYTON (DENT, 1965).

Wladyslaw Sikorski (Polish, 1881–1943): politician. Active in the Polish independence movement from 1908, Sikorski saw Poland achieve independence in 1918 and from 1922 to 1923 was Premier of the democratic Government, destroyed after Pilsudski's (q.v.) coup d'etat in 1926. Banned

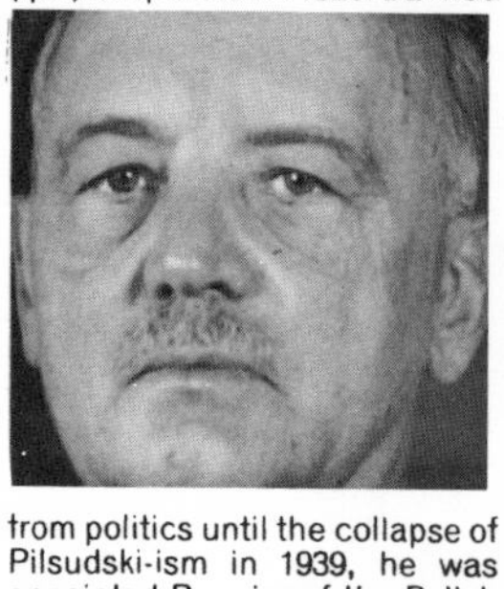

from politics until the collapse of Pilsudski-ism in 1939, he was appointed Premier of the Polish Government-in-exile in France immediately after the fall of Poland, and moved to London after the fall of France. He tried desperately to moderate his colleagues' hostility towards the Soviet Union: after the Nazi attack on Russia he negotiated an agreement with Soviet Ambassador Maisky whereby Polish prisoners in Russia were released and a Polish Army formed in Russia under General Anders. He was severely criticised for this by anti-Soviet extremists and was unable to prevent a Polish-Soviet breach after the discovery of the Katyn Woods murders in April 1943. Sikorski was killed on July 4, 1943, in an aeroplane crash at Gibraltar (later the subject of Rolf Hochhuth's controversial play *The Soldiers*). While he lived Sikorski was the one chance for preserving reasonable Polish-Soviet relations, which deteriorated after his death. **N. B.**

'A HISTORY OF MODERN POLAND', BY HANS ROOS (EYRE AND SPOTTISWOODE, 1966).

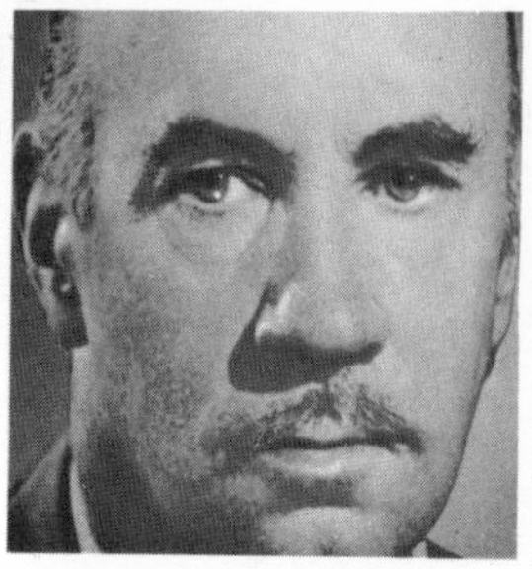

Igor Sikorsky (U.S., ex-Russian, b. 1889): aeronautical engineer. Sikorsky has had three careers, any one of which would have been enough to ensure his fame. Although best known as the builder of the first successful helicopter, he also built a highly successful series of flying-boats, and designed the first four-engined aeroplane, which also boasted an enclosed cabin and upholstered chairs – luxuries for 1913. Sikorsky was his own test pilot, using his practical experience in the air to modify and improve his designs. After the 1917 Revolution he left Russia, and designed a bomber for the Allies which was still unbuilt by the time of the Armistice. He went to the United States, and taught and lectured until 1923, when he formed the Sikorsky Aero Engineering Corporation. Later this company became part of United Aircraft, and produced a series of flying-boats designed by Sikorsky. But his most enduring fame dates from the day in 1939 when he made the first successful helicopter flight. The first of many production models, the Sikorsky R4, followed in 1943, and vertical take-off and landing was born. **N. J. M. H.**

'THE STORY OF THE WINGED S', BY IGOR SIKORSKY (ROBERT HALE, 1940).

Georges Simenon (Belgian, b. 1903): novelist. "The greatest story-teller of our day," one of his admirers boldly says. Well, certainly the most versatile. Simenon's range of characters is astonishing. He writes about thousands of very different peo-

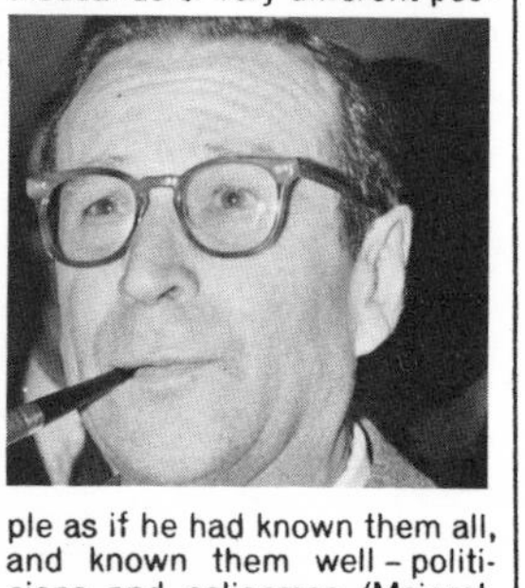

ple as if he had known them all, and known them well – politicians and policemen (Maigret, of course, being the most celebrated), aristos, clerks and peasants, whores and housewives, factory workers, concierges, inexperienced girls. The list is almost endless. And every important character is shown in a setting visualised with such depth and clarity that each time one would swear the author had spent years in the place he describes. Understanding goes with vision. Simenon understands always what makes his people commit crimes, hide secrets, preserve over years a vision of revenge. He is hardly ever unjust to one character in relation to another. The books, or the best of them, are remarkably even in quality, although in general the books written in the Thirties and Forties are better than the later ones. Perhaps not the greatest story-teller, but rather the finest social recorder among modern novelists. **J. G. S.**

'PEDIGREE'- AUTOBIOGRAPHY (PENGUIN, 1965); 'SIMENON IN COURT', BY JOHN RAYMOND (HAMMOND, 1968).

Wallis Simpson, later Duchess of Windsor (U.S., b. 1896): socialite. Wallis Warfield was said by her cousin Upton Sinclair to be a descendant of the legendary Princess Pocahontas. In 1936 her romance with Edward VIII (q.v.) sparked off one of the most dramatic constitutional crises, if the briefest, in the history of the British monarchy. Her first marriage – to a pilot – was short-lived; her second to American born, naturalised British stockbroker Ernest Simpson

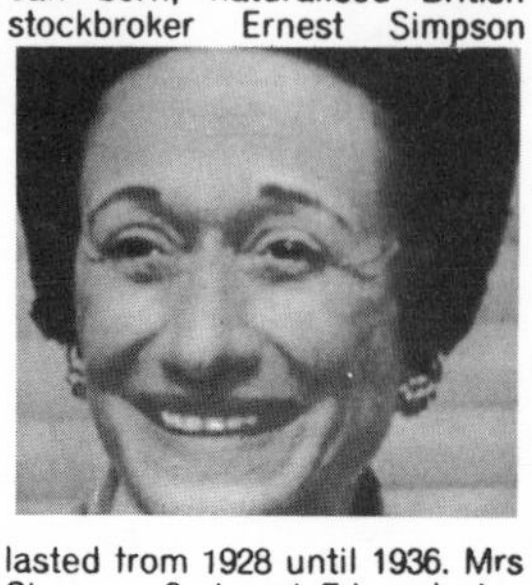

lasted from 1928 until 1936. Mrs Simpson first met Edward at a house party in 1930, but it was not until 1934 that they "crossed the line that marked the indefinable frontier between friendship and love". Attractive, lively, above all independent in spirit, she was eventually to be described simply by Edward as "the woman I love". After she was granted a divorce on October 27, 1936, Baldwin (q.v.) made it clear to the still uncrowned King that he must either renounce Mrs Simpson or abdicate. He chose abdication and left the country on December 11. Most of the main issues of the crisis had been posed behind the scenes before the British public knew anything about them. Mrs Simpson became Duchess (but not Her Royal Highness) after her marriage to Edward in 1937, and their exile continues long after the issues have been forgotten. **A. B.**

'THE HEART HAS ITS REASONS', BY THE DUCHESS OF WINDSOR (MICHAEL JOSEPH, 1956); 'A KING'S STORY', BY THE DUKE OF WINDSOR (CASSELL, 1951); 'ABDICATION', BY BRIAN INGLIS (HODDER, 1966).

Frank Sinatra (U.S., b. 1915): singer and actor. A great singer, yes. A good actor, too, embodying the coolhead hipster. Do-gooder and demon. Yet his legend is infinitely more than the sum of his achievements. As a singer, he was the nearest thing to a teenage idol before the age of rock 'n' roll. Now, for the generation which worshipped him in the 1940s, he has become the symbol of middle-aged nostalgia for adolescence. Through him the 45-year-olds are still, as his best-selling album has it, Swinging Lovers. They dream again, in a world stridently filled with the Clamour of Youth, of being Strangers in the Night. He may wear toupees; he may have kept some allegedly dubious company; his career may have been marked by brawls and controversy; he may be much-married. No matter. He is untouchable, hero of the Sunset Strip era, Super Star. Sinatra learned his art with the big dance bands of Harry James and Tommy Dorsey. In this unbeatable *conservatoire* for a popular singer, he polished his genius for musical phrasing, for impeccable choice of songs, for dramatic timing. In 1942–43 he went solo, sexy and soulful. Women screamed, swooned, rioted for him. From these early days of *Nancy* and *I Couldn't Sleep a Wink Last Night*, the records have kept coming, sung in a deceptively lazy, gradually rusting voice which is brilliantly inimitable. So have the movies, some fine (like his Maggio in *From Here to Eternity*) and some

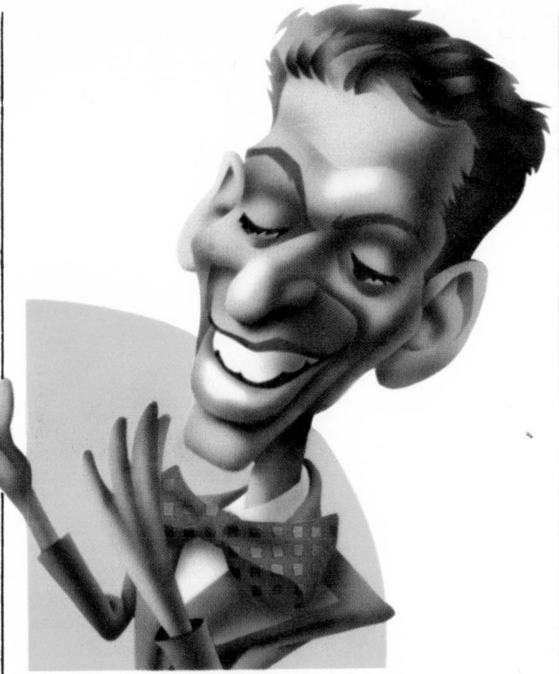

awful. He is, of course, a multi-millionaire with stakes in hotels, recording companies, real estate and all that. But what matters is that he is the most richly-equipped popular singer of the century, an artist who transcended his material as the myth transcended its maker. **D. J.**

'SINATRA', BY ARNOLD SHAW (W. H. ALLEN, 1968); RECORDS: 'THE ESSENTIAL FRANK SINATRA' (3 VOLS., CBS 63172/3/4); 'SWING EASY' (CAPITOL, T20577); 'CYCLES' (REPRISE, RLP 1027 AND RSLP 1207).

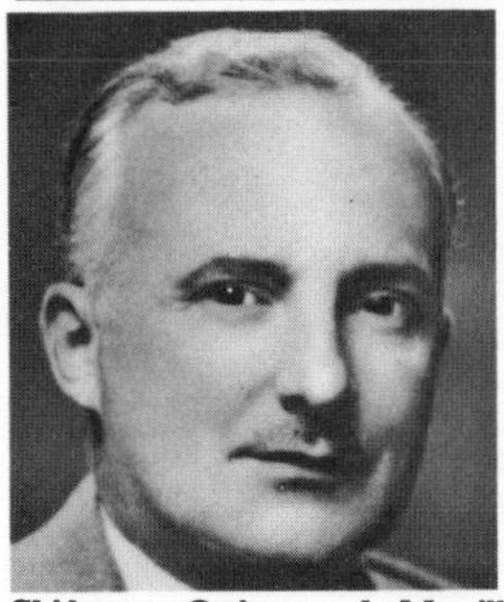

Skidmore, Owings and Merrill (U.S., Louis Skidmore, above, 1897–1962; Nathaniel Owings, b. 1903; John Merrill, b. 1896): architects. In visually expressing the managerial revolution as architects laureate to U.S. big business, SOM are themselves big business – a massive exercise in the teamwork tradition of Gropius (q.v.), with a design partner and an administrative partner jointly responsible for each job. In the Fifties the SOM style was sleek and glassy, Gordon Bunshaft of the New York office designing the offices of Lever (1952), Pepsi Cola (1959), Union Carbide (1960) and Chase Manhattan (1961); even finer was Inland Steel (1954) by Bruce Graham of the Chicago office. SOM landscaped romantic country house settings of parkland for Connecticut General Life Insurance (1957) and the Air Force Academy, Colorado Springs (1959). In the Sixties there has been a more sculptural approach, as in Bunshaft's Rare Book Library at Yale (1960–3) and Banque Lambert at Brussels (1958–64), in the Mauna Kea hotel at Hawaii (1963–5) by Edward Bassett of the San Francisco office, in Graham's 1100-ft tower of tapered brown steel for the John Hancock Centre, Chicago (1966–9), and in the vast Illinois University campus by Walter Netsch of the Chicago office (1964–). Specially notable are the concrete structures of SOM's Chicago engineer, Myron Goldsmith (Brunswick Building, 1963–5). **N. J. W. T.**

'SOM: ARCHITECTURE OF SKIDMORE, OWINGS AND MERRILL, 1950–1962', BY DANZ AND HITCHCOCK (ARCHITECTURAL PRESS, 1963).

Burrhus Frederic Skinner (U.S., b. 1904): psychologist. It was watching his own daughter in arithmetic class in 1953 that encouraged B. F. Skinner to apply his behaviourist principles to education. From that was generated programmed learning and the teaching machine. Skinner believes that learning by mistakes is highly inefficient, and merely spraying information at pupils, however rich, is hopeless. His view is that if a creature is to learn it must be immediately rewarded when it re-

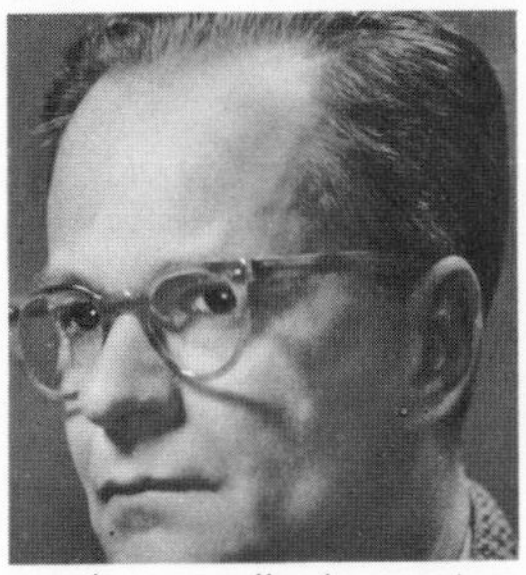

sponds correctly to a given stimulus. This reward reinforces the conditioning. Therefore the teaching must be broken down into such minute steps that wrong responses hardly ever happen (95 per cent. correct is the target), and the correct responses build up powerfully. The teacher has to put hours into a programme for every minute that the pupil takes out. So it involves both an unprecedented scrutiny of normal teaching sequences and a very high initial cost. His discovery is unnervingly ambiguous. Like H. G. Wells (q.v.) he feels that man is engaged in a final "race between education and catastrophe". And he knows more than most people how important – as an instrument of control – educational technology may be to future governments. He has given the world either the method which will remove huge and needless blockages in our logical thought or a conditioning technique which could greatly shrink our humanity if systematically applied. **B. J.**

'SCIENCE AND HUMAN BEHAVIOUR', BY B. F. SKINNER (MACMILLAN, N. Y., 1953).

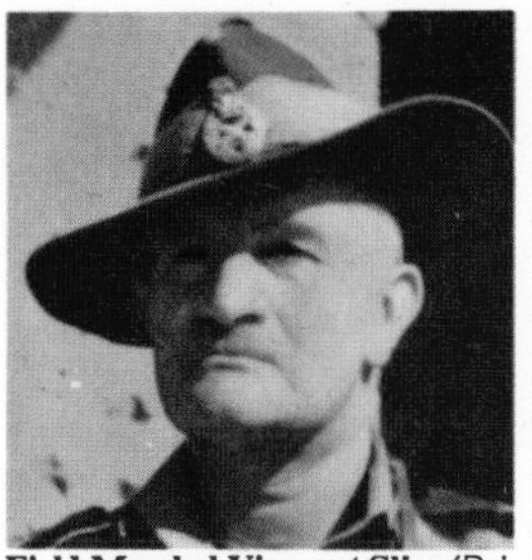

Field Marshal Viscount Slim (British, 1891–1970): soldier. Unable to gain a place at Sandhurst, William Slim began the First World War as a lance-corporal, and ended it an officer in the Indian army. By 1940 he was a Brigadier, and commanded the 10th Indian Brigade in the unimpressive attack on Gallebat. Surviving its failures and developing brilliantly, he was selected in 1942 as the "most suitable candidate" for the dangerous honour, shared with Alexander (q.v.), of bringing order to the chaos of the forces in Burma. Three and a half months later he led 'Burcorps', decimated by battle, racked by tropical fevers, half-starved and short of every *matériel* of war, into Imphal at the end of the longest fighting retreat in the history of the British Army. At Imphal and Kohima he barred the road to India. When, in March 1944, Yamaguchi launched the Japanese army for "the day when the Rising Sun shall proclaim our definite victory in India", Slim broke it in five savage months. 'The Disaster of Imphal' is the greatest land defeat ever suffered by the Japanese. From there, Slim launched the advance to the Irrawaddy. Mandalay recaptured, Rangoon recovered, the 14th Army welded into a great fighting machine, Slim won back Burma as a soldier's soldier. **D. D.**

'DEFEAT INTO VICTORY', BY VISCOUNT SLIM (CASSELL, 1956); 'SLIM AS MILITARY COMMANDER', BY SIR GEOFFREY EVANS (BATSFORD, 1969).

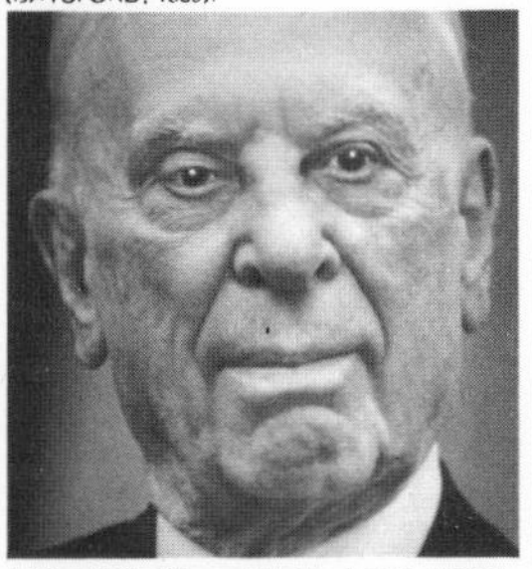

Alfred P. Sloan (U.S., 1875–1966): businessman. Sloan is generally credited with the invention of the basic management tool of big business – decentralised operating divisions to give managers the incentives and opportunities they would otherwise lack in a big business, combined with strict central financial control. This formula he applied with devastating success at General Motors which outstripped Ford within three years of Sloan's accession to power, and is now the world's largest business. He started with G.M. when the component-making company he ran was absorbed in 1918 and developed his theory while G.M. was being built up out of many disparate companies by William Durant. After financial troubles had led to Durant's departure, Sloan became President (managing director) of G.M. in 1923 and, until he retired as chief executive in 1946, developed and refined his management techniques. After 20 years as chairman (1937–56) he retired to write the influential book *My Years with General Motors*, describing his theory in action. What the book omitted was his ability to persuade difficult and important men like Charles Kettering (who invented the self-starter) and William Olds (mobile) to work for him. **A. N. F.**

'MY YEARS WITH GENERAL MOTORS', BY ALFRED P. SLOAN JR., ED JOHN MCDONALD AND CATHARINE STEVENS (SIDGWICK AND JACKSON, 1965).

Bessie Smith (U.S., 1894–1937): singer and songwriter. Billed as 'Empress of the Blues', Bessie Smith more than anyone elevated the blues of the American Negro into an accepted art form, influencing the whole stream of 20th-century popular music thereafter. She was also among the first black Americans to become a nationally famous entertainer. In her heyday (the middle 1920s) she was, indeed, the most successful Negro entertainer in the USA. Born in harsh Mississippi poverty, she toured with carnival-type shows in her teens, and in 1923 broke through to the black mass market with her blues recordings. For a few years she was at the top, recording with Louis Armstrong (q.v.) and other big names, but from 1928 onwards she went steadily downhill. Public taste was changing, she had problems with song-material, she was drinking heavily. By 1931 she had stopped recording (except for one nostalgic session in 1933) and in 1937 she died after a car smash – sadly, just at the time when her artistry was beginning to be accepted as towering by white as well as black Americans. She had a majestic stage appearance, dominating her listeners with a voice of immense power, harsh and beautiful at once. John Hammond, the American critic and producer, called her "the greatest artist American jazz ever produced". **D. J.**

'THE ENCYCLOPAEDIA OF JAZZ', BY LEONARD FEATHER (ARTHUR BARKER, REV. ED., 1961); 'JAZZ ON RECORD', BY ALBERT McCARTHY ET. AL. (HANOVER BOOKS, 1968); RECORDS: THE BESSIE SMITH STORY (4 VOLUMES, CBS).

David Smith (U.S., 1906–1965): sculptor. Born in Decatur, Indiana, into a blacksmith's family, Smith personified the idea of the American artist as an open-hearted giant with direct and colossal appetites: a man at one with his materials, his environment, and his century. Trained as a painter from 1927–32, he found that "the painting developed into raised levels from the canvas. Gradually the canvas was the base and the painting was a sculpture . . .".

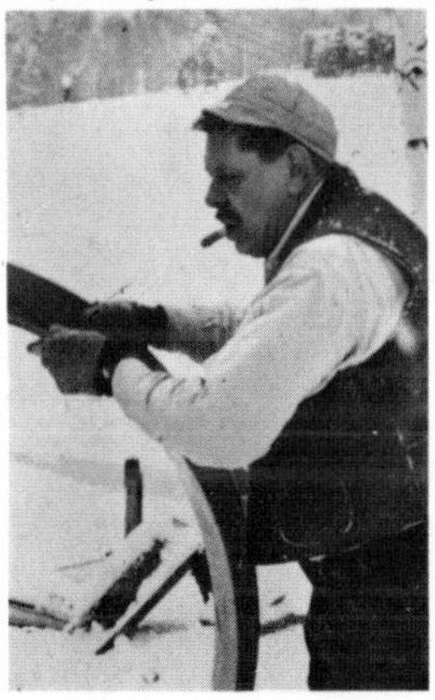

In 1933 Smith saw reproductions of the iron sculptures of Gonzalez and Picasso (q.v.) and realised that his inherited oneness with iron and steel could be put to creative use. Thereafter he worked in these materials with an ever greater freedom and assurance and on a more and more monumental scale. His work embraced a wide range of feeling and subject-matter: social criticism (the caustic *Medals of Dishonour* of 1937–40), poetic fantasy (the *Interiors* inspired by Giacometti [q.v.] in his Surrealist phase), and a full-hearted affirmation in the late *Cubi* of the virtues of the unafraid vertical man. Smith's use of standard industrial units was an inspiration to Anthony Caro (q.v.) and others, and his distant and isolated studio at Bolton Landing, N.Y., strewn as it and its surroundings were with emblems of an unforced and triumphant masculinity, became in the end one of the sacred places of American art. **J. R.**

'DAVID SMITH: SCULPTURE AND WRITINGS', ED. C. GRAY (THAMES AND HUDSON, 1968).

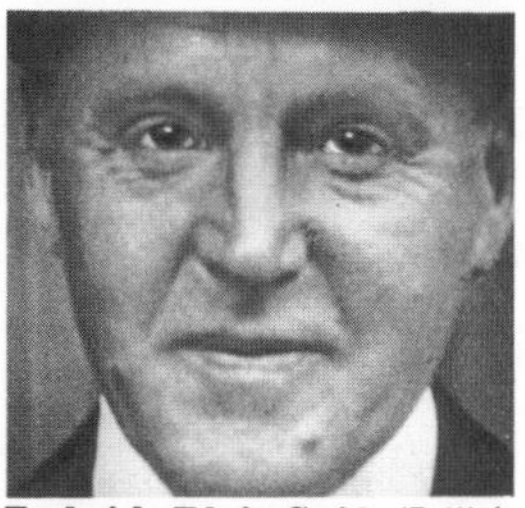

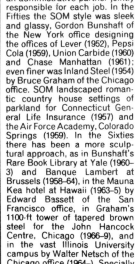

Frederick Edwin Smith (British, 1872–1930): barrister and politician. Beaverbrook (q.v.) rated F. E. Smith, who became Lord Birkenhead in 1919, "the cleverest man in the kingdom", and Churchill (q.v.) gave him a place of honour in his *Great Contemporaries*. He is best remembered for his words rather than his deeds – for his anecdotes and his fluent, coruscating wit. Elected in 1906 to a predominantly Liberal House of Commons, he dazzled his hearers with his first speech. "I am old, but you have beaten me at my own game," he was told by the Irish Nationalist Tim Healy. Smith had already been earning a fantastic £6000 a year at the Bar. He loved pleasure, but his power of concentration was as remarkable as his gift for vituperation. He was ranged with the Lords against the Liberals in 1910 and 1911 and with the Ulstermen against Asquith (q.v.) and Redmond in 1913 and 1914. He held office for the first time during the War – as Solicitor-General in 1915 – and from 1919 to 1922 was Lord Chancellor, in the thick of Coalition politics. Without his efforts, the Anglo-Irish Treaty of 1921 might never have been signed. He had no sympathy with the "second-class brains" who led the Conservatives out of the Coalition, and though he served somewhat restlessly with Baldwin (q.v.) he quit Westminster for the City in 1928. **A. B.**

'F. E.: THE LIFE OF F. E. SMITH, FIRST EARL OF BIRKENHEAD', BY LORD BIRKENHEAD (EYRE AND SPOTTISWOODE, 1969).

Ian Smith (Rhodesian, b. 1919): politician. The supersession by Ian Smith of Lord Malvern, Sir Roy Welensky and Sir Edgar Whitehead as the principal white leader of the Rhodesians has been seen as one of the tragedies of British Central Africa but as the Prime Minister responsible for Rhodesia's unilateral declaration of independence in 1965 he must be given priority. A politician of limited outlook, Smith never gave emphasis to 'inter-racial partnership' as a policy goal but rather stressed the dangers of 'premature' African advancement and the importance of long-term white leadership. His success since 1964 derives from the break-up of the Federation of Rhodesia and Nyasaland, the nature of the electorate – a

dominant minority conscious of isolation and exposure on a major frontier – and his own capacity for simple, direct and stubborn repetition of his electors' fears and aspirations. As the first Rhodesian-born Prime Minister and a wounded airman of the Second World War his position has been reinforced. World history has seen many examples of otherwise second-rate men in positions of crucial importance, but few have occupied a post more critical than that of Ian Smith in this century's great issue of race relations. **K. K.**

Jan Christiaan Smuts (South African, 1870–1950): statesman, Boer general turned British Field Marshal, Empire and world statesman and Chancellor of

Cambridge University, Smuts was also a mountaineer, lawyer, scientist and Holist philosopher. As a brilliant student he identified Africa's major problem of 'black-white' relations, but confessed an inability to see light; as a young graduate he was bitterly critical of British Imperial policy, and published *A Century of Wrong*. A brave, resourceful commando general and a practical advocate of conciliation with Britain after defeat, he drafted the 1909 South Africa Act, a unitary constitution with power in white hands. A British general and a member of the Imperial War Cabinet, he was a founder of the Royal Air Force, the Commonwealth of Nations and the League of Nations. As a deputy, he co-operated in enacting Hertzog's (q.v.) segrega-

tion laws in 1936 despite the opposition of J. H. Hofmeyr (later to be his Second World War deputy), whom Smuts described as "South Africa's conscience". He became Prime Minister for the second time in 1939 (and as an international leader, he was a confidant of Churchill and a founder-mem-

ber of the United Nations), but he neglected internal South African politics and was defeated by Malan (q.v.) and apartheid in 1948. A brilliant, charismatic, paradoxical statesman-politician-philosopher, he won the acclaim of Britain and the respect of world leaders, but failed to come to grips with the racial issues of his homeland – the crucial test for any Prime Minister of South Africa. **K. K.**

'SMUTS', BY W. K. HANCOCK, 2 VOLS. (CAMBRIDGE U.P., 1962-1968), 'AFRICA AND SOME WORLD PROBLEMS', BY J. C. SMUTS (CLARENDON PRESS, OXFORD, 1930).

Philip Snowden (British, 1864–1937): politician. Snowden, together with MacDonald and Arthur Henderson (qq.v.), dominated the Labour Party from 1911 to 1931. During the First World War he was a pacifist, but it was as a puritanical

Chancellor of the Exchequer (1924, 1929–1931) that he made his mark on his times. He certainly looked the part – emaciated, thin-lipped, cramped, suffering (he had been crippled by a cycling accident), and he stood for the traditional virtues of hard work, thrift, frugality, foresight. In economic

with the League of Decency to procure the censorship of unsuitable films, and was adept at ferreting out Reds in the labour unions. Liberals have liked to represent him as an ecclesiastical McCarthy (q.v.). **E. R. N.**
'THE CARDINAL SPELLMAN STORY', BY ROBERT I. GANNON (DOUBLEDAY, TORONTO, 1962); 'OUR AMERICAN PRINCES', BY F. B. THORNTON (PUTMAN, N. Y., 1963).

Oswald Spengler (German, 1880–1936): philosopher. To some thinkers the apparent randomness of history is the outward shell of a deeper orderliness. For Hegel and Marx the deep structure was the dialectic, a process involving a thesis, antithesis and synthesis. Spengler saw the organic cycle of birth, growth and death as the underlying pattern of all civilisations. The first volume of his massive work *The Decline of the West* was published in 1918. In it he compared Indian, Classical, Arabian and Western civilisations and claimed to show how each passed through a spring, a summer, an autumn and a winter. Western civilisation was seen as currently being in the winter. The timing was apt, as Spengler seemed to offer an explanation to those bewildered by the enormity and carnage of the First World War. This big, obtuse volume sold about 100,000 copies. During the next decade it became a favourite academic pastime to list the errors that Spengler had made and he unsuccessfully attempted to use his popular acclaim to gain influence as a commentator on political events. Even though the general argument of *The Decline of the West* now seems poor, it produced at the time a conviction of inevitable doom that many have never lost. **B. R. O.**
'THE DECLINE OF THE WEST', BY O. SPENGLER (ALLEN AND UNWIN, 1926-9).

terms this meant an absolute adherence to the gold standard, free trade, economy and deflation – exactly the opposite of what was needed in a situation of depression and mass unemployment. Nor did his Socialism suggest an alternative. For him it was moral, not economic, and so far was he from understanding any Socialist economic policy that after he joined the National Government in 1931 he condemned the Labour Party's mildly expansionary programme as "Bolshevism run mad". Though warm and humorous in private, a vein of bitterness ran deep in him and in his last writings he denounced the associates of a lifetime. A 19th-century figure, he was baffled by the problems of the 20th century. **R. Sk.**
AN AUTOBIOGRAPHY', BY VISCOUNT SNOWDEN, 2 VOLS. (NICHOLSON AND WATSON, 1934); 'PHILIP SNOWDEN', BY COLIN CROSS (BARRIE AND ROCKLIFF, 1966).

Frederick Soddy (British, 1877–1956): chemist. In the age of the H-bomb, the radioactive disintegration of elements causes little surprise. Around the turn of the century this new phenomenon appeared to contradict all the accepted canons of physical law, especially ideas about the irreducible funda-

an element undergoes radioactive decay, subatomic particles are ejected from the nucleus and new elements are formed. A demonstration of this was provided by Soddy and Ramsay when they showed that helium, already noticed in the sun's chromosphere or illuminated disc, was given off by the decay of radium compounds. Later, as Professor of Chemistry at Glasgow, Soddy evolved the concept of isotopes, elements that are virtually identical yet have different atomic cores. A Nobel Prize winner in 1921, Soddy shaped our ideas of atomic constitution and profoundly influenced all following researches. **P. J. F.**
'A LIFE OF SIR WILLIAM RAMSAY', BY M. W. TRAVERS (ARNOLD, 1956); 'NOBEL LECTURES: CHEMISTRY 1901–1921' (ELSEVIER, 1966).

Georges Sorel (French, 1847–1922): philosopher. A self-taught road engineer from Normandy, Sorel derived his ideas from a wide variety of sources (Hegel, Marx, Bergson) but maintained a great originality. He rejected society as he knew it and he despised bourgeois morality and culture; he thought that there was no hope of ever attaining Socialism by parliamentary means; he did not think that a

result of violence. Violence was both necessary. and salutary (his *Reflections on Violence,* published in 1908, is the only one of his books to have been translated into English). He believed that men were moved by irrational ideas and passions; the proletariat needed a myth that would inspire and sustain them. The general strike would be the epic of the working class. Though Sorel had little influence on French trade-unionism, his ideas were important for Lenin, Mussolini (qq.v.) and Rosenberg. Similar considerations to his on violence are popular in some quarters even now. **D. W. J. J.**
'THE GENESIS OF GEORGES SOREL', BY JAMES H. MEISEL (GEORGE WAHR, ANN ARBOR, MICHIGAN, 1951); 'CONSCIOUSNESS AND SOCIETY', BY H. STUART HUGHES MACGIBBON AND KEE, 1959).

Cardinal Francis Spellman (U.S., 1889–1967): religious leader. One of the last of the American ultramontanist prelates, Spellman was a Vatican official for 20 years, starting as the supervisor of the playgrounds established by the Knights of Columbus in Italy. His flair for eliciting large charitable donations from rich fellow-countrymen did not go unrecognised. He was sent back to America in purple, and

mental particles of matter. The investigation in depth of the precise events accompanying radioactive decay is the monument to a few groups of chemists and physicists, among them Soddy, who was a collaborator of Rutherford (q.v.) in Canada and of Sir William Ramsay at University College London. If

model of an ideal society could ever be devised and then attained by a series of gradual reforms; nor did he believe in the overthrow of capitalism by any economic inevitability. For Sorel – possibly the philosopher most often referred to and least often read – the revolution could only come about as the

from 1939 presided over the archdiocese of New York. In post-war America he emerged as an articulate defender of Catholic and national morality – a vocation which involved him in a famous altercation with Mrs Roosevelt over the question of state aid to Catholic schools in 1949. He also worked intimately

Benjamin Spock (U.S., b. 1903): paediatrician. The well-thumbed copy of Dr Spock's book *Baby and Child Care* found in many homes might be called The Paperback Granny. The small nuclear family without the help and support of near – and nearby – relatives can be peculiarly ignorant.and intimidated by a new baby. The Paperback Granny has advice to offer on everything, from abscesses via knock-knees to zwieback. The advice is well received; as a best-seller Spock's book is outnumbered only by the Bible (which is usually given away). Spock's success reflects both the social need and his skill in answering it. Before Spock the natural uncertainty of young parents was made worse by conflicting expert opinions: much unhappiness was caused by slavish following of unsuitable but fashionable methods. Spock insists that parents can use their own judgment and gives the information necessary for reasonable decisions. He is able to do this by drawing on his extensive experience and knowledge. Spock does not find social eminence and social responsibility incompatible. He became leader of the National Committee against the Vietnam War and was arrested in 1967 for civil disobedience. He received a two-year sentence (which was quashed on appeal), and many parents felt betrayed by him – though many more of them understood the logic of his position. **B. R. O.**

'BABY AND CHILD CARE', BY BENJAMIN SPOCK (REVISED ED., BODLEY HEAD, 1969).

Axel Springer (German, b. 1912): newspaper proprietor. Starting from scratch after the war, Springer has built up the biggest newspaper publishing organisation on the European continent. He publishes nearly 40 per cent of the total circulation of West Germany's daily newspapers. If the lurid popular daily *Bild Zeitung* (4.5 million) is taken into account, his share of the national – as distinct from the regional or local – press is as high as 88 per cent. Apart from *Bild*, he publishes four dailies, including the internationally respected *Die Welt*, two Sundays and two radio and

television weeklies. Springer adopted four guiding principles by which all his publications are supposed to abide: support for the re-unification of Germany; reconciliation of Germans and Jews; rejection of every form of totalitarianism; and promotion of the social market economy. Politically his newspapers, while providing a platform for a variety of views, are national, conservative and often intolerant of minorities. His offices have been attacked by Left-wing demonstrators. His main contribution has been to create lively newspapers in Germany. **H. N. C.**

Constance Spry (British, 1886–1960): flower arranger and cookery writer. "Constance Spry made us see things to which we had grown blind with custom," said one admirer of this doyenne of flower arrangement, and indeed she made her skills accessible to women of all classes all over the English-speaking world. Brought up in Ireland, she spent her youth as a nurse, as secretary to the Lord Lieutenant's wife, as a personnel officer and as a school principal; she was 42 before she started her flower decoration business in London in the mid-Twenties.

She once stopped the traffic in Bond Street with a display of purple cabbages and red roses; professionally she was in no way hidebound and was the first to use hot-house with garden or hedgerow flowers – a combination unthought of before. She won considerable fame as a lecturer in Britain, America and Australia; her books brought her more. Yet today she is a household word not only for her shops, the finishing school she opened after the Second World War, and her books on flower arrangement – but also for *The Constance Spry Cookery Book*, written with Rosemary Hume, and published when she was 70. **S. M.**

'THE CONSTANCE SPRY COOKERY BOOK', (DENT, 1956); 'FLOWER DECORATION', BY CONSTANCE SPRY (DENT, 1934).

Joseph Vissarionovich Stalin (Russian, 1879–1953): head of state. The man who forged the shape of modern Soviet Russia was a Georgian, born the son of a poor cobbler named Dzhugashvili. Expelled at 19 from the theological seminary where he was educated, he became a Marxist in 1901 and under the pseudonym Stalin (Man of Steel) a leader of the underground Bolshevik organisation. His part in 1917 was not prominent, but his administrative ability made him indispensable, and in 1922 he became General Secretary of the Party. Consistently underrated by his rivals ("just a small-town politician", one called him), he gradually gained control of Party and Government. After Lenin's (q.v.) death he removed Trotsky, Zinoviev and Bukharin (qq.v.) from the leadership, and by 1929 held undisputed power. Then, at immense cost – low living standards, elimination of freedom of expression, purges in which millions perished – Stalin within a decade made Russia an industrial nation. This enabled her to withstand Hitler's attack in 1941, and to recover from devastation (some 25 million Russians died during the War) to become the world's second greatest industrial power. The Red Army now

occupied Eastern Europe, and Stalin established Communist regimes there – the beginning of the Cold War. His closing years were marked by gross adulation and by even more arbitrary repression. Neither long survived him, but, although Khrushchev (q.v.) denounced Stalin's errors and measures of liberalisation followed which significantly changed Soviet society, the political habits which flourished under Stalin are dying hard. **A. Q. D.**

'STALIN, A POLITICAL BIOGRAPHY', BY I. DEUTCHER (O.U.P., 1949); 'STALIN', BY L. D. TROTSKY (HOLLIS AND CARTER, 1947).

Konstantin Stanislavsky (Russian, 1865–1938): actor, writer and theatrical director. Stanislavsky reacted against the rhetorical and highly romantic style of the 19th-century Russian theatre. He introduced a naturalistic interpretation of the ordinary surfaces of life that was penetrated with gentle shafts of poetic perception. It was this underlying poetic sense that distinguished his work from that of André Antoine at the Théâtre Libre in Paris. Stanislavsky's first notable production was Tolstoy's *Fruits of Enlightenment*, but his chief triumphs were in his Chekhov productions, which, however, Chekhov himself did not always approve, thinking them too tragic. Some

of these productions can still be seen at the Moscow Art Theatre, where they remain in the current repertory. Stanislavsky's influence on the modern theatre has been very great, especially in America, where his work led to the development of The Method. He wrote several books, which remain the principal authorities on his work. **H. H.**

BOOKS BY STANISLAVSKY: 'AN ACTOR PREPARES' (GEOFFREY BLES, 1937; PENGUIN 1967); 'MY LIFE IN ART' (GEOFFREY BLES, 1924; PENGUIN, 1948)

Wendell Stanley (U.S., 1904–1971): biochemist. In the 1930s John Northrop (q.v.) had excited the chemical world by substantiating Sumner's (q.v.) work: enzymes were proteins and no longer mysterious. But what about the viruses which were considered living entities because they reproduce and mutate, but whose structure – carbohydrate, fat, protein, hydrocarbon or inorganic – was completely unknown? Stanley attacked this problem, using the tobacco mosaic virus. He grew tobacco, infected it, let it grow more, mashed the plant and used the Northrop and Sumner techniques for extracting pro-

tein. In 1935 he found needle-like crystals with the infective properties of the virus in high concentration – and they proved to be protein in nature. The biochemical world found it hard to accept that a living entity could have a crystalline structure (they thought it should be either non-living and crystalline, or non-crystalline and living) but since then many other viruses have been crystalised, and all have turned out to be nucleoproteins. The nucleic acid portion was shown to contain the virus activity, so Stanley's isolation of the first virus set the scene for the investigation of the virus problems which merged with gene theory and the molecular biology of Crick and Watson (qq.v.). **P. G. R.**

Prince Ernst Rüdiger Starhemberg (Austrian, 1899–1956): politician. Heir to one of the oldest aristocratic families, Starhemberg did much to undermine the first Austrian republic, without being able to profit from its downfall. He was an enthusiastic soldier in the First World War, being much decorated. After 1918 he sought to escape from a dull social-democratic future and embraced the cause of German nationalism. He met Hitler (q.v.), and played a part in the Munich *Putsch* of 1923. After its failure he returned to Austria and led the *Heimwehr* ('Home Guard') a local Fascist body. In 1930 he made an alliance with the Austrian conservative Party under Dollfuss, and swung it towards dictatorship; and in 1934 he organised an attack by the army on the Vienna Social Democrats, in which artillery was used against the workers' flats. Gradually Starhemberg came to see the wickedness of German Nazism, and adopted the cause of pure Austrian patriotism, joining the Catholic Fatherland Front and seeking Mussolini's (q.v.) protection against Hitler. But day-to-day politics bored him – he was basically a mere playboy. He retired from politics, which had eaten up his fortune, in 1936, married an actress, and had to stay away from Austria when it was occupied by the Germans. On the outbreak of war in 1939, he volunteered for the French air force after feeble attempts at exile politics, but later emigrated to South America. He returned to Austria shortly before his death in 1955. **N. S.**

THE AUSTRIAN ODYSSEY', BY GORDON SHEPHERD (MACMILLAN, 1961); 'DOLLFUSS', BY GORDON BROOK-SHEPHERD (MACMILLAN, 1961).

Hermann Staudinger (German, 1881–1965): chemist. Plastics have become common, accepted materials, yet relatively few of us realise how they come to possess their useful properties. In the same way, there was by the 1920s a reasonably active international plastics industry without its members having much knowledge about the nature of the materials they produced. Staudinger's signal

contribution to science and technology was to clarify the underlying principles of a large group of compounds, the polymers, to which plastics belong, and create conditions where further development could take place. The building blocks of plastics are giant molecules, composed of a small range of reasonably simple substances.

The pattern in which polymers are built up controls the final properties of the material – a determining factor not only in plastics but also in biologically important materials like proteins and nucleic acids. Staudinger's achievements won him the Nobel Prize in 1953, and were in no small measure responsible for the strides of the German plastics industry before the war and for the international achievments in plastics ever since. **P. J. F.**

'CHEMISTRY CREATES A NEW WORLD', BY BERNARD JAFFE (PYRAMID PUBLICATIONS, REV. ED., N.Y., 1962); 'PLASTICS IN THE MODERN WORLD', BY E. G. COUZENS AND V. E. YARSLEY (PENGUIN, REV. ED., 1969).

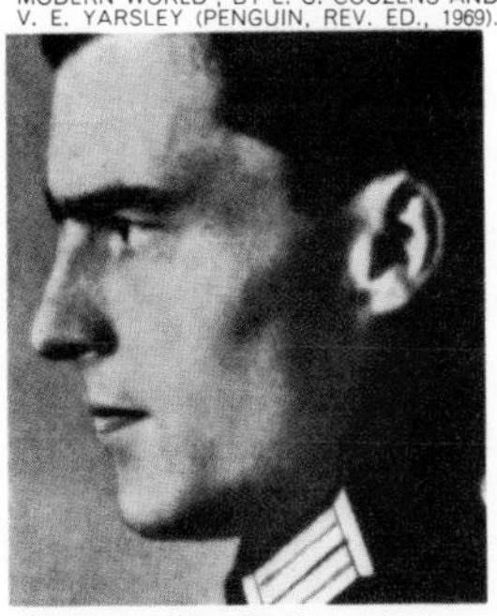

Claus von Stauffenberg (German, 1907–1944): resistance leader. Had the time bomb concealed in Stauffenberg's brief case at Hitler's (q.v.) conference room in the Wolf's Lair at Rastenburg done its job more thoroughly the pattern of contemporary Europe might look very different today. A Swabian aristocrat and officer, Stauffenberg's revolutionary temperament was fired by the writings of Stefan George (q.v.) and matured into a form of Christian Socialism. Disturbed by the persecution of the Jews in 1938, first-hand experience of the atrocities committed in occupied Russia convinced him of the need to destroy the man responsible. After many abortive attempts Stauffenberg finally set off his bomb on July 20, 1944, and departed for Berlin to await the moment to announce the liberation of Germany. The moment never came. Hitler escaped the full force of the blast, his hair scorched and with "a backside like a baboon", his communications with the Reich intact. Stauffenberg was shot the next day; some colleagues committed suicide, others were hanged a month later. **S. S.**

'STAUFFENBERG', BY JOACHIM KRAMARZ (ANDRE DEUTSCH, 1967); 'TROUBLED LOYALTY', BY CHRISTOPHER SYKES (COLLINS, 1968); 'THE CONSPIRACY AGAINST HITLER IN THE TWILIGHT WAR', BY HAROLD DEUTSCH (O.U.P., 1968).

Gertrude Stein (U.S., 1874–1946): writer. Gertrude Stein's fame and influence centre on a new way of thinking about the art of writing. In books, lectures, and conversations stretching over the 40 years of her expatriate life in France, she mapped out an insistently repetitive, anti-associational style designed to render

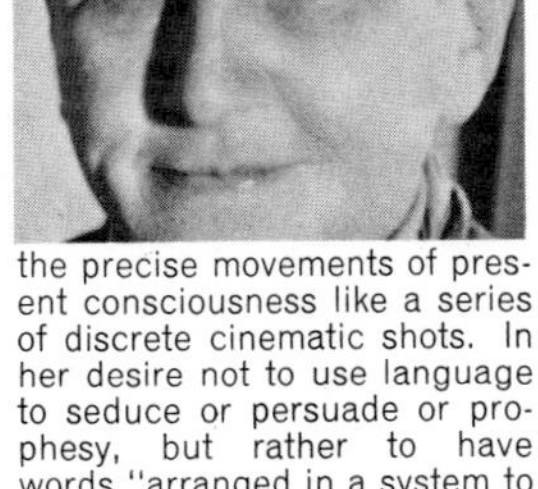

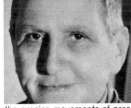

the precise movements of present consciousness like a series of discrete cinematic shots. In her desire not to use language to seduce or persuade or prophesy, but rather to have words "arranged in a system to pointing", she applied to literature an equivalent of what Mondrian discovered in art, and Wittgenstein (qq.v.) in philosophy. Her famous circular motto, "A rose is a rose is a rose is a rose", was a reminder that things are only what they are, despite Symbolist and other attempts to extend 19th-century habits of association and 'depth' into the 20th century. From the fairly traditional prose of *Three Lives* (1909) and *The Autobiography of Alice B. Toklas* (1933), her work ranges out widely into criticism (*Lectures in America*), the novel (*The Making of Americans*), poetry (*Stanzas in Meditation*), and some startling plays and proto-happenings, in all of which her disputed but still seminal linguistic structures are deployed. "Not to the future, but to the fuchsia." **E. G. M.**

'GERTRUDE STEIN: A BIOGRAPHY OF HER WORK', BY DONALD SUTHERLAND (O.U.P., 1951); 'GERTRUDE STEIN: HER LIFE AND WORK', BY ELIZABETH SPRIGGE (HAMISH HAMILTON, 1957); 'GERTRUDE STEIN AND THE PRESENT', BY ALLEGRA STEWART (HARVARD U.P./O.U.P., 1967).

John Stephen (British, b. 1938): fashion designer. A major influence in the renaissance of men's ready-to-wear, a pioneer of pop clothing and the uncrowned King of Carnaby Street, Stephen came to London from Glasgow at 19 to work in the Military Department at Moss Bros. He left after a year to work for Bill Green who ran Vince Shops, specialising in adventurous leisurewear for men, and later he and a friend opened the Nicholas Perry Boutique in Notting Hill. After a year he decided to set up on his own in Soho's Beak Street, and when fire destroyed the premises three months later his landlord offered him a shop in a sleepy backwater behind Regent Street called Carnaby Street. Here he opened his first shop in 1957 – and the Carnaby boom began. He cut, altered, changed and took chances with imaginative and daring merchandise. Men

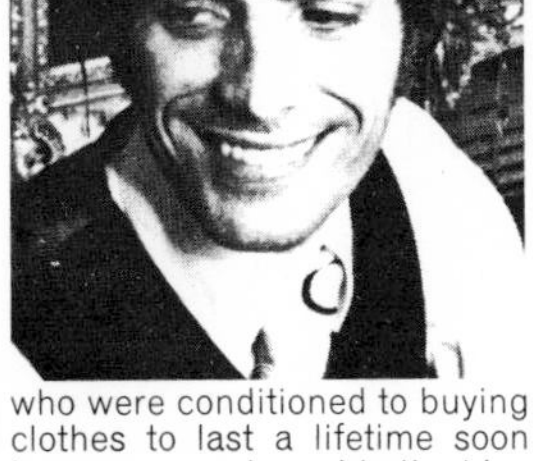

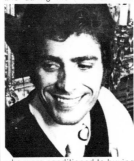

who were conditioned to buying clothes to last a lifetime soon became accustomed to the idea of cheap clothes and seasonal obsolescence. Pop groups patronised his shop, the pop fans followed and music blared while customers tried on clothes – slim-line trousers, kipper ties, floral shirts, suede and leather jackets. Soon Stephen had eight shops and the street became a tourist attraction. Journalists referred to it as 'the birthplace of swinging London': shop rents rose from £10 a week to around £100. In 1967 Stephen started selling women's clothes – clothes for 'dolly birds'. He now has seven shops in Carnaby Street alone, and he also supplies clothes to shops all over the country, as well as in America, Canada, Sweden, Norway, France, Germany and Switzerland. **M. McC.**

Wallace Stevens (U.S., 1879–1955): poet. The publication of Stevens's first book, *Harmonium* (1922), coincided with Eliot's (q.v.) *The Waste Land*. Eliot's recognition blocked Stevens's. The latter came to feel that "Eliot and I are dead opposites", and contrast between them shows why: Eliot's poetry

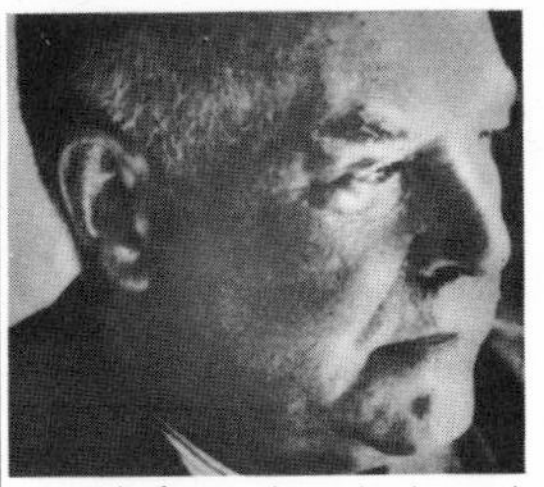

moved from despair towards religious transcendence ("The point of intersection of the timeless With time"); for Stevens the human imagination was the only means of transcendence. He began in 'Sunday Morning' (*Harmonium*) with the death of Christianity and a probing of the adequacy of sensuous and imaginative experience. In the long poems of meditation that followed over the years, 'The Man with the Blue Guitar', 'Notes toward a Supreme Fiction', 'The Auroras of Autumn'. 'The Rock', Stevens's sense of the relation between imagination and reality deepened. He came to realise that men "do not create in light and warmth alone". This and the increasing awareness of all that is concerned in the act of meditation when the human mind confronts a godless world stamped Stevens's often lonely poetry with the mark of his time. Deliberately facing a single issue (the dance, marriage, divorce, remarriage of imagination and its universe), he developed from the aesthete of the early journals into a strong-minded connoisseur of chaos. **C. T.**

'CONNOISSEURS OF CHAOS', BY DENIS DONOGHUE (FABER, 1966); 'WALLACE STEVENS', BY FRANK KERMODE (OLIVER AND BOYD, 1960); 'POETS OF REALITY', BY J. HILLIS MILLER (O.U.P., 1966).

Adlai Stevenson (U.S., 1900–1965); politician. Stevenson is remembered as the liberal hope of the 1950s. His humanity, humility and wit contrasted with the blandness of Eisenhower and the viciousness of McCarthy (qq.v.) Derisively called an 'egghead' by critics, he responded: "Eggheads of the world unite! You have nothing to lose but your yolks." After Princeton and Harvard Law School, Stevenson entered private practice in Chicago. In 1933 he served a brief tour in Washington with the New Deal. His active internationalism led him back to Washington in 1940 and in 1945 he played a

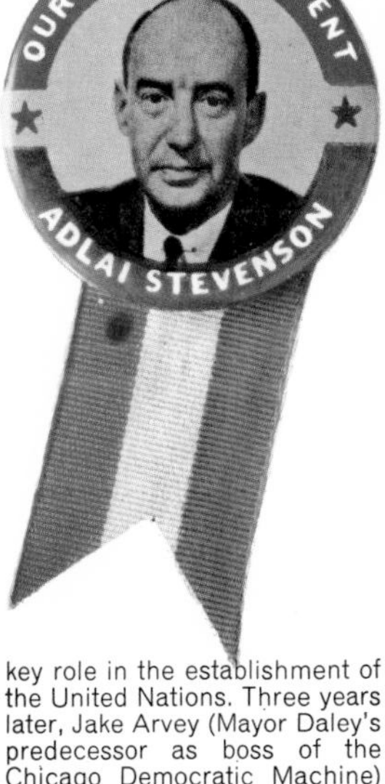

key role in the establishment of the United Nations. Three years later, Jake Arvey (Mayor Daley's predecessor as boss of the Chicago Democratic Machine) picked Stevenson to run for the governorship of Illinois, which he won with the largest majority in Illinois history. His four years as a progressive Governor of a major state projected him on to the national scene and, despite his unwillingness to run, his long-remembered welcoming speech to the Democratic Convention in Chicago led to his selection as one of the few dark horses to be nominated in this century. But his campaign was doomed. Eisenhower's victory left Stevenson as 'titular leader' of the Democratic party, but he soon came into conflict with the Democratic congressional leaders, Sam Rayburn and Lyndon Johnson (q.v.) His renomination in 1956 was accepted as being a lost cause; he ran an uninspired and uninspiring campaign. Four years later, although John Kennedy had said that he "assumed" any Democratic president would make Stevenson Secretary of State, the new President relegated him to the United Nations. His four years as Ambassador witnessed the signing of the Test Ban Treaty, but also saw his dutiful defence of presidential action at the Bay of Pigs, in the Dominican Republic and in Vietnam. His sudden death in London came before the riots at home and the escalation in Vietnam left bankrupt the civilised liberalism he had represented. **W. H. J.**

'PUTTING FIRST THINGS FIRST: A DEMOCRATIC VIEW', BY ADLAI STEVENSON (HART-DAVIS, 1960); 'ADLAI STEVENSON; A STUDY IN VALUES', BY HERBERT JOSEPH MULLER (HAMISH HAMILTON, 1968).

Karlheinz Stockhausen (German, b. 1928): compcser. John Cage (q.v.) apart, there is no other figure on the contemporary scene who has aroused as widespread controversy as Stockhausen. Some musicians still find it difficult to regard him as a composer at all, while others, our own Roger Smalley included, feel (a little defensively, perhaps) that he is the greatest composer since Beethoven. His influence, in any case, is far-reaching and profound; in the main, it centres on three innovatory aspects of his work – his electronic techniques, his use of space, and his drawing the performer, and even the listener, into the creative process by way of aleatoric music and indeterminacy. With

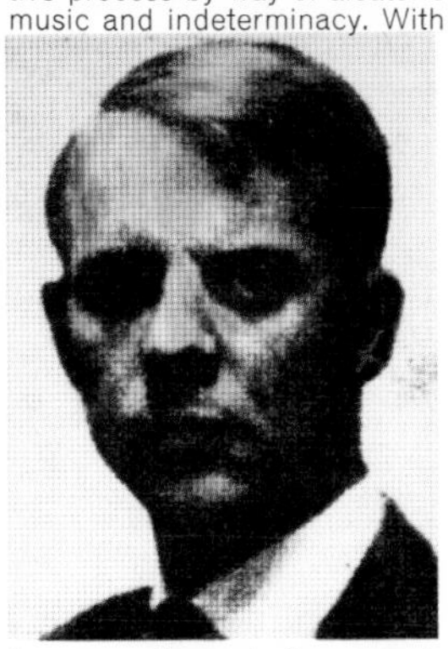

the recording of *Gruppen* (a spatial work for three chamber orchestras, 109 instruments in all) and *Carré* (for four orchestras and choruses, equally spatial), virtually all his important works are now available on disc – a unique feat for an avant-garde composer, and one which seems to turn aggressive crusades on his behalf into a cultural luxury. To deny his creative presence, on the other hand, is to say, "Stop the musical world: I want to get off." Even some of those who hate his approach have, unwittingly, come under its influence – the surest proof of historical importance. **H. K.**

'STOCKHAUSEN'S GRUPPEN', BY ROGER SMALLEY (THE MUSICAL TIMES, SEPTEMBER, 1967).

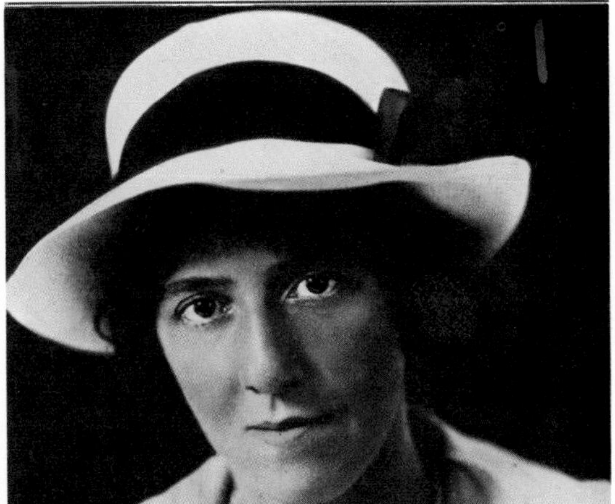

Marie Stopes (British, 1880–1958): birth control pioneer. A sexually unhappy marriage, and the search for information it provoked, inspired Marie Stopes to write "a book on marriage and sex [which] would teach a man and a woman how to understand each other's sexual problems". This was *Married Love* (1918). It sold 2000 copies in its first fortnight, and after her marriage to the man who helped her publish it, Humphrey Verdon Roe, she wrote *Wise Parenthood* (1918), which included descriptions of various methods of birth control; and in 1921 she opened Britain's first birth control clinic, in Islington, London. At the age of 40, after an earlier career as a scientist, she had embarked on her life's work. The medical profession was, as usual hostile. The Roman Catholics attacked her even more fiercely: in 1922 a Dr Halliday Sutherland wrote of her work so venomously that Marie Stopes sued him for libel – a famous trial in which she was awarded a derisory £100 damages by the jury, was found against by the judge, won in the Court of Appeal and finally lost in the House of Lords. It was the first of many legal battles – some she won, some she lost – which served to spread her fame to the millions of women she wanted to reach. She was not only a brilliant propagandist – she even wrote a play about birth control which ran for three months – but a woman prepared to put her vision into practice. **S. M. R.**

'MARIE STOPES', BY KEITH BRIANT (THE HOGARTH PRESS, 1962); 'THE BIRTH CONTROLLERS', BY PETER FRYER (SECKER AND WARBURG, 1965).

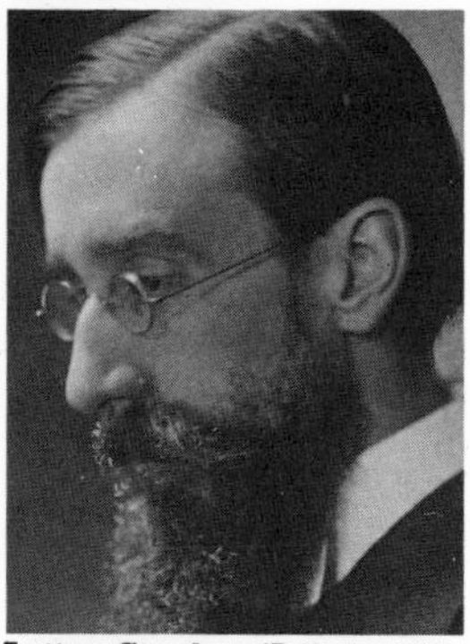

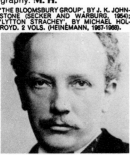

Lytton Strachey (British, 1880–1932): biographer. As an 'Apostle' at Cambridge, Strachey proclaimed a fierce antagonism to the dogmatic requirements of Christianity, and to the worldly religion of success. As a member of the Bloomsbury Group and in his complex personal life, he set an example of forbearance in human relationships. As an essayist and a conscientious objector in the First World War, he campaigned for an end to barbarism and the re-introduction of civilised standards. But it was not until the spring of 1918, when his great polemic *Eminent Victorians* was published, that, overnight, his views became notorious. The impact of this book was tremendous. The world was weary of big guns and big phrases, and Strachey's witty, ironic sifting of those Victorian pretensions that seemed to have led to war was especially appealing to the jaded palate of the younger generation. Three years later Strachey reverted from the anarchist to his natural romanticism, and produced in *Queen Victoria* a perfectly-constructed biography that playfully enhanced the legend of the little old lady on the throne. In 1928 came his last biography, *Elizabeth and Essex*, a beautiful tapestry depicting scenes of theatrical drama, that was much frowned upon by professional historians. Strachey's battles as a polemicist are now all won, but his influence persists as the man who revitalised modern biography. **M. H.**

'THE BLOOMSBURY GROUP', BY J. K. JOHNSTONE (SECKER AND WARBURG, 1954); 'LYTTON STRACHEY', BY MICHAEL HOLROYD, 2 VOLS. (HEINEMANN, 1967-1968).

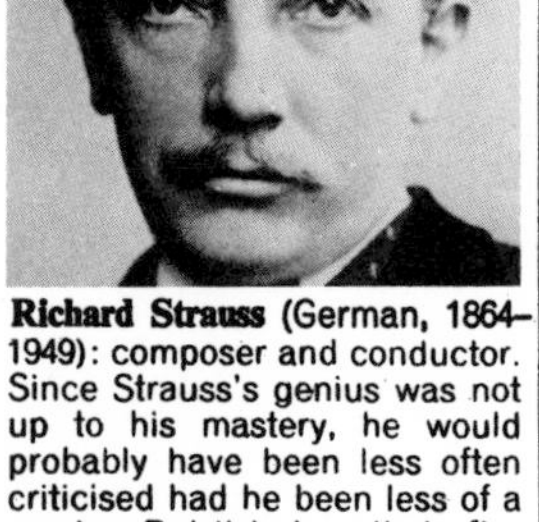

Richard Strauss (German, 1864–1949): composer and conductor. Since Strauss's genius was not up to his mastery, he would probably have been less often criticised had he been less of a master. But it is true that after the stunningly novel achievements of the symphonic poems *Don Juan* (1888) and *Till Eulenspiegels lustige Streiche* (1894–5), or the operas *Salome* (1904–5) and *Elektra* (1906–8), Strauss renounced any temptation further to contribute to the 20th-century revolution. This is not to denigrate masterpieces like *Der Rosenkavalier* – which, however, by now feels like a 19th-century classic. It is, in fact, 20th-century composers rather than audiences that are hard on Strauss's mellifluous textures: where he blends and fills in, they contrast and weed out. Even Schoenberg (q.v.), who is sometimes thought to have been influenced by him, had come to the conclusion by 1914 that what he had learnt from Strauss he had misunderstood. Where our century has pursued truth, Strauss decided to chase beauty – and very successfully so, until the end: the four orchestral songs of 1948 are held in deep and general esteem, even though many musicians think them half a century out of date; but then, so is half of our century's population, anyway. **H. K.**

'RICHARD STRAUSS: A CRITICAL COMMENTARY ON HIS LIFE AND WORKS', BY NORMAN DEL MAR, 2 VOLS. (BARRIE AND ROCKLIFF, 1962-1969).

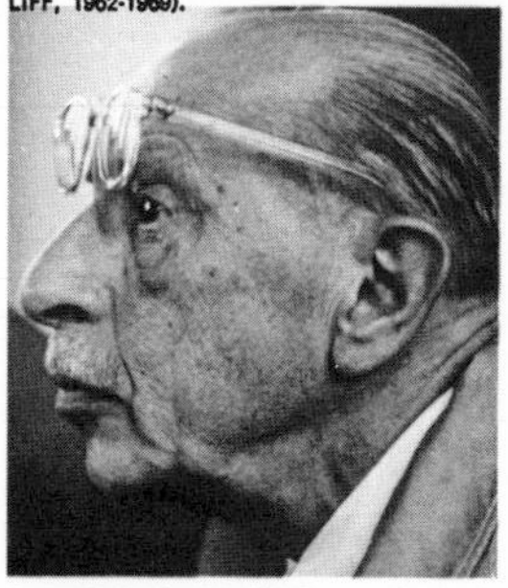

Igor Stravinsky (U.S., ex-French, ex-Russian, 1882–1971): composer. The most persistently influential composer this century, he learned from his father (a renowned operatic bass in St Petersburg) and from Rimsky-Korsakov, but mainly from his own never-satisfied ears. Stravinsky rocketed to fame with the blazing colour and vitality of his scores for the Diaghilev (q.v.) Ballet, of which the last (*Rite of Spring*, 1913) also sealed his reputation as an incorrigible modernist. Expatriate from Russia after the Revolution, Stravinsky lived in France and Switzerland before finally settling (1945) in California. His transition from vivid nationalism to the outwardly nonchalant neo-classicism of his mid-career disconcerted those who had learned to love the ballets. Later, those who discerned a musical passion at work amid the dry textures of works like the *Symphony in C* (1940) or the apparent stylistic mockery of *The Rake's Progress* (1951), were disquieted to find the ever-exploratory septuagenarian quarrying Webern's (q.v.) serialism with a calculating zeal (e.g. *Movements for Piano and Orchestra*, 1959) apparently quite unspontaneous. But however enigmatic Stravinsky may have been artistically, the creative excitement he engendered is unparalleled in modern music. **S. C. V. D.**

'EXPOSITIONS AND DEVELOPMENTS', BY I. STRAVINSKY, WITH R. CRAFT (FABER, 1962); 'DIALOGUES AND A DIARY', BY I. STRAVINSKY, WITH R. CRAFT (FABER, 1968); 'STRAVINSKY', BY E. W. WHITE (FABER, 1966); 'STRAVINSKY', BY ROMAN VLAD (O.U.P., 1960).

Gustav Stresemann (German, 1878–1929): statesman. Foreign minister of the German Republic from 1923 to 1929, Stresemann believed that Germany must fulfil the terms of the Versailles Treaty. He hoped to restore Germany's world position by German good conduct abroad. This policy meant tacit acceptance of the 'guilt clause' and provoked wild opposition in German nationalist circles. He was no dreamy idealist. From 1902 to 1918, as the General Secretary of the Union of Saxon Industrialists, he had belonged to the very groups which now howled for his scalp. Defeat, revolution, inflation and civil war gradually transformed him into a moderate, if not enthusiastic, republican. In 1919 he formed the

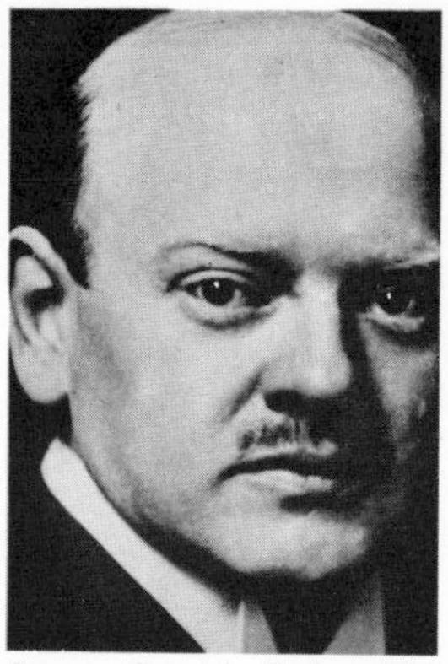

German People's Party, which he led through the 1920s by sheer force of personality. After a brief period as Chancellor, he became foreign minister and so outstanding a statesman that he survived from one unstable cabinet to the next, because there was no-one to replace him. He died three weeks before the market crash of 1929 put an end to the golden years of the Weimar Republic. **J. St.**

'A HISTORY OF THE WEIMAR REPUBLIC,' 2 VOLS. BY ERICH EYCK (WILEY, 1968); 'STRESEMANN AND THE POLITICS OF THE WEIMAR REPUBLIC', BY H. A. TURNER (PRINCETON U.P., 1963).

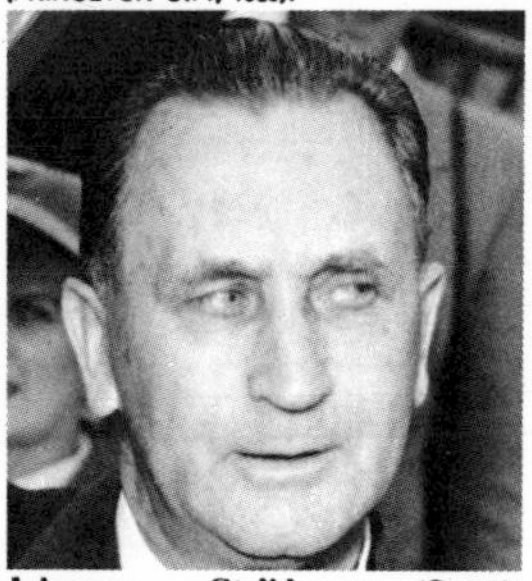

Johannes Strijdom (South African, 1893–1958): politician. A Transvaal Nationalist Leader, who succeeded Dr Malan (q.v.) as Prime Minister in 1954, Strijdom is chiefly known for his blunt defence of *baasskap* (domination) as the leading principle of *apartheid*: "The only way the European can maintain supremacy is by domination." His importance stems from this stark frankness. As the leader in the Senate of the Nationalist Party he was a foremost advocate of the Bantustan policy. He served as an essential transitional Afrikaner-nationalist leader between Malan and the urbane, confident, unyielding Verwoerd. **K. K.**

Erich von Stroheim (German, 1885–1957): actor and film director. Stroheim was one of the great non-conformists of the cinema, who paid the penalty of scorning the studio system. Born in Austria, the son of a Prussian-born Jew, he played a bit part in D. W. Griffith's (q.v.) *Birth of a Nation*, and subsequently persuaded Carl Laemmle, head of Universal Studios, to employ him as star and director of his own script, *Blind Husbands*. It was a box-office success and established him as a mordant observer of society, with a cynical eye for sexual foibles. His shooting methods were eccentric, leisurely and expensive. In his passion for realism he dressed actors playing Austrian soldiers in authentic uniforms imported from Vienna, and drilled them for days until they were parade-ground smart. Once, it was said, he kept three hundred people waiting on a set for three days while trying to induce a dog to sneeze. He fell foul of Irving Thalberg, one of the industry's new creative book-keepers, and as a result, his greatest film,

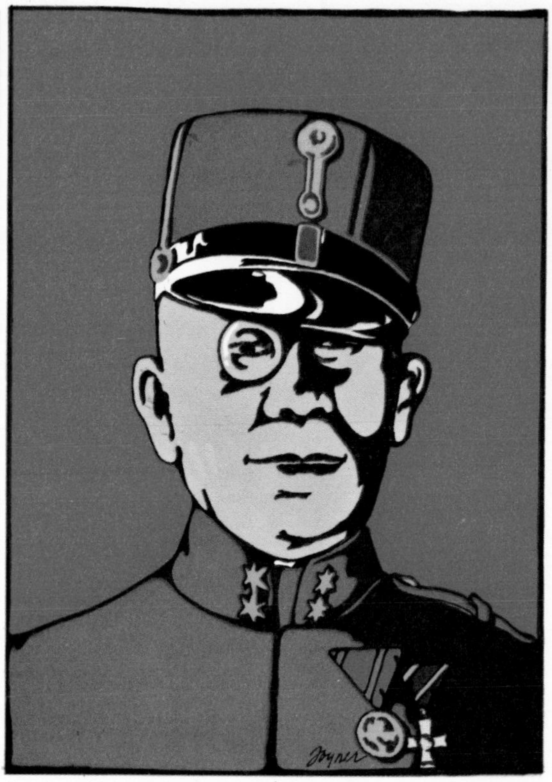

ERICH VON STROHEIM BY JERRY JOYNER

Greed – which ran ten hours in the original version, and had taken two years to make – was cut and mutilated, to be written off on the studio books as a tax loss. The surplus negative was burned, said Stroheim, to reclaim forty-three cents' worth of silver. As an actor he specialised in playing sabre-scarred Prussian officers (most notably in Renoir's [q.v.] *La Grande Illusion*) and was commonly billed as 'the man you love to hate'. In 1950, seven years before his death, he played his best Hollywood role, almost a self-portrait, as a one-time great director turned butler to an ageing movie queen, in Billy Wilder's *Sunset Boulevard*. Its irony was perfect. Its contempt for the system which allowed its finest talents to rot was absolute. **P. O.**

'HOLLYWOOD SCAPEGOAT', BY PETER NOBLE (FORTUNE PRESS, 1950).

Preston Sturges (U.S., 1898–1959): film writer and director. A rare bird of the American screen, this brilliant, volatile comedy writer-director of the 1940s gave the impression of putting only a fraction of his life into his films. Preston Sturges's mother, a friend of Isadora Duncan (q.v.), sent him to school in Chicago wearing a Greek tunic, and when he was 16 left him in charge of the Deauville branch of her cosmetics business, the Maison

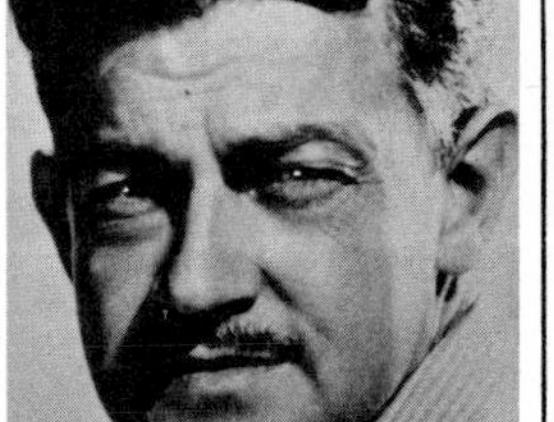

Desti. Here he is said to have devised a kiss-proof lipstick, the beginning of a career of insatiable, playful and practical inventions, which also included a library filing system and a vertical take-off technique. He was a playwright and screen-writer before he took up film direction in 1940. Sturges's best films (*The Miracle of Morgan's Creek*, *Palm Beach Story*, *Hail the Conquering Hero*, *Sullivan's Travels*) are unique in their combination of speed, chaos, wayward literacy and optimistic and distracted imposture. A typical Sturges situation: the Hollywood director setting out in painstaking tramp disguise to lock for Real Life, but first asking the butler to ascertain where hoboes might be expected to board freight trains. Satirist, iconoclast, sleight-of-hand artist, raucous but elegant stylist, Preston Sturges annexed a corner of the American screen for a world of timeless and imperishable absurdity, inhabited by a stock company of spry ancients, shy millionaires, distraught officials and indefatigable small-town gossips. **P. H.**

Sukarno (Indonesian, 1901–1970): politician. The foremost advocate of Indonesian nationalism, Sukarno proclaimed the Republic of Indonesia as its first President on August 17, 1945. Following independence, he occupied a figurehead role but with the breakdown of parliamentary democracy in the 1950s he moved to the centre of the political stage. In 1959, he set his stamp on the Indonesian political scene with the inauguration of the period of Guided Democracy, notable for its symbol-mongering and economic decline. With the abortive

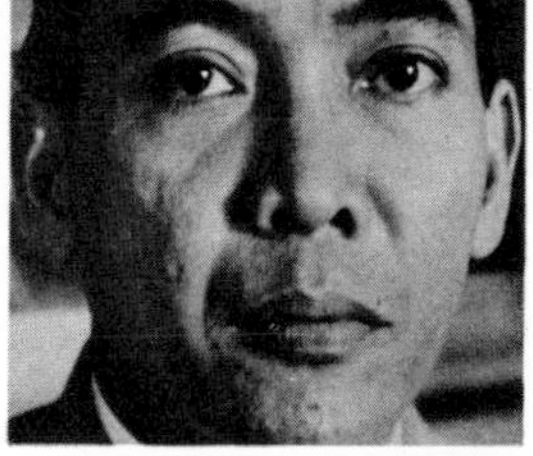

coup of October 1965 the army, under General Suharto, assumed increasing power and in March 1967 Sukarno was eased from office to live in seclusion. The only nationalist figure with an Indonesia-wide appeal, he enjoyed remarkable oratorical powers. He ruled in the style of a Javanese King and sought to provide the heterogeneous

Indonesian people with an ideological anchorage. He favoured an heroic stance to substantive policy making and combined a revolutionary style with a social conservatism. In international affairs he sought pre-eminence for Indonesia behind the slogan of the New Emerging Forces; a two-camp interpretation of world conflict. His political prancing, however, left him with a notoriety one associates with Mussolini (q.v.) rather than with Mazzini. **M. L.**

'SUKARNO, AN AUTOBIOGRAPHY' (BOBBS-MERRILL, N. Y., 1965); 'EIGHT NATION MAKERS', BY WILLARD A. HANNA (MACMILLAN, 1964).

James Batcheller Sumner (U.S., 1887–1955): biochemist. One of the striking attributes of living organisms is the rapidity and precision with which essential chemical reactions are carried out. That this is due to the activity of a group of catalysts named enzymes had been known since the early 19th century, but their chemical structure remained a complete mystery. Willstatter (q.v.) had produced negative evidence that enzymes were not protein (his tests weren't delicate enough) but Sumner wasn't convinced. In 1926 he was extracting the enzyme content of the jack

bean – a rich source of the enzyme called urease. He used various solvents to isolate the different chemical characteristics. Eventually he found crystals had appeared overnight in one of his fractions. He redissolved the crystals in water and found he had highly concentrated urease activity. He could not separate the enzyme activity from the crystals: the crystals were the enzyme. And the crystals were, in fact, shown to be protein. This was the first time an enzyme had been isolated in pure crystalline form and characterised as a protein. But Sumner's work received great opposition, and it was not until John Northrop (q.v.) extended and confirmed Sumner's work that the protein nature of enzymes was accepted.

The immediate result of Sumner's work was to stimulate further research: Northrop and Stanley (q.v.) went on to work in the related fields of viruses and virus deseases. All three shared the 1946 Nobel Prize for Chemistry. **P. G. R.**

Sun Yat-sen (Chinese, 1866–1925): statesman. The decline of the Manchu Empire and the humiliation of its defeat by Japan in 1895 prompted Sun to seek a solution to China's problems beyond the premise of dynastic preservation. In this patriotic effort he had the support of the urban fringe groups, secret societies, and modernised scholars, and through them the newly organised armies, who ushered in the Republic in 1912. As Sun alone could represent his civilian following, he was naturally chosen as the President; but the lack of military power, financial resources and well-organised party reduced him to a helpless on-looker after the failure of China's first democratic experiment. His programme for China, the Three Principles of the People (nationalism, democracy, and people's livelihood), remained nevertheless the most coherent of the time. The Russian Revo-

lution gave him new hopes, and in 1923 Sun made an alliance with Russia, co-operated with the young Chinese Communist Party, reorganised his own party and trained a new army in preparation for another revolution against the despotic warlord regime in Peking. The Chinese on the Asian continent as well as on Formosa admire his struggle for national interests; Western commentators, on the other hand, persistently undervalue him because of his unscrupulous choice of allies and methods and because of the ambiguity of his theory. Yet he more than anyone else helped to spread nationalism among the Chinese and design a plan for its fulfilment. **J. C.**

'SUN YAT-SEN, HIS LIFE AND ITS MEANING', BY LYON SHARMAN (STANFORD U.P., 1968).

Gideon Sundback (U.S., ex-Swedish, 1880–1954): engineer. It was not until 1914 that the zip fastener came on to the market, perfected by a young Swedish engineer, Gideon Sundback. He came straight from designing turbo-generators to the help of the American Automatic Hook & Eye Co., the partners in which had had the idea of a line of such fasteners which could be opened or closed in a single movement. Unfortunately, their 'C-Curity' was found by purchasers embarrassingly unreliable, suddenly springing open or remaining oyster-tight when a quick disengagement was required. Sundback fastened to the edge of a tape "a series of tiny cups". They interlocked, holding each other in place, and the fastener fastened.

But it was not until the First World War that zippers (a later trade-name) came into wide use. A tailor used them for U.S. sailor's money belts, and then they appeared on flying suits and civilian garments. Sundback held the world rights for his invention, apart from the U.S., where Talon Inc. succeeded the original company. A British firm, Lightning Fasteners Ltd., took up the world rights with Sundback as a shareholder. The world output of zips is now over a quarter of a million miles a year. **G. P. G. N.**

Gloria Swanson (U.S., b. 1899): film actress. Throughout the Twenties Gloria Swanson was at once the supreme movie queen and an international ideal of feminine sophistication. More than two decades later, in Billy Wilder's (q.v.) *Sunset Boulevard,* she created the enduring myth and archetype of the one-time silent diva, with her character of Norma Desmond, preserving the Babylonian splendours of a vanished Hollywood. The Norma Desmond myth, potent as it is, has sometimes been too closely identified with the star herself, who in fact survived her film career as a notably sane and healthy woman. At 15 she was an extra; after the First World War and a boisterous spell at Keystone, she was starred by De Mille (q.v.) in his comedies of sophisticated manners and became the ideal wish-dream of post-war womanhood. Her costumes and deportment were everywhere copied as a model of elegance and chic, while her marriage to a European title gave Hollywood new confidence and aspirations. Almost incidentally, it seemed, she was a good actress and a great comedienne. A spell as producer gave her her most distinguished roles (in *Sadie Thompson* and the ill-fated Stroheim [q.v.] *Queen Kelly*), but proved financially disastrous. Despite her gifts as an actress, talking pictures did not comfortably accommodate a creature of her super-human stature; and only in *Sunset Boulevard* has she found an appropriate role since the demise of the silent film to which she contributed so much. **D. R.**

'HOLLYWOOD IN THE TWENTIES', BY DAVID ROBINSON (ZWEMMER-BARNES, 1968); 'THE PARADE'S GONE BY', BY KEVIN BROWNLOW (SECKER AND WARBURG, 1969).

John Millington Synge (Irish, 1871–1909): dramatist. "Go to the Aran Islands. Live there as if you were one of the people themselves." That was Yeats's advice in 1898 to a B.A. second class of Trinity College, Dublin. It led to Synge's plays, a film masterpiece by Flaherty (q.v.), a pilgrimage by Artaud (q.v.),

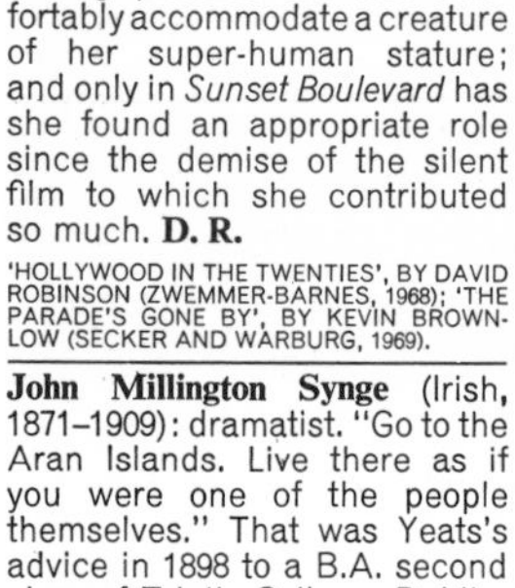

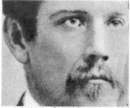

and today's flow of tourists. All sprang from *The Aran Islands* in which Synge described folklore, poverty and stoicism on the Atlantic outpost. He had found his subject and a primitive idiom ready for shaping. Add to this Synge's hard-edged comic attitude to love, death, sex, religion, and you have *The Playboy of the Western World.* This play is now scarcely visible through a fog of imitations, though once it caused riots. As good is *Riders to the Sea* which piles the destructiveness of poverty and the ocean combined on to one island family, with every line and stage direction increasing the weight. To have spanned extremes of experience, the articulate and the dumb, is Synge's achievement. **L. K.**

'J. M. SYNGE AND THE IRISH THEATRE', BY M. BOURGEOIS (BLOM, 1965); 'SYNGE AND THE ANGLO-IRISH DRAMA', BY A. PRICE (METHUEN, 1961).

Albert von Szent-Györgi (U.S., ex-Hungarian, b. 1893): biochemist. Szent-Györgi has made important contributions to three areas of cell chemistry. He was the first to isolate a vitamin, extracting crystals of ascorbic acid (Vitamin C) from paprika. Subsequently he studied respiration at the cellular level: most forms of life obtain energy by oxidising their foodstuffs and

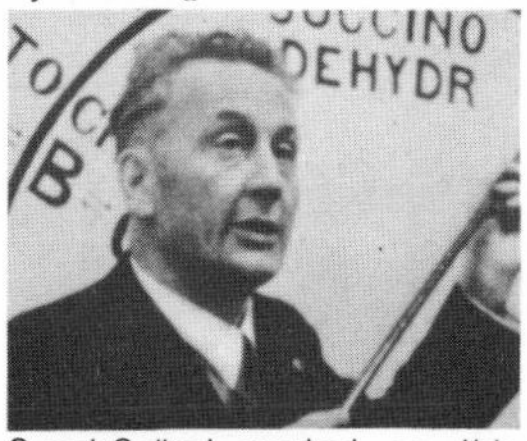

Szent-Györgi worked on this oxidative metabolism, which involves chains of reactions involving complex substances that act to transfer hydrogen. He analysed several steps in what was later discovered – by Krebs (q.v.) – to be the cyclic final pathway for energy extraction from carbohydrates, fats and proteins. Recently he has worked at Woods Hole, in the U.S., on muscle physiology, showing the effect magnesium has on the behaviour of myosin and actin, the functional units of muscle. His most fundamental discoveries, however, have been in respiratory physiology. **J. B. M.**

Joseph Szigeti (U.S., ex-Hungarian, b. 1892): violinist. "In development of our art," Carl Flesch (q.v.) says in his analysis of Szigeti's achievement, "he represents the great outsider, neither member nor – owing to his highly individual style – founder of a school, whose innovating programmes have had a highly stimulating, if not indeed a revolutionary effect." Outsider as a virtuoso (whose

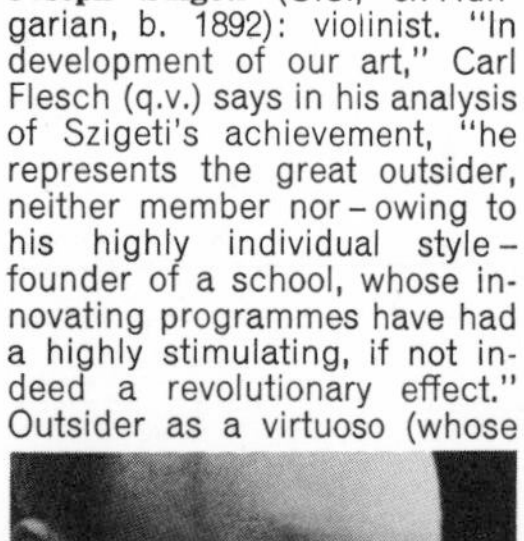

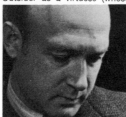

low right upper arm belongs to the 19th century), he is, as a musician, our century's greatest insider amongst great virtuosos: duo partner of Busoni and Bartók (qq.v.) – Bartók's *Rhapsody No. 1* and *Contrasts* are dedicated to him – close friend and collaborator of Stravinsky (q.v.), Bloch, and other outstanding composers, he has done more for contemporary music than any other player of his stature – selflessly so: "I have never commissioned any work for my own exclusive use: I somehow always managed to have my hands full without that." What Flesch calls his occasional "scratchy noises" are part of Szigeti's prophetic 20th-century style: Flesch's essentially 19th-century sound-ideals did not yet include the barbaric. But as early as 1906, Joseph Joachim, perhaps the profoundest musician amongst the last century's violin virtuosos, had predicted a great future for the 14-year-old. **H. K.**

'WITH STRINGS ATTACHED: REMINISCENCES AND REFLECTIONS', BY JOSEPH SZIGETI (CASSELL, 1949); 'THE MEMOIRS OF CARL FLESCH', TRANS. AND ED. HANS KELLER (ROCKLIFF, 1957); 'VIOLINS AND VIOLINISTS', BY FRANZ FARGA, TRANS. EGON LARSEN (BARRIE AND ROCKLIFF, 1969).

Leo Szilard (U.S., ex-Hungarian, 1898–1964): physicist. With Enrico Fermi (q.v.) on December 2, 1942, Szilard achieved the first nuclear chain reaction in the famous 'squash court' plutonium pile. In 1933 he fled from the Nazis to Vienna, then to London where, at St. Bartholomew's Hospital, he started his work in nuclear physics. Between 1935 and 1937 he worked at Oxford, but soon opted for the States. Upon the discovery of nuclear fission in 1939, Szilard, with Einstein (q.v.) and Wigner, approached Roosevelt (q.v.) to urge the U.S. Government to begin work on the atom bomb. At the Metallurgical Laboratory, Chicago, he devised ways to purify the plutonium which made possible the first chain reaction. After this success he remained at Chicago, working towards techniques for the commercial production of plu-

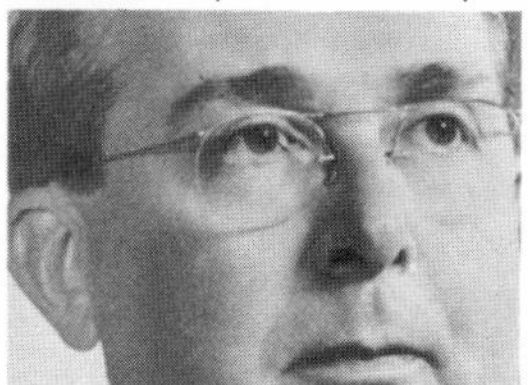

tonium, while Fermi went to work under Oppenheimer (q.v.) at Los Alamos on the atom bomb project which came to grisly fruition at Nagasaki and Hiroshima in 1945. Szilard subsequently became involved in the political aspects of nuclear weapons. He campaigned tirelessly for peace and greater public knowledge about atomic energy and the bomb, and was largely instrumental in forming the Federation of Atomic Scientists devoted to these ends. **P. H. S. S.**

T

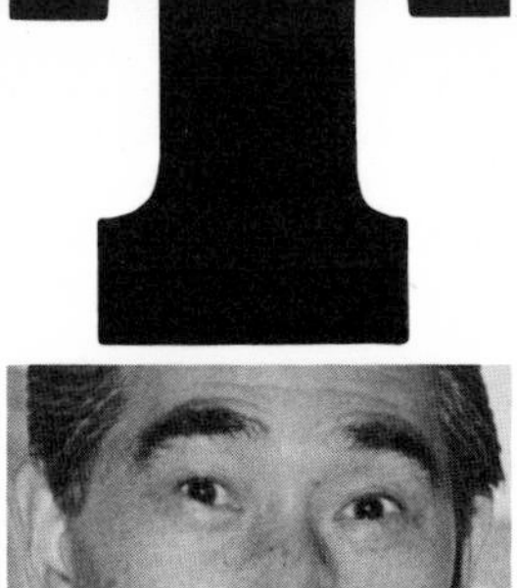

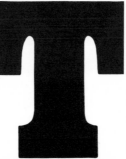

Kenzo Tange (Japanese, b. 1913): architect. Unquestionably the most exciting architect of the Sixties – Japan being at a Victorian stage of unbridled inventiveness and capitalist expansion – Tange combines elements of Brutalism, in the rough concrete manner of Le Corbusier's (q.v.) later works, both with native traditions of monumental log-built temples and with the latest pop fantasies of science fiction. He started quietly enough with the Peace Centre at Hiroshima (1949–56) and Tokyo City Hall (1952–7), but the Kagawa Prefectural Offices (1958) introduced the motif of twinned concrete beams, derived from logs. Decisive monumentality followed with Kurashiki Town Hall (1960–2) and the grandiose suspension-bridge roofs of the Olympic Gymnasia in Tokyo (1963–5). Tange is a visionary town planner and he co-ordinated the 1970 Osaka Expo. In the Dentsu flats, Tokyo (1965–7), he put into practice the Constructivist fantasy of buildings acting as bridges in mid-air; while in the Yamanashi Broadcasting Centre (1965–7) the proliferation of mechanical services was expressed in an array of streamlined Futurist clip-on packages. **N. J. W. T.**

'KENZO TANGE', BY ROBIN BOYD (PRENTICE-HALL, 1962).

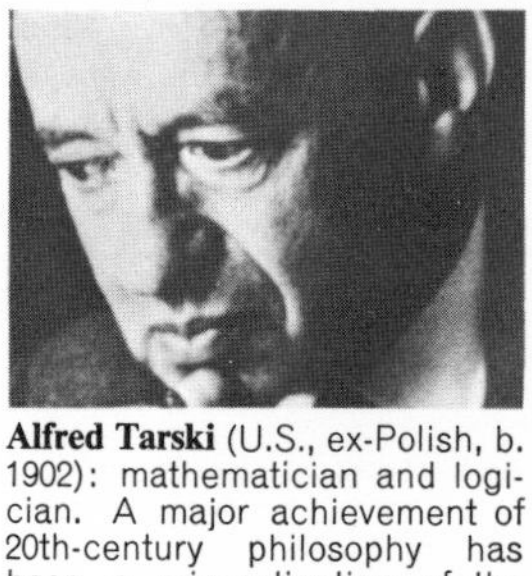

Alfred Tarski (U.S., ex-Polish, b. 1902): mathematician and logician. A major achievement of 20th-century philosophy has been a reinvestigation of the nature of logic and the construction of rigorous systems that resemble mathematics in their economy. Tarski is one of the founders, and probably the major developer, of the particular branch called metamathematics which investigates formal theories. His most important achievement was establishing the semantic method, a technique for investigating the relations between expressions and the objects they denote. This in turn led him to a valuable understanding of what was implied by logical consequence and, most importantly, to a definition of truth. Much of his work was in decision theory and he was extremely successful in demonstrating a way of deciding which kinds of sentences could be proved. **W. A. O.**

'LOGIC, SEMANTICS, METAMATHEMATICS,' BY A. TARSKI (O.U.P., 1956); 'A DECISION METHOD FOR ELEMENTARY ALGEBRA AND GEOMETRY', BY A. TARSKI (SANTA MONICA, CALIFORNIA, 1948).

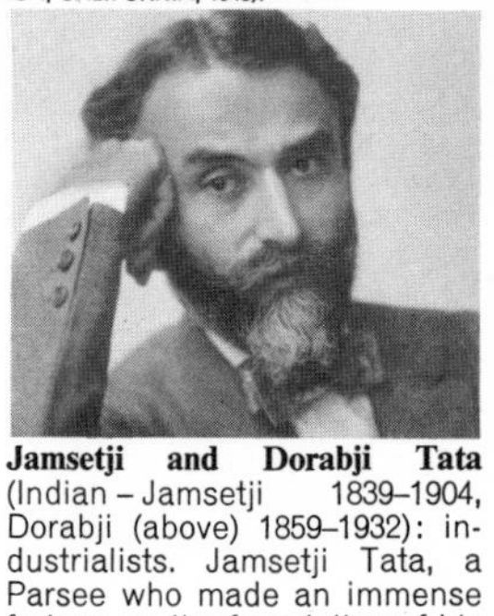

Jamsetji and Dorabji Tata (Indian – Jamsetji 1839–1904, Dorabji (above) 1859–1932): industrialists. Jamsetji Tata, a Parsee who made an immense fortune on the foundation of his Bombay cotton mills, was the visionary who saw that an independent India would have to be economically strong. His son Dorabji went out into the jungles of Orissa and the mountains of the Western Ghats to make the dream come true. In 1903, in face of virtually total scepticism from the British authorities and his fellow Indians, he found a hill of almost solid (65 per cent.) iron ore near Nagpur, raised £1.45 million of capital on the Indian market, and finally built a steel town employing nearly 70,000 men. Just before his death the Tata enterprises provided jobs for over 250,000 Indians; they were a vital adjunct to the work of Gandhi and Nehru (qq.v.). **P. W.**

Edward Tatum (U.S., b. 1909): biochemist and geneticist. Tatum shared the 1958 Nobel Prize for the discovery that genes regulate certain definite chemical processes. In working out how far we are controlled by hereditary factors, Tatum and his colleagues, Beadle and

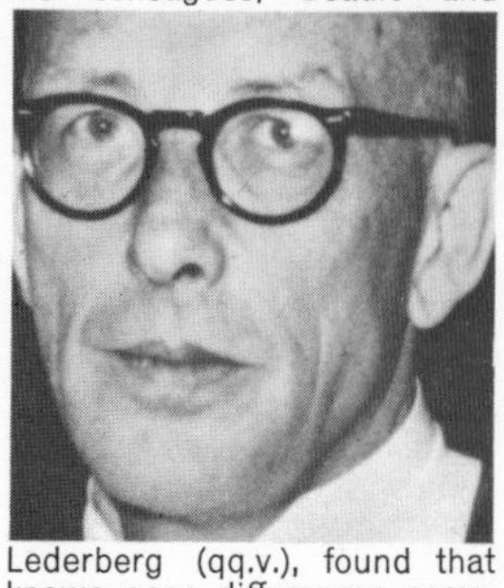

Lederberg (qq.v.), found that known gene differences correlated exactly with the cell's ability to perform primary chemical reactions, like those involved in growth. By systematically adjusting the diet of mutant strains of bacteria the exact nature of their growth requirements could be found, and the final cross-breeding with the original strain showed that this was dependent on mutation in single genes. Tatum concluded that each gene controls the production, function and specificity of particular enzymes, and hinted that every biochemical reaction is theoretically alterable by gene mutation. The most significant impact of his work lay in showing that inherited abnormalities resulting from disturbance of metabolic processes may be treated by a supplemental diet. This gives new hope for mentally or otherwise defective children, and points towards a new world in which genetic manipulation becomes possible. **P. G. R.**

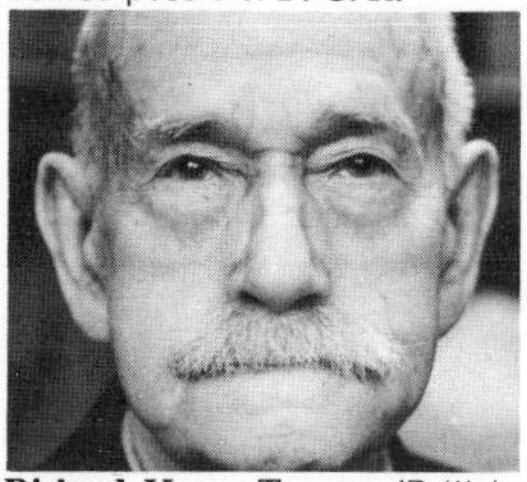

Richard Henry Tawney (British, 1880–1962); historian. R. H. Tawney, 'apostle of equality', became Professor of Economic History at the London School of Economics at 50, in the same year that his book *Equality* appeared. Two other books he wrote influenced not only historians but a far wider public. *The Acquisitive Society* (1921) was in the tradition of Carlyle, Ruskin and Morris; *Religion and the Rise of Capitalism* (1926) was a distinctively English contribution to an international controversy about the origins of the value system of the modern world. Tawney was never in doubt concerning his own values. He objected fiercely to "private ownership divorced from work"; treated education as a right to which everyone was entitled; and demanded that the political programmes of the Labour Party should be imbued with moral sense and social purpose. His style was more distinctive than his message – rich, complex, abounding in compelling imagery; his humility was respected by all who knew him. His influence outlives his scholarship: he stands with Cole and Laski as a formative intellectual influence on the British Labour movement. **A. B.**

'R. H. TAWNEY: A PORTRAIT BY SEVERAL HANDS', ED. J. R. WILLIAMS (SHENVAL PRESS, 1960); 'THE ATTACK', BY R. H. TAWNEY (ALLEN AND UNWIN, 1953).

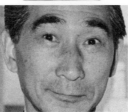

MODEL OF ELIZABETH TAYLOR BY SASKIA DE BOER; PHOTOGRAPH BY DAVID MONTGOMERY

Elizabeth Taylor (British, ex-U.S., b. 1932): film actress. Beautiful, capricious, endowed with qualities sometimes clouded in her much publicised career – five marriages, three divorces and a million dollars for playing Cleopatra in the age of the Common Man she is defiantly a star in the grand manner. Born in England of American parents, who in 1939 moved to California, she played her first part of any note in one of MGM's doggie films, *Lassie Come Home*, and soon afterwards won a leading role in *National Velvet*. The temperament of a true actress began to show itself in her performance as the society girl in *A Place in the Sun* (a version of Dreiser's *An American Tragedy*); she was still in her early twenties when in *Giant* she played for the same director a role ranging from girlhood to middle age. Two Tennessee Williams films, *Cat on a Hot Tin Roof* and *Suddenly, Last Summer*, displayed her exceptional sensibility in the portrayal of nervous tension; but it was a performance in an inferior piece, *Butterfield 8*, which won her an Oscar. *Cleopatra* did not enhance her reputation; however, in *Who's Afraid of Virginia Woolf?* she played, opposite her fifth husband Richard Burton, with savage brilliance. Her appearances under Joseph Losey's direction (*Boom!* and *Secret Ceremony*) have brought further evidence that it is possible to be paid a million dollars for a film and still be an actress as well as a star. **D. P.**

'ELIZABETH TAYLOR: AN INFORMAL MEMOIR', BY ELIZABETH TAYLOR (HARPER AND ROW, N.Y., 1964).

Pierre Teilhard de Chardin (French, 1881–1955): theologian. The most eloquent Christian visionary of the age of science. All matter seemed to him like wood about to flame up into glory, all life a prologue to the finale already foreshadowed in the triumphant humanity of Jesus Christ. Educated by, and immediately recruited into, the Jesuit order, he was equally devout before the presence of God in the countryside and in science. Even experience of war and exile did not really disturb his cosmic optimism. Exile came because he specialised in the study of the early origins of man, and in 1926 the Jesuits found it prudent to send him to China for research, forbidding him to publish his theological speculations. He continued to do respected scientific work and to write a prose-poetry all his own. Published after his death in New York, his books won immense popularity in the France where he had not been allowed to teach. Sir Julian Huxley (q.v.) commended *The Phenomenon of Man* for its panorama of evolution. This and other writings have won devotees in English; for Teilhard held God's creation and man's progress together in a picture of a universe evolving towards perfection. **D. L. E.**

'TEILHARD DE CHARDIN,' BY BERNARD TOWERS (LUTTERWORTH PRESS, 1966); 'TEILHARD DE CHARDIN', BY ROBERT SPEAIGHT (COLLINS, 1967).

Edward Teller (U.S., ex-Hungarian, b. 1908): physicist. Although he was one of the prominent physicists associated with the manufacture of the A-bomb, Teller will be remembered for his later association with the much more powerful H-bomb. He was born in Budapest, studied at Leipzig and Göttingen before working in Copenhagen and London, and in 1935 went to the U.S. to continue theoretical studies on nuclear, atomic and molecular physics. During the war years he worked on the atomic bomb with Fermi (q.v.) at Columbia and Chicago Universities and subsequently with Oppenheimer (q.v.) at California University and the Los Alamos Laboratory. Between 1949 and 1951 he carried out theoretical work with the U.S. team which established the possibility of making the hydrogen bomb, based on the energy released by the fusion of light atomic nuclei, in contrast to the fission bomb in which heavy nuclei split apart. He has been director of the U.S. Atomic Energy Commission's Lawrence Radiation Laboratory, and its Livermore Radiation Laboratory. With Fermi and others in the 1950s he developed the theory of controlled nuclear fusion. And he initiated the study of atomic explosions for peaceful purposes – the so-called Project Plowshare. Teller came to be recognised as the arch-proponent of the hydrogen bomb, believing that the security of the Western world depended upon stock-piling nuclear weapons. **P. H. S. S.**

'BRIGHTER THAN A THOUSAND SUNS', BY ROBERT JUNGK (GOLLANCZ, 1958); 'THE RELUCTANT REVOLUTIONARY', BY E. TELLER (UNIVERSITY OF MISSOURI PRESS, 1964).

Shirley Temple (U.S., b. 1928): film actress. Shirley Temple was, without doubt, the greatest child star in the history of Hollywood. Her vogue lasted from 1934 until 1939 with films such as *Dimples, Rebecca of Sunnybrook Farm, Curly Top, Poor Little Rich Girl* and Kipling's *Wee Willie Winkie* – whom the studio changed to a girl so that their star could play the part. Graham Greene's review of the film in the magazine *Night and Day* brought an action for libel ("a gross outrage", adjudged Lord Stewart) which resulted in damages of £2000. It was a popular decision. Everyone loved Shirley. Her professionalism was total. At six she won an Oscar as the most outstanding personality of the year, and her song *On the Good Ship Lollipop* became better known than the *Internationale*. As an adult she appeared unmemorably in several films, and hosted a television series. She divorced her first husband, John Agar; she is now married to businessman Charles Black, and is active on the Right wing of Republican politics. Her worst review appeared in *Pravda* when she announced her intention to stand as a Republican candidate. The former child star, said the Russian reporter, had "decided to sit at the controls of the militarist bombers", and her public pronouncements amounted to a "fearful hawk-like screaming". Nobody sued. **P. O.**

SHIRLEY TEMPLE BY BARRY ZAID/PUSH-PIN

Archbishop William Temple (British, 1881–1944): religious leader. Born to the purple, Temple was ordained only after a period of suspense and doubt. While still a layman he formed lasting interests in educational and social work, but a Canonry of Westminster, after a brief headmastership, brought him into the central counsels of the Anglican Church. He became prominent among those who called for a degree of autonomy for the Church of England, and contributed substantially to a new statement of her doctrine. As Bishop of Manchester (1921–29) and later as Archbishop of York (1929–42) he became increasingly respected in national life, especially through his vigorous concern with social, economic and international questions, while remaining independent of party. He was a strong supporter of the Ecumenical Movement and although his short period as Archbishop of Canterbury was overshadowed by war and his own ill-health, Temple was tireless in the search for Christian principles with which to guide the post-war world. Trained as a philosopher, Temple developed into an independent thinker, but it was as a prophet, a man of God and an enlightened bishop that he won and held the affection of the English people. **R. M. H.**

'WILLIAM TEMPLE, ARCHBISHOP OF CANTERBURY, HIS LIFE AND LETTERS' BY F. A. IREMONGER (O.U.P. 1948).

William Templeman (British, 1911–1970): agricultural scientist. Templeman joined ICI's Jealott's Hill Research Station at Bracknell, Berks., in 1933, to study recently discovered plant growth regulators ('plant hormones'). While experimenting to see whether these substances could increase crop yields, he noticed the selective weedkilling action

of a man-made one – alpha naphthyl acetic acid. Weak doses applied to oats sown with yellow charlock killed the weeds without harming the oats. He made a systematic search for cheaper synthetic chemicals with the same selectivity, in collaboration with an ICI colleague, Dr W. A. Sexton, and was rewarded by the discovery of two particularly effective ones: MCPA (1941) and 2,4-D (1942). Further research, jointly with the Rothamsted Experimental Station, followed. Its practical value was confirmed in a crash programme of field trials throughout Britain in 1945. MCPA was introduced commercially by ICI in 1946, and 2,4-D was developed independently in the U.S. following similar researches there. Herbicidal chemicals are now available for virtually any weed/crop situation. **S. L.**

Valentina Tereshkova (Russian, b. 1937): cosmonaut. The first (and so far the only) woman to go into space punctured the myth that space travellers need to be strapping ex-fighter pilots. When Yuri Gagarin (q.v.) made the first manned flight in 1961, Valentina Tereshkova was an enthusiastic member of the Young Communist League working in a textile mill at her home town of Yaroslovl. Her only experience of the air had been parachuting with the local club. After Gagarin's flight, Valentina applied for cosmonaut training, and spent most of 1962 in preparation for her flight. Finally she was launched in her Vostok spacecraft in June 1963, two days after Valery Bykovsky had gone into orbit in a similar capsule. "This is Seagull," she reported; "I feel fine and cheerful. I see the horizon, a pale blue, blue stripe. It's the Earth. How beautiful it is." Valentina stayed up for 48 orbits, then landed on June 19. Later in the year, she was married to Andrian Nikolayev, another cosmonaut, and in 1964 she had a daughter. **N. J. M. H.**

Luisa Tetrazzini (Italian, 1871–1940): singer. Probably the most brilliant coloratura soprano of the century, Tetrazzini first appeared in 1890 in Florence, her native city. But her world fame dates from a foggy Saturday night at Covent Garden in 1907, when an audience with no particular expectations recognised an unmistakable star. Tetrazzini's success was due to qualities well attested by her many records: a rounded beauty of tone and an unsurpassed flexibility and brilliance in rapid scales, staccato arpeg-

gios, and all such kinds of florid singing. By the time of her greatest fame, an ample figure and a round, jolly face precluded all notions of dramatic plausibility in such roles as the consumptive Violetta, the fragile Amina (in *La Sonnambula*) or the exotic Lakmé. "This jovial old lady, with her still undefeated vocal technique" made concert appearances as late as 1934, but her last years were clouded by an unwise marriage and the threat of poverty. **D. S.-T.**

'MY LIFE OF SONG', BY LUISA TETRAZZINI (CASSELL, 1921).

Dylan Thomas (British, 1914–1953): poet. A highly-gifted Welshman, the self-styled "Rimbaud of Cwmdonkin Drive", Thomas achieved greater popularity than any other poet in English since Yeats (q.v.). His first book, *18 Poems* (1934), appeared when he was only 20; much of his best work was written while he was still a young man. He played the role of *enfant terrible* in life and, to some extent, on the page – see the stories in *Portrait of the Artist as a Young Dog* (1940) – with a determination that led to excessive drinking, nervous exhaustion and an early death. His popularity thrived on the myths surrounding him. He did much by his public readings to increase his reputation as a writer. His poems, though often obscure and difficult, always sound well. The dense style of his early work associated him with the English Surrealist movement of the 1930s, and attempts an exploration of unconscious feeling on such subjects as birth, sex and death. Later work degenerates into sentiment and rhetoric, as in *Under Milk Wood*, perhaps the most successful radio play ever written. **M. D.**

'THE LIFE OF DYLAN THOMAS', BY CONSTANTINE FITZGIBBON (J. M. DENT, 1965).

Thomson has frequently claimed that his only interest in newspapers is in their balance sheets. Unlike Hearst, Northcliffe or Beaverbrook (qq.v.), Thomson never seems to have thought of newspapers as personal instruments of political and social power but to have found satisfaction in his late-flowering talents as a businessman. He has done more than most to give independent quality journalism a viable commercial framework. **F.-W.**

Maurice Thorez (French, 1900–1964): politician. The most famous of French Communists, Thorez, the son and grandson of miners, went into the pits at the age of 12. After the First World War he became a Socialist and later a Communist. From 1923 he was a full-time party worker, and from 1930 Secretary-General. The French Communists developed a cult for his personality; the Party became the party of

Maurice Thorez. He led it successfully through the period of isolation to the period of co-operation with other parties; his policy was that of the outstretched hand. After the Second World War his contribution to Communism was his rigid loyalty to Stalin (q.v.) and the Soviet Union. It was because the Russians did not want a Communist revolution in France that he sought to come to power by constitutional means. He served in a number of Governments until 1947 and seems to have impressed de Gaulle with his patriotism. After 1947 he was the leader of a Revolutionary Party which had ceased to believe in revolution. He suffered a stroke in 1950, but no-one ever questioned his leadership. He preached loyalty and received it. **D. W. J. J.**

'COMMUNISM AND THE FRENCH INTELLECTUALS, 1914–1960', BY DAVID CAUTE (DEUTSCH, 1964).

cessful responses tend to drop out. The behaviour becomes streamlined and the cat learns to operate the catch immediately. Thorndike's concern with observable behaviour and the use of animal subjects became predominant features of psychology. The connections strengthened were thought to be specific to the task and this specificity in the theory gave it ready application in education where objectives could be defined concretely. **B. R. O.**

'PSYCHOLOGY AND THE SCIENCE OF EDUCATION', BY G. M. JONICH (COLUMBIA U.P., 1962).

James Thurber (U.S., 1894–1961): writer and cartoonist. Encouraged by *The New Yorker's* editor, Harold Ross (q.v.), Thurber became one of the great humorists. Readers in America and Britain built a cult around his world of gentle desperation. As a stylist, concerned with the perfection of the language, he took Henry James as his master. His range included front-line despatches from the war between men and women (*A Couple of Hamburgers* and *The Secret Life of Walter Mitty*), satirical fantasy (*Fables For Our Time*, 1939), surgical reporting (*Soapland*), verbal knockabout (*The Thirteen Clocks*, 1951) and classic situation comedy (*The Night the Bed Fell On Father*). Thurber fought bravely against eventual blindness. He claimed that most editors thought his

economical and intuitive cartoons were drawn "by moonlight or under water". Their usual protagonists are a Thurber man (round-shouldered, bald and twitchy) and a Thurber woman (lank-haired and laser-eyed) watched by a Thurber dog crouching in the background. Captions one-line *mal mots* like: "All right, have it your way – you heard a seal bark", and "Well, I'm disenchanted, too. We're all disenchanted." He shared his mother's gift: "a sure grasp of confusion". The mournful note in his laughter was a reaction to the savagery of the 20th century. **A. Mi.**

BOOKS BY THURBER: 'MY LIFE AND HARD TIMES' (HAMISH HAMILTON, 1950); 'THE YEARS WITH ROSS' (HAMISH HAMILTON, 1959).

Paul Tillich (U.S., ex-German, 1886–1965): theologian. When he was a German army chaplain in the First World War, Tillich witnessed hundreds of deaths, and experienced the death of his liberally optimistic creed. In academic life after the war he set himself both to widen theology's concern for the whole life of society (he was a leader of the Religious Socialist movement) and to deepen theology's basis in philosophy. In 1933 he was forced by the Nazis to begin a second life as a professor in New York. He became prominent only in the 1950s, but then he was one of America's favourite pundits. His books contained some difficult philosophy in the German style, but Tillich

preached his vision of life with power, entranced students, and protested effectively against the triviality of American church talk in the Eisenhower (q.v.) years. In 1963, Bishop John Robinson's paperback *Honest to God* popularised his thought as the best clue to theological reconstruction. **D. L. E.**

'PAUL TILLICH', BY JOHN HEYWOOD THOMAS (LUTTERWORTH/CAREY KINGS-GATE, 1965); 'THE SHAKING OF THE FOUNDATIONS', BY PAUL TILLICH (S.C.M. PRESS, 1949, PELICAN, 1962).

Nikolas Tinbergen (Dutch, b. 1907): zoologist. Tinbergen is best known for his study of the social behaviour of animals in their natural environment. Together with Konrad Lorenz (q.v.), he felt that it was far too simple to explain all animal behaviour in terms of rigid inherited instincts modified by the geographical environment of various individual experiences. He concentrated on the way different species of animals, chiefly birds, react to each other or to other species. A robin, he found, will choose another from its territory at the sight of its red breast alone. In this way he isolated and carefully tested stimulus-response processes which form social behaviour. He added interesting comments on some birds' complicated courtship behaviour, holding that these social displays are the result of dual motivation causing conflict (love/hate, etc.). His studies took him to the Arctic and the African plains, thus promoting the importance of international study. **P. G. R.**

BOOKS BY TINBERGEN: 'A STUDY OF INSTINCT' (O.U.P., 1951); 'SOCIAL BEHAVIOUR IN ANIMALS' (METHUEN, 1953); 'BIRD LIFE' (O.U.P., 1954); 'ANIMAL BEHAVIOUR' (CLARENDON PRESS, OXFORD, 1965).

Alfred von Tirpitz (German, 1849–1930): admiral. For 19 years following his appointment in 1897 as State Secretary of the Imperial Naval Office, Tirpitz dominated the development of German naval power with his impressive battleship construction programmes. He made Germany the second most formidable naval power in the world. Unfortunately, he also provoked a bitter arms race with Britain and helped to isolate Germany in world affairs. Tirpitz brought to his office a developed naval strategy, a complete foreign policy, a commitment to modern technology and management, a flair for politics and the liberal outlook of the comfortable middle class into which he had been born. This unusual combination of attributes made him the most consistently effective political figure in late Wilhelmine Germany. Yet it was not enough. He could never control the mercurial Kaiser (q.v.) nor the conduct of foreign affairs. The quiet

James Henry Thomas (British, 1874–1949): politician. A working man who became Cabinet minister and stamped a distinctive middle-of-the-road image on the modern Labour Party. After his elementary school days Thomas was an errand-boy at the age of nine, and subsequently became an engine-cleaner and engine-driver. As a Cabinet minister – known as Rt. Hon. Dress Shirt – he preserved his exaggerated working-class accent and served as a symbol of working-class aspirations in the 20th century. Not a Socialist, but a strong believer in independent labour representation, his greatest services to the Labour movement were before the First World War when he encouraged reluctant trade unions to put their weight and wealth behind the struggling infant Labour Party. As General Secretary of the National Union of Railwaymen, 1918-24, he held to the moderate course through a period of revolutionary fervour, and after the General Strike (1926) he worked successfully for better employer-worker relations. His affable, conciliatory qualities were useful in steering the Statute of Westminster through Parliament in 1931, but his record as a minister was not otherwise distinguished. His attempts to find orders for shipyards in 1930 were rightly derided as "ships that pass in the night"; Thomas finally resigned after a Budget indiscretion. Personifying the hard-living, non-intellec-

tual 'plain man', J. H. Thomas was a pioneer of the independent, but essentially moderate, Labour Party; his attitudes foreshadowed modern consensus politics. **A. M.**

'J. H. THOMAS: A LIFE FOR UNITY', BY GREGORY BLAXLAND (MULLER, 1964); 'A HISTORY OF THE LABOUR PARTY FROM 1914', BY G. D. H. COLE (ROUTLEDGE, 1948); 'LABOUR AND POLITICS 1900–1906', BY F. BEALEY AND H. PELLING (MACMILLAN, 1958).

Lord Thomson of Fleet (British, ex-Canadian, b. 1894): newspaper publisher. Born in Toronto, the son of a barber, Roy Thomson started work at 14 as a clerk in a coal yard and now owns more newspapers spread across more countries than any other man in the world. He also controls many radio and television stations, a large number of periodicals and important book publishing interests. Thomson was 40 before he developed an interest in communications and then almost by accident: as an unsuccessful dealer in auto-

mobile spares in North Bay, Ontario, he took on an agency for radio sets. He started up a small local radio station on borrowed capital in order to help sales. Over the next 20 years he built up a chain of small local newspapers and radio stations. At 60, when many men are taking things easy, he came to Britain and began his spectacular advance as a newspaper publisher. Purchase of *The Scotsman*, rapidly followed by a contract for Scottish Television which gave him funds for expansion, led to control of the former Kemsley newspaper empire including *The Sunday Times*. In 1966 he added *The Times* to his constantly expanding interests all over the world.

Edward Thorndike (U.S., 1874–1949): psychologist. The ideas of Thorndike dominated American psychology for the first half of the century, arousing the opposition of the Gestalt school – e.g. Kohler (q.v.). Thorndike's theory – Connectionism – is best explained by a typical experiment: a hungry cat is placed in a puzzle box with a catch it can manipulate to escape and get food outside. The cat eventually operates the catch and gets the food. Thorndike's Law of Effect stated that this satisfactory outcome strengthened the connection between the stimulus and the response. The connection is further strengthened over a series of trials, while unsuc-

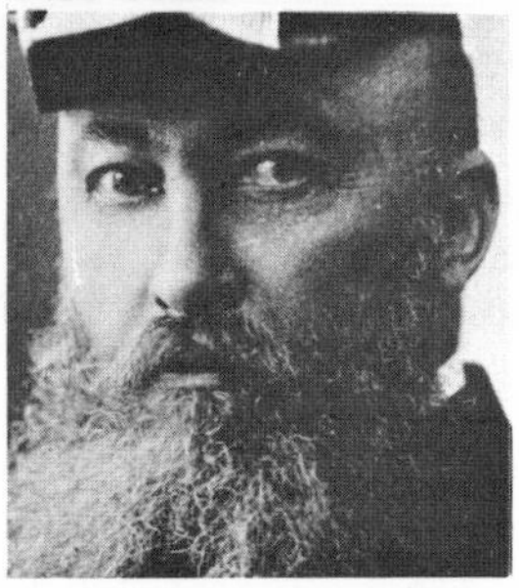

foreign policy on which the peaceful growth of German naval power rested could never be realised, and Tirpitz watched as his fleet became itself the cause of acute international unrest. He fell from office on the issue of submarine warfare, a weapon he had neglected in his pre-war plans. **J. St.**

'TIRPITZ AND THE BIRTH OF THE GERMAN BATTLE FLEET', BY JONATHAN STEINBERG (MACDONALD, 1968); 'GREAT BRITAIN AND THE GERMAN NAVY', BY E. L. WOODWARD (O.U.P., 1935).

Arne Tiselius (Swedish, b. 1902): chemist. Tiselius developed important chemical methods for separating the large molecules which go to make up living organisms. He carried out most of his researches at Uppsala University. In 1930 he succeeded in separating protein molecules by the so-called 'moving boundary' method of electrophoresis. Others had tried to separate large molecules in solutions by applying a voltage to persuade them to move at differing rates dependent upon their sizes. But it was Tiselius who discovered the exact conditions under which the method would work, and who evolved the optical techniques necessary to measure the effect. He used the technique in 1937 to separate the proteins in blood serum for the first time. Electrophoresis, now widely used in biochemical research, is a gentle method of separating compounds which differ only slightly in chemical composition. In 1940, Tiselius began work on another biochemical separa-

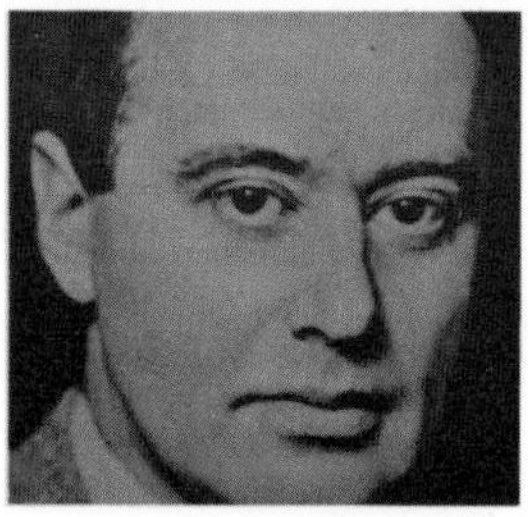

tion technique of far-reaching significance – chromatography, in which the big molecules are separated by absorbing them selectively on a column of suitable material (blotting paper in the simplest case). He received the Nobel Prize for Chemistry in 1948, and in 1965 he was appointed to the chairmanship of the Nobel Committee for Chemistry. Tiselius provided two of the key weapons in the modern biochemist's armoury. **P. H. S. S.**

Josip Broz Tito (Yugoslav, b. 1892): statesman. A professional Communist and official of the Comintern before the Second World War, Tito became a national hero through his leadership of the armed resistance to the German occupation. By 1943 he had organised an army 300,000 strong and exercised effective control over considerable areas of Yugoslavia, although he had received no material help from the Russians and was not recognised by the Western Allies. By 1945, 800,000 Partisans were keeping 17 German divisions fully occupied. After the war, as the only Communist leader in Eastern Europe who did not owe his position to Russian influence, Tito's confidence in his popular support enabled him to resist Stalin's (q.v.) attempts to dictate policy to Yugoslavia. Russian efforts to overthrow Tito by subverting party officials, expelling Yugoslavia from the Cominform and applying economic pressure, failed. Tito's subsequent skilful exploitation of his position between East and West to secure economic and even military aid

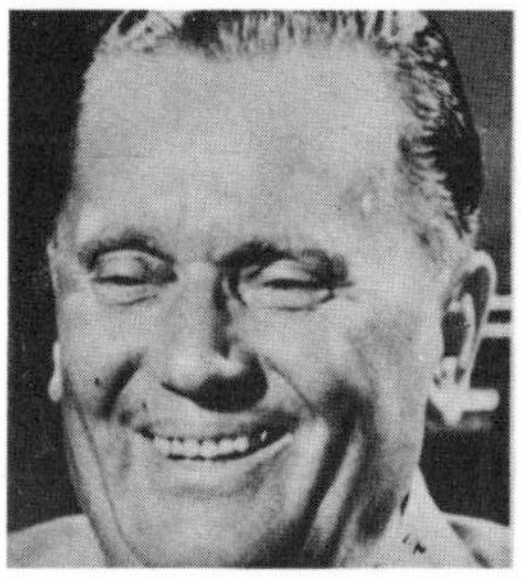

from the United States, without compromising either his party's claim to be Marxist or Yugoslavia's national independence, have enabled him to consolidate a regime which is Communist but free from Russian suzerainty and which thus constitutes, by example, a standing threat to Russian influence on Communist leaders in Eastern Europe. **J. M. K.**

'TITO SPEAKS', BY VLADIMIR DEDIJER (WEIDENFELD AND NICOLSON, 1953); 'DISPUTED BARRICADE: THE LIFE AND TIMES OF JOSIP BROZ TITO, MARSHAL OF YUGOSLAVIA', BY SIR FITZROY MACLEAN (JONATHAN CAPE, 1957).

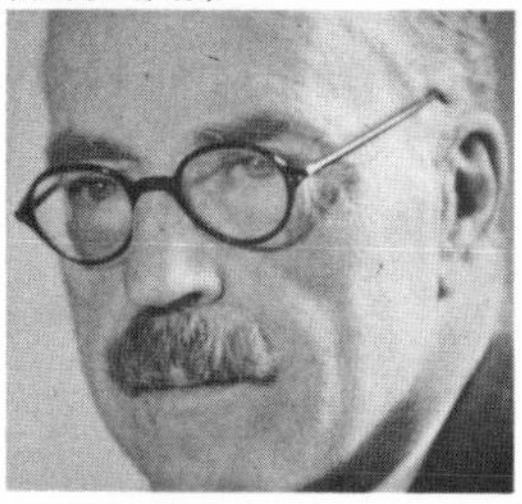

Sir Henry Tizard (British, 1885–1959): scientist. Tizard, an Oxford scientist, joined the Royal Flying Corps in the First World War and was much engaged, as was his friend and later rival, Lindemann, in a variety of flying experiments. After the war, with this first-hand knowledge of flying and airmen, Tizard became, in his own phrase, a "scientist in and out of the Civil Service" and was specially concerned with aeronautical research. In 1935 he became Chairman of the Committee for Scientific Survey of Air Defence. The problem was to devise means of effectively safeguarding the country against future German air attack. The Tizard Committee proposed to adapt Watson-Watt's (q.v.) brilliant invention, later to be known as 'radar', and thus provide British fighters with early warning of approach and location of enemy. A successful demonstration in 1936 was followed by the construction of a radar early warning chain. Tizard was particularly effective in making it suitable to the operation requirements of Fighter Command. Thus, by 1940, Britain possessed the most efficient system of air defence in the world. Credit for its operational effectiveness is due largely to Tizard. Without it, Germany would have had a real chance of winning the Battle of Britain and so the war. **N. F.**

'TIZARD', BY R. W. CLARK (METHUEN, 1965); 'THE PROFESSOR IN TWO WORLDS', BY THE SECOND EARL OF BIRKENHEAD (COLLINS, 1964).

Joe Hin Tjio (U.S., ex-Indonesian, b. 1919): geneticist. Tjio showed in 1956, with Levan in Sweden, that man has 46 chromosomes and not 48, as believed since Painter's work in 1924. Confusion about human chromosomes, years after the structure of DNA had been elucidated, was due to inadequate technique. Tjio applied new methods to a study of cultured cells, and so filled an astonishing gap in man's knowledge of himself. Ford, at Harwell, confirmed the observation. Barr's (q.v.) discovery of sex chromatin focused attention on

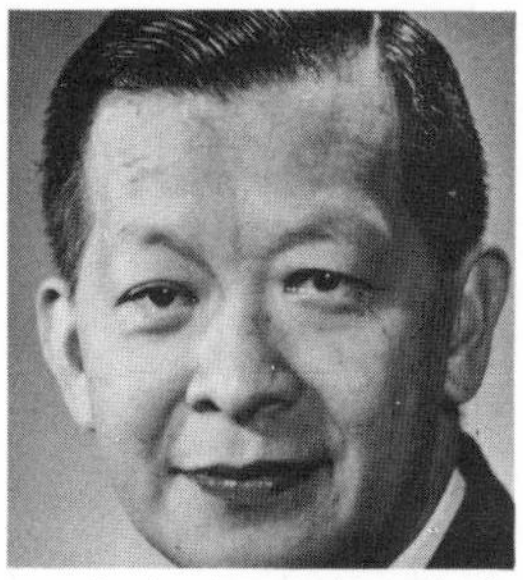

sexual development and, in Edinburgh, Patricia Jacobs found that some infertile males have an extra X chromosome. Lejeune in Paris found an extra chromosome in children with Down's syndrome (more commonly known as mongolism). Advances rapidly followed in fields as diverse as mental retardation, infertility, industrial medicine, malformations, cancer, behaviour and criminology. Tjio, born in Java in 1919 but now a citizen of the U.S., was trained in Indonesia and was interned there by the Japanese. He studied in Denmark and the United States and, while head of cytogenetics in Zaragoza, Spain, spent summers in Sweden. After a period in Colorado, he moved to the National Institutes of Health, Maryland, where he is still working and producing valuable results. **D. G. H.**

'GENETICS IN MEDICINE', BY J. W. THOMSON AND M. W. THOMSON (SAUNDERS, PHILADELPHIA, 1966); 'HUMAN GENETICS', BY V. A. MCKUSICK (PRENTICE HALL, 1964).

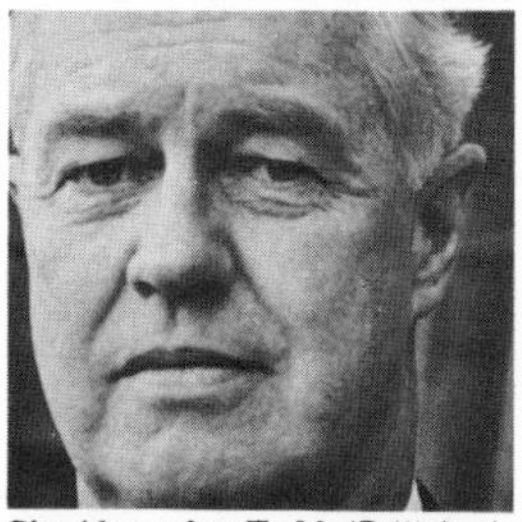

Sir Alexander Todd (British, b. 1907): chemist. Lord Todd has established an international scientific reputation by his work on a range of chemical substances that are of great interest in all living organisms. Among these are enzymes and coenzymes which have an important role in the activity of the cell nucleus, a number of vitamins and other physiologically important materials. In addition to his scientific work, Todd has also taken a prominent part in both national and international scientific affairs, and he has also been Chairman of the Advisory Council on Scientific Policy. His best known work is in the field of the structure of nucleotides – substances intimately connected with genetic inheritance – in establishing a knowledge of their constituents and the ways in which they are arranged. This was vital to knowledge of how DNA works. He was awarded a Nobel Prize in 1957. **P. J. F.**

'NOBEL LECTURES IN CHEMISTRY, 1942–62', (ELSEVIER, LONDON, 1964).

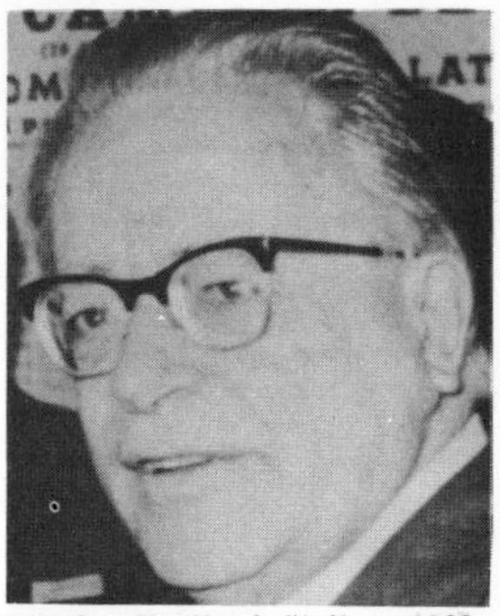

Palmiro Togliatti (Italian, 1893–1964): politician. The most eminent Communist outside Russia and China, Togliatti was also the ablest politician in post-war Italy. A founder member in 1921 of the tiny Italian Communist Party, he ended by attracting the support of one voter in every four. As a loyal Stalinist he escaped successive purges, and in 1935 became Secretary of the Comintern. Later he fought in Spain. Returning to Italy in 1944 he astonished everyone by entering the Government alongside bourgeois conservatives, until expelled from the Cabinet in 1947. The new Italian constitution owed much to his conciliatory attitude towards the Vatican, and he disagreed with Russian practice by insisting that atheist propaganda would merely antagonise other Italians. After 1944 he realistically accepted democratic methods, rejecting violence and hoping to win power by constitutional means. He also advocated 'polycentrism', whereby individual Communist parties would adapt doctrine to suit conditions even though still remaining loyal to the international movement. His posthumously published political testament, the 'Yalta Memorandum', urged Russian Communists to allow more freedom; and, though siding with Russia against China, it also criticised the Russians for not handling Mao (q.v.) with more tact. **D. M. S.**

'UNITY IN DIVERSITY: ITALIAN COMMUNISM AND THE COMMUNIST WORLD,' BY DONALD L. M. BLACKMER (M.I.T. PRESS, 1968).

Hideki Tojo (Japanese, b. 1884–1948): military leader. Lieutenant-General Tojo was prepared to accept the tremendous gamble of fighting the United States rather than make the concessions demanded by Washington as the price for lifting the economic embargo imposed on Japan in July 1941. As Japan's Premier at the time of Pearl Harbour he came to rank with the European dictators in the demonology of

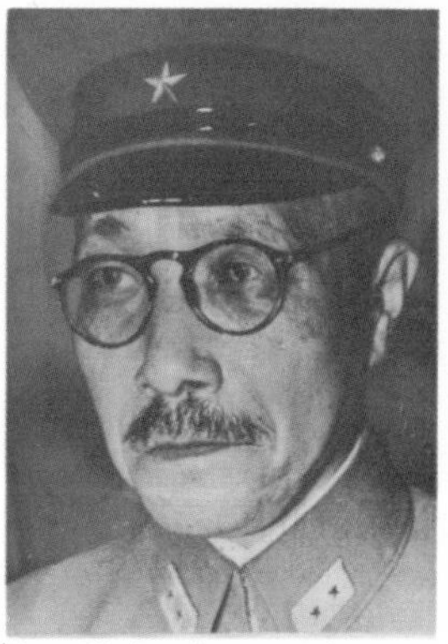

the allied nations; and among the Japanese after the war he was the scapegoat for the ruin brought upon them by the follies of militarist leadership. But although very powerful (he was War Minister as well as Premier) Tojo was never a dictator. He resigned in July 1944, after the Imphal disaster and the loss of Saipan. Summoned to await trial after Japan's surrender as a major war criminal suspect, he tried but failed to kill himself. He redeemed himself in Japanese eyes, to some extent, by his dignified bearing at the International Military Tribunal, when he accepted full responsibility for taking the nation into war, and by showing himself under cross-examination to be at least the intellectual equal of the American chief prosecutor. Sentenced to death, he was executed at Sugamo, Tokyo. **G. R. S.**

'TOJO AND THE COMING OF THE WAR', BY ROBERT J. C. BUTOW (PRINCETON U.P./O.U.P., 1961).

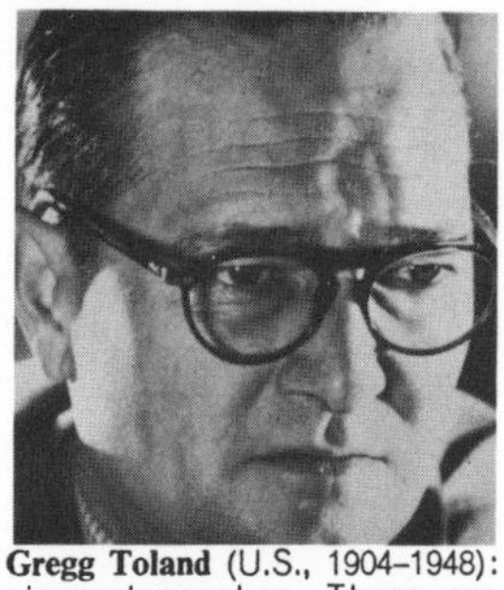

Gregg Toland (U.S., 1904–1948): cinematographer. There are few film cameramen who have taken a recognisable style from film to film. Toland was one of them. He worked from the late 1920s through the 1930s, principally with Sam Goldwyn on movies like *Tugboat Annie, These Three, Dead End* and *The Goldwyn Follies*, culminating in an Oscar for *Wuthering Heights* in 1939. Toland worked most frequently with William Wyler, and Wyler's best films, like *The Best Years of Our Lives*, were those that he photographed. Toland was fascinated by the possibilities of extending the depth of field in movie photography. He used lenses of short focal lengths (wide angles) to keep everything, background as well as foreground, in sharp focus. This tended to free the eye of the spectator within the action, so that he could absorb the image himself rather than be forced into an emotional response by the use of intercut close-ups, particularly in moments of tension. André Bazin called it "one-shot montage": in which the spectator does his own cutting from face to object to setting. This style worked in the realistic *Grapes of Wrath* and in the theatrical *Little Foxes*. And it worked on a scale still unequalled in the cinema in *Citizen Kane:* a total style, ranging from cinéma-vérité documentary to surrealist still-life. **P. Ma.**

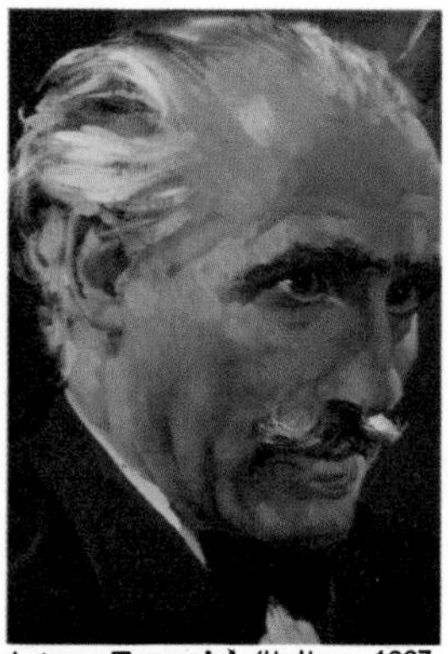

Arturo Toscanini (Italian, 1867–1957): conductor. Toscanini, a native of Parma, was the best-known conductor of the first half of the century. Many considered him to be the greatest. At 19, in Rio de Janeiro, he stepped up to the conductor's desk in an emergency and conducted Verdi's *Aida* from memory. He never looked back. He conducted the first performances of several famous scores: Verdi's *Quattro Pezzi Sacri*, Leoncavallo's *I Pagliacci*, Puccini's *La Bohème* as well as his posthumous *Turandot*. To his native Italy he introduced Wagner's *Götterdämmerung*, *Siegfried* and *Tristan and Isolde*. He became chief conductor at La Scala in Milan in 1898, and of the New York Metropolitan Opera in 1907. In 1928 he became chief conductor of the New York Philharmonic Orchestra, bringing it to Europe in 1930, the occasion of his London debut with them, and in 1936 he directed the NBC Orchestra. He left Italy in 1928 after refusing to conduct the Fascist song *Giovanezza*. He resigned from the Salzburg Festival after the Austrian *Anschluss*. Toscanini was in his 80th year when he returned to Europe for several concerts in which a younger generation was able to experience his prodigious and passionate musicianship. **F. A.**

'THE TOSCANINI LEGACY', BY S. HUGHES (PUTNAM, 1959).

Charles Hard Townes (U.S., b. 1915): physicist. Simultaneously with two Russians, Basov and Prokhorov, Townes invented the maser, a device with which it is possible to produce trains of continuous, ordered, electromagnetic waves, similar to radio waves, but at substantially shorter wavelengths. The physical principle which Townes employed, known as stimulated emission of radiation, has been applied both in the microwave and optical parts of the spectrum, in the latter case giving rise to the celebrated laser. In 1953 he and his co-workers devised the first ammonia maser operating at a wavelength of 1.25 cm. He, and his two Russian counterparts, with whom he shared the Nobel Prize in 1964, were thus the first to realise in practice the important atomic process of stimulated emission anticipated by Einstein (q.v.) in 1917. Since 1964, the maser, and even more particularly the laser, has found enormous and growing applications in the field of communications, for fundamental physics, spectroscopy, sensitive measurements and extremely precise ranging (a laser-ranging device was planted on the Moon by the Apollo 11 astronauts). **P. H. S. S.**

Arnold Toynbee (British, b. 1889): historian. For every thousand persons who have heard of the life-cycle of civilisations, perhaps a hundred have read Somerville's abridgement of *The Study of History*; ten some part of that work's 12 volumes; and one the Chatham House annual *Survey of International Affairs*. Yet the enduring value of Toynbee's work probably runs the other way. His influence as an historian has been small, his impact as systematiser and prophet very great. Twice he rose to the occasion. In the England of the 1930s and in the U.S. and Germany after the war, when his forecasts about the inevitable

TROTSKY BY BURTON SILVERMAN

fates of nations filled a gap left by the decay of religion. However, the effects wore off quite quickly. The great scheme is marred for the scholar by its demonstrable indifference to historical fact, and for the generality by the cloudy religiosity which intruded at the second stage and subverted the argument of the first. Despite the range of vision and the massive learning, patchily gathered from dozens of literatures, the interpreting mind rarely penetrates deeply. Still, for good or ill, Toynbee has left his footprint on the historical thinking of two generations and has taught the West to abandon its self-centred superiority to other civilisations. **G. R. E.**

'COMPARING NOTES', BY ARNOLD AND PHILIP TOYNBEE (WEIDENFELD AND NICOLSON, 1963); 'EXPERIENCES', BY ARNOLD TOYNBEE (O.U.P., 1969).

G. M. Trevelyan (British, 1876–1962): historian. Trevelyan looked like an eagle, talked like a raven, and wrote like a turtledove. He loved Northumberland and George Meredith and should have been a poet. Instead, he spent his life writing an enormous amount of history which was very widely read in the belief that it represented the

real thing. Actually, it fulfilled his ambition to reunite history and literature by sacrificing the essence of the first. His history remained on the surface and practically never asked searching questions. This weakness of intellectual attack especially damaged his most famous and most successful book, his *Eng-lish Social History* (1944). The book sired nothing: when English historians came really to concern themselves with the history of their society, they had to begin by forgetting the smooth sentimentalities of Trevelyan's "history with the politics left out". Trevelyan held the Cambridge Regius chair of history for 13 years without ever having taught anyone before, and his tenure left few marks. Industrious, fluent and kind, interested in all he read, a writer of frequent skill, he possessed an unoriginal mind; and all the rows of volumes cannot disguise his failure to advance historical understanding. However, the pleasure he gave to so many provides a more cheering memorial. **G. R. E.**

'CLIO, A MUSE, AND OTHER ESSAYS', BY G. M. TREVELYAN (LONGMANS, NEW ED. 1930); 'FREEDOM AND THE HISTORIAN', BY OWEN CHADWICK (CAMBRIDGE U.P., 1969).

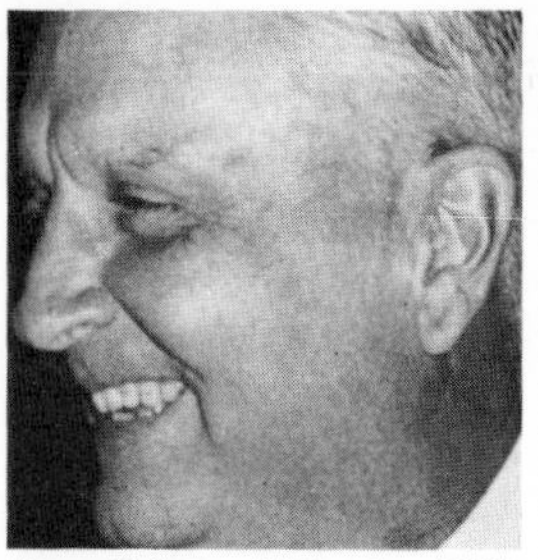

Juan Trippe (U.S., b. 1899): airline chief. Trippe moved into the brand-new aviation industry in 1922 as president of the then tiny Long Island Airways. As air transport boomed, his plans mushroomed, and in 1927 he founded Pan American World Airways. Trippe knew the way his company should go. The story is that he drew a set of pencil lines on the office map, showing the main international routes he intended to go for, and within 10 years they were all realities. Pan Am was never the world's biggest airline under his rule – United, sticking mainly to the domestic U.S. market, has a bigger fleet and flies more route miles – but it led the international pack. Back in 1962 there was a chance that Trippe might really scoop the pool – a merger was all but fixed up between Pan Am and Howard Hughes's (q.v.) Trans-World Airways, but fell through. Meanwhile, however, Trippe acquired from the British property developer Jack Cotton the Pan Am Building over New York's Grand Central Station. The negotiations were typical of the secrecy and toughness which characterise Trippe's management methods: the Pan Am men wore masks at the meetings, and Trippe himself was known throughout the deal only by his code-name, 'The Traveller'. He retired in 1968. **P. W.**

Lev Davidovich Trotsky (Russian, 1879–1940): politician. Trotsky was the first in the line of brilliant, romantic and tragic revolutionaries of this century. Of Jewish origins, he sprang into prominence during the 1905 Revolution as leader of the St Petersburg Soviet. He was the only Russian Marxist who could approach Lenin (q.v.) in both intellectual grasp and leadership. He nonetheless for years opposed him, believing Lenin's concept of party organisation tended to one-man dictatorship. But in the Russia of 1917 Trotsky saw that the Bolsheviks were the only effective revolutionary party and joined them. With Lenin in hiding in Finland, he led the seizure of power; then, as Commissar of War, he created the Red Army and was the chief architect of Soviet victory in the Civil War. But as the emphasis switched to more gradual construction, his impatience with normal administrative processes, his contempt for political manoeuvring and his flamboyant style enabled opponents to make charges of Bonapartist ambitions sound plausible. Although the obvious successor to Lenin, a coalition of his rivals denied him power. In the mid-1920s, Trotsky provoked the most violent debate in Soviet history over Stalin's policy of building Socialism in Russia at the expense of promoting world revolution, and over his own proposals for rapid industrialisation (later adopted by Stalin). Expelled from the Party in 1927 and from the USSR in 1929, he tried in exile to build an international Socialist revolutionary movement opposed to Stalinist Communism (the Fourth International). This attempt failed, but he did create the first clear revolutionary alternative to official Soviet ideology. As such, though politically powerless, Trotsky remained a threat: and finally in exile in Mexico, he was assassinated by a Stalinist agent. **A. Q. D.**

'A HISTORY OF SOVIET RUSSIA', BY E. H. CARR, 10 VOLS. (MACMILLAN, 1950–1969); 'THE PROPHET ARMED', 'THE PROPHET UNARMED', 'THE PROPHET OUTCAST', BY I. DEUTSCHER (O.U.P., 1954, 1959, 1963); 'REVOLUTIONARY SILHOUETTES', BY A. V. LUNACHARSKY (ALLEN LANE, THE PENGUIN PRESS, 1968).

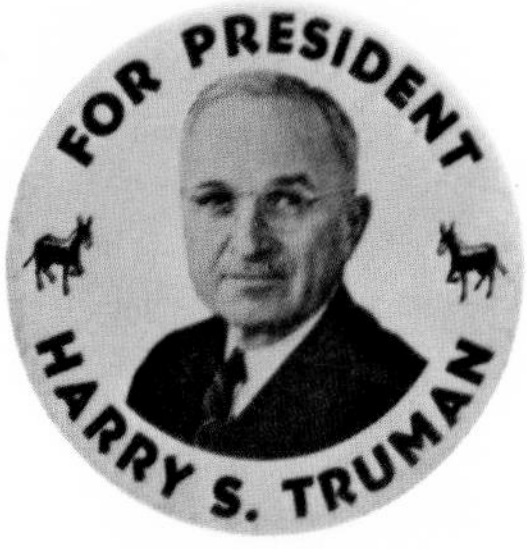

Harry S. Truman (U.S., b. 1884): statesman. President Truman continued and developed the progressive domestic policies of the New Deal and the support given by his predecessor, Franklin D. Roosevelt (q.v.), to democracy in the outside world. A Missouri farm boy, First World War major, failed haberdasher, reader of history, and machine-sponsored politician, United States Senator Harry Truman (the S is only an initial and stands for nothing) was chosen as Vice-Presidential candidate in 1944 as a liberal Democrat with a good Congressional war record. Not much was expected of him when he succeeded to the Presidency on the death of Roosevelt on April 12, 1945. He turned out to be, if not one of the great, at least one of the near-great Presidents. He presided over the readjustment of America from war to peace while continuing the reforms of what he now called the 'Fair Deal'. Against all the odds and virtually unanimous opinion of the newly powerful public-opinion pollsters, he won the Presidential election of 1948. More important, he inaugurated the American policy of the containment of international Communism, in the successive stages of the enunciation of the Truman Doctrine, the formation of Nato and the fighting of the Korean War. **H. C. A.**

'MEMOIRS', BY HARRY S. TRUMAN 2 VOLS. (DOUBLEDAY, N. Y., 1955–56); 'THE MAN FROM MISSOURI', BY ALFRED STEINBERG (PUTNAM, N. Y., 1962).

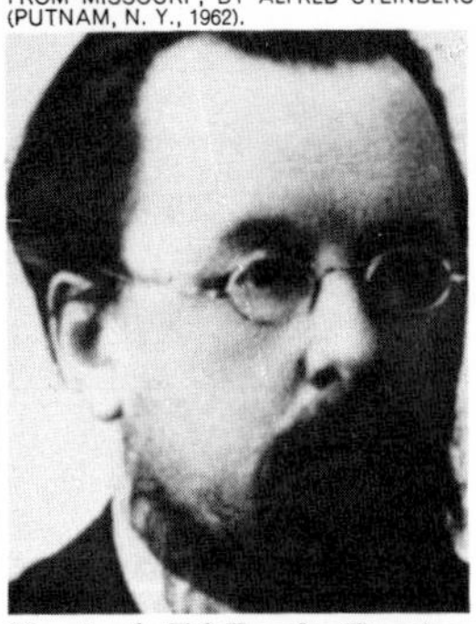

Konstantin Tsiolkovsky (Russian, 1857–1935): physicist. Tsiolkovsky, who is remembered as the father of space travel, was a self-taught physicist of enormous ability before he turned his attention to space. Hampered by conditions in Tsarist Russia and by his own deafness, Tsiolkovsky was unfortunate enough to devise the kinetic theory of gases 10 years too late, unaware of the work of Maxwell. When this was pointed out to him, he observed philosophically that it had been good experience. From 1883, when he first worked out the principle of the rocket in detail, he devoted himself to a remarkably advanced theoretical analysis of space travel. His rockets were to have been propelled by a mixture of liquid hydrogen and liquid oxygen, and he realised that the only way of escaping earth's gravity was by using the multi-stage principle – a single rocket would have needed too much fuel to be practicable. Starved of funds, Tsiolkovsky did no experimental work but this did not inhibit his imagination, and in a series of articles published in 1911 in a Russian magazine he gave a comprehensive survey of the theory of space flight. Later in life, his genius was recognised, and Sputnik 1 was timed to go into orbit on the hundredth anniversary of his birth (it was 29 days late). His tombstone carries the words "Mankind will not remain tied to Earth forever". **N. J. M. H.**

Mikhail Tswett (Russian, 1872–1919): biologist. Tswett laid the foundations of chromatography, whose impact on chemistry several decades later has been compared with that of computers on mathematics. Chromatography allows the separation of minute and sometimes labile amounts of substances: it can serve as a diagnostic and also as a preparative method. It depends on the ability of a surface to absorb different substances more or less strongly. Thus a mixture of compounds dissolved in a suitable carrier will be deposited at different places on a particular phase and components can be individually removed. Tswett discovered this effect in his work on plant pigments which he separated by pouring their solutions

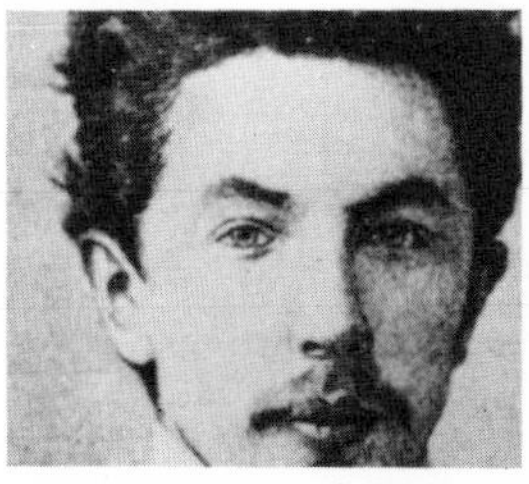

through columns of powdered chalk. Today chromatography has been developed both in the use of materials and the sophistication of its techniques — from the automatic control of factory processes to the details of biochemical research. **P. J. F.**

U

Walter Ulbricht (German and Russian, b. 1893): head of state. Until his ill-health in 1971, Ulbricht had been ruler and virtually dictator of East Germany since it was granted statehood by Russia in 1949. In theory he served at first under two figureheads, Pieck and Grotewohl. In practice, he controlled the political life of the country as Chairman of the mixed Communist-Socialist SED Party (Socialist Unity). He has been responsible for creating a 'People's Socialist' state on the Soviet model, for pursuing Stalinist policies until long after Stalin's death, and for the brutal repression of the East German rising of 1953 and the building of the Berlin Wall in 1961. Up to its building, over three million East Germans had fled to the West. He was a Social Democrat in his early years, became a Communist at the time of the Spanish Civil War after fleeing from Nazi Germany, and carried out the liquidation of anti-Stalinists in Spain. Nicknamed 'Comrade Cell', he became a

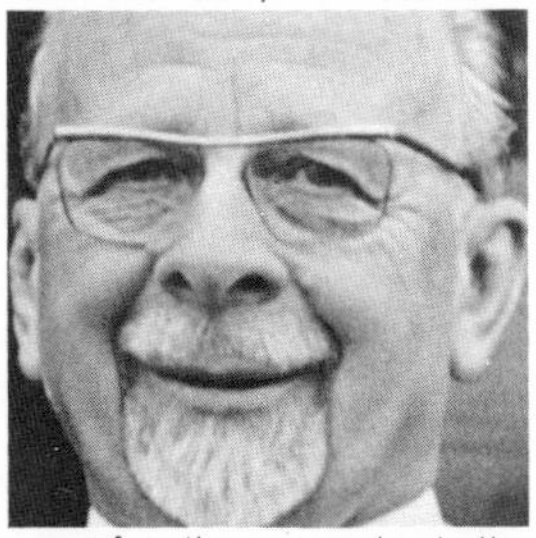

super-functionary and at the same time a brilliant organiser and executor of Communist policies. During the war he was given Soviet citizenship. After the war, he helped found the SED (which he purged on three different occasions), carried out the socialisation of industry and agriculture, repressed all political opposition, persecuted the Christian churches persistently, and built up a powerful East German Army. **T. C. F. P.**

'GERMANY BEYOND THE WALL: PEOPLE, POLITICS AND PROSPERITY', BY JEAN EDWARD SMITH (LITTLE, BROWN, BOSTON 1969); 'WALTER ULBRICHT', BY CAROLA STERN (PALL MALL, 1965); 'PROFILE OF EAST GERMANY', BY ALEX HORNSBY (COLLETTS, 1966).

Ullstein Brothers (German): publishers. The five sons of Leopold Ullstein (d. 1899) developed the publishing house he founded until it became the largest pri-

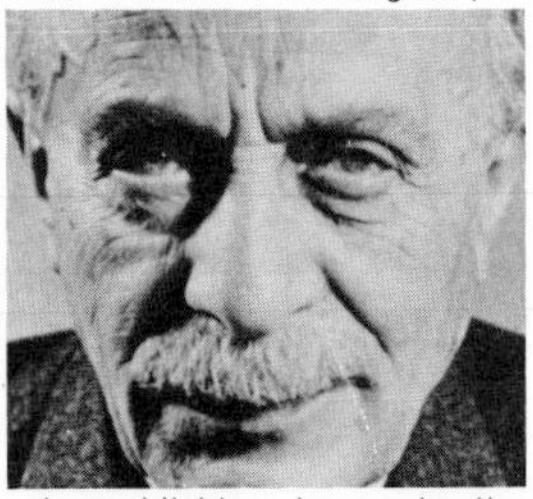

vate publishing house in the world. Hans (1859–1935); Louis (1863–1933); Franz (1868–1944); Rudolf (1874–1964) and Hermann (1875–1943) ran the House of Ullstein as a family concern. Each had some speciality; Rudolf (above) was the expert on printing machinery. From their building in the heart of Berlin they controlled a chain of newspapers, illustrated magazines which sold in millions, and their book publishing interest, which just before Hitler's coming to power published over 2 million copies a year. Before the First World War, the brothers had taken the lead in the picture magazine field, and their position was a dominant one in German publishing under the Weimar republic. As a Jewish business they were soon expropriated by the Nazis, who forced the brothers to sell out for a nominal sum in 1934. Ullstein, renamed Deutscher Verlag, then became a Nazi party publisher for Goebbels's (q.v.) propaganda. The brothers went into exile, and only Rudolf returned to Germany after the war. In 1952 the remnants of the business were restored to the Ullsteins, but eventually it was absorbed into the Springer (q.v.) empire. **H. N. C.**

'THE RISE AND FALL OF THE HOUSE OF ULLSTEIN', BY HERMANN ULLSTEIN (NICHOLSON AND WATSON, 1944).

V

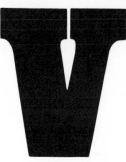

Rudolph Valentino (U.S., ex-Italian, 1895–1926): film actor. The Great Lover, he was called in the 1920s: identifying him with the characters he played, succumbing to his dark, smooth, Mediterranean charm, millions of women adopted him as their romantic idol. An immigrant from southern Italy, a professional dancing partner before he was an actor, he began his film career as a heavy and made little headway until in 1921 he was cast, less for his playing than for his dancing and his looks, in *The Four Horsemen of the Apocalypse.* The film made the bolero and the tango fashionable and Valentino an adored public figure. But it was his performance as the conquering male of *The Sheik* which introduced a new, arrogant kind of lover to the world. *Blood and Sand, Monsieur Beaucaire, The Eagle* and *Son of the Sheik* (his last film) were among his triumphs. His career owed something to the influence of the dancer and art director Natacha Rambova, to whom he was briefly married. But his popularity should not obscure the fact that as an actor he had a certain subtlety as well as personal magnetism. **D. P.**

'VALENTINO', BY ALAN ARNOLD (HUTCHINSON, 1952).

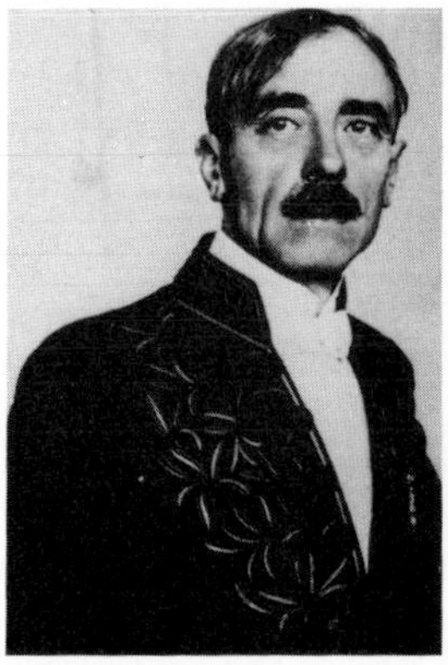

Paul Valéry (French, 1871–1945): poet, essayist, critic. With Proust, Valéry was the dominating intelligence of the first half of the French 20th century, the writer who bridged the world of science with that of art. His intellectual preference was for the scientific virtues – clarity, objectivity, truth – and this inhibited him from devoting his life completely to literature, whose motives are suspect. Half his time was spent in writing about writing and the creative act, out of which occupation poems were formed like crystals. His deeply original work can be condensed into two or three of his long prose essays, of which the most important was *La Soirée avec M. Teste,* his great poem *La Jeune Parque* (1917), and *Charmes* (1922). Valéry was a profound humanist, witty, a wonderful talker, a lover of women and the glitter of the world, yet without vanity. The purity of the early mornings when he did his original thinking clung to him through the heat of the day. **C. C.**

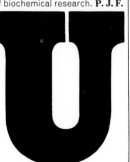

RUDOLPH VALENTINO
IN "THE EAGLE"
'FAMOUS CINEMA STAR' SERIES.

Dame Ninette de Valois (British, b. 1898): dancer and choreographer. Ninette de Valois joined Diaghilev (q.v.) in 1923, dancing as a soloist in 13 ballets. In 1926 she opened an Academy in London to lay the foundation for a British ballet: she and her pupils performed in Dublin, Cambridge, and in London at the Old Vic in Shakespeare. In 1931 she became Director of the Vic-Wells Ballet at Lilian Baylis's new Sadler's Wells Theatre: the small company, of which she was ballerina, gave occasional evenings of ballet. The company became the Sadler's Wells Ballet in 1935 with Frederick Ashton as resident choreographer and Constant Lambert as musical director. Markova and Dolin were the principal dancers, succeeded by Robert Helpmann and Margot Fonteyn (q.v.). De Valois's own ballets included *Job, The Rake's Progress, The Gods go a'Begging, Checkmate, The Prospect Before Us*. But her greatest role has been as teacher and administrator. The Sadler's Wells Ballet transferred to Covent Garden after the war and became The Royal Ballet in 1957. De Valois was directly responsible for the founding of the major British ballet company, and nurtured it in conjunction with Ashton, to whom she relinquished the Directorship. **R. B.**

THE SADLER'S WELLS BALLET', BY MARY CLARKE (A. AND C. BLACK, 1955).

Edgar Varèse (U.S., ex-French, 1885–1965): composer. Varèse has become a father-figure to the musical *avant garde* of today, thanks to his experiments in the use of new sonorities and his concern with the spatial effect of sounds. He studied at the Paris Schola Cantorum with d'Indy and Roussel between 1904 and 1906, without, perhaps benefiting much from their musical instruction. Similarly, he attended Widor's classes at the Paris Conservatoire in 1907. He won a civic prize and con-

L. VARÈSE.

ducted a workers' choir in Paris before moving to Berlin where he lived till 1914. All the music he wrote up to that time was destroyed during the Great War. In 1915 Varèse went to New York, where he became involved in organising concerts of modern music. There he evolved his own atonal style of composition in which he could speculatively indulge his undoubted flair for combining and juxtaposing outré instrumental colours and contrasts of pitch and dynamics—for instance in *Octandre* (1924) and *Arcana* (1926). A 15-year period of creative silence was broken by *Déserts* (1954) in which Varèse introduced electronic tapes. He collaborated with Le Corbusier (q.v.) in providing a *Poème Electronique* (1958) for the Brussels Exhibition. **F. A.**

José Vasconcelos (Mexican, 1882–1959): politician. Vasconcelos's career is inseparably connected with that of the Mexican Revolution, which he helped to mould. A lawyer by training, he found a niche as confidential agent abroad for the early revolutionary movement. He was named to the newly created post of Secretary of Public Education by President Obregón (q.v.). Above all, he launched the campaign against illiteracy which brought the Mexican Indian majority into effective contact with their new rulers. It was for them that the walls of public buildings were, on Vasconcelos's authority, given over to the great Mexican muralists to record the triumph of the Revolution for all to see. Vasconcelos's belief that Obregón's successor was betraying the cause led him into a disastrous campaign for the Presidency in 1929, after which he retired from public life. Foremost Mexican spokesman for the liberation of the Indian, his work was widely influential in South America. **P. A. R. C.**

'A MEXICAN ULYSSES, AN AUTOBIOGRAPHY', BY J. VASCONCELOS, TRANS. W. REX CRAWFORD (INDIANA U.P., 1963).

Ralph Vaughan Williams (British, 1872–1958): composer. Vaughan Williams was 40 before *A Sea Symphony* and *Fantasia on a Theme of Thomas Tallis* established him as the foremost British composer of his generation, and very influential in promoting a national pride in native music to match that in literature and architecture. His editorship of *The English Hymnal* (supplying some now famous tunes himself), his lifelong association with the English Folksong and Dance Society, and his founding (1905) and directorship of the Leith Hill Festival at Dorking (where he lived) all influenced his own work as much as he influenced society through them. Personally modest and of notable independence, he gradually won wide and affectionate respect. Since his death the sobriquets of 'VW' and (worse) 'Uncle Ralph' and all they stood for have somewhat encumbered his standing. The three central symphonies (4, 5 and 6) and *Job* (a masque for dancing after Blake) perhaps represent the crown of his achievement in the larger forms. "He realised that all art which is worthwhile must spring from its own soil," Vaughan Williams once wrote of Stanford, but these words are still truer of himself. **S. C. V. D.**

'NATIONAL MUSIC AND OTHER ESSAYS', BY R. VAUGHAN WILLIAMS (O.U.P., 1963); 'VAUGHAN WILLIAMS', BY A. E. F. DICKINSON (FABER, 1963).

Thorstein Veblen (U.S., 1857–1929): economist and sociologist. Veblen ranks among the founding fathers of the modern social sciences. While his contemporaries accepted a harmonious and archaic economic system in which the typical firm remained small, he moved ahead, anticipating the prospect of industrial giantism. The business system, he perceived in 1904, was moving towards the creation of the massive corporation, the extension of mass-production and the limitation of competition. This development carried within it the risk of *over*-production and depression, and the greater risk that the big corporations would combat such problems by using their considerable political power to promote armament programmes and nationalistic causes. As a reformer he achieved little, but as a prophet – generally of doom – he was remarkably accurate. Between 1904 and 1915 his economic theories led him to predict: Germany's defeat in the First World War, Japanese imperialism, German Fascism, the giant corporation and the Great Depression. **R. C. T.**

'THORSTEIN VEBLEN', BY D. F. DOWD (WASHINGTON SQUARE PRESS, N.Y., 1966).

Eleutherios Venizelos (Greek, 1864–1936): statesman. The greatest political figure of modern Greece, Venizelos started and finished life as a rebel. At 17, from his native Crete, he led a revolt against the Sultan, and at 71 (a year before his death), back in Crete, he joined a disastrous military coup against the Greek Government and the Constitution he himself had moulded. Eight times Prime Minister of Greece, it was during

his first term in office, in 1910, that he dazzled the European diplomatic world by his brilliant rhetoric, his intelligence, his infectious patriotism. Lloyd George (q.v.) was one of his fervent admirers. "He had but to ask, and all was given to him . . ." Led by the tall handsome Cretan, Greece momentarily united, gained territories, grew in importance and prestige. The First World War shattered the image. Venizelos, faithful to the Allies, opposed pro-German King Constantine, and Greece was divided again. By turns monarchist or republican, a democrat with an autocrat under his skin, Venizelos, after instigating wars against Bulgaria and Turkey, in one last stroke of genius led the way to peace between Greece and her neighbours. **H. V.**

'A SHORT HISTORY OF MODERN GREECE', BY E. S. FORSTER (METHUEN, 1968).

Michael Ventris (British, 1922–1956): cryptographer. "During the last few weeks, I have come to the conclusion that the Knossos and Pylos tablets must, after all, be written in Greek." With these simple words, broadcast in 1952, Ventris announced the achievement that has given him a place beside Champollion and Rawlinson. He chose to be an architect, but never

abandoned a boyhood resolution to find the key to the Linear B script of Late Bronze Age Crete and Greece. With tenacity, a photographic memory and an extraordinary gift for languages, he did what had been held impossible: deciphered the script without the aid of a 'bilingual'. It could now no longer be doubted that a Mycenaean Greek dynasty had come to rule in Knossos. More important, the tablets brought news about the Greek tongue and social and religious life many centuries before Homer. Their value for Homeric, classical and linguistic studies is still not exhausted. **J. J. Ha.**

'THE DECIPHERMENT OF LINEAR B', BY JOHN CHADWICK (C.U.P., 1958).

Jean Vigo (French, 1905–1934): film director. One of the true revolutionaries in the French cinema, son of a pacifist who died – murdered, it is said – in prison, Vigo was brought up by family connections who, since the year was 1917 and war continued, at first had to conceal the identity of this "son of the traitor". Life at boarding school – indeed all his early experiences, including a visit to his adored father in prison – formed him for revolt. At 23 he made his first film, *A Propos de Nice*, a savage commentary, setting squalid poverty beside decadent wealth, on the French Riviera. A documentary study of a swimmer, *Jean Taris, Champion de Natation*, imaginatively used underwater photography and slow and reverse-motion shots. Then came the splendid surrealist *Zéro de Conduite* with its picture of a boys' school – a forerunner of *If . . .* – as a breeder of anarchy (naturally it was banned by the censor); and *L'Atalante* with its hallucinatory symbols and its love story, a story to be mutilated by commercial distributors but still unforgettable, still adorned by Michel Simon's fantastic performance. Vigo was 29 when he died; he had made only four films. Yet he was two decades ahead of the New Wave in the French cinema. **D. P.**

'JEAN VIGO' (BRITISH FILM INSTITUTE NEW INDEX SERIES NO. 4).

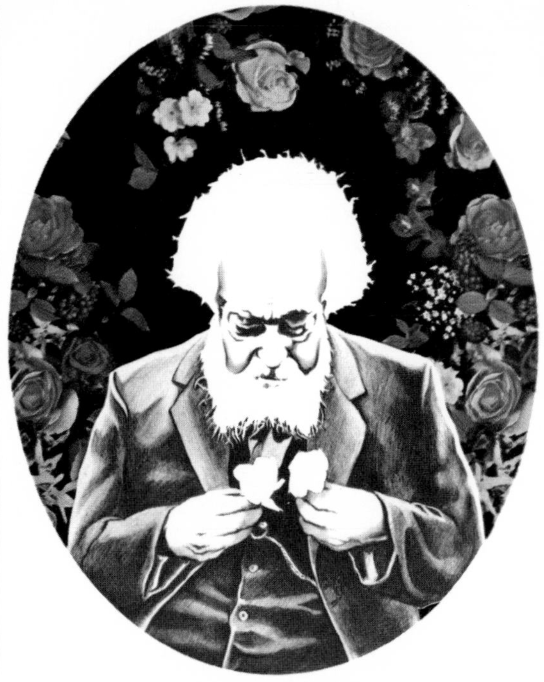

Hugo de Vries (Dutch, 1845–1935): botanist. Darwin's postulate, 'the survival of the fittest', has become a well accepted slogan in evolution theory. De Vries wondered about the 'arrival' of the fittest; why there were variations between species of plants and between individuals of the same species. Secondary factors like climate and nutrition, which were said to account for these differences, were rejected when he was struck one day by the sight of what he took to be two distinct species of Evening Primrose growing side by side. By careful comparison and breeding de Vries and his contemporary von Tschermak developed a theory of mutation, duplicating, it was seen later, the work of Gregor Mendel. He believed that a new species could arise spontaneously by gene mutation – that the mutant would rapidly establish itself as a complete new distinct species of plant. This was a violent swing away from Darwin's hypothesis of extremely slow cumulative change: more recent work on gene mutation and development of new strains synthesises both approaches. This sort of thing had always been known to herdsmen and farmers who had frequently seen the production of freaks or 'sports'. Some freak characteristics had even been put to use, like the short-legged breed of sheep, observed in 1791, that could not jump over fences and was therefore preserved by breeding. Most importantly, de Vries and von Tschermak showed that it was possible to isolate part of the evolutionary process for the purpose of careful study and heralded some of the results of a study of genetics and heredity. **P. G. R.**

W

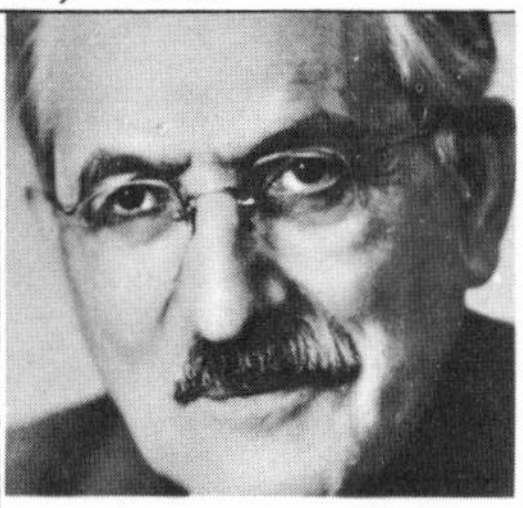

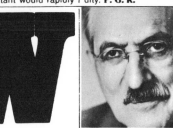

Selman Waksman (U.S., ex-Russian, b. 1888): chemist. In 1944, with Albert Schatz and Elizabeth Bugie, Waksman published the discovery of streptomycin, an antibiotic from a soil microbe of the group actinomycetes. This was the first winner from the technique of systematic test-tube screening of antibiotics against micro-organisms, which in this case fortunately included the tubercle bacillus. Low toxicity distinguished streptomycin from many previous antibiotics, and its introduction into medicine, particularly for tuberculosis, was speeded by the know-how of penicillin manufacture and by the rapid production of a reliable clinical assessment by the British Medical Research Council. Hopes were dimmed when tubercle bacilli resistant to the drug emerged during treatment; but soon its combination with PAS (*para*-aminosalicylic acid), a synthetic drug introduced in 1946 by Lehmann in Sweden, and later with isoniazid, reduced this hazard. Combinations of these drugs are still major routine. Streptomycin represented the first breakthrough in drug treatment of tuberculosis, but the chief triumphs of it and the latest drugs have been in technically advanced nations. Much remains to be done for this disease in the developing countries. **P. D'A. H.**

'NOBEL PRIZE WINNERS IN MEDICINE AND PHYSIOLOGY 1901-1965', BY T. L. SOURKES (ABELARD-SCHUMAN, 1967); 'STREPTOMYCIN', BY S. A. WAKSMAN (BAILLIERE, TINDALL AND COX, 1949).

DeWitt Wallace (U.S., b. 1889): publisher. Multiple wounds from a German shrapnel burst in October 1918 put DeWitt Wallace, a Minnesota college professor's unacademic son, on his back in hospital for months. He read copiously, and concluded that most articles in magazines were far too long. He began to practise condensing them, convinced that there was a future for a monthly reprint publication which did just that to articles which were "of lasting interest". He married Lila Bell Acheson,

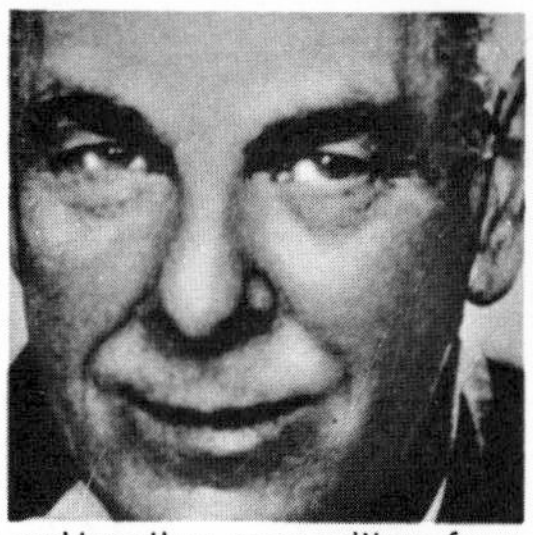

and together, as co-editors, founders and owners, they solicited mail order subscriptions. *The Reader's Digest* first appeared in February 1922. It contained no advertising (introduced in the U.S. edition only in 1954). Today, the monthly world sales are over 29 million copies, and the Wallaces have an empire which includes the publishers Funk and Wagnalls, records, and the Condensed Book Club. Articles are chosen, sifted, pruned and pruned again with the mechanical sureness of a flour mill by an army of editors. The huge resources of the *Digest* are irresistible – often now articles are commissioned direct, sold to magazines, and then digested after publication. Its surefire success is due to its conservative, implacably middle-brow stance, exactly reflecting the values of American suburbia. Its international editions are potent weapons in the world propaganda battle (the Russians have imitated the format) and the *Digest* appears, apparently of its own volition, in areas as they become sensitive, a front-line soldier for free enterprise. **G. P. G. N.**

'OF LASTING INTEREST: THE STORY OF THE READER'S DIGEST', BY JAMES PLAYSTED WOOD (DOUBLEDAY, N. Y., REV. ED., 1967).

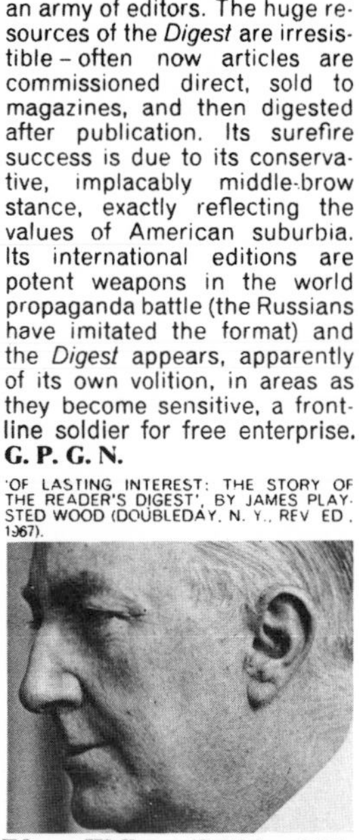

Edgar Wallace (British, 1875–1932): writer. One hundred and seventy books in 27 years, sales running into millions, 17 plays produced in six years, eight films from his books in as many months, hundreds of thousands made and spent, in debt to the tune of £140,000 when he died in 1932: what was Edgar Wallace beyond a personality with a big cigar, a lazy but speedy writer of forgettable fiction? Something, undoubtedly. The conversation in his half-dozen best crime stories crackles with life. The best plays, like *The Ringer* (1926) and *On the Spot* (1930), are efficiently plotted, and the dialogue again is brilliant. Unconcerned with literature, he had a genuine feeling for the theatre. But most of the success came in the last decade of his life, after years as hack journalist, racing tipster, crime reporter, writer of almost anything for almost anybody. It was too late for him to bother about anything except cash. He remains not as a writer but as a symbol of the Good Life vulgarised: the archetypal Big Spender who happened to make his money with his pen. **J. G. S.**

'EDGAR WALLACE', BY MARGARET LANE (HEINEMANN, 1938).

Henry Agard Wallace (U.S., 1888–1965): agriculturalist. The man who pioneered the exploitation of hybrid vigour was born into a dynasty of agricultural leaders. His father was Secretary of Agriculture under Presidents Harding and Coolidge, and he himself edited the in-

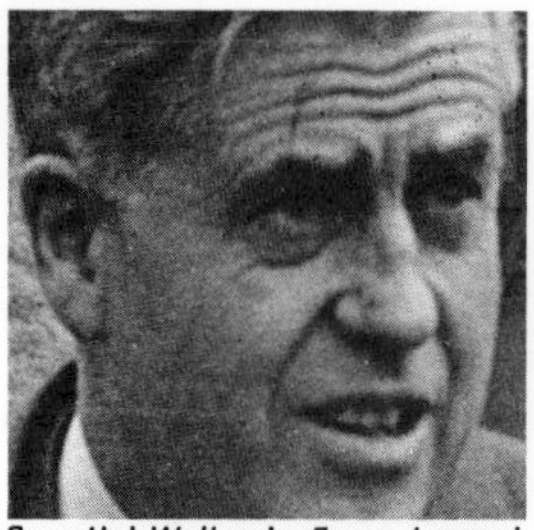

fluential *Wallace's Farm Journal*, founded by his grandfather, became Secretary of Agriculture in 1933 and was elected Vice President in 1940. He retired from public life in 1948. His principal contribution to 20th-century agriculture was that he saw the potential value of early researches on hybrid corn (maize). Shull in 1908 had demonstrated the increased vigour in corn plants obtained by crossing two inbred lines. The snag – poor seed output of inbred parents – was overcome by F. D. Jones in 1918 when he used vigorous single-cross parents. Wallace formed a seed company to pioneer development of this 'double cross' breeding system. He consolidated farm acceptance of hybrid corn during his term as Secretary of Agriculture, and U.S. corn yields rose by between 40 and 50 per cent. His son pioneered the development of hybrid chickens. Results: more corn from fewer acres in all corn-growing countries and the growth of factory farming for eggs, poultry, meat, pigs. **S. L.**

'CORN AND CORN GROWING', BY H. A. WALLACE AND E. N. BRESSMAN, 5TH EDN (CHAPMAN AND HALL, 1949); 'CORN AND CORN IMPROVEMENT', ED. G. F. SPRAGUE (ACADEMIC PRESS, 1955).

Sir Barnes Wallis (British, b. 1887): engineer. A man whose brilliance is undimmed in old age, Wallis trained originally as a marine engineer, but soon turned to designing airships. Unhappily his R100, a successful design, was grounded after a government-designed rival, the R101, crashed. He pioneered geodetic construction for aircraft – a system in which the framework of the aircraft was stressed, so that they were both

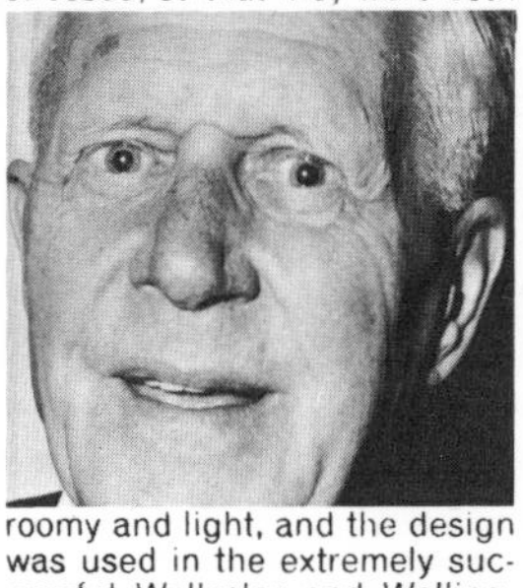

roomy and light, and the design was used in the extremely successful Wellesley and Wellington bombers. Another invention was the 'bouncing bomb', a bomb designed to travel nearly horizontally along the water contained by a dam and thus breach these tempting but difficult targets. Two other inventions apply to high-speed flight and long-distance transport. One of the problems of reconciling supersonic flight over the sea and subsonic flight over land is that two quite different wingshapes are needed. Barnes Wallis's radical suggestion was that the wing should pivot from a position suitable for low speed to one for high speed. The idea was subsequently developed in America. Another idea was that Britain should build a fleet of containerised cargo-carrying submarines. These would travel under the polar ice cap, taking weeks less than a conventional cargo boat. **W. A. O.**

'VICKERS AIRCRAFT SINCE 1908', BY C. F. ANDREWS (PUTNAM, 1969).

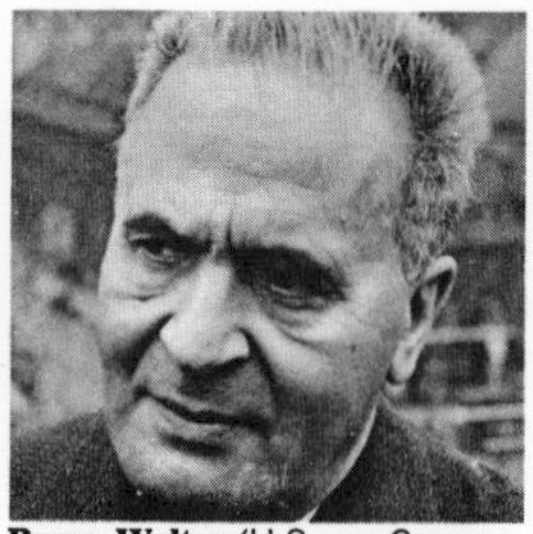

Bruno Walter (U.S., ex-German, 1876–1962): conductor. In the 1920s and 1930s, educated taste in symphonic music and opera was both broadened and standardised by radio and records. By those means as well as through live performances, Walter's work as interpreter had an effect comparable to Toscanini's (q.v.) His special field was the German and Austrian classics; his speciality-within-a-speciality, Mahler (q.v.), whose assistant conductor he had been at the pre-1914 Vienna Opera. His main centres were Munich, Berlin, Salzburg, and Vienna (musical director of the State Opera, 1936–38), but his many guest appearances in London began as early as 1909 and continued till 1955. As a Jew, he was barred by the Nazis from working in Germany, then in Austria; took French, later American, nationality, settling in California. In 1947 he began the association with Kathleen Ferrier – as coach, piano accompanist, and conductor – which propelled her to international stature. **A. J.**

'THEME AND VARIATIONS', AUTOBIOGRAPHY (LONDON, 1947).

Ernest Walton (British, b. 1903): physicist. Walton's name is linked with that of Cockcroft (q.v.) as the pair who made the first successful atom-smashing machine. In 1927 he became one of the famous group conducting research under Rutherford (q.v.) at the Cavendish Laboratory, Cambridge. After starting work on hydrodynamics, his interest turned to accelerators for elementary particles. At the Cavendish he met Cockcroft, who was already studying the problem of how to split atomic nuclei, using

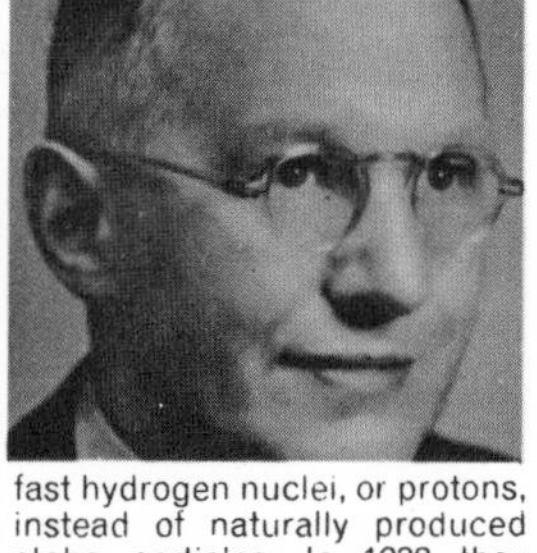

fast hydrogen nuclei, or protons, instead of naturally produced alpha particles. In 1932 they produced the first accelerator, an electrical machine which produced the necessary high voltages by rectifying high-voltage alternating currents derived from a transformer. Later the method was superseded by Lawrence and Livingstone's cyclotron, the ancestor of the present big synchrotons employed by particle physicists all over the world. Walton's pioneering work helped to set the scene for today's frontier research in physics. **P. H. S. S.**

'THE WORLD OF THE ATOM', ED. HENRY A. BOORSE AND LLOYD MOTZ (BASIC BOOKS, 1966).

Sir William Walton (British, b. 1902): composer. Precision, passion, and parody: Walton is a Sitwell musician. He collaborated at times with all three (Edith, Osbert, Sacheverell): his *Facade*, on Edith's verses (rhythmically declaimed against a sextet which includes alto saxophone), remains fresh after 50

years, its nostalgia no less appealing than its keen wit. *Belshazzar's Feast* (1931, with Osbert) revived English oratorio. A violin concerto – for Heifetz (q.v.) – viola concerto, two symphonies and *Variations on a Theme by Hindemith* have contributed greatly to his stature; his grandiose opera *Troilus and Cressida* rather less. He has also proved himself a skilled practitioner of film music, notably for Olivier's (q.v.) *Henry V* (1944). Sir William sometimes conducts his own work, not always to its advantage. Tuneful, with propulsive rhythms and romantic surges, this work has nothing in common with today's new music – a situation at which the composer, living comfortably on the island of Ischia, can afford to smile. **A. J.**

'THE MUSIC OF WILLIAM WALTON', BY FRANK HOWES (O.U.P., 1965).

Aby Warburg (German, 1866–1929): art historian. Warburg was a scholar of profound erudition who saw himself as a psychologist of civilisation, basing his diagnosis on an intensive study of individual images or symbols. Starting from an investigation of painters and patrons in the Florence of the Medicis, he aimed to assess the meaning of the transition from Quattrocento realism to Cinquecento idealism. This led him to study the ways by which the High Renaissance rediscovered the authentic appearance of the ancient gods whose image had been corrupted and disguised in the mythological and astrological illustrations of the preceding eras. For Warburg these corruptions were symptomatic

of the primitive mental states reflected in astrological superstitions, only to be conquered by the rational detachment of science or the restraint of classic art. Thus the history of the elements which Western civilisation derived from classical antiquity became his principal concern. In the 1920s Fritz Saxl turned his library into a centre for humanistic studies which incidentally drew Erwin Panofsky (q.v.) into its orbit. The subsequent diaspora spread Warburg's influence to Anglo-Saxon countries, hitherto more concerned with connoisseurship or the appreciation of form. The Warburg Institute is now part of the University of London. **E. H. G.**

'LECTURES', BY FRITZ SAXL. 2 VOLS. (THE WARBURG INSTITUTE, 1957).

Andy Warhol (U.S., b. 1930): artist and film-maker. Warhol came to New York from Pittsburgh in 1952, worked for a time as a commercial artist and by 1959 was making hand-painted pictures of comic-book characters. In 1962 he began on a new

ACTRESS SHOOTS ANDY WARHOL

Cries 'He Controlled My Life'

Guest From London Shot With Pop Art Movie Man

Shot in attack on underground movie producer Andy Warhol, Valerie Solanis art gallery owner Mario Amaya, wounded by one of his female stars, Valerie Solanis 28, the "girl on the staircase" in one of his recent films. She walked into Andy's sixth-floor office at 33 Union Square West late yesterday afternoon and got off at least five shots. Valerie later surrendered.—*Stories on page 3*

Warhol is I was doing his thing with friend in Village spot recently.

tack: the mechanical reproduction of familiar images, sometimes intact, sometimes adjusted, embellished or 'deteriorated'. The intention was to let feeling come through directly and without the superimposition of style; but, paradoxically, these agglomerations of soup-cans and Coke bottles and familiar heads already look stylish. The communication game takes a new turn, and a multiple por-

trait by Warhol turns out to have the rigid grandeur of an iconostasis. Warhol later turned film-maker. Beginning with films in which boredom and immobility were made welcome as trusted friends and allies, he went on to explore areas of feeling and behaviour hitherto out of bounds. **J. R.**

CATALOGUE OF EXHIBITION AT MODERNA MUSEET, STOCKHOLM (1968); 'ANDY WARHOL'S INDEX BOOK' (RANDOM HOUSE, N. Y., 1967).

Earl Warren (U.S., b. 1891): lawyer. As Chief Justice of the United States, Warren was primarily responsible for the fact that the Supreme Court in the 1950s and 1960s probably played a more positive role in American national life than it had done since the early days of the Republic. He became an efficient, reforming Republican Governor of California running for three terms, then Chief Justice from 1953 until June 1969. He gave a decisively liberal and progressive lead to the Court, especially on the issues of civil liberties, race, and electoral reform. In a series of far-reaching decisions, beginning with the unanimous judgment in *Brown v. Board of Education* in 1954 which declared that "separate educational facilities are inherently unequal", the Court became for a period the most active and in some ways the most effective reforming agency of the Federal government. **H. C. A.**

'EARL WARREN: A POLITICAL BIOGRAPHY', BY LEO KATCHER (McGRAW-HILL, N. Y., 1967).

James Dewey Watson (U.S., b. 1928): molecular biologist. The brilliant deductions of Watson and Francis Crick (q.v.) finally determined the double helical structure of the DNA molecule, and showed how this theory was compatible with the known laws of stereochemistry, the X-ray crystallography of Wilkins (q.v.) and chemical data. The interwoven spirals form templates for one another: when they separate in genetic reproduction each half can replicate the other. This is how genetic information is passed from one cell to another, from one being to another, and this discovery started molecular genetics. Watson was the ebullient member of the team. *The Double Helix*, his account of the discovery, aroused controversy because it recounts the daily lives of the scientists involved – and how he wangled his way to the Cavendish Laboratory, met Crick there and started to urge him on the DNA structure course, and how the race to beat Linus Pauling (q.v.) in California was won with the unknown help of Wilkins at King's College, Cambridge. **P. G. R.**

'THE DOUBLE HELIX', BY J. D. WATSON (WEIDENFELD AND NICOLSON, 1968).

Tom Watson (U.S., 1874–1956): computer tycoon. In 1914 Tom Watson, fired as sales manager of National Cash Register, and under a suspended jail sentence for unprincipled trade practices, joined a little company then called Computer-Tabulating-Recording. Now International Business Machines, its assets and annual sales are both rapidly approaching 8 billion dollars, and it is responsible for building and selling some four out of every five computers manufactured in the Western world. Watson was a dedicated salesman – dedicated as probably no salesman has ever been. At the head of his swelling battalion of clean-shaven, impeccably-dressed, non-drinking young executives, singing the company anthem 'Ever Onward IBM' and never forgetting for one moment the injunction "Think!" which decorated every desk and office in the organisation, he drove the business forward, inexorably, through slump, boom, war and peace, never in its history failing at least to double in size every four years. Anyone wise enough to purchase 100 shares in 1916, at the then-current price of 550 dollars, would now possess a fortune approaching £20 million. **P. W.**

James Dewey Watson — see above column.

Sir Robert Watson-Watt (British, b. 1892): physicist and engineer. The man who developed radar was a research engineer who in 1919 filed a patent concerned with radio direction-finding. After a time in the Meteorological Office he became superintendent of the radio section of the National Physical Laboratory, and in 1935 was appointed head of a team recruited to design practical systems of locating aircraft by radio waves – what was to become generally known as radar. They started work at Orfordness and then in 1936 went to nearby Bawdsey Manor where their work was to give Britain a valuable lead in this technology. Early in the Second World War Watson-Watt and his team had provided Britain with a radio screen to detect and locate attacking planes in all weathers and by day or by night. The Battle of Britain was won as much on the TV-like screens of the radar stations as in the air. Watson-Watt was knighted in 1942; after the war he worked on the development of radar for peaceful uses. **P. O. W.**

BOOKS BY WATSON-WATT: 'THREE STEPS TO VICTORY' (ODHAMS, 1958); 'THE PULSE OF RADAR' (DIAL PRESS, 1959); 'MAN'S MEANS TO HIS END' (HEINEMANN, 1967).

Evelyn Waugh (British, 1903–1966): novelist. The first phase of Waugh's reputation was as a brilliant though heartless satirist of the social scene of the late Twenties. This formed the subject of his first two novels, *Decline and Fall* (1928) and *Vile Bodies* (1930). In *A Handful of Dust* (1934) he showed himself capable of wistful longings for a romantic ideal of gentlemanly conduct, but he was regarded primarily as a satirist until *Brideshead Revisited* (1945). This

novel startled many of Waugh's admirers with a solemn, nostalgic celebration of aristocratic ideals, in which Waugh's intensely conservative brand of Roman Catholicism became for the first time a major theme in his fiction. In *Sword of Honour* (1965) Waugh combined the elements of farce and nostalgia in a long novel about the Second World War which is one of the few masterpieces of recent English fiction. Waugh went out of his way to display provocatively unpopular attitudes on social and religious issues. Nevertheless, a great many readers who were quite out of sympathy with his views readily responded to his superb imaginative inventiveness and the lucidity and elegance of his prose. **B. B.**

'EVELYN WAUGH', BY MALCOLM BRADBURY (OLIVER AND BOYD, 1964).

Warren Weaver (U.S., b. 1894): mathematician. For computers to have wider applications than mere calculation, it was necessary to develop the study of communication and control. This science is known as cybernetics, and it is mainly the product of investigations by Shannon, Weaver, and Wiener (q.v.). Once developed, cybernetics was found to be vital for the extension of automation, for translating machines and for the study of the way that the brain works: Weaver's book *The Mathematical Theory of Communica-*

tion has proved invaluable to biologists and psychologists as well as to physicists and engineers. Weaver will also be remembered for his energetic campaigning for the popularisation of science, in particular so that both government and the electorate should be able to make rational decisions where scientific issues are concerned. For this reason, he was an early opponent of secrecy in research: one of his most valuable tasks was acting as chairman of the Genetics Panel for the influential National Academy of Sciences report on the biological effects of atomic radiation. **W. A. O.**

'THE MATHEMATICAL THEORY OF COMMUNICATION', BY C. SHANNON AND W. WEAVER (UNIVERSITY OF ILLINOIS, 1949).

Beatrice Webb (British, 1858–1943) and **Sidney Webb** (British, 1859–1947): social reformers. The Webbs were a formidable intellectual partnership and pillars of the Fabian Society – the intellectual coterie which in 1884 set out to reform society, preferably through 'permeation' of existing parties. The Webbs published a series of heavyweight studies which provided the basic information without which social reform was impossible. Though their part in founding the Labour Party in 1900 was negligible, their brand of moderate, reformist 'socialism from above' increasingly influenced the policies of the party. They founded the London School of Economics for the scholarly study of economic and social problems, and the *New Statesman* as a forum for intellectual socialism. Sidney was principal author of Labour's moderate Socialist programme of 1918 and held office in both MacDonald (q.v.) Labour administrations; when he was created Baron Passfield, Beatrice, with true upper-class nonchalance, refused to change her name. The Webbs were the real progenitors of the modern paternalist, bureaucratic Welfare State. **A. M.**

'FABIAN SOCIALISM AND ENGLISH POLITICS', BY A. M. MCBRIAR (C.U.P., 1966).

Max Weber (German, 1864–1920): sociologist. Weber ranks with Durkheim (q.v.) as a founder of modern sociology. He began his career as a lawyer and economist but his academic interests progressively broadened, partly as a result of his involvement in the socio-political problems of Wilhelmine Germany, and ultimately embraced a wide range of questions concerning capitalist society and culture. The essay by which he is best known—*The Protestant Ethic and the Spirit of Capitalism* – was, however, only the start of a series of studies of the interrelations between religious values, social stratification and economic institutions, which Weber extended to the societies of China, India and ancient Palestine. The central theoretical arguments of this work remain of major relevance for present-day problems of economic development. Weber also made fundamental contributions on questions of method. His analyses of the nature of sociological explanation and of the place of 'values' in social science have been refined and elaborated (and often misunderstood) but not superseded. Moreover, embodied in Weber's methodological arguments is a philosophy of the relationship between science and politics, knowledge and action. **J. H. G.**

'LEONARDO, DESCARTES, MAX WEBER', BY KARL JASPERS (ROUTLEDGE, 1965); 'MAX WEBER: AN INTELLECTUAL PORTRAIT', BY R. BENDIX (HEINEMANN, 1960).

Anton von Webern (Austrian, 1883–1945): composer. No sooner had *Grove's Dictionary* (1954) said that "he is unlikely to have any direct followers in his specialised methods" than they became the most important single influence on Western music for a decade or so – whence Webern's significance for what promise to be music's several

simultaneous futures may well be overestimated. The fact remains that he applied the twelve-tone method more consistently than its discoverer – his teacher Schoenberg (q.v.), for whom thematic invention, old-fashioned inspiration, invariably came first: if the method didn't like it, it could lump it. Altogether, Webern's mastery was simpler and more didactic than Schoenberg's. Like his own master, he has become a 20th-century classic; but his musical – as distinct from his methodological – subtleties remain to be fully explored. An idealistic socialist, he dropped his prefix of nobility. He was accidentally shot dead; had he lived to counter his misapprehending imitators, one or two of those futures of music might have come to sound a little different. Humphrey Searle is his outstanding pupil. **H. K.**

'ANTON WEBERN: AN INTRODUCTION TO HIS WORKS', BY WALTER KOLNEDER, TRANS. HUMPHREY SEARLE (FABER, 1968).

Alfred Wegener (German, 1880–1930): meteorologist. Wegener is regarded as the founder of the theory of continental drift. Although more limited versions of the hypothesis had been previously advanced by others, notably F. B. Taylor in 1908, his *The Origin of Continents and Oceans*, published in 1915, was the first detailed analysis of the evidence for and against this hotly debated proposal. Wegener was born in Berlin and educated at the Universities of Heidelberg, Innsbruck and Berlin. His life's work was largely concerned with meteorology which led him to take part in several expeditions to Greenland, where he eventually died on the ice cap. He published his theory of continental drift in 1912 but it was his book, an attempt to reconcile the evidence of geophysicists with that of geographers and geologists, that three years later divided earth scientists into two sharply defined camps. To explain anomalies in such matters as worldwide distribution of fossils and the evidence for past climates, Wegener advanced the idea that the continents were previously joined together as one super-continent which later broke into fragments that drifted to their present positions. His highly imaginative picture of past events has now been largely vindicated. **P. H. S. S.**

'THE ORIGIN OF CONTINENTS AND OCEANS', BY A. WEGENER (METHUEN, 4TH ED., 1968).

Kurt Weill (U.S., ex-German, 1900–1950): composer. Brecht's (q.v.) collaborator wanted to bring opera out of its plush-and-romanticism phase, to make it sharp, socially aggressive, and didactic – an aim he achieved pre-eminently (with Brecht) in *The Threepenny Opera.* This clever updating of the idea of *The Beggar's Opera* (1728) enjoyed two waves of success – in the 1930s and in the 1950s, when *Mack the Knife* captured the pop taste. Also successful, though to a more specialised audience, was *The Rise and Fall of the City of Mahagonny,* (1927, revised 1930), a satire on get-rich-quick capitalism in which the German text is interrupted by hopefully-American verses to jazz-influenced music.

Banned by the Nazis as a Jew, Weill composed music for shows in Paris, London, and New York – including *Street Scene* (Elmer Rice), and *Knickerbocker Holiday* (Maxwell Anderson). He persevered in combining highly sophisticated musical skills with an immediate, 'popular' directness, but the gap between institutional opera and Broadway now seems as wide as ever. His widow (and famed interpreter) is Lotte Lenya. **A. J.**

Chaim Weizmann (Israeli, ex-Russian, 1874–1952): statesman. Without Dr Weizmann there would have been no Israel. He was in every sense its father: instrumental in its conception in the Balfour Declaration of 1917; its guide and teacher in infancy; the object of resentment in later years and veneration as first President in his old age. The statesman in him saw a national home, the growth of many generations, living in peace and amity with the Arabs. The scientist saw a barren land transformed by the Jews into a fertile and humane country. Weizmann came to Manchester University in 1904. Soon with the help of men like C. P. Scott and Harry Sacher he had turned Manchester into the fulcrum of practical Zionism. Radiating great intellectual force and charm he came close enough to Balfour, Lloyd George, Churchill and Truman (qq.v.) to play a crucial part in most decisions affecting Palestine. Zionist militancy and Hitler's persecution undid Weizmann's hopes for an evolutionary state,

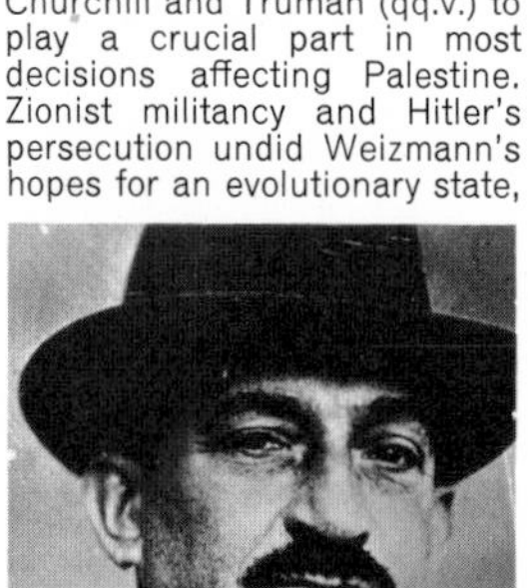

and Arab intransigence destroyed his optimism for settlement without harming their interests. **S. S.**

'TRIAL AND ERROR', BY CHAIM WEIZMANN (HAMISH HAMILTON, 1949); 'CHAIM WEIZMANN – A BIOGRAPHY BY SEVERAL HANDS', ED. MEYER WEISGAL AND JOEL CARMICHAEL (WEIDENFELD AND NICOLSON, 1962).

Sir Henry Wellcome (British, ex-U.S., 1856–1938): pharmaceutical tycoon. Wellcome, born in Frontier Dakota (he was in the Great Sioux War), came to Britain in 1880 and set up Burroughs, Wellcome to mass-produce drugs in the 'Tabloid' form – a trade-name which the firm jealously protected. By 1924 they had made him (Burroughs having dropped out early) one of the richest men in London. He had enormously wide interests – he personally led expeditions to explore the Upper Nile and the Biblical sites in Palestine and built up a world-famous art collection. But his real addiction was to medicine and pharmacy, from primitive herbal techniques to advanced modern research. He founded the Wellcome Physiological Research Laboratories, the Wellcome Chemical Re-

search Laboratories, the Wellcome Tropical Research Laboratories in Khartoum, and, in London, the Historical Medical Museum, probably the most comprehensive anywhere. In 1924 he handed over the business to the non-profit-making Wellcome Foundation, devoting its whole income to the furtherance of medical knowledge, and in 1931 its work was centralised as the world-wide Wellcome Research Institute. **P. W.**

Orson Welles (U.S., b. 1915): film actor and director. Welles was 25 when he made *Citizen Kane* (1941), a film which landed like a thunderbolt on a dozing Hollywood, and one of the most prodigious displays of creative zest and energy in cinema history. Earlier, Welles had acted and directed in Ireland (a 17-year-old Ghost in *Hamlet* at the Dublin Gate Theatre), had founded with John Houseman his Mercury Theatre company, and in 1938 jolted New York with his radio adaptation of *The War of the Worlds*, persuading a surprising number of sane citizens that the Earth was under invasion from space. In Citizen Kane's Xanadu, Welles created one of the cinema's most mesmerising images of absolute and corrupting power. He has pursued power and its use and misuse from *The Magnificent Ambersons* through baroque melodrama (*Touch of Evil*) and Shakespearian adaptation (*Othello*) to the almost patriarchal calm of *The Immortal Story.* As actor he brought into cinema mythology the massively corrupt and alluring figure of Harry Lime. Welles has said of himself, "I'm a man of the Middle Ages, with certain implications due to the barbarism of America." **P. H.**

'THE CINEMA OF ORSON WELLES', BY PETER COWIE (ZWEMMER, 1965).

Herbert George Wells (British, 1866–1946): writer and visionary. Although Wells was a dominant intellectual influence in the early 20th century, in many ways he remained a man of the late Victorian age. This was apparent in the encyclopaedic breadth of his interests, his passion for popular education and his belief in evolutionary progress. Wells, who studied in the Eighties under Thomas Huxley, was one of the very few English men of letters to have received a scientific education. In his earliest writings – the scientific romances of the Nineties – Wells saw the possibilities of science in largely sensational and pessimistic terms, but after the turn of the century he embarked on a series of utopian projections of a future where technological advance and large-scale social engineering have abolished most of the traditional ills of mankind. There was an uncomfortably totalitarian element in these visions. Yet Wells was by no means single-minded: in his entertaining realistic novels of the 1900s, like *Tono-Bungay* and *The History of Mr Polly*, he showed a Dickensian affection for ordinary fallible humanity, and it is these books, together with his early scientific romances, that are most likely to endure. **B.B.**

'THE EARLY H. G. WELLS', BY BERNARD BERGONZI (MANCHESTER U.P., 1961); 'H. G. WELLS, JOURNALISM AND PROPHECY, 1893–1946', ED. W. W. WAGAR (BODLEY HEAD, 1966); 'H. G. WELLS, HIS TURBULENT LIFE AND TIMES', BY LOVAT DICKSON (MACMILLAN, 1969).

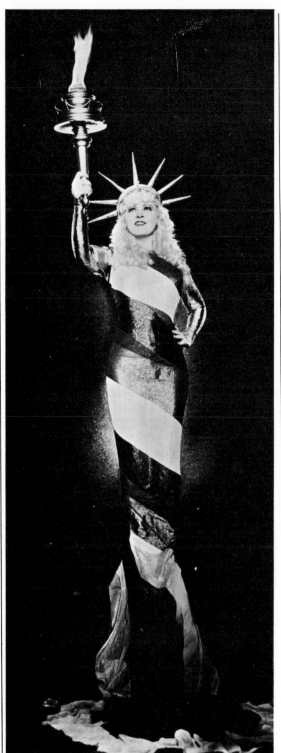

Sir Frank Whittle (British, b. 1907): engineer. Whittle pioneered the development of the jet engine. From earliest childhood he was "mad on aeroplanes". At 16 he got into Cranwell and after remarkable success in an engineering course was sent in 1934 to read engineering at Cambridge. He had already, at the age of 22, taken out a patent on a turbo-jet engine design (turned down by the Air Ministry because the materials required to withstand the very high temperatures were not then available). Power-Jets Ltd. was at last formed in 1936, and the Air Ministry let him devote a few hours a week to his work for the company. They made a jet engine work, and from 1937 Whittle worked full-time on the project. The war hastened progress – and a Gloster jet engined plane flew at over 350 mph in 1941. **P. O. W.**

'JET: THE STORY OF A PIONEER', BY SIR FRANK WHITTLE (F. MULLER, 1953).

Mae West (U.S., b. 1892): film actress. "I'm a fast-moving girl that likes 'em slow." "It's not the men in my life, it's the life in my men." Mae West was the most original Hollywood sex symbol of all, because she was self-made. No studio in the 1930s (the decade in which she made most of her movies) would have had the guts or imagination to invent her: because Mae mixed her sex with comedy. Her major films, *Night after Night, She Done Him Wrong* and *I'm No Angel*, were basically her inventions. She wrote most of her own material, perhaps because she came from vaudeville. She was not the creation of a director – like Dietrich – or a studio – like Monroe. She was never a creature under control. She was 40 when she got to Hollywood. She came prepared. Mae was no victim although she was defeated by her greatest enemy, hypocrisy, in the guise of the Catholic League of Decency, who made her producers care more about so-called morals than real money. "My goodness, what beautiful diamonds." *Goodness had nothing to do with it.* "I've been places and seen things." *I've been things and seen places.* "One of the finest women ever to walk the streets." *I have excited and stimulated, but I have never demoralised.* **P. Ma.**

'GOODNESS HAD NOTHING TO DO WITH IT', BY MAE WEST (W. H. ALLEN, 1959).

Sir Mortimer Wheeler (British, b. 1890): archaeologist. Wheeler has contributed more to British archaeology than any one man this century. In the 1890s and 1900s General Pitt Rivers and Sir Flinders Petrie (q.v.) worked to bring order to archaeology through the typological study of artefacts, the accurate examination of an entire site, and a grasp of the importance of the totality of the phenomena present. In the 1920s Wheeler expanded their groundwork and became, along with Sir Cyril Fox and O. G. S. Crawford, the pioneer field archaeologist of the day. His digs at Segontium, Caerleon, Verulamium, Maiden Castle and in India established his reputation and the value of accurate fieldwork. In the post-war years Wheeler has worked to bring archaeology to the consciousness of the public, on whom it depends for its financial life-blood, through television, books, and the Press. His life-work paved the way for archaeologists today. **P. G. St. B. C.**

'STILL DIGGING', BY MORTIMER WHEELER (MICHAEL JOSEPH, 1955).

John Rex Whinfield (British, 1901–1966): chemist. Whinfield's invention of polyester, the first all-British synthetic fibre, better known as Terylene, led to one of the greatest post-war successes of British industry. Unlike nylon, an incidental product of fundamental research, Terylene was derived from Carother's (q.v.) earlier work and arose from a specific attempt to create a polyester fibre. It was in the Lancashire laboratories of Calico Printers' Association, in 1941, that Whinfield invented Terylene in association with Dr J. T. Dickson. The Ministry of Supply declared the invention a secret during the war and it took until 1950 to develop to the point where a commercial plant could be sanctioned. The world licence, outside America, went to ICI, and Whinfield became a Director of ICI's Fibres Division. He retired in 1963 and died three years later, but he had lived to see his work become the basis of a huge world-wide industry. Terylene yarns are now used for every form of clothing for men and women and for a great range of household and industrial textiles, and world capacity for all polyester fibre is estimated at over 3000 million lb. per year and is still growing. **P. C. A.**

Alfred North Whitehead (British, 1861–1947): philosopher and mathematician. As a mathematics tutor at Trinity College, Cambridge, Whitehead first taught Russell (q.v.) and then collaborated with him on *Principia Mathematica*, the great work in which they tried to show that all pure mathematics is a continuation of formal logic. As professor at London between 1910 and 1924 Whitehead turned to the examination of the fundamental ideas of physical science. At Harvard he began the series of ambitious metaphysical works for which he is best known. In them he argues that the standard scientific picture of the world, derived from Descartes and Newton, rests on the mistake of supposing the theoretical abstractions of science, rather than the data from which they are constructed, to be the real stuff of the world ("the fallacy of misplaced concreteness"). For him the world is a stream of events, which are of the nature of feelings or experiences, overlapping and continuous with one another; not an array of stable, enduring, mutually exclusive substances. Although often memorable and witty, Whitehead is persistently obscure. For all his gifts and the arcane fascination of his system he has had little influence on the main stream of philosophy. **A. Q.**

BOOKS BY WHITEHEAD: 'SCIENCE AND THE MODERN WORLD' (C.U.P., 1927); 'PROCESS AND REALITY' (C.U.P., 1929); 'ADVENTURES OF IDEAS' (C.U.P., 1933).

Paul Whiteman (U.S., 1890–1967): bandleader. Popularly called 'The King of Jazz', which he certainly was not. Beside Ellington or Armstrong (qq.v.) he is scarcely a starter. He was a very good musician who was the first to realise the commercial potential of a popular music influenced by jazz. He picked up jazz traits of syncopation, phrasing and instrumentation and proceeded to polish and orchestrate them in a manner highly pleasing to the frenetic 1920s. The paradox of Whiteman is that he wasted good jazzmen like Bix Beiderbecke (q.v.), Jack Teagarden and Red Norvo in his orchestra, yet proclaimed their talents to the world. They and many others owed their start to him. He also played poor jazz, but launched Gershwin's (q.v.) *Rhapsody in Blue* in a New York concert hall in 1924. His hits included *Whispering, Avalon, Japanese Sandman, Song of India*. He went out of fashion in the 1930s, and ended up as a disc jockey and a successful musical director with the American Broadcasting Company. **D. J.**

'THE BIG BANDS', BY GEORGE T. SIMON (COLLIER-MACMILLAN, 1968); RECORD: PAUL WHITEMAN'S 50TH ANNIVERSARY RECORD (MUSIC FOR PLEASURE, MFP 1183).

Norbert Wiener (U.S., 1894–1964): mathematician. Wiener, the founder of cybernetics, was a child prodigy. He graduated at 14 and gained his Ph.D. at Harvard at 18, then studied logic under Bertrand Russell (q.v.) at Cambridge University and under Hilbert at Göttingen. In 1919 Wiener settled at Massachusetts Institute of Technology where he worked till his death. After carrying out important studies in analytical and applied mathematics, he became interested in computers. During the Second World War, following investigations of fire-control for anti-aircraft guns, he evolved electronic 'feedback' systems which led him to consider analogous systems in the brain. He delved deeper into brain functions and applied statistical methods to them. Eventually he came to consider the complete relationship between control, organisation and communication in the very general terms he called 'cybernetics'. The growth of the computer and its applications has led to widespread adoption of Wiener's way of thinking. **P. H. S. S.**

'CYBERNETICS', BY N. WIENER (CHAPMAN & HALL, 1949); 'I AM A MATHEMATICIAN', BY N. WIENER (GOLLANCZ, 1956).

Sir Vincent Wigglesworth (British, b. 1899): biologist. Wigglesworth's name is linked, rather dramatically, with that of *Rhodinius prolixus* – a South American blood-sucking bug. His fascinating discoveries about insect metamorphosis – the change from larva to mature insect – are set amid detailed and comprehensive studies of insect life: the way they hatch, the action of adhesive organs in walking on various surfaces, the function of sense organs, and the healing of wounds. He discovered that the endocrine gland situated in the head of an insect secretes a hormone which prevents the development of adult characteristics until the insect is fully grown. By grafting on the head of another insect he could arrest development, produce over-large larvae, and reverse the changes in some organs. In addition to head-grafting he joined various parts of insects together and studying the effects of different organs on growth and function in each insect in the search to discover what controls the various phases of its life. Comparatively little was known about insects until the work of Wigglesworth and others began to unravel their complex organisation. **P. G. R.**

BOOKS BY VINCENT WIGGLESWORTH: 'INSECT PHYSIOLOGY' (METHUEN, 1934); 'THE PRINCIPLES OF INSECT PHYSIOLOGY' (METHUEN, 1963).

Billy Wilder (U.S., ex-Austrian, b. 1906): film director. Wilder enjoys full artistic control on his films – a privilege accorded few directors in Hollywood's history. A newspaper reporter in Vienna and Berlin, he had by the time of Hitler's (q.v.) accession written 20 German films. A refugee, he arrived in Hollywood in 1934 and after lean years established a screenwriting partnership with Charles Brackett – their work included *Bluebeard's Eighth Wife* and *Ninotchka* for Lubitsch (q.v.), *Ball of Fire* and *A Song is Born* for Hawks (q.v.). Wilder's debut as a director was with *The Major and the Minor* (1942), first of a distinguished list of films that included *Double Indemnity*, *The Lost Weekend* and *Sunset Boulevard*. His great qualities are an astringent wit, forever teetering on the edge of bad taste with an acrobatic insolence, a scorn for the obvious and an acute sense of audience interest. His patience is also legendary – he extracted fine comic performances from Marilyn Monroe (q.v.) in two films, *The Seven Year Itch* and *Some Like it Hot*. A decade later, his study of New York office sex, *The Apartment*, remains unequalled. His 1970 film, *The Private Life of Sherlock Holmes*, exposed a hidden side to the great detective. **G. C. P.**

'BILLY WILDER', BY AXEL MADSEN (CINEMA ONE/SECKER AND WARBURG, 1968).

Wilhelm II (German, 1859 1941): head of state. Known as 'Kaiser Bill' by the British, Wilhelm II was in fact an impetuous but intelligent, well-meaning man with a stunted arm who tried to behave as he thought the Germans expected. Moreover, the constitution devised by Bismarck when he united Germany in 1871 failed to define the relative rights of the Emperor and his chief minister, the Chancellor, who was responsible to him, not to Parliament. Two years after Wilhelm's accession, his refusal to allow Bismarck a free hand led to the latter's resignation. Thereafter the Kaiser took decisions when he thought fit or was available, but otherwise left them to his officials. Largely in consequence of this, Germany found herself by 1914 with only one reliable ally, Austria-Hungary, and so lost the war precipitated by the need to save that ally from collapse. On defeat, Wilhelm fled to Holland where he died. **M. L. G. B.**

ESSAY 'THE EX-KAISER' IN 'GREAT CONTEMPORARIES', BY WINSTON CHURCHILL (COLLINS, 1937); 'THE KAISER AND HIS TIMES', BY MICHAEL BALFOUR (CRESSET PRESS, 1964).

Queen Wilhelmina (Dutch 1880–1962): head of state. Is remembered as the living symbol of Dutch resistance. Wilhel-

mina's greatest achievement was to reconcile the dramatic economic and social changes taking place in the Netherlands with the continuity of the monarchy. From 1898 to 1948, when she abdicated in favour of her daughter, her long reign was characterised by a stern Calvinist piety and a sense of divine mission. Although deferential to parliamentary sovereignty, Wilhelmina exercised great influence on policy: preserving Dutch neutrality during the First World War and offering an asylum to the defeated Kaiser afterwards. Nipping a Communist rising in the bud in 1918, she encouraged the great social reforms of the post-war years which inaugurated the Dutch welfare state and guided her ministers along the path of an economic reconstruction compatible with the federalist tastes of the Dutch people. With the German occupation of May 1940, she fled to London with her ministers and remained there until the liberation, broadcasting on Radio Orange to one of the most daring and energetic resistance groups in Europe. Her jubilee, like Victoria's before her, marked a farewell to the old Dutch life. But, more like Queen Mary than Victoria, her simplicity and transparent virtue had brought the Orange monarchy into the homes of all her subjects. **S. S.**

Maurice Wilkins (British, ex-New Zealander, b. 1916): biophysicist. Maurice Wilkins provided most of the hard information on which Francis Crick and J. D. Watson (qq.v.) based their structure for deoxyribonucleic acid (DNA), the key chemical of life. He will be remembered for his application of the methods of physics to the molecules of life. The Braggs (qq.v.) had shown that X-rays are diffracted by regular arrays of atoms in a crystal structure, and Wilkins was one of those who extended the technique to more

complex biological molecules. The most exciting of these was DNA, the molecule which holds the key to heredity. Almost by accident, Wilkins had found that DNA could be formed into very fine fibres, whose perfection and uniformity suggested a regular molecular arrangement. An X-ray diffraction picture was an immediate success: the very first one showed that DNA had a highly regular spiral structure. On the basis of pictures like these, with the help of chemical information. Watson and Crick were able to make inspired guesses about the detailed structure of DNA, hitting the right answer in the spring of 1953. The result was the exceedingly pretty double helix structure. **N. J. M. H.**

'THE DOUBLE HELIX', BY J. D. WATSON (WEIDENFELD AND NICOLSON, 1968); 'NOBEL LECTURES: PHYSIOLOGY OR MEDICINE', 1942-1962' (ELSEVIER, 1964).

Richard Willstätter (German, 1872–1942): chemist. A tragic figure, Willstätter spans the period between the heroic age of von Baeyer and Thiele and modern research in biochemistry. He achieved spectacular results in elucidating the constitution of plant materials and a number of alkaloids such as cocaine and atropine. He also successfully investigated the constitution of chlorophyll, the green pigment in plants, and haemoglobin, the oxygen carrier in blood, and his work on enzymes contributed in a large measure to the emergence of modern biochemistry. Yet all his life he was dogged both by personal misfortune and by the enmity of the quasi-feudal and largely anti-Semitic German academic establishment – he resigned his chair in Munich in 1924 as a protest against anti-Semitism. He refused offers outside Germany but in 1938 was hounded out by the Gestapo and found refuge in Switzerland. Willstätter's work represents a major contribution to some of the most interesting areas of molecular science. **P. L. F.**

'FROM MY LIFE', BY RICHARD WILLSTATTER (W. A. BENJAMIN. N. Y., 1965).

Edmund Wilson (U.S., b. 1895): critic. Wilson has been American literature's great representative, in this century, of the White Anglo-Saxon Protestant

mind. Since the war, Jewish and then Black writers have been dominant, and before the war his only challengers are Hemingway and Faulkner (qq.v.). It was Wilson who confronted Symbolism, in *Axel's Castle*, and Marxism, in *To the Finland Station*, and reduced them to commonsense American terms. It was Wilson who embodied old-fashioned intellectual virtues, but his significance can be seen in particular relationships to American writers, for instance to Mary McCarthy and Scott Fitzgerald (q.v.). These relationships have been personal – he was married to Mary McCarthy – but also ideological. When, in *Memories of a Catholic Girlhood*, she endorses the Protestant strain in her heritage against the Irish and Jewish strains, she also endorses Wilson. Her Protestant lawyer grandfather Preston, the hero of that book, reflects Wilson, reflects the triumph of his kind of WASP integrity in her mind over the rebellious romanticisms she was also attracted to. **M. G.**

'EDMUND WILSON', BY SHERMAN PAUL (UNIVERSITY OF ILLINOIS PRESS, 1965).

Charles Thomson Rees Wilson (British, 1869–1959): physicist. C. T. R. Wilson's invention of the cloud chamber made possible the first observations of the behaviour of the fundamental particles. When a volume of moist air is expanded very rapidly, a cloud of tiny water particles

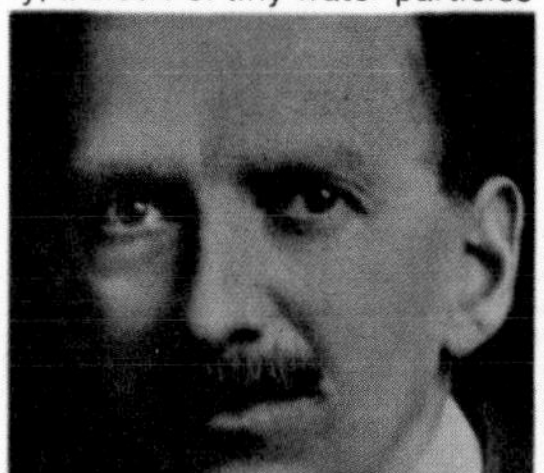

forms; Wilson decided that each droplet was forming around a free ion in the chamber, and realised that the passage of X-rays, which would release many more ions, would produce much denser clouds. This effect was extended in 1911 to the first observation of the tracks of alpha and beta particles and electrons. As the particles travelled across the chamber they produced, Wilson said, "wisps and threads of clouds", exactly like the paths predicted theoretically by W. H. Bragg (q.v.) some years before. In the years that followed the cloud chamber was very widely used, and became, in Rutherford's opinion, "the most original and wonderful instrument in scientific history". **N. J. M. H.**

'NOBEL LECTURES IN PHYSICS, 1922-1941' (ELSEVIER, 1965).

Harold Wilson (British, b. 1916). politician. "Dull, devious, diligent, and deliberate," said one of his enemies. Yet it was Wilson who said that when Macmillan (q.v.) landed from a foreign trip at London airport Butler went forward and gripped him warmly by the throat. No-one who can dream up a phrase like that can be truly dull. The other things, maybe. Wilson is an archetypal *middle*-class meritocrat; his father, an industrial chemist, ran a Jowett car before the war. He is of Yorkshire, non-conformist, Lib-Lab stock; as a King's Scout he once preached at the local Baptist Chapel. He went up to Oxford on a history exhibition, got 17 alphas out of a possible 18 in Philosophy, Politics and Economics. "All facts, no bloody ideas," concluded Aneurin Bevan (q.v.). M.P. at 29, President of the Board of Trade at 31, all he needed as a

boy wonder was friends; but he would quote Kipling: "All men must count with you but none too much." In 1960 he lost against Gaitskell (q.v.) for the leadership; to his enemies it was the worst in a long list of betrayals, to his friends an act of courage. Gaitskell's premature death made him leader in 1963 and then Premier in October 1964; a plentiful supply of fish fingers, HP sauce, and three Gannex macs moved with him into No. 10. He was soon plunged by the communications roller-coaster from whizz-kid to guilty man as de Gaulle and Ian Smith (qq.v.) said no and the pound was humiliatingly devalued. Yet the social reforms have gone forward and it is far too soon to judge him. Before Wilson, Prime Ministers in 20th-century Britain assumed office at an average age of 60; he was 48 and, despite his shock election defeat in 1970, could well be back for more. **G. S.**

Kemmons Wilson (U.S., b. 1913): hotelier. The motel reached its apotheosis in Holiday Inns of America, Inc., the first of which went up in Memphis in 1952. Motor hotels, lodges and inns sprang up in America as the motor car became the overwhelmingly dominant form of transport, but many of them at first were shabby shacks. By the late 1940s a better class of motel had begun to appear, but the long distance traveller had still to take pot-luck, both in the quality of his accommodation and in the price he had to pay. Wilson changed that. Born poor, he started up in business with slot machines, afterwards owning a small cinema chain. The legend is that he returned from a lousy vacation and decided from that piece of primitive market research that the motels were wide open for development. Right from the start he planned a nation-wide chain, with exactly the same standards in each Inn. "Inexpensive luxury" would be absolutely predictable; each room would have two double beds, one for Mom and Pop, the other for the kids (for whom there would be no extra charge). Today a new Holiday Inn opens every $2\frac{1}{2}$ days – it is the largest hotel group in the world, with over 1100 units at the last count. **G. P. G. N.**

1000

WIG-WOO

Woodrow Wilson (U.S., 1856–1924): statesman. A professor and President of Princeton University and a dazzling Governor of New Jersey, Wilson was President of the U.S. from 1913–1921, a Democratic gentleman-reformer mainly concerned with domestic issues. By an irony he himself recognised, Wilson was plunged into foreign crisis. Determined to restore peace, and to preserve American neutrality, he found himself leading the U.S. into war. His dream, embodied in his Fourteen Points and in the League of Nations Covenant, was to fashion a world free from conflict. But the Paris peacemakers thought him unworldly, in several senses; and he offended the U.S. Senate ("Why will he persist in stroking the cat the wrong way?" asked Lord Bryce). Wilson's dream turned sour. He suffered a physical breakdown, and the Senate refused to ratify the Treaty. If not quite a martyr Wilson was a victim of circumstance. For all his tactical errors and his priggish airs he was wiser than his critics in insisting that without some quasi-religious vision the world might well blow itself to bits. **M. F. C.**

'WOODROW WILSON AND THE POLITICS OF MORALITY', BY JOHN M. BLUM (LITTLE, BROWN, BOSTON, 1956); WOODROW WILSON: A PROFILE, ED. ARTHUR S. LINK (HILL AND WANG, N.Y., 1968).

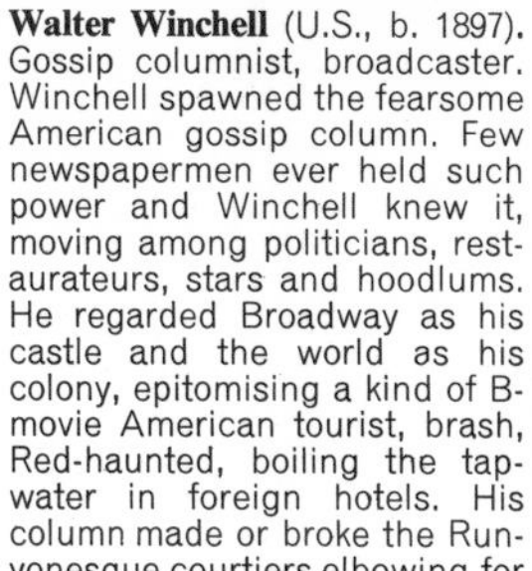

Walter Winchell (U.S., b. 1897). Gossip columnist, broadcaster. Winchell spawned the fearsome American gossip column. Few newspapermen ever held such power and Winchell knew it, moving among politicians, restaurateurs, stars and hoodlums. He regarded Broadway as his castle and the world as his colony, epitomising a kind of B-movie American tourist, brash, Red-haunted, boiling the tap-water in foreign hotels. His column made or broke the Runyonesque courtiers elbowing for favour, but politically it was less assured, whipping up All-American causes. Before the War he was isolationist but he vociferously changed tack in the early Forties, calling isolationist Colonel Lindbergh (q.v.) "Berlindbergh". Son of poor New York Jewish parents, Winchell ran away from home at 12, became a vaudeville dancer, and turned newsman in 1922. His closest friends have included Edgar Hoover (q.v.) and 'Lucky' Luciano. Winchell hated Britain for its "Brutish" behaviour in Palestine; he murdered the English language with words like 'infanticipating', meaning pregnant. In February 1969 he retired, his column almost dead in an increasingly sophisticated market. **P. Du.**

'WALTER WINCHELL', BY ST CLAIR McKELWAY (CHAPMAN AND HALL, 1941).

Orde Wingate (British, 1903–1944): soldier. Wingate formed the first Jewish special night squads for village defence in Palestine in 1938, and is now revered by the Israelis as the founder of their army and the architect of their victories. In the Second World War he led the successful Ethiopian guerrilla movement against the Italians. But Wingate is best known for the Chindit operations in Burma (1943–44), which taught British and Gurkha troops that they could move and defeat the Japanese in the jungle. He pioneered dependence on air supply for armies in areas lacking communications, thus pointing the way to the defence of Imphal and reconquest of Burma (q.v. Slim), but was killed in an air crash returning from a visit to the Chindits inside Burma. He had all the qualities and eccentricities of a great leader and prophet; Roosevelt (q.v.) gave him direct personal American air support, and he was regarded by Churchill (q.v.) as "a man of destiny". He did not suffer fools of higher rank gladly. Much to the annoyance of the orthodox, he is one of the few generals whose reputation will outlive the 20th century. **R. G. K. T.**

'ORDE WINGATE', BY CHRISTOPHER SYKES (COLLINS, 1959).

Stephen Wise (U.S., ex-Hungarian, 1874–1949): rabbi. Wise was less the traditional rabbi (='teacher') than the fiery prophet, raising his powerful voice as one of the greatest orators of his day against injustice and oppression. He refused the influential pulpit of Temple Emanuel as it was controlled by a board of trustees. From the pulpit of his Free Synagogue ("pewless and dueless") he fearlessly advocated Zionism (very unusual for a Reform Rabbi in the first quarter of the 20th century), civil rights, the ad-

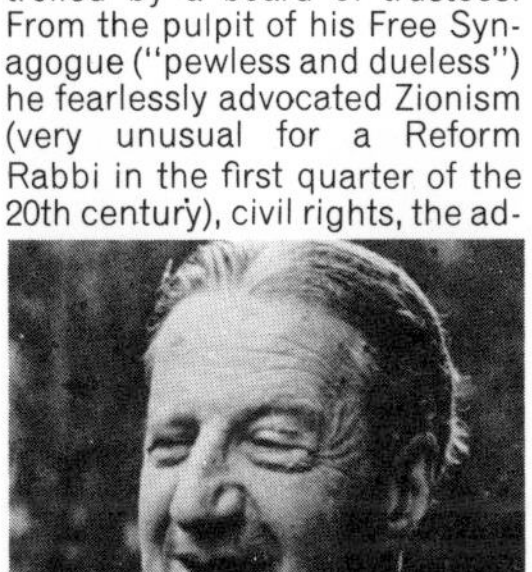

vancement of coloured people, protection of the weak, higher wages for workers. Wise studied under Jellinek ("Judaism is a wonderful religion. It is a pity the Jews spoil it") in Vienna and Neubauer in Oxford. In 1922 he founded the Jewish Institute of Religion, the seminary in an undogmatic cast for the training of rabbis of every denomination. His favourite story: Wise to Freud: "Who is the greatest living Jew?" Freud: "What about you?" Wise: "No, no, no!" Freud: "One 'no' would have been enough." **L. J.**

'CHALLENGING YEARS', AUTOBIOGRAPHY (PUTMAN, N.Y., 1949); 'RABBI AND MINISTER', BY C. H. VOSS (WORLD PUBLISHING CO., CLEVELAND, 1964).

Sergei Witte (Russian, 1849–1915): politician. Russia in 1890 was under-developed, barely 30 years out of serfdom, its society wholly hostile to any form of modernisation. Yet within a decade Witte set in motion the juggernaut of Russian heavy industry. As Finance Minister he used foreign capital and expertise, allied with the autocratic power of the Tsarist State, to substitute for Russia's lack of more usual development materials. And he produced one of the highest industrial growth rates in modern economic experience. Russia paid heavily. Witte inaugurated the practice of raiding agriculture in order

to finance industry, squeezing out every ear of exportable grain. And to this he added fearsome taxes and tariffs. But by pulling Russia forcibly out of backwardness, he unleashed on its career one of the world's greatest industrial powers. By instigating a deliberate crash on living standards, he aggravated the growing unrest within Russia and thus unwittingly contributed to the 1917 Revolution. Ironically, he has been extensively imitated in post-Imperial Russia. **R. C. T.**

'SERGEI WITTE AND THE INDUSTRIALISATION OF RUSSIA', BY T. H. VON LAUE (COLUMBIA U. P., 1963).

Ludwig Wittgenstein (British, ex-Austrian, 1889–1951): philosopher. Wittgenstein's two philosophies have been profoundly influential: his *Tractatus* was the sacred text of the logical positivists and his later writings determined the methods and subject-matter of the 'ordinary-language' philosophy of the post-war years. Born in Vienna, he came to England in 1908 and to Cambridge in 1912 to study with Russell (q.v.). The war interrupted their brilliantly fertile collaboration but Wittgenstein found time in the Austrian artillery to write his *Tractatus Logico-Philosophicus*. It is an account of the logical structure that any possible language must possess, however much it may be obscured by surface detail. He abandoned philosophy for various forms of simple, self-denying life until his return in 1929 to Cambridge, where he was professor from 1939 to 1947. In *Philosophical Investigations*, his chief later work, he rejected the *Tractatus*, arguing that its rigid logical structure was something he had imposed on, not discovered in, language. **A. Q.**

BOOKS BY WITTGENSTEIN: 'TRACTATUS LOGICO-PHILOSOPHICUS', TRANS. PEARS AND MCGUINESS (ROUTLEDGE AND KEGAN PAUL, 1961); 'PHILOSOPHICAL INVESTIGATIONS', TRANS G. E. M. ANSCOMBE (BLACKWELL, OXFORD, 1967). 'LUDWIG WITTGENSTEIN – A MEMOIR', BY NORMAN MALCOLM (O.U.P., 1962).

Pelham Grenville Wodehouse (U.S., ex-British, b. 1881): writer. P. G. Wodehouse created a garden-party of immortal characters – Bertie Wooster, Clarence Earl of Emsworth, Jeeves, Ukridge, Mr Mulliner, Webster the pious cat, scores of fierce or sporting aunts, heavy uncles, young men in spats – all of them suspended in the mellow atmosphere of a sunny 1925. They and Wodehouse's style, which draws on boarding school slang as much as on Shakespeare, can move some individuals to a peptic rage but most people to a delight increased by annotation. Wodehouse has written about 100 books and produces one more every year; and, living most of the time in America, he has made a fortune. Apart from a streak of pain during the last war, when he was abused for innocently broadcasting from Berlin, his personal life has been uneventful: typing and a little golf. **P. N.**

'WODEHOUSE AT WORK', BY RICHARD USBORNE (HERBERT JENKINS, 1960); 'OVER SEVENTY', BY P. G. WODEHOUSE (HERBERT JENKINS, 1957).

Sir Henry Wood (British, 1869–1944): conductor. The father-figure of Promenade Concerts (though by no means their originator) learned his trade as conductor of a travelling opera company. Then, in 1895, he was engaged by the impresario Robert Newman to conduct a series of Promenade Concerts at London's newly built Queen's Hall. In 1927 the BBC took over management, in 1941 the bombing of Queen's Hall forced a

transfer to the Albert Hall, but Wood retained his conductorship of the Proms until the year of his death, not even accepting an assistant conductor until 1939. Active also in other concert series, he was a tremendous disciplinarian (known to his musicians as 'Timber'). He ended the pernicious system by which orchestral players freely sent in deputies to do their work. He also pioneered much new music (Schoenberg's [q.v.] totally strange *Five Orchestral Pieces* as early as 1912) and made many orchestral arrangements himself, some under the name Klenovsky. The high international reputation of London orchestral players today for teamwork and quickness of learning is Wood's memorial, second only to the Proms themselves. **A. J.**

'MY LIFE OF MUSIC', BY HENRY WOOD (GOLLANCZ, 1938); 'THE LAST YEARS OF HENRY J. WOOD', BY JESSIE WOOD (GOLLANCZ, 1954).

Robert Woodruff (U.S., 1890): Coca-Cola magnate. Woodruff, an urbane, astute, enormously wealthy Georgian, built Coca-Cola (concocted in 1886) into an international synonym for the American way of life. His banker father headed a group of companies which bought control in 1919; Robert became President in 1923 with the ambition (which he only marginally failed to fulfil) that there should be no place on earth too remote, geographically or culturally, to enjoy the benefits of Coca-Cola. He ran the business like an army (complete with perpetual

enemy, in the shape of Pepsi-Cola) and in 1941 he clinched his climacteric deal – he ensured (and it sometimes took the U.S. Navy, Marines and General 'Blood and Guts' Patton to do it) that the famous refresher should be available to every member of the U.S. forces wherever he might be at a nickel a bottle. "It's a religion as well as a business," he once said. **P. W.**

'THE BIG DRINK', BY E. J. KAHN (REINHARDT, 1960).

Virginia Woolf (British, 1882–1941): critic and novelist. In her writing, her critical taste, and her style of life, Virginia Woolf is very nearly the prime representative of the literary culture – part Victorian, part Bloomsbury, and part Cambridge – that was most fashionable and most influential in England between 1914 and 1939. Her critical essays, first collected in the *Common Reader* (1925 and 1932), are in the 'appreciative' style of an earlier generation. Sensitive, eager to seize the essence

of writers as various as Joyce, Lawrence, and Hemingway (qq.v.), the critic is closely related to the novelist. Her first novel, *The Voyage Out* (1915), though of a traditional type, has occasional moments of intense perception that anticipate her later fictional mode. The form that emerges in *Mrs Dalloway* (1925) is a highly controlled type of metaphorical fiction. In *To the Lighthouse*, a minor masterpiece, she brought the novel as far toward the lyric poem as it can go. In *The Waves* she pushed her method still further. The last novels, *The Years* (1937), and *Between the Acts* (1941), show her struggling to escape the impasse her genius led her into. **R. A. Br.**

'A WRITER'S DIARY', BY V. WOOLF, ED. LEONARD WOOLF (HOGARTH PRESS, 1953); 'VIRGINIA WOOLF', BY JOAN BENNET (C.U.P., 2ND ED., 1964); 'VIRGINIA WOOLF', BY DAVID DAICHES (NICHOLSON AND WATSON, 1945).

Earl of Woolton (British, 1883–1964): businessman and politician. The first political post of Frederick Marquis, who had already earned a barony outside politics, was as Minister of Food in 1940. He had the matchless gift of a human touch in his appeals to the British housewife. Soon she was thinking of fighting the war on the "kitchen front", making "Woolton Pie" (meatless). Woolton she regarded as her friend, who by his unorthodox methods would see to it that she fed the family. Born in Manchester, he went to university there, and full-time social work followed (this always remained an interest). He became Controller of Civilian Boots in the First World War, so successfully that Cohen of Lewis's stores asked him ("the first not of my faith and family") to join their board. In 1936 he became chairman, and was simultaneously heavily involved in public life. He professed no party affiliation, however, until he joined the defeated Conservatives in 1945. The next year he was made Chairman of the Tory Party organisation. 'Uncle Fred' galvanised the party, raising its spirits and giving it a democratic air. Woolton was, with R. A. Butler (q.v.), the chief architect of what was to be 13 years of Tory rule. **G. P. G. N.**
'MEMOIRS OF THE RT. HON. LORD WOOLTON' (CASSELL, 1959).

Wilbur Wright (U.S., 1867–1912) and **Orville Wright** (U.S., 1871–1948): aviation pioneers. The Wright brothers made the first powered sustained and controlled flights in an aeroplane. This was on December 17, 1903, in a machine of their own design and manufacture. The first actual flight on this occasion had Orville at the controls and the longest (on one of Wilbur's turns in piloting) was a second under one minute over a distance of about a quarter of a mile. Two years later. their Flyer III was the first practical aeroplane capable of flights of over half an hour and with the ability to turn, bank, circle and fly in a figure of eight. Their achievements brought world fame and the resources to continue their researches into flying. Wilbur died in 1912, and in 1915 Orville retired to devote much of his time to protecting their priority in making the earliest aeroplane flight. Ironically, their own country in the shape of the Smithsonian Institution (regarded as giving the 'official' view of U.S. science) was niggardly in this respect and it was not until 1942 that the Wrights' first flight claim was finally recognised. **P. O. W.**

'THE INVENTION OF THE AEROPLANE', BY C. H. GIBBS-SMITH (FABER AND FABER, 1966); 'THE WRIGHT BROTHERS', BY F. C. KELLY (HARRAP, 1944); 'CONTACT', BY H. S. VILLARD (ARTHUR BARKER, 1969).

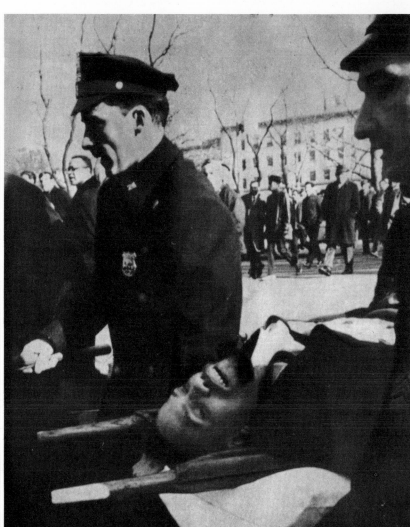

Frank Lloyd Wright (U.S., 1867–1959): architect. The 20th century's most fertile romantic in any art, Wright's 70-year career began in Louis Sullivan's Chicago office and ended on the frontier of Pop Art. His first career (1893–1909) was as the great master of the Prairie School of domestic design: long low houses with strip windows, hipped roofs and overhanging eaves. In the air-conditioned Larkin offices at Buffalo (1904), Wright developed a blocky style in concrete, further rationalised in the Imperial Hotel, Tokyo (1916–22). After disastrous personal upheavals, he returned to the forefront of International Modern with the cantilevered balconies of Falling Water (1936) and the mushroom-columned offices for Johnson Wax at Racine (1936–1939). In his old age, Wright's output ranged from the neo-Victorian extravagances of the Mile High City project (1958) to the streamlined Expressionist curves of the Guggenheim Museum, New York and what can now be seen prophetically as Pop Art in the painted concrete 'spaceship' of the Marin County Offices (begun 1957). **N. J. W. T.**
'FRANK LLOYD WRIGHT: AUTOBIOGRAPHY (FABER, 1945); 'FRANK LLOYD WRIGHT', BY V. SCULLY (MAYFLOWER, 1960).

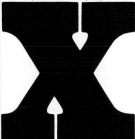

Malcolm X (U.S., 1925–1965): hoodlum, minister, leader. Malcolm Little was born on May 19, 1925 in Omaha, Nebraska. His father, a nationalist black minister, was murdered by whites, his mother spent 26 years in a mental hospital. Rejecting the black middle-class, Malcolm passed through the Boston ghetto to become 'Big Red', a Harlem hoodlum who led a band of armed robbers to a ten-year jail sentence. Malcolm X was born in the Norfolk Prison Colony in 1948. On release, he transformed the Black Muslims into a major force for self-discipline and self-help among ghetto blacks. By 1963 he was second only to Elijah Muhammed; as the Muslims' spokesman, he preached total rejection and hatred of all white men and their works. El-Hajj Malik El-Shabazz was born in April 1964 on the pilgrimage to Mecca. Elijah Muhammed's power mania had shattered Malcolm X's faith. The colour-blindness of world Islam offered an alternative to the Muslims' racist response to white racism. He preached a new message of bi-racial action and non-racial hope until, on February 21, 1965, he was assassinated by Black Muslims. Although a true believer always,

– first in the jungle ethics of the ghetto, then in the counter-racism of the Muslims, finally in the brotherhood of Islam – the man beneath the names kept growing both in self and social awareness. For many Americans, black and white, he remains Malcolm X, the violent trouble-maker who saw "chickens coming home to roost" in the assassination of John F. Kennedy (q.v.). For others there remains the progress towards freedom from hate recorded in his autobiography and enacted in his life. **W. H. J.**
'THE AUTOBIOGRAPHY OF MALCOLM X (PENGUIN, 1968).

Isoroku Yamamoto (Japanese, 1884–1943): admiral. Profoundly opposed to the belligerence of Japan's ruling military clique, Admiral Yamamoto planned the Pearl Harbour attack as the one hope of breaking American sea-power before it broke Japan. He had few illusions about power and none about America and Britain. In 1940 he told his Prime Minister, Prince Konoye, "I can

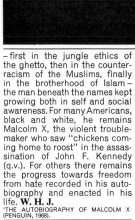

raise havoc against them for one year or at most 18 months..." He did exactly that. Pearl Harbour, planned after the Royal Navy's triumph at Taranto in 1940, was labelled infamous. Timed to coincide with the end of negotiations, negotiation continued too long. An overwhelming victory, it was also, paradoxically, a disaster. By eliminating the slow battleships, missing the carriers, and ignoring the vital strategic fuel reserves, it forced the fast U.S. carrier strategy which, with the submarines, finally shattered Japan. Yamamoto imposed control ruthlessly, but at Midway, attempting to complete what should have been achieved at Pearl, the Japanese Navy broke under his hand. Despite victories in the Solomons, defeat was already apparent. Yamamoto died, shot down because of an intercepted signal. American cryptoanalysis of Japanese codes was a primary factor both in his defeat at Midway and in his death. **D. D.**
'ADMIRAL OF THE PACIFIC', BY JOHN DEANE POTTER (HEINEMANN, 1965); 'DEATH OF A NAVY', BY A. D'ALBAS (HALE, 1957).

William Butler Yeats (Irish, 1865–1939): poet and playwright. Turning at 21 from art to a study of mystical religions and Irish legend, and inspired by his love for the beautiful revolutionary Maud Gonne, Yeats sought to reawaken the spirit of his people with poems on traditional and nationalist themes. In the service of the same cause he and Lady Gregory founded the Abbey Theatre, and writing for the stage purged his style of its Pre-Raphaelite diction. Yeats's mounting disillusionment with Irish politics came to a head in 1912 with the controversy over the Lane bequest of French Impressionist paintings, but the Easter Rising of 1916 restored his faith in the heroic character of Ireland. The discovery, on his honeymoon the following year, of his wife's talent for automatic writing profoundly affected his life and work. Her 'communicators' provided him with a system of symbolism that was to underlie many of his finest poems and plays. The writings that followed his mar-

1000

WOO-ZEP

riage have a spare, colloquial lyricism, wholly unlike his earlier manner, although many of his early themes reached their full flowering in the later period. The work of these years, eloquent, passionate, and complex, earned him the Nobel Prize and a position second to none among English-speaking poets of this century. **J. H. S.**

'W. B. YEATS 1865–1939', BY JOSEPH HONE (MACMILLAN, 1962); 'THE LONELY TOWER', BY T. R. HENN (METHUEN, 1950); 'THE IDENTITY OF YEATS', BY RICHARD ELLMANN (MACMILLAN, 1954).

Charles Tyson Yerkes (U.S., 1837–1905): financier. London's tube system is largely the crea-

tion of an American financier. Yerkes came to London in 1900, 63 years old, with personal resources of 20 million dollars. Early in his career he had been jailed for embezzlement; later he had electrified horse tramways, constructed elevated railways, and bribed the aldermen of Chicago with over a million dollars. Yerkes gloried in London's overcrowding, for he had a maxim: "It is the straphanger that pays the dividends." With only three short tube lines existing, he took over the company constructing the Hampstead tube (now the Northern Line), extending it to open country at Golders Green. In the USA, he said, people and houses followed the railway. He took over the District, Piccadilly, and the Baker Street and Waterloo, which were then under construction. All these interests were financially consolidated in 1902 in the Underground Electric Railway Co. of London Ltd. The group managed to manoeuvre their plans through Parliament. Then came a successful call for vast amounts of capital, not only for the tubes, which were extended, but also for Lots Road power station. Yerkes did not live to see the opening, between 1905–7, of the system he so energetically organised and which was to grow into the world's most extensive underground network. **G. P. G. N.**

'RAILS THROUGH THE CLAY', BY A. A. JACKSON AND D. F. CROOME (ALLEN AND UNWIN, 1962).

Nikolai Ivanovich Yezhov (Russian, 1895–c. 1939): police chief. Yezhov was the obscure provincial party official whom Stalin chose to be the agent of his worst purges. Appointed head of the NKVD, the Soviet secret police, in 1936, the two years of his rule (known to the Russians as Yezhovshchina – the years of Yezhov) were the height of the terror. On Stalin's instructions, he purged the army of 30,000 senior officers, staged the show trials of 1937–38 which liquidated

the remnants of Stalin's former rivals, eliminated all those who had any connection with them, and even removed many of Stalin's own supporters. In 1937–38 alone, possibly 12 million people were under arrest; how many perished is still unknown. Yezhov was the ideal instrument for Stalin. He possessed the bureaucrat's hatred of the old Bolshevik intelligentsia, together with an imagination too narrow to be disloyal. He was also too obsessed with punishing the enemies of the people to see that he could be used to attract blame away from Stalin. By 1938 it seems that Yezhov was getting out of hand. But by then he had served his purpose – to extinguish any potential opposition to Stalin, whether political, military or even mental. In December 1938 he was replaced by Beria (q.v.), and two months later disappeared, probably to suffer the same violent and unannounced fate as many of his victims. With his removal the worst excesses of the purges ended, but the machine of terror which he had perfected survived as an integral part of Stalinist Russia. **A. Q. D.**

'THE GREAT TERROR', BY ROBERT CONQUEST (MACMILLAN, 1968); 'INTO THE WHIRLWIND', BY EVGENIA S. GINZBURG (COLLINS/HARVILL, 1967); 'THE COMMUNIST PARTY OF THE SOVIET UNION', BY L. B. SCHAPIRO (EYRE AND SPOTTISWOODE, 1960).

Shigeru Yoshida (Japanese, 1878–1967): politician. Yoshida, the Grand Old Man of post-war

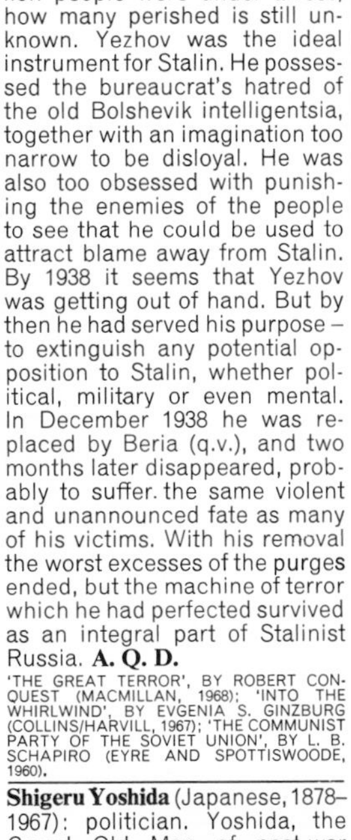

Japanese politics, was Prime Minister five times between early 1946 and the end of 1954; and after his retirement he was influential behind the scenes, as adviser to successive conservative premiers. Before entering politics his life had been spent in the diplomatic service, including a spell as ambassador in London. Reputedly Anglophile, he had a pronounced liking for English clothes and cars; and as a liberal and peace advocate he was held in custody by the Japanese military police towards the end of the war. This made him acceptable to MacArthur (q.v.). He has been called 'the Adenauer of Japan'. Like Adenauer (q.v.) he combined a posture of rugged independence, comforting to his compatriots' morale, with an ability to retain the goodwill of the Americans, whose demands in the last resort were irresistible. He presided over the recovery of his nation and signed, on behalf of Japan, the San Francisco Peace Treaty of 1951. His experience, robust physique, and great intelligence enabled him to dominate the political scene, his often dictatorial and occasionally irascible manner earning him the nickname 'One-man Yoshida'. **G. R. S.**

'THE YOSHIDA MEMOIRS', BY SHIGERU YOSHIDA (HEINEMANN, 1961).

Lester Young (U.S., 1909–1959): jazz musician. Young first became known on his appearance with Count Basie's (q.v.) orchestras around 1936. He was the first tenor saxophonist to become known for his complete rejection of the almost univer-

sally adopted 'romantic' style instigated by Coleman Hawkins (q.v.), which he replaced with a more economical line and a bone-dry sound. He was the first jazzman to teach his contemporaries, many of them wallowing in an ocean of newly-found virtuosity, that it is part of the technique of the great jazz improviser to know what to leave out as well as what to put in. Curiously, many of his great extemporisations were not fully appreciated till 10 or 15 years after their performance on record, and the Lester Young style, until fairly recently the basis of so many tenor saxophone players' conceptions (as was Hawkins's [q.v.] in the Thirties), gained a real foothold in about 1950 after its instigator had well passed the high points of his own career. **J. P. W. D.**

Z

Mildred Didrikson Zaharias (U.S., 1914–1956): sportswoman. Babe Didrikson was the most amazing woman athlete the world has ever seen. She was nicknamed Babe for her skill at baseball as a child at a time when Babe Ruth (q.v.) was at his zenith. She stood 5 ft. 6 in. and excelled at *all* track and field events, basketball and golf. In 1932, when she was 18, she burst into the headlines when she won, singlehanded, the *team* title at the 1932 American Women's Athletics Championships and Olympic trials, capturing five of eight events. Two weeks later, at the Los Angeles Olympics, she won two of the three events she was allowed to enter, the javelin and 80-metre hurdles, setting world records in each. But it is as a golfer, with a longest drive of 315 yards, that she is best remembered. In 1947 she won 17 major tournaments in a row,

culminating in the British Women's Amateur championships, an unsurpassed record. At one time she earned $100,000 a year from golf, and towards the end of her life sometimes played while suffering from intense pain, illness and physical handicaps. Importantly, Babe Zaharias, who hugged life to herself, helped to emancipate her sex in sport, though not all women have wanted to emulate her entirely. Asked to wear a brassiere under her shirt in a 1933 basketball game, she replied: "What do you think I am? A sissy?" In 1953 she was first stricken with cancer; in 1956 she died of it, and people discovered that Babe Zaharias could make them cry as well as smile. **Jo. L.**

'THIS LIFE I'VE LED', BY BABE ZAHARIAS (ROBERT HALE, 1956).

Emiliano Zapata (Mexican, 1879–1919): revolutionary. Peasant, horse-coper, cock-fighting enthusiast, dandy, Zapata took over the leadership of a group of villages in the State of Morelos, south of Mexico City, in protest against land-stealing by local sugar-planters. In 1911 he joined the rebellion against President Diaz's dictatorship but continued in revolt against its leader, Madero, who did not share Zapata's passionate interest in agrarian reform and justice for the villagers. A guerrilla leader ruling by what he called love, he showed extraordinary tenacity in his nine-year revolt against all those leaders of the Mexican Revolution who would not accept the rights of Morelos to self-government. His alliance with the ex-bandit Pancho Villa seriously embarrassed the ruling President Carranza, but Villa showed little interest in agrarian reform or Zapata in national politics. Zapata was led into a trap and assassinated in April 1919. Though his interests were largely local and though he remained a provincial revolutionary, his agrarian programme made him a symbol of justice. **R. Ca.**

'ZAPATA AND THE MEXICAN REVOLUTION', BY J. WOMACK JR. (KNOPF, N.Y., 1968).

Pieter Zeeman (Dutch, 1865–1943): physicist. Zeeman was awarded a Nobel Prize in 1902 for his discovery that the lines produced by passing the light from a flame through a diffraction grating – the spectral lines – were multiplied by a powerful magnetic field. Each line was replaced by a triplet, the two additional lines having slightly lower and higher frequencies

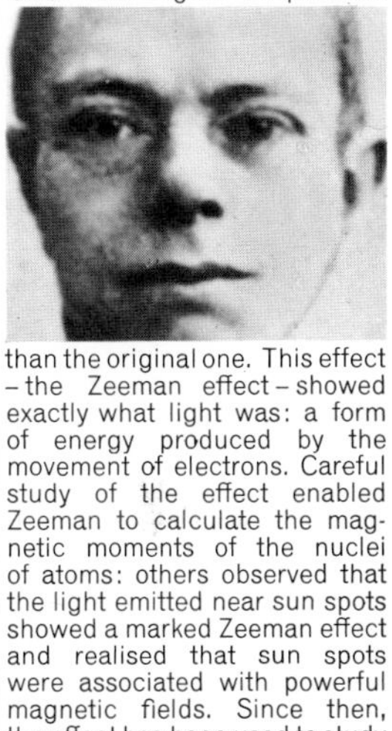

than the original one. This effect – the Zeeman effect – showed exactly what light was: a form of energy produced by the movement of electrons. Careful study of the effect enabled Zeeman to calculate the magnetic moments of the nuclei of atoms: others observed that the light emitted near sun spots showed a marked Zeeman effect and realised that sun spots were associated with powerful magnetic fields. Since then, the effect has been used to study the magnetic field of other stars. Zeeman was essentially the first person to demonstrate a link between magnetism and light, and thus to show that light was part of a spectrum that also included radio waves and X-rays. **W. A. O.**

Ferdinand von Zeppelin (German, 1838–1917): aeronautical pioneer. Zeppelin built the first practical and manoeuvrable airships where the gas bags were carried in a rigid frame rather than comprising the actual body as in earlier balloons. This work was based on the ideas of an Austrian engineer called Schwartz who unsuccessfully tried to build an aluminium airship in 1897. Zeppelin, a German aristocrat, left the army in the late 1880s to devote his energies to aeronautics. In 1894 his proposals for a lighter-than-air flying machine were examined by a commission

appointed by the Kaiser but turned down. Nothing daunted, at the age of 60 he put virtually all his capital into a company for producing airships. His first model, completed in 1900, weighed 12 tons and contained 400,000 cubic feet of hydrogen in a structure some 40 feet by 400; it was not a success. By 1906, however, his third ship

proved manoeuvrable in flight and would travel at about 35 m.p.h. Zeppelin's efforts were now recognised by a government award and orders for two airships. Most of the successful rigid airships built were based on Zeppelin's work. **P. O. W.**

'FAMOUS AIRSHIPS OF THE WORLD', BY J. A. SINCLAIR (MULLER, 1956); 'MY ZEPPELINS', BY H. ECKENER (PUTNAM, 1958).

Georgi Zhukov (Russian, b. 1896): soldier. Born in a peasant's hut at Strelkovka, Zhukov was a furrier's apprentice before he made himself the hammer of Germany. The Russian general who never lost a battle, he began his military career as a Tsarist conscript. Adopting the Bolshevik cause at the outset of the revolution in 1917, he rapidly achieved command of a cavalry regiment and won distinction defending Tsaritsyn – later renamed Stalingrad. In the peace which followed the civil war he studied the potentials of the newly invented tank and in 1939, applying theories which he had evolved, he destroyed the Japanese 6th Army at Khalkhingol in Mongolia, Japan's heaviest defeat before the Second World War. Already a Hero of the Soviet Union when Germany attacked in 1941, he organised the defence of Leningrad, returned to command the Moscow front, and became a folk hero by the splendour of that defence. In the autumn of 1942 he was despatched to the Stalingrad front. He sustained its bitter defence, and with the surrender of the German 6th Army under Paulus, shattered the ambitions of Hitler (q.v.). Liberator of Poland (and sharing in the deplorable story of the Warsaw betrayal), Zhukov commanded the Russians' final victorious thrust to Berlin. He was discredited as Stalin's general during the Khrushchev (q.v.) era, but he was rehabilitated in 1965. **D. D.**

'MARSHAL ZHUKOV'S GREATEST BATTLES', BY G. K. ZHUKOV (MACDONALD, 1969).

Florenz Ziegfeld (U.S., 1867–1932): impresario. Ziegfeld was the last and the most gorgeous exponent of comparatively harmless sensual beauty that the stage has known. He took the shapeliest female contours that he could find; adorned them with sumptuous scantiness at enormous expense; and then paraded them in seemingly endless succession in a series of harmlessly aphrodisiac shows called the Ziegfeld Follies that endured for 24 editions until the advent of the all-talking, all-dancing, all-singing film killed them in 1931. With sincere patriotic and moral fervour, he called this exercise in good taste libidinousness ''Glorifying the American Girl''. Ziegfeld was the last stage champion of uncomplicated, unleering, innocuous, heterosexual sex. Already before he died the exquisite and dangerous acrobat Barbette had introduced a more equivocal note into expensive popular entertainment. Many celebrated artists worked for Ziegfeld – Mae Murray, Marion Davies, Paulette God-

dard, Eddie Cantor, Fanny Brice, and Maurice Chevalier among them. **H. H.**

Karl Ziegler (German, b. 1898): chemist. Ziegler's most important discovery was that it was possible to control the structure of the very large molecules of plastics by making a careful choice of the catalyst used to assist the process of manufacture. Previously plastics had been made by joining together large numbers of small molecules – that is, by polymerising them – but the atoms in the polymers that resulted often formed chains with branches and not straight chains. Ziegler showed that there were stereospecific catalysts that controlled the arrangement of the molecules as they joined. It was

particularly applied to the manufacture of polyethylene when it gave a product that was harder and more resistant to heat than that made by the conventional process. In addition, the method was simpler as it did not need high pressures. Similar catalysts are used for making polypropylene, as well as higher alcohols which are important ingredients in detergents and in many other organic processes. This was the work that won him a Nobel Prize in 1963. Ziegler also discovered a method of making chemicals that contained large rings of atoms and that exist in perfumes, and he revealed the chemical processes involved in the manufacture of synthetic rubber. After studying at the University of Marburg, he later became Professor of Chemistry at Heidelberg and then Director of the Max Planck Institute for Coal Research. **W. A. O.**

Grigori Zinoviev (Russian, 1883–1936): politician. Next to Lenin and Trotsky (qq.v.), Zinoviev was the best known of the early leaders of Bolshevik Russia. He was one of Lenin's earliest supporters and his closest collaborator for the decade preceding 1917. In the Revolution he was second only to Trotsky as an orator – but his judgment was poor, courage weak and intellect shallow. In October 1917 he opposed Lenin's proposal to seize power, and after the Revolution briefly resigned from the Party leadership. Recanting immediately, he was made Party chief in Petrograd and, in 1919, head of the Communist International – a prestigious post in an age of expected world revolution. As such, his name was associated with the forged letter instructing British Communists to prepare an uprising, which contributed to the fall of the first Labour Government in 1924. During Lenin's incapacity in 1922–23, Zinoviev was effectively leader of the Party, but he lacked both political shrewdness and respect. Outmanoeuvred by Stalin (q.v.), he was removed from his posts in 1926. Recantation followed, but Stalin finally had him shot after the first of the great show trials. **J. D. B.**

'THE CONSCIENCE OF THE REVOLUTION', BY R. V. DANIELS (O.U.P., 1961); 'TROTSKY: THE PROPHET UNARMED, 1921–29', BY I. DEUTSCHER (O.U.P., 1959); 'A HISTORY OF SOVIET RUSSIA', BY E. H. CARR, 10 VOLS. (MACMILLAN, 1950–69).

Bernhard Zondek (German, 1891–1968): gynaecologist. The first person to extract from the urine and from the ovaries a potent preparation of the ovarian hormone, Zondek, with Aschheim, demonstrated in 1927 that the urine of pregnant women contained a hormone derived from the placenta. This discovery formed the basis of the original Aschheim-Zondek pregnancy test. They subsequently showed that this hormone was similar to one elaborated by the pituitary gland that controls the activity of the gonads (ovaries or testes) and consequently known as gonadotrophin. These fundamental pioneer discoveries laid the foundations of reproductive physiology and led eventually to the introduction of the modern so-called fertility drugs used by Carl Gemzell (q.v.) and others. **P. M. F. B.**

Emile Zuckerkandl (French, ex-Austrian, b. c. 1906): biochemist. Zuckerkandl has brought a new dimension to the study of evolution in man and other animals by his investigations of their chemical differences. At the California Institute of Technology, with the Nobel Laureate Linus Pauling (q.v.), he laid some of the foundations of what is known as molecular anthropology. Zoologists have always had difficulty in fitting individual plants and animals into the evolutionary picture simply by observing their gross physical differences and similarities. Zuckerkandl has brought a new precision to this field by showing that evolution can also be studied chemically. His particular interest has been in the protein molecules common to most animals, such as the haemoglobin molecule found in red blood cells. His study of the way these molecules differ between species promises to sharpen our knowledge of evolution and the ways in which it operates. **J. H.**

'CLASSIFICATION AND HUMAN EVOLUTION', ED. SHERWOOD L. WASHBURN (METHUEN, 1964).

Vladimir Zworykin (U.S., ex-Russian, b. 1889): engineer and physicist. Zworykin studied at the Technological Institute of Leningrad and was a pupil of Boris Rosing who, as long ago as 1907, took out the first patent for the use of a cathode ray tube as the receiving element for a TV system. In 1919 Zworykin settled in the U.S. where he worked on the development of an all-electronic television system. At the vast RCA Victor Laboratories, where fellow Russian emigré David Sarnoff (q.v.) put powerful facilities at his disposal, Zworykin's successful Iconoscope TV Camera tube was patented before the announcement of the Emi-

tron by the EMI team working independently in the U.K. In 1929 his system was demonstrated, but the standards were still not high enough to assure the immediate enthusiasm of the public. So, despite this initial American lead in the race for a workable electronic TV system, it was for Britain to start the world's first high definition public service in 1936. Zworykin relates wryly an incident early in his career: after one demonstration of his TV pictures, a director advised his boss: ''Put this guy to work on something more useful''. **P. O. W.**

'TELEVISION IN SCIENCE AND INDUSTRY', BY ZWORYKIN, ROMBERG AND FLOREY (CHAPMAN AND HALL, 1958); 'TELEVISION', BY G. A. MORTON AND V. ZWORYKIN (CHAPMAN AND HALL, 1940).

Sir Solly Zuckerman (British, b. 1904): anatomist. Sir Solly was Chief Scientific Adviser to Wilson's Government and chaired the Central Advisory Council for Science and Technology. As Professor of Anatomy at Birmingham University from 1943 to 1968, his scientific work has been largely concerned with primates, their reproduction and social life, and the functional relationships between man, monkeys and apes. However, it is as a prominent scientific administrator and committee man that his impact has been greatest. During the Second World War he served as scientific adviser to Combined Operations, RAF. He has worked on many advisory councils and committees covering such diverse fields as defence, resources, agriculture, manpower, and the BBC. His contribution has been to bring to political thinking a greater awareness of the potentialities and limitations of science and technology. **P. H. S. S.**

'THE IMAGE OF TECHNOLOGY', BY SIR SOLLY ZUCKERMAN (O.U.P., 1967); 'SCIENTISTS AND WAR', BY SIR SOLLY ZUCKERMAN (HAMISH HAMILTON, 1966).

1000

MAKERS OF THE TWENTIETH CENTURY

SUBJECT INDEX

Some names appear in more than one category.

Architecture and Design
Aalto, Bakst, Behrens, Breuer, le Corbusier, Eames, Fuller, Geddes, Gropius, Howard, Philip Johnson, Kahn, Loewy, Lutyens, Martin and Matthew, Moholy-Nagy, Nervi, Pevsner, Rietveld, Mies van der Rohe, Saarinen, Skidmore, Owings and Merrill, Tange, Frank Lloyd Wright.

Art
Arp, Bacon, Bakst, Boccioni, Bomberg, Bonnard, Brancusi, Braque, Caro, de Chirico, Dali, Dubuffet, Duchamp, Ernst, Giacometti, Heartfield, Johns, Kandinsky, Kirchner, Klee, de Kooning, Léger, Magritte, Malevich, Matisse, Miró, Moholy - Nagy, Mondrian, Henry Moore, Newman, Nicholson, Oldenburg, Panofsky, Pevsner, Picasso, Pollock, Rauschenberg, Rothko, Schwitters, David Smith, Warburg, Warhol.

Anthropology and Sociology
Bateson, Dart, Durkheim, Geddes, Heyerdahl, Leakey, Leiris, Lévi-Strauss, Malinowski, Mead, Pareto, Parsons, Thorndike, Weber, Veblen, Zuckerkandl.

Biology
Adrian, Bawden, Beadle, Biffen, Dobzhansky, Eccles, Elton, Gray, Haldane, Hammond, Hodgkin, Hopkins, J. Huxley, Jacob, Kendrew, Krebs, Lederberg, Lorenz, Medawar, Monod, Morgan, Hermann Muller, Northrop, Perutz, Petersen, Pincus, Pirie, Sherrington, Stanley, Sumner, Szent-Györgi, Tatum Templeman, Tinbergen, Tiselius, Tjio Tswett, de Vries, H. A. Wallace, J. D. Watson, Wigglesworth, Wilkins, Zuckerman.

Business and Industry
Agnelli, Arden, Beaverbrook, Birdseye, Benton, Biro, Boot, Burton, Butlin, Chambers, Cullen, Dassault, Dior, Eastman, Ferguson, Ferrari, Flick, Henry Ford, Gluckstein, Haas, de Havilland, Hefner, Hilton, Honda, W. H. Hoover, Hughes, Iwazaki, Howard Johnson, Junkers, Kearton, Korda, Krupp, Lever, Marks, Mattei, Mayer, Moores, Niarchos, Northcliffe, Norman, Nuffield, Ogilvy, Onassis, Ernest Oppenheimer, Philips, Porsche, Quant, Rank, Rathenau, Reeves, Rockefeller, Rolls and Royce, Rothapfel, Helena Rubinstein, Samuel, Sassoon, Saunders, Scholl, Sloan, Springer, the Tatas, Thomson, Trippe, Ullstein, DeWitt Wallace, Tom Watson, Wellcome, Kemmons Wilson, Yerkes, Zeppelin, Woodruff.

Chemistry
Alder, Baekeland, Bosch, Brode, Calvin, Carothers, Chain, Crick, Ehrlich, Fischer, Haber, Haworth, Hinshelwood, Ingold, Karrer, Kendall, Kuhn, Libby, Midgley, Paul Muller, Natta, Ostwald, Paneth, Pauling, Sir Robert Robinson, Frederick Sanger, Schrader, Seaborg, Semenov, Soddy, Staudinger, Todd, Whinfield, Willstätter, Ziegler.

Cinema
Antonioni, Astaire, Bardot, Bass, Beatles, Bergman, Berkeley, Bogart, Bow, Brando, Buñuel, Cagney, Chaplin, Clair, Crosby, Bette Davis, Dietrich, Disney, Dovzhenko, Dreyer, Eisenstein, Fairbanks, Feuillade, W. C. Fields, Flaherty, John Ford, Gable, Garbo, Gish, Godard, Griffith, Harlow, Hawks, Hepburn, Hitchcock, Hughes, Keaton, Korda, Kubrick, Kurosawa, Lang, Laurel and Hardy, Lubitsch, Marx Brothers, Mayer, Méliès, De Mille, Monroe, Olivier, Pickford, Pudovkin, Rank, Renoir, Resnais, Robbe-Grillet, Rossellini, Rothapfel, Sinatra, Stroheim, Sturges, Swanson, Taylor, S. Temple, Toland, Valentino, Vigo, Warhol, Welles, West, Wilder.

Communications
Avedon, Baird, Bartholomew, Bass, Beaverbrook, Benton, Bottomley, Buchman, Capa, Cartier-Bresson, Cassandre, Christiansen, Croly, Eastman, Gallup, Gill, Goebbels, Goldberg, Billy Graham, Haley, Hearst, Hefner, Hemingway, William Joyce, Kauffer, Kirby, Lane, Lippmann, London, Lorant, Low, Luce, Murrow, Northcliffe, Ogilvy, Dorothy Parker, Priestley, Reith, Ross, Salomon, Sarnoff, Springer, Thomson, Ullstein, DeWitt Wallace, Winchell.

Dance
Astaire, Balanchine, Diaghilev, Duncan, Fokine, Fonteyn, Martha Graham, Nijinsky, Pavlova, Rambert, de Valois.

Education and Emancipation
Baden-Powell, Binet, Melville Dewey, Dick-Read, Ellis, Kinsey, Montessori, Neill, Pankhurst, Piaget, Margaret Sanger, Skinner, Spock, Stopes.

Engineering
Aiken, Baird, Biró, von Braun, Bush, Carrier, de la Cierva, Cockerell, Dornberger, Ferguson, Goldmark, de Havilland, Hinton, Holland, Hutchison, Issigonis, Junkers, Langmuir, Mitchell, George Mueller, Oberth, Poulsen, Shoenberg, Sikorsky, Sundback, Tsiolkovsky, Wallis, Watson-Watt, Whittle, Wright Brothers, Zeppelin, Zworykin.

Fashion
Arden, Avedon, Balenciaga, Chanel, Courrèges, Dior, Poiret, Quant, Helena Rubinstein, Sassoon, Schiaparelli, Shrimpton, Stephen.

Exploration and Adventure
Amundsen, Blériot, Sir Malcolm Campbell, Cobb, Cousteau, Gagarin, Heyerdahl, Hillary, Amy Johnson, Lindbergh, Piccard, Scott, Shackleton, Tereshkova.

History and Archaeology
Childe, Leakey, Namier, Panofsky, Petrie, Pevsner, Spengler, Tawney, Toynbee, Trevelyan, Ventris, Warburg, Wheeler.

Jazz and Pop
Andersen, Armstrong, Basie, Beatles, Beiderbecke, Berlin, Coleman, Crosby, Dylan, Ellington, Gracie Fields, Ella Fitzgerald, Gershwin, Gillespie, Goodman, Hawkins, Hines, Holiday, Jolson, Kern, La Rocca, Glenn Miller, Oliver, Charlie Parker, Piaf, Porter, Presley, Redding, Django Reinhardt, Rodgers, Sinatra, Bessie Smith, Whiteman, Young.

Literature
D'Annunzio, Apollinaire, Auden, Babel, Barrie, Beckett, Bellow, Blok, Blyton, Brecht, Breton, Brooke, Camus, Chandler, Christie, Cocteau, Colette, Conrad, Coward, Douglas, Dreiser, Ehrenburg, Eliot, Faulkner, Scott Fitzgerald, Forster, Frost, Galsworthy, Genet, George, Gide, Gorky, Grass, Graves, Greene, Zane Grey, Hemingway, Aldous Huxley, James Joyce, Kafka, Kipling, D. H. Lawrence, T. E. Lawrence, Leavis, Leiris, Sinclair Lewis, London, Lukács, Malamud, Malraux, Mann, Marinetti, Maurras, Mayakovsky, Henry Miller, de Montherlant, Musil, Nabokov, O'Casey, O'Neill, Orwell, Osborne, Dorothy Parker, Pasternak, Pirandello, Potter, Pound, Priestley, Proust, Frank Richards, Rilke, Robbe-Grillet, Salinger, Sartre, Senghor, Shaw, Simenon, Stein, Stevens, Strachey, Synge, Dylan Thomas, Thurber, Valéry, Edgar Wallace, Waugh, Wells, Edmund Wilson, Wodehouse, Woolf, Yeats.

Mathematics
Dirac, Sir Ronald Fisher, Neumann, Russell, Weaver, Whitehead, Wiener.

Music
Bartók, Beecham, Berg, Boulez, Britten, Busoni, Cage, Callas, Caruso, Casals, Chaliapin, Debussy, Delius, Elgar, Flagstad, Flesch, Furtwängler, Heifetz, Hindemith, Holst, Huberman, Kodály, Kreisler, Mahler, Melba, Messiaen, Milhaud, Poulenc, Prokofiev, Puccini, Rachmaninov, Ravel, Rostal, Artur Rubinstein, Shoenberg, Segovia, Shostakovich, Sibelius, Stockhausen, Strauss, Stravinsky, Szigeti, Tetrazzini, Toscanini, Varèse, Vaughan Williams, Walter, William Walton, Webern, Weill, Wood.

Medicine and Psychology
Banting, Barnard, Barr, von Behring, Binet, Bovet, Burnet, Calmette, Cannon, Carrell, Dale, Dick-Read, Domagk, Eijkmann, Einthoven, Enders, Sir Alexander Fleming, Florey, Flynn, Forssman, Freud, Gemzell, Haas, Hauser, Huggins, Isaacs, Jung, Kohler, Kolff, Landsteiner, Laing, Mering, Minot, Moniz, Papanicolaou, Pavlov, Reich, Richet, Rorschach, Sabin, Scholl, Schweitzer, Shea, Spock, Waksman, Zondek.

Philosophy, Theology and Religion
Adler, Austin, Barth, Bergson, Bonhoeffer, Buber, Buchman, Carnap, Chomsky, Croce, J. A. Dewey, Freud, Billy Graham, Heidegger, Huddleston, Husserl, Jaurès, John XXIII, Kautsky, Martin Luther King, Kohler, Maritain, Merleau-Ponty, G. E. Moore, Paul VI, Pius XII, Popper, Rasputin, Russell, Schweitzer, Sorel, Spellman, Spengler, Tarski, Teilhard de Chardin, William Temple, Tillich, Whitehead, Wise, Wittgenstein, Malcolm X.

Physics
Appleton, Aston, Baade, Bethe, Bohr, Bondi, Lawrence Bragg, William Bragg, de Broglie, Carlson, Chadwick, Cockcroft, Curie, Diels, Dirac, Einstein, Fermi, John Fleming, De Forest, Franck, Gabor, Geiger, Goddard, Guillaume, Hahn, Heisenberg, Hess, Hillier, Hoyle, Hubble, Jansky, Kamerlingh-Onnes, Land, Landau, Langevin, von Laue, Lovell, McMillan, Marconi, Meitner, Millikan, Mosely, Erwin Mueller, J. Robert Oppenheimer, Pauli, Piccard, Planck, Powell, Raman, Reber, Runcorn, Rutherford, Ryle, Schrödinger, Szilard, Teller, Tizard, Townes, Walton, Wegener, C. T. R. Wilson, Zeeman.

Politics and Administration
Abdullah, Acheson, Addison, Adenauer, Aga Khan, Alexander, Asquith, Ataturk, Attlee, Baldwin, Balfour, Beaverbrook, Beneš, Ben Gurion, Beria, Bethmann-Hollweg, Bevan, Beveridge, Bevin, Bidault, Blum, Bose, Bottomley, Bourguiba, Brandeis, Brandt, Brezhnev, Briand, Bukharin, Butler, Byrnes, Capone, Carson, Casement, Castro, Austen Chamberlain, Neville Chamberlain, Chambers, Chiang Kai-shek, Chou En-lai, Churchill, Clemenceau, Collins, Cripps, Curzon, Cushing, Darlan, Denning, De Valéra, Diem, Djilas, Dubcek, Du Bois, Dulles, Ebert, Eden, Edward VII, Edward VIII, Eichmann, Eisenhower, Elizabeth II, Erhard, Farouk, John Fisher, Warren Fisher, Franco, Gaitskell, Indira Gandhi, Mahatma Gandhi, de Gaulle, Gheorghiu-Dej, Giolitti, Goebbels, Goering, Gomulka, Sir Edward Grey, Guevara, Hallstein, Hammerskjöld, Hardie, Henderson, Hertzog, Herzl, Himmler, Hindenburg, Hirohito, Hitler, Ho Chi Minh, H. Hoover, J. Edgar Hoover, Horthy, Huddleston, Hugenberg, Jaurès, Jinnah, John XXIII, Lyndon B. Johnson, Kautsky, John F. Kennedy, Robert Kennedy, Kenyatta, Kerensky, Keynes, Khrushchev, Mackenzie King, Martin Luther King, Kosygin, Kun, La Follette, La Guardia, Lansbury, Laurier, Laval, T. E. Lawrence, Lenin, John L. Lewis, Lie, Lloyd George, Long, Lugard, Luthuli, Luxemburg, Lyautey, McCarthy, MacDonald, Macmillan, McNamara, Makarios, Malan, Malraux. Mandela, Maniu, Mansholt, Mao Tse-tung, Marshall, Masaryk, Meir, Mendes-France, Menzies, Metaxas, Mollet, Molotov, Monnet, Morant, Mosley, Mountbatten, Mussolini, Nagy, Nasser, Nehru, Nixon, Nkrumah, Nyerere, Orr, Pankhurst, Pašić, la Pasionaria, Paul VI, Perón, Pétain, Pilsudski, Pius XII, Poincaré, Primo de Rivera, Quisling, Rapacki, Rasputin, Rathenau, Reith, Ribbentrop, F. D. Roosevelt, Theodore Roosevelt, Russell, Salan, Salazar, Schacht, Schleicher, Senghor, Sikorski, F. E. Smith, Ian Smith, Smuts, Snowden, Spellman, Stalin, Starhemberg, Stauffenberg, Stevenson, Stresemann, Strijdom, Sukarno, Sun Yat-sen, William Temple, J. H. Thomas, Thorez, Tito, Togliatti, Tojo, Townes, Trotsky, Truman, Ulbricht, Vasconcelos, Venizelos, H. A. Wallace, Warren, the Webbs, Weizmann, Wilhelm II, Wilhelmina, Harold Wilson, Woodrow Wilson, Witte, Woolton, Malcolm X, Yezhov, Yoshida, Zapata, Zinoviev, Zuckerman.

Sport
Ali, Anquetil, Bannister, Barnes, Bradman, Brundage, Busby, Charlton, Crapp, Culbertson, Joe Davis, Fangio, Fry, Herrera, Hobbs, Igloi, Jack Johnson, Jones, Killy, Kramer, Lenglen, Louis, Lunn, Manolete, Matthews, Moss, Naismith, Nepia, Nurmi, Nuvolari, Owens, Palmer, Pelé, Piggott, Gordon Richards, Rimet, Sugar Ray Robinson, Ruth, Shoemaker, Zaharias.

Theatre and Music Hall
Artaud, Bergman, Brook, Mrs Patrick Campbell, Cochran, Cocteau, Copeau, Coward, Craig, Evans, Gielgud, Grock, Houdini, Lee, Mistinguett, Olivier, Piscator, Max Reinhardt, Stanislavsky, Ziegfeld.

War
Alexander, Baden-Powell, Castro, Chiang Kai-shek, Darlan, Doenitz, Douhet, Dowding, Eisenhower, Lord Fisher, Giap, Goering, Guderian, Guevara, Haig, Kitchener, T. E. Lawrence, Liddell Hart, Ludendorff, Lyautey, MacArthur, Mao Tse-tung, Marshall, Metaxas, von Moltke, Montgomery, Nimitz, Pétain, Raborn, Rickover, Salan, Schleicher, Seeckt, Slim, Tirpitz, Tito, Wingate, Yamamoto, Zhukov.

Miscellaneous
Atlas, Cavell, Crippen, Crowley, Curnonsky, David, Frank, Hinds, Jekyll, Mata Hari, Oswald, Philby, Simpson, Spry.

EDITORIAL STAFF

Editor
Godfrey Smith
Editorial Committee
THE SUNDAY TIMES MAGAZINE
Bill Cater, Associate Editor
David King, Art Editor
Robert Lacey, Features Assistant
Meriel McCooey, Assistant Editor
Nicholas Mason, Production Editor
Philip Norman, Features writer
Graham Norton, Writer/researcher
Tony Osman, Science Editor
George Perry, Assistant Editor
Michael Rand, Art Director and Managing Editor
Susan Raven, Assistant Editor
June Stanier, Picture Editor
Francis Wyndham, Assistant Editor
ADVISORY PANEL
Dr Alfred Byrne, Sunday Times Medical Correspondent
David Divine, Sunday Times Defence Correspondent
Derek Jewell, Sunday Times Jazz/Pop critic
J. W. Lambert, Sunday Times Literary Editor
John Lovesey, Sunday Times Sports Features Editor
Christopher Ricks, Professor of English, Bristol University
John Russell, Sunday Times Art Critic
Simon Schama, Fellow of Christ's College, Cambridge
Nicholas Taylor, Sunday Times Environmental Correspondent
Peter Wilsher, Editor, Sunday Times Business News
Art Department
Gilvrie Misstear, Assistant Art Editor
Andrew Dark
Terence Seago
Sub-Editors
Suzanne Hodgart
Clive Ranger
Christine Verity
Photographic Research
Doris Bryen
Célestine Dars
Erica Kirtley
Research
Gilda Archer
Eve Chard
Terry Sain
Production
Stanley Daw, Production Manager
Kenneth Hall, Assistant Production Manager

CONTRIBUTORS

A. A.: Alison Adburgham, author and Fashion Editor, *The Guardian* (Balenciaga, Schiaparelli).

C. H. A.: Sir Christopher Andrewes, virologist, formerly Deputy Director, National Institute for Medical Research, Mill Hill (Isaacs, Sabin).

C. M. A.: Dr C. M. Andrew, Fellow and Director of Studies in History, Corpus Christi College, Cambridge (Blum, Briand).

D. A.: Daniel Aaron, Visiting Professor, Department of English and American Studies, Sussex University (Dreiser, Sinclair Lewis).

E. P. A.: E. P. Abraham, Professor of Chemical Pathology, Oxford University (Florey).

F. A.: Felix Aprahamian, *Sunday Times* music critic (Beecham, Callas, Caruso, Debussy, Delius, Elgar, Messiaen, Milhaud, Poulenc, Ravel, Toscanini, Varese).

G. D. A.: Gilda Archer, *Sunday Times Magazine* (Bass).

G. E. A.: Gillian Avery, authority on children's books (Blyton, Potter).

H. C. A.: H. C. Allen, Director, Institute of U.S. Studies, London University, and Commonwealth Fund Professor of American History, University College, London (Acheson, Brandeis, Du Bois, J. Edgar Hoover, MacArthur, McNamara, Truman, Warren).

H. H. A.: pseudonym, for political reasons (King Abdullah of Jordan).

H. J. B. A.: Sir Hedley Atkins, Professor of Surgery, London University (Huggins).

J. A.: Joe Avrach, author and journalist (Buchman, Gill, Grock, Hillary, Loewy, Moholy-Nagy, Scott).

K. A.: Kenneth Allsop, author and journalist (Bottomley).

L. A.: Larry Adler, harmonica virtuoso (Berlin, Gershwin, Kern, Porter, Rodgers).

P. C. A.: Sir Peter Allen, Chairman, ICI (Carothers Whinfield).

S. P. A.: Stephen Aris, *Sunday Times Business News* (Marks, Niarchos, Onassis, Samuel).

A. B.: Asa Briggs, Vice-Chancellor and Professor of History, Sussex University (Asquith, Balfour, Austen Chamberlain, Neville Chamberlain, Edward VIII, Hardie, Lloyd George, Pankhurst, Simpson, F. E. Smith, Tawney).

B. B.: Bernard Bergonzi, critic and Senior Lecturer in English, Warwick University (Brooke, Galsworthy, Waugh, Wells).

Br. Br.: Brigid Brophy, novelist and non-fiction writer (Colette, Henry Miller).

C. L. B.: C. L. Boltz, former Scientific Editor, *Financial Times* (Bush, Gabor, Goldmark, Land, Langevin, Langmuir, Shockley).

D. B.: Donald Burke, sports writer and foreign correspondent for Time-Life (Ruth).

D. A. K. B.: D. A. K. Black, Professor of Medicine, Manchester University (Kolff).

D. H. V. B.: Hugh Brogan, Assistant Lecturer in American History and Fellow of St John's College, Cambridge (Croly, Lyndon Johnson, John Kennedy, Robert Kennedy, Lippmann, Nixon, Theodore Roosevelt).

E. A. B.: Dr E. A. Bennet, Physician Emeritus, The Bethlem Royal Hospital and the Maudsley Hospital (Ellis, Jung).

H. J. B.: Humphry Berkeley, Chairman, UNA of Great Britain and Northern Ireland (Hammarskjöld, Lie).

J. B.: John Ballantine, sports writer (Jones).

J. A. B.: Jonas A. Barish, Professor of English, University of California, Berkeley (Genet, Pirandello).

J. D. B.: John Barber, Research Fellow of Jesus College, Cambridge (Bukharin, Kerensky, Lenin, Zinoviev).

J. E. B.: James Boswell painter, illustrator and journalist (Kirchner).

J. M. B.: Maxwell Boyd, *Sunday Times* motoring correspondent (Nuvolari).

J. R. B.: J. R. Busvine, Professor in Entomology as Applied to Hygiene, London School of Hygiene and Tropical Medicine (Paul Müller).

M. B.: Michael Bateman, *The Sunday Times* (Low).

M. L. G. B.: Michael Balfour, Reader in European History, University of East Anglia (Bethmann Hollweg, Hindenburg, Ludendorff, von Moltke, Wilhelm II).

M. S. B.: Malcolm Bradbury, Senior Lecturer in English and American Literature, University of East Anglia (Forster).

N. B.: Lord Bethell, writer on East European affairs (Gomulka, Sikorski).

P. B.: Mrs Pat Besford, *Daily Telegraph* swimming correspondent (Crapp).

P. H. E. B.: Peter H. E. Borwick, Staff Officer, Education Services, The Machine Tool Trades Association (Cockerell, Issigonis).

P. M. F. B.: Dr Peter Bishop, consultant endocrinologist and medical consultant to the Family Planning Association (Gemzell, Zondek).

R. B.: Richard Buckle, *Sunday Times* ballet critic (Balanchine, Diaghilev, Duncan, Fokine, Fonteyn, Martha Graham, Nijinsky, Pavlova, Rambert, de Valois).

R. A. B.: Lord Butler, Master of Trinity College, Cambridge (Nehru).

R. A. Br.: Reuben A. Brower, Professor of English, Harvard University; visiting Professor at Oxford University, 1968–9 (Frost, Woolf).

S. G. B.: Dr S. G. Browne, Director of the Leprosy Study Centre (Schweitzer).

T. J. B.: T. J. Binyon, Lecturer in Russian, Oxford University (Blok, Mayakovsky).

A. C.: August Closs, Emeritus Professor of German, Bristol University (George, Grass, Rilke).

A. C. C.: Alexander Cockburn, writer and journalist (Amundsen, Bleriot, Sir Malcolm Campbell, Cobb, Lindbergh, Petrie, Quisling).

A. L. C.: Tony Clifton, *The Sunday Times* (Hilton).

A. O. C.: Angela Carter, novelist, winner of the Somerset Maugham award, 1969 (Zane Grey).

B. C.: Barbara Cartland, author (Gipsy Rose Lee).

C. C.: Cyril Connolly, author and *Sunday Times* literary critic (Douglas, Scott Fitzgerald, Valery).

C. A. C.: C. A. Clarke, Professor of Medicine and Director of the Nuffield Unit of Medical Genetics, Liverpool University (Landsteiner).

C. J. C.: Christopher Chataway, M.P. and former 5000-metre world record holder (Bannister).

F. L. C.: F. L. Carsten, Masaryk Professor of Central European History, London University (Ebert, Kautsky, Luxemburg).

G. R. A. C.: Robert Conquest, poet and political writer (Babel, Pasternak).

H. C.: Harry Carpenter, BBC boxing correspondent (Louis).

H. N. C.: Norman Crossland, *Guardian* Bonn correspondent (Springer, Ullstein).

J. C.: Dr Jerome Ch'en, Senior Lecturer in Asian History, Leeds University (Chiang Kai-shek, Chou En-lai, Mao Tse-tung, Sun Yat-sen).

J. Cr.: John Cruickshank, Professor of French, Sussex University (Camus, Sartre).

J. J. H. C.: John Cavill, formerly *Sunday Times Business News* (Ernest Oppenheimer).

M. C.: Milton Caniff, American cartoonist, creator of Steve Canyon (Goldberg, Kirby).

M. C. C.: Colin Cowdrey, Kent and England cricketer (Hobbs).

M. F. C.: Marcus Cunliffe, Professor of American Studies, Sussex University (Dulles, Eisenhower, La Follette, La Guardia, John L. Lewis, Long, McCarthy, Marshall, Franklin D. Roosevelt, Woodrow Wilson).

M. M. C.: Margaret Costa, *Sunday Times Magazine* cookery writer (Curnonsky, David).

N. C.: Sir Neville Cardus, *Guardian* music critic and cricket writer (Fry).

P. A. R. C.: Dr P. A. R. Calvert, Lecturer in Latin American Studies, Southampton University (Vasconcelos).

P. C.: Peter Coveney, Lecturer in History, Nottingham University (James Barrie).

P. G. St. B. C.: Patricia Connor, *Sunday Times* archaeological correspondent (Childe, Heyerdahl, Wheeler).

R. C.: Sir Robert Cockburn, Director, Royal Aircraft Research Establishment (von Braun).

R. Ca.: Raymond Carr, Warden of St Antony's College and formerly Professor of History of Latin America, Oxford University (Castro, Franco, Guevara, La Pasionaria, Primo de Rivera, Zapata).

S. M. C.: Susan Cooper, author, journalist and biographer (Priestley).

T. F. C.: Terry Coleman, *Guardian* feature writer (Birdseye, Amy Johnson, Dorothy Parker, Django Reinhardt, Frank Richards).

V. Z. C.: Sir Zachary Cope, Consulting Surgeon to St Mary's Hospital, Paddington (Sir Alexander Fleming).

W. H. C.: Harry Carr, racehorse breeder and former Royal jockey (Piggott).

A. C.-M.: Arthur Calder-Marshall, novelist, biographer and critic (London).

A. Q. D.: pseudonym, for political reasons (Brezhnev, Ehrenburg, Khrushchev, Kosygin, Stalin, Trotsky, Yezhov).

D. D.: David Divine, author and *Sunday Times* defence correspondent (Alexander, Doenitz, Dornberger, Haig, Holland, Nimitz, Raborn, Rickover, Slim, Yamamoto, Zhukov).

D. Do.: Denis Donoghue, Professor of Modern English and American Literature, University College, Dublin (Joyce, Nabokov, O'Neill).

D. A. D.: Dudley Doust, *Sunday Times* sports contributor (Naismith).

J. P. W. D.: John Dankworth, musician and composer (Coleman, Goodman, Hawkins, Charlie Parker, Young).

M. D.: Martin Dodsworth, Lecturer in English, Royal Holloway College, London University (Dylan Thomas).

P. D.: Polly Devlin, Associate Features Editor, American *Vogue* (Shrimpton).

P. Du.: Peter Dunn, *The Sunday Times* (Winchell).

S. C. V. D.: Stephen Dodgson, composer (Hindemith, Holst, Sibelius, Stravinsky, Vaughan Williams).

T. D.: Terry Delaney, sports writer and radio producer (Charlton).

A. E.: Alistair Elliot, Assistant Librarian, Newcastle University Library (Melville Dewey, Faulkner, Gorky).

C. E.: Clive Everton, Editor, *Billiards and Snooker* (Joe Davis).

D. G. E.: David G. Evans, Professor of Bacteriology, London School of Hygiene and Tropical Medicine (Enders).

D. L. E.: The Rev. David L. Edwards, Dean of King's College, Cambridge (Barth, Bonhoeffer, John XXIII, Paul VI, Pius XII, Teilhard de Chardin, Tillich).

E. J. E.: John Ezard, *The Guardian* (Cavell).

G. R. E.: G. R. Elton, Professor of English Constitutional History, Cambridge University (Namier, Toynbee, Trevelyan).

H. M. E.: Harold Evans, Editor, *The Sunday Times* (Martin Luther King).

R. T. E.: Robert Elson, Time Inc. historian and journalist (Luce).

A. C. F.: Dr A. C. Frazer, Director-General, British Nutrition Foundation (Hauser).

A. M. F.: Andrew Forge, Head of Painting, Goldsmiths' School of Art (Bomberg).

A. N. F.: Nicholas Faith, Deputy Editor, *Sunday Times Business News* (Honda, Sloan).

J. L. F.: John Fuller, Fellow of Magdalen College, Oxford (Auden, Eliot).

J. W. F.: John W. Fairclough, Assistant General Manager and Data Processing Director, I.B.M. United Kingdom Ltd. (Aiken).

J. W. J. F.: Dr John Fletcher, Reader in French, University of East Anglia (Cocteau).

N. F.: Noble Frankland, Director, Imperial War Museum (Douhet, Dowding, Mitchell, Tizard).

P. F.: Paul Fairest, Tutor, Selwyn College, Cambridge (Denning).

P. J. F.: Dr. Peter Farago, Editor, *Chemistry in Britain* (Baekeland, Brode, Chain, Diels, Fischer, Haber, Hinshelwood, Ingold, Midgley, Natta, Ostwald, Paneth, Pauling, Raman, Sir Robert Robinson, Seaborg, Semenov, Soddy, Staudinger, Todd, Tswett, Willstätter.

P. N. F.: Philip French, critic, author and broadcaster (Brando, Lang, Marx Brothers, Mayer, Monroe).

W. F.: W. Feldberg, Emeritus Professor of Physiology and Head of the Laboratory of Neuro-pharmacology, National Institute for Medical Research, Mill Hill (Dale).

F.-W.: Lord Francis-Williams, author and journalist (Thomson).

B. G.: Brian Glanville, *Sunday Times* football correspondent (Herrera, Pele).

C. H. G.: Charles Gray, Professor of Chemical Pathology, London University, King's College Hospital Medical School (Kendall).

E. H. G.: E. H. Gombrich, Professor of the History of the Classical Tradition, London University, and Director of The Warburg Institute (Warburg).

F. J. G.: John Gillingham, Professor of Neurological Surgery, Edinburgh University (Moniz).

F. T. R. G.: Frank Giles, Deputy Editor, *The Sunday Times* (Elizabeth II).

J. H. G.: John H. Goldthorpe, Official Fellow, Nuffield College, Oxford (Durkheim, Pareto, Parsons, Weber).

M. G.: Martin Green, Professor of English, Tufts University, U.S.A. (Salinger, Edmund Wilson).

P. G. H. G.: P. G. H. Gell Professor of Experimental Pathology, Birmingham University (Burnet).

Ph. G.: Philip Granville, Director of Lord's Gallery, London (Cassandre, Kauffer).

R. D. G.: Dr Ronald Gray, University Lecturer in German and Fellow of Emmanuel College, Cambridge (Brecht, Kafka).

R. H. G.: R. H. Girdwood, Professor of Therapeutics, Edinburgh University (Minot).

R. M. G.: Dr Richard Griffiths, Fellow of Brasenose College, Oxford (Darlan, Laval, Petain).

A. H.: Dr Alex Herxheimer, Senior Lecturer in Pharmacology and Therapeutics, London Hospital Medical College (Bovet).

A. H. H.: Albert Hourani, Director of the Middle East Centre and Fellow of St Antony's College, Oxford (Aga Khan, Ataturk, Bourguiba, Farouk, T. E. Lawrence, Nasser).

C. H.: Carol Hogben, Deputy Keeper, Circulation Department, Victoria & Albert Museum (Cartier-Bresson).

C. B. H.: Colin Haycraft, Director, Gerald Duckworth & Co. (Lane).

C. D. H.: C. D. Hamilton, Editor in Chief, Times Newspapers, and wartime infantry battalion commander under Field Marshal Montgomery (Montgomery).

D. G. H.: D. G. Harnden, Professor of Cancer Studies, Birmingham University (Tjio).

D. J. H.: Douglas Hewitt, Staff Tutor, Oxford University Delegacy for Extra-Mural Studies (Conrad).

H. H.: Harold Hobson, *Sunday Times* theatre critic (Artaud, Brook, Mrs Patrick Campbell, Cochran, Copeau, Coward, Craig, Evans, Gracie Fields, Gielgud, Mistinguett, Olivier, Piscator, Max Reinhardt, Stanislavsky, Ziegfeld).

H. P. H.: Sir Harold Himsworth, former Secretary, Medical Research Council (Banting).

I. H.: Ian Hamilton, Editor, *The Review* (Graves).

J. H.: Janine Hill, freelance journalist (Dart, Dobzhansky, Leakey, Levi-Strauss, Zuckerkandl).

J. J. H.: John Hennessy, Sports Editor, *The Times* (Brundage).

J. J. Ha.: Jacquetta Hawkes, author and archaeologist (Ventris).

M. H.: Michael Holroyd, biographer of Lytton Strachey (Strachey).

N. J. M. H.: Nigel Hawkes, Science Editor, *Science Journal* (Hillier, Junkers, Krebs, von Laue, Mosely, Edwin Mueller, George Mueller, Oberth, Sikorsky, Tereshkova, Tsiolkovsky, Wilkins, C. T. R. Wilson).

P. H.: Penelope Houston, Editor, *Sight & Sound* (Antonioni, Bogart, Hepburn, Hitchcock, Keaton, Kubrick, Resnais, Sturges, Welles).

P. D'A. H.: Dr P. D'Arcy Hart, former Director, Medical Research Council's Tuberculosis Research Unit (Waksman).

R. H.: Robert Harling, Editor, *House & Garden* (Breuer, Eames).

R. H.: Rayner Heppenstall, novelist and critic (Orwell).

R. M. H.: The Rev. R. M. Hardy, Fellow and Chaplain of Selwyn College, Cambridge (William Temple).

T. H.: Tom Hopkinson, author and journalist (Avedon, Capa, Lorant, Northcliffe, Salomon).

A. J.: Arthur Jacobs, Professor at the Royal Academy of Music and Associate Editor, *Opera* (Walter, William Walton, Weill, Wood).

B. J.: Brian Jackson, Director, Advisory Centre for Education (Montessori, Neill, Piaget, Skinner).

C. M. J.: C. M. Jones, Editor, *Lawn Tennis* (Kramer).

C. T. J.: Timothy Johnson, *Sunday Times* technology correspondent (Philips).

D. J.: Derek Jewell, Publishing Director of Times Newspapers and *Sunday Times* jazz/pop critic (Andersen, Beatles, Crosby, Dylan, Ellington, Jolson, Glenn Miller, Moores, Piaf, Presley, Redding, Sinatra, Bessie Smith, Whiteman).

D. S. J.: Denis Jenkinson, *Motor Sport* foreign correspondent (Ferrari).

D. W. J. J.: Douglas Johnson, Professor of French History, University College, London (Bidault, Clemenceau, de Gaulle, Jaures, Lyautey, Malraux, Maurras, Poincare, Sorel, Thorez).

L. J.: Louis Jacobs, Rabbi of the New London Synagogue and author (Buber, Wise).

V. G. J. J.: Vivian Jenkins, *Sunday Times* chief rugby correspondent (Nepia).

W. H. J.: William Janeway, Marshall Scholar and Research Student in Economics, Cambridge University (Byrnes, Herbert Hoover, Oswald, Stevenson, Malcolm X).

H. K.: Hans Keller, musician and writer (Bartok, Berg, Boulez, Britten, Casals, Flesch, Furtwängler, Heifetz, Huberman, Kodaly, Kreisler, Mahler, Rostal, Schoenberg, Shostakovich, Stockhausen, Strauss, Szigeti, Webern).

J. M. K.: J. Michael Kitch, Lecturer in History, School of Slavonic and East European Studies, London University (Djilas, Gheorghiu-Dej, Maniu, Tito).

K. K.: Kenneth Kirkwood, Rhodes Professor of Race Relations, Oxford University (Hertzog, Luthuli, Malan, Mandela, Nyerere, Ian Smith, Smuts, Strijdom).

L. K.: Laurence Kitchin, Lecturer in Drama, Bristol University, and broadcaster (O'Casey, Synge).

T. P. K.: Terence Kelly, broadcaster and film-maker (Rank).

L.: Lord Longford, former leader of the House of Lords and Lord Privy Seal (Attlee, Bevan, Bevin, Gaitskell).

A. L.: Dr Aubrey Leatham, physician to St George's Hospital and the National Heart Hospital and Dean of the Institute of Cardiology (Einthoven).

H. R. A. L.: Humphrey Lyttelton, jazz musician, broadcaster and journalist (Armstrong, Beiderbecke, Gillespie, La Rocca, Oliver).

J. L.: James Laver, former Keeper of Prints and Drawings, Victoria & Albert Museum (Courreges, Poiret).

Jo. L.: John Lovesey, Sports Features Editor, *The Sunday Times* (Igloi, Zaharias).

M. L.: Dr Michael Leifer, Lecturer in Political Studies and member of the Centre for South-East Asian Studies, Hull University (Diem, Ho Chi Minh, Sukarno).

S. L.: Mrs Sylvia Laverton, agricultural journalist (Biffen, Ferguson, Hammond, Petersen, Schrader, Templeman, H. A. Wallace).

V. L.: Vivian Lewis, *Sunday Times Business News* Paris correspondent (Dassault).

E. L.-S.: Edward Lucie-Smith, poet and art critic (Marinetti).

G. M. MacB.: George MacBeth, poet (Hemingway).

M. McC.: Meriel McCooey, *Sunday Times Magazine* (Chanel, Stephen).

K. McL.: Karen McLeod, Tutor, Oxford University Delegacy for Extra-Mural Studies (D. H. Lawrence).

J. McM.: Sir John McMichael, Emeritus Professor of Medicine, London University (Forssman).

T. McN.: Tom McNab, AAA National Coach (Owens).

N. McW.: Norris McWhirter, BBC TV athletics commentator, and compiler and editor of *The Guinness Book of Records* (Nurmi).

A. M.: Arthur Marwick, Professor of History, The Open University (Addison, Beveridge, Cripps, Sir Warren Fisher, Henderson, Lansbury J. H. Thomas, the Webbs).

A. Mi.: Adrian Mitchell, writer (Thurber).

A. W. M.: Andrew W. Morrison, Ear, Nose and Throat Surgeon, The London Hospital and the Royal National Throat, Nose and Ear Hospital (Shea).

D. L. M.: Doris Langley Moore, Founder of and Adviser to the Museum of Costume, Bath (Quant).

E. G. M.: Edwin Morgan, poet and Senior Lecturer in English, Glasgow University (Apollinaire, Stein).

G. W. M.: Ged Martin, Charles Kingsley Bye-Fellow, Magdalene College, Cambridge (Mackenzie King, Laurier).

J. B. M.: Dr John B. Messenger, Lecturer in Zoology, Sheffield University (Adrian, Bateson, Bawden, Cannon, Crick, Eccles, Elton, Gray, Julian Huxley, Jacob, Neumann, Pirie, Sherrington, Szent-Györgi).

J. L. M.: J. L. Mongar, Professor of Pharmacology, University College, London (Richet).

P. M.: Sir Philip Magnus, biographer of Edward VII (Edward VII).

P. Ma.: Paul Mayersberg, author and screenwriter (Hawks, Lubitsch, Toland, West).

R. F. M.: Ruddock F. Mackay, naval historian and Lecturer in Modern History, St Andrews University (Lord Fisher).

R. F. M.: Roger Mortimer, *Sunday Times* racing correspondent (Sir Gordon Richards).

R. G. M.: Robin Marlar, former Cambridge University and Sussex cricketer and *Sunday Times* cricket correspondent (Bradman).

S. M.: Sheila Macqueen, flower arrangement expert and author (Spry).
S. C. M.: Stirling Moss, former Grand Prix racing driver (Fangio).
T. M.: Tom Milne, film critic and Associate Editor, *Sight and Sound* (Bergman, Buñuel, Dreyer, Feuillade, John Ford, Godard, Griffith, Kurosawa, Renior).
B. N.: Bobby Neill, boxing manager, former Featherweight Champion of Great Britain (Sugar Ray Robinson).
E. R. N.: Dr E. R. Norman, Lecturer in History and Fellow of Jesus College, Cambridge (Carson, Casement, Collins, Cushing, De Valéra, Spellman).
G. P. G. N.: Graham Norton, *Sunday Times Magazine* (Baden-Powell, Bartholomew, Beaverbrook, Biró, Burton, Butlin, Cullen, Flynn, Gluckstein, Haas, Hefner, W. H. Hoover, Morant, Reith, Ross, Sarnoff, Sundback, DeWitt Wallace, Kemmons Wilson, Woolton, Yerkes).
N. N.: Nigel Nicolson, former M.P. for Bournemouth East and Christchurch (Churchill, Eden, Macmillan).
P. N.: Philip Norman, *Sunday Times Magazine* (Atlas, Mata Hari, Wodehouse).
B. R. O.: Brian Osman, educational psychologist (Adler, Binet, Cousteau, Dewey, Husserl, Kohler, Laing, Malinowski, Maritain, Mead, Pavlov, Reich, Rorschach, Spengler, Spock, Thorndike).
D. O.: David Owen, motoring journalist (Porsche).
I. O.: Dr Ian Oswald, Department of Psychiatry, Edinburgh University (von Mering).
P. O.: Philip Oakes, poet, novelist and *Sunday Times* columnist (Astaire, Cagney, Fairbanks, W. C. Fields, Flaherty, Gable, Laurel and Hardy, De Mille, Rossellini, Stroheim, Shirley Temple).
R. O.: Roland Oliver, Professor of African History, London University (Kenyatta, Lugard, Nkrumah, Senghor).
R. M. O.: R. M. Ogorkiewicz, Lecturer in Engineering, Imperial College, London (Guderian, Liddell Hart).
W. A. O.: Tony Osman, Science Editor, *Sunday Times Magazine* (Sir Ronald Fisher, Haldane, Aldous Huxley, Orr, Tarski, Wallis, Weaver, Zeeman, Ziegler).
A. S. P.: Professor Sir Alan Parkes, Fellow of Christ's College, Cambridge, and Editor, *Journal of Biosocial Science* (Pincus).
B. P.: Bruce Page, *Sunday Times* (Philby).
B. J. P.: Dr Bernard Porter, Lecturer in History, Hull University (Curzon, Kitchener, Menzies, Mountbatten).
D. P.: Dilys Powell, *Sunday Times* film critic (Chaplin, Clair, Dietrich, Disney, Korda, Pickford, Elizabeth Taylor, Valentino, Vigo).
G. C. P.: George Perry, *Sunday Times Magazine* (Bardot, Berkeley, Hughes, Howard Johnson, Rothapfel, Wilder).
G. P.: Gabriel Pearson, Lecturer in Literature, Essex University (Lukács, Mann).
H. J. P.: Dr H. J. Parish, former Clinical Director, Wellcome Research Laboratories (von Behring, Calmette).
I. A. R. P. Ian Peebles, former Middlesex and England cricketer, and *Sunday Times* cricket correspondent (Barnes).
J. P.: Joan Price, beauty journalist (Helena Rubinstein, Sassoon).
J. B. P.: J. B. Priestley, author and dramatist (Shaw).
L. F. P.: Dr L. Peter, Lecturer in Hungarian History, London University (Kun, Nagy).
L. v. d. P.: Lucia van der Post, *The Sunday Times* (Huddleston).
M. P.: Michael Parkinson, *Sunday Times* sports columnist (Sir Matt Busby).
M. I. P.: Dr Michael Podro, Lecturer in the Philosophy of Art, Warburg Institute (Panofsky).
P. G. J. P.: Peter Pulzer, Tutor in Politics, Christ Church, Oxford (Goebbels, Goering, Himmler, Hitler).
R. A. P.: Sir Rudolph Peters, Emeritus Professor of Biochemistry, Oxford University (Hopkins).
T. C. F. P.: The Hon. Terence Prittie, *Guardian* diplomatic correspondent (Adenauer, Brandt, Erhard, Meir, Ulbricht).
V. P.: Valerie Pitt, Head of Division of the Humanities, Woolwich Polytechnic (Billy Graham).
W. H. P.: William H. Pritchard, Associate Professor of English, Amherst College, Massachusetts (Greene, Leavis).
A. Q.: Anthony Quinton, University Lecturer in Philosophy and Fellow of New College, Oxford (Austin, Bergson, Carnap, Heidegger, Merleau-Ponty, G. E. Moore, Popper, Bertrand Russell, Whitehead, Wittgenstein).
P. Q.: Peter Quennell, author and critic (de Montherlant).
A. B. R.: Andrew Robertson, economist and journalist (Manolete).
A. P. R.: A. P. Ryan, Assistant Editor, *The Times* (Haley).
C. R.: Christopher Ricks, Professor of English, Bristol University (Beckett).
C. H. R.: C. H. Rolph, *New Statesman* legal correspondent (Hinds).
D. R.: David Robinson, *Financial Times* film critic (Bow, Bette Davis, Dovzhenko, Eisenstein, Garbo, Gish, Harlow, Méliès, Pudovkin, Swanson).
D. N. R.: Donald Ross, Cardiac and Thoracic Surgeon, National Heart and Guy's Hospitals (Barnard).
E. M. V. R.: Mary Raine, BBC Newsroom staff (Stanley Matthews).
F. R.: Frederic Raphael, writer (Culbertson).
I. R.: Dr Ismond Rosen, Consultant Psychiatrist, Paddington Clinic and Research Psychoanalyst, Hampstead Clinic (Kinsey).
J. R.: John Russell, *Sunday Times* art critic (Arp, Bacon, Bakst, Boccioni, Bonnard, Brancusi, Braque, Breton, Cage, Caro, de Chirico, Dali, Dubuffet, Duchamp, Ernst, Giacometti, Johns, Kandinsky, Klee, de Kooning, Leger, Magritte, Malevich, Matisse, Miró, Mondrian, Henry Moore, Newman, Nicholson, Oldenburg, Pevsner, Picasso, Pollock, Rauschenberg, Rothko, Schwitters, David Smith, Warhol).
L. R.: Lanning Roper, *Sunday Times* gardening correspondent (Jekyll).
P. G. R.: Paul Redfern, medical writer (Eijkman, Hodgkin, Kendrew, Lederberg, Lorenz, Medawar, Monod, Morgan, Northrop, Perutz, Sanger, Stanley, Sumner, Tatum, Tinbergen, de Vries, J. D. Watson, Wigglesworth).
S. A. R.: Stanley Reynolds, *Guardian* television critic (Muhammad Ali).
S. F. R.: Sir Stanley Rous, President, *Fédération Internationale de Football Association* and Chairman, Central Council of Physical Recreation (Rimet).
S. M. R.: Susan Raven, *Sunday Times Magazine* (Dick-Read, Sanger, Stopes).
W. J. R.: James Riddell, author and Olympic skier (Lunn).
W. R.-M. William Rees-Mogg, Editor, *The Times* (Butler).
A. S.: Dr Anil Seal, Lecturer in History and Fellow of Trinity College, Cambridge (Bose, Indira Gandhi, Mahatma Gandhi, Jinnah).
A. A. S.: Andrew Sinclair, historian, novelist and publisher (Hearst).
A. H. S.: Alan Huw Smith, *The Guardian* (Scholl, Shackleton).
C. A. S.: Anthony Storr, author and psychiatrist (Freud).
D. M. S.: Denis Mack Smith, historian and Fellow of All Souls College, Oxford (d'Annunzio, Croce, Giolitti, Mussolini, Togliatti).
E. F. S.: E. F. Scowen, Professor of Medicine, London University and Director of the Medical Professorial Unit, St Bartholomew's Hospital (Domagk).
E. M. S.: Dr Enid Starkie, Reader Emeritus in French Literature and Fellow of Somerville College, Oxford (Gide, Proust).
G. S.: Godfrey Smith, Editor, *Sunday Times Magazine* (Moss, Harold Wilson).
G. R. S.: Richard Storry, historian and Fellow of St Antony's College, Oxford (Hirohito, Tojo, Yoshida).
H. S.: H. Swinburne, Editor, *Heating and Ventilating Engineer* (Carrier).
J. S.: Jack Solomons, international boxing promoter (Jack Johnson).
J. S.: Dr John Street, Director, Centre of Latin American Studies, Cambridge (Perón).
J. St.: Dr Jonathan Steinberg, Lecturer in History and Fellow of Trinity Hall, Cambridge (Schleicher, Seeckt, Stresemann, Tirpitz).
J. A. S.: J. A. Strong, Professor of Medicine, Edinburgh University (Barr).
J. G. S.: Julian Symons, crime novelist, social historian and literary critic (Chandler, Christie, Simenon, Edgar Wallace).
J. H. S.: Jon Stallworthy, poet and critic (Yeats).
J. P. S.: Dr J. P. Stern, Lecturer in Modern Languages and Fellow of St John's College, Cambridge (Musil).
L. B. S.: L. B. Schapiro, Professor of Political Science (with special reference to Russian studies), London University (Beria).
M. A. S.: Dr Martin Sherwood, scientific writer and editor (Alder, Bosch, Haworth, Karrer, Kuhn, Libby).
N. S.: Norman Stone, Assistant Lecturer in History and Fellow of Gonville and Caius College, Cambridge (Horthy, Hugenberg, Starhemberg).
P. H. S. S.: Dr Peter Stubbs, Science Editor, *New Scientist* (Appleton, Aston, Beadle, Bethe, Bondi, Chadwick, Cockroft, Dirac, Franck, Geiger, Hess, Hoyle, Hubble, Jansky, Kamerlingh-Onnes, Landau, Lovell, Meitner, Hermann Muller, J. Robert Oppenheimer, Pauli, Planck, Powell, Runcorn, Ryle, Szilard, Teller, Tiselius, Townes, Ernest Walton, Wegener, Wiener, Zuckerman).
R. S.: Ronnie Scott, musician (Basie, Fitzgerald, Hines, Holiday).
R. Sk.: Robert Skidelsky, Research Fellow of the British Academy (Baldwin, MacDonald, Mosley, Snowden).
R. J. E. S.: Robert Silvey, former head of BBC Audience Research (Gallup).
S. S.: Simon Schama, Fellow of Christ's College, Cambridge, and Editor, *The Cambridge Review* (Ben Gurion, Eichmann, Frank, Hallstein, Herzl, Mansholt, Rasputin, Salazar, Stauffenberg, Weizmann, Wilhelmina).
A. S.-J.: Anne Scott-James, journalist and former Editor, *Harper's Bazaar* (Arden, Dior).
D. S.-T.: Desmond Shawe-Taylor, *Sunday Times* music critic (Busoni, Chaliapin, Flagstad, Melba, Prokofiev, Puccini, Rachmaninov, Tetrazzini).
H. S.-W.: Hugh Seton-Watson, Head of Department of History, School of Slavonic and East European Studies, London University (Beneš, Masaryk, Pašić, Pilsudski).
T.: Lord Thomson, Chairman, The Thomson Organisation (Rockefeller).
C. T.: Charles Tomlinson, poet and Reader in English Poetry, Bristol University (Pound, Stevens).
C. G. T.: Colin Tilney, harpsichordist (Artur Rubinstein, Segovia).
D. H. T.: Diana Tomkinson, Olympic skier (Killy).
G. W. T.: G. W. Taylor, Professor of Surgery, St Bartholomew's Hospital (Carrell).
J. L. M. T.: John L. M. Trim, Head of the Department of Linguistics and Fellow of Selwyn College, Cambridge (Chomsky).
J. R. T.: John Russell Taylor, author and *The Times* film critic (Osborne).
M. T.: Mildred Temple, *Sunday Times* New York bureau (Saunders).
N. T.: Dr Nathaniel Tarn, poet and anthropologist (Leiris).
N. J. W. T.: Nicholas Taylor, *Sunday Times* environmental correspondent (Aalto, Behrens, Le Corbusier, Fuller, Geddes, Gropius, Howard, Philip Johnson, Kahn, Lutyens, Martin and Matthew, Nervi, Rietveld, Mies van der Rohe, Saarinen, Skidmore, Owings and Merrill, Tange, Frank Lloyd Wright).
N. O. T.: Nicholas Tomalin, *The Sunday Times* (Murrow).
R. C. T.: Clive Trebilcock, Lecturer in Economic History and Fellow of Pembroke College, Cambridge (Keynes, Rathenau, Schacht, Veblen, Witte).
R. F. T.: R. F. Tredwen, Kodak International (Eastman).
R. G. K. T.: Sir Robert Thompson, airman, author and administrator (Giap, Wingate).
T. T.: Tony Tanner, Lecturer in English and Fellow of King's College, Cambridge (Bellow, Malamud).
T. Ti.: Teddy Tinling, designer of sports clothes and tennis umpire (Lenglen).
M. U.: Marc Ullmann, Deputy Editor, *L'Express* (Mendès-France, Mollet, Monnet, Salan).
H. V.: Helen Vlachos, journalist and publisher (Makarios, Metaxas, Venizelos).
N. V.: Nicholas Valery, Deputy Editor, *Science Journal* (Baade, Bohr, Sir Lawrence Bragg, Sir William Bragg, de Broglie, Calvin, de la Cierva, Curie, Einstein, Fermi, Gagarin, Goddard, Guillaume. Hahn, Heisenberg, McMillan, Millikan, Piccard, Reber, Rutherford, Schrödinger).
B. W.: Ben Wright, golf writer and commentator (Palmer).
C. W.: Colin Wilson, writer (Capone, Crippen, Crowley, Houdini, Joyce).
D. C. W.: Donald C. Watt, Reader in International History, London University (Sir Edward Grey, Molotov, Rapacki, Ribbentrop).
F. P. W.: Frank Whitford, writer and art historian (Heartfield).
J. B. W.: John Wadley, Editor, *International Cycle Sport* (Anquetil).
J. G. W.: J. G. Weightman, Professor of French, London University (Robbe-Grillet).
L. W.: Leonard Woolf, author (Kipling).
M. R. W.: M. R. Werner, author and Associate Editor, *Sports Illustrated* (Shoemaker).
P. W.: Peter Wilsher, Editor, *Sunday Times Business News* (Agnelli, Benton, Boot, Carlson, Chambers, Flick, Henry Ford, de Havilland, Iwazaki, Kearton, Krupp, Lever, Mattei, Norman, Reeves, Tata, Trippe, Tom Watson, Wellcome, Woodruff).
P. O. W.: Peter Wymer, Information Adviser, Council of Engineering Institutions (Baird, Sir John Fleming, De Forest, Hinton, Hutchison, Marconi, Nuffield, Poulsen, Rolls and Royce, Shoenberg, Watson-Watt, Whittle, Wright Brothers, Zeppelin, Zworykin).
R. W.: Robin Wright, Advertising Creative Director, Richard Cope and Partners (Ogilvy).
R. G. W.: R. G. White, Gardiner Professor of Bacteriology and Immunology, Glasgow University (Ehrlich).
R. P. W.: Roger Wood, former Editor, *Daily Express* (Christiansen).
S. W.: Stanley Way, Lecturer in Gynaecological Ontology, University of Newcastle upon Tyne (Papanicolaou).
Z. A. B. Z.: Z. A. B. Zeman, Lecturer in History, St Andrews University (Dubcek).

ILLUSTRATORS

Julian Allen (Crick, Fairbanks, Helena Rubinstein, Segovia, Zworykin).
Candy Amsden (Auden).
Saskia de Boer (Muhammad Ali, Brando, Dylan, Marx Brothers, Redding, Taylor – all models photographed by David Montgomery).
David Bomberg (self-portrait).
Mike Brownfield (Matthews).
Philip Castle (Artaud, Balenciaga, Bannister, Barrie, Bartholomew, Boulez, Brook, de la Cierva, Collins, Corbusier, Dior).
Seymour Chwast/Push Pin Studios (Dulles, Franco, Mahatma Gandhi, Holiday, J. Edgar Hoover, Laurel and Hardy, McCarthy, Scholl, Bessie Smith, Warren).
Cosmos/Push Pin Studios (Malraux, Piaget, Pirandello, Porter, Stockhausen, Varèse, Yeats).
Andrew Dark (Presley).
Paul Davis (Guevara).
Jim Dine (Bardot).
Anthony Donaldson (Pickford, Swanson).
Pauline Ellison (Hardie, Julian Huxley).
John Farman (Antonioni, Balanchine, Bidault, Chadwick, Cripps, Denning, Dubcek, Duncan, Eliot, Ferguson, Flaherty, Sir John Fleming).
Raymond Gabbott (Himmler, Toscanini).
Robert Grossman (Acheson, Armstrong, Atlas, Benton, von Braun, Capone, Coleman, Lyndon Johnson, Robert Kennedy, Onassis, Ruth, Sinatra, Ziegfeld).
Terry Gilliam (Agnelli, Beaverbrook, Bondi).
Milton Glazer (Shaw).
Richard Hamilton (Duchamp).
John Heartfield (Goering, Hitler, MacDonald).
Jerry Joyner/Push Pin Studios (Schweitzer, Stroheim, Wells).
Howie Kanovitz (Bacon, Cartier-Bresson).
David King/Kelpra Studios (Baird, Blériot, Brooke, Crowley, Gish, Hughes, Mata Hari).
R. B. Kitaj (Pound, Primo de Rivera, La Pasionaria).
Edda Köchl (Adenauer, Bartók, Brecht, Bünuel, Pavlova, Orwell, Renoir, Sartre, Schoenberg).
Roger Law (Adler, Alexander, Basie, Ben Gurion, Bethmann Hollweg, Bosch, Eastman).
Brian Love (Baden-Powell, Cage, Crippen, Darlan, Joe Davis, Doenitz, Guderian, De Mille, Owens, Piggott).
Mike McInnerney (Kafka, Lang, Prokofiev, Rilke).
Charlie Nichol (Addison, Burton).
Gabriel Pascalini (Gide, Palmer).
Picasso (Apollinaire).
Alan Rickards (de Vries, Wiener).
Arnold Schwartzman (Mussolini, Nimitz, Pavlov, Potter, Rasputin).
Terence Seago (Busby, Crosby, Hefner, Jolson, Krupp, Ian Smith).
Burton Silverman (Castro, Ho Chi Minh, Lenin, Mao Tsetung, Trotsky).
Gilbert Stone (Eichmann, Freud, Pius XII, Dylan Thomas).
Richard Weigand (Aalto, Adrian, Babel, Beiderbecke, Britten, Caruso, Austen Chamberlain, Christiansen, Dale, Eijkmann, Fangio, Haig, Hines, London, front and back cover).
Oliver Williams (Kenyatta, Laing, Mandela, Rockefeller).
Barry Zaid/Push Pin Studios (Kern, La Guardia, Lee, Mayer, Poiret, Spock, Shirley Temple, Whiteman, Wilhelm II).

PHOTOGRAPHERS AND PICTURE AGENCIES

Martin Breese
Tony Evans
Lewinski
Lotte Meitner-Graf
David Montgomery

Kevin Brownlow Collection
Camera Press
Imperial War Museum
John Kobal Collection
London Express Features
Magnum
Mander and Mitchenson Collection
Mansell Collection
Nobel Foundation
Paul Popper
Radio Times-Hulton Picture Library
Ullstein
Roger Viollet
Wide World

We are particularly grateful to the following for their assistance.
Architectural Press
G. Argent
Bowker Publishing Co. Ltd.
British Film Institute
British Museum
C.B.S. Records
Dobell's Jazz Record Shop
E.M.I.
Farmers Weekly
Paul Hamlyn Books Ltd.
Holborn Public Library
London Library
McGraw-Hill Publishing Co.
Music for Pleasure
National Book League
Penguin Books
R.C.A.-Victor
R.I.B.A.
Science Museum
Tate Gallery
United States Embassy Reference Library
University of London Library
Victoria and Albert Museum
Wellcome Foundation
Westminster Central Reference Library
J. Whitaker & Sons Ltd.
Wiener Library

No doubt at all about the winner: in a poll of some 1250 votes, Neil Armstrong always held a commanding lead and finally romped away with roughly 13.2 per cent of the total – more than four times as much as his closest challenger. (To be fair, Armstrong was *not* a name we wanted to leave out; if the first man on the Moon had been called Williams we would undoubtedly have included him. As it was, we were irreversibly past the As before Apollo 11 was launched.) There were also a number of fair-minded votes for the Armstrong-Aldrin-Collins trio.

The variety of choice was enormous. The 1250 votes were divided among 534 separate candidates – 373 of them with one vote only.

Indeed, only 12 candidates managed to achieve double figures. Leading the runners-up (and frequently accompanied by angry notes alleging "insults to Scotsmen") came racing driver Jim Clark with 40 votes; third was Yehudi Menuhin with 27, followed at a respectful distance by Rabindranath Tagore, Professor J. R. R. Tolkien, The Unknown Warrior (15 votes here), Judy Garland, John Steinbeck, Kathleen Ferrier, Sir Malcolm Sargent and Dr. L. L. Zamenhof (*who?* . . . he invented Esperanto).

Nobody else managed, so to speak, to save their deposits. But Bob Hope did surprisingly well; so did Prince Philip, Rudolf Steiner, Field Marshal Rommel, Helen Keller and Gavrilo Princip, the student who shot Franz Ferdinand at Sarajevo.

Arthur Koestler had the same number of supporters (six) as Spike Milligan and Ian Fleming. Mary Baker Eddy and Moshe Dayan had the same number (five) as Richard Dimbleby, David Frost and – thanks to a faithful and persistent group from West London – Dame Sybil Thorndike.

Four people wanted Jimmy Greaves, who shared this spot with, among others, Haile Selassie, Sir Michael Tippett, Emil Zatopek, Marshall McLuhan, Gary Sobers and John Buchan.

For the rest, the entries ranged from Myself (two votes, presumably from different selves), Kilroy (the one who Was Here), God (who presumably Is Here), the British Taxpayer and the space-dog Laika, to Prince Charles, King George VI, King Hussein and Lady Spencer Churchill.

Enoch Powell had five times as many votes as Edward Heath, which must prove something, Bernadette Devlin had the same number as Ian Paisley (and two more than Terence O'Neill), Christine Keeler twice as many as Stephen War, Len Hutton the same as Denis Compton. The remainder range across as wide a range as the original 1000, from the inventors of Moulton bicycles and catseyes, through pop (Herb Alpert, Shirley Bassey, Buddy Holly, the Rolling Stones), sport (George Best, Ron Clarke, Rod Laver, Tommy Simpson), the cinema (Robert Donat, James Dean, Francois Truffaut, Peter Sellers) and literature (Arnold Bennett, George Gissing, Tennessee Williams) to the wilder shores of world politics (Lee Kuan Yew, Lumumba, Lin Piao, Hastings Banda, Pierre Trudeau).

Finally – the Burton affair. Richard Burton got 107 votes, easily enough to boost him into second place. However, as 106 of them were written in the same hand and received in envelopes unmistakably addressed with the same typewriter, we decided to abide as far as possible by democratic principles, and regretfully invalidated 105 of them. Still, he has the consolation that somebody who lives in London W.1 must love him very much.

Neil Armstrong (U.S., b. 1930: astronaut. At 3.56 a.m. on July 21 this year, Armstrong became the first man to set foot on the Moon. His flight to the Sea of Tranquillity was a triumph for American technology in space and a massive fillip for small-town middle-class Americans who fear their society is being overwhelmed by demonstrators who don't believe in haircuts. Armstrong represents all the virtues of the old American success story – modest, diligent, brave, clean-cut, he is himself a small-town man born in Wapakoneta, Ohio. In public he is painfully shy, prone to blushing; in private he has been one of the smarter operators in NASA's tortuous office politics. It is well known in NASA that Armstrong's companion aboard the lunar module Eagle, Air Force Colonel Edward 'Buzz' Aldrin, was originally chosen to be the first man on the Moon but that Armstrong manoeuvred himself into the vital role. Armstrong lives for flying and is a brilliantly cool jet pilot, though inclined to suffer from gremlins: he had close shaves as a Navy pilot in Korea, during his Gemini 8 flight when the spacecraft began to spin wildly, and again when he baled out while testing a lunar landing trainer. On all three occasions Armstrong kept his head, just as he did when Eagle swooped in to land on the Moon with an overloaded computer and had to be steered manually away from a perilously rocky crater. As with many picture-book success stories, Armstrong has been lucky with his wife, Jan. Mrs. Armstrong, an athletic, strong-minded woman, lives and breathes for her husband's career. She used to watch him test-flying the X-15 rocket plane, standing on the roof of her home, following the plane through binoculars; and during the Moon landing she followed Eagle on a lunar navigation chart saying: "Good. Good. Good," as the module neared the cratered surface. **P. Du.**

'MAN ON THE MOON', BY JOHN M. MANSFIELD (CONSTABLE, 1969); 'JOURNEY TO TRANQUILLITY', BY HUGO YOUNG, BRYAN SILCOCK AND PETER DUNN (CAPE, 1969).